A·N·N·U·A·L E·D·I·T·I·O·N·S

CHILD GROWTH AND DEVELOPMENT

99/00

Sixth Edition

Editors

Ellen N. Junn
California State University, Fullerton

Ellen Junn is a professor of child development, administrative fellow in the Office of the Vice President of Academic Affairs, and director of the Office of Educational Equity at California State University, Fullerton. She received a B.S. in experimental psychology from the University of Michigan and her M.A. and Ph.D. in cognitive and developmental psychology from Princeton University. In addition to her work on educational equity issues, Dr. Junn's research and publications focus on developments in children's conceptions regarding adult social relationships and on college teaching effectiveness.

Chris J. Boyatzis
Bucknell University

Chris Boyatzis is an assistant professor of psychology at Bucknell University. He received a B.A. in psychology from Boston University and his M.A. and Ph.D. in developmental psychology from Brandeis University. Many of his research interests lie at the intersection of social and cognitive development in early childhood. Dr. Boyatzis has published research on children's nonverbal behavior and social status, media effects on children, symbolic development, and play and art. He has also written on the use of literature and film to teach developmental psychology.

Dushkin/McGraw-Hill
Sluice Dock, Guilford, Connecticut 06437

Visit us on the Internet
http://www.dushkin.com/annualeditions/

Credits

1. Conception to Birth
Facing overview—courtesy UNICEF photos.
2. Cognition, Language, and Learning
Facing overview—© 1998 by PhotoDisc, Inc.
3. Social and Emotional Development
Facing overview—© 1998 by Cleo Freelance Photography.
4. Parenting and Family Issues
Facing overview—© 1998 by Cleo Freelance Photography.
5. Cultural and Societal Influences
Facing overview—© 1998 by Cleo Freelance Photography.

Copyright

Cataloging in Publication Data
Main entry under title: Annual Editions: Child growth and development. 1999/2000.
    1. Child psychology—Periodicals. I. Junn, Ellen N., *comp.* II. Boyatzis, Chris J., *comp.* III.
Title: Child growth and development.
ISBN 0-07-040122-5   155.4'.05   ISSN 1075-5217

Sixth Edition

Cover image © 1999 PhotoDisc, Inc.

Printed in the United States of America   1234567890BAHBAH54321098   Printed on Recycled Paper

Members of the Advisory Board are instrumental in the final selection of articles for each edition of ANNUAL EDITIONS. Their review of articles for content, level, currentness, and appropriateness provides critical direction to the editor and staff. We think that you will find their careful consideration well reflected in this volume.

To the Reader

In publishing ANNUAL EDITIONS we recognize the enormous role played by the magazines, newspapers, and journals of the public press in providing current, first-rate educational information in a broad spectrum of interest areas. Many of these articles are appropriate for students, researchers, and professionals seeking accurate, current material to help bridge the gap between principles and theories and the real world. These articles, however, become more useful for study when those of lasting value are carefully collected, organized, indexed, and reproduced in a low-cost format, which provides easy and permanent access when the material is needed. That is the role played by ANNUAL EDITIONS.

New to ANNUAL EDITIONS is the inclusion of related World Wide Web sites. These sites have been selected by our editorial staff to represent some of the best resources found on the World Wide Web today. Through our carefully developed topic guide, we have linked these Web resources to the articles covered in this ANNUAL EDITIONS reader. We think that you will find this volume useful, and we hope that you will take a moment to visit us on the Web at *http://www.dushkin.com/* to tell us what you think.

We are delighted to welcome you to this fifth volume of *Annual Editions: Child Growth and Development 99/00.* The amazing sequence of events of prenatal development that lead to the birth of a baby is an awe-inspiring process. Perhaps more intriguing is the question of what the future may hold for this newly arrived baby—for instance, will this child become a doctor, a lawyer, an artist, a beggar, or a thief? Although philosophers and prominent thinkers such as Charles Darwin and Sigmund Freud have long speculated about the importance of infancy on subsequent development, not until the 1960s did the scientific study of infants and young children flourish. Since then, research and theory in infancy and childhood have exploded, resulting in a wealth of new knowledge about child development.

Past accounts of infants and young children as passive, homogeneous organisms have been replaced with investigations aimed at studying infants and young children at a "microlevel"—as active individuals with many inborn competencies, who are capable of shaping their own environment—as well as at a "macrolevel," by considering the larger context surrounding the child. In short, children are not "blank slates," and development does not take place in a vacuum; children arrive with many skills and grow up in a complex web of social, historical, political, economic, and cultural spheres.

As was the case for previous editions, we hope to achieve at least four major goals with this volume. First, we hope to present you with the latest research and thinking to help you better appreciate the complex interactions that characterize human development in infancy and childhood. Second, in light of the feedback we received on previous editions, we have placed greater emphasis on important contemporary issues and challenges, exploring topics such as understanding development in the context of current societal and cultural influences. Third, attention is given to articles that also discuss effective, practical applications. Finally, we hope that this anthology will serve as a catalyst to help students become more effective future professionals and parents.

To achieve these objectives, we carefully selected articles from a variety of sources, including scholarly research journals and texts as well as semiprofessional journals and popular publications. Every selection was scrutinized for readability, interest level, relevance, and currency. In addition, we listened to the valuable input and advice from members of our advisory board, consisting of faculty from a range of institutions of higher education, including community and liberal arts colleges as well as research and teaching universities. We are most grateful to the advisory board as well as to the excellent editorial staff of Dushkin/McGraw-Hill Publishers.

Annual Editions: Child Growth and Development 99/00 is organized into five major units. Unit 1 focuses on conception, prenatal development, and childbirth. Unit 2 presents information regarding developments in cognition, language, and learning. Unit 3 focuses on social and emotional development. Unit 4 is devoted to parenting and family issues such as child care issues, divorce and marital transitions, and parenting and discipline. Finally, unit 5 focuses on larger cultural and societal influences (such as the influence of popular culture and violent media on children, after-school care, and international child labor) and on special challenges (such as poverty, childhood victimization and abuse, resilience, and children with attention deficits).

Instructors for large lecture courses may wish to adopt this anthology as a supplement to a basic text, whereas instructors for smaller sections might also find the readings effective for promoting student presentations or for stimulating discussions and applications. Whatever format is utilized, it is our hope that the instructor and the students will find the readings interesting, illuminating, and provocative.

As the title indicates, *Annual Editions: Child Growth and Development* is by definition a volume that undergoes continual review and revision. Thus, we welcome and encourage your comments and suggestions for future editions of this volume. Simply fill out and return the comment card found at the end of this book. Best wishes, and we look forward to hearing from you!

Ellen N. Junn

Chris J. Boyatzis
Editors

Contents

UNIT 1

Conception to Birth

Four articles discuss the development of the child from
the prenatal stage to birth.

The concepts in bold italics are developed in the article. For further expansion please refer to the Topic Guide and the Index.

UNIT 2

Cognition, Language, and Learning

Eight selections consider the growth of children's cognitive and language abilities and their experiences in the learning process in school.

The concepts in bold italics are developed in the article. For further expansion please refer to the Topic Guide and the Index.

UNIT 3

Social and Emotional Development

Seven articles follow a child's emotional development into the larger social world.

The concepts in bold italics are developed in the article. For further expansion please refer to the Topic Guide and the Index.

UNIT 4

Parenting and
Family Issues

Five articles assess the latest
implications of child development
with regard to attachment, marital
transitions, day care, and discipline.

The concepts in bold italics are developed in the article. For further expansion please refer to the Topic Guide and the Index.

UNIT 5

Cultural and Societal Influences

Eight selections examine the impact that society and culture have on the development of the child.

The concepts in bold italics are developed in the article. For further expansion please refer to the Topic Guide and the Index.

The concepts in bold italics are developed in the article. For further expansion please refer to the Topic Guide and the Index.

Topic Guide

This topic guide suggests how the selections and World Wide Web sites found in the next section of this book relate to topics of traditional concern to child growth & development students and professionals. It is useful for locating interrelated articles and Web sites for reading and research. The guide is arranged alphabetically according to topic.

The relevant Web sites, which are numbered and annotated on pages 4 and 5, are easily identified by the Web icon (◎) under the topic articles. By linking the articles and the Web sites by topic, this ANNUAL EDITIONS reader becomes a powerful learning and research tool.

TOPIC AREA	TREATED IN	TOPIC AREA	TREATED IN
Aggression/ Violence	1. Politics of Biology 17. Children without Friends 18. Teacher Response to Superhero Play 23. When to Spank 24. Boys Will Be Boys 28. Of Power Rangers and V-Chips 30. Victimization of Children ◎ *4, 14, 18, 19, 24, 27, 32*	**Developmental Disabilities and Challenges**	7. Genetics of Cognitive Abilities and Disabilities 32. Boy without a Penis ◎ *13, 30*
		Discipline	23. When to Spank
Attachment	15. How Kids Mourn 21. Problem with Day Care 22. What Matters? What Does Not? ◎ *17, 20, 22, 23, 24, 25*	**Divorce/ Adoption/ Stepparents**	22. What Matters? What Does Not? ◎ *19, 20, 22, 23, 24, 25, 26*
Attention Deficit/Hyperac-tivity Disorder	7. Genetics of Cognitive Abilities and Disabilities ◎ *13*	**Drug Abuse**	1. Politics of Biology 4. Hope for 'Snow Babies' ◎ *3, 4, 19, 27*
Birth and Birth Defects/ Reproduction/ Teratogens	2. Multiplying the Risks 3. Putting a New Spin on the Birth of Human Birth 4. Hope for 'Snow Babies' 20. Why Johnny Can't Sleep 32. Boy without a Penis ◎ *5, 7, 19, 22*	**Economic Issues/Poverty**	27. Child Labor in Pakistan 29. Effects of Poverty on Children ◎ *11, 28, 29, 31*
Brain and Physical Development	3. Putting a New Spin on the Birth of Human Birth 4. Hope for 'Snow Babies' 5. Fertile Minds 6. How to Build a Baby's Brain 13. Early Experience and Emotional Development ◎ *5, 7, 13, 15, 18*	**Emotional Development**	1. Politics of Biology 4. Hope for 'Snow Babies' 11. What Have We Learned about Developmentally Appropriate Practice? 13. Early Experience and Emotional Development 15. How Kids Mourn 16. EQ Factor 17. Children without Friends 20. Why Johnny Can't Sleep 22. What Matters? What Does Not? 23. When to Spank 31. Resilience in Development ◎ *4, 6, 14, 15, 16, 17, 18, 19, 21, 24, 25, 26*
Child Abuse	4. Hope for 'Snow Babies' 5. Fertile Minds 23. When to Spank 30. Victimization of Children ◎ *7, 9, 11, 13*		
Cognitive Development	4. Hope for 'Snow Babies' 6. How to Build a Baby's Brain 7. Genetics of Cognitive Abilities and Disabilities 9. How Do Infants Learn about the Physical World? 10. Categories in Young Children's Thinking 11. What Have We Learned about Developmentally Appropriate Practice? 12. How Asian Teachers Polish Each Lesson to Perfection ◎ *7, 9, 10, 11, 13*	**Family/ Parenting**	11. What Have We Learned about Developmentally Appropriate Practice? 15. How Kids Mourn 21. Problem with Day Care 22. What Matters? What Does Not? 23. When to Spank 24. Boys Will Be Boys 25. Buried Alive 26. It's 4:00 p.m. Do You Know Where Your Children Are? 28. Of Power Rangers and V-Chips 30. Victimization of Children 31. Resilience in Development ◎ *19, 20, 21, 22, 23, 24, 25, 26*
Creativity	25. Buried Alive	**Gender Issues/Sexual Orientation**	1. Politics of Biology 19. Girls and Boys Together . . . but Mostly Apart 32. Boy without a Penis ◎ *7, 19, 23*
Cross-Cultural Issues	12. How Asian Teachers Polish Each Lesson to Perfection 27. Child Labor in Pakistan ◎ *31*	**High-Risk Infants/Children**	4. Hope for 'Snow Babies' 7. Genetics of Cognitive Abilities and Disabilities 17. Children without Friends

DUSHKIN ONLINE

● AE: Child Growth and Development

The following World Wide Web sites have been carefully researched and selected to support the articles found in this reader. If you are interested in learning more about specific topics found in this book, these Web sites are a good place to start. The sites are cross-referenced by number and appear in the topic guide on the previous two pages. Also, you can link to these Web sites through our DUSHKIN ONLINE support site at *http://www.dushkin.com/online/*.

The following sites were available at the time of publication. Visit our Web site—we update DUSHKIN ONLINE regularly to reflect any changes.

General Sources

1. American Academy of Pediatrics
http://www.aap.org/
This organization provides data for optimal physical, mental, and social health for all children.

2. CYFERNet
http://www.cyfernet.mes.umn.edu/
The Children, Youth, and Families Education Research Network is sponsored by the Cooperative Extension Service and USDA's Cooperative State Research Education and Extension Service. This site provides practical research-based information in areas including health, child care, family strengths, science, and technology

3. KidsHealth at the AMA
http://www.ama-assn.org/KidsHealth/
This site was developed to help parents find reliable children's health information. Click on the topic bars: Baby's Development, Nutrition, Pediatric News, Safety and Accident Prevention, and Childhood Infections.

4. National Institute of Child Health and Human Development
http://www.nih.gov/nichd/home2_home.html
The NICHD conducts and supports research on the reproductive, neurobiological, developmental, and behavioral processes that determine and maintain the health of children, adults, families, and populations.

Conception to Birth

5. Babyworld
http://www.babyworld.com/
Extensive information on caring for infants can be found at this site. There are also links to numerous other related sites.

6. Children's Nutrition Research Center (CNRC)
http://www.bcm.tmc.edu/cnrc/
CNRC, one of six USDA/ARS (Agricultural Research Service) facilities, is dedicated to defining the nutrient needs of healthy children, from conception through adolescence, and of pregnant and nursing mothers. The *Nutrition and Your Child* newsletter is of general interest and can be accessed from this site.

7. Zero to Three: National Center for Infants, Toddlers, and Families
http://www.zerotothree.org/
This national organization is dedicated solely to infants, toddlers, and their families. It is headed by recognized experts in the field and provides technical assistance to communities, states, and the federal government. The site provides information that the organization gathers and disseminates through its publications.

Cognition, Language, and Learning

8. Educational Resources Information Center (ERIC)
http://www.ed.gov/pubs/pubdb.html
This Web site is sponsored by the U.S. Department of Education and will lead to numerous documents related to elementary and early childhood education, as well as other curriculum topics and issues.

9. I Am Your Child
http://iamyourchild.org/
Information regarding early childhood development is provided on this site. Resources for parents and caregivers are provided.

10. National Association for the Education of Young Children (NAEYC)
http://www.naeyc.org/
The National Association for the Education of Young Children provides a useful link from its home page to a "parent information" site.

11. Results of NICHD Study of Early Child Care
http://www.nih.gov/nichd/html/news/rel4top.htm
This study indicates that the quality of child care for very young children does matter for their cognitive development and their use of language. Quality child care also leads to better mother-child interaction, the study finds.

12. Vandergrift's Children's Literature Page
http://www.scils.rutgers.edu/special/kay/childlit.html
This site provides information about children's literature and links to a variety of resources related to literacy for children.

13. Project Zero
http://pzweb.harvard.edu/
Harvard Project Zero, a research group at the Harvard Graduate School of Education, has investigated the development of learning processes in children and adults for 30 years. Today, Project Zero is building on this research to help create communities of reflective, independent learners; to enhance deep understanding within disciplines; and to promote critical and creative thinking. Project Zero's mission is to understand and enhance learning, thinking, and creativity in the arts and other disciplines for individuals and institutions.

Social and Emotional Development

14. Counseling for Children
http://montgomery-al.com/cfc/
This site discusses parents' questions about child counseling: What children would benefit? How is counseling of children different from that of adults? What about testing? It also offers a toy guide, homework hints, how to foster creativity, and a discussion of the power of play.

15. Help Children Work with Feelings
http://www.aha4kids.com/index.html
New multimedia materials that deal with emotional intelligence are available at this Web site.

16. Max Planck Institute for Psychological Research
http://www.mpipf-muenchen.mpg.de/BCD/bcd_e.htm
Several behavioral and cognitive development research projects are available on this site.

17. National Child Care Information Center (NCCIC)
http://www.nccic.org/
Information about a variety of topics related to child care and development is available on this site. Links to the *Child Care Bulletin*, which can be read online, and to the ERIC database of online and library-based resources are available.

18. Serendip
http://serendip.brynmawr.edu/serendip/
Organized into five subject areas (brain and behavior, complex systems, genes and behavior, science and culture, and science education), Serendip contains interactive exhibits, articles, links to other resources, and a forum area for comments and discussion.

Parenting and Family Issues

19. Facts for Families
http://www.aacap.org/web/aacap/factsFam/
The American Academy of Child and Adolescent Psychiatry here provides concise, up-to-date information on issues that affect teenagers and their families. Fifty-six fact sheets include issues concerning teenagers, such as coping with life, sad feelings, inability to sleep, getting involved with drugs, or not getting along with family and friends.

20. Families and Work Institute
http://www.familiesandworkinst.org/
Resources from the Families and Work Institute, which conducts policy research on issues related to the changing workforce and operates a national clearinghouse on work and family life, are provided.

21. The National Academy for Child Development
http://www.nacd.org/
This international organization is dedicated to helping children and adults reach their full potential. Its home page presents links to various programs, research, and resources in topics related to the family and society.

22. National Council on Family Relations
http://www.ncfr.com/
This NCFR home page will lead you to articles, research, and a lot of other resources on important issues in family relations, such as stepfamilies, couples, and divorce.

23. The National Parent Information Network (NPIN)
http://ericps.ed.uiuc.edu/npin/
The National Parent Information Network contains resources related to many of the controversial issues faced by parents raising children in contemporary society. In addition to articles and resources, discussion groups are also available.

24. Parenting and Families
http://www.cyfc.umn.edu/Parenting/parentlink.html
The University of Minnesota's Children, Youth, and Family Consortium site will lead you to many organizations and other resources related to divorce, single parenting, and stepfamilies, as well as information about other topics of interest in the study of children's development and the family.

25. Parentsplace.com: Single Parenting
http://www.parentsplace.com/family/singleparent/
This resource focuses on issues concerning single parents and their children. Although the articles range from parenting children from infancy through adolescence, most of the articles deal with middle childhood.

26. Stepfamily Association of America
http://www.stepfam.org/
This Web site is dedicated to educating and supporting stepfamilies and to creating a positive family image.

Cultural and Societal Influences

27. Ask NOAH About: Mental Health
http://www.noah.cuny.edu/illness/mentalhealth/mental.html
This enormous resource contains information about child and adolescent family problems, mental conditions and disorders, suicide prevention, and much more, all organized in a "clickable" outline form.

28. Association to Benefit Children (ABC)
http://www.a-b-c.org/
ABC presents a network of programs that includes child advocacy, education for disabled children, care for HIV-positive children, employment, housing, foster care, and day care.

29. Children Now
http://www.childrennow.org/
Children Now focuses on improving conditions for children who are poor or at risk. Articles include information on education, influence of media, health, and security.

30. Council for Exceptional Children
http://www.cec.sped.org/
This is the home page for the Council for Exceptional Children, a large professional organization that is dedicated to improving education for children with exceptionalities, students with disabilities, and/or the gifted child. It leads to the ERIC Clearinghouse on disabilities and gifted education and the National Clearinghouse for Professions in Special Education.

31. National Black Child Development Institute
http://www.nbcdi.org
Resources for improving the quality of life for African American children through public education programs are provided.

32. National Committee to Prevent Child Abuse (NCPCA)
http://www.childabuse.org/
Dedicated to their child abuse prevention efforts, the NCPCA provides statistics, parenting tips, chapter data, and other resources at this site.

We highly recommend that you review our Web site for expanded information and our other product lines. We are continually updating and adding links to our Web site in order to offer you the most usable and useful information that will support and expand the value of your Annual Editions. You can reach us at: *http://www.dushkin.com/annualeditions/*.

Unit 1

Key Points to Consider

❖ Where do you stand on the nature/nurture issue? Does it comfort you—or unsettle you—to know that the genes you inherited influence your mental health or sexual orientation, and so on? Given the information in the article "Politics of Biology," how would you respond to someone who claimed that a person's mental health or sexual orientation is "determined" by their genes?

❖ How would you balance the personal wish for a child and the expense and ethical complications of available reproductive technology? Assuming that new procedures continue to be developed, what options might be available to parents in the future?

 **Links**   **www.dushkin.com/online/**

These sites are annotated on pages 4 and 5.

6

Our understanding of conception and prenatal development is not what it used to be. We are now witness to dramatic changes in reproductive technology. Advances in this new "prenatal science" include fertility treatments for couples who have difficulty conceiving and a host of prenatal diagnostic tests, such as amniocentesis and alpha-fetoprotein testing, which assess the well-being of the fetus as well as detect genetic or chromosomal problems. These technological developments result in both benefits and risks that are discussed in the article "Multiplying the Risks."

Perhaps the oldest debate in the study of human development is the "nature versus nurture" question. Scientists have moved beyond thinking of development as due to either genetics *or* environment, now recognizing that nature *and* nurture interact to shape us. Each human is a biological organism, and each is surrounded, from the moment of conception, by environmental forces. According to "Politics of Biology," recent research highlights the contributions of genes and experience in influencing mental illness, violence, sexual orientation, and alcoholism. This selection is especially valuable because it helps the reader appreciate that findings from the nature/nurture debate both contribute to and reflect the trends of broader societal values and may in turn have ethical, political, legal, and societal consequences.

Students of child development should realize that the classic nature/nurture controversy applies as much to prenatal development as to other stages of childhood. While prenatal development is largely the result of the unfolding of an individual's genetic blueprint, the fetus is also in an environment within the mother's womb. Hence, the fetus is vulnerable to teratogens, hazards from the environment that interfere with normal prenatal development. We are learning more about potential harm to the developing fetus due to increasing rates of maternal use of illegal drugs. For example, the Effects of prenatal exposure to cocaine on babies is discussed in "Hope for 'Snow Babies.'"

Our notions of childbirth have themselves evolved throughout history. "Putting a New Spin on the Birth of Human Birth" provides readers with an anthropological perspective on the possible evolutionary significance of human birth and its relation to neonate head size and development.

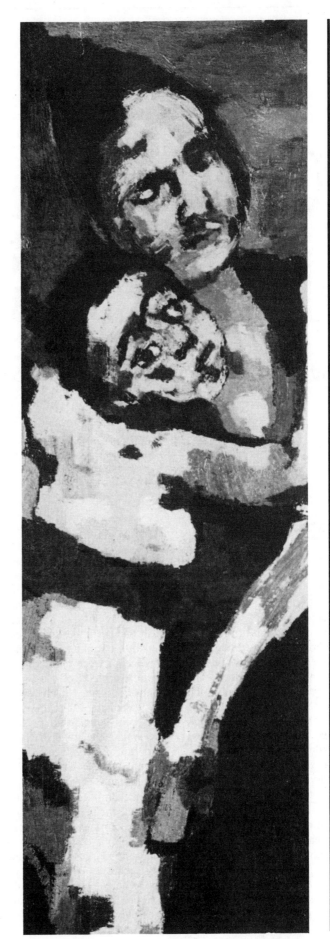

Conception to Birth

POLITICS OF BIOLOGY

How the nature vs. nurture debate shapes
public policy—and our view of ourselves

BY WRAY HERBERT

Laurie Flynn uses the technology of neuroscience to light up the brains of Washington lawmakers. As executive director of the National Alliance for the Mentally Ill, she marshals everything from cost analysis to moral pleading to make the case for laws banning discrimination against people with mental illness. But her most powerful advocacy tool by far is the PET scan. She takes a collection of these colorful brain images up to Capitol Hill to put on a show, giving lawmakers a window on a "broken" brain in action. "When they see that it's not some imaginary, fuzzy problem, but a real physical condition, then they get it: 'Oh, it's in the brain'."

The view of mental illness as a brain disease has been crucial to the effort to destigmatize illnesses such as schizophrenia and depression. But it's just one example of a much broader biologizing of American culture that's been going on for more than a decade. For both political and scientific reasons—and it's often impossible to disentangle the two—everything from criminality to addictive disorders to sexual orientation is seen today less as a matter of choice than of genetic destiny. Even basic personality is looking more and more like a genetic legacy. Nearly every week there is a report of a new gene for one trait or another. Novelty seeking, religiosity, shyness, the tendency to divorce, and even happiness (or the lack of it) are among the traits that may result in part from a gene, according to new research.

This cultural shift has political and personal implications. On the personal level, a belief in the power of genes necessarily diminishes the potency of such personal qualities as will, capacity to choose, and sense of responsibility for those choices—if it's in your genes, you're not accountable. It allows the alcoholic, for example, to treat himself as a helpless victim of his biology rather than as a willful agent with control of his own behavior. Genetic determinism can free victims and their families of guilt—or lock them in their suffering.

On the political level, biological determinism now colors all sorts of public-policy debates on issues such as gay rights, health care, juvenile justice, and welfare reform. The effort to dismantle social programs is fueled by the belief that government interventions (the nurturing side in the nature-nurture debate) don't work very well—and the corollary idea that society can't make up for every unfortunate citizen's bad luck. It's probably no coincidence that the biologizing of culture has accompanied the country's shift to the political right, since conservatives traditionally are more dubious about human perfectability than are liberals. As Northeastern University psychologist Leon Kamin notes, the simplest way to discover someone's political leanings is to ask his or her view on genetics.

 From *U.S. News & World Report*, April 21, 1997, pp. 72-80. © 1997 by U.S. News & World Report. Reprinted by permission.

Even so, genetic determinism can have paradoxical consequences at times, leading to disdain rather than sympathy for the disadvantaged, and marginalization rather than inclusion. Cultural critics are beginning to sort out the unpredictable politics of biology, focusing on four traits: violence, mental illness, alcoholism, and sexual orientation.

The nature of violence. To get a sense of just how thorough—and how politicized—the biologizing of culture has been, just look at the issue of urban gang violence as it is framed today. A few years ago, Frederick Goodwin, then director of the government's top mental health agency, was orchestrating the so-called Federal Violence Initiative to identify inner-city kids at biological risk for criminal violence, with the goal of intervening with drug treatments for what are presumed to be nervous-system aberrations. Goodwin got himself fired for comparing aggressive young males with primates in the jungle, and the violence initiative died in the resulting furor. But even to be proposing such a biomedical approach to criminal justice shows how far the intellectual pendulum has swung toward biology.

The eugenics movement of the 1930s was fueled at least in part by a desire to get rid of habitual criminals, and many attempts have been made over the years to identify genetic roots for aggression, violence, and criminality. A

As with many psychopathologies, criminal aggression is difficult to define precisely for research. Indeed, crime and alcohol abuse are so entangled that it's often difficult to know whether genetic markers are associated with drinking, criminality—or something else entirely, like a personality trait. A 1993 National Research Council study, for example, reported strong evidence of genetic influence on antisocial personality disorder, but it also noted that many genes are probably involved. Getting from those unknown genes to an actual act of vandalism or assault—or a life of barbaric violence—requires at this point a monstrous leap of faith.

Yet it's a leap that many are willing to make. When geneticist Xandra Breakefield reported a possible genetic link to violent crime a few years ago, she immediately started receiving phone inquiries from attorneys representing clients in prison; they were hoping that such genetic findings might absolve their clients of culpability for their acts.

Mutations and emotions. Just two decades ago, the National Institute of Mental Health was funding studies of economic recession, unemployment, and urban ills as possible contributors to serious emotional disturbance. A whole branch of psychiatry known as "social psychiatry" was dedicated to helping the mentally ill by rooting out such pathogens as poverty and racism. There is no

tating emotional and mental disorder was caused by cold and distant mothering, itself the result of the mother's unconscious wish that her child had never been born. A nationwide lobbying effort was launched to combat such unfounded mother blaming, and 20 years later that artifact of the Freudian era is entirely discredited. It's widely accepted today that psychotic disorders are brain disorders, probably with genetic roots.

But this neurogenetic victory may be double edged. For example, family and consumer groups have argued convincingly that schizophrenia is a brain disease like epilepsy, one piece of evidence being that it is treatable with powerful antipsychotic drugs. Managed-care companies, however, have seized upon the disease model, and now will rarely authorize anything but drug treatment; it's efficient, and justified by the arguments of biological psychiatry. The American Psychiatric Association just this month issued elaborate guidelines for treating schizophrenia, including not only drugs but an array of psychosocial services—services the insurance industry is highly unlikely to pay for.

The search for genes for severe mental disorders has been inconclusive. Years of studies of families, adoptees, and twins separated at birth suggest that both schizophrenia and manic-depressive illness run in families. But if that family pattern is the result of genes, it's

VIOLENCE. How can an act of vandalism or a bank robbery be rooted in DNA? There are a lot of choices involved in living a life of crime.

1965 study, for instance, found that imprisoned criminals were more likely than other people to have an extra Y chromosome (and therefore more male genes). The evidence linking this chromosomal aberration to crime was skimpy and tenuous, but politics often runs ahead of the evidence: Soon after, a Boston hospital actually started screening babies for the defect, the idea being to intervene early with counseling should personality problems become apparent. The screening was halted when further study showed that XYY men, while slightly less intelligent, were not unusually aggressive.

longer much evidence of these sensibilities at work today. NIMH now focuses its studies almost exclusively on brain research and on the genetic underpinnings of emotional illnesses.

The decision to reorder the federal research portfolio was both scientific and political. Major advances in neuroscience methods opened up research that wasn't possible a generation ago, and that research has paid off in drugs that very effectively treat some disorders. But there was also a concerted political campaign to reinterpret mental illness. A generation ago, the leading theory about schizophrenia was that this devas-

clearly very complicated, because most of the siblings of schizophrenics (including half of identical twins, who have the same genes) don't develop the disorder. Behavioral geneticists suspect that several genes may underlie the illness, and that some environmental stress—perhaps a virus or birth complications—also might be required to trigger the disorder.

On several occasions in the past, researchers have reported "linkages" between serious mental illness and a particular stretch of DNA. A well-known study of the Amish, for example, claimed a link between manic-depression and an aberration on chromosome 11. But none of these findings has held up when other researchers attempted to replicate them.

Even if one accepts that there are genetic roots for serious delusional illnesses, critics are concerned about the biologizing of the rest of psychiatric illness. Therapists report that patients come in asking for drugs, claiming to be victims of unfortunate biology. In one case, a patient claimed he could "feel his neurons misfiring"; it's an impossibility, but the anecdote speaks to the thorough saturation of the culture with biology.

Some psychiatrists are pulling back from the strict biological model of mental illness. Psychiatrist Keith Russell Ablow has reintroduced the idea of "character" into his practice, telling depressed patients that they have the responsibility and capacity to pull themselves out of their illness. Weakness of character, as Ablow sees it, allows mental illness to grow. Such sentiment is highly controversial within psychiatry, where to suggest that patients might be responsible for some of their own suffering is taboo.

Besotted genes. The best that can be said about research on the genetics of alcoholism is that it's inconclusive, but that hasn't stopped people from using genetic arguments for political purposes. The disease model for alcoholism is practically a secular religion in this

ently; or they may have inherited a certain personality type that's prone to risk-taking or stimulus-seeking. While studies of family pedigrees and adoptees have on occasion indicated a familial pattern for a particular form of alcoholism (early-onset disorder in men, for example), just as often they reveal no pattern. This shouldn't be all that surprising, given the difficulty of defining alcoholism. Some researchers identify alcoholics by their drunk-driving record, while others focus on withdrawal symptoms or daily consumption. This is what geneticists call a "dirty phenotype"; people drink too much in so many different ways that the trait itself is hard to define, so family patterns are all over the place, and often contradictory.

Given these methodological problems, researchers have been trying to locate an actual gene (or genes) that might be involved in alcoholism. A 1990 study reported that a severe form of the disorder (most of the subjects in the study had cirrhosis of the liver) was linked to a gene that codes for a chemical receptor for the neurotransmitter dopamine. The researchers even developed and patented a test for the genetic mutation, but subsequent attempts to confirm the dopamine connection have failed.

The issues of choice and responsibility come up again and again in discussions of alcoholism and other addictive

character flaw, many are concerned that the widely accepted disease model of alcoholism actually provides people with an excuse for their destructive behavior. As psychologist Stanton Peele argues: "Indoctrinating young people with the view that they are likely to become alcoholics may take them there more quickly than any inherited reaction to alcohol would have."

Synapses of desire. It would be a mistake to focus only on biological explanations of psychopathology; the cultural shift is much broader than that. A generation ago, the gay community was at war with organized psychiatry, arguing (successfully) that sexual orientation was a lifestyle choice and ought to be deleted from the manual of disorders. Recently the same community was celebrating new evidence that homosexuality is a biological (and perhaps genetic) trait, not a choice at all.

Three lines of evidence support the idea of a genetic basis for homosexuality, none of them conclusive. A study of twins and adopted siblings found that about half of identical twins of homosexual men were themselves gay, compared with 22 percent of fraternal twins and 11 percent of adoptees; a similar pattern was found among women. While such a pattern is consistent with some kind of genetic loading for sexual orientation, critics contend it also could be explained by the very similar experi-

MENTAL ILLNESS. Are psychiatric disorders diseases? The answer influences everything from insurance coverage to new research funding.

country, embraced by psychiatry, most treatment clinics, and (perhaps most important) by Alcoholics Anonymous. What this means is that those seeking help for excessive drinking are told they have a disease (though the exact nature of the disease is unknown), that it's probably a genetic condition, and that the only treatment is abstinence.

But the evidence is not strong enough to support these claims. There are several theories of how genes might lead to excessive drinking. A genetic insensitivity to alcohol, for example, might cause certain people to drink more; or alcoholics might metabolize alcohol differ-

disorders. Even if scientists were to identify a gene (or genes) that create a susceptibility to alcoholism, it's hard to know what this genetic "loading" would mean. It certainly wouldn't lead to alcoholism in a culture that didn't condone drinking—among the Amish, for example—so it's not deterministic in a strict sense. Even in a culture where drinking is common, there are clearly a lot of complicated choices involved in living an alcoholic life; it's difficult to make the leap from DNA to those choices. While few would want to return to the time when heavy drinking was condemned as strictly a moral failing or

ences many twins share. And, of course, half the identical twins did not become gay—which by definition means something other than genes must be involved.

A well-publicized 1991 study reported a distinctive anatomical feature in gay men. Simon LeVay autopsied the brains of homosexual men and heterosexual men and women and found that a certain nucleus in the hypothalamus was more than twice as large in heterosexual men as in gay men or heterosexual women. Although LeVay couldn't explain how this neurological difference might translate into homosexuality, he speculates that the nucleus is somehow related to sexual orientation. The hypothalamus is known to be involved in sexual response.

The only study so far to report an actual genetic connection to homosexuality is a 1993 study by Dean Hamer, a National Institutes of Health biologist who identified a genetic marker on the X chromosome in 75 percent of gay brothers. The functional significance of this piece of DNA is unknown, and subsequent research has not succeeded in duplicating Hamer's results.

Homosexuality represents a bit of a paradox when it comes to the intertwined issues of choice and determinism. When Hamer reported his genetic findings, many in the gay community celebrated, believing that society would be more tolerant of behavior rooted in biology and DNA rather than choice. LeVay, himself openly gay, says he undertook his research with the explicit agenda of furthering the gay cause. And Hamer testified as an expert witness in an important gay-rights case in Colorado where, in a strange twist, liberals found themselves arguing the deterministic position, while conservatives insisted that homosexuality is a choice. The argument of gay-rights advocates was that biological status conveyed legal status—and protection under the law.

History's warning. But history suggests otherwise, according to biologist and historian Garland Allen. During the

blemindedness," pauperism, and mental illness. The ultimate outcome of the eugenics craze in Europe is well known; homosexuals were not given extra sympathy or protection in the Third Reich's passion to purify genetic stock.

Allen is concerned about the possibility of a "new eugenics" movement, though he notes that it wouldn't be called that or take the same form. It would more likely take the form of rationing health care for the unfortunate. The economic and social conditions today resemble conditions that provided fertile ground for eugenics between the wars, he argues; moreover, in Allen's view, California's Proposition 187 recalls the keen competition for limited resources (and the resulting animosity toward immigrants) of the '20s. Further, Allen is quick to remind us that eugenics was not a marginal, bigoted movement in either Europe or the United States; it was a Progressive program, designed to harness science in the service of reducing suffering and misfortune and to help make society more efficient.

These concerns are probably justified, but there are also some signs that we may be on the crest of another important cultural shift. More and more experts, including dedicated biologists, sense that the power of genetics has been oversold and that a correction is needed. What's more, there's a glimmer of evidence that the typical American

no role whatsoever in homosexuality, and a similar percentage think heredity is irrelevant to drug addiction and criminality. Across the board, most believe that people's lives are shaped by the choices they make.

These numbers can be interpreted in different ways. It may be that neurogenetic determinism has become the "religion of the intellectual class," as one critic argues, but that it never really caught the imagination of the typical American. Or we may be witnessing a kind of cultural self-correction, in which after a period of infatuation with neuroscience and genetics the public is becoming disenchanted, or perhaps even anxious about the kinds of social control that critics describe.

Whatever's going on, it's clear that this new mistrust of genetic power is consonant with what science is now beginning to show. Indeed, the very expression "gene for" is misleading, according to philosopher Philip Kitcher, author of *The Lives to Come.* Kitcher critiques what he calls "gene talk," a simplistic shorthand for talking about genetic advances that has led to the widespread misunderstanding of DNA's real powers. He suggests that public discourse may need to include more scientific jargon—not a lot, but some—so as not to oversimplify the complexity of the gene-environment interaction. For example, when geneticists say they've

ALCOHOLISM. Heredity might be involved in some kinds of alcoholism. But no gene can make you buy a bottle of Scotch, pour a glass, and toss it down.

eugenics movement of the 1920s and 1930s, both in the United States and Europe, society became less, not more, tolerant of human variation and misfortune. Based on racial theories that held Eastern Europeans to be genetically inferior to Anglo-Saxon stock, Congress passed (and Calvin Coolidge signed) a 1924 law to restrict immigration, and by 1940 more than 30 states had laws permitting forced sterilization of people suffering from such conditions as "fee-

may not be buying it entirely. According to a recent *US. News*/Bozell poll, less than 1 American in 5 believes that genes play a major role in controlling behavior; three quarters cite environment and society as the more powerful shapers of our lives. Whether the behavior under question is a disorder like addiction, mental illness, or violence, or a trait like homosexuality, most believe that heredity plays some role, but not a primary one. Indeed, 40 percent think genes play

found a gene for a particular trait, what they mean is that people carrying a certain "allele"—a variation in a stretch of DNA that normally codes for a certain protein—will develop the given trait in a standard environment. The last few words—"in a standard environment"—are very important, because what scientists are *not saying* is that a given allele will necessarily lead to that trait in every environment. Indeed, there is mounting evidence that a particular allele will not

U.S. News/Bozell poll of 1,000 adults conducted by KRC Research Feb. 6–9, 1997. Margin of error: plus or minus 3.1 percent.

produce the same result if the environment changes significantly; that is to say, the environment has a strong influence on whether and how a gene gets "expressed."

It's hard to emphasize too much what a radical rethinking of the nature-nurture debate this represents. When most people think about heredity, they still think in terms of classical Mendelian genetics: one gene, one trait. But for most complex human behaviors, this is far from the reality that recent research is revealing. A more accurate view very likely involves many different genes, some of which control other genes, and many of which are controlled by signals from the environment. To complicate matters further, the environment is very complicated in itself, ranging from the things we typically lump under nurture (parenting, family dynamics, schooling, safe housing) to biological encounters like viruses and birth complications, even biochemical events within cells.

The relative contributions of genes and the environment are not additive, as in such-and-such a percentage of nature, such-and-such a percentage of experience; that's the old view, no longer credited. Nor is it true that full genetic expression happens once, around birth, after which we take our genetic legacy into the world to see how far it gets us. Genes produce proteins throughout the lifespan, in many different environ-

loading that gives some people a susceptibility—for schizophrenia, for instance, or for aggression. But the development of the behavior or pathology requires more, what National Institute of Mental Health Director Stephen Hyman calls an environmental "second hit." This second hit operates, counterintuitively, through the genes themselves to "sculpt" the brain. So with depression, for example, it appears as though a bad experience in the world—for example, a devastating loss—can actually create chemical changes in the body that affect certain genes, which in turn affect certain brain proteins that make a person more susceptible to depression in the future. Nature or nurture? Similarly, Hyman's own work has shown that exposure to addictive substances can lead to biochemical changes at the genetic and molecular levels that commandeer brain circuits involving volition—and thus undermine the very motivation needed to take charge of one's destructive behavior. So the choice to experiment with drugs or alcohol may, in certain people, create the biological substrate of the addictive disorder. The distinction between biology and experience begins to lose its edge.

Nurturing potentials. Just as bad experiences can turn on certain vulnerability genes, rich and challenging experiences have the power to enhance life, again acting through the genes.

chologist Urie Bronfenbrenner. Everything from lively conversation to games to the reading of stories can potentially get a gene to turn on and create a protein that may become a neuronal receptor or messenger chemical involved in thinking or mood. "No genetic potential can become reality," says Bronfenbrenner, "unless the relationship between the organism and its environment is such that it is *permitted* to be expressed." Unfortunately, as he details in his new book, *The State of Americans,* the circumstances in which many American children are living are becoming more impoverished year by year.

If there's a refrain among geneticists working today, it's this: The harder we work to demonstrate the power of heredity, the harder it is to escape the potency of experience. It's a bit paradoxical, because in a sense we end up once again with the old pre-1950s paradigm, but arrived at with infinitely more-sophisticated tools: Yes, the way to intervene in human lives and improve them, to ameliorate mental illness, addictions, and criminal behavior, is to enrich impoverished environments, to improve conditions in the family and society. What's changed is that the argument is coming not from left-leaning sociologists, but from those most intimate with the workings of the human genome. The goal of psychosocial interventions is optimal gene expression.

HOMOSEXUALITY. Gay-rights advocates once argued that homosexuality was a matter of lifestyle choice. Now they stress genes and destiny.

ments, or they don't produce those proteins, depending on how rich or harsh or impoverished those environments are. The interaction is so thoroughly dynamic and enduring that, as psychologist William Greenough says, "To ask what's more important, nature or nurture, is like asking what's more important to a rectangle, its length or its width."

The emerging view of nature-nurture is that many complicated behaviors probably have some measure of genetic

Greenough has shown in rat studies that by providing cages full of toys and complex structures that are continually rearranged—"the animal equivalent of Head Start"—he can increase the number of synapses in the rats brains by 25 percent and blood flow by 85 percent. Talent and intelligence appear extraordinarily malleable.

Child-development experts refer to the life circumstances that enhance (or undermine) gene expression as "proximal processes" a term coined by psy-

So assume for a minute that there is a cluster of genes somehow associated with youthful violence. The kid who carries those genes might inhabit a world of loving parents, regular nutritious meals, lots of books, safe schools. Or his world might be a world of peeling paint and gunshots around the corner. In which environment would those genes be likely to manufacture the biochemical underpinnings of criminality? Or for that matter, the proteins and synapses of happiness?

Multiplying the Risks

More group births mean more preemies and, often, more problems

BOBBI AND KENNY MCCAUGHEY seem thrilled to have seven new babies in tow, and last week's headlines show the world is happy for them. But amid the hoopla, it's worth keeping in mind that multiple birth is rarely a joyous accident. It's a growing health crisis. Driven by the aggressive use of fertility drugs and reproductive technology, the annual number of multiple births has quadrupled since the 1970s. The trouble is, kids born in groups are almost always born prematurely. And though intensive-care units can often keep them alive, the medical consequences can be devastating. As Dr. Peter Heyl of Eastern Virginia Medical School observes, "The human uterus is not meant to carry litters."

Under normal conditions, it almost never does. Women's hormonal rhythms are choreographed to ensure that the ovaries release one—and only one—fertile egg every month. Early in the menstrual cycle, a drop in circulating estrogen and progesterone prompts the body to release other hormones (GRF, FSH and LH). When stimulated by those hormones, egg-bearing sacs, or follicles, within the ovaries start to swell. After a week or so, a follicle will mature to the point where it's ready to release its egg into the fallopian tube for fertilization. But before doing that, it spurts estrogen into the bloodstream—shutting down the cascade of ovulation hormones and halting the growth of other follicles.

Fertility treatments can easily disrupt that arrangement. When supercharged by a drug like Pergonal or Metrodin (the treatment McCaughey received), a woman's ovaries can release as many as 40 eggs in one cycle. Doctors may extract them for in vitro fertilization (IVF) or leave them to be fertilized naturally. Though multiple births are rare under normal conditions, a third of all IVF pregnancies, and up to 20 percent of those achieved with fertility drugs, involve two or more babies.

That wouldn't be a problem if humans had the carrying capacity of, say, cats. But they don't. Women carrying multiple fetuses risk anemia, hypertension and labor complications that can require Caesarean delivery. And their babies are often born prematurely. On average, each additional fetus shortens the usual 40-week gestation period by three and one-half weeks. A pair of twins born at 36 weeks may do fine. But as the number of fetuses increases, the kids' gestation times and birth weights decline.

So do their health prospects. Even if they're born alive, triplets, quadruplets and quintuplets are 12 times more likely than other babies to die within a year. Many suffer from respiratory and digestive problems. They're also prone to a range of neurological disorders, including blindness, cerebral palsy and mental retardation. Until a fetus reaches about 36 weeks, its developing brain maintains a delicate cell factory known as the germinal matrix. The matrix normally finishes its job before a child is born. But if it's still active at the time of delivery, normal fluctuations in blood pressure can cause a hemorrhage that not only stalls neuron production but injures existing brain tissue. By selectively reducing the number of fetuses in a woman's womb—i.e., killing two of four quadruplets by lethal injection—a specialist can avert such problems. But couples can't always stomach that prospect, so doctors are often left struggling to postpone a dangerous delivery as long as possible.

These crises are not inevitable. After giving a woman fertility drugs, specialists can use imaging tests to monitor the behavior of her ovaries. If the tests show that numerous eggs have been released, the doctors can advise against sex or sperm injections and try a lower dose on the next cycle. And in newly adopted guidelines, the American Society for Reproductive Medicine agrees that IVF specialists should limit the number of viable embryos they place in patients' wombs. But fertility clinics are unregulated, and as long as their clients demand success at any cost, the boom in multiple births is likely to continue. Would-be parents should realize that more is not always merrier.

GEOFFREY COWLEY *and* KAREN SPRINGEN

When Fertility Drugs Work Too Well

Women's hormonal rhythms normally ensure production of just one viable egg every month. By forcing the release of numerous eggs at once, fertility drugs raise the chance of multiple birth.

The Normal Ovary

Under ordinary conditions, an ovary is the size of a grape. Inside there are fluid-filled sacs called follicles, each housing an egg, or ovum. During normal ovulation, one follicle matures, releasing its egg for fertilization in the fallopian tube.

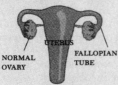

NORMAL OVARY · UTERUS · FALLOPIAN TUBE

The Ovary on Drugs

Fertility drugs jump-start follicle development, increasing the likelihood that more than one follicle will release a fertile egg. Drug treatment can make the ovaries swell up to 10 times their normal volume—roughly the size of a grapefruit.

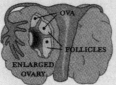

OVA · FOLLICLES · ENLARGED OVARY

Multiple Birth

The human uterus isn't designed to hold numerous fetuses. When it is forced to, the crowding causes early delivery. The consequences for babies can range from brain damage to death.

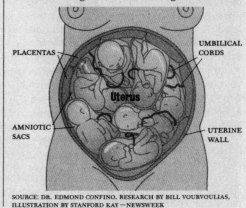

PLACENTAS · UMBILICAL CORDS · Uterus · AMNIOTIC SACS · UTERINE WALL

SOURCE: DR. EDMOND CONFINO. RESEARCH BY BILL VOURVOULIAS, ILLUSTRATION BY STANFORD KAY—NEWSWEEK

Putting a New Spin on the Birth of Human Birth

Humans do any number of things better than other animals, but giving birth is not one of them. Among the apes, our closest relatives, females bring infants into the world through a roomy birth canal with little fuss. In contrast, human babies often spend hours corkscrewing their way down a narrow birth canal, finally emerging head down, away from the mother—the only primates to do so. That makes human birth a risky business. Because babies don't bend backward, mothers can't pull them out without risk of serious injury, nor can they clear their newborns' airways if they are in trouble. Says University of Delaware anthropologist Karen Rosenberg wryly, "it's not the type of system you would invent if you were designing it today."

The process wasn't invented today, of course; it evolved over millions of years. But exactly when and how it did so has for decades perplexed anthropologists, who lacked **the fossil evidence that could answer those questions. Over the past 8 years, however, they have been able to reconstruct a few bones associated with the birth canal from human ancestors dating as far back as 3 million years. At a symposium at last month's meeting of the American Association of Physical Anthropologists in Denver, researchers used those bones to begin tracing the evolution of human birth.**

Those reconstructed bones, however, haven't given birth to a single scenario. In fact, they've produced a pair of decidedly nonidentical twins: Some researchers at the symposium presented new evidence that modern birth developed only very recently in our evolutionary history, while others countered with an intriguing speculation that it developed very early on.

Resolving this "when" question is important, says Wenda Trevathan, an anthropologist at New Mexico State University in Las Cruces, because of the insights it can produce about the social abilities of the creatures who evolved into human beings. "Human birth is so painful and risky," explains Trevathan, whose analysis puts her into the early camp, "that mothers need help from others to deliver a baby successfully." As a result, its development created a powerful selective force for empathy, communication, and cooperation—skills important to being human. And when those traits emerged is another date that anthropologists would love to pin down.

One thing researchers do know is why modern birth gives women such a difficult turn. The human pelvis, which surrounds the birth canal, crimps that canal partway down. At the top, the canal is widest from side to side. The longest dimension of a baby's head is from the nose to the back of the skull, and so the baby enters the canal facing sideways. But lower down, the canal changes its shape so that the longest dimension is from front to back. As a result, the infant must rotate 90 degrees. And there's one more twist: The baby's head is broadest at the back, but the lower canal is a bit broader at the front. So the infant enters the world facing down.

Apes, which have small heads and relatively larger pelves, don't have to go through these gyrations. In 1960, anthropologist Sherwood Washburn of the University of California, Berkeley, speculated that humans took this turn for the worse because the lineage was caught in an "obstetrical dilemma." The pelvis narrowed in response to two-legged walking, since this helps center our legs under our bodies. But as babies' heads and brains started getting bigger, the fit became really tight. The theory seemed sound, but the first hard evidence of when and how the pelvic girdle changed didn't come until 1986.

That was the year Owen Lovejoy of Kent State University in Ohio and Robert Tague, now at Louisiana State University, reconstructed the pelves of two australopithecines (the oldest known nonape human forerunners), including one belonging to "Lucy," the famous 3-million-year-old fossil female. They found that the australopithecine pelvis had changed from an apelike pattern. The back, which supports most of the upper body, had moved closer to the hip joints, giving the pelvis the shape of an oval stretched from hip to hip. The change helped "to adjust posture in a biped," says Tague.

But it also had implications for how australopithecine babies were born. Unlike newborn apes, which can ride into the world facing up all the way, australopithecine babies had to face sideways, Tague and Lovejoy argued. Only then could the head pass through the birth canal.

In Denver, Chris Ruff of the Johns Hopkins University School of Medicine argued that's probably the way hominid babies came into the world until just a few hundred thousand years ago. He based this conclusion on an analysis of two different parts of the skeleton of early *Homo*, human ancestors who appeared at least 2 million years ago, and some of their successors. First, Ruff measured the curve of the iliac brim, a bony feature that forms part of the start of the birth canal, and extrapolated from it the overall shape of the birth canal opening in early *Homo*. He concluded that the canal of this ancestor was oval, much like its shape in australopithecines.

The second feature Ruff examined was related to the width at the lower end of the canal: the shape of the thigh bones just below where some muscles attach them to the side of the pelvis. Bones change shape in response to the force of muscle tugs. And Ruff noted that in nine early *Homo* specimens, ranging in age from 1.9 to 0.7 million years old, the thigh bone shapes indicated these muscles were pulling very hard. "They would only do that if the hip joints were wider apart" than in modern humans, Ruff says. The muscles pull to counterbalance the weight of the airborne hip and leg during a step; the farther away that hip is, the harder they have to pull. The wide pelvis implied by these muscle actions also implies a wide birth canal "broadened to fit the head sideways all the way down," Ruff says. In other words, no rotation.

In fact, he continues, there's no evidence that the lower pelvis changed much from the australopithecine pattern until the last few hundred thousand years, with early modern humans and the Neanderthals. By that time, average brain size had shot up from about 800 milliliters in early *Homo* to more than 1200 milliliters (modern human brains are about 1400 milliliters, though there is a huge range of variation). "The head had become a critical component" in birth, says Ruff. To let it through, the lower end of the bony birth canal had to enlarge. It couldn't get any wider from side to side than it already was, because that would splay the legs out, Ruff says, and so it elongated from front to back.

And that change meant that human infants had to spin as they traversed the canal, first facing sideways, then turning so that they emerge face down.

Aware of the fragmentary nature of the fossils that Ruff used, other researchers were reserved in their reactions, although many found the argument plausible. "This is a very creative approach, because there are so few [whole pelves]," says Tague. "And Ruff is always very thorough in his work." One who does disagree is Lovejoy, who, though he did not hear Ruff's talk, says that in general "there's too much slop in the relationship between the [top of the thigh bone] and the birth canal to draw a reliable conclusion."

Another demurral comes from Trevathan, though for different reasons: She thinks rotation may have arisen very early—even in the australopithecines. She pointed out that if australopithecine babies did face sideways as they came through the canal, the next part of their anatomy coming through would cause problems: the shoulders, which would stretch across the narrowest diameter of the oval. "The shoulders are rigid, and they'd get caught," she says. The best way out, Trevathan suggests, was a rotational birth. The anthropologist, who was trained as a midwife, points out that even in modern humans the shoulders are a problem, particularly in larger babies.

As with Ruff's work, this notion was greeted with caution, but not rejection. Anthropologist Alan Mann of the University of Pennsylvania noted that "Obstetricians have been telling me for years about the great difficulty in fitting the shoulders through," yet anthropologists seem to have left them out of the evolutionary picture. Rosenberg, who likes the idea, says, however, that "I worry a bit that we may be exaggerating the importance of the shoulders. I'm not saying it's wrong, but Wenda only suggested it was a real problem with big babies," and australopithecine babies could have been rather small. And Ruff simply suggests that the babies could have turned their necks, lining

their heads up with their shoulders and avoiding the problem altogether.

The time when this rotation entered the picture might seem like a detail, but anthropologists feel that it's a crucial one, because that's when mothers began to need outside help. "Chimps hide at the time of birth; humans do exactly the opposite and seek assistance," Rosenberg says. The pain and difficulty of labor put a premium on companionship, Trevathan contends; studies by Marshall Klaus at Children's Hospital in Oakland, California, have shown that the presence of a support person during labor reduces the rate of Caesarean sections and other birth complications. Since aid at birth increases the chance of reproductive success, traits that support this aid become products of natural selection. Emotional empathy, communication, and responsiveness all fall into this category. "Of course, birth isn't the only pressure for social relationships, but it's got to be an important one," Rosenberg says.

Mann adds that "if a female needs assistance, it means complex interaction between mother and assistant. If this was occurring in australopithecines, it would suggest they are more complicated than the field appears to view them at the moment—something more than simple apes." He has argued that australopithecine babies went through a prolonged period of dependence, and this too would put a premium on social cooperation. "Of course," Rosenberg notes, "if Wenda's idea isn't true, then it means that rotation and cooperation probably didn't arrive until much later."

How, then, can this timing issue be resolved? "I hate to say this, because anthropologists always say it," Rosenberg says, "but we need more fossils. We have two female australopithecines, and I'd like some female early *Homo* pelves as well." There are none at present, preventing scientists from getting a more direct look at the birth canal and all it entails. Researchers are waiting for that chance—expectantly.

—Joshua Fischman

Hope for 'Snow Babies'

A mother's cocaine use may not doom her child after all

BY SHARON BEGLEY

THE EPIDEMIC OF CRACK COCAINE HAD just hit the inner cities in the mid-1980s when pediatricians and hospital nursery workers began reporting truly harrowing observations: babies born to women who had used cocaine while pregnant were not like other infants. They were underweight. They trembled. As newborns they were as rigid as plastic dolls. They cried inconsolably, seeming to recoil from hugs or touches and startled at the slightest sound. As they approached school age, it seemed that many could not sit still or focus, even on activities they enjoyed. For schools and for society, warned the press and the legions of anti-drug crusaders, cocaine babies would be a lost generation.

Well, scientists have found this generation. The snow babies, it seems, are neither the emotional and cognitive cripples that many predicted—nor the perfectly normal kids that biological revisionists have lately been claiming. Last week, at a landmark conference in Washington convened by the New York Academy of Sciences, more than three dozen neurologists, pediatricians and other researchers presented studies suggesting that the effects of cocaine on a fetus are far from simple, let alone predictable. They depend not only on such obvious things as how much of the drug the mother took and when but also on what sort of environment the baby grows up in. Although studies on large numbers of school-age children are only beginning, research on toddlers suggests that "most cocaine-exposed children do very well," says Dr. Barry Kosofsky of Har-

vard Medical School, co-chair of the conference. "Cocaine is not a sledgehammer to the fetal brain."

But neither is it a prenatal vitamin. Experiments show that rats, rabbits and monkeys exposed to cocaine in utero are profoundly messed up. Their brains develop abnormally. Neurons are too long or too short. "Receptors" to which brain chemicals attach are too many or too few or too sensitive. The animals' behavior reflects these aberrations: they typically act impulsively, have trouble learning and can't block out extraneous sights and sounds when learning a task. The challenge, obviously, is to figure out why the human and animal data tell such a "on the one hand, on the other hand" story it takes a human octopus to keep it all straight.

One reason cocaine-exposed children do not seem to be faring worse may reflect how human studies are done. To get a clean result, scientists must compare children who are as similar as possible on every measure except the one being studied—cocaine exposure. It is a fact of life, and thus of science, that the women and children who wind up in these studies are not the wealthy Wall Street traders sniffing a line at the end of a hard day. Instead they are poor, and often single, and the home they bring their baby to can be chaotic. These children have so many strikes against them that adding cocaine to the mix may not hurt them much more. Or as Prof. Barry Lester of Brown University puts it, "If you grow up in such a lousy environment, things are so bad al-

ready that cocaine exposure doesn't make much difference." That may be the case in a study at Philadelphia's Albert Einstein Medical Center. At the age of 4, cocaine-exposed kids score 70 on IQ tests; their peers in the impoverished neighborhood score 82. The U.S. average is 90 to 109.

Studies of coke-exposed children may also be looking for the wrong thing. "It is possible that what is being tested are not areas where these children are most vulnerable," says Lester. In tests at Einstein, for instance, cocaine-exposed children figure out the locks and secret compartments in a box holding little toys. And at the University of Illinois, Dr. Ira Chasnoff finds in his study of 170 children that the coke-exposed ones had roughly the same IQ scores at the age of 6 as those whose mothers were clean. But children take IQ tests, and do puzzles for scientists, in quiet rooms with few distractions. All the animal data suggest that the brain systems most damaged by cocaine are those that control attention and, especially, screen out irrelevant sights and sounds. "The children do fine in a quiet room by themselves," says neuroscientist Pat Levitt of the University of Pittsburgh. "But there is no question they have alterations in their brain structure and function which, while not keeping them from learning a task in isolation, could well hurt them in real life."

Real life is the classroom as multimedia madhouse, with posters covering every wall and kiddie art dangling from lights. It is not clear how cocaine-exposed children will fare in such environments. Of the 119 studies on how cocaine affects a child's development, reports Lester, only six have followed the children beyond the age of 3. One is already setting off alarm bells. A pilot study at Wayne State University in Detroit finds that teachers rated 27 cocaine-exposed 6-year-olds as having significantly more trouble paying attention than 75 non-exposed children (the teachers did not know who was who).

There is little debate that distractibility hinders learning. That's why thousands of parents put their hyperactive children on Ritalin. And that's why cocaine-exposed children who seem to be OK now may fare worse as they make their way through school. Dr. Gideon Koren of Toronto's Hospital for Sick Children is following 47 cocaine-exposed children who were adopted as infants. Their new families "can't tell the difference" between these children and others,

says Koren. But he can. When the children were 3 years old, their language skills were developing a little more slowly than that of nonexposed children; there were no IQ differences. But at the ages of 5 and 6, an IQ gap of 10 points has opened up. The older the children get, says Koren, "the more likely there will be [cognitive] differences" compared with other kids. "These must be biological differences."

It's too soon to draw final conclusions. Clearly the legions of crack babies have not burned out as badly as was feared, but the damage assessment is continuing. Most likely, the effects of cocaine are real but small. How starkly those effects show up depends, argues Kosofsky, on myriad factors, including the environment in which the child is raised. In Toronto, Koren's cocaine-exposed kids have, at the ages of 5 and 6, lower IQ scores than their otherwise healthy siblings. But their average score of 106 is still more than 20 points higher than typical

scores of children raised in disadvantaged homes.

There will be plenty of time for further study. Even though the crisis has left the front pages, every year at least 40,000 babies are born to women who took cocaine while pregnant, according to a 1995 estimate by the National Institute on Drug Abuse. For years these children have been demonized and written off. But as the results of studies show, few are beyond the help that a loving and stress-free home can provide. As last week's conference broke up, scientists who spend their nights tracking neurotransmitters and their days running underfunded clinics for cocaine-exposed kids raised a very different question: is labeling these babies "hopeless and lost" just a handy excuse to avoid helping them and their mothers?

With MARY HAGER *in Washington*

Unit 2

Unit Selections

Key Points to Consider

❖ Given that infants are more cognitively competent than once thought, what do you think about accelerated, formalized efforts to speed up infants' cognitive skills? What advantages or disadvantages do you envision for infants who are exposed to teaching and drilling at early ages? Do you think that there are "critical periods" in the very early years of development that will forever determine later cognitive growth? Imagine that you are a parent; would you rush to expose your infant to classical music or mathematics? Why or why not?

❖ Would knowing that learning disabilities have a genetic component make you think twice about having children with someone with a strong family history of learning disorders? Suppose that your child is diagnosed as having a learning disorder. Given the genetic studies, does this mean that there is little you can do to ameliorate your child's condition?

❖ Imagine that you have an hour to teach a group of students a simple geography lesson. Now suppose you must teach this lesson with a class of adults versus a class of 3- and 4-year-old children. What would be the first thing you would have to change about your teaching style for these two groups? Describe how you would employ "developmentally appropriate" practice in working with the children.

❖ How would you rate American versus Asian teachers in terms of their ability to help children learn? What things would you change about our educational system? Why is it that parents from these two cultures have such different values and expectations of teachers and education? What would your expectations be?

DUSHKINONLINE **Links** | **www.dushkin.com/online/**

These sites are annotated on pages 4 and 5.

We have come a long way from the days when the characterization of cognition of infants and young children included phrases like "tabula rasa" and "booming, buzzing confusion." Infants and young children are no longer viewed by researchers as blank slates, passively waiting to be filled up with knowledge. Today, experts in child development are calling for a reformulation of assumptions about children's cognitive abilities, as well as calling for reforms in the ways we teach children in our schools. Hence, the articles in the first subsection highlight some of the new knowledge of the cognitive abilities of infants and young children.

Recent brain development research indicates that babies possess a number of impressive abilities. The essays "Fertile Minds," "How to Build a Baby's Brain," "How Do Infants Learn about the Physical World?" and "Categories in Young Children's Thinking" describe how scientists are discovering, by employing ingenious experimental techniques, that infants possess many heretofore unrealized skills that are heavily influenced by both nature and early experiences. "The Genetics of Cognitive Abilities and Disabilities" presents data from recent studies showing that specific cognitive skills are influenced powerfully by the complex interaction of both environment and heredity.

The word "infant" is derived from Latin, meaning "without speech." "Baby Talk" discusses the remarkable new research on the precursors to early language acquisition in infancy and continued linguistic developments in early childhood. This research demonstrates that although the human brain is wired for language, it is exquisitely responsive to the language environment.

As Erik Erikson noted, from about age 6 to 12 years, children enter the period of "industry versus inferiority" and become preoccupied with learning the tools of their culture. In our culture, these tools are the "three R's"—learning to read, write, and do arithmetic in school. Thus, the second subsection of this unit addresses developments in school-age children.

Teachers of young children recognize that children's learning in school is influenced by educational philosophies and practices. The authors of "What Have We Learned about Developmentally Appropriate Practice?" review the evidence on how best to teach young children. Given the rapidly developing cognitive abilities of young children, teachers must be very aware of employing developmentally appropriate methods in helping children learn.

Similarly, "How Asian Teachers Polish Each Lesson to Perfection" presents very interesting cultural differences in attitudes and practices regarding education and teaching practices in the United States versus Asia. These articles offer much food for thought for those who believe that the United States should change its educational values and practices.

Cognition, Language, and Learning

FERTILE MINDS

From birth, a baby's brain cells proliferate wildly,
making connections that may shape a lifetime of experience.
The first three years are critical

By J. MADELEINE NASH

RAT-A-TAT-TAT. RAT-A-TAT-TAT. RAT-A-tat-tat. If scientists could eavesdrop on the brain of a human embryo 10, maybe 12 weeks after conception, they would hear an astonishing racket. Inside the womb, long before light first strikes the retina of the eye or the earliest dreamy images flicker through the cortex, nerve cells in the developing brain crackle with purposeful activity. Like teenagers with telephones, cells in one neighborhood of the brain are calling friends in another, and these cells are calling their friends, and they keep calling one another over and over again, "almost," says neurobiologist Carla Shatz of the University of California, Berkeley, "as if they were autodialing."

But these neurons—as the long, wiry cells that carry electrical messages through the nervous system and the brain are called—are not transmitting signals in scattershot fashion. That would produce a featureless static, the sort of noise picked up by a radio tuned between stations. On the contrary, evidence is growing that the staccato bursts of electricity that form those distinctive rat-a-tat-tats arise from coordinated waves of neural activity, and that those pulsing waves, like currents shifting sand on the ocean floor, actually change the shape of the brain, carving mental circuits into patterns that over time will enable the newborn infant to perceive a father's voice, a mother's touch, a shiny mobile twirling over the crib.

Of all the discoveries that have poured out of neuroscience labs in recent years, the finding that the electrical activity of brain cells changes the physical structure of the brain is perhaps the most breathtaking. For the rhythmic firing of neurons is no longer assumed to be a by-product of building the brain but essential to the process, and it begins, scientists have established, well before birth. A brain is not a computer. Nature does not cobble it together, then turn it on. No, the brain begins working long before it is finished. And the same processes that wire the brain before birth, neuroscientists are finding, also drive the explosion of learning that occurs immediately afterward.

At birth a baby's brain contains 100 billion neurons, roughly as many nerve cells as there are stars in the Milky Way. Also in place are a trillion glial cells, named after the Greek word for glue, which form a kind of honeycomb that protects and nourishes the neurons. But while the brain contains virtually all the nerve cells it will ever have, the pattern of wiring between them has yet to stabilize. Up to this point, says Shatz, "what the brain has done is lay out circuits that are its best guess about what's required for vision, for language, for whatever." And now it is up to neural activity—no longer spontaneous, but driven by a flood of sensory experiences—to take this rough blueprint and progressively refine it.

During the first years of life, the brain undergoes a series of extraordinary changes. Starting shortly after birth, a baby's brain, in a display of biological exuberance, produces trillions more connections between neurons than it can possibly use. Then, through a process that resembles Darwinian competition, the brain eliminates connections, or synapses, that are seldom or never used. The excess synapses in a child's brain undergo a draconian pruning, starting around the age of 10 or earlier, leaving behind a mind whose patterns of emotion and thought are, for better or worse, unique.

Deprived of a stimulating environment, a child's brain suffers. Researchers at Baylor College of Medicine, for example, have found that children who don't play much or are rarely touched develop brains 20% to 30% smaller than normal for their age. Laboratory animals provide another provocative parallel. Not only do young rats reared in toy-strewn cages exhibit more complex behavior than rats confined to sterile, uninteresting boxes, researchers at the University of Illinois at Urbana-Champaign have found, but the brains of these rats contain as many as 25% more synapses per neuron. Rich experiences, in other words, really do produce rich brains.

The new insights into brain development are more than just interesting science. They have profound implications for parents and policymakers. In an age when mothers and fathers are increasingly pressed for time—and may already be feeling guilty about how many hours they spend away from their children—the results coming out of the labs are likely to increase concerns about leaving very young children in the care of others. For the data underscore the importance of

 From *Time*, February 3, 1997, pp. 48-56. © 1997 by Time Inc. Magazine Company. Reprinted by permission.

hands-on parenting, of finding the time to cuddle a baby, talk with a toddler and provide infants with stimulating experiences.

The new insights have begun to infuse new passion into the political debate over early education and day care. There is an urgent need, say child-development experts, for preschool programs designed to boost the brain power of youngsters born into impoverished rural and inner-city households. Without such programs, they warn, the current drive to curtail welfare costs by pushing mothers with infants and toddlers into the work force may well backfire. "There is a time scale to brain development, and the most important year is the first," notes Frank Newman, president of the Education Commission of the States. By the age of three, a child who is neglected or abused bears marks that, if not indelible, are exceedingly difficult to erase.

But the new research offers hope as well. Scientists have found that the brain during the first years of life is so malleable that very young children who suffer strokes or injuries that wipe out an entire hemisphere can still mature into highly functional adults. Moreover, it is becoming increasingly clear that well-designed preschool programs can help many children overcome glaring deficits in their home environment. With appropriate therapy, say researchers, even serious disorders like dyslexia may be treatable. While inherited problems may place certain children at greater risk than others, says Dr. Harry Chugani, a pediatric neurologist at Wayne State University in Detroit, that is no excuse for ignoring the environment's power to remodel the brain. "We may not do much to change what happens before birth, but we can change what happens after a baby is born," he observes.

Strong evidence that activity changes the brain began accumulating in the 1970s. But only recently have researchers had tools powerful enough to reveal the precise mechanisms by which those changes are brought about. Neural activity triggers a biochemical cascade that reaches all the way to the nucleus of cells and the coils of DNA that encode specific genes. In fact, two of the genes affected by neural activity in embryonic fruit flies, neurobiologist Corey Goodman and his colleagues at Berkeley reported late last year, are identical to those that other studies have linked to learning and memory. How thrilling, exclaims Goodman, how intellectually satisfying that the snippets of DNA that embryos use to build their brains are the very same ones that will later allow adult organisms to process and store new information.

As researchers explore the once hidden links between brain activity and brain structure, they are beginning to construct a sturdy bridge over the chasm that previously separated genes from the environment. Experts now agree that a baby does not come into

Wiring Vision

WHAT'S GOING ON Babies can see at birth, but not in fine-grained detail. They have not yet acquired the knack of focusing both eyes on a single object or developed more sophisticated visual skills like dept perception. they also lack hand-eye coordination.

WHAT PARENTS CAN DO There is no need to buy high-contrast black-and-white toys to stimulate vision. But regular eye exams, starting as early as two weeks of age, can detect problems that, if left uncorrected, can cause a weak or unused eye to lose its functional connections to the brain.

WINDOW OF LEARNING Unless it is exercised early on, the visual system will not develop.

AGE (in years)	Birth 1 2 3 4 5 6 7 8 9 10
Visual acuity	
Binocular vision	

the world as a genetically preprogrammed automaton or a blank slate at the mercy of the environment, but arrives as something much more interesting. For this reason the debate that engaged countless generations of philosophers—whether nature or nurture calls the shots—no longer interests most scientists. They are much too busy chronicling the myriad ways in which genes and the environment interact. "It's not a competition," says Dr. Stanley Greenspan, a psychiatrist at George Washington University. "It's a dance."

THE IMPORTANCE OF GENES

THAT DANCE BEGINS AT AROUND THE THIRD week of gestation, when a thin layer of cells in the developing embryo performs an origami-like trick, folding inward to give rise to a fluid-filled cylinder known as the neural tube. As cells in the neural tube proliferate at the astonishing rate of 250,000 a minute, the brain and spinal cord assemble themselves in a series of tightly choreographed steps. Nature is the dominant partner during this phase of development, but nurture plays a vital supportive role. Changes in the environment of the womb—whether caused by maternal malnutrition, drug abuse or a viral infection—can wreck the clockwork precision of the neural assembly line. Some forms of epilepsy, mental retardation, autism and schizophrenia appear to be the results of developmental processes gone awry.

But what awes scientists who study the brain, what still stuns them, is not that things occasionally go wrong in the devel-

oping brain but that so much of the time they go right. This is all the more remarkable, says Berkeley's Shatz, as the central nervous system of an embryo is not a miniature of the adult system but more like a tadpole that gives rise to a frog. Among other things, the cells produced in the neural tube must migrate to distant locations and accurately lay down the connections that link one part of the brain to another. In addition, the embryonic brain must construct a variety of temporary structures, including the neural tube, that will, like a tadpole's tail, eventually disappear.

What biochemical magic underlies this incredible metamorphosis? The instructions programmed into the genes, of course. Scientists have recently discovered, for instance, that a gene nicknamed "sonic hedgehog" (after the popular video game Sonic the Hedgehog) determines the fate of neurons in the spinal cord and the brain. Like a strong scent carried by the wind, the protein encoded by the hedgehog gene (so called because in its absence, fruit-fly embryos sprout a coat of prickles) diffuses outward from the cells that produce it, becoming fainter and fainter. Columbia University neurobiologist Thomas Jessell has found that it takes middling concentrations of this potent morphing factor to produce a motor neuron and lower concentrations to make an interneuron (a cell that relays signals to other neurons, instead of to muscle fibers, as motor neurons do).

Scientists are also beginning to identify some of the genes that guide neurons in their long migrations. Consider the problem faced by neurons destined to become part of the cerebral cortex. Because they arise relatively late in the development of the mammalian brain, billions of these cells must push and shove their way through dense colonies established by earlier migrants. "It's as if the entire population of the East Coast decided to move en masse to the West Coast," marvels Yale University neuroscientist Dr. Pasko Rakic, and marched through Cleveland, Chicago and Denver to get there.

But of all the problems the growing nervous system must solve, the most daunting is posed by the wiring itself. After birth, when the number of connections explodes, each of the brain's billions of neurons will forge links to thousands of others. First they must spin out a web of wirelike fibers known as axons (which transmit signals) and dendrites (which receive them). The objective is to form a synapse, the gap-like structure over which the axon of one neuron beams a signal to the dendrites of another. Before this can happen, axons and dendrites must almost touch. And while the short, bushy dendrites don't have to travel very far, axons—the heavy-duty cables of the nervous system—must traverse distances that are the microscopic equivalent of miles.

What guides an axon on its incredible voyage is a "growth cone," a creepy, crawly sprout that looks something like an amoeba. Scientists have known about growth cones since the turn of the century. What they didn't know until recently was that growth cones come equipped with the molecular equivalent of sonar and radar. Just as instruments in a submarine or airplane scan the environment for signals, so molecules arrayed on the surface of growth cones search their surroundings for the presence of certain proteins. Some of these proteins, it turns out, are attractants that pull the growth cones toward them, while others are repellents that push them away.

THE FIRST STIRRINGS

UP TO THIS POINT, GENES HAVE CONTROLLED the unfolding of the brain. As soon as axons make their first connections, however, the nerves begin to fire, and what they do starts to matter more and more. In essence, say scientists, the developing nervous system has strung the equivalent of telephone trunk lines between the right neighborhoods in the right cities. Now it has to sort out which wires belong to which house, a problem that cannot be solved by genes alone for reasons that boil down to simple arithmetic. Eventually, Berkeley's Goodman estimates, a human brain must forge quadrillions of connections. But there are only 100,000 genes in human DNA. Even though half these genes—some 50,000—appear to be dedicated to constructing and maintaining the nervous system, he observes, that's not enough to specify more than a tiny fraction of the connections required by a fully functioning brain.

In adult mammals, for example, the axons that connect the brain's visual system arrange themselves in striking layers and columns that reflect the division between the left eye and the right. But these axons start out as scrambled as a bowl of spaghetti, according to Michael Stryker, chairman of the physiology department at the University of California at San Francisco. What sorts out the mess, scientists have established, is neural activity. In a series of experiments viewed as classics by scientists in the field, Berkeley's Shatz chemically blocked neural activity in embryonic cats. The result? The axons that connect neurons in the retina of the eye to the brain never formed the left eye–right eye geometry needed to support vision.

But no recent finding has intrigued researchers more than the results reported in October by Corey Goodman and his Berkeley colleagues. In studying a deceptively simple problem—how axons from motor neurons in the fly's central nerve cord establish connections with muscle cells in its limbs—the Berkeley researchers made an

Wiring Feelings

WHAT'S GOING ON Among the first circuits the brain constructs are those that govern the emotions. Beginning around two months of age, the distress and contentment experienced by newborns start to evolve into more complex feelings: joy and sadness, envy and empathy, pride and shame.
WHAT PARENTS CAN DO Loving care provides a baby's brain with the right kind of emotional stimulation. Neglecting a baby can produce brainwave patterns that dampen happy feelings. Abuse can produce heightened anxiety and abnormal stress responses.
WINDOW OF LEARNING Emotions develop in layers, each more complex than the last.

AGE (in years)	Birth 1	2	3	4	5	6	7	8	9	10
Stress Response										
Empathy, Envy										

unexpected discovery. They knew there was a gene that keeps bundles of axons together as they race toward their muscle-cell targets. What they discovered was that the electrical activity produced by neurons inhibited this gene, dramatically increasing the number of connections the axons made. Even more intriguing, the signals amplified the activity of a second gene—a gene called CREB.

The discovery of the CREB amplifier, more than any other, links the developmental processes that occur before birth to those that continue long after. For the twin processes of memory and learning in adult animals, Columbia University neurophysiologist Eric Kandel has shown, rely on the CREB molecule. When Kandel blocked the activity of CREB in giant snails, their brains changed in ways that suggested that they could still learn but could remember what they learned for only a short period of time. Without CREB, it seems, snails—and by extension, more developed animals like humans—can form no long-term memories. And without long-term memories, it is hard to imagine that infant brains could ever master more than rudimentary skills. "Nurture is important," says Kandel. "But nurture works through nature."

EXPERIENCE KICKS IN

WHEN A BABY IS BORN, IT CAN SEE AND HEAR and smell and respond to touch, but only dimly. The brain stem, a primitive region that controls vital functions like heartbeat and breathing, has completed its wiring. Elsewhere the connections between neurons are wispy and weak. But over the first few

months of life, the brain's higher centers explode with new synapses. And as dendrites and axons swell with buds and branches like trees in spring, metabolism soars. By the age of two, a child's brain contains twice as many synapses and consumes twice as much energy as the brain of a normal adult.

University of Chicago pediatric neurologist Dr. Peter Huttenlocher has chronicled this extraordinary epoch in brain development by autopsying the brains of infants and young children who have died unexpectedly. The number of synapses in one layer of the visual cortex, Huttenlocher reports, rises from around 2,500 per neuron at birth to as many as 18,000 about six months later. Other regions of the cortex score similarly spectacular increases but on slightly different schedules. And while these microscopic connections between nerve fibers continue to form throughout life, they reach their highest average densities (15,000 synapses per neuron) at around the age of two and remain at that level until the age of 10 or 11.

This profusion of connections lends the growing brain exceptional flexibility and resilience. Consider the case of 13-year-old Brandi Binder, who developed such severe epilepsy that surgeons at UCLA had to remove the entire right side of her cortex when she was six. Binder lost virtually all the control she had established over muscles on the left side of her body, the side controlled by the right side of the brain. Yet today, after years of therapy ranging from leg lifts to math and music drills, Binder is an A student at the Holmes Middle School in Colorado Springs, Colorado. She loves music, math and art—skills usually associated with the right half of the brain. And while Binder's recuperation is not 100%—for example, she has never regained the use of her left arm—it comes close. Says UCLA pediatric neurologist Dr. Donald Shields: "If there's a way to compensate, the developing brain will find it."

What wires a child's brain, say neuroscientists—or rewires it after physical trauma—is repeated experience. Each time a baby tries to touch a tantalizing object or gazes intently at a face or listens to a lullaby, tiny bursts of electricity shoot through the brain, knitting neurons into circuits as well defined as those etched onto silicon chips. The results are those behavioral mileposts that never cease to delight and awe parents. Around the age of two months, for example, the motor-control centers of the brain develop to the point that infants can suddenly reach out and grab a nearby object. Around the age of four months, the cortex begins to refine the connections needed for depth perception and binocular vision. And around the age of 12 months, the speech centers of the brain are poised to produce what is perhaps the most magical moment of childhood: the first word that marks the flowering of language.

When the brain does not receive the right information—or shuts it out—the result can be devastating. Some children who display early signs of autism, for example, retreat from the world because they are hypersensitive to sensory stimulation, others because their senses are underactive and provide them with too little information. To be effective, then, says George Washington University's Greenspan, treatment must target the underlying condition, protecting some children from disorienting noises and lights, providing others with attention-grabbing stimulation. But when parents and therapists collaborate in an intensive effort to reach these abnormal brains, writes Greenspan in a new book, *The Growth of the Mind* (Addison-Wesley, 1997), three-year-olds who begin the descent into the autistic's limited universe can sometimes be snatched back.

Indeed, parents are the brain's first and most important teachers. Among other things, they appear to help babies learn by adopting the rhythmic, high-pitched speaking style known as Parentese. When speaking to babies, Stanford University psychologist Anne Fernald has found, mothers and fathers from many cultures change their speech patterns in the same peculiar ways. "They put their faces very close to the child," she reports. "They use shorter utterances, and they speak in an unusually melodious fashion." The heart rate of infants increases while listening to Parentese, even Parentese delivered in a foreign language. Moreover, Fernald says, Parentese appears to hasten the process of connecting words to the objects they denote. Twelve-month-olds, directed to "look at the ball" in Parentese, direct their eyes to the correct picture more frequently than when the instruction is delivered in normal English.

In some ways the exaggerated, vowel-rich sounds of Parentese appear to resemble the choice morsels fed to hatchlings by adult birds. The University of Washington's Patricia Kuhl and her colleagues have conditioned dozens of newborns to turn their heads when they detect the *ee* sound emitted by American parents, vs. the *eu* favored by doting Swedes. Very young babies, says Kuhl, invariably perceive slight variations in pronunciation as totally different sounds. But by the age of six months, American babies no longer react when they hear variants of *ee,* and Swedish babies have become impervious to differences in *eu.* "It's as though their brains have formed little magnets," says Kuhl, "and all the sounds in the vicinity are swept in."

TUNED TO DANGER

EVEN MORE FUNDAMENTAL, SAYS DR. BRUCE Perry of Baylor College of Medicine in Houston, is the role parents play in setting

Wiring Language

WHAT'S GOING ON Even before birth, an infant is tuning into the melody of its mother's voice. Over the next six years, its brain will set up the circuitry needed to decipher—and reproduce—the lyrics. A six-month-old can recognize the vowel sounds that are the basic building blocks of speech.

WHAT PARENTS CAN DO Talking to a baby a lot, researchers have found, significantly speeds up the process of learning new words. The high-pitched, singsong speech style known as Parentese helps babies connect objects with words.

WINDOW OF LEARNING Language skills are sharpest early on but grow throughout life.

AGE (in years)	Birth	1	2	3	4	5	6	7	8	9	10
Recognition of speech											
Vocabulary											

up the neural circuitry that helps children regulate their responses to stress. Children who are physically abused early in life, he observes, develop brains that are exquisitely tuned to danger. At the slightest threat, their hearts race, their stress hormones surge and their brains anxiously track the nonverbal cues that might signal the next attack. Because the brain develops in sequence, with more primitive structures stabilizing their connections first, early abuse is particularly damaging. Says Perry: "Experience is the chief architect of the brain." And because these early experiences of stress form a kind of template around which later brain development is organized, the changes they create are all the more pervasive.

Emotional deprivation early in life has a similar effect. For six years University of Washington psychologist Geraldine Dawson and her colleagues have monitored the brain-wave patterns of children born to mothers who were diagnosed as suffering from depression. As infants, these children showed markedly reduced activity in the left frontal lobe, an area of the brain that serves as a center for joy and other lighthearted emotions. Even more telling, the patterns of brain activity displayed by these children closely tracked the ups and downs of their mother's depression. At the age of three, children whose mothers were more severely depressed or whose depression lasted longer continued to show abnormally low readings.

Strikingly, not all the children born to depressed mothers develop these aberrant brain-wave patterns, Dawson has found. What accounts for the difference appears to be the emotional tone of the exchanges between mother and child. By scrutinizing hours of videotape that show depressed mothers interacting with their babies, Dawson has attempted to identify the links between maternal behavior and children's brains. She found that mothers who were disengaged, irritable or impatient had babies with sad brains. But depressed mothers who managed to rise above their melancholy, lavishing their babies with attention and indulging in playful games, had children with brain activity of a considerably more cheerful cast.

When is it too late to repair the damage wrought by physical and emotional abuse or neglect? For a time, at least, a child's brain is extremely forgiving. If a mother snaps out of her depression before her child is a year old, Dawson has found, brain activity in the left frontal lobe quickly picks up. However, the ability to rebound declines markedly as a child grows older. Many scientists believe that in the first few years of childhood there are a number of critical or sensitive periods, or "windows," when the brain demands certain types of input in order to create or stabilize certain long-lasting structures.

For example, children who are born with a cataract will become permanently blind in that eye if the clouded lens is not promptly removed. Why? The brain's visual centers require sensory stimulus—in this case the stimulus provided by light hitting the retina of the eye—to maintain their still tentative connections. More controversially, many linguists believe that language skills unfold according to a strict, biologically defined timetable. Children, in their view, resemble certain species of birds that cannot master their song unless they hear it sung at an early age. In zebra finches the window for acquiring the appropriate song opens 25 to 30 days after hatching and shuts some 50 days later.

WINDOWS OF OPPORTUNITY

WITH A FEW EXCEPTIONS, THE WINDOWS OF opportunity in the human brain do not close quite so abruptly. There appears to be a series of windows for developing language. The window for acquiring syntax may close as early as five or six years of age, while the window for adding new words may never close. The ability to learn a second language is highest between birth and the age of six, then undergoes a steady and inexorable decline. Many adults still manage to learn new languages, but usually only after great struggle.

The brain's greatest growth spurt, neuroscientists have now confirmed, draws to a close around the age of 10, when the balance between synapse creation and atrophy abruptly shifts. Over the next several years, the brain will ruthlessly destroy its weakest synapses, preserving only those that have been magically transformed by experience. This magic, once again, seems to be encoded in the genes. The ephemeral bursts of electricity that travel through the brain, creating everything from visual images and pleasurable sensations to dark dreams and wild thoughts, ensure the survival of synapses by stimulating genes that promote the release of powerful growth factors and suppressing genes that encode for synapse-destroying enzymes.

By the end of adolescence, around the age of 18, the brain has declined in plasticity but increased in power. Talents and latent tendencies that have been nurtured are ready to blossom. The experiences that drive neural activity, says Yale's Rakic, are like a sculptor's chisel or a dressmaker's shears, conjuring up form from a lump of stone or a length of cloth. The presence of extra material expands the range of possibilities, but cutting away the extraneous is what makes art. "It is the overproduction of synaptic connections followed by their loss that leads to patterns in the brain," says neuroscientist William Greenough of the University of Illinois at Urbana-Champaign. Potential for greatness may be encoded in the genes, but whether that potential is realized as a gift for mathematics, say, or a brilliant criminal mind depends on patterns etched by experience in those critical early years.

Wiring Movement

WHAT'S GOING ON At birth babies can move their limbs, but in a jerky, uncontrolled fashion. Over the next four years, the brain progressively refines the circuits for reaching, grabbing, sitting, crawling, walking and running.
WHAT PARENTS CAN DO Give babies as much freedom to explore as safety permits. Just reaching for an object helps the brain develop hand-eye coordination. As soon as children are ready for them, activities like drawing and playing a violin or piano encourage the development of fine motor skills.
WINDOW OF LEARNING Motor-skill development moves from gross to increasingly fine.

AGE (in years)	Birth 1 2 3 4 5 6 7 8 9 10
Basic motor skills	
Fine motor ability	
Musical fingering	

Psychiatrists and educators have long recognized the value of early experience. But their observations have until now been largely anecdotal. What's so exciting, says

Matthew Melmed, executive director of Zero to Three, a nonprofit organization devoted to highlighting the importance of the first three years of life, is that modern neuroscience is providing the hard, quantifiable evidence that was missing earlier. "Because you can see the results under a microscope or in a PET scan," he observes, "it's become that much more convincing."

What lessons can be drawn from the new findings? Among other things, it is clear that foreign languages should be taught in elementary school, if not before. That remedial education may be more effective at the age of three or four than at nine or 10. That good, affordable day care is not a luxury or a fringe benefit for welfare mothers and working parents but essential brain food for the next generation. For while new synapses continue to form throughout life, and even adults continually refurbish their minds through reading and learning, never again will the brain be able to master new skills so readily or rebound from setbacks so easily.

Rat-a-tat-tat. Rat-a-tat-tat. Rat-a-tat-tat. Just last week, in the U.S. alone, some 77,000 newborns began the miraculous process of wiring their brains for a lifetime of learning. If parents and policymakers don't pay attention to the conditions under which this delicate process takes place, we will all suffer the consequences—starting around the year 2010.

THE BRAIN

A baby is born with a head on her shoulders and a mind primed for learning. But it takes years of experience—looking, listening, playing, interacting with parents—to wire the billions of complex neural circuits that govern language, math, music, logic and emotions.

How to Build a Baby's Brain

By Sharon Begley

YOU CANNOT SEE WHAT IS GOING ON INSIDE YOUR newborn's brain. You cannot see the electrical activity as her eyes lock onto yours and, almost instantaneously, a neuron in her retina makes a connection to one in her brain's visual cortex that will last all her life. The image of your face has become an enduring memory in her mind. And you cannot see the explosive release of a neurotransmitter—brain chemical—as a neuron from your baby's ear, carrying the electrically encoded sound of "ma," connects to a neuron in her auditory cortex. "Ma" has now commandeered a cluster of cells in the infant's brain that will, as long

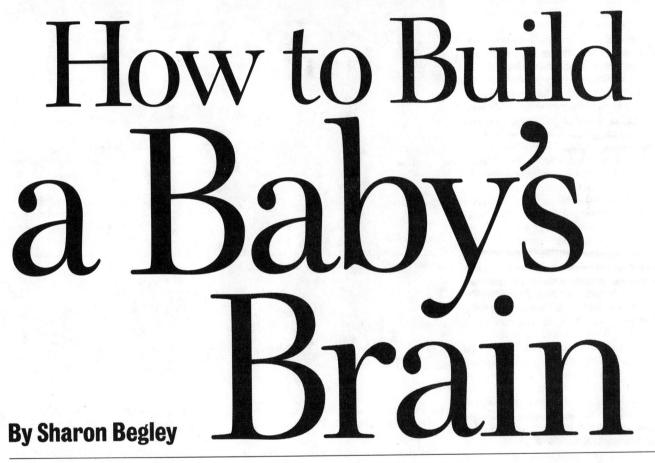

53% of all **parents** say that they read to their child every day; 55% of parents say they sing to or play music for their child every day

as the child lives, respond to no other sound.

You cannot see any of this. But Dr. Harry Chugani can come close. With positron-emission tomography (PET), Chugani, a pediatric neurobiologist at Wayne State University in Detroit, watches the regions of a baby's brain turn on, one after another, like city neighborhoods having their electricity restored after a blackout. He can measure activity in the primitive brain stem and sensory cortex from the moment the baby is born. He can observe the visual cortex burn with activity in the second and third months of life. He can see the frontal cortex light up at 6 to 8 months. He can see,

The native languages a baby hears will cr

in other words, that the brain of a baby is still forming long after the child has left the womb—not merely growing bigger, as toes and livers and arms do, but forming the microscopic connections responsible for feeling, learning and remembering. For doing, in short, everything that a brain is born to do but that it is born without knowing how to do.

Scientists are just now realizing how experiences after birth, rather than something innate, determine the actual wiring of the human brain. "Only 15 years ago," reports the Families and Work Institute in the just-released study "Rethinking the Brain," "neuroscientists assumed that by the time babies are born, the structure of their brains [had been] genetically determined." But by last year researchers knew that was wrong. Instead, early-childhood experiences exert a dramatic and precise impact, physically determining how the intricate neural circuits of the brain are wired (NEWSWEEK, Feb. 19, 1996). Since then they have been learning how those experiences shape the brain's circuits.

At birth, the brain's 100 billion or so neurons form more than 50 trillion connections (synapses). The genes the baby carries—from the egg and sperm that made him—have already determined his brain's basic wiring. They have formed the connections in the brain stem that will make the heart beat and the lungs respire. But that's all. Of a human's 80,000 different genes, fully half are believed to be involved in forming and running the central nervous system. Yet even that doesn't come close to what the brain needs. In the first months of life, the number of synapses will increase 20-fold—to more than 1,000 trillion. There simply are not enough genes in the human species to specify so many connections.

That leaves experience—all the signals that a baby receives from the world. Experience seems to exert its effects by strengthening synapses. Just as a memory will fade if it is not accessed from time to time, so synapses that are not used will also wither away in a process called pruning. The way to reinforce these wispy connections has come to be known as stimulation. Contrary to the claims of entrepreneurs preying on the anxieties of new parents, stimulation does not mean subjecting a toddler to flashcards. Rather, it is something much simpler—sorting socks by color or listening to the soothing cadences of a fairy tale. In the most extensive study yet of what makes a difference, Craig Ramey of the University of Alabama found that it was blocks, beads, peekaboo and other old-fashioned measures

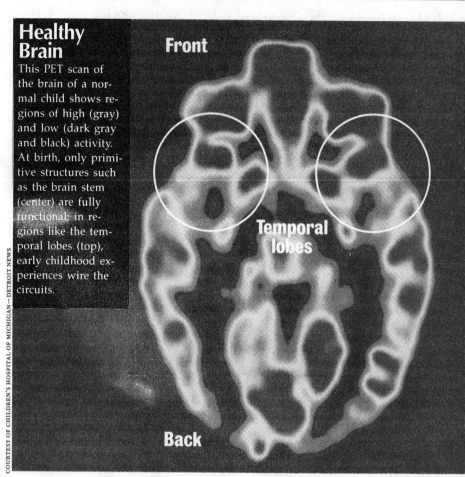

Healthy Brain
This PET scan of the brain of a normal child shows regions of high (gray) and low (dark gray and black) activity. At birth, only primitive structures such as the brain stem (center) are fully functional; in regions like the temporal lobes (top), early childhood experiences wire the circuits.

Front

Temporal lobes

Back

that enhance cognitive, motor and language development—and, absent traumas, enhance them permanently.

The formation of synapses (synaptogenesis) and their pruning occurs at different times in different parts of the brain. The sequence seems to coincide with the emergence of various skills. Synaptogenesis begins in the motor cortex at about 2 months. Around then, infants lose their "startle" and "rooting" reflexes and begin to master purposeful movements. At 3 months, synapse formation in the visual cortex peaks; the brain is fine-tuning connections allowing the eyes to focus on an object. At 8 or 9 months the hippocampus, which indexes and files memories, becomes fully functional; only now can babies form explicit memories of, say, how to move a mobile. In the second half of the first year, finds Chugani, the prefrontal cortex, the seat of forethought and logic, forms synapses at such a rate that it consumes twice as much energy as an adult brain. That furious pace continues for the child's first decade of life.

Research on language has shown how "neuroplastic" an infant's brain is, and how that plasticity lessens with age. Patricia Kuhl of the University of Washington studies the "auditory maps" that infants' brains construct out of phonemes (the smallest units of sound in a language, such as "ee" or "l"). At first, neurons in the auditory cortex are like laborers to whom jobs have not yet been assigned. But as a newborn hears, say, the patter of English, a different cluster of neurons in the auditory cortex is recruited to respond to each phoneme. Each cluster then fires only when a nerve from the ear carries that particular sound, such as "pa" or "ma." If one sound is clearly distinct from another, as "ra" and "la" are in English, then the neurons whose job it is to hear one will lie far from those whose job it is to hear the other. (Kuhl makes noninvasive electrical measurements, through the babies' scalps, to identify which neurons fire in response to a particular sound.) But if the sounds are nearly identical, as "ra" and "la" are in Japanese, then the two sets of neu-

te a permanent auditory map in his brain

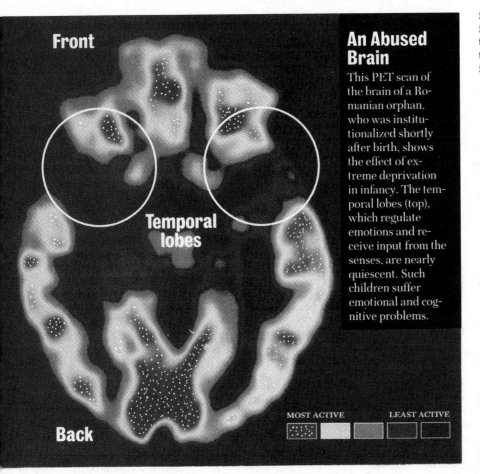

Front

Temporal lobes

Back

MOST ACTIVE   LEAST ACTIVE

An Abused Brain

This PET scan of the brain of a Romanian orphan, who was institutionalized shortly after birth, shows the effect of extreme deprivation in infancy. The temporal lobes (top), which regulate emotions and receive input from the senses, are nearly quiescent. Such children suffer emotional and cognitive problems.

ies, and "later" if it is attached to a frustrating wait for a trip to the playground, than if the word is presented in isolation from things the baby cares about. There is nothing mysterious about this: adults form a memory much more readily if it has emotional content (how did you hear that the space shuttle had exploded?) than if it doesn't (what's the difference between a sine and a cosine?). Causality, a key component of logic, is also best learned through emotion: if I smile, Mommy smiles back. A sense that one thing causes another forms synapses that will eventually support more abstruse concepts of causality. Feelings, concepts and language begin to be linked in this way in the months from 7 through 12.

Another route to brain wiring seems to be tapping into its natural harmonies. In the last year, new studies have nailed down how music affects spatial-temporal reasoning—the ability to see a disassembled picture of, say, a rabbit and mentally piece it back together. Such reasoning underlies math, engineering and chess. In a study published in February in the journal Neurological Research, scientists report how spatial-temporal reasoning in 3- and 4-year-olds was affected by weekly piano lessons. After six months, the budding Horowitzes—all of whom scored at the national average on tests of spatial recognition—scored 34 percent *above* average on this reasoning skill. None of the other children (who had received computer keyboard and mouse lessons, singing lessons or nothing at all) had improved. What explains the effect? Physicist Gordon Shaw of the University of California, Irvine, suspects that in playing the piano, "you are seeing how patterns work in space and time." When sequential finger and key patterns make melodies, neural circuits that connect positions (keys) to sounds in space and time (the melody) are strengthened. "Music training produces long-term modifications in neural circuitry," says Shaw. What scientists do not know is whether the effects of early music training endure—whether the preschoolers will be math wizards in high school.

The downside of the brain's great plasticity is that it is acutely vulnerable to trauma. "Experience may alter the behavior of an adult," says Dr. Bruce Perry of Baylor College of Medicine, but it "literally provides the organizing framework" for the brain of a child. If the brain's organization reflects its experience, and the experience of the traumatized child is fear and stress, then the neurochemical responses to fear and stress become the most powerful architects of the brain. "If you have experiences that

rons are so close that the baby will have trouble distinguishing the two phonemes. By 12 months, an infant's auditory map is formed. He will be unable to pick out phonemes he has not heard thousands of times for the simple reason that no cluster of neurons has been assigned the job of responding to that sound. And the older he gets, the more he will struggle to learn a new language: fewer unassigned neurons are available for the job of hearing new phonemes.

Experience counts in building vocabulary, too, and at a very young age. The size of a toddler's vocabulary is strongly correlated with how much a mother talks to the child, reports Janellen Huttenlocher of the University of Chicago. At 20 months, children of chatty mothers averaged 131 more words than children of less talkative mothers; at 2 years, the gap had more than doubled, to 295 words. "The critical factor is the number of times the child hears different words," says Huttenlocher. The effect holds for the complexity of sentence struc-

ture, too, she finds. Mothers who used complex sentences (those with dependent clauses, such as "when ..." or "because ...") 40 percent of the time had toddlers who did so 35 percent of the time; mothers who used such sentences in only 10 percent of their utterances had children who did so only 5 percent of the time.

NLY "LIVE" LANGUAGE, not television, produced these vocabulary- and syntax-boosting effects. Why doesn't all the gabbing on TV stimulate language development? Huttenlocher suspects that "language has to be used in relation to ongoing events, or it's just noise." That may hold for other sorts of cognition, too. Information embedded in an emotional context seems to stimulate neural circuitry more powerfully than information alone. A child will more readily learn the concept of "more" if it refers to the happy prospect of more cook-

are overwhelming, and have them again and again, it changes the structure of the brain," says Dr. Linda Mayes of the Yale Child Study Center. Here's how:

■ Trauma elevates stress hormones, such as cortisol, that wash over the tender brain like acid. As a result, regions in the cortex and in the limbic system (responsible for emotions, including attachment) are 20 to 30 percent smaller in abused children than in normal kids, finds Perry; these regions also have fewer synapses.

■ In adults who were abused as children, the memory-making hippocampus is smaller than in nonabused adults. This effect, too, is believed to be the result of the toxic effects of cortisol.

■ High cortisol levels during the vulnerable years of zero to 3 increase activity in the brain structure involved in vigilance and arousal. (It's called the locus ceruleus.) As a result the brain is wired to be on hair-trigger alert, explains Perry: regions that were activated by the original trauma are immediately reactivated whenever the child dreams of, thinks about or is reminded of the trauma (as by the mere presence of the abusive person). The slightest stress, the most inchoate fear, unleashes a new surge of stress hormones. This causes hyperactivity, anxiety and impulsive behavior. "The kids with the higher cortisol levels score lowest on inhibitory control," says neuroscientist Megan Gunnar of the University of Minnesota. "Kids from high-stress environments [have] problems in attention regulation and self-control."

Trauma also scrambles neurotransmitter signals, ratcheting up some and depressing others. Since neurotransmitters play key roles in telling growing neurons where to go and what to connect to, children exposed to chronic and unpredictable stress—a mother's boyfriend who lashes out in fury, an alcoholic uncle who is kind one day and abusive the next—will suffer deficits in their ability to learn. "Some percentage of capacity is lost," says Perry. "A piece of the child is lost forever."

That is tragedy enough, of course, but it is made even greater by the loss of what could have been. Babies are born into this world with their brain primed to learn. But they cannot do it alone.

With ANDREW MURR *in Los Angeles*

Rooting for Intelligence

Breast-feeding is good for health and bonding. And mother's milk may have another payoff: boosting a child's IQ scores.

BY DANIEL GLICK

BREAST MILK MAY be Mother Nature's ultimate food. It's potent enough to keep babies alive for the first 16 weeks of life. It contains antibodies to ward off illness; breast-fed babies suffer fewer ear infections, respiratory infections, rashes and allergies than bottle-fed babies. For mothers, nursing lowers the chance of getting breast cancer later in life, accelerates weight loss after pregnancy and may act as a natural (though imperfect) contraceptive.

But can breast-feeding also make a baby smarter?

The answer is still uncertain. But a series of studies shows everything from "small but still detectable" increases in cognitive development to an eight-point IQ difference between breast- and bottle-fed babies. Various measurements, including standard infant testing and even report cards from grade-school children, all give a statistically significant nod to babies who nursed. In one widely publicized 1992 study by Alan Lucas of the Dunn Nutrition Unit in Cambridge, Mass., preterm infants who were tube-fed breast milk scored much higher on developmental tests than babies who were tube-fed formula. "It's hard to come out and say, 'Your baby is going to be stupider or sicker if you don't breast-feed'," says Dr. Lawrence Gartner, chair of the American Academy of Pediatrics' working group on breast-feeding. "But that's what the literature says." (The academy recommends that infants be fed breast milk for the first 6 to 12 months of life, with appropriate solid foods added between the ages of 4 and 6 months.)

No one can explain exactly why breast milk may be such good brain food. The precise mix of enzymes, long-chain fatty acids and proteins that make up breast milk is so complex that no human engineer could ever duplicate it. And each ingredient has a purpose. Specific fatty acids found in breast milk have been shown to be critical for neurological development. Certain amino acids are a central component for the development of the retina, which could account for breast-fed babies' increased visual acuity—another way of measuring advanced brain development.

Critics say that trying to quantify the developmental advantages of breast-feeding is an epidemiologist's nightmare. Confounding factors include race, age, socioeconomic status and parental intelligence. But even formula makers acknowledge that their product will always be a pale imitation. Cow's-milk-based formula, even fortified with iron or fatty acids, simply can't match the complexity of nature's own. "Breast milk gives you things we don't even know about," says Dr. William Goldman, medical director of Wyeth Nutritionals International. The U.S. Food and Drug Administration is currently assessing a fierce debate over adding to formula a polyunsaturated fat that has been shown in some studies to stimulate eye and brain development—and in others to stunt growth.

Food for thought: The controversy will likely get louder, as breast-feeding advocates seize on the latest studies to bolster their case. Some researchers, on the other hand, suggest that different factors, like a loving home environment, may ultimately prove to be more important than what a child is fed. In a 1996 commentary in the British journal Lancet, William and Mark Feldman of the Hospital for Sick Children in Toronto wrote: "The best evidence is that intelligent, loving and caring mothers are more likely to have intelligent children, irrespective of how they feed their babies." But wouldn't it be something if mother's milk turns out to be, ahem, the mother's milk of intelligence?

The Genetics of Cognitive Abilities and Disabilities

Investigations of specific cognitive skills can help clarify how genes shape the components of intellect

by Robert Plomin and John C. DeFries

People differ greatly in all aspects of what is casually known as intelligence. The differences are apparent not only in school, from kindergarten to college, but also in the most ordinary circumstances: in the words people use and comprehend, in their differing abilities to read a map or follow directions, or in their capacities for remembering telephone numbers or figuring change. The variations in these specific skills are so common that they are often taken for granted. Yet what makes people so different?

It would be reasonable to think that the environment is the source of differences in cognitive skills—that we are what we learn. It is clear, for example, that human beings are not born with a full vocabulary; they have to learn words. Hence, learning must be the mechanism by which differences in vocabulary arise among individuals. And differences in experience—say, in the extent to which parents model and encourage vocabulary skills or in the quality of language training provided by schools—must be responsible for individual differences in learning.

Earlier in this century psychology was in fact dominated by environmental explanations for variance in cognitive abilities. More recently, however, most psychologists have begun to embrace a more balanced view: one in which nature and nurture interact in cognitive development. During the past few decades, studies in genetics have pointed to a substantial role for heredity in molding the components of intellect, and researchers have even begun to track down the genes involved in cognitive function. These findings do not refute the notion that environmental factors shape the learning process. Instead they suggest that differences in people's genes affect how easily they learn.

Just how much do genes and environment matter for specific cognitive abilities such as vocabulary? That is the question we have set out to answer. Our tool of study is quantitative genetics, a statistical approach that explores the causes of variations in traits among individuals. Studies comparing the performance of twins and adopted children on certain tests of cognitive skills, for example, can assess the relative contributions of nature and nurture.

In reviewing several decades of such studies and conducting our own, we have begun to clarify the relations among specialized aspects of intellect, such as verbal and spatial reasoning, as well as the relations between normal cognitive function and disabilities, such as dyslexia. With the help of molecular genetics, we and other investigators have also begun to identify the genes that affect these specific abilities and disabilities. Eventually, we believe, knowledge of these genes will help reveal the biochemical mechanisms involved in human intelligence. And with the insight gained from genetics, researchers may someday develop environmental interventions that will lessen or prevent the effects of cognitive disorders.

Some people find the idea of a genetic role in intelligence alarming or, at the very least, confusing. It is important to understand from the outset, then, what exactly geneticists mean when they talk about genetic influence. The term typically used is "heritability": a statistical measure of the genetic contribution to differences among individuals.

Verbal and Spatial Abilities

Heritability tells us what proportion of individual differences in a population—known as variance—can be ascribed to genes. If we say, for example, that a trait is 50 percent heritable, we are in effect saying that half of the variance in that trait is linked to heredity. Heritability, then, is a way of explaining what makes people different, not what constitutes a given individual's intelligence. In general, however, if heritability for a trait is high, the influence of genes on the trait in individuals would be strong as well.

Attempts to estimate the heritability of specific cognitive abilities began with family studies. Analyses of similarities between parents and their children and between siblings have shown that cognitive abilities run in families. Results of the largest family study done on specific cognitive abilities, which was conducted in Hawaii in the 1970s, helped to quantify this resemblance.

The Hawaii Family Study of Cognition was a collaborative project between researchers at the University of Colorado at Boulder and the University of Hawaii and involved more than 1,000 families and sibling pairs. The study determined correlations (a statistical measure of resemblance) between relatives on tests of verbal and spatial ability. A correlation of 1.0 would mean that the scores of family members were identical; a correlation of zero would indicate that the scores were no more similar than those of two people picked at random. Because children on average share half their genes with each parent and with siblings, the highest correlation in test scores that could be expected on genetic grounds alone would be 0.5.

The Hawaii study showed that family members are in fact more alike than unrelated individuals on measures of specific cognitive skills. The actual correlations for both verbal and spatial tests were, on average, about 0.25. These correlations alone, however, do not disclose whether cognitive abilities run in families because of genetics or because of environmental effects. To explore this distinction, geneticists rely on two "experiments": twinning (an experiment of nature) and adoption (a social experiment).

Twin studies are the workhorse of behavioral genetics. They compare the resemblance of identical twins, who have the same genetic makeup, with the resemblance of fraternal twins, who share only about half their genes. If cognitive abilities are influenced by genes, identical twins ought to be more alike than fraternal twins on tests of cognitive skills. From correlations found in these kinds of studies, investigators can estimate the extent to which genes account for variances in the general population. Indeed, a rough estimate of heritability can be made by doubling the difference between identical-twin and fraternal-twin correlations.

Adoption provides the most direct way to disentangle nature and nurture in family resemblance, by creating pairs of genetically related individuals who do not share a common family environment. Correlations among these pairs enable investigators to estimate the contribution of genetics to family resemblance. Adoption also produces pairs of genetically unrelated individuals who share a family environment, and their correlations make it possible to estimate the contribution of shared environment to resemblance.

Twin studies of specific cognitive abilities over three decades and in four countries have yielded remarkably consistent results [see illustration, "Twin Studies"]. Correlations for identical twins greatly exceed those for fraternal twins on tests of both verbal and spatial abilities in children, adolescents and adults. Results of the first twin study in the elderly—reported last year by Gerald E. McClearn and his colleagues at Pennsylvania State University and by Stig Berg and his associates at the Institute for Gerontology in Jönköping, Sweden—show that the resemblances between identical and fraternal

---

TESTS OF VERBAL ABILITY

1. VOCABULARY: In each row, circle the word that means the same or nearly the same as the underlined word. There is only one correct choice in each line.

    a. arid   coarse   clever   modest   dry
    b. piquant   fruity   pungent   harmful   upright

2. VERBAL FLUENCY: For the next three minutes, write as many words as you can that start with F and end with M.

3. CATEGORIES: For the next three minutes, list all the things you can think of that are FLAT.

JENNIFER C. CHRISTIANSEN

How Do Cognitive Abilities Relate to General Intelligence?

by Karen Wright

Since the dawn of psychology, experts have disagreed about the fundamental nature of intelligence. Some have claimed that intelligence is an inherent faculty prescribed by heredity, whereas others have emphasized the effects of education and upbringing. Some have portrayed intelligence as a global quality that permeates all facets of cognition; others believe the intellect consists of discrete, specialized abilities—such as artistic talent or a flair for mathematics—that share no common principle.

In the past few decades, genetic studies have convinced most psychologists that heredity exerts considerable influence on intelligence. In fact, research suggests that as much as half of the variation in intelligence among individuals may be attributed to genetic factors.

And most psychologists have also come to accept a global conceptualization of intelligence. Termed general cognitive ability, or "g," this global quality is reflected in the apparent overlap among specific cognitive skills. As Robert Plomin and John C. DeFries point out, people who do well on tests of one type of cognitive skill also tend to do well on tests of other cognitive abilities. Indeed, this intercorrelation has provided the rationale for IQ (intelligence quotient) tests, which yield a single score from combined assessments of specific cognitive skills.

Because specific and general cognitive abilities are related in this manner, it is not surprising that many of the findings regarding specific abilities echo what is already known about general ability. The heritabilities found in studies of specific cognitive abilities, for example, are comparable with the heritability determined for g. The developmental trend described by the authors—in which genetic influence on specific cognitive abilities seems to increase throughout childhood, reaching adult levels by the mid-teens—is also familiar to researchers of general cognitive ability.

And because measures of g are derived from intercorrelations of verbal and spatial abilities, a gene that is linked with both those traits is almost guaranteed to have some role in general cognitive ability as well—and vice versa. This month in the journal *Psychological Science*, Plomin and various collaborators report the discovery of the first gene associated with general cognitive ability. Although the finding should further understanding of the nature of cognition, it is also likely to reignite debate. Indeed, intelligence research may be one realm where understanding does little to quell disagreement.

KAREN WRIGHT is a freelance writer living in New Hampshire.

twins persist even into old age. Although gerontologists have assumed that genetic differences become less important as experiences accumulate over a lifetime, research on cognitive abilities has so far demonstrated otherwise. Calculations based on the combined findings in these studies imply that in the general population, genetics accounts for about 60 percent of the variance in verbal ability and about 50 percent of the variance in spatial ability.

Investigations involving adoptees have yielded similar results. Two recent studies of twins reared apart—one by Thomas J. Bouchard, Jr., Matthew McGue and their colleagues at the University of Minnesota, the other an international collaboration headed by Nancy L. Pedersen at the Karolinska Institute in Stockholm—have implied heritabilities of about 50 percent for both verbal and spatial abilities.

In our own Colorado Adoption Project, which we launched in 1975, we have used the power of adoption studies to further characterize the roles of genes and environment, to assess developmental trends in cognitive abilities and to explore the extent to which specific cognitive skills are related to one another. The ongoing project compares the correlations between more than 200 adopted children and their birth and adoptive parents with the correlations for a control group of children raised by their biological parents [see illustration, "Colorado Adoption Project"].

These data provide some surprising insights. By middle childhood, for example, birth mothers and their children who were adopted by others are just as similar as control parents and their children on measures of both verbal and spatial ability. In contrast, the scores of adopted children do not resemble those of their adoptive parents at all. These results join a growing body of evidence suggesting that the common family environment generally does not contribute to similarities in family members. Rather family resemblance on such measures seems to be controlled almost entirely by genetics, and environmental factors often end up making family members different, not the same.

The Colorado data also reveal an interesting developmental trend. It appears that genetic influence increases during childhood, so that by the mid-teens, heritability reaches a level comparable with that seen in adults. In correlations of verbal ability, for example, resemblance between birth parents and their children who were adopted by others increases from about

TESTS OF SPATIAL ABILITY

1. IMAGINARY CUTTING: Draw a line or lines showing where the figure on the left should be cut to form the pieces on the right. There may be more than one way to draw the lines correctly.

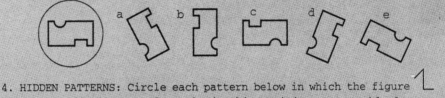

2. MENTAL ROTATIONS: Circle the two objects on the right that are the same as the object on the left.

3. CARD ROTATIONS: Circle the figures on the right that can be rotated (without being lifted off the page) to exactly match the one on the left.

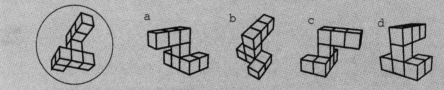

4. HIDDEN PATTERNS: Circle each pattern below in which the figure appears. The figure must always be in this position, not upside down or on its side.

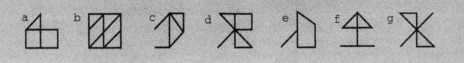

JENNIFER C. CHRISTIANSEN

0.1 at age three to about 0.3 at age 16. A similar pattern is evident in tests of spatial ability. Some genetically driven transformation in cognitive function seems to take place in the early school years, around age seven. The results indicate that by the time people reach age 16, genetic factors account for 50 percent of the variance for verbal ability and 40 percent for spatial ability—numbers not unlike those derived from twin studies of specific cognitive abilities.

The Colorado Adoption Project and other investigations have also helped clarify the differences and similarities among cognitive abilities. Current cognitive neuroscience assumes a modular model of intelligence, in which different cognitive processes are isolated anatomically in discrete modules in the brain. The modular model implies that specific cognitive abilities are also genetically distinct—that genetic effects on verbal ability, say, should not overlap substantially with genetic effects on spatial ability.

Psychologists, however, have long recognized that most specialized cognitive skills,

TESTS OF SPECIFIC ABILITIES administered to adolescents and adults include tasks resembling the ones listed here. The tests gauge each cognitive ability in several ways, and multiple tests are combined to provide a reliable measure of each skill. (Answers appear on last page.)

including verbal and spatial abilities, intercorrelate moderately. That is, people who perform well on one type of test also tend to do well on other types. Correlations between verbal and spatial abilities, for example, are usually about 0.5. Such intercorrelation implies a potential genetic link.

From Abilities to Achievement

Genetic studies of specific cognitive abilities also fail to support the modular model. Instead it seems that genes are responsible for most of the overlap between cognitive skills. Analysis of the Colorado project data, for example, indicates that genetics governs 70 percent of the correlation between verbal and spatial ability. Similar results have been found in twin studies in childhood, young adulthood and middle age. Thus, there is a good chance that when genes associated with a particular cognitive ability are identified, the same genes will be associated with other cognitive abilities.

Research into school achievement has hinted that the genes associated with cognitive abilities may also be relevant to academic performance. Studies of more than 2,000 pairs of high school–age twins were done in the 1970s by John C. Loehlin of the University of Texas at Austin and Robert C. Nichols, then at the National Merit Scholarship Corporation in Evanston, Ill. In these studies the scores of identical twins were consistently and substantially more similar than those of fraternal twins on all four domains of the National Merit Scholarship Qualifying Test: English usage, mathematics, social studies and natural sciences. These results suggest that genetic factors account for about 40 percent of the variation on such achievement tests.

Genetic influence on school achievement has also been found in twin studies of elementary school–age children as well as in our work with the Colorado Adoption Project. It appears that genes may have almost as much effect on school achievement as they do on cognitive abilities. These results are surprising in and of themselves, as educators have long believed that achievement is more a product of effort than of ability. Even more interesting, then, is the finding from twin studies and our adoption project that genetic effects overlap between different

categories of achievement and that these overlapping genes are probably the very same genetic factors that can influence cognitive abilities.

This evidence supports a decidedly nonmodular view of intelligence as a pervasive or global quality of the mind and underscores the relevance of cognitive abilities in real-world performance. It also implies that genes for cognitive abilities are likely to be genes involved in school achievement, and vice versa.

Given the evidence for genetic influence on cognitive abilities and achievement, one might suppose that cognitive disabilities and poor academic achievement must also show genetic influence. But even if genes are involved in cognitive disorders, they may not be the same genes that influence normal cognitive function. The example of mental retardation illustrates this point. Mild mental retardation runs in families, but severe retardation does not. Instead severe mental retardation is caused by genetic and environmental factors—novel mutations, birth complications and head injuries, to name a few—that do not come into play in the normal range of intelligence.

Researchers need to assess, rather than assume, genetic links between the normal and the abnormal, between the traits that are

What Heritability Means

The implications of heritability data are commonly misunderstood. As the main text indicates, heritability is a statistical measure, expressed as a percentage, describing the extent to which genetic factors contribute to variations on a given trait among the members of a population.

The fact that genes influence a trait does not mean, however, that "biology is destiny." Indeed, genetics research has helped confirm the significance of environmental factors, which generally account for as much variance in human behavior as genes do. If intelligence is 50 percent heritable, then environmental factors must be just as important as genes in generating differences among people.

part of a continuum and true disorders of human cognition. Yet genetic studies of verbal and spatial disabilities have been few and far between.

Genetics and Disability

Most such research has focused on reading disability, which afflicts 80 percent of children diagnosed with a learning disorder. Children with reading disability, also known as dyslexia, read slowly, show poor comprehension and have trouble reading aloud [see "Dyslexia," by Sally E. Shaywitz, SCIENTIFIC AMERICAN, November 1996]. Studies by one of us (DeFries) have shown that reading disability runs in families and that genetic factors do indeed contribute to the resemblance among family members.

TWIN STUDIES have examined correlations in verbal *(top)* and in spatial (bottom) skills of identical twins and of fraternal twins. When the results of the separate studies are put side by side, they demonstrate a substantial genetic influence on specific cognitive abilities from childhood to old age; for all age groups, the scores of identical twins are more alike than those of fraternal twins. These data seem to counter the long-standing notion that the influence of genes wanes with time.

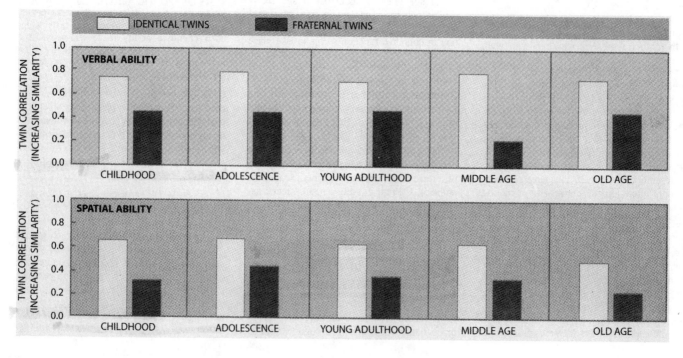

Moreover, even when genetic factors have an especially powerful effect, as in some kinds of mental retardation, environmental interventions can often fully or partly overcome the genetic "determinants." For example, the devastating effects of phenylketonuria, a genetic disease that can cause mental retardation, can often be nullified by dietary intervention.

Finally, the degree of heritability for a given trait is not set in stone. The relative influence of genes and environment can change. If, for instance, environmental factors were made almost identical for all the members of a hypothetical population, any differences in cognitive ability in that population would then have to be attributed to genetics, and heritability would be closer to 100 percent than to 50 percent. Heritability describes what is, rather than what can (or should) be. —*R.P. and J.C.D.*

The identical twin of a person diagnosed with reading disability, for example, has a 68 percent risk of being similarly diagnosed, whereas a fraternal twin has only a 38 percent chance.

Is this genetic effect related in any way to the genes associated with normal variation in reading ability? That question presents some methodological challenges. The concept of a cognitive disorder is inherently problematic, because it treats disability qualitatively—you either have it or you don't—rather than describing the degree of disability in a quantitative fashion. This focus creates an analytical gap between disorders and traits that are dimensional (varying along a continuum), which are by definition quantitative.

During the past decade, a new genetic technique has been developed that bridges the gap between dimensions and disorders by collecting quantitative information about the relatives of subjects diagnosed qualitatively with a disability. The method is called DF extremes analysis, after its creators, DeFries and David W. Fulker, a colleague at the University of Colorado's Institute for Behavioral Genetics.

For reading disability, the analysis works by testing the identical and fraternal twins of reading-disabled subjects on quantitative measures of reading, rather than looking for a shared diagnosis of dyslexia [see illustration, "Reading Scores"]. If reading disability is influenced by genes that also affect variation within the normal range of reading performance, then the reading scores of the identical twins of dyslexic children should be closer to those of the reading-disabled group than the scores of fraternal twins are. (A single gene can exert different effects if it occurs in more than one form in a population, so that two people may inherit somewhat different versions. The genes controlling eye color and height are examples of such variable genes.)

It turns out that, as a group, identical twins of reading-disabled subjects do perform almost as poorly as dyslexic subjects on these quantitative tests, whereas fraternal twins do much better than the reading-dis-

abled group (though still significantly worse than the rest of the population). Hence, the genes involved in reading disability may in fact be the same as those that contribute to the quantitative dimension of reading ability measured in this study. DF extremes analysis of these data further suggests that about half the difference in reading scores between dyslexics and the general population can be explained by genetics.

For reading disability, then, there could well be a genetic link between the normal and the abnormal, even though such links may not be found universally for other disabilities. It is possible that reading disability represents the extreme end of a continuum of reading ability, rather than a distinct disorder—that dyslexia might be quantitatively rather than qualitatively different from the normal range of reading ability. All this suggests that if a gene is found for reading disability, the same gene is likely to be associated with the normal range of variation in reading ability. The definitive test will come when a specific gene is identified that is associated with either reading ability or disability. In fact, we and other investigators are already very close to finding such a gene.

The Hunt for Genes

Until now, we have confined our discussion to quantitative genetics, a discipline that measures the heritability of traits without regard to the kind and number of genes involved. For information about the genes themselves, researchers must turn to molecular

COLORADO ADOPTION PROJECT, which followed subjects over time, finds that for both verbal *(top)* and spatial *(bottom)* abilities, adopted children come to resemble their birth parents *(white bars)* as much as children raised by their birth parents do *(gray bars)*. In contrast, adopted children do not end up resembling their adoptive parents *(black bars)*. The results imply that most of the family resemblance in cognitive skills is caused by genetic factors, not environment.

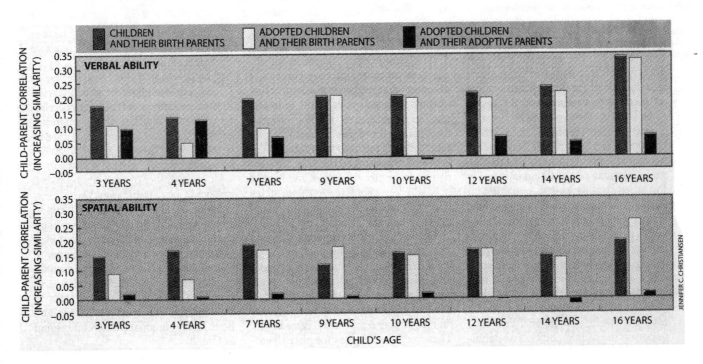

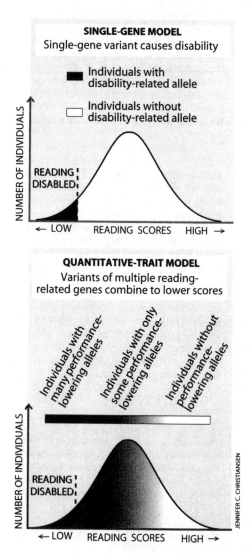

SINGLE-GENE MODEL
Single-gene variant causes disability

■ Individuals with disability-related allele

□ Individuals without disability-related allele

NUMBER OF INDIVIDUALS

READING DISABLED

← LOW   READING SCORES   HIGH →

QUANTITATIVE-TRAIT MODEL
Variants of multiple reading-related genes combine to lower scores

Individuals with many performance-lowering alleles

Individuals with only some performance-lowering alleles

Individuals without performance-lowering alleles

NUMBER OF INDIVIDUALS

READING DISABLED

← LOW   READING SCORES   HIGH →

JENNIFER C. CHRISTIANSEN

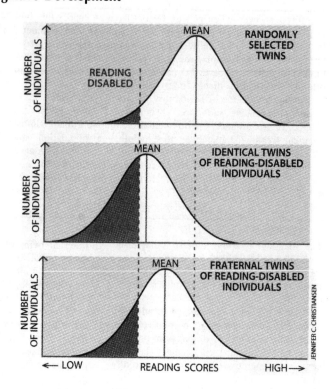

NUMBER OF INDIVIDUALS

MEAN   RANDOMLY SELECTED TWINS

READING DISABLED

MEAN   IDENTICAL TWINS OF READING-DISABLED INDIVIDUALS

NUMBER OF INDIVIDUALS

MEAN   FRATERNAL TWINS OF READING-DISABLED INDIVIDUALS

NUMBER OF INDIVIDUALS

← LOW   READING SCORES   HIGH →

JENNIFER C. CHRISTIANSEN

READING SCORES of twins suggest a possible genetic link between normal and abnormal reading skills. In a group of randomly selected members of twin pairs (top), a small fraction of children were reading disabled (gray). Identical (middle) and fraternal (bottom) twins of the reading-disabled children scored lower than the randomly selected group, with the identical twins performing worse than the fraternal ones. Genetic factors, then, are involved in reading disability. The same genes that influence reading disability may underlie differences in normal reading ability.

TWO MODELS illustrate how genetics may affect reading disability. In the classic view (top), a single variant, or allele, of a gene is able to cause the disorder; everyone who has that allele becomes reading disabled (graph). But evidence points to a different model (bottom), in which a single allele cannot produce the disability on its own. Instead variants of multiple genes each act subtly but can combine to lower scores and increase the risk of disability.

genetics—and increasingly, they do. If scientists can identify the genes involved in behavior and characterize the proteins that the genes code for, new interventions for disabilities become possible.

Research in mice and fruit flies has succeeded in identifying single genes related to learning and spatial perception, and investigations of naturally occurring variations in human populations have found mutations in single genes that result in general mental retardation. These include the genes for phenylketonuria and fragile X syndrome, both causes of mental retardation. Single-gene defects that are associated with Duchenne's mus-

cular dystrophy, Lesch-Nyhan syndrome, neurofibromatosis type 1 and Williams syndrome may also be linked to the specific cognitive disabilities seen in these disorders [see "Williams Syndrome and the Brain," by Howard M. Lenhoff, Paul P. Wang, Frank Greenberg and Ursula Bellugi; SCIENTIFIC AMERICAN, December 1997].

In fact, more than 100 single-gene mutations are known to impair cognitive development. Normal cognitive functioning, on the other hand, is almost certainly orchestrated by many subtly acting genes working together rather than by single genes operating in isolation. These collaborative genes are thought to affect cognition in a probabilistic rather than a deterministic manner and are called quantitative trait loci, or QTLs. The name, which applies to genes involved in a complex dimension such as cognition, emphasizes the quantitative nature of certain physical and behavioral traits. QTLs have already been identified for diseases such as diabetes, obesity and hypertension as well as for behavioral problems involving drug sensitivity and dependence.

But finding QTLs is much more difficult than identifying the single-gene mutations responsible for some cognitive disorders. Fulker addressed this problem by developing a method, similar to DF extremes analysis, in which certain known variations in DNA are correlated with sibling differences in quantitative traits. Because genetic effects are easier to detect at the extremes of a dimension, the method works best when at least one member of each sibling pair is known to be extreme for a trait. Investigators affiliated with the Colorado Learning Disabilities Research Center at the University of Colorado first used this technique, called QTL linkage, to try to locate a QTL for reading disability—and succeeded. The discovery was reported in 1994 by collaborators at Boulder, the University of Denver and Boys Town National Research Hospital in Omaha.

Like many techniques in molecular genetics, QTL linkage works by identifying differences in DNA markers: stretches of DNA that are known to occupy particular sites on chromosomes and that can vary somewhat from person to person. The different versions of a marker, like the different versions of a gene, are called alleles. Because people have two copies of all chromosomes (except for the gender-determining X and Y chromosomes in males), they have two alleles for any given DNA marker. Hence, siblings can share one, two or no alleles of a marker. In other words, for each marker, siblings can either be like identical twins (sharing both alleles), like fraternal twins (sharing half their alleles) or like adoptive siblings (sharing no alleles).

The investigators who found the QTL for reading disability identified a reading-disabled member of a twin pair and then obtained reading scores for the other twin—the "co-twin." If the reading scores of the co-twins were worse when they shared alleles of a particular marker with their reading-disabled twins, then that marker was likely to lie near a QTL for reading disability in the same chromosomal region. The researchers found such a marker on the short arm of chromosome 6 in two independent samples, one of fraternal twins and one of non-twin

siblings. The findings have since been replicated by others.

It is important to note that whereas these studies have helped point to the location of a gene (or genes) implicated in reading disability, the gene (or genes) has not yet been characterized. This distinction gives a sense of where the genetics of cognition stand today: poised on the brink of a new level of discovery. The identification of genes that influence specific cognitive abilities will revolutionize researchers' understanding of the mind. Indeed, molecular genetics will have far-ranging consequences for the study of all human behavior. Researchers will soon be able to investigate the genetic connections between different traits and between behaviors and biological mechanisms. They will be able to better track the developmental course of genetic effects and to define more precisely the interactions between genes and the environment.

The discovery of genes for disorders and disabilities will also help clinicians design more effective therapies and to identify peo-

ple at risk long before the appearance of symptoms. In fact, this scenario is already being enacted with an allele called Apo-E4, which is associated with dementia and cognitive decline in the elderly. Of course, new knowledge of specific genes could turn up new problems as well: among them, prejudicial labeling and discrimination. And genetics research always raises fears that DNA markers will be used by parents prenatally to select "designer babies."

We cannot emphasize too much that genetic effects do not imply genetic determinism, nor do they constrain environmental interventions. Although some readers may find our views to be controversial, we believe the benefits of identifying genes for cognitive dimensions and disorders will far outweigh the potential abuses.

TEST ANSWERS VERBAL:1a.dry; 1b. pungent
SPATIAL:1. 2.b,c; 3.a,c,d; 4.a,b,f

The Authors

ROBERT PLOMIN and JOHN C. DeFRIES have collaborated for more than 20 years. Plomin, who worked with DeFries at the University of Colorado at Boulder from 1974 to 1986, is now at the Institute of Psychiatry in London. There he is research professor of behavioral genetics and deputy director of the Social, Genetic and Developmental Psychiatry Research Center. DeFries directs the University of Colorado's Institute for Behavioral Genetics and the university's Colorado Learning Disabilities Research Center. The ongoing Colorado Adoption Project, launched by the authors in 1975, has so far produced three books and more than 100 research papers. Plomin and DeFries are also the lead authors of the textbook *Behavioral Genetics,* now in its third edition.

Further Reading

NATURE, NURTURE AND PSYCHOLOGY. Edited by Robert Plomin and Gerald E. McClearn. American Psychological Association, Washington, D.C., 1993.
GENETICS OF SPECIFIC READING DISABILITY. J. C. DeFries and Maricela Alarcón in *Mental Retardation and Developmental Disabilities Research Reviews,* Vol. 2, pages 39–47; 1996.
BEHAVIORAL GENETICS. Third edition. Robert Plomin, John C. DeFries, Gerald E. McClearn and Michael Rutter. W. H. Freeman, 1997.
SUSCEPTIBILITY LOCI FOR DISTINCT COMPONENTS OF DEVELOPMENTAL DYSLEXIA ON CHROMOSOMES 6 AND 15. E. L. Grigorenko, F. B. Wood, M. S. Meyer, L. A. Hart, W. C. Speed, A. Schuster and D. L. Pauls in *American Journal of Human Genetics,* Vol. 60, pages 27–39; 1997.

BABY TALK

Learning language, researchers are finding, is an astonishing act of brain computation—and it's performed by people too young to tie their shoes

By Shannon Brownlee

Inside a small, dark booth, 18-month-old Karly Horn sits on her mother Terry's lap. Karly's brown curls bounce each time she turns her head to listen to a woman's recorded voice coming from one side of the booth or the other. "At the bakery, workers will be baking bread," says the voice. Karly turns to her left and listens, her face intent. "On Tuesday morning, the people have going to work," says the voice. Karly turns her head away even before the statement is finished. The lights come on as graduate student Ruth Tincoff opens the door to the booth. She gives the child's curls a pat and says, "Nice work."

Karly and her mother are taking part in an experiment at Johns Hopkins University in Baltimore, run by psycholinguist Peter Jusczyk, who has

spent 25 years probing the linguistic skills of children who have not yet begun to talk. Like most toddlers her age, Karly can utter a few dozen words at most and can string together the occasional two-word sentence, like "More juice" and "Up, Mommy." Yet as Jusczyk and his colleagues have found, she can already recognize that a sentence like "the people have going to work" is ungrammatical. By 18 months of age, most toddlers have somehow learned the rule requiring that any verb ending in *-ing* must be preceded by the verb *to be*. "If you had asked me 10 years ago if kids this young could do this," says Jusczyk, "I would have said that's crazy.

Linguists these days are reconsidering a lot of ideas they once considered crazy. Recent findings like

Jusczyk's are reshaping the prevailing model of how children acquire language. The dominant theory, put forth by Noam Chomsky, has been that children cannot possibly learn the full rules and structure of languages strictly by imitating what they hear. Instead, nature gives children a head start, wiring them from birth with the ability to acquire their parents native tongue by fitting what they hear into a preexisting template for the basic structure shared by all languages. (Similarly, kittens are thought to be hard-wired to learn how to hunt.) Language, writes Massachusetts Institute of Technology linguist Steven Pinker, "is a distinct piece of the biological makeup of our brains." Chomsky, a prominent linguist at MIT, hypothesized in the 1950s that children are endowed from birth with "universal grammar," the fundamental rules that are common to all languages, and the ability to apply these rules to the raw material of the speech they hear—without awareness of their underlying logic.

The average preschooler can't tell time, but he has already accumulated a vocabulary of thousands of words—plus (as Pinker writes in his book, *The Language Instinct*,) "a tacit knowledge of grammar more sophisticated than the thickest style manual." Within a few months of birth, children have already begun memorizing words without knowing their meaning. The question that has absorbed—and sometimes divided—linguists is whether children need a special language faculty to do this or instead can infer the abstract rules of grammar from the sentences they hear, using the same mental skills that allow them to recognize faces or master arithmetic.

The debate over how much of language is already vested in a child at birth is far from settled, but new linguistic research already is transforming traditional views of how the human brain works and how language evolved. "This debate has completely changed the way we view the brain," says Elissa Newport, a psycholinguist at the University of Rochester in New York. Far from being an orderly, computer-like machine that methodically calculates step by step, the brain is now seen as working more like a beehive, its swarm of interconnected neurons sending signals back and forth at lightning speed. An infant's brain, it turns out, is capable of taking in enormous amounts of information and finding the regular patterns contained within it. Geneticists and linguists recently have begun to challenge the common-sense assumption that intelligence and language are inextricably linked, through research on a rare genetic disorder called Williams syndrome, which can seriously impair cognition while leaving language nearly intact (box, Rare Disorder Reveals Split between Language and Thought). Increasingly sophisticated technologies such as magnetic resonance imaging are allowing re-

searchers to watch the brain in action, revealing that language literally sculpts and reorganizes the connections within it as a child grows.

Little polyglots. An infant's brain can perceive every possible sound in every language. By 10 months, babies have learned to screen out foreign sounds and to focus on the sounds of their native language.

The path leading to language begins even before birth, when a developing fetus is bathed in the muffled sound of its mother's voice in the womb. Newborn babies prefer their mothers' voices over those of their fathers or other women, and researchers recently have found that when very young babies hear a recording of their mothers' native language, they will suck more vigorously on a pacifier than when they hear a recording of another tongue.

At first, infants respond only to the prosody—the cadence, rhythm, and pitch—of their mothers' speech, not the words. But soon enough they home in on the actual sounds that are typical of their parents' language. Every language uses a different assortment of sounds, called phonemes, which combine to make syllables. (In English, for example, the consonant sound "b" and the vowel sound "a" are both phonemes, which combine for the syllable *ba*, as in *banana*.) To an adult, simply perceiving, much less pronouncing, the phonemes of a foreign language can seem impossible. In English, the p of *pat* is "aspirated," or produced with a puff of air; the p of *spot* or *tap* is unaspirated. In English, the two p's are considered the same; therefore it is hard for English speakers to recognize that in many

other languages the two p's are two different phonemes. Japanese speakers have trouble distinguishing between the "l" and "r" sounds of English, since in Japanese they don't count as separate sounds.

Polyglot tots. Infants can perceive the entire range of phonemes, according to Janet Werker and Richard Tees, psychologists at the University of British Columbia in Canada. Werker and Tees found that the brains of 4-month-old babies respond to every phoneme uttered in languages as diverse as Hindi and Nthlakampx, a Northwest American Indian language containing numerous consonant combinations that can sound to a nonnative speaker like a drop of water hitting an empty bucket. By the time babies are 10 months to a year old, however, they have begun to focus on the distinctions among phonemes of their native language and to ignore the differences among foreign sounds. Children don't lose the ability to distinguish the sounds of a foreign language; they simply don't pay attention to them. This allows them to learn more quickly the syllables and words of their native tongue.

An infant's next step is learning to fish out individual words from the nonstop stream of sound that makes up ordinary speech. Finding the boundaries between words is a daunting task, because people don't pause ... between ... words ... when ... they speak. Yet children begin to note word boundaries by the time they are 8 months old, even though they have no concept of what most words mean. Last year, Jusczyk and his colleagues reported results of an experiment in which they let 8-month-old babies listen at home to recorded stories filled with unusual words, like *hornbill* and *python*. Two weeks later, the researchers tested the babies with two lists of words, one composed of words they had already heard in the stories, the other of new unusual words that weren't in the stories. The infants listened, on average, to the familiar list for a second longer than to the list of novel words.

The cadence of language is a baby's first clue to word boundaries. In most English words, the first syllable is accented. This is especially noticeable in words known in poetry as trochees—two-syllable words stressed on the first syllable—which parents repeat to young children (BA-by, DOG-gie, MOM-my). At 6 months, American babies pay equal amounts of attention to words with different stress patterns, like gi-RAFFE or TI-ger. By 9 months, however, they have heard enough of the typical first-syllable-stress pattern of English to prefer listening to trochees, a predilection that will show up later, when they start ut-

tering their first words and mispronouncing giraffe as *raff* and banana as *nana*. At 30 months, children can easily repeat the phrase "TOM-my KISS-ed the MON-key," because it preserves the typical English pattern, but

Discriminating minds. Toddlers listen for bits of language like <u>the</u>, which signals that a noun will follow. Most 2-year-olds can understand "Find the dog," but they are stumped by "Find gub dog."

they will leave out the *the* when asked to repeat "Tommy patted the monkey." Researchers are now testing whether French babies prefer words with a second-syllable stress—words like *be-RET* or *ma-MAN*.

Decoding patterns. Most adults could not imagine making speedy progress toward memorizing words in a foreign language just by listening

to somebody talk on the telephone. That is basically what 8-month-old babies can do, according to a provocative study published in 1996 by the University of Rochester's Newport and her colleagues, Jenny Saffran

and Richard Aslin. They reported that babies can remember words by listening for patterns of syllables that occur together with statistical regularity.

The researchers created a miniature artificial language, which consisted of a handful of three-syllable nonsense words constructed from 11 different syllables. The babies heard a computer-generated voice repeating

WILLIAMS SYNDROME

Rare disorder reveals split between language and thought

Kristen Aerts is only 9 years old, but she can work a room like a seasoned pol. She marches into the lab of cognitive neuroscientist Ursula Bellugi, at the Salk Institute for Biological Studies in La Jolla, Calif., and greets her with a cheery, "Good morning Dr. Bellugi. How are you today?" The youngster smiles at a visitor and says, "My name is Kristen. What's yours?" She looks people in the eye when

she speaks and asks questions—social skills that many adults never seem to master, much less a third grader. Yet for all her poise, Kristen has an IQ of about 79. She cannot write her address; she has trouble tying her shoes, drawing a simple picture of a bicycle, and subtracting 2 from 4; and she may never be able to live independently.

Kristen has Williams syndrome, a rare genetic disorder that affect both

body and brain, giving those who have it a strange and incongruous jumble of deficits and strengths. They have diminished cognitive capacities and heart problems, and age prematurely, yet they show outgoing personalities and a flair for language. "What makes Williams syndrome so fascinating," says Bellugis, "is it shows that the domains of cognition and language are quite separate."

Genetic gap. Williams syndrome, which was first described in 1961, results when a group of genes on one copy of chromosome 7 is deleted during embryonic development. Most people with Williams resemble each other more than they do their families, with wide-set hazel eyes, upturned noses, wide mouths. They also share a peculiar set of mental impairments. Most stumble over the simplest spa-

these words in random order in a monotone for two minutes. What they heard went something like "bidakupadotigolabubidaku." *Bidaku*, in this case, is a word. With no cadence or pauses, the only way the babies could learn individual words was by remembering how often certain syllables were uttered together. When the researchers tested the babies a few minutes later, they found that the infants recognized pairs of syllables that had occurred together consistently on the recording, such as *bida*. They did not recognize a pair like *kupa*, which was a rarer combination that crossed the boundaries of two words. In the past, psychologists never imagined that young infants had the mental capacity to make these sorts of inferences. "We were pretty surprised we could get this result with babies, and with only brief exposure," says Newport. "Real language, of course, is much more complicated, but the exposure is vast."

Learning words is one thing; learning the abstract rules of grammar is another. When Noam Chomsky first voiced his idea that language is hardwired in the brain, he didn't have the benefit of the current revolution in cognitive science, which has begun to pry open the human mind with so-

phisticated psychological experiments and new computer models. Until recently, linguists could only parse languages and marvel at how quickly

children master their abstract rules, which give every human being who can speak (or sign) the power to express an infinite number of ideas from a finite number of words.

There also are a finite number of ways that languages construct sentences. As Chomsky once put it, from a Martian's-eye view, everybody on Earth speaks a single tongue that has thousands of mutually unintelligible

dialects. For instance, all people make sentences from noun phrases, like "The quick brown fox," and verb phrases, like "jumped over the fence."

Masters of pattern. Researchers played strings of three-syllable nonsense words to 8-month-old babies for two minutes. The babies learned them by remembering how often syllables occurred together.

And virtually all of the world's 6,000 or so languages allow phrases to be moved around in a sentence to form questions, relative clauses, and passive constructions.

Statistical wizards. Chomsky posited that children were born knowing these and a handful of other basic laws of language and that they learn their parents' native tongue with the help of a "language acquisition de-

tial tasks, such as putting together a puzzle, and many cannot read or write beyond the level of a first grader.
In spite of these deficits, Bellugi has found that children with the disorder are not merely competent at language but extraordinary. Ask normal kids to name as many animals as possible in 60 seconds, and a string of barnyard and pet-store examples will tumble out. Ask children with Williams, and you'll get a menagerie or rare creatures, such as ibex, newt, yak, and weasel. People with Williams have the gift of gab, telling elaborate sto-

ries with unabashed verve and incorporating audience teasers such as "Gadzooks!" and "Lo and behold!"
This unlikely suite of skills and inadequacies initially led Bellugi to surmise that Williams might damage the right hemisphere of the brain, where spatial tasks are processed, while leaving language in the left hemisphere intact. That has not turned out to be true. People with Williams excel at recognizing faces, a job that enlists the visual and spatial-processing skills of the right hemisphere. Using functional brain imaging, a tech-

nique that shows the brain in action, Bellugi has found that both hemispheres of the brains of people with Williams are shouldering the tasks of processing language.
Bellugi and other researchers are now trying to link the outward characteristics of people with Williams to the genes they are missing and to changes in brain tissue. They have begun concentrating on the neocerebellum, a part of the brain that is enlarged in people with Williams and that may hold clues to their engaging personalities and to the evolution of language. The neocerebel-

lum is among the brain's newest parts, appearing in human ancestors about the same time as the enlargement of the frontal cortex, the place where researchers believe rational thoughts are formulated. The neocerebellum is significantly smaller in people with autism, who are generally antisocial and poor at language, the reverse of people with Williams. This part of the brain helps make semantic connections between words, such as *sit* and *chair*, suggesting that it was needed for language to evolve.

vice," preprogrammed circuits in the brain. Findings like Newport's are suggesting to some researchers that perhaps children can use statistical regularities to extract not only individual words from what they hear but also the rules for cobbling words together into sentences.

This idea is shared by computational linguists, who have designed computer models called artificial neural networks that are very simplified versions of the brain and that can "learn" some aspects of language. Artificial neural networks mimic the way that nerve cells, or neurons, inside a brain are hooked up. The result is a device that shares some basic properties with the brain and that can accomplish some linguistic feats that real children perform. For example, a neural network can make general categories out of a jumble of words coming in, just as a child learns that certain kinds of words refer to objects while others refer to actions. Nobody has to teach kids that words like *dog* and *telephone* are nouns, while *go* and *jump* are verbs; the way they use such words in sentences demonstrates that they know the difference. Neural networks also can learn some aspects of the meaning of words, and they can infer some rules of syntax, or word order. Therefore, a computer that was fed English sentences would be able to produce a phrase like "Johnny ate fish," rather than "Johnny fish ate," which is correct in Japanese. These computer models even make some of the same mistakes that real children do, says Mark Seidenberg, a computational linguist at the University of Southern California. A neural network designed by a student of Seidenberg's to learn to conjugate verbs sometimes issued sentences like "He jumped me the ball," which any parent will recognize as the kind of error that could have come from the mouths of babes.

But neural networks have yet to come close to the computation power of a toddler. Ninety percent of the sentences uttered by the average 3-year-old are grammatically correct. The mistakes they do make are rarely random but rather the result of following the rules of grammar with excessive zeal. There is no logical reason for being able to say "I batted the ball" but not "I holded the rabbit," except that about 180 of the most commonly used English verbs are conjugated irregularly.

Strict grammarians. Most 3-year-olds rarely make grammatical errors. When they do, the mistakes they make usually are the result of following the rules of grammar with excessive zeal.

Yet for all of grammar's seeming illogic, toddlers' brains may be able to spot clues in the sentences they hear that help them learn grammatical rules, just as they use statistical regularities to find word boundaries. One such clue is the little bits of language called grammatical morphemes, which among other things tell a listener whether a word is being used as noun or as a verb. *The,* for instance, signals that a noun will soon follow, while the suffix *ion* also identifies a word as a noun, as in vibration. Psycholinguist LouAnn Gerken of the University of Arizona recently reported that toddlers know what grammatical morphemes signify before they actually use them. She tested this by asking 2-year-olds a series of questions in which the grammatical morphemes were replaced with other words. When asked to "Find the dog for me," for example, 85 percent of children in her study could point to the right animal in a picture. But when the question was "Find *was* dog for me," they pointed to the dog 55 percent of the time. "Find *gub* dog for me," and it dropped to 40 percent.

Fast mapping. Children may be noticing grammatical morphemes when they are as young as 10 months and have just begun making connections between words and their definitions. Gerken recently found that infants' brain waves change when they are listening to stories in which grammatical morphemes are replaced with other words, suggesting they begin picking up grammar even before they know what sentences mean.

Such linguistic leaps come as a baby's brain is humming with activity. Within the first few months of life, a baby's neurons will forge 1,000 trillion connections, an increase of 20-fold from birth. Neurobiologists once assumed that the wiring in a baby's brain was set at birth. After that, the brain, like legs and noses, just grew bigger. That view has been demolished, says Anne Fernald, a psycholinguist at Stanford University, "now that we can eavesdrop on the brain." Images made using the brain-scanning technique positron emission tomography have revealed, for instance, that when a baby is 8 or 9 months old, the part of the brain that stores and indexes many kinds of memory becomes fully functional. This is precisely when babies appear to be able to attach meaning to words.

Other leaps in a child's linguistic prowess also coincide with remarkable changes in the brain. For instance, an adult listener can recognize *eleph* as *elephant* within about 400 milliseconds, an ability called "fast mapping" that demands that the brain process speech sounds with phenomenal speed. "To understand strings of words, you have to identify individual words rapidly," says Fernald. She and her colleagues have found that around 15 months of age, a child needs more than a second to recognize even a familiar word, like *baby*. At 18 months, the child can get the picture slightly before the word is ending. At 24 months, she knows the word in a mere 600 milliseconds, as soon as the syllable *bay* has been uttered.

Fast mapping takes off at the same moment as a dramatic reorganization of the child's brain, in which language-related operations, particularly grammar, shift from both sides of the brain into the left hemisphere. Most adult brains are lopsided when it comes to language, processing grammar almost entirely in the left temporal lobe, just over the left ear. Infants and toddlers, however, treat language in both hemispheres, according to Debra Mills, at the University of California–San Diego, and Helen Neville, at the University of Oregon. Mills and Neville stuck electrodes to toddlers' heads to find that processing of words that serve special grammatical functions, such as prepositions, conjunctions, and articles, begins to shift into the left side around the end of the third year.

From then on, the two hemispheres assume different job descriptions. The right temporal lobe continues to perform spatial tasks, such as following the trajectory of a baseball and predicting where it will land. It also pays attention to the emotional information contained in the cadence and pitch of speech. Both hemispheres know the meanings of many words, but the left temporal lobe holds the key to grammar.

This division is maintained even when the language is signed, not spoken. Ursula Bellugi and Edward Klima, a wife and husband team at the Salk Institute for Biological Studies in La Jolla, Caiif., recently demonstrated this fact by studying deaf people who were lifelong signers of American Sign Language and who also had suffered a stroke in specific areas of the brain. The researchers found, predictably, that signers with damage to the right hemisphere had great difficulty with tasks involving spatial perception, such as copying a drawing of a geometric pattern. What was surprising was that right hemisphere damage did not hinder their fluency in ASL, which relies on movements of the hands and body in space. It was signers with damage to the left hemisphere who found they could no longer express themselves in ASL or understand it. Some had trouble producing the specific facial expressions that convey grammatical information in ASL. It is not just speech that's being processed in the left hemisphere, says MIT's Pinker, or movements of the mouth, but abstract language.

Nobody knows why the left hemisphere got the job of processing language, but linguists are beginning to surmise that languages are constructed the way they are in part because the human brain is not infinitely capable of all kinds of computation. "We are starting to see how the universals among languages could arise out of constraints on how the brain computes and how children learn," says Johns Hopkins linguist Paul Smolensky. For instance, the vast majority of the world's languages favor syllables that end in a vowel, though English is an exception. (Think of a native Italian speaking English and adding vowels where there are none.) That's because it is easier for the auditory centers of the brain to perceive differences between consonants when they come before a vowel than when they come after. Human brains can easily recognize *pad, bad,* and *dad* as three different words; it is much harder to distinguish *tab, tap,* and *tad.* As languages around the world were evolving, they were pulled along paths that minimize ambiguity among sounds.

Birth of a language. Linguists have never had the chance to study a spoken language as it is being constructed, but they have been given the opportunity to observe a new sign language in the making in Nicaragua. When the Sandinistas came to power in 1979, they established schools where deaf people came together for the first time. Many of the pupils had never met another deaf person, and their only means of communication at first was the expressive but largely unstructured pantomime each had invented at home with their hearing families. Soon the pupils began to pool their makeshift gestures into a system that is similar to spoken pidgin, the form of communication that springs up in places where people speaking mutually unintelligible tongues come together. The next generation of deaf Nicaraguan children, says Judy Kegl, a psycholinguist at Rutgers University, in Newark, N.J., has done it one better, transforming the pidgin sign into a full-blown language complete with regular grammar. The birth of Nicaraguan sign, many linguists believe, mirrors the evolution of all languages. Without conscious effort, deaf Nicaraguan children have created a sign that is now fluid and compact, and which contains standardized rules that allow them to express abstract ideas without circumlocutions. It can indicate past and future, denote whether an action was performed once or repeatedly, and show who did what to whom, allowing its users to joke, recite poetry, and tell their life stories.

Linguists have a long road ahead of them before they can say exactly how a child goes from babbling to banter, or what the very first languages might have been like, or how the brain transforms vague thoughts into concrete words that sometimes fly out of our mouths before we can stop them. But already, some practical conclusions are falling out of the new research. For example, two recent studies show that the size of toddlers' vocabularies depends in large measure on how much their mothers talk to them. At 20 months, according to a study by Janellen Huttenlocher of the University of Chicago, the children of talkative mothers had 131 more words in their vocabularies than children whose mothers were more taciturn. By age 2, the gap had widened to 295 words.

In other words, children need input and they need it early, says Newport. Parking a toddler in front of the television won't improve vocabulary, probably because kids need real human interaction to attach meaning to words. Hearing more than one language in infancy makes it easier for a child to hear the distinctions between phonemes of more than one language later on.

Newport and other linguists have discovered in recent years that the window of opportunity for acquiring language begins to close around age 6, and the gap narrows with each additional candle on the birthday cake. Children who do not learn a language by puberty will never be fluent in any tongue. That means that profoundly deaf children should be exposed to sign language as early as possible, says Newport. If their parents are hearing, they should learn to sign. And schools might rethink the practice of waiting to teach foreign languages until kids are nearly grown and the window on native command of a second language is almost shut.

Linguists don't yet know how much of grammar children are able to absorb simply by listening. And they have only begun to parse the genes or accidents of brain wiring that might give rise, as Pinker puts it, to the poet, the raconteur, or an Alexander Haig, a Mrs. Malaprop. What is certain is that language is one of the great wonders of the natural world, and linguists are still being astonished by its complexity and its power to shape the brain. Human beings, says Kegl, "show an incredible enthusiasm for discourse." Maybe what is most innate about language is the passion to communicate.

How Do Infants Learn About the Physical World?

Renée Baillargeon

Renée Baillargeon is a Professor of Psychology at the University of Illinois at Urbana-Champaign. Address correspondence to Renée Baillargeon, Department of Psychology, University of Illinois, 603 East Daniel, Champaign, IL 61820.

Until recently, young infants were assumed to lack even the most fundamental of adults' beliefs about objects. This conclusion was based largely on analyses of young infants' performance in object manipulation tasks. For example, young infants were said to be unaware that an object continues to exist when masked by another object because they consistently failed tasks that required them to search for an object hidden beneath or behind another object.[1]

In time, however, researchers came to realize that young infants might fail tasks such as search tasks not because of limited physical knowledge, but because of difficulties associated with the planning and execution of action sequences. This concern led investigators to seek alternative methods for exploring young infants' physical knowledge, methods that did not depend on the manipulation of objects.

Infants' well-documented tendency to look longer at novel than at familiar events[2] suggested one alternative method for investigating young infants' beliefs about objects.

In a typical experiment, infants are presented with two test events: a possible and an impossible event. The possible event is consistent with the expectation or belief examined in the experiment; the impossible event, in contrast, violates this expectation. The rationale is that if infants possess the belief being tested, they will perceive the impossible event as more novel or surprising than the possible event, and will therefore look reliably longer at the impossible than at the possible event.

Using this violation-of-expectation method, investigators have demonstrated that even very young infants possess many of the same fundamental beliefs about objects as adults do.[3,4] For example, infants aged 2.5 to 3.5 months are aware that objects continue to exist when masked by other objects, that objects cannot remain stable without support, that objects move along spatially continuous paths, and that objects cannot move through the space occupied by other objects.

The repeated demonstration of sophisticated physical knowledge in early infancy has led investigators in recent years to focus their efforts in a new direction. In addition to exploring what infants know about the physical world, researchers have become interested in the question of how infants attain their physical knowledge.

My colleagues and I have begun to build a model of the development of young infants' physical reasoning.[5–7] The model is based on the assumption that infants are born not with substantive beliefs about objects (e.g., intuitive notions of impenetrability, continuity, or force), as researchers such as Spelke[8] and Leslie[9] have proposed, but with highly constrained mechanisms that guide the development of infants' reasoning about objects. The model is derived from findings concerning infants' intuitions about different physical phenomena (e.g., support, collision, and unveiling phenomena). Comparison of these findings points to two developmental patterns that recur across ages and phenomena. We assume that these patterns reflect, at least indirectly, the nature and properties of infants' learning mechanisms. In this review, I describe the patterns and summarize some of the evidence supporting them.

FIRST PATTERN: IDENTIFICATION OF INITIAL CONCEPT AND VARIABLES

The first developmental pattern is that, when learning about a new physical phenomenon, infants first form a preliminary, all-or-none concept that captures the essence of the phenomenon but few of its details. With further experience, this *initial concept* is progressively elaborated. Infants slowly identify discrete and continuous *variables* that are relevant to the initial concept, study the

From *Current Directions in Psychological Science*, October 1994, pp. 133-140. © 1994 by the American Psychological Society. Reprinted by permission of Cambridge University Press.

effects of those variables, and incorporate this accrued knowledge into their reasoning, resulting in increasingly accurate predictions over time.

To illustrate the distinction between initial concepts and variables, I summarize experiments on the development of young infants' reasoning about support phenomena (conducted with Amy Needham, Julie DeVos, and Helen Raschke), collision phenomena (conducted with Laura Kotovsky), and unveiling phenomena (conducted with Julie DeVos).[3,5-7]

Support Phenomena

Our experiments on young infants' ability to reason about support phenomena have focused on simple problems involving a box and a platform. Our results indicate that by 3 months of age, if not before, infants expect the box to fall if it loses all contact with the platform and to remain stable otherwise. At this stage, any contact between the box and the platform is deemed sufficient to ensure the box's stability. At least two developments take place between 3 and 6.5 months of age. First, infants become aware that the locus of contact between the box and the platform must be taken into account when judging the box's stability. Infants initially assume that the box will remain stable if placed either on the top or against the side of the platform. By 4.5 to 5.5 months of age, however, infants come to distinguish between the two types of contact and recognize that only the former ensures support. The second development is that infants begin to appreciate that the amount of contact between the box and the platform affects the box's stability. Initially, infants believe that the box will be stable even if only a small portion (e.g., the left 15%) of its bottom surface rests on the platform (see Fig. 1). By 6.5 months of age, however, infants expect the box to fall unless a significant portion of its bottom surface lies on the platform.

These results suggest the following developmental sequence. When learning about the support relation between two objects, infants first form an initial concept centered on a distinction between contact and no contact. With further experience, this initial concept is progressively revised. Infants identify first a discrete (locus of contact) and later a continuous (amount of contact) variable and incorporate these variables into their initial concept, resulting in more successful predictions over time.

Collision Phenomena

Our experiments on infants' reasoning about collision events have focused on simple problems involving a moving object (a cylinder that rolls down a ramp) and a stationary object (a large, wheeled toy bug resting on a track at the bottom of the ramp). Adults typically expect the bug to roll down the track when hit by the cylinder. When asked how far the bug will be displaced, adults are generally reluctant to hazard a guess (they are aware that the length

Fig. 1. Paradigm for studying infants' understanding of support phenomena. In both events, a gloved hand pushes a box from left to right along the top of a platform. In the possible event (top), the box is pushed until its leading edge reaches the end of the platform. In the impossible event (bottom), the box is pushed until only the left 15% of its bottom surface rests on the platform.

of the bug's trajectory depends on a host of factors about which they have no information). After observing that the bug rolls to the middle of the track when hit by a medium-size cylinder, however, adults readily predict that the bug will roll farther with a larger cylinder and less far with a smaller cylinder made of identical material.

Our experiments indicate that by 2.5 months of age, infants already possess clear expectations that the bug should remain stationary when not hit (e.g., when a barrier prevents the cylinder from contacting the bug) and should be displaced when hit. However, it is not until 5.5 to 6.5 months of age that infants are able to judge, after seeing that the medium cylinder causes the bug to roll to the middle of the track, that the bug should roll farther with the larger but not the smaller cylinder (see Fig. 2). Younger infants are not surprised to see the bug roll to the end of the track when hit by either the larger or the smaller cylinder, even though all three of the cylinders are simultaneously present in the apparatus, so that their sizes can be readily compared, and even though the infants have no difficulty remembering (as shown in other experiments) that the bug rolled to the middle of the track with the medium cylinder. These results suggest that prior to 5.5 to 6.5 months of age, infants are unaware that the size of the cylinder can be used to reason about the length of the bug's trajectory.

One interpretation of these findings is that when learning about collision events between a moving and a stationary object, infants first form an initial concept centered on a distinction between impact and no impact. With further experience, infants begin to identify variables that influence this initial concept. By 5.5 to 6.5 months of age, infants realize that the size of the moving object can be used to predict how far the stationary object will be displaced. After seeing how far a stationary object travels with a moving object of a given size, infants readily use this information to calibrate their predictions about how far the stationary object will travel with moving objects of different sizes.

Unveiling Phenomena

Our experiments on unveiling phenomena have involved problems in which a cloth cover is removed to reveal an object. Our results indicate that by 9.5 months of age, infants realize that the presence (or absence) of a protuberance in the cover signals the presence (or absence) of an object beneath the cover. Infants are surprised to see a toy retrieved from under a cover that lies flat on a surface, but not from under a cover that displays a marked protuberance.

At this stage, however, infants are not yet aware that the size of the protuberance in the cover can be used to infer the size of the object beneath the cover. When shown a cover with a small protuberance, they are not surprised to see either a small or a large toy retrieved from under the cover. Furthermore, providing infants with a reminder of the protuberance's size has no effect on their performance. In one experiment, for example, infants saw two identical covers placed side by side; both covers displayed a small protuberance (see Fig. 3). After a few seconds, a screen hid the left cover; the right cover remained visible to the right of the screen. Next, a hand reached behind the screen's right edge twice in succession, reappearing first with the cover and then with a small (possible event) or a large (impossible event) toy dog. Each dog was held next to the visible cover, so that their sizes could be readily compared. At 9.5 months of age, infants judged that either dog could have been hidden under the cover behind the screen. At 12.5 months of age, however, infants showed reliable surprise at the large dog's retrieval.

Together, these results suggest the following developmental sequence.

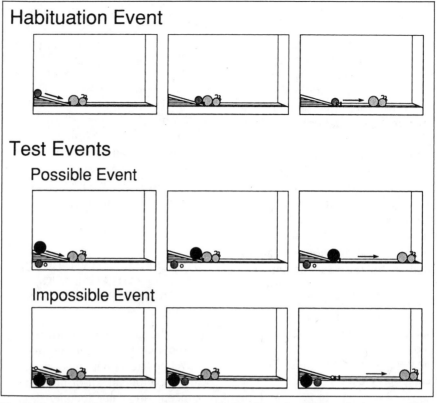

Fig. 2. Paradigm for studying infants' understanding of collision phenomena. First, infants are habituated to (i.e., repeatedly shown) an event in which a blue, medium-size cylinder rolls down a ramp and hits a bug resting on one end of a track; the bug then rolls to the middle of the track. In the test events, two new cylinders are introduced, and the bug now rolls to the end of the track. The cylinder used in the possible event is a yellow cylinder larger than the habituation cylinder; the cylinder used in the impossible event is an orange cylinder smaller than the habituation cylinder.

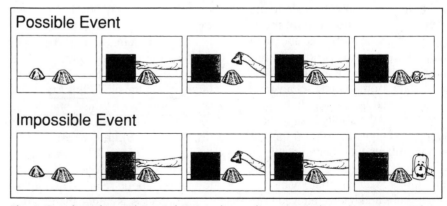

Fig. 3. Paradigm for studying infants' understanding of unveiling phenomena. Infants first see two identical covers placed side by side; both covers display a small protuberance. Next, a screen hides the left cover, and a gloved hand reaches behind the screen twice in succession, reappearing first with the cover and then with a small (top) or a large (bottom) toy dog. Each dog is held next to the visible cover, so that their sizes can be readily compared.

When learning about unveiling phenomena, infants first form an initial concept centered on a distinction between protuberance and no protuberance. Later on, infants identify a continuous variable that affects this concept: They begin to appreciate that the size of the protuberance in the cover can be used to infer the size of the object under the cover.

Comments

How can the developmental sequences described in this section be explained? As I mentioned earlier, we assume that these sequences reflect not the gradual unfolding of innate beliefs, but the application of highly constrained, innate learning mechanisms to available data. In this approach, the problem of explaining the age at which specific initial concepts and variables are understood is that of determining (a) what data—observations or manipulations—are necessary for learning and (b) when these data become available to infants.

For example, one might propose that 3-month-old infants have already learned that objects fall when released in midair because this expectation is consistent with countless observations (e.g., watching their caretakers drop peas in pots, toys in baskets, clothes in hampers) and manipulations (e.g., noticing that their pacifiers fall when they open their mouths) available virtually from birth. Furthermore, one might speculate that it is not until 6.5 months that infants begin to appreciate how much contact is needed between objects and their supports because it is not until this age that infants have available pertinent data from which to abstract such a variable. Researchers have reported that the ability to sit without support emerges at about 6 months of age; infants then become able to sit in front of tables (e.g., on a parent's lap or in a high chair) with their upper limbs and hands relieved from the encumbrance of postural maintenance and thus free to manipulate objects.[10] For the first time, infants may have the opportunity to deposit objects on tables and to note that objects tend to fall unless significant portions of their bottom surfaces are supported. In the natural course of events, infants would be unlikely to learn about such a variable from observation alone because caretakers rarely deposit objects on the edges

of surfaces. There is no a priori reason, however, to assume that infants could not learn such a variable if given appropriate observations (e.g., seeing that a box falls when released on the edge of a platform). We are currently conducting a "teaching" experiment to investigate this possibility; our preliminary results are extremely encouraging and suggest that very few observations may be necessary to set infants on the path to learning.

SECOND PATTERN: USE OF QUALITATIVE AND QUANTITATIVE STRATEGIES

In the previous section, I proposed that when learning about a novel physical phenomenon, infants first develop an all-or-none initial concept and later identify discrete and continuous variables that affect this concept. The second developmental pattern suggested by current evidence concerns the strategies infants use when reasoning about continuous variables. Following the terminology used in computational models of everyday physical reasoning,[11] a strategy is said to be *quantitative* if it requires infants to encode and use information about absolute quantities (e.g., object A is "this" large or has traveled "this" far from object B, where "this" stands for some absolute measure of A's size or distance from B). In contrast, a strategy is said to be *qualitative* if it requires infants to encode and use information about relative quantities (e.g., object A is larger than or has traveled farther than object B). After identifying a continuous variable, infants appear to succeed in reasoning about the variable qualitatively before they succeed in doing so quantitatively.

To illustrate the distinction between infants' use of qualitative and quantitative strategies, I report experiments on the development of infants' ability to reason about collision phenomena (conducted with

Laura Kotovsky), unveiling phenomena (conducted with Julie DeVos), and barrier phenomena.[3,5-7]

Collision Phenomena

As I explained earlier, 5.5- to 6.5-month-old infants are surprised, after observing that a medium-size cylinder causes a bug to roll to the middle of a track, to see the bug roll farther when hit by a smaller but not a larger cylinder. Such a finding suggests that by 5.5 to 6.5 months of age, infants are aware that the size of the cylinder affects the length of the bug's trajectory.

In these initial experiments, the small, medium, and large cylinders were placed side by side at the start of each event, allowing infants to compare their sizes directly. In subsequent experiments, only one cylinder was present in the apparatus in each test event. Under these conditions, 6.5-month-old infants were no longer surprised when the small cylinder caused the bug to roll to the end of the track; only older, 7.5-month-old infants showed surprise at this event.

Our interpretation of these results is that at 5.5 to 6.5 months of age, infants are able to reason about the cylinder's size only qualitatively: They can predict the effect of modifications in the cylinder's size only when they are able to encode such modifications in relative terms (e.g., "this cylinder is smaller than the one used in the last trial"). When infants are forced to encode and compare the absolute sizes of the cylinders, because the cylinders are never shown side by side, they fail the task. By 7.5 months of age, however, infants have already overcome this initial limitation and succeed in the task even when they must rely on their representation of the absolute size of each cylinder to do so.[12]

Unveiling Phenomena

In the previous section, I reported that 9.5-month-old infants are not surprised to see either a small or a large toy dog retrieved from under a cover with a small protuberance, even when a second, identical cover is present. Unlike these younger infants, however, 12.5-month-old infants *are* surprised when the large dog is brought into view. This last finding suggests that by 12.5 months of age, infants are aware that the size of the protuberance in a cloth cover can be used to infer the size of the object under the cover.

In our initial experiment, 12.5-month-old infants were tested with the second cover present to the right of the screen (see Fig. 3). Subsequent experiments were conducted without the second cover (see Fig. 4, top panel) or with the second cover placed to the left, rather than to the right, of the screen (see Fig. 4, bottom panel); in the latter condition,

infants could no longer compare in a single glance the size of the dog to that of the cover. Our results indicated that 12.5-month-old infants fail both of these conditions: They no longer show surprise when the large dog is retrieved from behind the screen. By 13.5 months of age, however, infants are surprised by the large dog's retrieval even when no second cover is present.

These results suggest that at 12.5 months of age, infants are able to reason about the size of the protuberance in the cover only qualitatively: They can determine which dog could have been hidden under the cover only if they are able to compare, in a single glance, the size of the dog with that of a second, identical cover (e.g., "the dog is bigger than the cover"). When infants are forced to represent the absolute

size of the protuberance in the cover, they fail the task. By 13.5 months of age, however, infants have already progressed beyond this initial limitation; they no longer have difficulty representing the absolute size of the protuberance and comparing it with that of each dog.

Barrier Phenomena

Our experiments on barrier phenomena have focused on problems involving a moving object (a rotating screen) and a stationary barrier (a large box). In the test events, infants first see the screen lying flat against the apparatus floor; the box stands clearly visible behind the screen. Next, the screen rotates about its distant edge, progressively occluding the box. At 4.5 months of age, infants expect the screen to stop when it reaches the occluded box; they are surprised if the screen rotates unhindered through a full 180° arc. However, infants are initially poor at predicting at what point the screen should encounter the box and stop. When shown a possible event in which the screen stops against the box (112° arc) and an impossible event in which the screen stops after rotating through the top 80% of the space occupied by the box (157° arc), 6.5-month-old infants give evidence of detecting this 80% violation, but 4.5-month-old infants do not: They judge both the 112° and the 157° stopping points to be consistent with the box's height and location (see Fig. 5).

In subsequent experiments, we examined whether 4.5-month-old infants would succeed in detecting the 80% violation if provided with a second, identical box. In one condition, this second box was placed to the right of and in the same fronto-parallel plane as the box behind the screen (see Fig. 6, left panel). In the possible event, the screen stopped when aligned with the top of the second box; in the impossible event, the screen rotated past the top of the second box. In another condition,

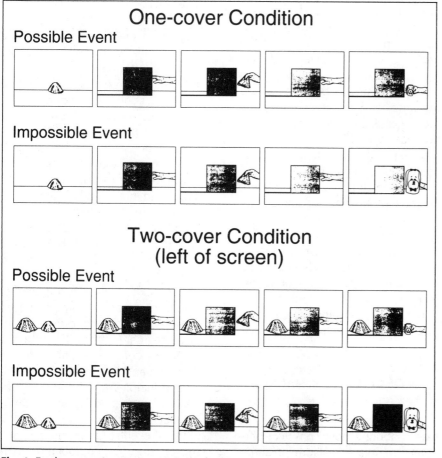

Fig. 4. Further experiments examining infants' understanding of unveiling phenomena. These test events are identical to those depicted in Figure 3 except that only one cover is used (top) or the second, identical cover is placed to the left of the screen (bottom). In the latter condition, infants can no longer compare in a single glance the height of the dog to that of the second cover.

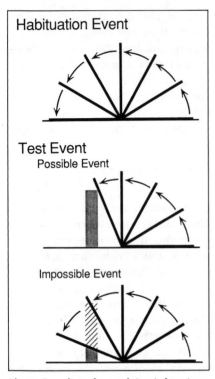

Fig. 5. Paradigm for studying infants' understanding of barrier phenomena. Infants are first habituated to a screen that rotates through a 180° arc, in the manner of a drawbridge. Next, a large box is placed behind the screen. In the possible event, the screen stops when it encounters the box (112° arc); in the impossible event, the screen stops after rotating through the top 80% of the space occupied by the box (157° arc).

the second box was placed to the right of but slightly in front of the box behind the screen (see Fig. 6, right panel). In this condition, the screen rotated past the top of the second box in each test event. The infants succeeded in detecting the 80% violation in the first but not the second condition.

These results suggest that at 4.5 months of age, infants are able to reason about the box's height and location only qualitatively: They can predict the screen's stopping point only when they are able to rely on a simple alignment strategy (e.g., "the screen is aligned with the top of the visible box"). By 6.5 months of age, however, infants have already progressed beyond this point; they can use their representations of the occluded box's height and distance

from the screen to estimate, within broad limits, at what point the screen will stop.

Comments

How should the developmental sequences described in this section be explained? We think it unlikely that these sequences reflect the maturation of infants' general quantitative reasoning or information processing because the same pattern recurs at different ages for different phenomena. What phenomenon-specific changes could account for the findings reported here? At least two hypotheses can be advanced. On the one hand, it could be that when first reasoning about a continuous variable, infants either do not spontaneously encode information about this variable or do not encode this information swiftly enough or precisely enough for it to be of use in the tasks examined here (e.g., infants do not encode the size of the protuberance in the cover and hence are unable to judge which dog could have been hidden beneath it). On the other hand, infants could encode the necessary quantitative information but have difficulty accessing or processing this information in the context of deriving new and unfamiliar predictions (e.g., infants encode the protuberance's size and realize that they must compare it with that of the dog, but are thwarted in performing this comparison by the added requirement of having to retrieve part of the information from memory). Future research will no doubt help determine which, if either, of these hypotheses is correct.

CONCLUDING REMARKS

I have argued that in learning to reason about a novel physical phenomenon, infants first form an all-or-none concept and then add to this initial concept discrete and continuous variables that are discovered to affect the phenomenon. Further-

more, I have proposed that after identifying continuous variables, infants succeed in reasoning first qualitatively and only later quantitatively about the variables.

This sketchy description may suggest a rather static view of development in which accomplishments, once attained, are retained in their initial forms. Nothing could be further from the truth, however. Our data suggest that the variables infants identify evolve over time, as do the qualitative and quantitative strategies infants devise. When judging whether a box resting on a platform is stable, for example, infants initially focus exclusively on the amount of contact between the box's bottom surface and the platform, and as a consequence treat symmetrical and asymmetrical boxes alike. By the end of the 1st year, however, infants appear to have revised their definition of this variable to take into account the shape (or weight distribution) of the box.[5] Similarly, evidence obtained with the rotating-screen paradigm suggests that infants' quantitative reasoning continues to improve over time (e.g., 6.5-month-old infants can detect 80% but not 50% violations, whereas 8.5-month-old infants can detect both), as does their qualitative reasoning (e.g., 6.5-month-old infants will make use of a second box to detect a violation even if this second box differs markedly in color from the box behind the screen, whereas 4.5-month-old infants will not).[3]

The model of the development of infants' physical reasoning proposed here suggests many questions for future research. In particular, what are the innate constraints that guide this development? Are infants born with core principles (e.g., intuitive notions of impenetrability and continuity) that direct their interpretations of physical events? Or are infants, as I suggested earlier, equipped primarily with learning mechanisms that are capable, when applied to coherent sets of observations, of producing appropriate generalizations? What

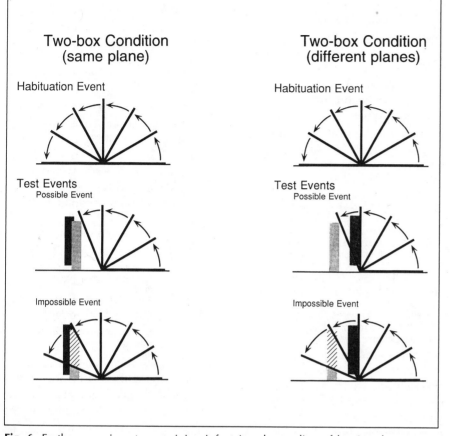

Two-box Condition (same plane)

Habituation Event

Test Events
Possible Event

Impossible Event

Two-box Condition (different planes)

Habituation Event

Test Events
Possible Event

Impossible Event

Fig. 6. Further experiments examining infants' understanding of barrier phenomena. These events are identical to those depicted in Figure 5 except that a second, identical box stands to the right of and in the same fronto-parallel plane as the box behind the screen (left) or to the right and in front of the box behind the screen (right).

evidence would help distinguish between these two views?

Some insight into this question may be gained by considering two predictions that proponents of the innate-principles view might offer. The first prediction is that when reasoning about a physical event involving a core principle, infants should succeed at about the same age at detecting all equally salient violations of the principle. Thus, researchers who deem impenetrability a likely core principle might expect infants who realize that a small object cannot pass through a gapless surface to understand also that a large object cannot pass through a small gap; provided that the two situations violate the impenetrability principle to a similar degree, they would be expected to yield identical interpretations. The second prediction is that infants should succeed at

about the same age at reasoning about different physical events that implicate the same underlying core principle. Thus, it might be proposed that infants who are successful at reasoning about objects' passage through gaps should be just as adept at reasoning about objects' entry into containers, because both phenomena would trigger the application of the impenetrability principle.

The model presented here departs systematically from the two predictions just described. First, the model predicts explicitly that when reasoning about physical events, infants succeed in detecting certain types of violations before others. Thus, in contrast to the innate-principles view, the model would expect infants to recognize that a small object cannot pass through a gapless surface before they recognize that a

large object cannot pass through a smaller gap. This developmental sequence would be cast in terms of the formation of an initial concept centered on a distinction between gap and no gap, followed by the identification of size as a continuous variable relevant to the phenomenon.

Second, the present model also diverges from the prediction that different physical events that implicate the same core principle should be understood at about the same age. The results summarized in the preceding sections and elsewhere[6]—such as the finding that unveiling tasks yield the same developmental patterns as rotating-screen tasks, but at much later ages—suggest that infants respond to physical events not in terms of abstract underlying principles, but in terms of concrete categories corresponding to specific ways in which objects behave or interact. Thus, according to our model, it would not be at all surprising to find that infants succeed in reasoning about gaps several weeks or months before they do containers; the order of acquisition of the two categories would be expected to depend on the content of infants' daily experiences. The model does not rule out the possibility that infants eventually come to realize that superficially distinct events—such as those involving gaps and containers, or rotating screens and cloth covers—can be deeply related; unlike the innate-principles view, however, the model considers such a realization a product, rather than a point of departure, of learning.

One advantage of the view that infants process physical events in terms of concrete categories focusing on specific types of interactions between objects is that this view makes it possible to explain incorrect interpretations that appear to stem from miscategorizations of events. Pilot data collected in our laboratory suggest that young infants expect a moving object to stop when it encounters a tall, thin box but not a short, wide box, even when the latter is considerably larger in volume than the former. We suspect that infants are led by the dominant vertical axis of the tall box to perceive it as a wall-like, immovable object, and hence categorize the event as an instance of a barrier phenomenon; in contrast, infants tend to view the wide box as a movable object, and hence categorize the event as an instance of a collision phenomenon, resulting in incorrect predictions.

The foregoing discussion highlighted several types of developmental sequences that would be anticipated in an innate-mechanisms view but not (without considerable elaboration) in an innate-principles view. To gain further insight into the nature and origins of these developmental sequences, we have adopted a dual research strategy. First, we are examining the development of infants' understanding of additional physical phenomena (e.g., gap, containment, and occlusion phenomena) to determine how easily these developments can be captured in terms of the patterns described in the model and to compare more closely the acquisition time lines of phenomena that are superficially distinct but deeply related. Second, as was alluded to earlier, we are attempting to teach infants initial concepts and variables to uncover what kinds of observations, and how many observations, are required for learning. We hope that the pursuit of these two strategies will eventually allow us to specify the nature of the learning mechanisms that infants bring to the task of learning about the physical world.

Acknowledgments—This research was supported by grants from the Guggenheim Foundation, the University of Illinois Center for Advanced Study, and the National Institute of Child Health and Human Development (HD-21104). I would like to thank Jerry DeJong, for his support and insight, and Susan Carey, Noam Chomsky, Judy DeLoache, Cindy Fischer, John Flavell, Laura Kotovsky, Brian Ross, and Bob Wyer, for many helpful comments and suggestions.

Notes

1. J. Piaget, *The Construction of Reality in the Child* (Basic Books, New York, 1954).

2. E.S. Spelke, Preferential looking methods as tools for the study of cognition in infancy, in *Measurement of Audition and Vision in the First Year of Postnatal Life*, G. Gottlieb and N. Krasnegor, Eds. (Ablex, Norwood, NJ, 1985).

3. R. Baillargeon, The object concept revisited: New directions in the investigation of infants' physical knowledge, in *Visual Perception and Cognition in Infancy*, C.E. Granrud, Ed. (Erlbaum, Hillsdale, NJ, 1993).

4. E.S. Spelke, K. Breinlinger, J. Macomber, and K. Jacobson, Origins of knowledge, *Psychological Review*, 99, 605–632 (1992).

5. R. Baillargeon, L. Kotovsky, and A. Needham, The acquisition of physical knowledge in infancy, in *Causal Understandings in Cognition and Culture*, G. Lewis, D. Premack, and D. Sperber, Eds. (Oxford University Press, Oxford, in press).

6. R. Baillargeon, A model of physical reasoning in infancy, in *Advances in Infancy Research*, Vol. 9, C. Rovee-Collier and L. Lipsitt, Eds. (Ablex, Norwood, NJ, in press).

7. R. Baillargeon, Physical reasoning in infants, in *The Cognitive Neurosciences*, M.S. Gazzaniga, Ed. (MIT Press, Cambridge, MA, in press).

8. E.S. Spelke, Physical knowledge in infancy: Reflections on Piaget's theory, in *The Epigenesis of Mind: Essays on Biology and Cognition*, S. Carey and R. Gelman, Eds. (Erlbaum, Hillsdale, NJ, 1991).

9. A.M. Leslie, ToMM, ToBy, and Agency: Core architecture and domain specificity, in *Causal Understandings in Cognition and Culture*, G. Lewis, D. Premack, and D. Sperber, Eds. (Oxford University Press, Oxford, in press).

10. P. Rochat and A. Bullinger, Posture and functional action in infancy, in *Francophone Perspectives on Structure and Process in Mental Development*, A. Vyt, H. Bloch, and M. Bornstein, Eds. (Erlbaum, Hillsdale, NJ, in press).

11. K.D. Forbus, Qualitative process theory, *Artificial Intelligence*, 24, 85–168 (1984).

12. This example focused exclusively on the size of the cylinder, but what of the distance traveled by the bug in each event? It seems likely that infants encode this information not in quantitative terms (e.g., "the bug traveled x as opposed to y distance"), but rather in qualitative terms, using as their point of reference the track itself (e.g., "the bug rolled to the middle of the track"), their own spatial position (e.g., "the bug stopped in front of me"), or the brightly decorated back wall of the apparatus (e.g., "the bug stopped in front of such-and-such section of the back wall").

Categories in Young Children's Thinking

Susan A. Gelman

The world is potentially a bewildering place for young children. Every day a child's senses are bombarded by countless different sights, sounds, tastes, and smells. Furthermore, all this variety is constantly changing, since the world is not a static place: people move, voices come and go, TV images flit across the screen, and new smells waft in as meals are served. In the nineteenth century William James (1890) suggested that infants and young children are overwhelmed by all this diversity, and they experience the world as a "blooming, buzzing confusion." Over the past few decades, however, researchers have discovered that even young children are able to make sense of the world by forming categories. A *category* is any grouping of things that are different in some way. Every time children use a word, put away a toy in the toy box, recognize a person's gender, or decide that a particular food is "yucky," they are using categories to organize their experience. Simple words like "doggie," "milk," or "ball" are among children's earliest categories of the world around them.

> **Researchers have consistently found that even newborns form sensible categories of simple sights, sounds, tastes, and smells. In some ways babies seem to be born knowing how to carve up the world into categories.**

This article will review some of the research on children's early categories. One of the most important findings from recent studies is that children can be quite sophisticated in how they group objects and think about those groupings. Children certainly do view the world somewhat differently from adults. However, the picture that emerges from recent research is that young children's categories are extremely important for guiding how they think about the world at large.

Early errors

Many past studies have shown that preschool children's categories differ from those of older children or adults. One primary difference is that the preschooler is more focused on superficial properties: how things look or where they can be found. We can see this with children's earliest words. Children younger than about age two-and-a-half typically "overextend" their words by applying them in overly broad ways, such as calling any round object a ball or any four-legged animal a dog (Clark 1973). These overextension errors have been documented in children learning a variety of languages across many different cultures.

Piaget's own observations suggest that throughout early childhood children form categories that seem immature from the standpoint of an adult (Inhelder & Piaget 1964). For example, if a five-year-old is asked to sort a set of plastic shapes, he might arrange them into a picture (such as putting a triangle on top of a square to form a house) rather than place together those of the same shape (such as separating all the triangles from all the squares). Likewise, preschool children often tend to put together items that go together in a scene rather than items that are alike in more fundamental ways. For instance, if a four-year-old is given pictures of a spider, a grasshopper, and a web and is asked to "put together the ones that go together," she typically will place the spider with the web (a *thematic* grouping) rather than with the grasshopper (a *taxonomic* grouping) (Smiley & Brown 1979). At this age, children also typically find it difficult to group together things in two different ways at the same

***Susan A. Gelman**, Ph.D., is professor of psychology at the University of Michigan. She has received awards from the American Psychological Association, the J.S. Guggenheim Foundation, and the National Science Foundation for her research on concept and language learning in children.*

*This is one of a regular series of Research in Review columns. The column in this issue was invited by Research in Review Editor **Carol Seefeldt**, Ph.D., professor at the University of Maryland, College Park.*

Illustrations © by Patti Argoff.

time, such as realizing that someone can be *both* a boy *and* a brother (Piaget 1928; Markman 1989).

These kinds of difficulties are typical of preschool children and disappear as children get older. The same child who at age two is calling a tomato a ball will have no problem grouping it with other fruits and vegetables at age six, and may very well become a botanist as an adult! It is important to keep in mind, however, that the kinds of errors I've described above are not the only ways that young children classify. As described next, children are in some ways much more capable than these early errors would suggest.

Early abilities

One way to observe early capabilities is to study infants. In the past 20 years, researchers have devised ingenious experimental methods for gauging what infants know. Researchers measure the very simple behaviors that infants can do, such as head-turns, sucking on a pacifier, gazing, facial expressions, and even heartbeats. Using these methods, researchers have consistently found that even newborns form sensible categories of simple sights, sounds, tastes, and smells (Mehler & Fox 1985). One-month-old babies group together speech sounds in much the same way as adults do, for example, perceiving that "bay" and "day" are different sounds. Before they are six months of age, infants categorize faces and emotional expressions (happy, sad, angry). They perceive colors, objects, even kinds of animals—all well before they can even speak (Quinn, Eimas, & Rosenkrantz 1993). It seems clear, then, that simple categories are not beyond the capacity of young children. In some ways babies seem to be born knowing how to carve up the world into categories.

Perhaps even more impressive is the behavior of children who are "experts." Chi, Mervis, and their colleagues have studied young children who are exceptionally interested in a particular topic, such as dinosaurs, birds, or the game of chess. For example, one dinosaur expert who was studied at age four-and-a-half had been exposed to dinosaur information since turning three, and his parents read dinosaur books to him for an average of three hours per week (Chi & Koeske 1983). Another child became expert in identifying and naming birds and could identify 118 different kinds of birds by four years of age (Johnson & Mervis 1994). The general finding from this research is that when children know a great deal about a specialized domain, their categories look remarkably like the categories one would find with older children or even adults. Age seems to present few barriers for a child who has become an expert on a certain topic. Chi, Hutchinson, and Robin (1989) studied four-year-old children who were highly knowledgeable about the domain of dinosaurs and found

Children younger than about age two-and-a-half typically "overextend" their words by applying them in overly broad ways, such as calling any round object a ball or any four-legged animal a dog.

that their categories of dinosaurs were detailed, factually correct, and chock-full of information. These results tell us that even preschoolers can form mature categories.

We turn next to the question of how children use categories to think about information that is not immediately obvious.

Beyond the obvious

In *Beyond the Information Given*, Bruner (1973) points out that most of what we know about the world around us is not directly shown or visible. Instead, we make inferences from whatever information is available to go beyond what is most immediate. One can intuitively appreciate this point by considering a few familiar proverbs: "Don't judge a book by its cover," "Beauty is only skin deep," "Appearances can be deceiving." In real life, as in proverbs, how something looks can be misleading. Consider the trick-or-treater at Halloween who looks like a witch but is really the second-grader down the street; the apple that looks luscious on the outside but is full of worms inside; the animal that flies in the sky and looks like a bird but is really a bat.

Notice that these examples involve contrasting categories: witch versus girl, edible versus inedible, bird versus bat. Much of "going beyond the information given"

Preschool children typically find it difficult to group together things in two different ways at the same time, such as realizing that someone can be *both* a boy *and* a brother.

involves forming categories that are based on information that's neither obvious nor visible.

I would like to turn now to the question of how and when children realize that categories go beyond the obvious. I will review three areas of research evidence with preschool children: the appearance-reality distinction, the power of words, and the thinking on biological growth. The theme that will emerge is that by four years of age preschool children clearly understand that categories include nonobvious information. In the summary, I bring out the positive—and negative—implications of this understanding for young children.

The appearance-reality distinction

When do children realize that appearances can be deceiving? Past research finds that, although three-year-olds have some difficulties holding in mind the distinction between appearance and reality, these difficulties greatly subside during the preschool years. For example, some years ago deVries (1969) examined children's reactions to a docile cat wearing a dog mask. Children first saw that the cat was harmless; then the cat briefly disappeared behind a screen, reappearing a moment later with the dog mask in place. Some of the three-year-olds become quite frightened after viewing the transformation and insisted that the cat had turned into a dog. However, by age six the children typically reported that the animal wasn't really a dog; it was only a cat wearing a mask.

Flavell (1986) found a marked shift between ages three and four in how children reason about appearance-reality conflicts. He presented children with deceptive objects, such as a glass of milk taken from plain view and placed behind an orange filter. Even though children saw for themselves that the filter changed the appearance of the object, the three-year-olds typically insisted that appearance and reality were one and the same—for example, that the liquid looked orange and that it was "really and truly" orange juice. In contrast, the four-year-olds understood that even though the liquid looked orange, it was "really and truly" milk. Part of the difficulty for three-year-olds seems to be keeping both appearance and reality in mind at the same time.

Other researchers have found some awareness of the appearance-reality distinction at even younger ages. When children are able to view a costume change directly,

These are all tigers, even though they are wearing and doing different things.

even three-year-olds realize that wearing a costume doesn't affect identity (Keil 1989). So, for example, a horse wearing a zebra costume is still a horse.

In fact, by four years of age, children realize that the "insides" of an animal or object may be even more important than its "outsides" for identifying what it is. In our own work Wellman and I asked children to show us which items had the same outsides and which had the same insides (Gelman & Wellman 1991). By age four, children could tell us that items that were alike on the outside were not necessarily alike on the inside. For example, a piggy bank and a real pig were judged to be alike on the outside but not the inside. Conversely, a real pig and a cow were judged to be alike on the inside but not the outside. Furthermore, when we asked children what would happen if a dog, say, didn't have its blood and

---

When do children realize that appearances can be deceiving? Research finds that, although three-year-olds have some difficulties holding in mind the distinction between appearance and reality, these difficulties greatly subside during the preschool years. When appearance-reality distinctions (for example, you are still you even if you have on a mask) are complex or tricky, young children are still more likely than older children to get confused.

bones, four- and five-year-olds told us that it would no longer be a dog and would no longer bark or eat dog food. However, when we asked them what would happen if a dog didn't have its fur, they reported that it still would be a dog and still could bark. Even though children can't see an object's insides, they understand that insides can be more important than outward appearances.

One final note about the appearance-reality distinction: Although four-year-olds *can* appreciate the distinction, this does not mean that they always *do*. When appearance-reality distinctions are complex or tricky, young children still are more likely than older children to get confused. For example, early elementary school children continue to err when asked whether superficial changes affect animal identity, often reporting that operations, ingestion of pills, or injections that result in physical appearance changes also can change what an animal actually is (Keil 1989).

The power of words

Young children place great weight on the names we give to things. Piaget (1929) suggested that children at first think that names are linked to the "essence" of a category: "In learning the names of things the child at this stage believes it is doing much more." He observed that children have some difficulty recognizing that the words we assign to objects are arbitrary, and instead they attach special significance to the name itself.

More recently, research has shown that children use category names (bird, dinosaur, squirrel) as a guide to extending their knowledge and making inferences. Children tend to assume that animals with the same category name are alike in important, nonobvious ways (Gelman & Markman 1986). For example, preschool children as young as two-and-a-half years typically assume that different kinds of birds all live in nests, feed their babies the same kinds of food, and have the same kinds of bones inside. Even when we teach children biological facts that they've never heard before, three- and four-year-olds generalize these facts to other animals with the same name.

We found also that children make use of new names that they learn in the context of the research study. For example, Coley and I showed two-and-a-half-year-old children pictures of unfamiliar animals such as a pterodactyl and a leaf-insect (Gelman & Coley 1990). One group of children learned no names for these animals and tended to assume incorrect labels for them (for example, that the pterodactyl was a bird and the leaf-insect a leaf). A second group of children learned the correct category names for these animals, for example, "dinosaur" for the pterodactyl and "bug" for the leaf-insect. We then asked children various questions about the animals: whether or not the pterodactyl lived in a nest, whether or not the leaf-insect grew on a tree, and so forth. The children who had not learned the correct names typically answered the questions incorrectly, assuming that the pterodactyl lived in a nest (like other flying animals) or the leaf-insect grew on a tree. But the children who had learned the new category names made appropriate inferences based on the names. They said that the pterodactyl, like other dino-

saurs, did not live in a nest, for example. Simply providing a name for the animal changed how children thought about the animal and what inferences they made.

Preschool children pay close attention to the words we apply not just to categories of animals but also to categories of people. Hearing a child labeled "boy" or "girl" has vast implications for the kinds of inferences children form (Gelman, Collman, & Maccoby 1986). Preschoolers expect that a child's behaviors, preferences, goals, physical properties, and future identity can all be predicted based on whether the child is referred to as a boy or a girl. Children make such inferences even if they are thinking about a child whose appearance is atypical, such as a boy with long hair or a girl with very short hair.

What is important in these cases is that an adult supplies the gender category label (boy, girl). If an adult doesn't say whether the child in question is a boy or a girl, children often have difficulty coming up with the correct classification on their own and tend instead to make inferences based on appearances. So when they meet a long-haired boy, many four-year-olds will assume that the child is a girl and plays with dolls. As soon as they hear that he is a boy, however, their way of thinking about the child shifts.

Recently my colleagues and I have started to look at the kinds of generalizations children spontaneously express in their everyday talk and the kinds of generalizations that mothers express when talking with their children (Gelman et al. in press). Our focus was on statements and

---

Sample Generalizations Expressed in Spontaneous Talk

Some generalizations expressed by mothers

"Remember, I told you cats like balls of yarn?"

"That's a chipmunk. And they eat the acorns."

"Did you know when pigs get big, they're called hogs?"

"A wok is how people in China cook. Well, actually, a wok is how people in America cook like Chinese people."

Some generalizations expressed by children*

"That shirt's not for girls." (Ross, two years, seven months)

"Animals eat berries and they eat mushrooms." (Abe, two years, nine months)

"Indians live in Africa." (Adam, three years, three months)

"Bad guys have some guns." (Mark, three years, seven months)

*Bloom (1970), Brown (1973), Kuczaj (1976), Mac Whinney and Snow (1985, 1990), and Sachs (1983) have made their transcripts of adult-child interactions available through the Child Language Data Exchange System (CHILDES).

These are all pigs, even though they are wearing and doing different things.

questions referring to an entire category rather than those referring to only a portion of a category. For example, we examined those times that children and mothers talked about mice (as a general category) rather than *some* mice, *my* mouse, or *those* mice. In other words, we wished to see when children and parents go beyond the specific context they are in to think about the category as an abstract whole. The box on page 23 lists some examples.

Rodriguez and I are finding that children begin making broad generalizations about categories as early as two-and-a-half years of age, but that these generalizations increase rather dramatically between two-and-a-half and four years. This result suggests that children may become increasingly attentive to categories during this period. We are also finding that the sorts of generalizations that both children and parents express are especially frequent for categories of people and animals (for example, in the box on page 23 these categories include cats, chipmunks, pigs, girls, animals, Indians, and bad guys). Both mothers and children make many fewer generalizations about categories of inert objects such as shoes, books, chairs.

Children sometimes maintain these generalizations even in the face of conflicting information. For example, consider the conversation that I recently had with my three-and-a-half-year-old son:

Adam: Kids don't like coffee. Grown-ups do.

Me: I don't like coffee.

Adam: Yes, you do! You're not a kid.

Similarly, many children express strong gender-stereotyped beliefs in the preschool years, reporting, for example, that mommies can't be doctors or that boys can't play with dolls (Liben & Signorella 1987). These category-based generalizations seem somewhat rigid and inflexible at the preschool age and are not easily overcome simply by giving the child counterevidence.

It is not yet clear whether or how the talk that children hear from mothers and other caregivers affects the kinds of generalizations they form. Do children who hear many generalizations tend to generalize more broadly than children who do not? Do the sorts of categories that parents and other caregivers talk about in this way affect how children think about these particular categories? For example, if a caregiver expresses many generalizations about gender categories, does this lead children to notice gender more or to make more inferences based on gender? These are important questions that await future research.

Thinking about biological growth

Caterpillars turn into butterflies, tadpoles turn into frogs, babies become adults, and acorns become oak trees. These examples of growth and metamorphosis provide an interesting arena for looking at how children understand categories because in every case the category member undergoes dramatic change and yet in some sense remains the same.

Long before they have any detailed knowledge of biological processes children come to understand several fundamental points about growth (Rosengren et al. 1991; Hickling & Gelman 1995). Four-year-olds understand that an individual animal can change shape, color, and size over the course of growth yet still keep the same name and identity. They understand that every kind of plant comes from a specialized kind of seed; for example, apple trees come from apple seeds. They understand that the growth cycle is predictable and repeating: from seed to plant to fruit to seed to plant to fruit, and so on. They recognize that growth itself comes about due to natural processes (such as sunshine and rain) and not due to artificial processes (such as human activities).

Four-year-olds also realize that nature can "win out" over nurture. For example, if four-year-old children hear about an animal that is adopted by another species and raised in this atypical environment (e.g., a cow raised by pigs), they predict that the animal will continue to grow and develop just like the birth parents (Gelman & Wellman 1991)—the cow will moo and have a straight tail when it grows up, even though it has been raised by pigs.

When children know a great deal about a specialized domain, their categories look remarkably like the categories one would find with older children or even adults.

Preschoolers expect that a child's behaviors, preferences, goals, physical properties, and future identity can all be predicted based on whether the child is referred to as a boy or a girl. Children sometimes maintain these generalizations even in the face of conflicting information. Many children express strong gender-stereotyped beliefs in the preschool years, reporting, for example, that mommies can't be doctors or that boys can't play with dolls.

Preschool children make similar predictions about nature-nurture conflicts with seeds (e.g., a lemon seed planted in a cornfield) or people (e.g., a baby whose birth parents and adoptive parents differ in skin color or personality trait) (Hirschfeld 1996; Springer 1996; Taylor 1996).

Taken altogether, these studies suggest that four-year-old children view growth and development as natural processes (Gelman & Kremer 1991) unfolding inside the animal or plant rather than resulting from outside influences. They expect that a great deal of how an animal or plant grows and develops is fixed at birth in the infant animal or the seed of the plant.

Children at age three know a great deal less about biological growth (Gelman & Wellman 1991; Rosengren et al. 1991; Hickling & Gelman 1995). It may be that early experiences are contributing to the changes between ages three and four. One study found that children who care for a pet goldfish at home are more knowledgeable about biology than children who do not (Inagaki 1990). However, at this point little is known about the kinds of experiences that children have with growth and metamorphosis in their preschools and at home and how these experiences affect children's understanding of growth.

Summary

Children have an impressive understanding of categories by age four—they grasp the distinction between appearance and reality, they use names as a guide for making inferences, and they realize that growth is an orderly, natural process. To some extent, even two-and-a-half- and three-year-old children show some of these same early understandings. However, there are also developmental changes during the preschool period (especially between two-and-a-half and four years of age). The youngest children are apt to have more difficulties with the appearance-reality distinction, are less apt to form spontaneous generalizations using the categories that they have, and are easily confused about the growth process.

Altogether the lesson we have learned from studying children's early categories is that categories are tremendously important tools for young children and have implications for how they view the world. Like any tools, categories can be used in either useful or inappropriate ways. We have already seen some of the dangers in early

categories: children sometimes take names more seriously than they should and draw overly broad generalizations based on the categories that they know. Overall, however, we view the effects of categories as mostly positive. Children make use of categories to expand their knowledge. By simply naming objects we can encourage children to notice how different items are similar and help children gain new information about the world. Furthermore, because children expect items in a category to be alike in nonobvious ways, they are able to learn about "scientific" properties (such as the insides of animals) well before kindergarten age. Both of these implications illustrate that categories are the foundation for later learning in school.

References

Bloom, L. 1970. Language development: Form and function in emerging grammars. Cambridge, MA: MIT Press.

Brown, R.W. 1973. A first language: The early stages. Cambridge, MA: Harvard University Press.

Bruner, J.S. 1973. *Beyond the information given: Studies in the psychology of knowing.* New York: Norton.

Chi, M., J. Hutchinson, & A. Robin. 1989. How inference about novel domain-related concepts can be constrained by structured knowledge. Merrill-Palmer Quarterly 35: 27–62.

Chi, M.T.H., & R.D. Koeske. 1983. Network representation of a child's dinosaur knowledge. *Developmental Psychology* 19: 29–39.

Clark, E.V. 1973. What's in a word? On the child's acquisition of semantics in his first language. In *Cognitive development and the acquisition of language,* ed. T.E. Moore. New York: Academic.

deVries, R. 1969. *Constancy of generic identity in the years three to six.* Monographs of the Society for Research in Child Development, vol. 34, no. 3, serial no. 127. Chicago: University of Chicago Press.

Flavell, J.H. 1986. The development of children's knowledge about the appearance-reality distinction. *American Psychologist* 41: 418–25.

Gelman, S.A., & J.D. Coley. 1990. The importance of knowing a dodo is a bird: Categories and inferences in 2-year-old children. *Developmental Psychology* 26: 796–804.

Gelman, S.A., J.D. Coley, K. Rosengren, E. Hartman, & T. Pappas. In press. *Beyond labeling: The role of maternal input in the acquisition of richly-structured categories.* Monographs of the Society for Research in Child Development. Chicago: University of Chicago Press.

Gelman, S.A., P. Collman, & E.E. Maccoby. 1986. Inferring properties from categories versus inferring categories from properties: The case of gender. *Child Development* 57: 396–404.

Gelman, S.A., & K.E. Kremer. 1991. Understanding natural causes: Children's explanations of how objects and their properties originate. *Child Development* 62: 396–414.

Gelman, S.A., & E.M. Markman. 1986. Categories and induction in young children. *Cognition* 23: 183–209.

Gelman, S.A., & H.M. Wellman. 1991. Insides and essences: Early understandings of the non-obvious. *Cognition* 38: 213–44.

Hickling, A.K., & S.A. Gelman. 1995. How does your garden grow? Early conceptualization of seeds and their place in plant growth cycle. *Child Development* 66: 856–76.

Hirschfeld, L.A. 1996. *Race in the making: Cognition, culture, and the child's construction of human kinds.* Cambridge, MA: MIT Press.

Inagaki, K. 1990. The effects of raising animals on children's biological knowledge. *British Journal of Developmental Psychology* 8: 119–29.

Inhelder, B., & J. Piaget. 1964. *The early growth of logic in the child.* New York: Norton.

James, W. 1890. *The principles of psychology.* New York: Dover.

Johnson, K.E, & C.B. Mervis. 1994. Microge-netic analysis of first steps in children's acquisition of expertise on shorebirds. *Developmental Psychology* 30: 418–35.

Keil, F.C. 1989. *Concepts, kinds, and cognitive development.* Cambridge, MA: MIT Press.

Kuczaj, S. 1976. -ing, -s, and -ed: A study of the acquisition of certain verb inflections. Ph.D. diss., University of Minnesota.

Liben, L.S., & M.L. Signorella, eds. 1987. *Children's gender schemata.* San Francisco: Jossey-Bass.

MacWhinney, B., & C. Snow. 1985. The Child Language Data Exchange System. *Journal of Child Language* 12: 271–95.

MacWhinney, B., & C. Snow. 1990. The Child Language Data Exchange System: An update. *Journal of Child Language* 17: 457–72.

Markman, E.M. 1989. *Categorization and naming in children: Problems of induction.* Cambridge, MA: MIT Press.

Mehler, J., & R. Fox, eds. 1985. *Neonate cognition: Beyond the blooming, buzzing confusion.* Hillsdale, NJ: Erlbaum.

Piaget, J. 1928. *Judgement and reasoning in the child.* London: Routledge & Kegan Paul.

Piaget, J. 1929. *The child's conception of the world.* London: Routledge & Kegan Paul.

Quinn, P.C., P.D. Eimas, & S.L. Rosenkrantz. 1993. Evidence for representations of perceptually similar natural categories by 3-month-old and 4-month-old infants. *Perception* 22: 463–75.

Rosengren, K.S., S.A. Gelman, C.W. Kalish, & M. McCormick. 1991. As time goes by: Children's early understanding of growth in animals. *Child Development* 62: 1302–20.

Sachs, J. 1983. Talking about the there and then: The emergence of displaced reference in parent-child discourse. In *Children's language, vol. 4,* ed. K.E. Nelson. Hillsdale, NJ: Erlbaum.

Smiley, S.S., & A.L. Brown. 1979. Conceptual preference for thematic or taxonomic relations: A nonmonotonic age trend from preschool to old age. *Journal of Experimental Child Psychology* 28: 249–57.

Springer, K. 1996. Young children's understanding of a biological basis for parent-offspring relations. *Child Development* 67: 2841–56.

Taylor, M.G. 1996. The development of children's beliefs about social and biological aspects of gender differences. *Child Development* 67: 1555–71.

What Have We Learned about Developmentally Appropriate Practice?

Loraine Dunn and Susan Kontos

The National Association for the Education of Young Children's long-awaited revision of the developmentally appropriate practice guidelines (Bredekamp & Copple 1997) represents years of public and private discussion among early childhood professionals about the nature of best practice in our field. It functions as a record of consensus thinking on this topic at a point in time (Bredekamp 1997) and, as such, is a working document to stimulate and guide continuing (never-ending!) discussions of this crucial issue over the next decade or so, until it is time for a new version. It is also likely to stimulate a wave of new research that attempts to capture the nuances of the newly articulated guidelines as they are interpreted into beliefs and practices of professionals in the field. Because the past is always prologue to the present, it seems like a logical time to review the research that was generated by the first edition of the developmentally appropriate practice guidelines, which was published in 1987. This article assesses what we have learned from a decade of research on developmentally appropriate practice to help us chart our future course for early childhood practice and scholarship.

Reviewing previous studies on developmentally appropriate practices, as articulated in the first edition, gives us a sense of the research questions that it engendered. In this article, we focus on three issues that have received research attention: (1) How prevalent or common are developmentally appropriate practices in programs serving young children? (2) What do teachers and parents think about developmentally appropriate practice, and how do these beliefs influence teachers' practice? (3) How do appropriate and inappropriate practices influence children's development?

Loraine Dunn, *Ph.D., is an associate professor in the area of early childhood education at the University of Oklahoma in Norman. She teaches early childhood education courses for future teachers and conducts research on classroom practices and professional preparation.*

Susan Kontos, *Ph.D., is professor of child development and family studies at Purdue University in West Lafayette, Indiana, where she teaches courses in early childhood education for future teachers and conducts research on children in early childhood classrooms.*

How common are programs that use developmentally appropriopriate practices?

Since the original NAEYC developmentally appropriate practice guidelines were published, a considerable number of studies have examined the topic. Some of these studies took their definition of developmentally appropriate practice directly from the suggestions for appropriate practice (not the position statement per se) in the 1987 publication (Bredekamp). Questionnaires and observation tools were developed to discriminate between more and less appropriate beliefs and practices (e.g., Hyson, Hirsh-Pasek, & Rescorla 1990; Oakes & Caruso 1990; Charlesworth et al. 1993). Other studies used existing program evaluation tools, deriving scores representative of various features of appropriate practice (Bryant, Clifford, & Peisner 1991; Farran et al. 1993; Sherman & Mueller 1996). The Early Childhood Environment Rating Scale (ECERS) developed by Harms and Clifford (1980), and the developmentally appropriate caregiving (guidance, teacher-child interaction, time for child-initiated activity) and developmentally appropriate (materials and activities available) activities ECERS scores created for the National Child Care Staffing Study (Whitebook, Howes, & Phillips 1989) have been used frequently for this purpose.

What does the research tell us about the existence of developmentally appropriate practice in early childhood programs? Unfortunately, it suggests that few early childhood education classrooms exemplify developmentally appropriate practice—as little as one-third to one-fifth of the programs studied. This seems to be the case in settings serving both preschool-age children and children ages five through eight. Oakes and Caruso (1990) reported that the kindergarten teachers they observed rarely engaged in strategies consistent with developmentally appropriate practice (i.e., child-initiated activities, divergent questioning, small-group instruction). Hatch and Freeman (1988) noted a prevalence of didactic practices in kindergartens. Only 20% of the kindergarten classrooms observed by Bryant, Clifford, and Peisner (1991) were considered developmentally appropriate. Sherman and Mueller (1996) reported that the implementation of developmentally appropriate practice was modest at best

From *Young Children,* July 1997, pp. 4-13. © 1997 by the National Association for the Education of Young Children. Reprinted by permission.

(i.e., below the midpoint of the scale used) in kindergarten, first-grade, and second-grade classrooms, even though half of the teachers they observed had received training on delivering a developmentally appropriate program. Developmentally appropriate practices did occur with greater frequency in the classrooms of those teachers who had received the training.

The situation does not appear to be any better at the preschool level. Only one-third of the child care classrooms observed by Kontos and Dunn (1993) were characterized by a play-based, child-initiated curriculum consistent with developmentally appropriate practice. The teachers rarely elaborated on children's play or asked children divergent questions; instead, they spent a great deal of time placing limits on children's behavior. Few activities or materials to promote literacy, a component of developmentally appropriate practice, were seen in these classrooms during play times. In fact, one-third of the classrooms had no literacy-related activities or materials available during playtime. Literacy-related events, such as storytelling, did occur at other times of the day (Dunn, Beach, & Kontos 1994). In contrast, many of the public-school preschool classrooms observed by Farran and colleagues (1993) were considered developmentally appropriate. However, some types of appropriate practice were more prevalent than others. The teachers in these classrooms acted more appropriately in guiding and nurturing children than in providing activities and materials for learning. This is consistent with research in child care settings where developmentally appropriate caregiving has been more evident than developmentally appropriate activities (Whitebook, Howes, & Phillips 1989).

We appear to have a ways to go in making early childhood programs widely available that exemplify developmentally appropriate practice. This conclusion is consistent with accreditation data. When programs are denied accreditation by NAEYC's National Academy of Early Childhood Programs, their curriculum often does not meet the criteria for developmentally appropriate practice (Bredekamp & Apple 1986). Byrant, Clifford, and Peisner (1991) noted that teachers seem to know what appropriate practice is but need assistance in its implementation. The accredita-

tion guidelines can be helpful but are only a place to start. The NAEYC position statement on developmentally appropriate practice was specifically designed to help teachers in this task. Examples of appropriate and inappropriate practice were included in both the previous and current editions specifically to help teachers differentiate between appropriate and inappropriate practices (Bredekamp 1997). Other tools that may be helpful are the Early Childhood Environment Rating Scale (Harms & Clifford 1980) and the analogous rating scales for infant-toddler programs, school-age programs, and family child care. While these tools were specifically designed to help programs do self-evaluation, they focus on the environment as much as on curriculum per se or teacher-child interaction. Consequently, to round out the definition of developmentally appropriate practice, other sources should be consulted as well.

Beliefs and practices

It makes no sense to discuss developmentally appropriate practices without paying attention to how such practices are—or are not—put into place in classrooms. According to Hyson, practices in early childhood education are a reflection of teacher beliefs, parental expectations, administrative pressure, and "broad societal imperatives" (1991, 27). Most of the research in this area focuses on teachers and parents.

Teachers

It is frequently assumed that engaging in developmentally appropriate practices is primarily contingent on teachers' beliefs about early childhood education. But research indicates that the relationship between early childhood teachers' beliefs and practices may be more complex than that. Two research teams found moderate positive relationships between early childhood teachers' beliefs and practices—that is, the

One important aspect of developmentally appropriate education is having many daily opportunities for each child to make choices about what she will do and with whom she will do it. Of course, all available choices should have educational value. Do your children have big blocks of time for free choice and a variety of interesting activities to choose among?

© Subjects & Predicates

© Subjects & Predicates

What props, picture books, resource people, outings, music, carpentry, or art projects can you add to what you see children doing during playtime?

In developmentally appropriate preschool or primary programs, teachers expand upon children's play themes and interests. They deepen the educational value of the spontaneous experience.

more strongly teachers believed in developmentally appropriate practices, the more likely they were to implement those practices in their classrooms (Hyson, Hirsh-Pasek, & Rescorla 1990; Charlesworth et al. 1993). Oakes and Caruso (1990) reported that although most of the kindergarten teachers in their study rarely used developmentally appropriate teaching strategies, teachers who believed in sharing decisionmaking with children and supporting their autonomy were more likely to use developmentally appropriate teaching strategies than teachers who believed in controlling classroom decisions without input from the children. In contrast, Hatch and Freeman (1988) interviewed 36 kindergarten teachers and found that more than half of them demonstrated conflicts between their philosophy of early childhood education (which typically was either maturationist or constructivist) and their classroom practices (which were didactic and skill oriented). While the teachers espoused a philosophy consistent with child initiation, their classroom practices were academically oriented and didactic. In child care classrooms, Kontos and Dunn (1993) found no differences in the beliefs of teachers whose classrooms differed in developmental appropriateness (as measured by the amount and use of free play). In general, although we cannot say that teachers exhibit congruence of beliefs and behaviors in the classroom, we can say that teachers beliefs are more consistent with developmentally appropriate practices than their behaviors (Charlesworth et al. 1993). This may well reflect the gap between knowledge and application (Bryant, Clifford, & Peisner 1991).

Several studies have shown that training affects teachers' knowledge of developmentally appropriate practice and their likelihood of using these practices. According to Snider and Fu (1990), teachers with greater knowledge of developmentally appropriate practice had academic training in early childhood education and child development as well as breadth in the content of that training. Teachers with the highest developmentally appropriate practice knowledge scores were those with breadth of content in their training and supervised practical experience. Inservice training may also make a difference. Teachers who received inservice training on developmentally appropriate practices via work-

shops, site visits, and journal reflections reported a greater tendency to use these practices in the classroom (Mangione & Maniates 1993). Supporting this notion are data indicating that teachers who received training on implementing developmentally appropriate practice used appropriate practices with greater frequency than teachers without the training (Sherman & Mueller 1996). Although more studies clearly are needed, the available research indicates that both preservice and inservice training probably are important contributors to the prevalence of developmentally appropriate practices in early childhood classrooms.

Parents

Research on parents' beliefs about appropriate practices in early childhood programs helps us to examine the extent to which congruence exists between parents and professionals. Studies show that parents tend to empha-

All parents and teachers agree that learning to read and write is of central importance in the early years. We all want all children to have the ability to read by the age of eight. Yet many preschool, kindergarten, and primary classrooms do not have literacy-promoting materials such as books, paper and pencils, and notepads in their various play areas. How hard is it to do this? Can you take time to do this today?

size school-related skills more than teachers do and that this tendency may be greater for low-income and minority parents (Hess et al. 1981; Knudson-Lindauer & Harris 1989; Hyson et al. 1991; Stipek et al. 1992; Hyson & DeCsipkes 1993; Holloway et al. 1995). Parents of young children appear to be more concerned than teachers about teaching children to count, read, and write and to be less concerned about promoting independence or a positive self-concept. Holloway and colleagues (1995) found that low-income mothers did not view play as a context for learning, although they did perceive it as appropriate for enhancing emotional and physical development. These studies appear to highlight differences in the beliefs of parents and teachers about early childhood education.

Hyson and colleagues (1991) found that only one-third of middle- and upper-middle-class mothers endorsed early, formal academic instruction, while Hyson and DeCsipkes (1993)

found strong agreement with academic instruction among African American parents of kindergarten children. Interestingly, the African American parents also agreed with many developmentally appropriate practices, leading the researchers to infer that these parents did not perceive developmentally appropriate and didactic instruction as dichotomies. According to one study (Stipek et al. 1992), parents with less education more strongly endorse didactic methods of instruction for young children. Holloway and colleagues (1995) suggest that different cultural models of schooling and respect for authority are at the root of differences in parents' beliefs across various income and ethnic populations. They, like Hyson and DeCsipkes (1993), found that low-income mothers acknowledged a wide variety of activities as appropriate for learning. Parents from low-income, minority groups, even as they endorse didactic approaches, appear to be tolerant of a variety of pedagogical approaches, perhaps more so than do middle-class and White parents.

Overall, research suggests that parents' and teachers' beliefs about early childhood education are not congruent. The lack of congruence may not be salient to parents because teachers' practices, especially in kindergarten, are frequently more didactic than their beliefs. Two studies have shown that parents select early childhood programs that are consistent with their educational beliefs (Rescorla et al. 1990; Stipek et al. 1992). In other words, parents who endorse teacher-directed, didactic approaches tend to choose academic early childhood programs for their children, and vice versa. Thus, parents seem to exhibit some congruence between their own beliefs and behaviors.

Children's development

Those who advocate for developmentally appropriate practice do so based on convictions that these classroom practices enhance children's development and facilitate learning.

© The Growth Program

Many parents prefer a didactic (instructional) approach. Teachers and parents need to work closely together so that parents understand how children learn math and literacy skills through play, projects (such as the apple project you see here), conversation with other children, and casual (but purposeful!) small-group work with a teacher. No one wants children not to learn academic skills. The question is how children best learn them.

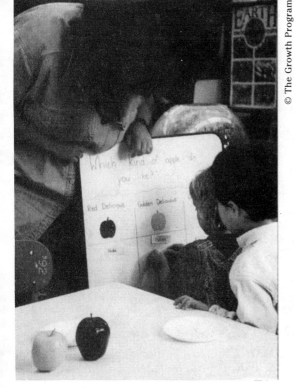

© The Growth Program

© The Growth Program

Social-emotional development

Given the context in which the original NAEYC position statement was released, namely Elkind's (1981) discussion of the "hurried child," it is not surprising that the earliest studies on developmentally appropriate practice focused on stress and emotional development. Two research teams (Hyson, Hirsh-Pasek, & Rescorla 1990; Burts et al., A comparison 1992) documented that children exhibit more stress in didactic environments than in child-initiated environments. In the Hyson, Hirsh-Pasek, and Rescorla study (1990), preschool children enrolled in child-initiated programs displayed lower levels of test anxiety than children enrolled in academic programs. This was the case regardless of parental preferences for classroom approaches.

The second research team led by Burts of Louisiana State University (Burts et al., A comparison 1992), found that kindergarten children exhibited lower levels of stress in the classroom when they were enrolled in developmentally appropriate programs. Specifically, children in inappropriate classrooms exhibited more total stress behaviors throughout the day and more stress behaviors during grouptimes and workbook/worksheet activities. Developmentally appropriate programs were not totally stress free, however; children in these settings displayed more stress during transitions and center times than children in inappropriate settings.

The Louisiana State team has continued their study of stress and developmentally appropriate practice, examining differences in gender, socioeconomic status (SES), and race in both preschool and kindergarten children. Their work suggests boys may be more vulnerable to inappropriate contexts because they display more stress than girls in inappropriate classrooms, and boys in inappropriate classrooms exhibit more stress than other boys in appropriate classrooms. Children from low-SES families responded more negatively to inappropriate environments by exhibiting more stress than

their counterparts in appropriate environments. Low-SES African American children exhibited higher levels of overall stress than low-SES European American children regardless of what type of program they attended (Burts et al., Observed activities 1992; Hart et al. 1996).

Consistent with the work on stress, beneficial effects were observed on children's motivation in developmentally appropriate environments as opposed to inappropriate environments (Stipek et al. 1995). Preschool and kindergarten children in child-centered classrooms had higher expectations for their own success, were less dependent on adult permission and approval, and were more willing to attempt challenging academic tasks. Approaching the motivation question from a slightly different angle, Hyson, Hirsh-Pasek, and Rescorla (1990) found children in appropriate classrooms had more positive attitudes about school. These findings on stress and motivation imply that developmentally appropriate practices are beneficial to children's emotional well-being, an important prerequisite to intrinsic motivation and optimal learning.

While the literature on emotional development clearly favors developmentally appropriate practice, studies of children's social development paint a less clear picture. On the one hand, some findings favor developmentally appropriate practices. Children in more appropriate classrooms are seen as more socially skilled and as having better social and work habits than children in less appropriate classrooms. These children view themselves as more cooperative than do children in inappropriate classrooms (Marcon 1992; Mantzicopoulos, Neuharth-Pritchett, & Morelock 1994).

On the other hand, some findings reveal no differences between children in appropriate and inappropriate classrooms or suggest appropriate practices may lead to less-than-desirable social outcomes. Children in appropriate and inappropriate classrooms rate themselves similarly with regard to their social competence (Mantzicopoulos,

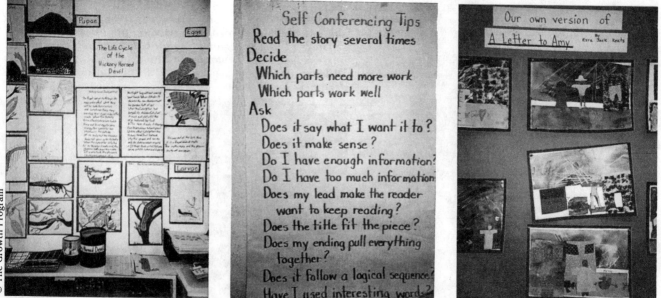

Children from developmentally appropriate backgrounds seem more motivated to learn and to have more positive attitudes toward learning. The majority of the studies that have been done indicate that a didactic approach is not necessary to promote children's learning of academic skills.

Neuharth-Pritchett, & Morelock 1994). Taken together these data seem confusing. However, each study approached social development from a very different angle; thus, the findings may reflect the complexity of social development and its varied relationships with classroom practices.

Cognitive development

Turning now to cognitive development, we focus on creativity, language development, children's perceptions of their cognitive competence, and traditional measures of achievement. Classrooms characterized by child initiation appear to facilitate children's creative development. The Hyson research team found that children in child-initiated classrooms scored higher on measures of creativity, or divergent thinking, than children in academically oriented classrooms (Hirsh-Pasek, Hyson, & Rescorla 1990; Hyson, Hirsh-Pasek, & Rescorla 1990). In two other studies on language development in child-initiated and academically focused programs, the developmentally appropriate, or child-initiated, programs were associated with better language outcomes. Progress reports from public-school preschool programs indicated children in child-initiated classrooms had better verbal skills than children in academically oriented programs (Marcon 1992). Children's receptive language was better in programs with higher-quality literacy environments and when developmentally appropriate activities were more prevalent (Dunn, Beach, & Kontos 1994). Young children in developmentally appropriate programs also seemed more confident in their own cognitive skills. Children described their cognitive competence more positively when they attended child-initiated rather than academically oriented programs (Mantzicopoulos, Neuharth-Pritchett, & Morelock 1994; Stipek et al. 1995).

When using the traditional measuring sticks of achievement tests and report card grades, it is difficult to say whether child-centered or didactic programs are superior. Similar to the state of affairs for social development, the available research is equivocal with regard to these assessments of cognitive development. The majority of the studies indicate that a didactic approach is *not* necessary to promote children's learning of academic skills. Supporting developmentally appropriate practice are studies by Sherman and Mueller (1996) and Marcon (1992). Sherman and Mueller (1996) observed better reading and mathematics achievement scores for children attending developmentally appropriate kindergarten through second grade. Preschool children in Marcon's (1992) study had more positive progress reports overall and specifically on math and science when they attended child-initiated programs. In contrast, Stipek and her colleagues (1995) found that the literacy achievement of preschool and kindergarten children was higher in didactic classrooms as opposed to child-initiated classrooms. Mathematics achievement was similar for children in both types of classrooms, however. Hyson, Hirsh-Pasek, and Rescorla (1990) found no differences in academic achievement as a function of the developmental appropriateness of the program preschool children attended.

Studies following children over time suggest there may be academic benefits to developmentally appropriate programs in the long run. Children experiencing preschool programs rating high on developmental appropriateness do well academically in first grade (Frede & Barnett 1992). In addition, children of low SES attending appropriate kindergarten classrooms tend to have better reading achievement scores in first grade than children attending inappropriate kindergarten classrooms (Burts et al. 1993). These are encouraging findings given

It appears that in the long run, there may be academic benefits to developmentally appropriate programs over academically oriented programs for young children. When children's own interests and successes motivate them, they tend to work hard. When academic skill learning is embedded in interesting activities, wouldn't you guess that most children would learn these skills more easily?

that the classroom children currently attend is also likely to influence their performance. The fact that differences between children in more- and less-appropriate classrooms are evident a year or more later suggests that children's learning environments during these early years are important.

What have we learned?

What have we learned from the research on developmentally appropriate practice? First, developmentally appropriate practices are not the norm in early childhood programs. Although teachers endorse this pedagogical method, they often struggle with implementation. Professional preparation designed to help teachers implement developmentally appropriate practice can be quite effective. We need to learn more about how to most effectively support teachers' implementation of developmentally appropriate practice.

Second, parents and teachers may not agree on the value of developmentally appropriate practice. Helping parents understand the link between developmentally appropriate practices and basic skill acquisition may prevent potential tensions between parents and teachers over instructional methods. The emotional costs of academically oriented classrooms, particularly for children from low-SES, minority groups, behoove us to make parents aware of the potential benefits of developmentally appropriate practice.

Third, developmentally appropriate practices create a positive classroom climate conducive to children's healthy emotional development. Emotional development is an area often neglected when making programming decisions. This literature reminds us that children's emotions and their participation in classroom activities are vitally linked.

Fourth, we have only scratched the surface in understanding how developmentally appropriate practices influence children's social development. While developmentally appropriate practices enhance children's social skills in general, additional data are needed to determine how these practices affect other facets of socialization. Finally, classroom practices and children's cognitive development interact in complex ways.

Taken together the research favors developmentally appropriate practice. In general, child-initiated environments were associated with higher levels of cognitive functioning. Coupling this information with the findings on stress and motivation provides a strong argument for developmentally appropriate practice, especially for low-income children—the very children whose parents may prefer academically oriented programs. While academic environments sometimes may result in higher levels of achievement, this achievement may come at emotional costs to the child. Given that similar cognitive advantages also occur in child-initiated environments, it would seem beneficial to explore ways to communicate more effectively how cognitive development is enhanced through developmentally appropriate practices.

Developmentally appropriate practices will continue to receive close scrutiny from both the practitioner and research communities. As both groups move forward with the new NAEYC guidelines, we will learn much more about teaching and learning in early childhood environments.

References

Bredekamp, S., ed. 1987. *Developmentally appropriate practice in early childhood programs serving children from birth through age 8.* Exp. ed. Washington, DC: NAEYC.

Bredekamp, S. 1997. NAEYC issues revised position statement on developmentally appropriate practice in early childhood programs. *Young Children* 52 (2): 34–40.

Bredekamp, S., & P.L. Apple. 1986. How early childhood programs get accredited: An analysis of accreditation decisions. *Young Children* 42 (1): 34–37.

Bredekamp, S., & C. Copple, eds. 1997. *Developmentally appropriate practice in early childhood programs.* Rev. ed. Washington, DC: NAEYC.

Bryant, D.M., R.M. Clifford, & E.S. Peisner. 1991. Best practices for beginners: Developmental appropriateness in kindergarten. *American Educational Research Journal* 28: 783–803.

Burts, D.C., C.H. Hart, R. Charlesworth, & L. Kirk. 1992. A comparison of frequencies of stress behaviors observed in kindergarten children in classrooms with developmentally appropriate versus developmentally inappropriate instructional practices. *Early Childhood Research Quarterly* 5: 407–23.

Burts, D.C., C.H. Hart, R. Charlesworth, P.O. Fleege, J. Mosely, & R.H. Thomasson. 1992. Observed activities and stress behaviors of children in developmentally appropriate and inappropriate kindergarten classrooms. *Early Childhood Research Quarterly* 7: 297–318.

Burts, D.C., C.H. Hart, R. Charlesworth, D.M. DeWolf, J. Ray, K. Manuel, & P.O. Fleege. 1993. Developmental appropriateness of kindergarten programs and academic outcomes in first grade. *Journal of Research in Childhood Education* 8: 23–31.

Charlesworth, R., C.H. Hart, D.C. Burts, R.H. Thomasson, J. Mosely, & P.O. Fleege. 1993. Measuring the developmental appropriateness of kindergarten teachers' beliefs and practices. *Early Childhood Research Quarterly* 8: 255–76.

Dunn, L., S.A. Beach, & S. Kontos. 1994. Quality of the literacy environment in day care and children's development. *Journal of Research in Childhood Education* 9: 24–34.

Elkind, D. 1981. *The hurried child.* Reading, MA: Addison-Wesley.

Farran, D.C., W. Son-Yarbough, B. Silveri, & A.M. Culp. 1993. Measuring the environment in public school preschools for disadvantaged children: What is developmentally appropriate? In *Perspectives in developmentally appropriate practice: Advances in early education and day care, vol. 5,* ed. S. Reifel, 75–93. Greenwich, CT: JAI Press.

Frede, E., & W.S. Barnett. 1992. Developmentally appropriate public school preschool: A study of implementation of the High/Scope curriculum and its effects on disadvantaged children's skills at first grade. *Early Childhood Research Quarterly* 7: 483–99.

Harms, T., & R. Clifford. 1980. *Early childhood environment rating scale.* New York: Teachers College Press.

Hart, C.H., R. Charlesworth, M.A. Durland, D.C. Burts, M. DeWolf, &

P.O. Fleege. 1996. Developmentally appropriate practice in preschool classrooms: Further support for SES and gender equity. Manuscript submitted for publication, Brigham Young University, Provo, Utah.

Hatch, J.A., & E.B. Freeman. 1988. Kindergarten philosophies and practices: Perspectives of teachers, principals, and supervisors. *Early Childhood Research Quarterly* 3: 151–66.

Hess, R.D., G.G. Price, W.P. Dickson, & M. Conroy. 1981. Different roles for mothers and teachers: Contrasting styles of child care. In *Advances in early education and day care, vol. 2,* ed. S. Kilmer, 1–28. Greenwich, CT: JAI Press.

Hirsh-Pasek, K., M.C. Hyson, & L. Rescorla. 1990. Academic environments in preschool: Do they pressure or challenge young children? *Early Education and Development* 1: 401–23.

Holloway, S.D., M.F. Rambaud, B. Fuller, & C. Eggers-Pierola. 1995. What is "appropriate practice" at home and in child care? Low-income mothers' views on preparing their children for school. *Early Childhood Research Quarterly* 10: 451–73.

Hyson, M.C. 1991. The characteristics and origins of the academic preschool. In *New directions for child development, no. 53, Academic instruction in early childhood: Challenge or pressure?* eds. L. Rescorla, M.C. Hyson, & K. Hirsh-Pasek, 21–29. New York: Jossey-Bass.

Hyson, M.C., & C. DeCsipkes. 1993. Educational and developmental belief systems among African-American parents of kindergarten children. Paper presented at the Biennial Conference of the Society for Research in Child Development, March, New Orleans. ERIC, ED 364336.

Hyson, M.C., K. Hirsh-Pasek, & L. Rescorla. 1990. The classroom practices inventory: An observation instrument based on NAEYC's guidelines for developmentally appropriate practices for 4- and 5-year-old children. *Early Childhood Research Quarterly* 5: 475–94.

Hyson, M.C., K. Hirsh-Pasek, L. Rescorla, J. Cone, & L. Martell-Boinske. 1991. Ingredients of parental pressure in early childhood. *Journal of Applied Developmental Psychology* 12: 347–65.

Knudson-Lindauer, S., & R. Harris. 1989. Priorities for kindergarten curricula: Views of parents and teachers. *Journal of Research on Childhood Education* 4: 51–61.

Kontos, S., & L. Dunn. 1993. Caregiver practices and beliefs in child care varying in developmental appropriateness and quality. In *Perspectives in developmentally appropriate practice: Advances in early education and day care, vol. 5,* ed. S. Reifel, 53–74. Greenwich, CT: JAI Press.

Mangione, P.L., & H. Maniates. 1993. Training teachers to implement developmentally appropriate practice. In *Perspectives in developmentally appropriate practice: Advances in early education and day care, vol. 5,* ed. S. Reifel, 145–66. Greenwich, CT: JAI Press.

Mantzicopoulos, P.Y., S. Neuharth-Pritchett, & J.B. Morelock. 1994. Academic competence, social skills, and behavior among disadvantaged children in developmentally appropriate and inappropriate classrooms. Paper presented at the Annual Meeting of the American Educational Research Association, April, New Orleans.

Marcon, R.A. 1992. Differential effects of three preschool models on inner-city 4-year-olds. *Early Childhood Research Quarterly* 7: 517–30.

Oakes, P.B., & D.A. Caruso. 1990. Kindergarten teachers' use of developmentally appropriate practices and attitudes about authority. *Early Education and Development* 1: 445–57.

Rescorla, L, M.C. Hyson, K. Hirsh-Pasek, & J. Cone. 1990. Academic expectations in mothers of preschool children: A psychometric study of the Educational Attitude Scale. *Early Education and Development* 1: 167–84.

Sherman, C.W., & D.P. Mueller. 1996. Developmentally appropriate practice and student achievement in inner-city elementary schools. Paper presented at Head Start's Third National Research Conference, June, Washington, D.C.

Snider, M.H., & V.R. Fu. 1990. The effects of specialized education and job experience on early childhood teachers' knowledge of developmentally appropriate practice. *Early Childhood Research Quarterly* 5: 69–78.

Stipek, D., R. Feiler, D. Daniels, & S. Milburn. 1995. Effects of different instructional approaches on young children's achievement and motivation. *Child Development* 66: 209–23.

Stipek, D., S. Milburn, D. Galluzzo, & D. Daniels. 1992. Parents' beliefs about appropriate education for young children. *Journal of Applied Developmental Psychology* 13: 293–310.

Whitebook, M., C. Howes, & D. Phillips. 1989. *Who cares? Child care teachers and the quality of care in America. Final report of the National Child Care Staffing Study.* Oakland, CA: Child Care Employee Project.

HOW ASIAN TEACHERS POLISH EACH LESSON TO PERFECTION

JAMES W. STIGLER AND HAROLD W. STEVENSON

James Stigler is associate professor of psychology at the University of Chicago. He was awarded the Boyd R. McCandless Young Scientist Award from the American Psychological Association and was awarded a Guggenheim Fellowship for his work in the area of culture and mathematics learning. Harold W. Stevenson is professor of psychology and director of the University of Michigan Program in Child Development and Social Policy. He is currently president of the International Society for the Study of Behavioral Development and has spent the past two decades engaged in cross-cultural research.

This article is based on a book by Harold W. Stevenson and James Stigler, entitled The Learning Gap *(1994).*

ALTHOUGH THERE is no overall difference in intelligence, the differences in mathematical achievement of American children and their Asian counterparts are staggering.[1]

Let us look first at the results of a study we conducted in 120 classrooms in three cities: Taipei (Taiwan); Sendai (Japan); and the Minneapolis metropolitan area. First and fifth graders from representative schools in these cities were given a test of mathematics that required compu-

tation and problem solving. Among the one hundred first-graders in the three locations who received the lowest scores, fifty-eight were American children; among the one hundred lowest-scoring fifth graders, sixty-seven were American children. Among the top one hundred first graders in mathematics, there were only fifteen American children. And only one American child appeared among the top one hundred fifth graders. The highest-scoring American classroom obtained an average score lower than that of the lowest-scoring Japanese classroom and of all but one of the twenty classrooms in Taipei. In whatever way we looked at the data, the poor performance of American children was evident.

These data are startling, but no more so than the results of a study that involved 40 first- and 40 fifth-grade classrooms in the metropolitan area of Chicago—a very representative sample of the city and the suburbs of Cook County—and twenty-two classes in each of these grades in metropolitan Beijing (China). In this study, children were given a battery of mathematics tasks that included diverse problems, such as estimating the distance between a tree and a hidden treasure on a map, deciding who won a race on the basis of data in a graph, trying to explain subtraction to visiting Martians, or calculating the sum of nineteen and forty-five. There was no area in which the American children were competitive with those from China. The Chinese children's superiority appeared in complex tasks involving the application of knowledge as well as in the routines of computation. When fifth graders were asked, for example, how many members of a stamp club with twenty-four members collected only foreign stamps if five-sixths of the members did so, 59 percent of Beijing children, but only 9 percent of the Chicago children produced the correct answer. On a computation test, only 2.2 percent of the Chinese fifth graders scored at or below the mean for their American counterparts. All of the twenty Chicago area schools had average scores on the fifth-grade geometry test that were below those of the Beijing schools. The results from all these tasks paint a bleak picture of American children's competencies in mathematics.[2]

The poor performance of American students compels us to try to understand the reasons why. We have written extensively elsewhere about the cultural differences in attitudes toward learning and toward the importance of effort vs. innate ability and about the substantially greater amounts of time Japanese and Chinese students devote to academic activities in general and to the study of math in particular.[3] Important as these factors are, they do not tell the whole story. For that we have to take a close look inside the classrooms of Japan, China, and the United States to see how mathematics is actually taught in the three cultures.

LESSONS NOT LECTURES

If we were asked briefly to characterize classes in Japan and China, we would say that they consist of coherent lessons that are presented in a thoughtful, relaxed, and nonauthoritarian manner. Teachers frequently rely on students as sources of information. Lessons are oriented toward problem solving rather than rote mastery of facts and procedures and utilize many different types of representational materials. The role assumed by the teacher is that of knowledgeable guide, rather than that of prime dispenser of information and arbiter of what is correct. There is frequent verbal interaction in the classroom as the teacher attempts to stimulate students to produce, explain, and evaluate solutions to problems. These characteristics contradict stereotypes held by most Westerners about Asian teaching practices. Lessons are not rote; they are not filled with drill. Teachers do not spend large amounts of time lecturing but attempt to lead the children in productive interactions and discussions. And the children are not the passive automata depicted in Western descriptions but active participants in the learning process.

We begin by discussing what we mean by the coherence of a lesson. One way to think of a lesson is by using the analogy of a story. A good story is highly organized; it has a beginning, a middle, and an end; and it follows a protagonist who meets challenges and resolves problems that arise along the way. Above all, a good story engages the reader's interest in a series of interconnected events, which are best understood in the context of the events that precede and follow it.

Such a concept of a lesson guides the organization of instruction in Asia. The curricula are defined in terms of coherent lessons, each carefully designed to fill a forty- to fifty-minute class period with sustained attention to the development of some concept or skill. Like a good story, the lesson has an introduction, a conclusion, and a consistent theme.

We can illustrate what we are talking about with this account of a fifth-grade Japanese mathematics class:

The teacher walks in carrying a large paper bag full of clinking glass. Entering the classroom with a large paper bag is highly unusual, and by the time she has placed the bag on her desk the students are regarding her with rapt attention. What's in the bag? She begins to pull items out of the bag, placing them, one-by-one, on her desk. She removes a pitcher and a vase. A beer bottle evokes laughter and surprise. She soon has six containers lined up on her desk. The children continue to watch intently, glancing back and forth at each other as they seek to understand the purpose of this display.

The teacher, looking thoughtfully at the containers, poses a question: "I wonder which one would hold the most water?" Hands go up, and the teacher calls on different students to give their guesses: "the pitcher," "the beer bottle," "the teapot." The teacher stands aside and ponders: "Some of you said one thing, others said something different. You don't agree with each other. There must be some way we can find out who is correct. How can we know who is correct?" Interest is high, and the discussion continues.

The students soon agree that to find out how much each container holds they will need to fill the containers with something. How about water? The teacher finds some buckets and sends several children out to fill them with water. When they return, the teacher says: "Now what do we do?" Again there is a discussion, and after several minutes the children decide that they will need to use a smaller container to measure how much water fits into each of the larger containers. They decide on a drinking cup, and one of the students warns that they all have to fill each cup to the same level—otherwise the measure won't be the same for all of the groups.

At this point the teacher divides the class into their groups (han) and gives each group one of the containers and a drinking cup. Each group fills its container, counts how many cups of water it holds, and writes the result in a notebook. When all of the groups have completed the task, the teacher calls on the leader of each group to report on the group's findings and notes the results on the blackboard. She has written the names of the containers in a column on the left and a scale from 1 to 6 along the bottom. Pitcher, 4.5 cups; vase, 3 cups; beer bottle, 1.5 cups; and so on. As each group makes its report, the teacher draws a bar representing the amount, in cups, the container holds.

Finally, the teacher returns to the question she posed at the beginning of the lesson: Which container holds the most water? She reviews how they were able to solve the problem and points out that the answer is now contained in the bar graph on the board. She then arranges the containers on the table in order according to how much they hold and writes a rank order on each container, from 1 to 6. She ends the class with a brief review of what they have done. No definitions of ordinate and abscissa, no discussion of how to make a graph preceded the example—these all became obvious in the course of the lesson, and only at the end did the teacher mention the terms that describe the horizontal and vertical axes of the graph they had made.

With one carefully crafted problem, this Japanese teacher has guided her students to discover—and most likely to remember—several important concepts. As this article unfolds, we hope to demonstrate that this example of how well-designed Asian class lessons are is not an isolated one; to the contrary, it is the norm. And as we hope to further demonstrate, excellent class lessons do not come effortlessly or magically. Asian teachers are not born great teachers; they and the lessons they develop require careful nurturing and constant refinement. The practice of teaching in Japan and China is more uniformly perfected than it is in the United States because their systems of education are structured to encourage teaching excellence to develop and flourish. Ours is not. We will take up the question of why and what can be done about this later in the piece. But first, we present a more detailed look at what Asian lessons are like.

COHERENCE BROKEN

Asian lessons almost always begin with a practical problem, such as the example we have just given, or with a word problem written on the blackboard. Asian teachers, to a much greater degree than American teachers, give coherence to their lessons by introducing the lesson with a word problem.

It is not uncommon for the Asian teacher to organize the entire lesson around the solution to this single problem. The teacher leads the children to recognize what is known and what is unknown and directs the students' attention to the critical parts of the problem. Teachers are careful to see that the problem is understood by all of the children, and even mechanics, such as mathematical computation, are presented in the context of solving a problem.

Before ending the lesson, the teacher reviews what has been learned and relates it to the problem she posed at the beginning of the lesson. American teachers are much less likely than Asian teachers to begin and end lessons in this way. For example, we found that fifth-grade teachers in Beijing spent eight times as long at the end of the class period summarizing the lessons as did those in the Chicago metropolitan area.

Now contrast the Japanese math lesson described above with a fifth-grade American mathematics classroom that we recently visited. Immediately after getting the students' attention, the teacher pointed out that today was Tuesday, "band day," and that all students in the band should go to the band room. "Those of you doing the news report today should meet over there in the corner," he continued. He then began the mathematics class with the remaining students by reviewing

It is not uncommon for the Asian teacher to organize the entire lesson around the solution to a single problem.

the solution to a computation problem that had been included in the previous day's homework. After this brief review, the teacher directed the students' attention to the blackboard, where the day's assignment had been written. From this point on, the teacher spent most of the rest of the period walking about the room monitoring the children's work, talking to individual children about questions or errors, and uttering "shushes" whenever the students began talking among themselves.

This example is typical of the American classrooms we have visited, classrooms where students spend more time in transition and less in academic activities, more time working on their own and less being instructed by the teacher; where teachers spend much of their time working with individual students and attending to matters of discipline; and where the shape of a coherent lesson is often hard to discern.

American lessons are often disrupted by irrelevant interruptions. These serve to break the continuity of the lesson and add to children's difficulty in perceiving the lesson as a coherent whole. In our American observations, the teacher interrupted the flow of the lesson with an interlude of irrelevant comments or the class was interrupted by someone else in 20 percent of all first-grade lessons and 47 percent of all fifth-grade lessons. This occurred less than 10 percent of the time at both grade levels in Sendai, Taipei, and Beijing. In fact, no interruptions of either type were recorded during the eighty hours of observation in Beijing fifth-grade classrooms. The mathematics lesson in one of the American classrooms we visited was interrupted every morning by a woman from the cafeteria who polled the children about their lunch plans and collected money from those who planned to eat the hot lunch. Interruptions, as well as inefficient transitions from one activity to another, make it difficult to sustain a coherent lesson throughout the class period.

Coherence is also disrupted when teachers shift frequently from one topic to another. This occurred often in the American classrooms we observed. The teacher might begin with a segment on measurement, then proceed to a segment on simple addition, then to a segment on telling time, and then to a second segment on addition. These segments constitute a math class, but they are hardly a coherent lesson. Such changes in topic were responsible for 21 percent of the changes in segments that we observed in American classrooms but accounted for only 4 percent of the changes in segments in Japanese classrooms.

Teachers frequently capitalize on variety as a means of capturing children's interest. This may explain why American teachers shift topics so frequently within the lesson. Asian teachers also seek variety, but they tend to

No one was leading instruction 9 percent of the time in Taiwan, 26 percent in Japan, and an astonishing 51 percent of the time in the United States.

introduce new activities instead of new topics. Shifts in materials do not necessarily pose a threat to coherence. For example, the coherence of a lesson does not diminish when the teacher shifts from working with numerals to working with concrete objects, if both are used to represent the same subtraction problem. Shifting the topic, on the other hand, introduces variety, but at the risk of destroying the coherence of the lesson.

CLASSROOM ORGANIZATION

Elementary school classrooms are typically organized in one of three ways: the whole class is working as a unit; the class is divided into a number of small groups; or children work individually. In our observations, we noted when the child was receiving instruction or assistance from the teacher and when the student was working on his own. The child was considered to be receiving instruction whenever the teacher was the leader of the activity, whether it involved the whole class, a small group, or only the individual child.

Looking at the classroom in this manner led us to one of our most pronounced findings: Although the number of children in Asian classes is significantly greater than the number in American classes, Asian students received much more instruction from their teachers than American students. In Taiwan, the teacher was the leader of the child's activity 90 percent of the time, as opposed to 74 percent in Japan, and only 46 percent in the United States. No one was leading instruction 9 percent of the time in Taiwan, 26 percent in Japan, and an astonishing 51 percent of the time in the United States (see Figure 1). Even American first graders actually spent more time on their own than they did participating in an activity led by the teacher.

One of the reasons American children received less instruction is that American teachers spent 13 percent of their time in the mathematics classes not working with any students, something that happened only 6 percent of the time in Japan and 9 percent in Taiwan. (As we will see later, American teachers have to steal class time to attend to the multitude of chores involving preparation, assessment, and administration because so little non-teaching time is available for them during the day.)

A much more critical factor in the erosion of instructional time was the amount of time American teachers were involved with individuals or small groups. American children spend 10 percent of their time in small groups and 47 percent of their time working individually. Much of the 87 percent of the time American teachers were working with their students was spent with

these individual students or small groups, rather than with the class as a whole. When teachers provide individual instruction, they must leave the rest of the class unattended, so instructional time for all remaining children is reduced.

Children can learn without a teacher. Nevertheless, it seems likely that they could profit from having their teacher as the leader of their activities more than half of the time they are in the classroom. It is the incredibly large amounts of time that American children are left unassisted and the effect that unattended time has on the coherence of the larger lesson that is the problem.

When children must work alone for long periods of time without guidance or reaction from the teacher, they begin to lose focus on the purpose of their activity. Asian teachers not only assign less seatwork than American teachers, they also use seatwork differently. Chinese and Japanese teachers tend to use short, frequent periods of seatwork, alternating between group discussion of problems and time for children to work problems on their own. Seatwork is thereby embedded into the lesson. After they work individually or in small groups on a problem, Asian students are called upon to present and defend the solutions they came up with. Thus, instruction, practice, and evaluation are tightly interwoven into a coherent whole. In contrast, the average length of seatwork in American fifth-grade classrooms was almost

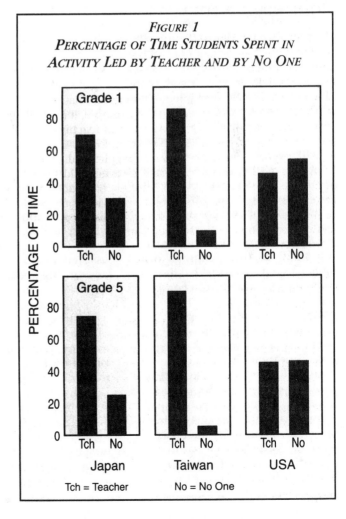

FIGURE 1
PERCENTAGE OF TIME STUDENTS SPENT IN ACTIVITY LED BY TEACHER AND BY NO ONE

PERCENTAGE OF TIME

Grade 1

Grade 5

Japan   Taiwan   USA

Tch = Teacher   No = No One

twice as long as it was in Asian classrooms. And, instead of embedding seatwork into the ongoing back and forth of the lesson, American teachers tend to relegate it to one long period at the end of the class, where it becomes little more than a time for repetitious practice. In Chicago, 59 percent of all fifth-grade lessons ended with a period of seatwork, compared with 23 percent in Sendai and 14 percent in Taipei. American teachers often do not discuss the work or its connection to the goal of the lesson, or even evaluate its accuracy. Seatwork was never evaluated or discussed in 48 percent of all American fifth-grade classes we observed, compared to less than 3 percent of Japanese classes and 6 percent of Taiwan classes.

Since Asian students spend so much of their time in whole-group work, we need to say a word about that format. Whole-class instruction in the United States has gotten a somewhat bad reputation. It has become associated with too much teacher talk and too many passive, tuned-out students. But as we will see in more detail as we continue our description of Asian classrooms, whole-class instruction in Japan and China is a very lively, engaging enterprise. Asian teachers do not spend large amounts of time lecturing. They present interesting problems; they pose provocative questions; they probe and guide. The students work hard, generating multiple approaches to a solution, explaining the rationale behind their methods, and making good use of wrong answers.

HANDLING DIVERSITY

The organization of American elementary school classrooms is based on the assumption that whole-group instruction cannot accommodate students' diverse abilities and levels of achievement; thus, large amounts of whole-class time are given up so that the teacher can work individually with students. Asian educators are

HOW WE MADE SURE WE WERE LOOKING AT REPRESENTATIVE SCHOOLS

FREQUENT REPORTS on television and in books and newspapers purport to depict what happens inside Japanese and Chinese classrooms. These reports usually are based on impressions gathered during brief visits to classrooms—most likely classrooms that the visitor's contacts in Asia have preselected. As a result, it is difficult to gauge the generality of what was seen and reported. Without observing large, representative samples of schools and teachers, it is impossible to characterize the teaching practices of any culture.

The descriptions that we present are based on two large observational studies of first- and fifth-grade classrooms that we conducted in Japan, Taiwan, China, and the United States. In contrast to informal observations, the strength of formal studies such as ours is that the observations are made according to consistent rules about where, when, and what to observe.

In the first study, our observers were in classrooms for a total of over four thousand hours—over a thousand class periods in 20 first- and fifth-grade classrooms in each of three cities: Sendai, Japan; Taipei, Taiwan; and Minneapolis, Minnesota.[1] Our second study took place in two hundred classrooms, forty each in Sendai and Taipei, plus forty in Beijing, China, and eighty in the

Chicago metropolitan area of the United States.[2] Care was taken to choose schools that were representative. Our Chicago metropolitan area sample—the urban and suburban areas that make up Cook County—included schools that are predominantly white, black, Hispanic, and ethnically mixed; schools that draw from upper, middle, and lower socioeconomic groups; schools that are public and private; and schools that are urban and suburban.

Observers visited each classroom four times over a one- to two-week period, yielding a total of eight hundred hours of observations. The observers, who were residents of each city, wrote down as much as they could about what transpired during each mathematics class. Tape recordings made during the classes assisted the observers in filling in any missing information. These detailed narrative accounts of what transpired in the classrooms yielded even richer information than we obtained in the first study, where the observers followed predefined categories for coding behavior during the course of observations.

After the narrative records had been translated into English, we divided each observation into segments, which we defined as beginning each time there was a change in topic, materials, or activity. For example, a segment began when

students put away their textbooks and began working on a worksheet or when the teacher stopped lecturing and asked some of the students to write their solutions to a problem on the blackboard.

Both studies focused on mathematics classes rather than on classes in subjects such as reading, where cultural differences in teaching practices may be more strongly determined by the content of what is being taught. For example, it is likely that the processes of teaching and learning about the multiplication of fractions transcend cultural differences, whereas teaching children how to read Chinese characters may require different approaches from those used to teach children to read an alphabetic language.

REFERENCES

[1]Stevenson, H.W., Stigler, J.W., Lucker, G.W., Lee, S.Y., Hsu, C.C., & Kitamura, S. (1987). Classroom behavior and achievement of Japanese, Chinese, and American children. In R. Glaser (Ed.), *Advances in instructional psychology.* Hillsdale NJ: Erlbaum.
[2]Stigler, J.W., & Perry, M. (1990). Mathematics learning in Japanese, Chinese, and American classrooms. In Stigler, J.W., Shweder, R.A., & Herdt, G. (Eds.), *Cultural psychology: Essays on comparative human development.* Cambridge, Cambridge University Press. Pp. 328-356.

more comfortable in the belief that all children, with proper effort, can take advantage of a uniform educational experience, and so they are able to focus on providing the same high-quality experience to all students. Our results suggest that American educators need to question their long-held assumption that an individualized learning experience is inherently a higher-quality, more effective experience than is a whole-class learning experience. Although it may be true that an equal amount of time with a teacher may be more effective in a one-on-one situation than in a large-group situation, we must realize that the result of individualized instruction, given realistic financial constraints, is to drastically reduce the amount of teacher instruction every child receives.

Japanese and Chinese teachers recognize individual differences among students, but they handle that diversity in a very different way. First, as we will see in more detail later, they have much greater amounts of non-teaching time than do American teachers, and part of that time is available for working with individual students. They may spend extra time with slower students or ask faster students to assist them, but they focus their lesson on teaching all children regardless of apparent differences in ability or developmental readiness. Before we discuss how they do that in a whole-group setting, we

---

Tracking does not exist in Asian elementary schools. This egalitarian philosophy carries over to organization within the classroom.

---

need to first address the question of whether American classrooms are more diverse than Asian ones, thus potentially rendering whole-class instruction more difficult.

Whenever we discuss our research on teaching practices, someone in the audience inevitably reminds us that Japan and China are nations with relatively homogeneous populations while the United States is the melting pot of the world. How could we expect that practices used in Asian societies could possibly be relevant for the American context, where diversity is the rule in race, ethnicity, language, and social class?

What impedes teaching is the uneven preparation of children for the academic tasks that must be accomplished. It is diversity in children's educational backgrounds, not in their social and cultural backgrounds, that poses the greatest problems in teaching. Although the United States is culturally more diverse than Japan or China, we have found no more diversity at the classroom level in the educational level of American than of Asian students. The key factor is that, in the United States, educational and cultural diversity are positively related, leading some persons to the inappropriate conclusion that it is ethnic and cultural diversity, rather than educational diversity, that leads to the difficulties faced by American teachers.

It is true, for example, that there is greater variability in mathematics achievement among American than among Japanese children, but this does not mean that the differences are evident in any particular classroom. Variability in the United States exists to a large extent across neighborhoods and schools (rather than within them). Within individual classrooms, the variability in levels of academic achievement differs little between the United States and Japan, Taiwan, or China. It is wrong to argue that diversity within classrooms is an American problem. Teachers everywhere must deal with students who vary in their knowledge and motivation.

Tracking does not exist in Asian elementary schools. Children are never separated into different classrooms according to their presumed levels of intellectual ability. This egalitarian philosophy carries over to organization within the classroom. Children are not separated into reading groups according to their ability; there is no division of the class into groups differentiated by the rate at which they proceed through their mathematics books. No children leave the classroom for special classes, such as those designed for children who have been diagnosed as having learning disabilities.

How do teachers in Asian classrooms handle diversity in students' knowledge and skills? For one thing, they typically use a variety of approaches in their teaching, allowing students who may not understand one approach the opportunity to experience other approaches to presenting the material. Periods of recitation are alternated with periods in which children work for short periods on practice problems. Explanations by the teacher are interspersed with periods in which children work with concrete materials or struggle to come up with their own solutions to problems. There is continuous change from one mode of presentation, one type of representation, and one type of teaching method to another.

Asian teaching practices thrive in the face of diversity, and some practices even depend on diversity for their effectiveness. Asking students to suggest alternative solutions to a problem, for example, works best when students have had experience in generating a variety of solutions. Incorrect solutions, which are typically dismissed by the American teacher, become topics for discussion in Asian classrooms, and all students can learn from this discussion. Thus, while American schools attempt to solve the problems of diversity by segregating children into different groups or different classrooms, and by spending large amounts of regular class time working with individual students, Asian teachers believe that the only way they can cope with the problem is by devising teaching techniques that accommodate the different interests and backgrounds of the children in their classrooms.

Asian teachers also exploit the fact that the same instruction can affect different students in different ways, something that may be overlooked by American teachers. In this sense, Asian teachers subscribe to what would be considered in the West to be a "constructivist" view of learning. According to this view, knowledge is regarded as something that must be constructed by the child rather than as a set of facts and skills that can be imparted by the teacher. Because children are engaged in their own construction of knowledge, some of the major tasks for the teacher are to pose provocative questions, to allow adequate time for reflection, and to vary teaching techniques so that they are responsive to differences in students' prior experience. Through such practices, Asian teachers are able to accommodate individual differences in learning, even though instruction is not tailored to each student.

USE OF REAL-WORLD PROBLEMS AND OBJECTS

Elementary school mathematics is often defined in terms of mathematical symbols and their manipulation; for example, children must learn the place-value system of numeration and the operations for manipulating numerals to add, subtract, multiply, and divide. In addition, children must be able to apply these symbols and operations to solving problems. In order to accomplish these goals, teachers rely primarily on two powerful tools for representing mathematics: language and the manipulation of concrete objects. How effectively teachers use these forms of representation plays a critical role in determining how well children will understand mathematics.

One common function of language is in defining terms and stating rules for performing mathematical operations. A second, broader function is the use of language as a means of connecting mathematical operations to the real world and of integrating what children know about mathematics. We find that American elementary school teachers are more prone to use language to define terms and state rules than are Asian teachers, who, in their efforts to make mathematics meaningful, use language to clarify different aspects of mathematics and to integrate what children know about mathematics with the demands of real-world problems. Here is an example of what we mean by a class in which the teacher defines terms and states rules:

An American teacher announces that the lesson today concerns fractions. Fractions are defined and she names the numerator and denominator. "What do we call this?" she then asks. "And this?" After assuring herself that the children understand the meaning of the terms, she spends the rest of the lesson teaching them to apply the rules for forming fractions.

Asian teachers tend to reverse the procedure. They focus initially on interpreting and relating a real-world problem to the quantification that is necessary for a mathematical solution and then to define terms and state rules. In the following example, a third-grade teacher in Japan was also teaching a lesson that introduced the notation system for fractions.

The lesson began with the teacher posing the question of how many liters of juice (colored water) were contained in a large beaker. "More than one liter," answered one child. "One and a half liters," answered another. After several children had made guesses, the teacher suggested that they pour the

juice into some one-liter beakers and see. Horizontal lines on each beaker divided it into thirds. The juice filled one beaker and part of a second. The teacher pointed out that the water came up to the first line on the second beaker—only one of the three parts was full. The procedure was repeated with a second set of beakers to illustrate the concept of one-half. After stating that there had been one and one-out-of-three liters of juice in the first big beaker and one and one-out-of-two liters in the second, the teacher wrote the fractions on the board. He continued the lesson by asking the children how to represent two parts out of three, two parts out of five, and so forth. Near the end of the period he mentioned the term "fraction" for the first time and attached names to the numerator and the denominator.

He ended the lesson by summarizing how fractions can be used to represent the parts of a whole.

In the second example, the concept of fractions emerged from a meaningful experience; in the first, it was introduced initially as an abstract concept. The terms and operations in the second example flowed naturally from the teacher's questions and discussion; in the first, language was used primarily for defining and summarizing rules. Mathematics ultimately requires abstract representation, but young children understand such representation more readily if it is derived from meaningful experience than if it results from learning definitions and rules.

Asian teachers generally are more likely than American teachers to engage their students, even very young ones, in the discussion of mathematical concepts. The kind of verbal discussion we find in American classrooms is more short-answer in nature, oriented, for example, toward clarifying the correct way to implement a computational procedure.

Teachers ask questions for different reasons in the United States and in Japan. In the United States, the purpose of a question is to get an answer. In Japan, teachers pose questions to stimulate thought. A Japanese teacher considers a question to be a poor one if it elicits an immediate answer, for this indicates that students were not challenged to think. One teacher we interviewed told us of discussions she had with her fellow teachers on how to improve teaching practices. "What do you talk about?" we wondered. "A great deal of time," she reported, "is spent talking about questions we can pose to the class— which wordings work best to get students involved in thinking and discussing the material. One good question can keep a whole class going for a long time; a bad one produces little more than a simple answer."

In one memorable example recorded by our observers, a Japanese first-grade teacher began her class by posing the question to one of her students: "Would you explain the difference between what we learned in yesterday's lesson and what you came across in preparing for today's lesson?" The young student thought for a long time, but then answered the question intelligently, a performance that undoubtedly enhanced his understanding of both lessons.

CONCRETE REPRESENTATIONS

Every elementary school student in Sendai possesses a "Math Set," a box of colorful, well-designed materials for teaching mathematical concepts: tiles, clock, ruler, checkerboard, colored triangles, beads, and many other attractive objects.

In Taipei, every classroom is equipped with a similar, but larger, set of such objects. In Beijing, where there is much less money available for purchasing such materials, teachers improvise with colored paper, wax fruit, plates, and other easily obtained objects. In all cases, these concrete objects are considered to be critically important tools for teaching mathematics, for it is through manipulating these objects that children can form important links between real-world problems and abstract mathematical notations.

American teachers are much less likely than Chinese or Japanese teachers to use concrete objects. At fifth grade, for example, Sendai teachers were nearly twice as likely to use concrete objects as the Chicago area teachers, and Taipei teachers were nearly five times as likely. There was also a subtle, but important, difference in the way Asian and American teachers used concrete objects. Japanese teachers, for example, use the items in the Math Set throughout the elementary school years and introduced small tiles in a high percentage of the lessons we observed in the first grade. American teachers seek variety and may use Popsicle sticks in one lesson, and in another, marbles, Cheerios, M&Ms, checkers, poker chips, or plastic animals. The American view is that objects should be varied in order to maintain children's interest. The Asian view is that using a variety of representational materials may confuse children, and thereby make it more difficult for them to use the objects for the representation and solution of mathematics problems. Having learned to add with tiles makes multiplication easier to understand when the same tiles are used.

Through the skillful use of concrete objects, teachers are able to teach elementary school children to understand and solve problems that are not introduced in American curricula until much later. An example occurred in a fourth-grade mathematics lesson we observed in Japan. The problem the teacher posed is a difficult one for fourth graders, and its solution is generally not taught in the United States until much later. This is the problem:

> There are a total of thirty-eight children in Akira's class. There are six more boys than there are girls. How many boys and how many girls are in the class?

This lesson began with a discussion of the problem and with the children proposing ways to solve it. After the discussion, the teacher handed each child two strips of paper, one six units longer than the other, and told the class that the strips would be used to help them think about the problem. One slip represented the number of girls in the class and the other represented the number of boys. By lining the strips next to each other, the children could see that the degree to which the longer one protruded beyond the shorter one represented 6 boys. The procedure for solving the problem then unfolded as the teacher, through skillful questioning, led the children to the solution: The number of girls was found by taking the total of both strips, subtracting 6 to make the strips of equal length, and then dividing by 2. The number of boys could be found, of course, by adding 6 to the number of girls. With this concrete visual representation of the problem and careful guidance from the teacher, even fourth graders were able to understand the problem and its solution.

STUDENTS CONSTRUCT MULTIPLE SOLUTIONS

A common Western stereotype is that the Asian teacher is an authoritarian purveyor of information, one who expects students to listen and memorize correct answers or correct procedures rather than to construct knowledge themselves. This may or may not be an accurate description of Asian high school teachers,[4] but, as we have seen in previous examples, it does not describe the dozens of elementary school teachers that we have observed.

Chinese and Japanese teachers rely on students to generate ideas and evaluate the correctness of the ideas. The possibility that they will be called upon to state their own solution as well as to evaluate what another student has proposed keeps Asian students alert, but this technique has two other important functions. First, it engages students in the lesson, increasing their motivation by making them feel they are participants in a group process. Second, it conveys a more realistic impression of how knowledge is acquired. Mathematics, for example, is a body of knowledge that has evolved gradually through a process of argument and proof. Learning to argue about mathematical ideas is fundamental to understanding mathematics. Chinese and Japanese children begin learning these skills in the first grade; many American elementary school students are never exposed to them.

We can illustrate the way Asian teachers use students' ideas with the following example. A fifth-grade teacher in Taiwan began her mathematics lesson by calling attention to a six-sided figure she had drawn on the blackboard. She asked the students how they might go about finding the area of the shaded region. "I don't want you to tell me what the actual area is, just tell me the approach you would use to solve the problem. Think of as many different ways as you can of ways you could determine the area that I have drawn in yellow chalk." She allowed the students several minutes to work in small groups and then called upon a child from each group to describe the group's solution. After each proposal, many of which were quite complex, the teacher asked members of the other groups whether the procedure described could yield a correct answer. After several different procedures had been suggested, the teacher moved on to a second problem with a different embedded figure and repeated the process. Neither teacher nor students actually carried out a solution to the problem until all of the alternative solutions had been discussed. The lesson ended with the teacher affirming the importance of coming up with multiple solutions. "After all," she said, "we face many problems every day in the real world. We have to remember that there is not only one way we can solve each problem."

American teachers are less likely to give students opportunities to respond at such length. Although a great deal of interaction appears to occur in American classrooms—with teachers and students posing questions and giving answers—American teachers generally pose questions that are answerable with a yes or no or with a short phrase. They seek a correct answer and continue calling on students until one produces it. "Since we can't subtract 8 from 6," says an American teacher, "we have to . . . what?" Hands go up, the teacher calls on a girl who says "Borrow." "Correct," the teacher replies. This kind of interchange does not establish the student as a valid source of information, for the final arbiter of the correctness of the student's opinions is still the teacher. The situation is very different in Asian classrooms, where children are likely to be asked to explain their answers and other children are then called upon to evaluate their correctness.

Clear evidence of these differing beliefs about the roles of students and teachers appears in the observations of how teachers evaluate students' responses. The most frequent form of evaluation used by American teachers was praise, a technique that was rarely used in either Taiwan or Japan. In Japan, evaluation most frequently took the form of a discussion of children's errors.

Praise serves to cut off discussion and to highlight the teacher's role as the authority. It also encourages children to be satisfied with their performance rather than informing them about where they need improvement. Discussing errors, on the other hand, encourages argument and justification and involves students in the exciting quest of assessing the strengths and weaknesses of the various alternative solutions that have been proposed.

Why are American teachers often reluctant to encourage students to participate at greater length during mathematics lessons? One possibility is that they feel insecure about the depth of their own mathematical training. Placing more emphasis on students' explanations necessarily requires teachers to relinquish some control over the direction the lesson will take. This can be a frightening prospect to a teacher who is unprepared to evaluate the validity of novel ideas that students inevitably propose.

USING ERRORS EFFECTIVELY

We have been struck by the different reactions of Asian and American teachers to children's errors. For Americans, errors tend to be interpreted as an indication of failure in learning the lesson. For Chinese and Japanese, they are an index of what still needs to be learned. These divergent interpretations result in very different reactions to the display of errors—embarrassment on the part of the American children, calm acceptance by Asian children. They also result in differences in the manner in which teachers utilize errors as effective means of instruction.

We visited a fifth-grade classroom in Japan the first day the teacher introduced the problem of adding fractions with unequal denominators. The problem was a simple one: adding one-third and one-half. The children were

> *The most frequent form of evaluation used by American teachers was praise, a technique that was rarely used in either Taiwan or Japan.*

told to solve the problem and that the class would then review the different solutions.

After everyone appeared to have completed the task, the teacher called on one of the students to give his answer and to explain his solution. "The answer is two-fifths," he stated. Pointing first to the numerators and then to the denominators, he explained: "One plus one is two; three plus two is five. The answer is two-fifths." Without comment, the teacher asked another boy for his solution. "Two point one plus three point one, when changed into a fraction adds up to two-fifths." The children in the classroom looked puzzled. The teacher, unperturbed, asked a third student for her solution. "The answer is five-sixths." The student went on to explain how she had found the common denominator, changed the fractions so that each had this denominator, and then added them.

The teacher returned to the first solution. "How many of you think this solution is correct?" Most agreed that it was not. She used the opportunity to direct the children's attention to reasons why the solution was incorrect. "Which is larger, two-fifths or one-half?" The class agreed that it was one-half. "It is strange, isn't it, that you could add a number to one-half and get a number that is smaller than one-half?" She went on to explain how the procedure the child used would result in the odd situation where, when one-half was added to one-half, the answer yielded is one-half. In a similarly careful, interactive manner, she discussed how the second boy had confused fractions with decimals to come up with his surprising answer. Rather than ignoring the incorrect solutions and concentrating her attention on the correct solution, the teacher capitalized on the errors the children made in order to dispel two common misperceptions about fractions.

We have not observed American teachers responding to children's errors so inventively. Perhaps because of the strong influence of behavioristic teaching that conditions should be arranged so that the learner avoids errors and makes only a reinforceable response, American teachers place little emphasis on the constructive use of errors as a teaching technique. It seems likely, however, that learning about what is wrong may hasten children's understanding of why the correct procedures are appropriate.

WHY NOT HERE?

Few who have visited urban classrooms in Asia would disagree that the great majority of Chinese and Japanese teachers are highly skilled professionals. Their dedication is legendary; what is often not appreciated is how thoughtfully and adroitly they guide children through the vast amount of material that they must master during the six years of elementary school. We, of course, witnessed examples of excellent lessons in American classrooms. And there are of course individual differences among Asian teachers. But what has impressed us in our personal observations and in the data from our observational studies is how remarkably well most Asian teachers teach. It is the *widespread* excellence of Asian class lessons, the high level of performance of the *average* teacher, that is so stunning.

The techniques used by Chinese and Japanese teachers are not new to the teaching profession—nor are they foreign or exotic. In fact, they are the types of techniques often recommended by American educators. What the Japanese and Chinese examples demonstrate so compellingly is that when widely implemented, such practices can produce extraordinary outcomes.

Unfortunately, these techniques have not been broadly applied in the United States. Why? One reason, as we have discussed, is the Asian belief that the whole-group lesson, if done well, can be made to work for every child. With that assumption, Asian teachers can focus on the perfection of that lesson. However, even if American educators shared that belief, it would be difficult for them to achieve anything near the broad-based high quality that we observed in Asian classrooms. This is not the fault of American teachers. The fault lies with a system that prepares them inadequately and then exhausts them physically, emotionally, and intellectually while denying them the collegial interaction that every profession relies upon for the growth and refinement of its knowledge base.

The first major obstacle to the widespread development and execution of excellent lessons in America is the fact that American teachers are overworked. It is inconceivable that American teachers, by themselves, would be able to organize lively, vivid, coherent lessons under a regimen that requires that they teach hour after hour every day throughout the school year. Preparing lessons that require the discovery of knowledge and the construction of understanding takes time. Teaching them effectively requires energy. Both are in very short supply for most American teachers.

Being an elementary school teacher in the United States at the end of the twentieth century is extraordinarily difficult, and the demands made by American society exhaust even the most energetic among them. "I'm dancing as fast as I can" one teacher summarized her feelings about her job, "but with all the things that I'm supposed to do, I just can't keep up."

The full realization of how little time American teachers have when they are not directly in charge of children became clear to us during a meeting in Beijing. We were discussing the teachers' workday. When we informed the Chinese teachers that American teachers are responsible for their classes all day long, with only an hour or less outside the classroom each day, they looked incredulous. How could any teacher be expected to do a good job when there is no time outside of class to prepare and correct lessons, work with individual children, consult

with other teachers, and attend to all of the matters that arise in a typical day at school! Beijing teachers teach no more than three hours a day, unless the teacher is a homeroom teacher, in which case, the total is four hours. During the first three grades, the teaching assignment includes both reading and mathematics; for the upper three grades of elementary school, teachers specialize in one of these subjects. They spend the rest of their day at school carrying out all of their other responsibilities to their students and to the school. The situation is similar in Japan. According to our estimate, Japanese elementary school teachers are in charge of classes only 60 percent of the time they are at school.

The large amounts of nonteaching time at school are available to Asian teachers because of two factors. The first concerns the number of teachers typically assigned to Asian schools. Although class sizes are considerably larger in Asia, the student-to-teacher ratio within a school does not differ greatly from that in the United States. By having more students in each class and the same number of teachers in the school, all teachers can have fewer teaching hours. Time is freed up for teachers to meet and work together on a daily basis, to prepare lessons for the next day, to work with individual children, and to attend staff meetings.

The second factor increasing the time available to Japanese and Chinese teachers at school is that they spend more hours at school each day than do American teachers. In our study, for example, teachers in Sendai and Taipei spent an average of 9.5 and 9.1 hours per day, respectively, compared to only 7.3 hours for the American teachers. Asian teachers arrive at school early and stay late, which gives them time to meet together and to work with children who need extra help. Most American teachers, in contrast, arrive at school shortly before classes begin and leave not long after they end. This does not mean a shorter work week for American teachers. What it does mean is that they must devote their evenings to working alone on the next day's lessons, further increasing their sense of isolation.

LEARNING FROM EACH OTHER

The second reason Asian class lessons are so well crafted is that there is a very systematic effort to pass on the accumulated wisdom of teaching practice to each new generation of teachers and to keep perfecting that practice by providing teachers the opportunities to continually learn from each other.

Americans often act as if good teachers are born, not made. We hear this from both teachers and parents. They seem to believe that good teaching happens if the teacher has a knack with children, gets along well with them, and keeps them reasonably attentive and enthusiastic about learning. It is a commonly accepted truism in many colleges of education that teaching is an art and that students cannot be taught how to teach.

Perhaps because of this belief, students emerge from American colleges of education with little training in how to design and teach effective lessons. It is assumed that teachers will discover this for themselves. Courses in teaching methods are designed to serve a different purpose. On the one hand, they present theories of learning and cognitive development. Although the students are able to quote the major tenets of the theorists currently in vogue, the theories remain as broad generalizations that are difficult to apply to the everyday tasks that they will face as classroom teachers. At the opposite extreme, these methods courses provide education students with lists of specific suggestions for activities and materials that are easy to use and that children should enjoy (for example, pieces of breakfast cereal make handy counters for teaching basic number facts). Teachers are faced, therefore, with information that is either too general to be applied readily or so specific that it has only limited usefulness. Because of this, American teachers complain that most of what they know had to be learned by themselves, alone, on the job.

In Asia, graduates of teacher training programs are still considered to be novices who need the guidance and support of their experienced colleagues. In the United States, training comes to a near halt after the teachers acquire their teaching certificates. American teachers may take additional coursework in the evenings or during summer vacations, or they may attend district or city-wide workshops from time to time. But these opportunities are not considered to be an essential part of the American system of teacher training.

In Japan, the system of teacher training is much like an apprenticeship under the guidance of experienced colleagues. The teacher's first year of employment marks the beginning of a lengthy and elaborate training process. By Japanese law, beginning teachers must receive a minimum of twenty days of inservice training during their first year on the job.[5] Supervising the inservice training are master teachers, selected for their teaching ability and their willingness to assist their young colleagues. During one-year leaves of absence from their own classrooms, they observe the beginner in the classroom and offer suggestions for improvement.

In addition to this early tutelage in teaching techniques, Japanese teachers, beginners as well as seasoned teachers, are required to continually perfect their teaching skills through interaction with other teachers. One mechanism is through meetings organized by the vice principal and head teachers of their own school. These experienced professionals assume responsibility for advising and guiding their young colleagues. The head teachers organize meetings to discuss teaching techniques and to devise lesson plans and handouts. These meetings are supplemented by informal districtwide study groups and courses at municipal or prefectural education centers.[6]

A glimpse at what takes place in these study groups is provided in a conversation we recently had with a Japanese teacher. She and her colleagues spend a good deal of their time together working on lesson plans. After they finish a plan, one teacher from the group teaches the lesson to her students while the other teachers look on. Afterward, the group meets again to criticize the teacher's performance and to make suggestions for how the lesson could be improved. In her school, there is an annual "teaching fair." Teachers from other schools are invited to visit the school and observe the lessons being taught. The visitors rate the lessons, and the teacher with the best lesson is declared the winner.

In addition, national television in Japan presents programs that show how master teachers handle particular lessons or concepts. In Taiwan, such demonstrations are available on sets of videotapes that cover the whole curriculum.

Making use of lessons that have been honed over time does not mean that the Asian teacher simply mimics what she sees. As with great actors or musicians, the substance of the curriculum becomes the script or the score; the goal is to perform the role or piece as effectively and creatively as possible. Rather than executing the curriculum as a mere routine, the skilled teacher strives to perfect the presentation of each lesson. She uses the teaching techniques she has learned and imposes her own interpretation on these techniques in a manner that she thinks will interest and motivate her pupils.

Of course, teachers find it easier to share helpful tips and techniques among themselves when they are all teaching the same lesson at about the same time. The fact that Taiwan, Japan, and China each has a national curriculum that provides a common focus is a significant factor in teacher interaction. Not only do we have no national curriculum in the United States, but the curriculum may not be consistent within a city or even within a single school. American textbooks, with a spiral curriculum that repeats topics year after year and with a profusion of material about each topic, force teachers to omit some of each year's material. Even when teachers use the same textbook, their classes differ according to which topics they choose to skip and in the pace with which they proceed through the text. As a result, American teachers have less incentive than Asian teachers to share experiences with each other or to benefit from the successes and failures that others have had in teaching particular lessons.

Adding further to the sense of isolation is the fact that American teachers, unlike other professionals, do not share a common body of knowledge and experience. The courses offered at different universities and colleges vary, and even among their required courses, there is often little common content from college to college. Student teaching, the only other activity in which all budding teachers participate, is a solitary endeavor shared only with the regular classroom teacher and perhaps a few fellow student teachers.

Opportunities for Asian teachers to learn from each other are influenced, in part, by the physical arrangements of the schools. In Japanese and Chinese schools, a large room in each school is designed as a teachers' room, and each teacher is assigned a desk in this room. It is here that they spend their time away from the classroom preparing lessons, correcting students' papers, and discussing teaching techniques. American teachers, isolated in their own classrooms, find it much harder to discuss their work with colleagues. Their desk and teaching materials are in their own classrooms, and the only common space available to teachers is usually a cramped room that often houses supplies and the school's duplicating facilities, along with a few chairs and a coffee machine. Rarely do teachers have enough time in their visits to this room to engage in serious discussions of educational policy or teaching practices.

* * *

Critics argue that the problems facing the American teacher are unique and that it is futile to consider what Japanese and Chinese teaching are like in seeking solutions to educational problems in the United States. One of the frequent arguments is that the students in the typical Asian classroom share a common language and culture, are well disciplined and attentive, and are not distracted by family crises and their own personal problems, whereas the typical American teacher is often faced with a diverse, burdened, distracted group of students. To be sure, the conditions encountered by teachers differ greatly among these societies. Week after week, American teachers must cope with children who present them with complex, wrenching personal problems. But much of what gives American classrooms their aura of disarray and disorganization may be traced to how schools are organized and teachers are trained as well as to characteristics of the children.

It is easy to blame teachers for the problems confronting American education, and this is something that the American public is prone to do. The accusation is unfair. We cannot blame teachers when we deprive them of adequate training and yet expect that on their own they will become innovative teachers; when we cast them in the roles of surrogate parents, counselors, and psychotherapists and still expect them to be effective teachers; and when we keep them so busy in the classroom that they have little time or opportunity for professional development once they have joined the ranks of the teaching profession.

Surely the most immediate and pressing task in educating young students is to create a new type of school environment, one where great lessons are a commonplace occurrence. In order to do this, we must ask how we can institute reforms that will make it possible for American teachers to practice their profession under conditions that are as favorable for their own professional development and for the education of children as those that exist in Asia.

Note: The research described in this article has been funded by grants from the National Institute of Mental Health, the National Science Foundation, and the W.T. Grant Foundation. The research is the result of collaboration with a large group of colleagues in China, Japan, Taiwan, and the United States who have worked together for the past decade. We are indebted to each of these colleagues and are especially grateful to Shinying Lee of the University of Michigan who has been a major contributor to the research described in this article.

REFERENCES

[1]The superior academic achievement of Chinese and Japanese children sometimes leads to speculation that they are brighter than American children. This possibility has been supported in a few reports that have received attention in the popular press and in several scientific journals. What has not been reported or widely understood is that, without exception, the studies contending that differences in intelligence are responsible for differences in academic performance have failed to meet acceptable standards of scientific inquiry. In fact, studies that have reported differences in I.Q. scores between Asian and American children have been flawed conceptually and methodologically. Their major defects are nonequivalent tests used in the different locations and noncomparable samples of children.

To determine the cognitive abilities of children in the three cultures, we needed tests that were linguistically comparable and culturally unbiased. These requirements preclude reliance on tests translated from one language to another or the evaluation of children in one country on the basis of norms obtained in another country. We assembled a team with members from each of the three cultures, and they developed ten cognitive tasks falling into traditional "verbal" and "performance" categories.

The test results revealed no evidence of overall differences in the cognitive functioning of American, Chinese, and Japanese children. There was no tendency for children from any of the three cultures to achieve significantly higher average scores on all the tasks. Children in each culture had strengths and weaknesses, but by the fifth grade of elementary school, the most notable feature of children's cognitive performance was the similarity in level and variability of their scores. [Stevenson, H.W., Stigler, J.W., Lee, S.Y., Lucker, G.W., Kitamura, S., & Hsu, C.C. (1985). Cognitive performance and academic achievement of Japanese, Chinese, and American children. *Child Development, 56,* 718-734.]

[2]Stevenson, H.W. (1990). Adapting to school: Children in Beijing and Chicago. *Annual Report.* Stanford CA: Center for Advanced Study in the Behavioral Sciences. Stevenson, H.W., Lee, S., Chen, C., Lummis, M., Stigler, J., Fan, L., & Ge, F. (1990). Mathematics achievement of children in China and the United States. *Child Development,* 61, 1053-1066. Stevenson, H.W., Stigler, J.W., & Lee, S.Y. (1986). Mathematics achievement of Chinese, Japanese, and American children. *Science,* 231, 693-699. Stigler, J.W., Lee, S.Y., & Stevenson, H.W. (1990). *Mathematical knowledge.* Reston: VA: National Council of Teachers of Mathematics.

[3]Stevenson, H.W., Lee, S.Y., Chen C., Stigler, J.W., Hsu, C.C., & Kitamura, S. (1990). Contexts of achievement. *Monographs of the Society for Research in Child Development.* Serial No. 221, 55, Nos. 1-2.

[4]Rohlen, T.P. (1983). *Japan's High Schools.* Berkeley: University of California Press.

[5]Dorfman, C.H. (Ed.) (1987). *Japanese Education Today.* Washington, D.C.: U.S. Department of Education.

[6]Ibid.

Unit 3

Unit Selections

Key Points to Consider

❖ What are some of the ways that friends can be beneficial or harmful to a child's self-concept and self-esteem? Why is it important for children to become members of a peer group? Can you think of popular books or movies that illustrate the values of friendship and peers?

❖ Do you think you have a high EQ? What sort of emotional characteristics do you think may go into having a high EQ? Do you think personality is something that is innately given or can one's personality be changed in significant ways? If you had a child with a very introverted personality, would it be advisable to try to help this child learn to become more extroverted? Why or why not?

❖ When you were a child, did you experience gender segregation—boys playing with boys, girls with girls? How might this have influenced your social and emotional development? Could gender segregation reinforce differences or create difficulties between boys and girls and between men and women? What could a teacher or parent do to influence gender segregation?

❖ Do you think children today experience high levels of aggression in their daily environment? Name some examples. As a parent or teacher, would you try to discourage children from acting out or playing aggressively, such as in the case of superhero play?

❖ Have you experienced a significant loss or death of a loved one as a child or as an adult? How would you help a child who has experienced this sort of profound loss?

 **Links**

www.dushkin.com/online/

14. **Counseling for Children**
    http://montgomery-al.com/cfc/

15. **Help Children Work with Feelings**
    http://www.aha4kids.com/index.html

16. **Max Planck Institute for Psychological Research**
    http://www.mpipf-muenchen.mpg.de/BCD/bcd_e.htm

17. **National Child Care Information Center (NCCIC)**
    http://www.nccic.org/

18. **Serendip**
    http://serendip.brynmawr.edu/serendip/

These sites are annotated on pages 4 and 5.

Social and Emotional Development

e of the truisms about our species is that we are
ial animals. From birth, each person's life is a
nstellation of relationships, from family at home to
nds in the neighborhood and school. This unit
dresses how children's social and emotional
velopment is influenced by important relationships
h parents, peers, and teachers.

When John Donne in 1623 wrote, "No man is
island . . . every man is . . . a part of the main,"
implied that all humans are connected to each
er and that these connections make us who we
. Early in this century, sociologist C. H. Cooley
hlighted the importance of relationships with the
ase "looking-glass self" to describe how people
d to see themselves as a function of how others
ceive them. Personality theorist Alfred Adler, also
ting in the early twentieth century, claimed that
sonal strength derived from the quality of one's
nectedness to others: The stronger the relation-
os, the stronger the person. The notion that a
son's self-concept arises from relations with others
o has roots in developmental psychology. As Jean
get once wrote, "There is no such thing as
ated individuals; there are only relations." The
cles in this unit respect these traditions by em-
asizing the theme that a child's development
urs within the context of relationships.

When most people think of children, words such
"carefree," "fun," "sheltered," and "happy" often
ne to mind—images of depression, sadness, and
urning are not typical. "How Kids Mourn" discusses

the sobering situations faced by children who have
experienced serious loss.

Having a high IQ is no guarantee of future life
success. Recent research indicates that "emotional
intelligence" as described in "The EQ Factor" may
be a vital ingredient in determining how successful
an individual becomes. This article describes how
researchers are delving into how to assess and
nurture children as they develop healthy and strong
emotional skills and abilities.

Another major influence in the landscape of
childhood is friendship. When do childhood
friendships begin? Friends become increasingly
important during the elementary school years. If
forming strong, secure attachments with family
members is an important task of early childhood,
then one of the major psychological achievements of
middle childhood is a move toward the peer group.
Across the elementary school years, children spend
ever-increasing time with peers in the neighborhood
and at school. Janis Bullock, in "Children without
Friends," examines children's relationships with peers
and describes different kinds of children—popular,
rejected, neglected. This article helps us understand
that friends are clearly a developmental and
psychological advantage.

An interesting characteristic of peer relations in
middle childhood is that boys and girls rarely play
together. Most of the time, boys play with boys and
girls play with girls. "Girls and Boys Together . . .
but Mostly Apart" discusses the central role of
gender in social and emotional development.

EARLY EXPERIENCE AND EMOTIONAL DEVELOPMENT:
The Emergence of Wariness of Heights

Joseph J. Campos,[1] Bennett I. Bertenthal,[2] and Rosanne Kermoian[1]
[1]*University of California at Berkeley,* [2]*University of Virginia*

Abstract—*Because of its biological adaptive value, wariness of heights is widely believed to be innate or under maturational control. In this report, we present evidence contrary to this hypothesis, and show the importance of locomotor experience for emotional development. Four studies bearing on this conclusion have shown that (1) when age is held constant, locomotor experience accounts for wariness of heights; (2) "artificial" experience locomoting in a walker generates evidence of wariness of heights; (3) an orthopedically handicapped infant tested longitudinally did not show wariness of heights so long as he had no locomotor experience; and (4) regardless of the age when infants begin to crawl, it is the duration of locomotor experience and not age that predicts avoidance of heights. These findings suggest that when infants begin to crawl, experiences generated by locomotion make possible the development of wariness of heights.*

Between 6 and 10 months of age, major changes occur in fearfulness in the human infant. During this period, some fears are shown for the first time, and many others show a step-function increase in prevalence (Bridges, 1932; Scarr & Salapatek, 1970; Sroufe, 1979). These changes in fearfulness occur so abruptly, involve so many different elicitors, and have such biologically adaptive value that many investigators propose maturational explanations for this developmental shift (Emde, Gaensbauer, & Harmon, 1976; Kagan, Kearsley, & Zelazo, 1978). For such theorists, the development of neurophysiological structures (e.g., the frontal lobes) precedes and accounts for changes in affect.

In contrast to predominantly maturational explanations of developmental changes, Gottlieb (1983, 1991) proposed a model in which different types of experiences play an important role in developmental shifts. He emphasized that new developmental acquisitions, such as crawling, generate experiences that, in turn, create the conditions for further developmental changes. Gottlieb called such "bootstrapping" processes probabilistic epigenesis. In contrast to most current models of developmental transition, Gottlieb's approach stresses the possibility that, under some circumstances, psychological function may precede and account for development of neurophysiological structures.

There is evidence in the animal literature that a probabilistic epigenetic process plays a role in the development of wariness of heights. Held and Hein (1963), for instance, showed that dark-reared kittens given experience with active self-produced locomotion in an illuminated environment showed avoidance of heights, whereas dark-reared littermates given passive experience moving in the same environment manifested no such avoidance. In these studies, despite equivalent maturational states in the two groups of kittens, the experiences made possible by correlated visuomotor responses during active locomotion proved necessary to elicit wariness of heights.

So long as they are prelocomotor, human infants, despite their visual competence and absence of visual deprivation, may be functionally equivalent to Held and Hein's passively moved kittens. Crawling may generate or refine skills sufficient for the onset of wariness of heights. These skills may include improved calibration of distances, heightened sensitivity to visually specified self-motion, more consistent coordination of visual and vestibular stimulation, and increased awareness of emotional signals from significant others (Bertenthal & Campos, 1990; Campos, Hiatt, Ramsay, Henderson, & Svejda, 1978).

There is anecdotal evidence supporting a link between locomotor experience and development of wariness of heights in human infants. Parents commonly report that there is a phase following the acquisition of locomotion when infants show no avoidance of heights, and will go over the edge of a bed or other precipice if the caretaker is not vigilant. Parents also report that this phase of apparent fearlessness is followed by one in which wariness of heights becomes quite intense (Campos et al., 1978).

In sum, both the kitten research and the anecdotal human evidence suggest that wariness of heights is not simply a maturational phenomenon, to be expected even in the absence of experience. From the perspective of probabilistic epigenesis, locomotor experience may operate as an organizer of emotional development, serving either to induce wariness of heights (i.e., to produce a potent emotional state that would never emerge without such experience) or to facilitate its emergence (i.e., to bring it about earlier than it otherwise would appear). The research reported here represents an attempt to determine whether

This research was supported by grants from the National Institutes of Health (HD-16195, HD-00695, and HD-25066) and from the John D. and Catherine T. MacArthur Foundation.

Address requests for reprints to Joseph J. Campos, Institute of Human Development, 1203 Tolman Hall, University of California at Berkeley, Berkeley, CA 94720.

locomotor experience is indeed an organizer of the emergence of wariness of heights.

Pinpointing the role of locomotion in the emergence of wariness of heights in human infants requires solution of a number of methodological problems. One is the selection of an ecologically valid paradigm for testing wariness of heights. Another is the determination of an outcome measure that can be used with both prelocomotor and locomotor infants. A third is a means of determining whether locomotion is playing a role as a correlate, an antecedent, an inducer, or a facilitator of the onset of wariness of heights.

The ecologically valid paradigm we selected for testing was the visual cliff (Walk, 1966; Walk & Gibson, 1961)—a large, safety-glass-covered table with a solid textured surface placed immediately underneath the glass on one side (the "shallow" side) and a similar surface placed some 43 in. underneath the glass on the floor below on the other side (the "deep" side).

To equate task demands for prelocomotor and locomotor infants, we measured the infants' wariness reactions while they were slowly lowered toward either the deep or the shallow side of the cliff. This descent procedure not only allowed us to assess differences in wariness reactions as a function of locomotor experience in both prelocomotor and locomotor infants but also permitted us to assess an index of depth perception, that is, a visual placing response (the extension of the arms and hands in anticipation of contact with the shallow, but not the deep, surface of the cliff [Walters, 1981]).

To assess fearfulness with an index appropriate to both pre- and postlocomoting infants, we measured heart rate (HR) responses during the 3-s period of descent onto the surface of the cliff. Prior work had shown consistently that heart rate decelerates in infants who are in a state of nonfearful attentiveness, but accelerates when infants are showing either a defensive response (Graham & Clifton, 1966) or a precry state (Campos, Emde, Gaensbauer, & Henderson, 1975).

To relate self-produced locomotion to fearfulness, we used a number of converging research operations. One was an *age-held-constant design,* contrasting the performance of infants who were locomoting with those of the same age who were not yet locomoting; the second was an analog of an experiential *enrichment* manipulation, in which infants who were otherwise incapable of crawling or creeping were tested after they had a number of hours of experience moving about voluntarily in walker devices; the third was an analog of an experiential *deprivation* manipulation, in which an infant who was orthopedically handicapped, but otherwise normal, was tested longitudinally past the usual age of onset of crawling and again after the delayed acquisition of crawling; and the fourth was a *cross-sequential lag design* aimed at teasing apart the effects of age of onset of locomotion and of duration of locomotor experience on the infant's avoidance of crossing the deep or the shallow side of the cliff to the mother.

EXPERIMENT 1: HR RESPONSES OF PRELOCOMOTOR AND LOCOMOTOR INFANTS

In the first study, a total of 92 infants, half locomoting for an average of 5 weeks, were tested at 7.3 months of age. Telemetered HR, facial expressions (taped from a camera under the deep side of the cliff), and the visual placing response were recorded. Each infant was lowered to each side of the cliff by a female experimenter, with the mother in another room.

As predicted from the work of Held and Hein (1963), locomotor infants showed evidence of wariness of heights, and prelocomotor infants did not. Only on deep trials did the HR of locomotor infants accelerate significantly from baselevels (by 5 beats/min), and differ significantly from the HR responses of prelocomotor infants. The HR responses of prelocomotor infants did not differ from baselevels on either the deep or shallow sides. Surprisingly, facial expressions did not differentiate testing conditions, perhaps because the descent minimized the opportunity to target these expressions to social figures.

In addition, every infant tested, regardless of locomotor status, showed visual placing responses on the shallow side, and no infant showed placing responses on the deep side of the cliff. Thus, all infants showed evidence for depth perception on the deep side, but only locomotor infants showed evidence of fear-related cardiac acceleration in response to heights.

EXPERIMENT 2: ACCELERATION OF LOCOMOTOR EXPERIENCE

Although correlated, the development of locomotion and the emergence of wariness of heights may be jointly determined by a third factor that brings about both changes. Disambiguation of this possibility required a means of providing "artificial" locomotor experience to infants who were not yet able to crawl. This manipulation was achieved by providing wheeled walkers to infants and testing them after their mothers had reported at least 32 hr of voluntary forward movement in the device.

Infants who received walkers were divided into two groups: prelocomotor walkers ($N = 9M, 9F$, Mean Age = 224 days, Walker Experience = 47 hr of voluntary forward movement) and locomotor walkers ($N = 9M, 7F$, Mean Age = 222 days, Walker Experience = 32 hr). The performance of infants in these two groups was compared with the performance of age-matched subjects, also divided into two groups: prelocomotor controls ($N = 9M, 9F$, Mean Age = 222 days) and locomotor controls ($N = 9M, 7F$, Mean Age = 222 days). The average duration of crawling experience was only 5 days in the locomotor walker and the locomotor control groups. All infants were tested using the same procedure as in the prior study. No shallow trials were administered in order to minimize subject loss due to the additional testing time required for such trials.

As revealed in Figure 1, the three groups of infants with any type of locomotor experience showed evidence of cardiac acceleration, whereas the prelocomotor control infants did not. It is noteworthy that all 16 infants in the locomotor walker group (who had a "double dosage" of locomotor experience consisting of walker training and some crawling) showed HR accelerations upon descent to the cliff. Planned comparisons revealed significant differences between (1) all walker infants and all controls, (2) all spontaneously locomoting infants and prelocomotor controls, and (3) prelocomotor walkers and prelocomotor controls. These findings show that the provision of "artificial" locomotor experience may facilitate or induce wariness of heights, even for infants who otherwise have little or no crawling experience. Locomotor experience thus appears to be an antecedent of the emergence of wariness.

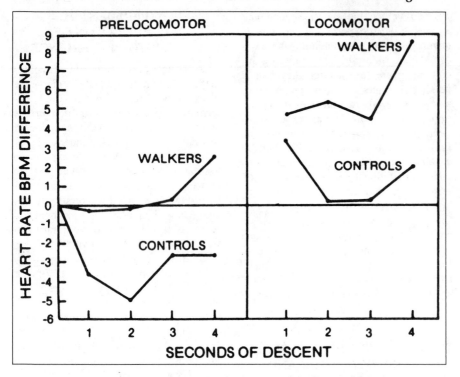

Fig. 1. Heart rate response while the infant is lowered toward the deep side of the visual cliff as a function of locomotor experience. The left panel contrasts the performance of prelocomotor infants with and without "artificial" walker experience. The right panel contrasts the performance of crawling infants with and without "artificial" walker experience. Heart rate is expressed as difference from baseline in beats/min.

sessed separately the effects of age of onset of crawling (early, normative, or late) and of duration of locomotor experience (11 or 41 days), as well as their interaction, using a longitudinal design.

The results of this study demonstrated a clear effect of locomotor experience independent of the age when self-produced locomotion first appeared. This effect of experience was evident with both nominal data (the proportion of infants who avoided descending onto the deep side of the cliff on the first test trial) and interval data (the latency to descend from the center board of the visual cliff onto the deep side on deep trials minus the latency to descend onto the shallow side on shallow trials). At whatever age the infant had begun to crawl, only 30% to 50% of infants avoided the deep side after 11 days of locomotor experience. However, after 41 days of locomotor experience, avoidance increased to 60% to 80% of infants. The latency data revealed a significant interaction of side of cliff with locomotor experience, but not a main effect of age, nor of the interaction of age with experience. The results of this study further suggest that locomotor experience paces the onset of wariness of heights.

EXPERIMENT 3: DEPRIVATION OF LOCOMOTOR EXPERIENCE

Although Experiment 2 showed that training in locomotion accelerates the onset of wariness of heights, it is possible that this response would eventually develop even in the absence of locomotor experience. To determine whether the delayed acquisition of crawling precedes the delayed emergence of wariness of heights, we longitudinally tested an infant with a peripheral handicap to locomotion. This infant was neurologically normal and had a Bayley Developmental Quotient of 126, but was born with two congenitally dislocated hips. After an early operation, he was placed in a full body cast. The infant was tested on the visual cliff monthly between 6 and 10 months of age using the procedures described above. While the infant was in the cast, he showed no evidence of crawling. At 8.5 months of age (i.e., 1.5 months after the normative age of onset of locomotion), the cast was removed, and the infant began crawling soon afterward.

This infant showed no evidence of dif-

ferential cardiac responsiveness on the deep versus shallow side of the cliff until 10 months of age, at which time his HR accelerated markedly on the deep side, and decelerated on the shallow. Although we cannot generalize from a single case study, these data provide further support for the role of self-produced locomotion as a facilitator or inducer of wariness of heights.

EXPERIMENT 4: AGE OF ONSET OF LOCOMOTION VERSUS LOCOMOTOR EXPERIENCE

In the studies described so far, HR was used as an imperfect index of wariness. However, we felt that a study using behavioral avoidance was needed to confirm the link between locomotor experience and wariness of heights. We thus used the locomotor crossing test on the visual cliff, in which the infant is placed on the center of the cliff, and the mother is instructed to encourage the infant to cross to her over either the deep or the shallow side. In this study, we also as-

PROCESSES UNDERLYING THE DEVELOPMENT OF WARINESS OF HEIGHTS

The pattern of findings obtained in these four studies, taken together with the animal studies by Held and Hein (1963), demonstrates a consistent relation between locomotor experience and wariness of heights. We propose the following interpretations for our findings.

We believe that crawling initially is a goal in itself, with affect solely linked to the success or failure of implementing the act of moving. Locomotion is initially not context dependent, and infants show no wariness of heights because the goal of moving is not coordinated with other goals, including the avoidance of threats. However, as a result of locomotor experience, infants acquire a sense of both the efficacy and the limitations of their own actions. Locomotion stops being an end in itself, and begins to be goal corrected and coordinated with the environmental surround. As a result, infants begin to show wariness of heights once locomotion becomes context dependent (cf. Bertenthal & Campos, 1990).

The context-dependency of the infants' actions may come about from falling and near-falling experiences that locomotion generates. Near-falls are particularly important because they are frequent, they elicit powerful emotional signals from the parent, and they set the stage for long-term retention of negative affect in such contexts.

There is still another means by which the infant can acquire a sense of wariness of depth with locomotion. While the infant moves about voluntarily, visual information specifying self-movement becomes more highly correlated with vestibular information specifying the same amount of self-movement (Bertenthal & Campos, 1990). Once expectancies related to the correlation of visual and vestibular information are formed, being lowered toward the deep side of the cliff creates a violation of the expected correlation. This violation results from the absence of visible texture near the infant when lowered toward the deep side of the cliff, relative to the shallow side. As a consequence, angular acceleration is not detected by the visual system, whereas it is detected by the vestibular system. This violation of expectation results in distress proportional to the magnitude of the violation. A test of this interpretation requires assessment of the establishment of visual-vestibular coordination as a function of locomotor experience and confirmation that wariness occurs in contexts that violate visual-vestibular coordination.

LOCOMOTOR EXPERIENCE AND OTHER EMOTIONAL CHANGES

The consequences of the development of self-produced locomotion for emotional development extend far beyond the domain of wariness of heights. Indeed, the onset of locomotion generates an entirely different emotional climate in the family. For instance, as psychoanalytic theories predict (e.g., Mahler, Pine, & Bergman, 1975), the onset of locomotion brings about a burgeoning of both positive and negative affect—positive affect because of the child's new levels of self-efficacy; negative affect because of the increases in frustration resulting from thwarting of the child's goals and because of the affective resonance that comes from increased parental expressions of prohibition (Campos, Kermoian, & Zumbahlen, in press). Locomotion is also crucial for the development of attachment (Ainsworth, Blehar, Waters, & Wall, 1978; Bowlby, 1973), because it makes physical proximity to the caregiver possible. With the formation of specific attachments, locomotion increases in significance as the child becomes better able to move independently toward novel and potentially frightening environments. Infants are also more sensitive to the location of the parent, more likely to show distress upon separation, and more likely to look to the parent in ambiguous situations.

Locomotion also brings about emotional changes in the parents. These changes include the increased pride (and sometimes sorrow) that the parents experience in their child's new mobility and independence and the new levels of anger parents direct at the baby when the baby begins to encounter forbidden objects. It seems clear from the findings obtained in this line of research that new levels of functioning in one behavioral domain can generate experiences that profoundly affect other developmental domains, including affective, social, cognitive, and sensorimotor ones (Kermoian & Campos, 1988). We thus propose that theoretical orientations like probabilistic epigenesis provide a novel, heuristic, and timely perspective for the study of emotional development.

REFERENCES

Ainsworth, M.D.S., Blehar, M., Waters, E., & Wall, S. (1978). *Patterns of attachment*. Hillsdale, NJ: Erlbaum.
Bertenthal, B., & Campos, J.J. (1990). A systems approach to the organizing effects of self-produced locomotion during infancy. In C. Rovee-Collier & L.P. Lipsitt (Eds.), *Advances in infancy research* (Vol. 6, pp. 1–60). Norwood, NJ: Ablex.
Bowlby, J. (1973). *Attachment and loss: Vol. 2. Separation*. New York: Basic Books.
Bridges, K.M. (1932). Emotional development in early infancy. *Child Development, 3*, 324–341.
Campos, J.J., Emde, R.N., Gaensbauer, T.J., & Henderson, C. (1975). Cardiac and behavioral interrelationships in the reactions of infants to strangers. *Developmental Psychology, 11*, 589–601.
Campos, J.J., Hiatt, S., Ramsay, D., Henderson, C., & Svejda, M. (1978). The emergence of fear of heights. In M. Lewis & L. Rosenblum (Eds.), *The development of affect* (pp. 149–182). New York: Plenum Press.
Campos, J.J., Kermoian, R., & Zumbahlen, R.M. (in press). In N. Eisenberg (Ed.), *New directions for child development*. San Francisco: Jossey-Bass.
Emde, R.N., Gaensbauer, T.J., & Harmon, R.J. (1976). Emotional expression in infancy: A biobehavioral study. *Psychological Issues* (Vol. 10, No. 37). New York: International Universities Press.
Gottlieb, G. (1983). The psychobiological approach to developmental issues. In P. Mussen (Ed.), *Handbook of child psychology: Vol. II. Infancy and developmental psychobiology* (4th ed.) (pp. 1–26). New York: Wiley.
Gottlieb, G. (1991). Experiential canalization of behavioral development: Theory. *Developmental Psychology 27*, 4–13.
Graham, F.K., & Clifton, R.K. (1966). Heartrate change as a component of the orienting response. *Psychological Bulletin, 65*, 305–320.
Held, R., & Hein, A. (1963). Movement-produced stimulation in the development of visually-guided behavior. *Journal of Comparative and Physiological Psychology, 56*, 872–876.
Kagan, J., Kearsley, R., & Zelazo, P.R. (1978). *Infancy: Its place in human development*. Cambridge, MA: Harvard University Press.
Kermoian, R., & Campos, J.J. (1988). Locomotor experience: A facilitator of spatial cognitive development. *Child Development, 59*, 908–917.
Mahler, M., Pine, F., & Bergman, A. (1975). *The psychological birth of the human infant*. New York: Basic Books.
Scarr, S., & Salapatek, P. (1970). Patterns of fear development during infancy. *Merrill-Palmer Quarterly, 16*, 53–90.
Sroufe, L.A. (1979). Socioemotional development. In J. Osofsky (Ed.), *Handbook of infant development* (pp. 462–516). New York: Wiley.
Walk, R. (1966). The development of depth perception in animals and human infants. *Monographs of the Society for Research in Child Development, 31*(Whole No. 5).
Walk, R., & Gibson, E. (1961). A comparative and analytical study of visual depth perception. *Psychological Monographs, 75*(15, Whole No. 5).
Walters, C. (1981). Development of the visual placing response in the human infant. *Journal of Experimental Child Psychology, 32*, 313–329.

Everybody knows a kid needs love. Now neuroscience is closing in on just how TLC shapes a child's brain and behavior.

BABIES, BONDS, AND BRAINS

BY KAREN WRIGHT

N TERMS OF BEHAVIORAL DEVEL-opment, I was something of a late bloomer. My mother reports that I slept away most of my infancy and toddlerhood, and even my adolescence was unremarkable. I didn't enter my angst-and-experimentation phase until my mid-20s, when, like a tortured teen, I blamed my parents for everything. Several years and several thousand dollars of psychotherapy later, I let my parents off the hook. I realized it couldn't all be their doing—my faults, my fears, my penchant for salty, cheese-flavored snack foods. I am not, after all, the simple product of my upbringing.

This healthy outlook threatened to come undone one recent afternoon as I stood outside the cages at the National Institutes of Health Animal Center in Poolesville, Maryland, watching Stephen Suomi's monkeys. Suomi, a primatologist at the National Institute of Child Health and Human Development, studies the effects of rearing environments on the behavior of young rhesus macaques. Fifty graduates of his program live in the center's five-acre enclosure; at the moment, they are gathered in a large chain-link cell with sawdust on the floor and monkey toys dangling from the ceiling. The arrival of human visitors stirs this cohort like dry leaves in a whirlwind, and its members quickly segregate into three factions. The boldest rush to get a cage-front view of the newcomers; a second phalanx hovers behind them, cautious but curious; and at the far end of the cage a third group forms a simian huddle of abject fear.

These monkeys are most definitely the products of their respective upbringings. The three groups were raised in three distinct settings. The bold monkeys spent the first six months of life being shuttled between monkey play groups and individual cages (and so were used to human handling); the sensibly cautious ones were reared by their natural families, with mothers, fathers, and siblings; and the fearful monkeys grew up parentless among same-age peers, to whom they retain an abnormally strong attachment.

Suomi is keenly interested in the spectrum of behavior among his macaques—from bold and aggressive to anxious and withdrawn—for it parallels the human trait known as temperament, the fundamental cast of personality that governs our propensity for hobnobbing, taking risks, or seeking thrills. He and other researchers have found that temperament is reflected in biology as well as behavior: heart rate, immune response, stress-hormone levels, and other physiological measures can be correlated with temperamental styles in humans and monkeys alike. And despite some investigators' assertions to the contrary, Suomi's experiments imply that temperament may be largely the result of a young monkey's home life.

"The patterns have some genetic heritability," says Suomi, jangling his car keys in front of the cage to get an even more exaggerated response. "But our work shows that you can modify these tendencies quite dramatically with certain types of early experiences."

Suomi belongs to the league of scientists who are studying the role that early childhood environment plays in determining adult behavior. He and his colleagues are working a bit beyond the pale, as late-twentieth-century science seems to savor the notion of genetic determinism. But the effects of childhood environment—specifically, the "environment" supplied by parenting—are coming under renewed scrutiny now, in large part because recent neurological studies have revealed that the structure of a child's brain remains surprisingly malleable months and even years after birth. The number of connections between nerve cells in an infant's brain grows more than 20-fold in the first few months of life, for example; a two-year-old's brain contains twice as many of these connections, called synapses, as an adult's brain. Throughout early childhood, synapses multiply and are pruned away at a furious pace. Something directs this dynamic rewiring, and researchers have concluded that that something is experience.

havioral researchers, who have long appreciated the importance of bonds between caregivers and children. "We know that little kids don't hop up and run away from lions—they don't deal directly with the world much," says Megan Gunnar, a developmental psychologist at the University of Minnesota in Minneapolis. "Their survival depends on their relationships." Hence, children are keenly at-

separated from their companions. Some peer-reared monkeys, mostly males, also have self-destructive tendencies toward impulsive behavior and aggression. They're the playground bullies, and they're often shunned by, or even kicked out of, their play groups.

Clearly, peer-rearing has unhappy consequences for an individual's social skills and ability to cope with stress. It has

"It's not just what happens to you that counts—it's what you think happens to you. And it's difficult to figure out what a child is thinking."

Of course, "experience" can come in all shapes and sizes. Childhood illness and diet, for example, count as experiences, too. But there's reason to believe that a child's experience of his parents is an especially potent sculptor of the parts of the brain involved in emotion, personality, and behavior. Some studies indicate that the strength of a child's bonding with his caregivers may increase his ability to learn and to cope with stress. Others show that childhood abuse and neglect can prime the brain for a lifetime of inappropriate aggression and scattered attention.

AS THE TWENTIETH century draws to a close, more than half of America's one-year-olds are spending their days with someone other than their mothers. This historic surge in day care has coincided with a rush of reports showing that early experiences may be more critical to brain development than anyone had previously imagined. Naturally, each new bulletin tweaks the guilty fears of working parents. So far, however, the news about kids and day care is pretty good. Children in day care appear to do just fine—provided the quality of the interactions between caregiver and child is high—and good day care may even enhance their social skills and performance in school. Low-quality day care, on the other hand, may compromise a child's adjustment and academic performance.

These results are not surprising to be-

tuned to the cues they receive from parents, says Gunnar, and they are especially sensitive to signs of indifference. Responsive, sensitive parents inspire trust in their children, giving rise to what behavioral scientists call secure attachment; insensitive or withdrawn parents can foster insecure attachment.

Nearly four decades of behavioral research has painted a dramatic picture of how important this attachment is to a child's emotional health. University of Wisconsin psychologist Harry Harlow's pioneering studies in the late fifties and early sixties found that monkeys reared in total isolation developed aberrant feeding, mating, parenting, and socializing behaviors. Developmental psychologists now believe that bonding with a parent or other caregiver is as essential to a normal childhood as learning to walk and talk. In the absence of a "good mother," children will attach as best they can to whatever figure presents itself—just as Harlow's infant monkeys became virtually inseparable from the cloth-and-wire surrogates in their cages.

Stephen Suomi's simian charges are another example of how behavior can be warped by bonding with a maladroit mom. The timid peer-reared monkeys at the NIH center are the victims of insecure attachment; their peers didn't provide the stability and sensitivity that make for a secure bond. (Imagine what a wreck you'd be if you were raised by a twin sister.) These monkeys are anxious and inhibited, and their temperaments are reflected in their reluctance to explore strange objects, their shyness with unfamiliar peers, their low status in monkey communities, and their distress on being

at least one other embarrassing side effect as well. "Every animal that's reared without a mother, no matter what its other social experience may be, turns out to be hyperoral," says Suomi. "They all suck their thumbs a lot."

Peer-rearing also leaves a distinctive stamp on the monkey's physiology. Samples of cerebrospinal fluid from Suomi's impulsive monkeys show that they grow up with lower levels of serotonin, a mood-regulating biochemical that has been linked with aggression, antisocial behavior, and depression in human beings. At the same time, turnover of norepinephrine, a chemical messenger associated with fearfulness, is unusually rapid in peer-reared monkeys. The monkeys' immune systems tend to be suppressed, while their levels of stress hormones are higher and their heart rates faster than those of mother-reared monkeys. Might these be the fruits of insecure attachment?

Megan Gunnar thinks so. Gunnar studies the relationship between attachment security and reactions to stress in human infants and toddlers. She's found that stressful circumstances such as vaccinations, the presence of strangers, and separation from mom produce elevations of the stress hormone cortisol in infants. By age two, however, children with secure attachments to their mothers don't get these cortisol rushes, even when they act stressed out. Children with insecure attachments, on the other hand, continue to show elevations of cortisol. It's as if secure attachment comforts the body more than the mind.

"In the animal literature, the contact with adult conspecifics—it doesn't have to be the mom, but it needs to be somebody who acts like a mom and that the baby is familiar with—has powerful effects at blocking the activity of stress-response systems," says Gunnar. "If the attachment figure is present, and the relationship has been reliable, then some aspect of the stress response just doesn't happen."

That's a good thing, says Gunnar, because a hyperactive stress-response system can wreak havoc on the body. The racing heartbeats and suppressed immune systems that Suomi sees in peer-reared monkeys, for example, are responses that would normally occur to help the young animal cope with a transient stress—such as being left alone while mom goes out and mates. But in peer-reared monkeys, the stress response

Kagan's view, before a child's environment would have exerted its effects. He has also found that up to 40 percent of four-month-olds have signs of a bold or fearless nature. These tendencies often mellow with time, however, so that by age four only 10 percent of children are either fearful or reckless.

Suomi finds virtually the same proportions of bold and fearful monkeys in his mother-reared troops—a fact that seems to argue for the genetic conservation of temperament. But Kagan contends that the rich inner life of the child may limit the relevance of animal studies, despite the seeming parallels in primate personalities. "It's not just what happens to you that counts—it's what you *think* happens to you," says Kagan. "And

ganization, trauma will create the problems we're talking about."

Many of the kids Perry sees have been exposed to domestic violence, and their unpredictable and threatening home lives, he says, can be read in both their physiology and their behavior. They seem to be in a perpetual state of arousal: their "fight or flight" response has somehow been permanently activated, and they have tense muscles, rapid heart rates, and trouble sleeping. Their stress-response systems may be irreparably altered. "These kids grow up with a neurophysiology that is perfectly adapted to survive in a chaotic, distressing environment," says Perry. "They develop this extreme hypervigilance because they never know what is going to happen next."

Growing up in even a mildly bad environment appears to affect your biology. The question is whether those changes can be reversed.

is cranked up day in, day out, and that super-responsiveness persists into adolescence—long past the age of primate attachment. Gunnar proposes that such a skewed stress-response system can promote lasting behavioral changes by interfering with brain development. In rat pups, she points out, chronic stress is known to disturb the development of the limbic system, frontal lobes, and hippocampus, parts of the brain that are involved in fearfulness and vigilance, attention focusing, learning, and memory. Gunnar suggests that secure attachment serves as a buffer against these disturbances, while insecure attachment leaves the brain open to insults that can result in lifelong anxiety, timidity, and learning difficulties.

OF COURSE, ANXIOUS, INhibited, or impulsive behavior isn't necessarily the result of early attachment problems. The extensive work of Harvard psychologist Jerome Kagan certainly suggests that such traits can be inborn. Kagan finds that 20 percent of human infants have the behavioral and physiological signs of an inhibited temperament at just four months of age—presumably, in

it is inordinately difficult to figure out what a child is thinking. Until we devise ways to measure what is in a child's head, we're not going to understand the child's environment."

The inner life of the child may help explain the phenomenon of so-called resilient children, those who somehow manage to rise above difficult home environments and live normal, even accomplished, lives. But these children are exceptional; it's clear that abusive or negligent parenting can have devastating effects on a child's emotional development. All the evidence suggests that physical abuse in childhood, for example, leads to a higher risk of drug use, mood disorders, violence, and criminality in adulthood. Girls who are sexually abused are more prone to depression, panic attacks, eating disorders, drug use, and suicide. And children reared in orphanages, without any parenting at all, often develop a disturbing array of social and behavioral problems. Researchers are beginning to explore the biological mechanisms for these associations, but it's not hard to imagine the psychological ones.

"I think there are people who, for genetic reasons, are more susceptible to certain kinds of stressful stimulation," says Bruce Perry, who studies the physiology of abused and neglected children at the Baylor College of Medicine in Houston. "But even with the optimum genetic or-

But the children of domestic violence are poorly adapted to life in a nonviolent world. Their vigilance can lead them to misinterpret other people's behavior and intentions, says Perry. Boys, for example, will perceive hostility and aggression in a look or an offhand remark and respond too readily in kind (think Robert DeNiro in *Taxi Driver*). Girls are more likely to shut down or withdraw completely from even mildly threatening circumstances. In school, both boys and girls tend to tune out verbal information and become hypersensitive to nonverbal cues. They might focus more on a teacher's hand gestures, for example, than the subject he's lecturing on.

Perhaps it's not surprising that severe stress in childhood leaves both biological and behavioral scars. But researchers are learning that even less extreme emotional stressors, such as parental conflict or depression, can also have an impact on kids' behavior and biology. The children of depressed mothers, for example, are at increased risk for depression themselves, and most psychologists think the risk cannot be ascribed entirely to genetics. EEG studies by psychologist Geraldine Dawson of the University of Washington in Seattle show that babies whose mothers are depressed have reduced activity in the left frontal region of the brain—the area implicated in joy, interest, and other positive emotions.

Growing up in even a mildly bad environment appears to affect your biology. The question, of course, is whether those changes can be reversed. Several lines of research suggest that they can be. Suomi, for example, has shown that even monkeys who are *born* anxious and inhibited can overcome their temperamental handicap—and even rise to the top of the dominance hierarchy in their troop—if they are raised by ultranurturing supermoms. Kagan's work confirms that mothering can alter the course of an inhibited child's development. A pioneering day-care program at the University of North Carolina at Chapel Hill has cut the incidence of mental retardation by as much as 80 percent among kids whose unstimulating home environment put them at high risk for low IQ. Dawson, too, has found that psychologically depressed mothers who manage to stay positive and engaged in caregiving can minimize the impact of their depression on their babies' brain waves. And her follow-up work revealed that, at age three, children's EEGs will return to normal if their mothers' depression lifts.

"So I wonder, how plastic is the brain?" says Dawson. "At what point in development do we start to see enduring effects as opposed to transient effects?"

The answer may be never. The new model of neural development holds that the primitive areas of the brain mature first: in the first three years of life, the regions in the cortex that govern our sensory and motor skills undergo the most dramatic restructuring, and these perceptual centers, along with instinctual ones such as the limbic system, will be strongly affected by early childhood experiences. This vulnerability is nothing to scoff at, says Robert Thatcher, a neuroscientist at the University of South Florida College of Medicine in Tampa. "The limbic system is where we live, and the cortex is basically a slave to that," he explains.

But the frontal cortex, which governs planning and decision making, and the cerebellum, a center for motor skills, are also involved in emotional development. And those parts of the brain don't get rewired until a person is five to seven years old. What's more, another major restructuring of the brain occurs between ages nine and eleven, says Thatcher. Suddenly, the brain is looking less like a sculpture in stone and more like a work in progress.

In fact, Thatcher's readings of the EEGs of adolescents and adults have revealed that some reorganization of the brain may occur about every two years from birth to death. He proposes that these reorganizations happen in response to waves of nerve growth factor that sweep across the cerebral hemispheres in two-year cycles, revamping up to one-fifth of the brain's synaptic connections at the leading edge of the wave. The idea of the traveling waves is just a theory now—but it's a theory that's making more sense to more scientists.

"The brain doesn't stop changing after three years," says Megan Gunnar. "For some things, the windows of influence are only beginning to close at that age, and for others they're only beginning to open." If Thatcher is right, the brain is, in fact, under lifelong renovation. Long-term studies are just now beginning to demonstrate that experiences later in life can redirect emotional and behavioral development, even in adulthood. Some of us—and our parents—are greatly relieved by the news.

Dealing with death: Let children grieve, the experts say. Don't shield them from loss, but help them express their fear and anger. BY JERRY ADLER

How Kids Mourn

THE PAIN NEVER GOES AWAY," SAYS Geoff Lake, who is 15 now, and was 11 when his mother, Linda, died of a rare form of cancer. He is only starting to realize it, but at each crucial passage of life—graduation, marriage, the birth of children—there will be a face missing from the picture, a kiss never received, a message of joy bottled up inside, where it turns into sorrow. His sleep will be shadowed by ghosts, and the bittersweet shock of awakening back into a world from which his mother is gone forever. If he lives to be 100, with a score of descendants, some part of him will still be the boy whose mother left for the hospital one day and never came home.

A child who has lost a parent feels helpless, even if he's a future King of England; abandoned, even in a palace with a million citizens wailing at the gates. But children have ways of coping with loss, if they are allowed to mourn in their own ways. Grief can be mastered, even if it is never quite overcome, and out of the appalling dysfunction of the Windsor family, one of the few positive signs psychologists could point to was the sight of William and Harry trudging manfully behind their mother's bier, both brushing away tears during the service. "There is something very healing," says Catherine Hillman, coordinator of the Westminster Bereavement Service, "about openly sharing pain."

The death of a parent can have devastating psychological consequences, including anxiety, depression, sleep disturbances, underachievement and aggression. But so can a lot of other things, and losing a parent is actually less devastating than divorce. "We know that children tend to do better after a parental death than a divorce," says sociolo-

gist Andrew Cherlin of Johns Hopkins, "and that's a stunning statistic, because you'd think death would be harder." Historically, people have always had mechanisms for coping with the early death of a parent, a fairly common event until recently.

As late as 1900, a quarter of all American children had lost at least one parent by the age of 15. The figure today is about 6 percent. A century ago most people lived on farms and died at home, so children had a fairly intimate, routine acquaintance with death. In the genteel, antiseptic suburban culture of midcentury, death became an abstraction for most American children, something that happened on television (and, in the case of cartoon characters, was infinitely reversible). Growing up as what psychologist Therese Rando calls "the first death-free generation," Americans forgot the rituals of grief so ancient that they predate civilization itself. So the mental-health profession has had to fill the gap. In the last few decades more then 160 "bereavement centers" have opened around the country, directed at allowing children to express and channel their grief over the death of a parent or sibling. The one thing they can't do is make the grief disappear, because it never does.

If they could enroll, William and Harry would be prime candidates for bereavement counseling. Experts consider them almost a case study in risk factors for future emotional problems, with the notable exception that, unlike many other children who have lost a parent, their social and financial status is not in any jeopardy. But children who experience "multiple family transitions"—such as a death on top of Charles and Diana's acrimonious and humiliatingly public divorce—"don't do as well as children who experience just one," Cherlin warns. David

Zinn, medical director of Beacon Therapeutic Center in Chicago, thinks this may be especially true if there is some causal connection, however remote, between the divorce and the death. It is not such a great leap of logic, for a child, to blame his father for the circumstances that put his mother in the back seat of a speeding car with a drunk at the wheel.

Moreover, the princes are each at an age that has been identified—by different experts—as being at particular risk when a parent dies. An adolescent, such as the 15-year-old William, is already undergoing difficult life changes, says Rabbi Earl Grollman, author of 25 books on coping with loss. "You're not only dealing with the death of a parent, you're dealing with the death of your own childhood," he says. "You thought you were beginning to know yourself, but now the road ahead is uncertain." "I think it's hardest when you're 9 to 12," says Maxine Harris, author of "The Loss That Is Forever." (Harry was just short of his 13th birthday when Diana died.) "You're not a little kid, so you feel more shy about crying or sitting on someone's lap, but you're also not an adolescent, with all the independence that comes with that."

Worse yet, in the opinions of most armchair specialists, is the famously reticent and undemonstrative temperament of the Windsor family. "The way to handle grief is to allow the expression of feelings and the sharing of sadness," declares Dr. Dennis Friedman, a psychiatrist who has written a book on the psyche of the British royal family. "This particular family doesn't allow the expression of grief. . . . There has been a pattern of deprivation of love beginning with Victoria, then gathering momentum, and ending up with Charles. [The princes] are

"Can't we just fly up to heaven and get her and bring her back when God isn't looking?"

COURTESY FERNSIDE, A CENTER FOR GRIEVING CHILDREN

Some mourning children draw or paint, others pound a toy in frustration

bereaved not only by the loss of a mother who was very close to them, but also for a father who is quite often unavailable to them because of his duties and temperament."

It will be hardest at night, when the routines of the day wind down and the memories crowd in. Nighttime is when 11-year-old Dennis Heaphy leaves his bedroom and pads down the hall of his home in New York's Long Island to take his place on the floor of the master bedroom. His 7-year-old sister, Catherine, is already sleeping in bed alongside their mother, Mary Beth, who lies awake with her own thoughts of Brian, the husband who died of a brain tumor last January. He was 37, a big, strong man until he got sick. Dennis remembers his father's teaching him to play basketball and the hockey games they would play in the street until 9 o'clock at night. The memories make him miss his father even more, but they are precious all the same. "My sister doesn't remember my dad as well," Dennis says. "She remembers him from when he was sick, when he would get mad at the littlest things and not act like himself. We have to help her out."

Children cling to their memories, try to fortify them against the passage of the years. "They're always afraid they're going to forget how their mother looked, what her voice sounded like, how she smelled," says Debby Shimmel, a volunteer at the St. Francis Center in Washington. They paint their memories

onto the quilts that are ubiquitous at bereavement centers, little shards of a shattered family, sharp enough to pierce the heart: "Mommy read Matty bedtime stories." "Leo and Mommy played Candyland." Or they draw their parents as angels in heaven. Envisioning what heaven is like for their dads, says Stefanie Norris of the Good Mourning program in Park Ridge, Ill., children sometimes draw a giant football stadium. At the end of each eight-week group session, children hold a memorial for their dead parents; they wear something their parent wore, or perhaps make one of their favorite dishes. This is a more concrete form of memorial than a church eulogy, and a lot more meaningful to a 7-year-old.

The other thing children can't do in church is get angry, but bereavement centers provide for that as well. The Dougy Center in Portland, Ore., the model for scores of bereavement houses around the country, includes a "splatter room," where kids throw violent sploches of paint, an innovation suggested by a child who came to the center after his father had been accidentally shot to death in his home by police. And most centers have some variation of the "volcano room," thickly padded with foam and supplied with large stuffed animals that are periodically pummeled into piles of lint. Barney is said to be the favorite of many teenagers.

This is, as it happens, almost the exact opposite of what was accepted wisdom a generation ago, when children were encouraged to get on with their lives and parents advised not to depress them with reminders of the departed. Lori Lehmann was 6 when her mother died of leukemia, 30 years ago. Lori was dropped off at a neighbor's house for the funeral, and afterward her father packed up all her mother's belongings and took down all her photographs, and no one ever talked about her. "He was so sad that you didn't feel like you could ask him about it," she remembers. Her father died himself nine years later, and now she is trying to reconstruct her parents, her mother especially, from relatives' memories. "It's the little things they tell me that I really love," she says. "Like what she cooked for dessert. I don't think my aunts realize how I cling to these things." Of course, by not talking to her, her father was sparing his own feelings as well; men of that generation didn't like to be seen crying.

And it's easy for parents to overlook the grief of young children. A child of 6, says New York psychiatrist Elliot Kranzler, is just on the cusp of mastering the four essential attributes of death: that is has a specific cause, involves the cessation of bodily function, is irreversible and is universal. Before that, children may nod solemnly when told of their father's death, and still expect him to be home for dinner. Young children process their loss a bit at a time; they may be sad for 10 minutes, then ask to go outdoors to play. And they are captives of childhood's inescapable solipsism. "It hits them over the head that they have needs to be met, and one key provider is gone," says Kranzler. "They pretty quickly tell their surviving parents to remarry." That isn't callous, merely practical on the child's part; and, of course, when the parent finally does remarry, it is one of the invariable rules of human psychology that the children will hate the new spouse. "There has not been a person I've interviewed who liked their stepparents when they were children," says Harris.

Children mourn piecemeal; they must return to it at each stage of maturity and conquer grief anew. Over the years, the sharp pang of loss turns to a dull ache, a melancholy that sets in at a certain time of year, a certain hour of the night. But every child who has lost a parent remains, in some secret part of his or her soul, a child forever frozen at a moment in time, crying out to the heedless heavens, as Geoff Lake did, when his mother died just days before his 12th birthday: "Mom, why did you die? *I had plans.*"

With PAT WINGERT *in Washington,* KAREN SPRINGEN *in Chicago,* BRAD STONE *in New York,* PATRICIA KING *in San Francisco,* CLAUDIA KALB *in Boston and* DONNA FOOTE *in London*

The EQ Factor

New brain research suggests that emotions, not IQ, may be the true measure of human intelligence

NANCY GIBBS

T TURNS OUT THAT A SCIENTIST can see the future by watching four-year-olds interact with a marshmallow. The researcher invites the children, one by one, into a plain room and begins the gentle torment. You can have this marshmallow right now, he says. But if you wait while I run an errand, you can have two marshmallows when I get back. And then he leaves.

Some children grab for the treat the minute he's out the door. Some last a few minutes before they give in. But others are determined to wait. They cover their eyes; they put their heads down; they sing to themselves; they try to play games or even fall asleep. When the researcher returns, he gives these children their hard-earned marshmallows. And then, science waits for them to grow up.

By the time the children reach high school, something remarkable has happened. A survey of the children's parents and teachers found that those who as four-year-olds had the fortitude to hold out for the second marshmallow generally grew up to be better adjusted, more popular, adventurous, confident and dependable teenagers. The children who gave in to temptation early on were more likely to be lonely, easily frustrated and stubborn. They buckled under stress and shied away from challenges. And when some of the students in the two groups took the Scholastic Aptitude Test, the kids who had held out longer scored an average of 210 points higher.

When we think of brilliance we see Einstein, deep-eyed, woolly haired, a thinking machine with skin and mismatched socks. High achievers, we imagine, were wired for greatness from birth.

But then you have to wonder why, over time, natural talent seems to ignite in some people and dim in others. This is where the marshmallows come in. It seems that the ability to delay gratification is a master skill, a triumph of the reasoning brain over the impulsive one. It is a sign, in short, of emotional intelligence. And it doesn't show up on an IQ test.

For most of this century, scientists have worshipped the hardware of the brain and the software of the mind; the messy powers of the heart were left to the poets. But cognitive theory could simply not explain the questions we wonder about most: why some people just seem to have a gift for living well; why the smartest kid in the class will probably not end up the richest; why we like some people virtually on sight and distrust others; why some people remain buoyant in the face of troubles that would sink a less resilient soul. What qual-

Children who aren't accepted by classmates are up to eight times more likely to drop out

ities of the mind or spirit, in short, determine who succeeds?

The phrase "emotional intelligence" was coined by Yale psychologist Peter Salovey and the University of New Hampshire's John Mayer five years ago to describe qualities like understanding one's own feelings, empathy for the feelings of others and "the regulation of emotion in a way that enhances living." Their notion is about to bound into the national conversation, handily shortened to EQ, thanks to a new book, *Emotional Intelligence* (Bantam; $23.95) by Daniel Goleman. Goleman, a Harvard psychology Ph.D. and a New York *Times* science writer with a gift for making even the chewiest scientific theories digestible to lay readers, has brought together a decade's worth of behavioral research into how the mind processes feelings. His goal, he announces on the cover, is to redefine what it means to be smart. His thesis: when it comes to predicting people's success, brainpower as measured by IQ and standardized achievement tests may actually matter less than the qualities of mind once thought of as "character" before the word began to sound quaint.

At first glance, there would seem to be little that's new here to any close reader of fortune cookies. There may be no less original idea than the notion that our hearts hold dominion over our heads. "I was so angry," we say, "I couldn't think straight." Neither is it surprising that "people skills" are useful, which amounts to saying, it's good to be nice. "It's so true it's trivial," says Dr. Paul McHugh, director of psychiatry at Johns Hopkins University School of Medicine. But if it were that simple, the book would not be quite so interesting or its implications so controversial.

This is no abstract investigation. Goleman is looking for antidotes to restore "civility to our streets and caring to our communal life." He sees practical applications everywhere for how companies should decide whom to hire, how couples can increase the odds that their marriages will last, how parents should raise their children and how schools should teach them. When street gangs substitute for families and schoolyard insults end in stabbings, when more than half

of marriages end in divorce, when the majority of the children murdered in this country are killed by parents and stepparents, many of whom say they were trying to discipline the child for behavior like blocking the TV or crying too much, it suggests a demand for remedial emotional education. While children are still young, Goleman argues, there is a "neurological window of opportunity" since the brain's prefrontal circuitry, which regulates how we act on what we feel, probably does not mature until mid-adolescence.

And it is here the arguments will break out. Goleman's highly popularized conclusions, says McHugh, "will chill any veteran scholar of psychotherapy and any neuroscientist who worries about how his research may come to be applied." While many researchers in this relatively new field are glad to see emotional issues finally taken seriously, they fear that a notion as handy as EQ invites misuse. Goleman admits the danger of suggesting that you can assign a numerical yardstick to a person's character as well as his intellect; Goleman never even uses the phrase EQ in his book. But he (begrudgingly) approved an "unscientific" EQ test in *USA Today* with choices like "I am aware of even subtle feelings as I have them," and "I can sense the pulse of a group or relationship and state unspoken feelings."

"You don't want to take an average of your emotional skill," argues Harvard psychology professor Jerome Kagan, a pioneer in child-development research. "That's what's wrong with the concept of intelligence for mental skills too. Some people handle anger well but can't handle fear. Some people can't take joy. So each emotion has to be viewed differently."

EQ is not the opposite of IQ. Some people are blessed with a lot of both, some with little of either. What researchers have been trying to understand is how they complement each other; how one's ability to handle stress, for instance, affects the ability to concentrate and put intelligence to use. Among the ingredients for success, researchers now generally agree that IQ counts for about 20%; the rest depends on everything from class to luck to the neural pathways that have developed in

the brain over millions of years of human evolution.

It is actually the neuroscientists and evolutionists who do the best job of explaining the reasons behind the most unreasonable behavior. In the past decade or so, scientists have learned enough about the brain to make judgments about where emotion comes from and why we need it. Primitive emotional responses held the keys to survival: fear drives the blood into the large muscles, making it easier to run; surprise triggers the eyebrows to rise, allowing the eyes to widen their view and gather more information about an unexpected event. Disgust wrinkles up the face and closes the nostrils to keep out foul smells.

Emotional life grows out of an area of the brain called the limbic system, specifically the amygdala, whence come delight and disgust and fear and anger. Millions of years ago, the neocortex was added on, enabling humans to plan, learn and remember. Lust grows from the limbic system; love, from the neocortex. Animals like reptiles that have no neocortex cannot experience anything like maternal love; this is why baby snakes have to hide to avoid being eaten by their parents. Humans, with their capacity for love, will protect their offspring, allowing the brains of the young time to develop. The more connections between limbic system and the neocortex, the more emotional responses are possible.

It was scientists like Joseph LeDoux of New York University who uncovered these cerebral pathways. LeDoux's parents owned a meat market. As a boy in Louisiana, he first learned about his future specialty by cutting up cows' brains for sweetbreads. "I found them the most interesting part of the cow's anatomy," he recalls. "They were visually pleasing—lots of folds, convolutions and patterns. The cerebellum was more interesting to look at than steak." The butchers' son became a neuroscientist, and it was he who discovered the short circuit in the brain that lets emotions drive action before the intellect gets a chance to intervene.

A hiker on a mountain path, for example, sees a long, curved shape in the grass out of the corner of his eye. He leaps out of the way before he realizes it is only a stick that looks like a snake. Then he calms down; his cortex gets the message a few milliseconds after his amygdala and "regulates" its primitive response.

Without these emotional reflexes, rarely conscious but often terribly powerful, we would scarcely be able to function. "Most decisions we make have a vast number of possible outcomes, and any attempt to analyze all of them would never end," says University of Iowa neurologist Antonio Damasio, author of *Descartes' Error: Emotion, Reason and the Human Brain*. "I'd ask you to lunch tomorrow, and when the appointed time arrived, you'd still be

Metamood is a difficult skill because emotions so often appear in disguise. A person in mourning may know he is sad, but he may not recognize that he is also angry at the person for dying—because this seems somehow inappropriate. A parent who yells at the child who ran into the street is expressing anger at disobedience, but the degree of anger may owe more to the fear the parent feels at what could have happened.

In Goleman's analysis, self-awareness is perhaps the most crucial ability because it allows us to exercise some self-control. The idea is not to repress feeling (the reaction

to resignation instead of perseverance. Over-worrying about failing increases the likelihood of failure; a salesman so concerned about his falling sales that he can't bring himself to pick up the phone guarantees that his sales will fall even further.

But why are some people better able to "snap out of it" and get on with the task at hand? Again, given sufficient self-awareness, people develop coping mechanisms. Sadness and discouragement, for instance, are "low arousal" states, and the dispirited salesman who goes out for a run is triggering a high arousal state that is incompatible with staying blue. Relaxation works better for

Anxiety is a rehearsal for danger. A little anxiety helps focus the mind; too much can paralyze it

thinking about whether you should come." What tips the balance, Damasio contends, is our unconscious assigning of emotional values to some of those choices. Whether we experience a somatic response—a gut feeling of dread or a giddy sense of elation—emotions are helping to limit the field in any choice we have to make. If the prospect of lunch with a neurologist is unnerving or distasteful, Damasio suggests, the invitee will conveniently remember a previous engagement.

When Damasio worked with patients in whom the connection between emotional brain and neocortex had been severed because of damage to the brain, he discovered how central that hidden pathway is to how we live our lives. People who had lost that linkage were just as smart and quick to reason, but their lives often fell apart nonetheless. They could not make decisions because they didn't know how they felt about their choices. They couldn't react to warnings or anger in other people. If they made a mistake, like a bad investment, they felt no regret or shame and so were bound to repeat it.

If there is a cornerstone to emotional intelligence on which most other emotional skills depend, it is a sense of self-awareness, of being smart about what we feel. A person whose day starts badly at home may be grouchy all day at work without quite knowing why. Once an emotional response comes into awareness—or, physiologically, is processed through the neocortex—the chances of handling it appropriately improve. Scientists refer to "metamood," the ability to pull back and recognize that "what I'm feeling is anger," or sorrow, or shame.

that has made psychoanalysts rich) but rather to do what Aristotle considered the hard work of the will. "Anyone can become angry—that is easy," he wrote in the *Nicomachean Ethics*. "But to be angry with the right person, to the right degree, at the right time, for the right purpose, and in the right way—that is not easy."

Some impulses seem to be easier to control than others. Anger, not surprisingly, is one of the hardest, perhaps because of its evolutionary value in priming people to action. Researchers believe anger usually arises out of a sense of being trespassed against—the belief that one is being robbed of what is rightfully his. The body's first response is a surge of energy, the release of a cascade of neurotransmitters called catecholamines. If a person is already aroused or under stress, the threshold for release is lower, which helps explain why people's tempers shorten during a hard day.

Scientists are not only discovering where anger comes from; they are also exposing myths about how best to handle it. Popular wisdom argues for "letting it all hang out" and having a good cathartic rant. But Goleman cites studies showing that dwelling on anger actually increases its power; the body needs a chance to process the adrenaline through exercise, relaxation techniques, a well-timed intervention or even the old admonition to count to 10.

Anxiety serves a similar useful purpose, so long as it doesn't spin out of control. Worrying is a rehearsal for danger; the act of fretting focuses the mind on a problem so it can search efficiently for solutions. The danger comes when worrying blocks thinking, becoming an end in itself or a path

high-energy moods like anger or anxiety. Either way, the idea is to shift to a state of arousal that breaks the destructive cycle of the dominant mood.

The idea of being able to predict which salesmen are most likely to prosper was not an abstraction for Metropolitan Life, which in the mid-'80s was hiring 5,000 salespeople a year and training them at a cost of more than $30,000 each. Half quit the first year, and four out of five within four years. The reason: selling life insurance involves having the door slammed in your face over and over again. Was it possible to identify which people would be better at handling frustration and take each refusal as a challenge rather than a setback?

The head of the company approached psychologist Martin Seligman at the University of Pennsylvania and invited him to test some of his theories about the importance of optimism in people's success. When optimists fail, he has found, they attribute the failure to something they can change, not some innate weakness that they are helpless to overcome. And that confidence in their power to effect change is self-reinforcing. Seligman tracked 15,000 new workers who had taken two tests. One was the company's regular screening exam, the other Seligman's test measuring their levels of optimism. Among the new hires was a group who flunked the screening test but scored as "superoptimists" on Seligman's exam. And sure enough, they did the best of all; they outsold the pessimists in the regular group by 21% in the first year and 57% in the second. For years after that, passing Selig-

In the corporate world, say personnel executives, IQ gets you hired, but EQ gets you promoted

man's test was one way to get hired as a MetLife salesperson.

Perhaps the most visible emotional skills, the ones we recognize most readily, are the "people skills" like empathy, graciousness, the ability to read a social situation. Researchers believe that about 90% of emotional communication is nonverbal. Harvard psychologist Robert Rosenthal developed the PONS test (Profile of Non-verbal Sensitivity) to measure people's ability to read emotional cues. He shows subjects a film of a young woman expressing feelings—anger, love, jealousy, gratitude, seduction—edited so that one or another nonverbal cue is blanked out. In some instances the face is visible but not the body, or the woman's eyes are hidden, so that viewers have to judge the feeling by subtle cues. Once again, people with higher PONS scores tend to be more successful in their work and relationships; children who score well are more popular and successful in school, even then their IQs are quite average.

Like other emotional skills, empathy is an innate quality that can be shaped by experience. Infants as young as three months old exhibit empathy when they get upset at the sound of another baby crying. Even very young children learn by imitation; by watch-

One Way to Test Your EQ

UNLIKE IQ, WHICH IS GAUGED BY THE FAMOUS STANFORD-Binet tests, EQ does not lend itself to any single numerical measure. Nor should it, say experts. Emotional intelligence is by definition a complex, multifaceted quality representing such intangibles as self-awareness, empathy, persistence and social deftness.

Some aspects of emotional intelligence, however, can be quantified. Optimism, for example, is a handy measure of a person's self-worth. According to Martin Seligman, a University of Pennsylvania psychologist, how people respond to setbacks—optimistically or pessimistically—is a fairly accurate indicator of how well they will succeed in school, in sports and in certain kinds of work. To test his theory, Seligman devised a questionnaire to screen insurance salesmen at MetLife.

In Seligman's test, job applicants were asked to imagine a hypothetical event and then choose the response (A or B) that most closely resembled their own. Some samples from his questionnaire:

You forget your spouse's (boyfriend's/girlfriend's) birthday.
A. I'm not good at remembering birthdays.
B. I was preoccupied with other things.

You owe the library $10 for an overdue book.
A. When I am really involved in what I am reading, I often forget when it's due.
B. I was so involved in writing the report, I forgot to return the book.

You lose your temper with a friend.
A. He or she is always nagging me.
B. He or she was in a hostile mood.

You are penalized for returning your income-tax forms late.
A. I always put off doing my taxes.
B. I was lazy about getting my taxes done this year.

You've been feeling run-down.
A. I never get a chance to relax.
B. I was exceptionally busy this week.

A friend says something that hurts your feelings.
A. She always blurts things out without thinking of others.
B. My friend was in a bad mood and took it out on me.

You fall down a great deal while skiing.
A. Skiing is difficult.
B. The trails were icy.

You gain weight over the holidays, and you can't lose it.
A. Diets don't work in the long run.
B. The diet I tried didn't work.

Seligman found that those insurance salesmen who answered with more B's than A's were better able to overcome bad sales days, recovered more easily from rejection and were less likely to quit. People with an optimistic view of life tend to treat obstacles and setbacks as temporary (and therefore surmountable). Pessimists take them personally; what others see as fleeting, localized impediments, they view as pervasive and permanent.

The most dramatic proof of his theory, says Seligman, came at the 1988 Olympic Games in Seoul, South Korea, after U.S. swimmer Matt Biondi turned in two disappointing performances in his first two races. Before the Games, Biondi had been favored to win seven golds—as Mark Spitz had done 16 years earlier. After those first two races, most commentators thought Biondi would be unable to recover from his setback. Not Seligman. He had given some members of the U.S swim team a version of his optimism test before the races; it showed that Biondi possessed an extraordinarily upbeat attitude. Rather than losing heart after turning in a bad time, as others might, Biondi tended to respond by swimming even faster. Sure enough, Biondi bounced right back, winning five gold medals in the next five races.

—By Alice Park

Why do some people remain buoyant in the face of troubles that would sink others?

ing how others act when they see someone in distress, these children acquire a repertoire of sensitive responses. If, on the other hand, the feelings they begin to express are not recognized and reinforced by the adults around them, they not only cease to express those feelings but they also become less able to recognize them in themselves or others.

Empathy too can be seen as a survival skill. Bert Cohler, a University of Chicago psychologist, and Fran Stott, dean of the Erikson Institute for Advanced Study in Child Development in Chicago, have found that children from psychically damaged families frequently become hypervigilant, developing an intense attunement to their parents' moods. One child they studied, Nicholas, had a horrible habit of approaching other kids in his nursery-school class as if he were going to kiss them, then would bite them instead. The scientists went back to study videos of Nicholas at 20 months interacting with his psychotic mother and found that she had responded to his every expression of anger or independence with compulsive kisses. The researchers dubbed them "kisses of death," and their true significance was obvious to Nicholas, who arched his back in horror at her approaching lips—and passed his own rage on to his classmates years later.

Empathy also acts as a buffer to cruelty, and it is a quality conspicuously lacking in child molesters and psychopaths. Goleman cites some chilling research into brutality by Robert Hare, a psychologist at the University of British Columbia. Hare found that psychopaths, when hooked up to electrodes and told they are going to receive a shock, show none of the visceral responses that fear of pain typically triggers: rapid heartbeat, sweating and so on. How could the threat of punishment deter such people from committing crimes?

It is easy to draw the obvious lesson from these test results. How much happier would we be, how much more successful as individuals and civil as a society, if we were more alert to the importance of emotional intelligence and more adept at teaching it? From kindergartens to business schools to corporations across the

country, people are taking seriously the idea that a little more time spent on the "touchy-feely" skills so often derided may in fact pay rich dividends.

In the corporate world, according to personnel executives, IQ gets you hired, but EQ gets you promoted. Goleman likes to tell of a manager at AT&T's Bell Labs, a think tank for brilliant engineers in New Jersey, who was asked to rank his top performers. They weren't the ones with the highest IQs; they were the ones whose E-mail got answered. Those workers who were good collaborators and networkers and popular with colleagues were more likely to get the cooperation they needed to reach their goals than the socially awkward, lone-wolf geniuses.

When David Campbell and others at the Center for Creative Leadership studied "derailed executives," the rising stars who flamed out, the researchers found that these executives failed most often because of "an interpersonal flaw" rather than a technical inability. Interviews with top executives in the U.S. and Europe turned up nine so-called fatal flaws, many of them classic emotional failings, such as "poor working relations," being "authoritarian" or "too ambitious" and having "conflict with upper management."

At the center's executive-leadership seminars across the country, managers come to get emotionally retooled. "This isn't sensitivity training or Sunday-supplement stuff," says Campbell. "One thing they know when they get through is what other people think of them." And the executives have an incentive to listen. Says Karen Boylston, director of the center's team-leadership group: "Customers are telling businesses, 'I don't care if every member of your staff graduated with honors from Harvard, Stanford and Wharton. I will take my business and go where I am understood and treated with respect.'"

Nowhere is the discussion of emotional intelligence more pressing than in schools, where both the stakes and the opportunities seem greatest. Instead of con-

stant crisis intervention, or declarations of war on drug abuse or teen pregnancy or violence, it is time, Goleman argues, for preventive medicine. "Five years ago, teachers didn't want to think about this," says principal Roberta Kirshbaum of P.S. 75 in New York City. "But when kids are getting killed in high school, we have to deal with it." Five years ago, Kirshbaum's school adopted an emotional literacy program, designed to help children learn to manage anger, frustration, loneliness. Since then, fights at lunchtime have decreased from two or three a day to almost none.

Educators can point to all sorts of data to support this new direction. Students who are depressed or angry literally cannot learn. Children who have trouble being accepted by their classmates are 2 to 8 times as likely to drop out. An inability to distinguish distressing feelings or handle frustration has been linked to eating disorders in girls.

Many school administrators are completely rethinking the weight they have been giving to traditional lessons and standardized tests. Peter Relic, president of the National Association of Independent Schools, would like to junk the SAT completely. "Yes, it may cost a heck of a lot more money to assess someone's EQ rather than using a machine-scored test to measure IQ," he says. "But if we don't, then we're saying that a

Deficient emotional skills may be the reason more than half of all marriages end in divorce

test score is more important to us than who a child is as a human being. That means an immense loss in terms of human potential because we've defined success too narrowly."

This warm embrace by educators has left some scientists in a bind. On one hand, says Yale psychologist Salovey, "I love the idea that we want to teach people a richer understanding of their emotional life, to help them achieve their goals." But, he adds, "what I would oppose is training conformity to social expectations." The danger is that any campaign to hone emotional skills in children will end up teaching that there is a "right" emotional response for any given situation—laugh at parades, cry at funerals, sit still at church. "You can teach self-control," says Dr. Alvin Poussaint, professor of psychiatry at Harvard Medical School. "You can teach that it's better to talk out your anger and not use violence. But is it good emotional intelligence not to challenge authority?"

 OME PSYCHOLOGISTS GO further and challenge the very idea that emotional skills can or should be taught in any kind of formal, classroom way. Goleman's premise that children can be trained to analyze their feelings strikes Johns Hopkins' McHugh as an effort to reinvent the

encounter group: "I consider that an abominable idea, an idea we have seen with adults. That failed, and now he wants to try it with children? Good grief!" He cites the description in Goleman's book of an experimental program at the Nueva Learning Center in San Francisco. In one scene, two fifth-grade boys start to argue over the rules of an exercise, and the teacher breaks in to ask them to talk about

Square Pegs in the Oval Office?

I F A HIGH DEGREE OF EMOTIONAL INTELLIGENCE IS A PREREQUISITE FOR OUT-standing achievement, there ought to be no better place to find it than in the White House. It turns out, however, that not every man who reached the pinnacle of American leadership was a gleaming example of self-awareness, empathy, impulse control and all the other qualities that mark an elevated EQ.

Oliver Wendell Holmes, who knew intelligence when he saw it, judged Franklin Roosevelt "a second-class intellect, but a first-class temperament." Born and educated as an aristocrat, F.D.R. had polio and needed a wheelchair for most of his adult life. Yet, far from becoming a self-pitying wretch, he developed an unbridled optimism that served him and the country well during the Depression and World War II—this despite, or because of, what Princeton professor Fred Greenstein calls Roosevelt's "tendency toward deviousness and duplicity."

Even a first-class temperament, however, is not a sure predictor of a successful presidency. According to Duke University political scientist James David Barber, the most perfect blend of intellect and warmth of personality in a Chief Executive was the brilliant Thomas Jefferson, who "knew the importance of communication and empathy. He never lost the common touch." Richard Ellis, a professor of politics at Oregon's Willamette University who is skeptical of the whole EQ theory, cites two 19th century Presidents who did not fit the mold. "Martin Van Buren was well adjusted, balanced, empathetic and persuasive, but he was not very successful," says Ellis. "Andrew Jackson was less well adjusted, less balanced, less empathetic and was terrible at controlling his own impulses, but he transformed the presidency."

Lyndon Johnson as Senate majority leader was a brilliant practitioner of the art of political persuasion, yet failed utterly to transfer that gift to the White House. In fact, says Princeton's Greenstein, L. B. J. and Richard Nixon would be labeled "worst cases" on any EQ scale of Presidents. Each was touched with political genius, yet each met with disaster. "To some extent," says Greenstein, "this is a function of the extreme aspects of their psyches; they are the political versions of Van Gogh, who does unbelievable paintings and then cuts off his ear."

History professor William Leuchtenburg of the University of North Carolina at Chapel Hill suggests that the 20th century Presidents with perhaps the highest IQs—Wilson, Hoover and Carter—also had the most trouble connecting with their constituents. Woodrow Wilson, he says, "was very high strung [and] arrogant; he was not willing to strike any middle ground. Herbert Hoover was so locked into certain ideas that you could never convince him otherwise. Jimmy Carter is probably the most puzzling of the three. He didn't have a deficiency of temperament; in fact, he was too temperate. There was an excessive rationalization about Carter's approach."

That was never a problem for John Kennedy and Ronald Reagan. Nobody ever accused them of intellectual genius, yet both radiated qualities of leadership with an infectious confidence and openheartedness that endeared them to the nation. Whether President Clinton will be so endeared remains a puzzle. That he is a Rhodes scholar makes him certifiably brainy, but his emotional intelligence is shaky. He obviously has the knack for establishing rapport with people, but he often appears so eager to please that he looks weak. "As for controlling his impulses," says Willamette's Ellis, "Clinton is terrible."   —*By Jesse Birnbaum*
Reported by James Carney/Washington and Lisa H. Towle/Raleigh

Some EQ is innate. Infants as young as three months show empathy

what they're feeling. "I appreciate the way you're being assertive in talking with Tucker," she says to one student. "You're not attacking." This strikes McHugh as pure folly. "The author is presuming that someone has the key to the right emotions to be taught to children. We don't even know the right emotions to be taught to adults. Do you really think a child of eight or nine really understands the difference between aggressiveness and assertiveness?"

The problem may be that there is an ingredient missing. Emotional skills, like intellectual ones, are morally neutral. Just as a genius could use his intellect either to cure cancer or engineer a deadly virus, someone with great empathic insight could use it to inspire colleagues or exploit them. Without a moral compass to guide people in how to employ their gifts, emotional intelligence can be used for good or evil. Columbia University psychologist Walter Mischel, who invented the marshmallow test and others like it, observes that the knack for delaying gratification that makes a child one marshmallow richer can help him become a better citizen or—just as easily—an even more brilliant criminal.

Given the passionate arguments that are raging over the state of moral instruction in this country, it is no wonder Goleman chose to focus more on neutral emotional skills than on the values that should govern their use. That's another book—and another debate.

—Reported by Sharon E. Epperson and Lawrence Mondi/New York, James L. Graff/Chicago and Lisa H. Towle/Raleigh

Children Without Friends

Who Are They and How Can Teachers Help?

This article highlights an area that should be of great concern to educators—children without friends. The author notes the serious implications of growing up friendless: "The uniqueness of peer relationships contributes to a child's normal development." Now, proven techniques of identification allow teachers and other professionals to help such children.—R.J.S.

Janis R. Bullock

Janis R. Bullock is Assistant Professor, Human Development and Counseling, Montana State University, Bozeman.

Children who have difficulty forming friendships and gaining acceptance among peers have received a tremendous amount of interest over the past decade. Research indicates that approximately 6 to 11 percent of elementary school-age children have no friends or receive no friendship nominations from peers (Hymel & Asher, 1977). This figure varies depending upon the assessment procedure used and it may be even higher in some subgroups. For example, children who have learning disabilities (Gresham, 1988) or are mildly retarded (Taylor, Asher & Williams, 1987) may experience even more difficulties forming so-cial relationships. Nonetheless, many average and above-average children are without friends. Consequently, research and intervention focusing on children with peer relationship problems are becoming more extensive.

Researchers continue to seek information that may contribute to the understanding and awareness of these children. Many children who experience poor peer relations are at risk and need support. Research on the consequences of peer rejection can provide teachers with the foundation and rationale for effective intervention. Teachers working closely with children who lack friends understand the frustration such students experience during attempts to interact with peers.

The uniqueness of peer relationships contributes to a child's normal development. Unlike adult-child relationships, child-child relations are more egalitarian and involve more reciprocal interactions. These interactions help children achieve competency in many areas. Therefore, children who lack friends do not enjoy many important benefits of interaction. Peer relations should be viewed as necessary for a child's healthy development.

Identifying Children Without Friends

In order to determine a child's status within the peer group, researchers often use two variations of sociometric measurement techniques. These measurements rely on children's perceptions of others and can identify those children who are rejected or neglected by their peer group. A widely used sociometric technique is the peer nomination method (Hymel & Rubin, 1985). In this technique, children are asked to pick from a list the names of three children with whom they like to play and three children with whom they do not like to play. In general, this procedure provides a useful means of assessing children's impact on their peers. Rejected children receive few positive nominations and many negative nominations, while neglected children receive few positive *or* negative nominations.

The rating scale measure (Singleton & Asher, 1977), a slightly different approach, is used to assess social acceptance or preference within the peer group. Children are asked to rate each classmate on a 1-5 Likert-type scale, in response to questions about how much they like to play or work with that class-

From *Childhood Education*, Winter 1992, pp. 92-96. © 1992 by the Association for Childhood Education International, 17904 Georgia Avenue, Suite 215, Olney, MD 20832. Reprinted by permission.

mate. Rejected children receive very low overall ratings, whereas ratings of neglected children do not differ from those of average children. Although neglected children are generally liked, they very often lack friends.

Sociometric Status and Behaviors in Children

Once researchers were able to identify rejected and neglected children, they became interested in determining the behaviors associated with each status. Information is typically gathered on child behavior in three ways: peer reports, teacher reports and direct observation. The behaviors of the children are then correlated with sociometric status.

Peers can provide an important perspective on the behavior norms within a peer group, providing insight on areas often unavailable or unknown to adults. A common technique requires children to characterize the behavior of peers (e.g., aggressive, helpful, cooperative, shy). A variety of behaviors attributed to children by their peers are related to their sociometric status (Carlson, Lahey & Neeper, 1984; Coie, Dodge & Coppotelli, 1982; Wasik, 1987). Across age groups, peers accept children who are considered helpful, friendly, cooperative, cheerful and prosocial. Peer rejection is generally associated with aggression, disruption and fighting. Shy, quiet children lacking social involvement are often neglected.

Because of their considerable contact with children, teachers can provide a valuable perspective on children's behavior. French and Waas (1988) obtained teacher ratings on popular, rejected and neglected 2nd- and 5th-grade children. Rejected children were characterized as aggressive, hostile and task avoidant, while neglected children were described as having more school behavior problems than popular children. Coie and Dodge (1988) asked teachers to rank 1st- and 2nd-grade boys of different sociometric statuses on a variety of peer aggression items. Well-accepted and neglected children were described as the least aggressive, whereas rejected children were described as the most aggressive. Rejected children also scored low in conformity to rules and interpersonal sensitivity. In general, teacher assessments coincided with children's perceptions.

Direct observational methods also contribute to research on the assessment of peer group behavior. Trained observers unacquainted with children can provide unbiased information on discrete behaviors of children. Various studies on school-age children (Dodge, Coie & Brakke, 1982; Gottman, Gonso & Rasmussen, 1975; Ladd, 1983) show a high degree of consistency in outcomes. Both popular and average-status children engage in more cooperative play and social conversation than do rejected children. Rejected children show many more inappropriate behaviors than any of the other status groups. Often alone, they wander around the room and are off-task during the work period. They are also more aggressive, argumentative and likely to engage in disruptive peer interactions.

Less observational information is available on neglected children. In general, they spend more time alone and make fewer social contacts. When they do attempt to make a social contact, they are often ignored. They are characterized as being neither aggressive nor disruptive and have difficulty integrating with peers. They engage in more solitary activities than other children (Dodge, Coie & Brakke, 1982). In general, research suggests that children who are rejected and neglected display certain behaviors that may contribute to their failure to interact with peers.

Children's Status and Dropping Out of School

Children who continually experience rejection are considered to be at risk for dropping out of school. Approximately 20 percent of children who enter school do not graduate for various reasons (Weiner, 1980). A small percentage leave reluctantly, generally due to family emergencies or crises. Others do so because of frustrations related to poor social adjustment. Yet, the majority of these students are considered at least average in intelligence with the ability to graduate.

Several studies provide support for the hypothesis that peer assessments of low acceptance can predict future dropouts. Gronlund and Holmlund (1958) reported that 54 percent of low-accepted boys dropped out of school, compared to 19 percent of high-accepted boys. Among girls, the dropout figure was 35 percent for low acceptance, compared to 4 percent for high acceptance. Barclay (1966) reported that low-accepted boys and girls were two to three times more likely to drop out of school.

These early studies did not distinguish between rejected and neglected children, a more recent concern. Kupersmidt's (1983) study does address the subclassification issue. In a 6-year longitudinal study of 5th-graders, she reports the dropout rate included 30 percent of the rejected, 10 percent of the neglected, 21 percent of the average and 4 percent of the popular sample. Although differences were only marginally significant, the rejected group did show a greater dropout rate. Kupersmidt suggests that perhaps only the rejected children are at risk.

In sum, evidence suggests that many adolescents who drop out of school experience poor peer adjustments in their earlier years of school. They are more likely to drop out of school than their more accepted peers. The effects appear to be stronger for boys than girls, yet patterns are consistent regardless of gender. Evidence suggests that peer rejection may be such an adverse experience that adolescents decide to leave school (Kupersmidt, Coie & Dodge, 1990). The relationship between neglected children and dropout rates is not so clear and needs further examination.

Considerations for Teachers

Children who are rejected by their peers often report feelings of loneliness and lower levels of self-esteem. A sensitive and supportive teacher will be aware of these feelings and will attempt to assess each child's situation. Teachers can begin by careful observation of the child. While observing the child who appears to be having difficulty interacting with peers, the teacher can ask:

- Do the children in the class seem to avoid, ignore and reject the child?
- Does the child lack certain social skills necessary for successful interaction with others?
- Does the child have difficulty interpreting other peoples' cues or requests?
- Does the child have difficulty communicating with others about his/her needs and desires?
- Does the child act aggressively while interacting with others?
- Is the child disruptive in the class?

Although there are no plans that work with every child, teachers can choose from several approaches found to be successful. Teachers will need to choose strategies that best fit the child's needs, are adaptable to the classroom and support their philosophy.

Some children are disliked by peers because they lack the skills necessary to get along with others.

Researchers (Oden & Asher, 1977) have developed techniques for coaching children in social skills. Coaching involves identifying the child's problem and providing some form of direct instruction regarding strategies for use when interacting with peers.

Children can be coached on specific concepts that will contribute to more positive interactions. Concepts that were used by Oden and Asher (1977) included participation (e.g., how to get started and the importance of paying attention), cooperation (e.g., the importance of

> *Evidence suggests that peer rejection may be such an adverse experience that adolescents decide to leave school.*

taking turns and sharing materials), communication (e.g., the importance of talking with others and listening) and being friendly and nice (e.g., the importance of smiling, helping and encouraging others). Coaches can assist children by:

- telling them why each concept is important to peer interaction
- asking for examples to assess children's understanding of the concept
- reinforcing the examples or providing suggestions when children have trouble finding their own examples
- discussing both positive and negative behavioral examples that are important to interactions

- trying out some of the ideas in a play situation
- assessing the situation afterward.

Some children may benefit from practice with younger age-mates. Coaching children has contributed to long-term changes in their behavior and sociometric status.

Children who have difficulty reading other children's cues may benefit by watching others who interact successfully. Low-status children can watch a variety of successful interactions on videotape or acted out by adults, other children or puppets. Studies (Gresham & Nagle, 1980; Jakibchuk & Smeraglio, 1976) indicate that low-status children exhibit an increase in positive interaction after viewing models, and the effects are maintained over time. Factors contributing to these positive outcomes seem to be:

- similarity of the model to the target child
- explicitly identifying the model's behavior to the target child
- using simple step-by-step narration to describe the purposes of the behavior (Asher, Renshaw & Hymel, 1982).

Children who act aggressively toward others are often the least liked in the classroom. Self-control training, also referred to as cognitive behavior modification, focuses on the maintenance of positive behaviors through internal cognitive control (Meichenbaum, 1985). In some cases, teaching aggressive children to self-regulate their behavior has proven more effective in reducing inappropriate behaviors than external reinforcers from teachers (Bolstad & Johnson, 1972).

Researchers (Camp, Blom, Herbert & Van Doornick, 1977) have taught children to reinforce themselves directly by following a thinking-out-loud strategy that was found to reduce disruptive behaviors and increase prosocial behaviors. When using the thinking-out-loud strategy, children are trained to say to themselves, first out loud and then silently, "What is my problem? What is my plan? Am I using my plan? How did I do?" This process helps children interrupt their impulsive behavior, keeps them on task and reminds them of the necessary steps to take when carrying out their task. This training often includes social problem-solving skills, whereby children are encouraged to suggest and evaluate solutions to problems (Spivak, Platt & Shure, 1976).

Disruptiveness is another behavior often related to peer rejection. Disruptive children are often off-task and engage in inappropriate classroom behavior. The percentage of rejected children described as disruptive by peers ranges from 36 percent to 38 percent (Coie & Koeppl, 1990). Two techniques for reducing disruptive behavior in the classroom are use of reinforcement and token incentives.

Positive reinforcement, often used in connection with modeling, has produced some immediate positive outcomes (Asher, Renshaw & Hymel, 1982). The behavior of a child or group of children can be subjected to direct reinforcement. Teachers can make a point of praising socially cooperative interactions, while ignoring any undesirable interactions deemed tolerable. Specific praise of a child immediately after a desirable behavior provides the strongest results. Other studies (e.g., Gresham, 1979) used reinforcement procedures to reduce the frequency of negative social behaviors, and these effects were found to maintain over time.

The use of tokens as a reward for desirable behavior, in conjunction with positive reinforcement, tends to reduce disruptiveness and increase on-task behavior (Kazdin, 1977). In a token economy, teachers identify those behaviors deemed desirable and undesirable. When students act in a desirable manner, they are rewarded with a token of the teacher's choice. Tokens can range from a point system, plastic disks or plastic cards that can be exchanged for toys, food or other privileges. Several variations of token economies exist in schools and institutions. Descriptions of procedures, rules and additional consid-

> **Not having friends contributes to loneliness, low self-esteem and inability to develop social skills.**

erations of this system can be found in Kazdin (1977).

Although token economies have shown success, they are not without their critics. This procedure focuses on the symptoms rather than the causes, and the effects of the program do not always generalize to other settings—such as home or play settings (Kazdin, 1977). In some cases, the system may not work at all. For example, Coie and Koeppl (1990) point out that children who lack basic skills or are unable to perform classroom tasks may need specific coaching in academic skills.

Communicating with parents will be especially important for teachers working with children who have difficulty interacting with peers. The increasing number of single-parent families or families with both parents working outside the home means that teachers will need to utilize a variety of approaches to maintain contact.

Options may include telephone calls, notes, letters and parent conferences. In order for children to benefit, parents need to have an understanding of their child's development and progress. Teachers can discuss their observations of the child and share what they are doing in the classroom that might also be reinforced at home. In addition, teachers can ask for parental input and suggestions. Teachers can also share information with parents on child guidance or parent discussion groups that might be available in the community.

In some cases, teachers may find that some children will need more assistance than is possible within the classroom. Not all children will respond to the techniques suggested. At some point, teachers must acknowledge the need for additional help. Teachers will need to work with the family and suggest other resources. A professional teacher will understand the importance of compiling resources and referrals that can be useful for families. This information might include services such as the school psychologist; community mental health clinics; child, family and marriage counselors; and developmental screening clinics.

Summary

A significant percentage of children are rejected or neglected during childhood. A lack of friends can put children at risk for later problems. More immediately, not having friends contributes to loneliness, low self-esteem and inability to develop social skills. Rejection or neglect by peers is a traumatic experience for some children. Research indicates that identification and intervention may help modify the negative experiences that some children encounter.

References

Asher, S., Renshaw, R., & Hymel, S. (1982). Peer relations and the development of social skills. In S. G. Moore & C. R. Cooper (Eds.), *The young child: Reviews of research*, Vol. 3, pp. 137-158. Washington, DC: NAEYC.

Barclay, J. (1966). Sociometric choices and teacher ratings as predictors of school dropout. *Journal of Social Psychology, 4*, 40-45.

Bolstad, O., & Johnson, S. (1972). Self-regulation in the modification of disruptive classroom behavior. *Journal of Applied Behavioral Analysis, 5*, 443-454.

Camp, B., Blom, G., Herbert, F., & Van Doornick, W. (1977). Think aloud: A program for developed self-control in young aggressive boys. *Journal of Abnormal Child Psychology, 5*, 157-169.

Carlson, C., Lahey, B., & Neeper, R. (1984). Peer assessment of the social behavior of accepted, rejected, and neglected children. *Journal of Abnormal Child Psychology, 12*, 189-198.

Coie, J., & Dodge, K. (1988). Multiple sources of data on social behavior and social status in the school: A cross-age comparison. *Child Development, 59*, 815-829.

Coie, J., Dodge, K., & Coppotelli, H. (1982). Continuities and changes in children's social status: A five-year longitudinal study. *Developmental Psychology, 18*, 557-570.

Coie, J., & Koeppl, G. (1990). Adapting intervention to the problems of aggressive and disruptive rejected children. In S. R. Asher & J. D. Coie (Eds.), *Peer rejection in childhood*, pp. 309-337. New York: Cambridge University Press.

Dodge, K., Coie, J., & Brakke, N. (1982). Behavior patterns of socially rejected and neglected preadolescents: The roles of social approach and aggression. *Journal of Abnormal Child Psychology, 10*, 389-410.

French, D., & Waas, G. (1985). Behavior problems of peer-neglected and peer-rejected elementary-age children: Parent and teacher perspectives. *Child Development, 56*, 246-252.

Gottman, J., Gonso, J., & Rasmussen, B. (1975). Social interaction, social competence, and friendship in children. *Child Development, 46*, 709-718.

Gresham, F. (1979). Comparison of response cost and time out in a special education setting. *Journal of Special Education, 13*, 199-208.

Gresham, F. (1988). Social competence and motivational characteristics of learning disabled students. In M. C. Luang, M. C. Reynolds & H. J. Walberg (Eds.), *Handbook of special education: Research and practice*, Vol. 2, pp. 283-302. Oxford: Pergamon.

Gresham, F., & Nagle, R. (1980). Social skills training with children: Responsiveness to modeling and coaching as a function of peer orientation. *Journal of Consulting and Clinical Psychology, 48*, 718-729.

Gronlund, N., & Holmlund, W. (1958). The value of elementary school sociometric status scores for predicting pupils' adjustment in high school. *Educational Administration and Supervision, 44*, 225-260.

Hymel, S., & Asher, S. (1977, March). *Assessment and training of isolated children's social skills*. Paper presented at the biennial meeting of the Society for Research in Child Development, New Orleans. (Eric Document Reproduction Service No. ED 136 930).

Hymel, S., & Rubin, K. (1985). Children with peer relationships and social skills problems: Conceptual, methodological, and developmental issues. In G. J. Whitehurst (Ed.), *Annals of child development*, Vol. 2, pp. 251-297. Greenwich, CT: JAI Press.

Jakibchuk, Z., & Smeraglio, V. (1976). The influence of symbolic modeling on the social behavior of preschool children with low levels of social responsiveness. *Child Development, 47*, 838-841.

Kazdin, A. (1977). *The token economy: A review and evaluation*. New York: Plenum.

Kupersmidt, J. (1983, April). Predicting delinquency and academic problems from childhood peer status. In J. D. Coie (Chair), *Strategies for identifying children at social risk: Longitudinal correlates and consequences*. Symposium conducted at the biennial meeting of the Society for Research in Child Development, Detroit, MI.

Kupersmidt, J., Coie, J., & Dodge, K. (1990). The role of poor peer relationships in the development of disorder. In S. R. Asher & J. D. Coie (Eds.), *Peer rejection in childhood*, pp. 253-273. New York: Cambridge University Press.

Ladd, G. (1983). Social networks of popular, average, and rejected children in school settings. *Merrill-Palmer Quarterly, 29*, 283-308.

Meichenbaum, D. H. (1985). *Stress innoculation training*. New York: Pergamon Press.

Oden, S., & Asher, S. (1977). Coaching children in social skills for friendship making. *Child Development, 48*, 495-506.

Singleton, L., & Asher, S. (1977). Peer preferences and social interaction among third-grade children in an integrated school district. *Journal of Educational Psychology, 69*, 330-336.

Spivak, G., Platt, J., & Shure, M. (1976). *The problem-solving approach to adjustment*. San Francisco: Jossey-Bass.

Taylor, A., Asher, S., & Williams, G. (1987). The social adaptation of mainstreamed, mildly retarded children. *Child Development, 58*, 1321-1334.

Wasik, B. (1987). Sociometric measures and peer descriptions of kindergarten children: A study of reliability and validity. *Journal of Clinical Child Psychology, 16*, 218-224.

Weiner, I. P. (1980). Psychopathology in adolescence. In J. Adelson (Ed.), *Handbook of adolescent psychology*, pp. 447-471. New York: Wiley.

Teacher Response to Superhero Play: To Ban or Not To Ban?

Brenda J. Boyd

Brenda J. Boyd is Assistant Professor, Department of Human Development, Washington State University, Pullman.

Superhero play has received a great deal of attention from parents and educators in recent years. As defined here, superhero play refers to the active, physical play of children pretending to be media characters imbued with extraordinary abilities, including superhuman strength or the ability to transform themselves into superhuman entities. While some view this play as violent and aggressive, it is not so by definition.

This kind of play is a fact of life for those of us directly responsible for young children or for the training and support of those who deal with young children. A look at a bibliographic database related to early childhood (e.g., ERIC) offers ample evidence that children's involvement in superhero play is of growing concern to early childhood educators—the number of articles classified under superhero play as a subject between 1990 and 1995 is twice that found for the years 1985-1990.

Teachers of young children have become increasingly vocal opponents of superhero play, voicing concern about the behavior in their classrooms. Articles in professional publications such as *Young Children*, *Child Care Information Exchange* and *Childhood Education* by such authors as Bergen (1994) and Carlsson-Paige and Levin (1995) report that more and more teachers are choosing to ban superhero play from their classrooms. Newspaper articles found in the *Seattle Times* (Henderson, 1994) and the *Wall Street Journal* (Pereira, 1994) indicate that this concern has gone beyond an academic debate about child behavior. Teachers are sincerely concerned for the safety of children and themselves; many worry about violence as children engaged in superhero play grow older.

As a former child care provider/early educator and current teacher educator, I also have concerns about reported increases in violent and aggressive behavior in preschool classrooms. I suggest, however, that banning superhero play may not be the most effective means for dealing with children's increasing exposure to inappropriate and poor quality television programming. I will suggest that 1) we do not yet have valid data on these "increases" in classroom superhero play, 2) this behavior may play some developmental function necessary for young children's healthy growth and 3) by banning superhero play, teachers may be denying themselves a powerful opportunity to teach about values, respect, safety and living in a democratic social group.

Teacher Estimates of Play and Aggression

I begin by examining the premise that aggressive, violent superhero play is on the rise in preschool classrooms. The published reports of this increase are based on anecdotal reports from teachers (Carlsson-Paige & Levin, 1991; Jennings & Gillis-Olion, 1979; Kostelnik, Whiren & Stein, 1986) and from limited surveys of teachers of young children (Carlsson-Paige

From *Childhood Education*, Fall 1997, pp. 23-28. © 1997 by the Association for Childhood Education International, 17904 Georgia Avenue, Suite 215, Olney, MD 20832. Reprinted by permission.

& Levin, 1995). These non-random samples are often drawn from participants at conference workshops on superhero and war play in the classroom, who may already be sensitized to and concerned about the issue of aggressive play. These reports lead us to believe that preschool children are spending the majority of their time karate chopping and pouncing on each other.

My own research, in which I collected time interval samples of preschool children's behavior, has led me to question this belief (Boyd, 1996). In one sample of a group of 3- to 5-year-old children at a laboratory preschool, I found that only 2 of 17 children exhibited superhero play during a 1-month observation period. The time spent in superhero play accounted for less than 1 percent of the 300 minutes of play observed. In a second sample, in which children in a full-day child care program were observed, only 5 percent of play time, on the average, could be classified as superhero play. In this group of 16 children, only 4 children exhibited superhero play. In both samples, boys were the only superhero players. Furthermore, my observers and I never witnessed a child being physically hurt by another child while involved in superhero play.

Although these findings are clearly preliminary, they suggest that teacher reports of the occurrence and nature of superhero play may not be entirely objective, and may lead to an inflated estimate of this behavior. Previous research about teachers' views of aggression offers two lines of evidence to support this hypothesis.

First, evidence suggests that children and teachers have differing perspectives on "play fighting" and "aggression." In a study published in 1985, Smith and Lewis showed videotapes of play episodes to preschool children, their teacher and the assistant teacher. The children were more likely to agree with each other or with an objective observer than with their teachers in assessing behavior as play or aggression.

These results suggest that teachers rely on some perspective not shared by children to differentiate aggression and play. This perspective is reflected in the criteria teachers reportedly used for determining aggression in this study. The assistant teacher, whose assessment of behavior was least often in agreement with the children, based her remarks on her knowledge of the children's personalities, as reflected in comments such as "Well, knowing those boys, I know they can't cooperate together. Chances are it wasn't playful, it was aggressive" (Smith & Lewis, 1985, p. 180).

Second, one study (Connor, 1989) suggests that teachers' perspectives often differ not only from children's perspectives, but also from other non-teaching adults', including teachers in training. That is, teachers tend to see behavior as aggressive, rather than playful, more often than non-teachers. In this study, three preschool teachers viewed video clips of child behavior; the teachers labeled all 14 clips as examples of aggressive behavior. When the clips were shown to psychology students, however, the majority rated only two incidents as aggressive, two as play and the rest were rated differentially, depending on the viewer's gender. Men were more likely to view behavior as playful, while women more often labeled behavior as aggression. Additionally, Connor reported that preservice teachers agreed more often with female college students than with inservice teachers when rating behavior as play or aggression.

These findings suggest two points. First, some aspect of working in child care/early education may lead teachers to view play as negative behavior, in general, and as aggression in particular. Perhaps teachers' sense of responsibility for children's behavior and their safety leads them to be overly sensitive to potential disruption and physical injury. Connor's study (1989) supports this hypothesis. Teachers reported concern with the potential for injury, noting that the children "were playing too rough and someone could get hurt" (p. 217).

As I discuss superhero play with teachers, however, I find that the sense of responsibility is not only limited to concern with immediate behavior, but also includes the long-term consequences of aggressive play. I am struck by the connection teachers make between preschool play behavior and that of adolescent gangs. Early childhood educators seem to be equating young children's pretend behaviors with the actual loss of life and violence on their streets. This equation seems premature. We have too little

> *P*erhaps teachers' sense of responsibility for children's behavior and their safety leads them to be overly sensitive to potential disruption and physical injury.

information about the importance and/or potential harm of such fantasy play.

Second, gender socialization may also influence how teachers of young children (predominantly women) view superhero play. As Connor (1989) has suggested, women may grow up with less desire and/or opportunity to be involved in super-hero and other physical play than men. This lack of involvement may lead them to be less accepting of such play. More-over, if girls are discouraged from involvement in physi-cal activity because they may get hurt, this may lead them to believe that rough play is dangerous and should be avoided. Taken together, the research on gender and my anecdotal information from teachers suggest that early childhood educators may be overreacting to su-perhero play because of their fears about an increasingly violent society, and because of gender bias about play.

The Developmental Function of Superhero Play

The possibility that superhero play may serve some devel-opmental purpose is the essence of my second concern about banning superhero play. Early childhood educa-tors have long held that pretend play is critical for young children's healthy emotional development. This belief has been used to defend involvement in superhero play. Specifically, scholars suggest children have a need to resolve feelings about power and control. Some have suggested that superhero play offers a sense of power to children in a world dominated by adults, thus helping children to cope with the frustrations of limited control (Carlsson-Paige & Levin, 1990; Curry, 1971; Ritchie & Johnson, 1982; Slobin, 1976; Walder, 1976). Similarly, by playing out scenarios focused on good and evil, children can work through feelings of anxiety and fear about their own safety (Peller, 1971). Additionally, such play may help children express their anger and aggression and become comfortable with these feel-ings, which may otherwise be frightening to the child (Carlsson-Paige & Levin, 1990; Ritchie et al., 1982).

While this theory is well-established in the child development literature, it is a weak argument for supporting the developmental function of superhero play without empirical research that directly examines its developmental relevance. Moreover, this set of hypotheses about the role of superhero play in provid-ing emotional security is not easily tested. Other perspectives for investigating the function of super-hero play, however, are available.

Although superhero play has received limited em-pirical attention, a related type of play, known as "rough-and-tumble play" (R&T), has been more thor-oughly researched. The term "rough-and-tumble play" is commonly used to refer to children's play fighting, wrestling and chasing behaviors, from preschool

> *B*y playing out scenarios focused on good and evil, children can work through feelings of anxiety and fear . . .

through adolescence (e.g., Costabile et al., 1991; Pellegrini, 1987). I argue that superhero play is a special case of R&T and that the similarity of these types of play allows us to develop hypotheses about the potential function of superhero play. I will describe the similari-ties between these types of play, outline some of the hypothesized functions of R&T and consider the impli-cations of this work for the study of superhero play.

R&T and superhero play share several characteris-tics. Both types of play can involve chasing, wrestling, kicking, mock battles and feigned attacks (Kostelnik et al., 1986). In addition, R&T frequently involves fantasy enactment or pretending (Smith & Connolly, 1987; Smith & Lewis, 1985), as does superhero play. Adults often confuse both R&T and superhero play with ag-gression (Kostelnik et al., 1986); furthermore, R&T play is often identified as pretend play in research studies (Pellegrini, 1987). Teachers' accounts of superhero play indicate that this play is routinely marked by play fighting, kicking and martial arts moves. In fact, these types of behavior seem to be the central cause for teachers' concern (Bergen, 1994; Carlsson-Paige & Levin, 1995; Henderson, 1994). These similarities suggest to me that superhero play can be conceptualized as a special case of R&T play, in which children assume the role of a superhero character.

The similarity in these types of play led researchers to examine the function of superhero play. This body of research suggests that R&T play may serve some im-portant developmental functions for young children, especially boys. R&T play serves three potential func-tions—specifically, affiliation, dominance and social skill facilitation (Smith & Boulton, 1990).

Affiliation. R&T play may help children form or

maintain friendships. R&T's positive social nature is underscored by the presence of children laughing and smiling, and by the absence of children inflicting pain (Blurton Jones, 1972; Smith, 1982). R&T partners are consistently found to be friends (Humphreys & Smith, 1987; Smith & Lewis, 1985). While this does not directly show that R&T play builds friendships, these results nevertheless suggest that R&T play helps children develop or maintain friendships (Smith & Boulton, 1990).

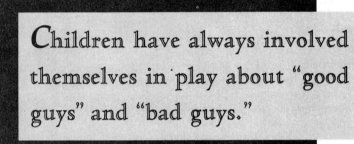

Children have always involved themselves in play about "good guys" and "bad guys."

Dominance. Animal researchers first used the concept of dominance to describe a hierarchical order of dominance within a species that controls access to resources such as space, food and mates (Wilson, 1975). They found that this hierarchy can reduce conflict, by clearly defining a power structure within a group (Hinde, 1974). Strayer and Strayer (1976) applied this concept to a group of children and observed a fairly stable hierarchy, with few conflicts.

Smith and Boulton (1990) suggest that through R&T play, children can maintain or improve their ranking within the hierarchy. A child can maintain her or his rank by picking worthy "opponents" who are equal in strength. Or, a child could safely improve her rank by picking a slightly stronger play partner, and suffer little if she was not successful.

Humphreys and Smith (1987) support the dominance maintenance hypothesis. When comparing class consensus rankings of 7- to 11-year-olds' strength, they found, in most cases, no consistent difference in the two participants of an R&T bout. Their findings suggest that children do select partners near to them in the dominance hierarchy.

Social Skill Facilitation. Some researchers have suggested that involvement in R&T offers children an opportunity to develop social skills, which consequently leads to successful peer interactions. Both parent-child play and peer play support this hypothesis. Parke, MacDonald and their colleagues report that children whose parents (especially fathers) engage in physical play with them are more likely to be popular with their peers (MacDonald, 1987; Parke,

MacDonald, Beitel & Bhavnagri, 1987). Power and Parke (1981) argue that physical play with parents helps children learn to regulate and interpret emotion by serving "as context for a wide range of communicative and affectively charged social interaction" (p. 160). Indeed, in one study, physical play did correlate with girls' ability to "read" facial expressions, suggesting some relationship between physical play and skill at reading social cues (Parke et al., 1987).

help w/ social cues

While the results are more numerous in terms of peer-peer R&T, they are also more mixed. Pellegrini (1988) found that children rejected by their peers were less successful than popular children at discriminating between serious fighting and R&T. In addition, for popular children, R&T served as a precursor to rule-oriented games, yet for rejected children, it led to aggression (Pellegrini, 1991). Several other researchers' findings indicate either no relation between R&T and popularity, or a negative correlation (Dodge, 1983; Ladd, 1983; Rubin, Daniels-Bierness & Hayvren, 1982). It is difficult to compare these results, however, because there is no uniform definition of R&T (Smith, 1989).

While the connection between superhero play and R&T is clearly speculative, an examination of how R&T play functions offers a measurable perspective on superhero play's possible contribution to development. The similarity between R&T and superhero play suggests that these types of play may also serve similar developmental functions. At the very least, this examination makes clear that it is premature to deny children the opportunity for involvement in superhero play. We first need to know more about the developmental implications of such a denial.

Sending Play Underground and a Lost Opportunity
This brings us to my third and final concern about banning superhero play. As other scholars of play have noted, banning has two possible effects (Carlsson-Paige & Levin, 1995). First, banning superhero play from the classroom sends children the message that they must hide their interests from adults, and that it is wrong for them to be interested in issues of power and control, good and evil, and so on. A related consequence is that teachers may lose an important opportunity to influence children's ideas about violence and the use of power, and about managing individual needs in a social community.

My concern about children's covert involvement in superhero play stems from the observation that children have always involved themselves in play about "good guys" and "bad guys." By telling children that such play is wrong or bad, we may be communicating that it is not acceptable to be interested in issues of control, nor is it acceptable to have fears about power. At the same time, we lose an opportunity to help children feel safe in a world that may be dangerous at times. While we need not expose children to inappropriate levels of violence, danger or fear, we should not expect that young children do not share adults' fears about violence, even if it is undeveloped. Part of the human condition is to fear and to desire mastery of that fear. Should we tell children that using a natural tool to conquer that fear, such as play, is wrong?

Second, I think that if teachers are truly concerned about exposing children to televised violence and aggression (or are concerned children will likely hear about such programming from friends anyway, even if they are not allowed to watch), are they not required to help children work through these issues in their play? When we ban superhero play (or any behavior children find interesting), we ignore a powerful opportunity for helping children learn valuable lessons in a familiar and appealing context.

Resources are available for helping teachers to use superhero play effectively in the classroom. Diane Levin (1994) has published practical suggestions for helping children to learn about establishing "peaceable" classroom communities; these ideas attend to all children's safety needs without simply banning superhero play. These suggestions can help teachers address their concerns about the children who do not like to play superheroes or who are frightened by others' superhero play. In addition, Gayle Gronlund (1992) offers interesting ideas for moving children beyond the scripted narratives they see on television, which she developed from working with her kindergarten class during the Ninja Turtle days. More recently, Julie Greenberg (1995) discussed ways to "make friends with the Power Rangers." Even when teachers decide to support superhero play in their classrooms, they may not know the best way to begin. These resources offer a starting point.

I believe that banning superhero play is not the most productive manner for dealing with our concerns about increased violence in our classrooms. Instead, educators should consider the best means for making positive use of this play; some of the resources I have described can be useful in this endeavor. Be assured that I am not advocating a free-for-all without teacher input into play. Each educator must decide, on the basis of information about their students and their needs, whether this sort of play is acceptable, at what level and with what supports in place. I encourage early childhood educators to take a broad and contextual view, as we do with all the behaviors we encounter, and to offer children the best supports we can in their daily lives.

References

Bergen, D. (1994). Should teachers permit or discourage violent play themes? *Childhood Education, 70*(5), 300-301.

Blurton Jones, N. (Ed.). (1972). *Ethological studies of child behavior* (pp. 97-129). London: Cambridge University Press.

Boyd, B. J. (1996). *Superhero play in the early childhood classroom.* Unpublished manuscript.

Carlsson-Paige, N., & Levin, D. E. (1995). Can teachers resolve the war-play dilemma? *Young Children, 50*(5), 62-63.

Carlsson-Paige, N., & Levin, D. (1991). The subversion of healthy development and play: Teachers' reactions to the Teenage Mutant Ninja Turtles. *Day Care and Early Education, 19*(2), 14-20.

Carlsson-Paige, N., & Levin, D. (1990). *Who's calling the shots? How to respond effectively to children's fascination with war play and war toys.* Philadelphia, PA: New Society Publishers.

Connor, K. (1989). Aggression: Is it in the eye of the beholder? *Play and Culture, 2,* 213-217.

Costabile, A., Smith, P. K., Matheson, L., Aston, J., Hunter, T., & Boulton, M. (1991). Cross-national comparison of how children distinguish serious and playful fighting. *Developmental Psychology, 27,* 881-887.

Curry, N. E. (1971). Five-year-old play. In N. E. Curry & S. Arnaud (Eds.), *Play: The child strives toward self-realization* (pp. 10-11). Washington, DC: National Association for the Education of Young Children.

Dodge, K. A. (1983). Behavioral antecedents of peer social status. *Child Development, 54,* 1383-1399.

Greenberg, J. (1995). Making friends with the Power Rangers. *Young Children, 50*(5), 60-61.

Gronlund, G. (1992). Coping with Ninja Turtle play in my kindergarten classroom. *Young Children, 48*(1), 21-25.

Henderson, D. (1994, December 14). No "morphing" allowed in class: Power Rangers play all the rage for kids. *The Seattle Times,* pp. A1, A21.

Hinde, R. A. (1974). *A biological basis of human social behavior.* New York: McGraw-Hill.

Humphreys, A. P., & Smith, P. K. (1987). Rough and tumble, friendship, and dominance in school children: Evidence for continuity and change with age. *Child Development, 58,* 201-212.

Jennings, C. M., & Gillis-Olion, M. (1979, November). *The impact of television cartoons on child behavior.* Paper presented at the meeting of the National Association for the Education of Young Children, Atlanta, GA.

Kostelnik, M., Whiren, A., & Stein, L. (1986). Living with He-Man: Managing superhero fantasy play. *Young Children, 41*(4), 3-9.

Ladd, G. (1983). Social networks of popular, average, and rejected children in a school setting. *Merrill-Palmer Quarterly, 29,* 283-307.

Levin, D. E. (1994). *Teaching young children in violent times: Building a peaceable classroom.* Cambridge, MA: Educators for Social Responsibility.

MacDonald, K. (1987). Parent-child physical play with rejected, neglected and popular boys. *Developmental Psychology, 23,* 705-711.

Parke, R. D., MacDonald, K. B., Beitel, A., & Bhavnagri, N.

(1987). The role of the family in the development of peer relationships. In R. Peters (Ed.), *Social learning and systems approaches to marriage and the family* (pp. 17-44). New York: Bruner/Mazel.

Pellegrini, A. D. (1991). A longitudinal study of popular and rejected children's rough-and-tumble play. *Early Education and Development, 2*(3), 205-213.

Pellegrini, A. D. (1988). Elementary-school children's rough-and-tumble play and social competence. *Developmental Psychology, 24*(6), 802-806.

Pellegrini, A. D. (1987). Rough-and-tumble play: Developmental and educational significance. *Educational Psychologist, 22,* 23-43.

Peller, L. (1971). Models of children's play. In R. Herron & B. Sutton-Smith (Eds.), *Child's play* (pp. 110-125). New York: Wiley.

Pereira, J. (1994, December 7). Caution: Morphing may be hazardous to your teacher. *Wall Street Journal,* pp. A1, A8.

Power, T. G., & Parke, R. D. (1981). Play as a context for early learning. In L. M. Laosa & I. E. Sigel (Eds.), *Families as learning environments for children* (pp. 147-178). New York: Plenum.

Ritchie, K. E., & Johnson, Z. M. (1982, November). *Superman comes to preschool: Superhero TV play.* Paper presented at the meeting of the National Association for the Education of Young Children, Washington, DC.

Rubin, K. H., Daniels-Bierness, T., & Hayvren, M. (1982). Social and social-cognitive correlates of sociometric status in preschool and kindergarten children. *Canadian Journal of Behavioral Science, 14,* 338-347.

Slobin, D. (1976). The role of play in childhood. In C. Shaefer (Ed.), *Therapeutic use of child's play* (pp. 95-118). New York: Aronson.

Smith, P. K. (1989). The role of rough-and-tumble play in the development of social competence: Theoretical perspectives and empirical evidence. In B. H. Schneider, G. Attili, J. Nadel & R. P. Weissberg (Eds.), *Social competence in developmental perspective* (pp. 239-258). Dordrect: Kluwer Academic Publishers.

Smith, P. K. (1982). Does play matter? Functional and evolutionary aspects of animal and human play. *The Behavioral and Brain Sciences, 5,* 139-184.

Smith, P. K., & Boulton, M. (1990). Rough-and-tumble play, aggression, and dominance: Perceptions and behavior in children's encounters. *Human Development, 33,* 271-282.

Smith, P. K., & Connolly, K. J. (1987). *The ecology of preschool behavior.* Cambridge, England: Cambridge University Press.

Smith, P. K., & Lewis, K. (1985). Rough-and-tumble play, fighting and chasing in nursery school children. *Ethology and Sociobiology, 6,* 175-181.

Strayer, F. F., & Strayer, J. (1976). An ethological analysis of social agonism and dominance relations among preschool children. *Child Development, 47,* 980-989.

Walder, R. (1976). Psychoanalytic theory of play. In C. Shaefer (Ed.), *Therapeutic use of child's play* (pp. 79-94). New York: Aronson.

Wilson, E. O. (1975). *Sociobiology. The new synthesis.* Cambridge, MA: Belknap Press of Harvard University Press.

Girls and Boys Together... But Mostly Apart: Gender Arrangements in Elementary Schools

Barrie Thorne

Michigan State University

Throughout the years of elementary school, children's friendships and casual encounters are strongly separated by sex. Sex segregation among children, which starts in preschool and is well established by middle childhood, has been amply documented in studies of children's groups and friendships (e.g., Eder & Hallinan, 1978; Schofield, 1981) and is immediately visible in elementary school settings. When children choose seats in classrooms or the cafeteria, or get into line, they frequently arrange themselves in same-sex clusters. At lunchtime, they talk matter-of-factly about "girls' tables" and "boys' tables." Playgrounds have gendered turfs, with some areas and activities, such as large playing fields and basketball courts, controlled mainly by boys, and others—smaller enclaves like jungle-gym areas and concrete spaces for hopscotch or jumprope—more often controlled by girls. Sex segregation is so common in elementary schools that it is meaningful to speak of separate girls' and boys' worlds.

Studies of gender and children's social relations have mostly followed this "two worlds" model, separately describing and comparing the subcultures of girls and of boys (e.g., Lever, 1976; Maltz & Borker, 1983). In brief summary: Boys tend to interact in larger, more age-heterogeneous groups (Lever, 1976; Waldrop & Halverson, 1975; Eder & Hallinan, 1978). They engage in more rough and tumble play and physical fighting (Maccoby & Jacklin, 1974). Organized sports are both a central activity and a major metaphor in boys' subcultures; they use the language of "teams" even when not engaged in sports, and they often construct interaction in the form of contests. The shifting hierarchies of boys' groups (Savin-Williams, 1976) are evident in their more frequent use of direct commands, insults, and challenges (Goodwin, 1980).

Fewer studies have been done of girls' groups (Foot, Chapman, & Smith, 1980; McRobbie & Garber, 1975), and—perhaps because categories for description and analysis have come more from male than female experience—researchers have had difficulty seeing and analyzing girls' social relations. Recent work has begun to correct this skew. In middle childhood, girls' worlds are less public than those of boys; girls more often interact in private places and in smaller groups or friendship pairs (Eder & Hallinan, 1978; Waldrop & Halverson, 1975). Their play is more cooperative and turn-taking (Lever, 1976). Girls have more intense and exclusive friendships, which take shape around keeping and telling secrets, shifting alliances, and indirect ways of expressing disagreement (Goodwin, 1980; Lever, 1976; Maltz & Borker, 1983). Instead of direct commands, girls more often use directives which merge speaker and hearer, e.g., "let's" or "we gotta" (Goodwin, 1980).

Although much can be learned by comparing the social organization and subcultures of boys' and of girls' groups, the separate worlds approach has eclipsed full, contextual understanding of gender and social relations among children. The separate worlds model essentially involves a search for group sex differences, and shares the limitations of individual sex difference research. Differences tend to be exaggerated and similarities ignored, with little theoretical attention to the integration of similarity and difference (Unger, 1979). Statistical findings of difference are often portrayed as dichotomous, neglecting the considerable individual variation that exists; for example, not all boys fight, and some have intense and exclusive friendships. The sex difference approach tends to abstract gender from its social context, to assume that males and females are qualitatively and permanently different (with differences perhaps unfolding through separate developmental lines). These assumptions mask the possibility that gender arrangements and patterns of similarity and difference may vary by situation, race, social class, region, or subculture.

Sex segregation is far from total, and is a more complex and dynamic process than the portrayal of separate worlds reveals. Erving Goffman (1977) has observed that sex segregation has a "with-then-apart" structure; the sexes segregate periodically, with separate spaces, rituals, groups, but they also come together and are, in crucial ways, part of the same world. This is certainly true in the social environment of elementary schools. Although girls and boys do interact as boundaried collectivities—an image suggested by the separate worlds approach—there are other occasions when they work or play in relaxed and integrated ways. Gender is less central to the organization and meaning of some situations than others. In short, sex segregation is not static, but is a variable and complicated process.

To gain an understanding of gender which can encompass both the "with" and the "apart" of sex segregation, analysis should start not with the individual, nor with a search for sex differences, but with social relationships. Gender should be conceptualized as a system of relationships rather than as an immutable and dichotomous given. Taking this approach, I have organized my research on gender and children's social relations around questions like the following: How and when does gender enter into group formation? In a given situation, how is gender made more or less salient or infused with particular meanings? By what rituals, processes, and forms of social organization and conflict do "with-then-apart" rhythms get enacted? How are these processes affected by the organization of institutions (e.g., different types of schools, neighborhoods, or summer camps), varied settings (e.g., the constraints and possibilities governing interaction on playgrounds vs. classrooms), and particular encounters?

METHODS AND SOURCES OF DATA

This study is based on two periods of participant observation. In 1976–1977 I observed for 8 months in a largely working-class elementary school in California, a school with 8% Black and 12% Chicano students. In 1980 I did fieldwork for 3 months in a Michigan elementary school of similar size (around 400 students), social class, and racial composition. I observed in several classrooms—a kindergarten, a second grade, and a combined fourth-fifth grade—and in school hallways, cafeterias, and playgrounds. I set out to follow the round of the school day as children experience it, recording their interactions with one another, and with adults, in varied settings.

Participant observation involves gaining access to everyday, "naturalistic" settings and taking systematic notes over an extended period of time. Rather than starting with preset categories for recording, or with fixed hypotheses for testing, participant-observers record detail in ways which maximize opportunities for discovery. Through continuous interaction between observation and analysis, "grounded theory" is developed (Glaser & Strauss, 1967).

The distinctive logic and discipline of this mode of inquiry emerges from: (1) theoretical sampling—being relatively systematic in the choice of where and whom to observe in order to maximize knowledge relevant to categories and analysis which are being developed; and (2) comparing all relevant data on a given point in order to modify emerging propositions to take account of discrepant cases (Katz, 1983). Participant observation is a flexible, open-ended and inductive method, designed to understand behavior within, rather than stripped from, social context. It provides richly detailed information which is anchored in everyday meanings and experience.

DAILY PROCESSES OF SEX SEGREGATION

Sex segregation should be understood not as a given, but as the result of deliberate activity. The outcome is dramatically visible when there are separate girls' and boys' tables in school lunchrooms, or sex-separated groups on playgrounds. But in the same lunchroom one can also find tables where girls and boys eat and talk together, and in some playground activities the sexes mix. By what processes do girls and boys separate into gender-defined and relatively boundaried collectivities? And in what contexts, and through what processes, do boys and girls interact in less gender-divided ways?

In the school settings I observed, much segregation happened with no mention of gender. Gender was implicit in the contours of friendship, shared interest, and perceived risk which came into play when children chose companions—in their prior planning, invitations, seeking-of-access, saving-of-places, denials of entry, and allowing or protesting of "cuts" by those who violated the rules for lining up. Sometimes children formed mixed-sex groups for play, eating, talking, working on a classroom project, or moving through space. When adults or children explicitly invoked gender—and this was nearly always in ways which separated girls and boys—boundaries were heightened and mixed-sex interaction became an explicit arena of risk.

In the schools I studied, the physical space and curricula were not formally divided by sex, as they have been in the history of elementary schooling (a history evident in separate entrances to old school buildings, where the words "Boys" and "Girls" are permanently etched in concrete). Nevertheless, gender was a visible marker in the adult-organized school day. In both schools, when the public address system sounded, the principal inevitably opened with: "Boys and girls . . . ," and in addressing clusters of children, teachers and aides regularly used gender terms ("Heads down, girls"; "The girls are ready and the boys aren't"). These forms of address made gender visible and salient, conveying an assumption that the sexes are separate social groups.

Teachers and aides sometimes drew upon gender as a basis for sorting children and organizing activities. Gender is an embodied and visual social category which roughly divides the population in half, and the separation of girls and boys permeates the history and lore of schools and playgrounds. In both schools—although through awareness of Title IX, many teachers had changed this practice—one could see separate girls' and boys' lines moving, like caterpillars, through the school halls. In the 4th-5th grade classroom the teacher frequently pitted girls against boys for spelling and math contests. On the playground in the Michigan school, aides regarded the space close to the building as girls' territory, and the playing fields "out there" as boys' territory. They sometimes shooed children of the other sex away from those spaces, especially boys who ventured near the girls' area and seemed to have teasing in mind.

In organizing their activities, both within and apart from the surveillance of adults, children also explicitly invoked gender. During my fieldwork in the Michigan school, I kept daily records of who sat where in the lunchroom. The amount of sex segregation varied: It was least at the first grade tables and almost total among sixth graders. There was also variation from classroom to classroom within a given age, and from day to day. Actions like the following heightened the gender divide:

> In the lunchroom, when the two second grade tables were filling, a high-status boy walked by the inside table, which had a scattering of both boys and girls, and said loudly, "Oooo, too many girls," as he headed for a seat at the far table. The boys at the inside table picked up their trays and moved, and no other boys sat at the inside table, which the pronouncement had effectively made taboo.

In the end, that day (which was not the case every day), girls and boys ate at separate tables.

Eating and walking are not sex-typed activities, yet in forming groups in lunchrooms and hallways children often separated by sex. Sex segregation assumed added dimensions on the playground, where spaces, equipment, and activities were infused with gender meanings. My inventories of activities and groupings on the playground showed similar patterns in both schools: Boys controlled the large fixed spaces designated for team sports (baseball diamonds, grassy fields used for football or soccer); girls more often played

closer to the building, doing tricks on the monkey bars (which, for 6th graders, became an area for sitting and talking) and using cement areas for jumprope, hopscotch, and group games like four-square. (Lever, 1976, provides a good analysis of sex-divided play.) Girls and boys most often played together in kickball, and in group (rather than team) games like four-square, dodgeball, and handball. When children used gender to exclude others from play, they often drew upon beliefs connecting boys to some activities and girls to others:

> A first grade boy avidly watched an all-female game of jump rope. When the girls began to shift positions, he recognized a means of access to the play and he offered, "I'll swing it." A girl responded, "No way, you don't know how to do it, to swing it. You gotta be a girl." He left without protest.

Although children sometimes ignored pronouncements about what each sex could or could not do, I never heard them directly challenge such claims.

When children had explicitly defined an activity or a group as gendered, those who crossed the boundary—especially boys who moved into female-marked space—risked being teased. ("Look! Mike's in the girls' line!"; " 'That's a girl over there,' a girl said loudly, pointing to a boy sitting at an otherwise all-female table in the lunchroom.") Children, and occasionally adults, used teasing—especially the tease of "liking" someone of the other sex, or of "being" that sex by virtue of being in their midst—to police gender boundaries. Much of the teasing drew upon heterosexual romantic definitions, making cross-sex interaction risky, and increasing social distance between boys and girls.

RELATIONSHIPS BETWEEN THE SEXES

Because I have emphasized the "apart" and ignored the occasions of "with," this analysis of sex segregation falsely implies that there is little contact between girls and boys in daily school life. In fact, relationships between girls and boys—which should be studied as fully as, and in connection with, same-sex relationships—are of several kinds:

1. "Borderwork," or forms of cross-sex interaction which are based upon and reaffirm boundaries and asymmetries between girls' and boys' groups;
2. Interactions which are infused with heterosexual meanings;
3. Occasions where individuals cross gender boundaries to participate in the world of the other sex; and
4. Situations where gender is muted in salience, with girls and boys interacting in more relaxed ways.

Borderwork

In elementary school settings boys' and girls' groups are sometimes spatially set apart. Same-sex groups sometimes claim fixed territories such as the basketball court, the bars, or specific lunchroom tables. However, in the crowded, multi-focused, and adult-controlled environment of the school, groups form and disperse at a rapid rate and can never stay totally apart. Contact between girls and boys sometimes lessens sex segregation, but gender-defined groups also come together in ways which emphasize their boundaries.

"Borderwork" refers to interaction across, yet based upon and even strengthening gender boundaries. I have drawn this notion from Fredrik Barth's (1969) analysis of social relations which are maintained across ethnic boundaries with-out diminishing dichotomized ethnic status.[1] His focus is on more macro, ecological arrangements; mine is on face-to-face behavior. But the insight is similar: Groups may interact in ways which strengthen their borders, and the maintenance of ethnic (or gender) groups can best be understood by examining the boundary that defines the group, "not the cultural stuff that it encloses" (Barth, 1969, p. 15). In elementary schools there are several types of borderwork: contests or games where gender-defined teams compete; cross-sex rituals of chasing and pollution; and group invasions. These interactions are asymmetrical, challenging the separate-but-parallel model of "two worlds."

Contests

Boys and girls are sometimes pitted against each other in classroom competitions and playground games. The 4th-5th grade classroom had a boys' side and a girls' side, an arrangement that re-emerged each time the teacher asked children to choose their own desks. Although there was some within-sex shuffling, the result was always a spatial moiety system—boys on the left, girls on the right—with the exception of one girl (the "tomboy" whom I'll describe later), who twice chose a desk with the boys and once with the girls. Drawing upon and reinforcing the children's self-segregation, the teacher often pitted the boys against the girls in spelling and math competitions, events marked by cross-sex antagonism and within-sex solidarity:

> The teacher introduced a math game; she would write addition and subtraction problems on the board, and a member of each team would race to be the first to write the correct answer. She wrote two score-keeping columns on the board: 'Beastly Boys' . . . 'Gossipy Girls.' The boys yelled out, as several girls laughed, 'Noisy girls! Gruesome girls!' The girls sat in a row on top of their desks; sometimes they moved collectively, pushing their hips or whispering 'pass it on.' The boys stood along the wall, some reclining against desks. When members of either group came back victorious from the front of the room, they would do the 'giving five' hand-slapping ritual with their team members.

On the playground a team of girls occasionally played against a team of boys, usually in kickball or team two-square. Sometimes these games proceeded matter-of-factly, but if gender became the explicit basis of team solidarity, the interaction changed, becoming more antagonistic and unstable:

> Two fifth-grade girls played against two fifth-grade boys in a team game of two-square. The game proceeded at an even pace until an argument ensued about whether the ball was out or on the line. Karen, who had hit the ball, became annoyed, flashed her middle finger at the other team, and called to a passing girl to join their side. The boys then called out to other boys, and cheered as several arrived to play. 'We got five and you got three!' Jack yelled. The game continued, with the girls yelling, 'Bratty boys! Sissy boys!' and the boys making noises—'weee haw' 'ha-ha-ha'-as they played.

Chasing

Cross-sex chasing dramatically affirms boundaries between girls and boys. The basic elements of chase and elude, capture and rescue (Sutton-Smith, 1971) are found in various kinds of tag with formal rules, and in informal episodes of chasing which punctuate life on playgrounds. These episodes begin with a provocation (taunts like "You can't get me!" or "Slobber monster!"; bodily pokes or the grabbing of possessions). A provocation may be ignored, or responded to by chasing. Chaser and chased may then alternate roles. In an ethnographic study of chase sequences on a school playground, Christine Finnan (1982) observes that chases vary in number of chasers to chased (e.g., one chasing one, or five chasing two); form of provocation (a taunt or a poke); outcome (an episode may end when the chased outdistances the chaser, or with a brief touch, being wrestled to the ground, or the recapturing of a hat or a ball); and in use of space (there may or may not be safety zones).

Like Finnan (1982), and Sluckin (1981), who studied a playground in England, I found that chasing has a gendered structure. Boys frequently chase one another, an activity which often ends in wrestling and mock fights. When girls chase girls, they are usually less physically aggressive; they less often, for example, wrestle one another to the ground.

Cross-sex chasing is set apart by special names— "girls chase the boys"; "boys chase the girls"; "the chase"; "chasers"; "chase and kiss"; "kiss chase"; "kissers and chasers"; "kiss or kill"—and by children's animated talk about the activity. The names vary by region and school, but contain both gender and sexual meanings (this form of play is mentioned, but only briefly analzyed, in Finnan, 1981; Sluckin, 1981; Parrott, 1972; and Borman, 1979).

In "boys chase the girls" and "girls chase the boys" (the names most frequently used in both the California and Michigan schools) boys and girls become, by definition, separate teams. Gender terms override individual identities, especially for the other team ("Help, a girl's chasin' me!"; "C'mon Sarah, let's get that boy"; "Tony, help save me from the girls"). Individuals may call for help from, or offer help to, others of their sex. They may also grab someone of their sex and turn them over to the opposing team: "Ryan grabbed Billy from behind, wrestling him to the ground 'Hey girls, get 'im,' Ryan called."

Boys more often mix episodes of cross-sex with same-sex chasing. Girls more often have safety zones, places like the girls' restroom or an area by the school wall, where they retreat to rest and talk (sometimes in animated postmortems) before new episodes of cross-sex chasing begin.

Early in the fall in the Michigan school, where chasing was especially prevalent, I watched a second grade boy teach a kindergarten girl how to chase. He slowly ran backwards, beckoning her to pursue him, as he called, "Help, a girl's after me." In the early grades chasing mixes with fantasy play, e.g., a first-grade boy who played "sea monster," his arms outflung and his voice growling, as he chased a group of girls. By third grade, stylized gestures—exaggerated stalking motions, screams (which only girls do), and karate kicks—accompany scenes of chasing.

Names like "chase and kiss" mark the sexual meanings of cross-sex chasing, a theme I return to later. The threat of kissing—most often girls threatening to kiss boys—is a ritualized form of provocation. Cross-sex chasing among sixth graders involves elaborate patterns of touch and touch avoidance, which adults see as sexual. The principal told the sixth graders in the Michigan school that they were not to play "pom-pom," a complicated chasing game, because it entailed "inappropriate touch."

Rituals of Pollution

Cross-sex chasing is sometimes entwined with rituals of pollution, as in "cooties," where specific individuals or groups are treated as contaminating or carrying "germs." Children have rituals for transfering cooties (usually touching someone else and shouting "You've got cooties!"), for immunization (e.g., writing "CV" for "cootie vaccination" on their arms), and for eliminating cooties (e.g., saying "no gives" or using "cootie catchers" made of folded paper) (described in Knapp & Knapp, 1976). While girls may give cooties to girls, boys do not generally give cooties to one another (Samuelson, 1980).

In cross-sex play, either girls or boys may be defined as having cooties, which they transfer through chasing and touching. Girls give cooties to boys more often than vice versa. In Michigan, one version of cooties is called "girl stain"; the fourth-graders whom Karkau, 1973, describes, used the phrase "girl touch." "Cootie queens," or "cootie girls" (there are no "kings" or "boys") are female pariahs, the ultimate school untouchables, seen as contaminating not only by virtue of gender, but also through some added stigma such as being overweight or poor.[2] That girls are seen as more polluting than boys is a significant asymmetry, which echoes cross-cultural patterns, although in other cultures female pollution is generally connected to menstruation, and not applied to prepubertal girls.

Invasions

Playground invasions are another asymmetric form of borderwork. On a few occasions I saw girls invade and disrupt an all-male game, most memorably a group of tall sixth-grade girls who ran onto the playing field and grabbed a football which was in play. The boys were surprised and frustrated, and, unusual for boys this old, finally tattled to the aide. But in the majority of cases, boys disrupt girls' activities rather than vice versa. Boys grab the ball from girls playing four-square, stick feet into a jumprope and stop an ongoing game, and dash through the area of the bars, where girls are taking turns performing, sending the rings flying. Sometimes boys ask to join a girls' game and then, after a short period of seemingly earnest play, disrupt the game:

> Two second-grade boys begged to "twirl" the jumprope for a group of second-grade girls who had been jumping for some time. The girls agreed, and the boys began to twirl. Soon, without announcement, the boys changed from "seashells, cockle bells'" to "hot peppers" (spinning the rope very fast), and tangled the jumper in the rope. The boys ran away laughing.

Boys disrupt girls' play so often that girls have developed almost ritualized responses: They guard their ongoing play, chase boys away, and tattle to the aides. In a playground cycle which enhances sex segregation, aides who try to spot potential trouble before it occurs sometimes shoo boys away from areas where girls are playing. Aides do not anticipate trouble from girls who seek to join groups of boys, with the exception of girls intent on provoking a chase sequence. And indeed, if they seek access to a boys' game, girls usually play with boys in earnest rather than breaking up the game.

A close look at the organization of borderwork—or boundaried interactions between the sexes—shows that the worlds of boys and girls may be separate, but they are not parallel, nor are they equal. The worlds of girls and boys articulate in several asymmetric ways:

1. On the playground, boys control as much as ten times more space than girls, when one adds up the area of large playing fields and compares it with the much smaller areas where girls predominate. Girls, who play closer to the building, are more often watched over and protected by the adult aides.

2. Boys invade all-female games and scenes of play much more than girls invade boys. This, and boys' greater control of space, correspond with other findings about the organization of gender, and inequality, in our society: compared with men and boys, women and girls take up less space, and their space, and talk, are more often violated and interrupted (Greif, 1982; Henley, 1977; West & Zimmerman, 1983).

3. Although individual boys are occasionally treated as contaminating (e.g., a third grade boy who both boys and girls said was "stinky" and "smelled like pee"), girls are more often defined as polluting. This pattern ties to themes that I discuss later: It is more taboo for a boy to play with (as opposed to invade) girls, and girls are more sexually defined than boys.

A look at the boundaries between the separated worlds of girls and boys illuminates within-sex hierarchies of status and control. For example, in the sex-divided seating in the 4th-5th grade classroom, several boys recurringly sat near "female space": their desks were at the gender divide in the classroom, and they were more likely than other boys to sit at a predominantly female table in the lunchroom. These boys—two nonbilingual Chicanos and an overweight "loner" boy who was afraid of sports—were at the bottom of the male hierarchy. Gender is sometimes used as a metaphor for male hierarchies; the inferior status of boys at the bottom is conveyed by calling them "girls":

> Seven boys and one girl were playing basketball. Two younger boys came over and asked to play. While the girl silently stood, fully accepted in the company of players, one of the older boys disparagingly said to the younger boys, 'You girls can't play.'[3]

In contrast, the girls who more often travel in the boys' world, sitting with groups of boys in the lunchroom or playing basketball, soccer, and baseball with them, are not stigmatized. Some have fairly high status with other girls. The worlds of girls and boys are assymetrically arranged, and spatial patterns map out interacting forms of inequality.

Heterosexual Meanings

The organization and meanings of gender (the social categories "woman/man," "girl/boy") and of sexuality vary cross-culturally (Ortner & Whitehead, 1981)—and, in our society, across the life course. Harriet Whitehead (1981) observed that in our (Western) gender system, and that of many traditional North American Indian cultures, one's choice of a sexual object, occupation, and one's dress and demeanor are closely associated with gender. However, the "center of gravity" differs in the two gender systems. For Indians, occupational pursuits provide the primary imagery of gender; dress and demeanor are secondary, and sexuality is least important. In our system, at least for adults, the order is reversed: heterosexuality is central to our definitions of "man" and "woman" ("masculinity"/"femininity"), and the relationships that obtain between them, whereas occupation and dress/demeanor are secondary.

Whereas erotic orientation and gender are closely linked in our definitions of adults, we define children as relatively asexual. Activities and dress/demeanor are more important than sexuality in the cultural meanings of "girl" and "boy." Children are less heterosexually defined than adults, and we have nonsexual imagery for relations between girls and boys. However, both children and adults sometimes use heterosexual language—"crushes," "like," "goin' with," "girlfriends," and "boyfriends"—to define cross-sex relationships. This language increases through the years of elementary school; the shift to adolescence consolidates a gender system organized around the institution of heterosexuality.

In everyday life in the schools, heterosexual and romantic meanings infuse some ritualized forms of interaction between groups of boys and girls (e.g., "chase and kiss") and help maintain sex segregation. "Jimmy likes Beth" or "Beth likes Jimmy" is a major form of teasing, which a child risks in choosing to sit by or walk with someone of the other sex. The structure of teasing, and children's sparse vocabulary for relationships between girls and boys, are evident in the following conversation which I had with a group of third-grade girls in the lunchroom:

> Susan asked me what I was doing, and I said I was observing the things children do and play. Nicole volunteered, 'I like running, boys chase all the girls. See Tim over there? Judy chases him all around the school. She likes him.' Judy, sitting across the table, quickly responded, 'I hate him. I like him for a friend.' 'Tim loves Judy,' Nicole said in a loud, sing-song voice.

In the younger grades, the culture and lore of girls contains more heterosexual romantic themes than that of boys. In Michigan, the first-grade girls often jumped rope to a rhyme which began: "Down in the valley where the green grass grows, there sat Cindy (name of jumper), as sweet as a rose. She sat, she sat, she sat so sweet. Along came Jason, and kissed her on the cheek . . . first comes love, then comes marriage, then along comes Cindy with a baby carriage. . . . Before a girl took her turn at jumping, the chanters asked her "Who do you want to be your boyfriend?" The jumper always proferred a name, which was accepted matter-of-factly. In chasing, a girl's kiss carried greater threat than a boy's kiss; "girl touch," when defined as contaminating, had sexual connotations. In short, starting at an early age, girls are more sexually defined than boys.

Through the years of elementary school, and increasing with age, the idiom of heterosexuality helps maintain the gender divide. Cross-sex interactions, especially when children initiate them, are fraught with the risk of being teased about "liking" someone of the other sex. I learned of several close cross-sex friendships, formed and maintained in neighborhoods and church, which went underground during the school day.

By the fifth grade a few children began to affirm, rather than avoid, the charge of having a girlfriend or a boyfriend; they introduced the heterosexual courtship rituals of adolescence:

In the lunchroom in the Michigan school, as the tables were forming, a high-status fifth-grade boy called out from his seat at the table: 'I want Trish to sit by me.' Trish came over, and almost like a king and queen, they sat at the gender divide—a row of girls down the table on her side, a row of boys on his.

In this situation, which inverted earlier forms, it was not a loss, but a gain in status to publically choose a companion of the other sex. By affirming his choice, the boy became unteasable (note the familiar asymmetry of heterosexual courtship rituals: the male initiated). This incident signals a temporal shift in arrangements of sex and gender.

Traveling in the World of the Other Sex

Contests, invasions, chasing, and heterosexually-defined encounters are based upon and reaffirm boundaries between girls and boys. In another type of cross-sex interaction, individuals (or sometimes pairs) cross gender boundaries, seeking acceptance in a group of the other sex. Nearly all the cases I saw of this were tomboys—girls who played organized sports and frequently sat with boys in the cafeteria or classroom. If these girls were skilled at activities central in the boys' world, especially games like soccer, baseball, and basketball, they were pretty much accepted as participants.

Being a tomboy is a matter of degree. Some girls seek access to boys' groups but are excluded; other girls limit their "crossing" to specific sports. Only a few—such as the tomboy I mentioned earlier, who chose a seat with the boys in the sex-divided fourth-fifth grade—participate fully in the boys' world. That particular girl was skilled at the various organized sports which boys played in different seasons of the year. She was also adept at physical fighting and at using the forms of arguing, insult, teasing, naming, and sports-talk of the boys' subculture. She was the only Black child in her classroom, in a school with only 8% Black students; overall that token status, along with unusual athletic and verbal skills, may have contributed to her ability to move back and forth across the gender divide. Her unique position in the children's world was widely recognized in the school. Several times, the teacher said to me, "She thinks she's a boy."

I observed only one boy in the upper grades (a fourth grader) who regularly played with all-female groups, as opposed to "playing at" girls' games and seeking to disrupt them. He frequently played jumprope and took turns with girls doing tricks on the bars, using the small gestures—for example, a helpful push on the heel of a girl who needed momentum to turn her body around the bar—which mark skillful and earnest participation. Although I never saw him play in other than an earnest spirit, the girls often chased him away from their games, and both girls and boys teased him. The fact that girls seek, and have more access to boys' worlds than vice versa, and the fact that girls who travel with the other sex are less stigmatized for it, are obvious asymmetries, tied to the asymmetries previously discussed.

Relaxed Cross-Sex Interactions

Relationships between boys and girls are not always marked by strong boundaries, heterosexual definitions, or by interacting on the terms and turfs of the other sex. On some occasions girls and boys interact in relatively comfortable ways. Gender is not strongly salient nor explicitly invoked, and girls and boys are not organized into boundaried collectivities. These "with" occasions have been neglected by those studying gender and children's relationships, who have emphasized either the model of separate worlds (with little attention to their articulation) or heterosexual forms of contact.

Occasions where boys and girls interact without strain, where gender wanes, rather than waxes in importance, frequently have one or more of the following characteristics:

1. The situations are organized around an absorbing task, such as a group art project or creating a radio show, which encourages cooperation and lessens attention to gender. This pattern accords with other studies finding that cooperative activities reduce group antagonism (e.g., Sherif & Sherif, 1953, who studied divisions between boys in a summer camp; and Aronson et al., 1978, who used cooperative activities to lessen racial divisions in a classroom).

2. Gender is less prominent when children are not responsible for the formation of the group. Mixed-sex play is less frequent in games like football, which require the choosing of teams, and more frequent in games like handball or dodgeball which individuals can join simply by getting into a line or a circle. When adults organize mixed-sex encounters—which they frequently do in the classroom and in physical education periods on the playground—they legitimize cross-sex contact. This removes the risk of being teased for choosing to be with the other sex.

3. There is more extensive and relaxed cross-sex interaction when principles of grouping other than gender are explicitly invoked—for example, counting off to form teams for spelling or kickball, dividing lines by hot lunch or cold lunch, or organizing a work group on the basis of interests or reading ability.

4. Girls and boys may interact more readily in less public and crowded settings. Neighborhood play, depending on demography, is more often sex and age integrated than play at school, partly because with fewer numbers, one may have to resort to an array of social categories to find play partners or to constitute a game. And in less crowded environments there are fewer potential witnesses to "make something of it" if girls and boys play together.

Relaxed interactions between girls and boys often depend on adults to set up and legitimize the contact.[4] Perhaps because of this contingency—and the other, distancing patterns which permeate relations between girls and boys—the easeful moments of interaction rarely build to close friendship. Schofield (1981) makes a similar observation about gender and racial barriers to friendship in a junior high school.

IMPLICATIONS FOR DEVELOPMENT

I have located social relations within an essentially spatial framework, emphasizing the organization of children's play, work, and other activities within specific settings, and in one type of institution, the school. In contrast, frameworks of child development rely upon temporal metaphors, using images of growth and transformation over time. Taken alone, both spatial and temporal frameworks have shortcomings; fitted together, they may be mutually correcting.

Those interested in gender and development have relied upon conceptualizations of "sex role socialization" and "sex differences." Sexuality and gender, I have argued, are more situated and fluid than these individualist and intrinsic models imply. Sex and gender are differently organized and defined across situations, even within the same institution. This situational variation (e.g., in the extent to which an encounter heightens or lessens gender boundaries, or is infused with sexual meanings) shapes and constrains individual behavior. Features which a developmental perspective might attribute to individuals, and understand as relatively internal attributes unfolding over time, may, in fact, be highly dependent on context. For example, children's avoidance of cross-sex friendship may be attributed to individual gender development in middle-childhood. But attention to varied situations may show that this avoidance is contingent on group size, activity, adult behavior, collective meanings, and the risk of being teased.

A focus on social organization and situation draws attention to children's experiences in the present. This helps correct a model like "sex role socialization" which casts the present under the shadow of the future, or presumed "endpoints" (Speier, 1976). A situated analysis of arrangements of sex and gender among those of different ages may point to crucial disjunctions in the life course. In the fourth and fifth grades, culturally defined heterosexual rituals ("goin' with") begin to suppress the presence and visibility of other types of interaction between girls and boys, such as nonsexualized and comfortable interaction, and traveling in the world of the other sex. As "boyfriend/girlfriend" definitions spread, the fifth-grade tomboy I described had to work to sustain "buddy" relationships with boys. Adult women who were tomboys often speak

of early adolescence as a painful time when they were pushed away from participation in boys' activities. Other adult women speak of the loss of intense, even erotic ties with other girls when they entered puberty and the rituals of dating, that is, when they became absorbed into the institution of heterosexuality (Rich, 1980). When Lever (1976) describes best-friend relationships among fifth-grade girls as preparation for dating, she imposes heterosexual ideologies onto a present which should be understood on its own terms.

As heterosexual encounters assume more importance, they may alter relations in same-sex groups. For example, Schofield (1981) reports that for sixth- and seventh-grade children in a middle school, the popularity of girls with other girls was affected by their popularity with boys, while boys' status with other boys did not depend on their relations with girls. This is an asymmetry familiar from the adult world; men's relationships with one another are defined through varied activities (occupations, sports), while relationships among women—and their public status—are more influenced by their connections to individual men.

A full understanding of gender and social relations should encompass cross-sex as well as within-sex interactions. "Borderwork" helps maintain separate, gender-linked subcultures, which, as those interested in development have begun to suggest, may result in different milieux for learning. Daniel Maltz and Ruth Borker (1983) for example, argue that because of different interactions within girls' and boys' groups, the sexes learn different rules for creating and interpreting friendly conversation, rules which carry into adulthood and help account for miscommunication between men and women. Carol Gilligan (1982) fits research on the different worlds of girls and boys into a theory of sex differences in moral development. Girls develop a style of reasoning, she argues, which is more personal and relational; boys develop a style which is more positional, based on separateness. Eleanor Maccoby (1982), also following the insight that because of sex segregation, girls and boys grow up in different environments, suggests implications for gender differentiated prosocial and antisocial behavior.

This separate worlds approach, as I have illustrated, also has limitations. The occasions when the sexes are together should also be studied, and understood as contexts for experience and learning. For example, assymetries in cross-sex relationships convey a series of messages: that boys are more entitled to space and to the nonreciprocal right of interrupting or invading the activities of the other sex; that girls are more in need of adult protection, and are lower in status, more defined by sexuality, and may even be polluting. Different types of cross-sex interaction—relaxed, boundaried, sexualized, or taking place on the terms of the other sex—provide different contexts for development.

By mapping the array of relationships between and within the sexes, one adds complexity to the overly static and dichotomous imagery of separate worlds. Individual experiences vary, with implications for development. Some children prefer same-sex groupings; some are more likely to cross the gender boundary and participate in the world of the other sex; some children (e.g., girls and boys who frequently play "chase and kiss") invoke heterosexual meanings, while others avoid them.

Finally, after charting the terrain of relationships, one can trace their development over time. For example, age variation in the content and form of borderwork, or of cross- and same-sex touch, may be related to differing cognitive, social, emotional, or physical capacities, as well as to age-associated cultural forms. I earlier mentioned temporal shifts in the organization of cross-sex chasing, from mixing with fantasy play in the early grades to more elaborately ritualized and sexualized forms by the sixth grade. There also appear to be temporal changes in same and cross-sex touch. In kindergarten, girls and boys touch one another more freely than in fourth grade, when children avoid relaxed cross-sex touch and instead use pokes, pushes, and other forms of mock violence, even when the touch clearly couches affection. This touch taboo is obviously related to the risk of seeming to *like* someone of the other sex. In fourth grade, same-sex touch begins to signal sexual meanings among boys, as well as between boys and girls. Younger boys touch one another freely in cuddling (arm around shoulder) as well as mock violence ways. By fourth grade, when homophobic taunts like "fag" become more common among boys, cuddling touch begins to disappear for boys, but less so for girls.

Overall, I am calling for more complexity in our conceptualizations of gender and of children's social relationships. Our challenge is to retain the temporal sweep, looking at individual and group lives as they unfold over time, while also attending to social structure and context, and to the full variety of experiences in the present.

ACKNOWLEDGMENT

I would like to thank Jane Atkinson, Nancy Chodorow, Arlene Daniels, Peter Lyman, Zick Rubin, Malcolm Spector, Avril Thorne, and Margery Wolf for comments on an earlier version of this paper. Conversations with Zella Luria enriched this work.

NOTES

1. I am grateful to Frederick Erickson for suggesting the relevance of Barth's analysis.

2. Sue Samuelson (1980) reports that in a racially mixed playground in Fresno, California, Mexican-American, but not Anglo children gave cooties. Racial, as well as sexual inequality, may be expressed through these forms.

3. This incident was recorded by Margaret Blume, who, for an undergraduate research project in 1982, observed in the California school where I earlier did fieldwork. Her observations and insights enhanced my own, and I would like to thank her for letting me cite this excerpt.

4. Note that in daily school life, depending on the individual and the situation, teachers and aides sometimes lessened, and at other times heightened, sex segregation.

REFERENCES

Aronson, E. et al. (1978). *The jigsaw classroom.* Beverly Hills, CA: Sage.

Barth, F. (Ed.). (1969). *Ethnic groups and boundaries.* Boston: Little, Brown.

Borman, K. M. (1979). Children's interactions in playgrounds. *Theory into Practice, 18,* 251–257.

Eder, D., & Hallinan, M. T. (1978). Sex differences in children's friendships. *American Sociological Review, 43,* 237–250.

Finnan, C. R. (1982). The ethnography of children's spontaneous play. In G. Spindler (Ed.), *Doing the ethnography of schooling* (pp. 358–380). New York: Holt, Rinehart & Winston.

Foot, H. C., Chapman, A. J., & Smith, J. R. (1980). Introduction. *Friendship and social relations in children* (pp. 1–14). New York: Wiley.

Gilligan, C. (1982). *In a different voice: Psychological theory and women's development.* Cambridge, MA: Harvard University Press.

Glaser, B. G., & Strauss, A. L. (1967). *The discovery of grounded theory.* Chicago: Aldine.

Goffman, E. (1977). The arrangement between the sexes. *Theory and Society, 4,* 301–336.

Goodwin, M. H. (1980). Directive-response speech sequences in girls' and boys' task activities. In S. McConnell-Ginet, R. Borker, & N. Furman (Eds.), *Women and language in literature and society* (pp. 157–173). New York: Praeger.

Greif, E. B. (1980). Sex differences in parent-child conversations. *Women's Studies International Quarterly, 3,* 253–258.

Henley. N. (1977). *Body politics: Power, sex, and nonverbal communication.* Englewood Cliffs, NJ: Prentice-Hall.

Karkau, K. (1973). *Sexism in the fourth grade.* Pittsburgh: KNOW, Inc. (pamphlet)

Katz, J. (1983). A theory of qualitative methodology: The social system of analytic fieldwork. In R. M. Emerson (Ed.), *Contemporary field research* (pp. 127–148). Boston: Little, Brown.

Knapp, M., & Knapp. H. (1976). *One potato, two potato: The secret education of American children.* New York: W. W. Norton.

Lever, J. (1976). Sex differences in the games children play. *Social Problems, 23,* 478–487.

Maccoby, E. (1982). *Social groupings in childhood: Their relationship to prosocial and antisocial behavior in boys and girls.* Paper presented at conference on The Development of Prosocial and Antisocial Behavior. Voss, Norway.

Maccoby, E., & Jacklin, C. (1974). *The psychology of sex differences.* CA: Stanford University Press.

Maltz, D. N., & Borker, R. A. (1983). A cultural approach to male-female miscommunication. In J. J. Gumperz (Ed.), *Language and social identity* (pp. 195–216). New York: Cambridge University Press.

McRobbie, A., & Garber, J. (1975). Girls and subcultures. In S. Hall and T. Jefferson (Eds.), *Resistance through rituals* (pp. 209–223). London: Hutchinson.

Ortner, S. B., & Whitehead, H. (1981). *Sexual meanings.* New York: Cambridge University Press.

Parrott, S. (1972). Games children play: Ethnography of a second-grade recess. In J. P. Spradley & D. W. McCurdy (Eds.), *The cultural experience* (pp. 206–219). Chicago: Science Research Associates.

Rich, A. (1980). Compulsory heterosexuality and lesbian existence. *Signs, 5,* 631–660.

Samuelson, S. (1980). The cooties complex. *Western Folklore, 39,* 198–210.

Savin-Williams, R. C. (1976). An ethological study of dominance formation and maintenance in a group of human adolescents. *Child Development, 47,* 972–979.

Schofield, J. W. (1981). Complementary and conflicting identities: Images and interaction in an interracial school. In S. R. Asher & J. M. Gottman (Eds.), *The development of children's friendships* (pp. 53–90). New York: Cambridge University Press.

Sherif, M., & Sherif, C. (1953). *Groups in harmony and tension.* New York: Harper.

Sluckin, A. (1981). *Growing up in the playground.* London: Routledge & Kegan Paul.

Speier, M. (1976). The adult ideological viewpoint in studies of childhood. In A. Skolnick (Ed.), *Rethinking childhood* (pp. 168–186). Boston: Little, Brown.

Sutton-Smith, B. (1971). A syntax for play and games. In R. E. Herron and B. Sutton-Smith (Eds.), *Child's Play* (pp. 298–307). New York: Wiley.

Unger, R. K. (1979). Toward a redefinition of sex and gender. *American Psychologist, 34,* 1085–1094.

Waldrop, M. F., & Halverson, C. F. (1975). Intensive and extensive peer behavior: Longitudinal and cross-sectional analysis. *Child Development, 46,* 19–26.

West, C., & Zimmerman, D. H. (1983). Small insults: A study of interruptions in cross-sex conversations between unacquainted persons. In B. Thorne, C. Kramarae, & N. Henley (Eds.), *Language, gender and society.* Rowley, MA: Newbury House.

Whitehead, H. (1981). The bow and the burden strap: A new look at institutionalized homosexuality in Native America. In S. B. Ortner & H. Whitehead (Eds.), *Sexual meanings* (pp. 80–115). New York: Cambridge University Press.

Unit 4

Unit Selections

Key Points to Consider

❖ Where did you get your ideas, values, and beliefs about how a parent behaves? If you were unsure about how to respond to a particular parenting situation, whom would you consult in order to make your decision? How do you think your own experience of parenting by your parents has affected your attitudes or possible parenting practices for your current or future children? Do you think your parents had a significant effect on your growing up? Do you think you or your child's friends will have a stronger influence on your child? Would this make you change the way you permit your children to make friends with others?

❖ Given the reality of dual career families and the research on the effects of day care, do you think that as a nation we should be developing national standards for day care programs? Why or why not? How would you go about searching for a high quality day care setting for your child?

❖ Divorce and remarriage are so common in the United States that virtually no one has a family network that has not been touched by these marital transitions. Have you experienced these transitions, and what was the outcome? Since divorce and remarriage affect boys and girls differently and at different ages, how might you handle these transitions in the best interests of a child?

❖ Were you ever spanked by a parent or teacher? If so, how did the experience make you feel? Now imagine being hit by your boss or spouse for disobeying or making a mistake. Why is this situation between adults unacceptable, while most people find it acceptable for a parent to strike a child? How do you see yourself altering your current or future disciplinary style with children? How might you teach your children to deal with conflict? If you decide not to use spanking, how would you discipline your child?

DUSHKIN ONLINE Links   www.dushkin.com/online/

These sites are annotated on pages 4 and 5.

Few people today realize that the potential freedom to *choose* parenthood—deciding whether to become a parent, deciding when to have children, or deciding how many children to have—is a development due to the advent of reliable methods of contraception and other recent sociocultural changes. Moreover, unlike any other significant job we may aspire to, few, if any, of us will receive any formal training or information about the lifelong responsibility of parenting. For most of us, our behavior is generally based on our own conscious and subconscious recollections of how we were parented as well as on our observations of the parenting practices of others around us. In fact, our society often behaves as if the mere act of producing a baby automatically confers upon the parents an innate parenting ability and as if a family's parenting practices should remain private and not be subjected to scrutiny or criticism by outsiders.

Given this climate, it is not surprising that misconceptions about many parenting practices continue to persist today. Only within the last 30 years or so have researchers turned their lenses on the scientific study of the family. Social, historical, cultural, and economic forces also have dramatically changed the face of the American family today. For example, the dual-career family is a reality of American life. James Collins highlights the link between the research on how day care influences young children and the effect these findings have for public policy and programs designed to give young children a "smart start." A related shift in parenting involves the fact that significant numbers of children in our country will experience the divorce and/or remarriage of their parents at some point during their lifetimes. In "What Matters? What Does Not? Five Perspectives on the Association between Marital Transitions and Children's Adjustment," Mavis Hetherington and colleagues describe the effects of divorce and remarriage on children.

As more women have entered the workforce, concerns have grown about the effects of day care

on very young children. "The Problem with Day Care" reviews many of these concerns and provides suggestions for parents.

All parents must sooner or later face the question of how to discipline their children. When a young child fails to obey, should the parent reach for the paddle? In "When to Spank" the author presents the research on the effects of various forms of discipline and suggests that parents utilize a variety of practices in disciplining their children.

Parenting and Family Issues

Why Johnny Can't Sleep

The notion that babies should spend the night apart from parents is widely accepted. Trouble is, it makes no sense

By ROBERT WRIGHT

EVERY NIGHT THOUSANDS OF PARENTS, following standard child-care advice, engage in a bloodcurdling ritual. They put their several-months-old infant in a crib, leave the room, and studiously ignore its crying. The crying may go on for 20 or 30 minutes before a parent is allowed to return. The baby may then be patted but not picked up, and the parent must quickly leave, after which the crying typically resumes. Eventually sleep comes, but the ritual recurs when the child awakes during the night.

The same thing happens the next night, except that the parent must wait five minutes longer before the designated patting. This goes on for a week, two weeks, maybe even a month. If all goes well, the day finally arrives when the child can fall asleep without fuss and go the whole night without being fed. For Mommy and Daddy, it's Miller time.

This is known as "Ferberizing" a child, after Richard Ferber, America's best-known expert on infant sleep. Many parents find his prescribed boot camp for babies agonizing, but they persist because they've been assured it's harmless. Ferber depicts the ritual as the child's natural progress toward nocturnal self-reliance. What sounds to the untrained ear like a baby wailing in desperate protest of abandonment is described by Ferber as a child "learning the new associations."

At this point I should own up to my bias: my wife and I are failed Ferberizers. When our first daughter proved capable of crying for 45 minutes without reloading, we gave up and let her sleep in our bed. When our second daughter showed up three years later, we didn't even bother to set up the crib.

How did we have the hubris to defy the mainstream of current child-care wisdom? That brings me to my second bias: Darwinism. For our species, the natural nighttime arrangement is for kids to sleep alongside their mothers for the first few years. At least, that's the norm in hunter-gatherer societies, the closest things we have to a model of the social environment in which humans evolved. Mothers typically nurse their children to sleep and then nurse on demand through the night. Sounds taxing, but it's not. When the baby cries, the mother starts nursing reflexively, often without really waking up. (And the father, as I can personally attest, never leaves Z-town.)

Just because Ferberization is unnatural doesn't necessarily mean it's bad. If parents find it ultimately worth the trouble, that's their prerogative. But Ferber goes further; he depicts his regime as a matter not just of parental convenience but of parental duty. He claims that children *need* to sleep alone. "Even if you and your child seem happy about his sharing your bed at night," he writes in *Solve your Child's Sleep Problems,* "and even if he seems to sleep well there, in the long run this habit will probably not be good for either of you."

Why, exactly, is it bad to sleep with your kids? Learning to sleep alone, says Ferber, lets your child "see himself as an independent individual." I'm puzzled. It isn't obvious to me how a baby would develop a robust sense of autonomy while confined to a small cubicle with bars on the side and rendered powerless to influence its environment. (Nor is it obvious these days, when many kids spend 40 hours a week in day care, that they need extra autonomy training.) I'd be willing to look at the evidence behind this claim, but there isn't any. Comparing Ferberized with non-Ferberized kids as they grow up would tell us nothing. After all, Ferberizing and non-Ferberizing parents no doubt tend to have broadly different approaches to child rearing, and they probably have different cultural milieus. We can't control our variables.

Lacking data, Ferber and other experts make creative assertions about what's going on inside the child's head. Ferber says that if you let a toddler sleep between you and your spouse, "in a sense separating the two of you, he may feel too powerful and become worried." Well, he may, I guess. Or he may just feel cozy. Hard to say (though he certainly looks cozy). Child-care guru T. Berry Brazelton tells us that when a child wakes up at night and you refuse to retrieve her from the crib, "she won't like it, but she'll understand." Oh.

According to Ferber, the trouble with letting a child who fears sleeping alone into your bed is that "you are not really solving the problem. There must be a reason why he is so fearful." Yes, there must. Here's one candidate. Maybe your child's brain was designed by natural selection over millions of years during which mothers slept with their babies. Maybe back then if babies found themselves alone at night it of-

ten meant bad news (that the mother had been eaten by a beast, say). Maybe the young brain is designed to respond to this situation by screaming so that any relatives within earshot will discover the child. Maybe, in short, the reason that kids left alone sound terrified is that kids left alone naturally get terrified. Just a theory.

A few weeks of nightly terror presumably won't scar a child for life. If Ferber's gospel harms kids, it's more likely doing so via a second route: the denial of mother's milk to the child at night. Breast milk, researchers are finding, is a kind of "external placenta," loaded with hormones masterfully engineered to assist development. One study found that it boosts IQ.

Presumably most, and perhaps all, breast-feeding benefits can be delivered via daytime nursing. Still, we certainly don't know that an 11-hour nightly gap in the feeding schedule isn't doing harm. And we do know that such a gap isn't part of nature's plan for a five-month-old child—at least, to judge by hunter-gatherer societies. Or to judge by the milk itself: it is thin and watery—typical of species that nurse frequently. Or to judge by mothers. Abruptly ending nighttime nursing can lead to painful engorgement or even breast infection. Meanwhile, as all available evidence suggests that nighttime feeding is natural, Ferber asserts the opposite. If after three months of age your baby wakes repeatedly, demanding to be fed, "she is developing a sleep problem."

As "family bed" boosters have noted, male physicians, who have no idea what motherhood is like, have cowed women for decades into doing unnatural and destructive things. For a while doctors said mothers shouldn't feed more than once every four hours. Now they admit they were wrong. For a while they pushed bottle feeding. Now they admit this was wrong. For a while they told pregnant women to keep weight gains minimal (and some women did so by smoking more cigarettes!). Wrong again.

There are signs that yet another well-advised retreat is under way. Though Ferber hasn't put out the white flag, Brazelton is sounding less and less dismissive of parents who sleep with their kids. (Not surprisingly, the least dismissive big-name child-care expert is a woman, Penelope Leach.) Better late than never. But in child care, as in the behavioral sciences generally, we could have saved ourselves a lot of time and trouble by recognizing at the outset that people are animals and pondering the implications of that fact.

This is excerpted from an article originally published in Slate™ *magazine,* **www.slate.com.** Slate™ *is a trademark of Microsoft Corp. Copyright 1997 Robert Wright. All rights reserved.*

From *Time*, April 14, 1997, pp. 74-76. © 1997 by Robert Wright. Reprinted by permission.

the problem with day care

Meryl Frank is an expert on child care. For five years she ran a Yale University program that studied parental leave.... Frank went back to work part time when her son, Isaac, was 5 months old, and in the two years since then she has changed childcare arrangements nine times.

Her travails began with a well-regarded day care center near her suburban New Jersey home. On the surface, it was great. One staff member for every three babies, a sensitive administrator, clean facilities. "But when I went in," Frank recalls, "I saw this line of cribs and all these babies with their arms out crying, wanting to be picked up. I felt like crying myself." She walked out without signing Isaac up and went through a succession of other unsatisfactory situations—a babysitter who couldn't speak English, a woman who cared for 10 children in her home at once—before settling on a neighborhood woman who took Isaac into her home. "She was fabulous," Frank recalls wistfully. Three weeks after that babysitter started, she got sick and had to quit. Frank advertised for help in the newspaper and got 30 inquiries but no qualified babysitter. (When Frank asked one prospective nanny about her philosophy of discipline, the woman replied: "If he touched the stove, I'd punch him.") A few weeks later she finally hired her tenth babysitter. "She's a very nice young woman," Frank says. "Unfortunately, she has to leave in May. And I just found out I'm pregnant again and due in June."

That's what happens when a *pro* tries to get help.

So begins a story in a special issue of *Newsweek* on family trends. While this many day care problems in two years is probably not average, it is by no means unusual. Mismatches, repeated disappointments, and occasional horror stories are the rule, not the exception, when it comes to hiring parental substitutes today—as you'll quickly discover once you start interviewing a cross-section of day care users about their actual experiences.

In a perfect world, there would be an abundance of intelligent, well-balanced, devoted individuals willing to attend lavishly and patiently to the demands of strangers' children—enough so that every family who wanted could have their own full-time loving surrogate. These dream workers would all be willing to provide their services so cheaply that

BY KARL ZINSMEISTER

there would be little or no strain on family finances. And they would remain with the same family year after year, meshing perfectly with child, parents, and surroundings.

But there are no dream caretakers. There is very little that even comes close. In real life, purchased care is rarely more than a stopgap. That's not my verdict. It's the verdict of parents themselves. Take Joanie Colquitt, mother and holder of a master's degree in social psychology. In a long letter she wrote me a few years ago, Ms. Colquitt details a quite typical set of experiences:

I can remember when I considered sending my own first child to day care. I had spent so long on my education and we did truly need the money. So I visited what was, at that time, the number-one day care chain in the country. What I saw there broke my heart. Babies were lined up, six in a row, crying, waiting for their meals. Toddlers were still in their cribs, some with tear-stained cheeks simply sitting there with no toys, no companionship, with looks of having given up any hope for personal attention a long time ago.... There was a bucket on the the floor next to the high chairs where several rags floated in dirty looking water. The helper pulled one out to wipe a baby's face. There were 15-month-old children who could not even walk, I believe because they had not been allowed out of their cribs enough to develop properly.

I have visited other day care centers that were cleaner, and had academic programs and activities galore. However, the atmosphere, to me, was still negative. The children were not loved the way they needed to be and you could tell. They looked tired and kind of washed out.

Author Linda Burton is another person who has described in detail what she came across while scouring her hometown (the Washington, D.C. area) for day care:

In one instance, I found the "absolutely marvelous" family day care

From a child's perspective, the typical day care arrangement is a puzzling, often chilly, slightly sad arrangement.

provider, recommended by trusted friends, sleeping on her sofa while 11 children (she had informed me that she only cared for five) wandered aimlessly around in front of the blaring TV. Another time, on an unannounced visit, I found that the "highly recommended" licensed day care provider confined seven preschoolers to her tiny dining room. I found them huddled together, leaning over a barricade to watch a TV program showing in the adjacent room.

These are not isolated anecdotes. Anyone investigating the world of full-time day care quickly amasses files of such testimony. A few years ago the Metropolitan Toronto Social Planning Council investigated a sample of 281 day care homes. They reported that a small number were genuinely stimulating, and another small number were out-and-out abusive. The large majority, however, provided care that was merely indifferent. Only a few of the caregivers studied were able to make themselves genuinely interested in each of their individual enrollees. In a significant minority of cases, youngsters were simply ignored most of the time.

How do parents react to the disappointing standards of most hired care? Very often, by lowering their expectations. I was struck by a conversation my wife and I once had with three of our Washington, D.C. neighbors who used significant amounts of substitute

care for their children. We asked them how they liked their current sitters. "This one's good with children," replied the first. "She's always proselytizing for the Jehovah's Witnesses, though, and sometimes that annoys me." Another volunteered about her sitter: "She's great. Except that she's really incredibly lazy." "_____ is nice, and we're happy with her," answered the third, "but she smokes all the time, and never has the TV off."

Day care-using parents make minor compromises like these by the millions. And some end up facing much larger worries. Like the dual-career Washington, D.C. couple (the mother actually worked as a child care researcher at one of the local universities) who discovered that the Spanish-speaking woman they were dropping their nine-month-old off with was taking in several other babies without their knowledge, and regularly leaving them with her 12-year-old daughter while she went out to clean houses. (They discovered this only when one of the infants swallowed 30 aspirin tablets and ended up in a hospital.)

A telling example of how difficult it can be to accurately judge a hired caregiver involves professor Sandra Scarr. Scarr is one of the most zealous academic defenders of day care in the country. She argues regularly and vociferously in her writing and in media interviews that "day care can actually be good for children." Yet when Scarr employed babysitters for her own children, her day care expertise and enthusiasm were not enough to avoid problems. One day she returned from work to find her 18-month-old weeping. "Kathy hit me! Kathy hit me!," the toddler cried simply. Scarr found large, red welts on her daughter's body—"the sitter had beaten her badly." She expressed great frustration when told by police that there could be no prosecution without witnesses. Apparently without any sense of irony, Scarr complained bitterly that "no one was there to prevent the abuse or to testify about it."

Karl Zinsmeister is editor in chief of The American Enterprise *and J.B. Fuqua Fellow at the American Enterprise Institute.*

But physical dangers and out-and-out abuse are not the major problems associated with substitute parenting. Despite the screaming headlines, these are fairly unusual occurrences, thank goodness. The commoner, deeper drawback is simply that it is an emotionally unsatisfying substitute for the natural attentions of mother and father. From a youngster's perspective, the typical day care arrangement is a puzzling, often chilly, slightly sad arrangement. Unfortunately, very few discussions of day care look at things from that angle. "We could do with another Charles Dickens," suggests family historian John Sommerville, "to give us a child's-eye view" of the world of day care.

DAY CARE AS IT REALLY IS

There's no need for anyone to write a book on what children encounter in a typical day care setting—because a writer named Deborah Fallows has already done that. Fallows (a Radcliffe graduate, linguist, and former assistant dean at Georgetown University who is married to *U.S. News* editor James Fallows) is not Charles Dickens. But in *A Mother's Work* she describes one-and-a-half years' worth of close observation in dozens of diverse day care centers scattered across Maryland, Washington, D.C., Texas, and Massachusetts.

While Fallows discovered no abuse, relatively little dirt, and adequate physical conditions in most centers, she nonetheless found the average child's experience frighteningly empty. This was a fairly typical visit:

I settled into an inconspicuous corner of the room and began to watch the children.... Often, one child would attach himself to me—maybe going off for a few minutes but always coming back to say a few words...point to a shoe that need tying...or show me his tummy.

The teacher watching the children tried her hardest, ad-libbing her way from one activity to the next. She put on a record and started to dance. One little blond boy started dancing along with her. A few others joined the group. Five or six gathered by some swinging cabinet doors that formed the partition between the play area and the rest of the room. One little girl sat by herself, crying softly in the corner. The rest wandered around....

Then a fight erupted between two little boys, and the teacher had to stop dancing to break it up. Without her example, the dancing died off. She tried again a few minutes later but was interrupted this time by a small couple who tripped over each other....

She gave up records then and tried reading a story. The same few eager dancers moved right in to listen, while the rest kept on swinging on the cabinet doors or aimlessly wandering. The little girl was still crying in her corner. After a short story, the teacher opened the large cabinet and pulled out some puppets. This immediately attracted the largest crowd of the morning. All but a few rushed right over to watch the show. But the brilliance of the idea dimmed after several moments. As her impromptu story line weakened, the toddlers drifted back to their swinging doors and wandering, shuffling their feet, chasing back and forth....

Here as at other centers I visited, you could almost feel the morning driving itself toward the grand finale—lunch.

Fallows gives wrenching descriptions of children referred to by their teachers as "little boy" or "hey little girl," of activities that cater to the group average but leave quiet toddlers behind, of desperate notes pinned to youngsters' coats in which parents plead for extra attention or special comforts. She tells of caretakers who can't remember babies by name and description just a few months after they've graduated to an older group ("I'm not sure which one it was. They all do that after a while..."). There is much tedium, much bewilderment, many unconsoled tears. Children clamoring to go "to mommy's house," are quieted with small fibs ("yeah, mommy will be here soon"). In a situation that human biology guarantees no natural parent would ever have to face (four to ten same-aged youngsters per adult), tired teachers do what they can to get by.

Fallows' testimony is cool, relentlessly detailed, and very convincing. For individuals who have never visited average day care centers or thought much about what group care of infants and toddlers comprises—and how many adults, even prospective parents, have?—her observations will come as an upsetting revelation.

Another disturbingly realistic portrait of full-day hired childcare is provided by William and Wendy Dreskin in their book *The Day Care Decision*. For five years, the Dreskins co-directed their own non-profit nursery school and then day care center in the San Francisco area. Theirs was a very high quality program: teachers had a B.A. plus one year of graduate training, child to adult ratios were low, there was lots of educational equipment, and an intelligent curriculum. I know the Dreskins myself and can testify that they are extremely warm, wise, gentle individuals who have raised two great kids of their own—the kind of people who are naturals with children.

They started out with a half-day preschool, which was very successful. But with more and more dual-career parents demanding day-long care they found that a facility in use only three hours a day was becoming uneconomic. So they decided to expand into a full-day operation. "We were going to offer a quality program. We did not have the slightest suspicion that there might be a serious problem with even the best day care programs," they write.

Then they began to notice changes in their children. "Some of the same boys and girls we had known as nursery schoolers became different children when they were subjected to the stress of full-time day care." The Dreskins cite numerous specific cases to illustrate the alterations in personality they observed. Three year-olds who had been happy in a morning program began to withdraw, lash out, or cry for hours at a time. In the individual journals that were a standard part of the Dreskin's program, they began to dictate poignant pleas for more time with their parents. Some children lost previously acquired skills. Others began to refuse to take their toys home at night. ("What's the use? I'm here more than at home.")

The parents changed too. As they subconsciously transferred more and more of the responsibility for their child to the center, they gradually stopped coming to school meetings. They didn't check books out of the lending library. They asked fewer questions and dropped in on classes less. They showed up after work badly overstressed. "We typically saw scenes like this," the Dreskins write:

> Carl's mother arrives at 6:00 P.M., tired and frazzled. Carl tries to show her a picture he has painted. 'Show me later. Get your lunch box. Come on.'

She is already halfway out the door. Carl trails after her, crying at the rebuff and at the effort of trying to balance his painting, his lunch box, his fire engine, and the cup of fruit salad he made in a cooking project that afternoon. We can tell from his mother's mood what sort of evening Carl will have. So much for the precious two hours he will get to spend with his mother between leaving day care and going to bed.

"For two years we watched day care children respond to the stresses of eight to ten hours a day of separation from their parents with tears, anger, withdrawal, or profound sadness," the Dreskins write, "and we found, to our dismay, that nothing in our own affection and caring for these children would erase this sense of loss and abandonment." They found themselves in a dilemma: "The problem was not with our facility.... It was obvious that there was a problem inherent in day care itself, a problem that hung like a dark storm over 'good' and 'bad' day care centers alike. The children were too young to be spending so much time away from their parents. They were like young birds being forced out of the nest and abandoned by their parents before they could fly, their wings undeveloped, unready to carry them out into the world." "We were so distressed by our observations," the Dreskins conclude, "that we closed the center."

The Dreskins may be more sensitive and braver than most day care practi-

The Importance of Early Childhood Attachme

Numerous studies conducted in varied settings show clearly that the only way to build strong independence in children is to indulge their strong needs for *dependence* when they are very young. As Margaret Mead put it, "we do not know—man has never known—how else to give a human being a sense of selfhood and identity, a sense of the worth of the world." The path to the sturdy self lies directly across the lap of mother and father. There is no other route.

Parents who push their children out into the world before they are ready do them no favors. In my years of working in parent-cooperative play groups and nursery schools I myself have seen a number of strikingly disturbed and protestful children in this situation. I remember one two-year-old in Washington, D.C., for instance, who would shake and whimper, frantically clutch her stuffed animal, and finally curl herself on the floor in a tight crouch, refusing to be comforted, on many mornings when she was dropped off. Usually it was her babysitter who delivered her, only occasionally her mother, never her father.

"Human attachment" research has demonstrated that the early relationship between infants and preschoolers and their parents is the "foundation stone" of all subsequent personality development. It has also shown that even very marginal parental care is better for a young child than institutional care. As John Bowlby, the only psychiatrist who has twice received the American Psychiatric Association's highest award, warned, "a home must be very bad before it is bettered by a good institution."

A classic investigation by psychiatrist René Spitz, for instance, compared the development of infants raised by nurses in children's homes with infants raised by mothers confined to prison. He found that the infants in institutional child care exhibited evidence of depression and were stunted in their development, while the mother-raised children developed normally, despite the inhospitable setting and the fact that every one of the mothers was either mentally retarded or emotionally disturbed.

In groundbreaking mid-1950s research, Yale professors Sally Provence and Rose Lipton examined infants who spent a considerable part of their first year in superior institutions. They found that these youngsters suffered incapacities in all areas of physical and mental development compared to home-reared children, and their deficits did not disappear when they were moved into home settings by age one. Follow-up work showed that these parent-deprived children never fully overcame their physical, cognitive, and emotional impairments. When it became clear how much these youngsters had withered, most of the group homes were shut down.

Another telling result came from the work of child analysts Anna Freud and Dorothy Burlingham. After arriving in London with her father Sigmund in 1938, Anna Freud helped set up the Hampstead Nurseries. During the war, the Nurseries provided care for infants and children who could not be looked after at home because their parents were working in the war effort, or because a parent had been lost, or because their homes were thought unsafe due to the German bombing blitz. Both Freud and Burlingham were already world-renowned child analysts at the time, and strong believers in the importance of good early relationships. They chose their staff carefully

tioners, but their experiences are not unusual. A vast body of skeptical testimony on hired child care is available from individuals right inside the profession. Several years ago, after I'd written a number of scholarly articles about day care, *Reader's Digest* reprinted a review of day care research I'd put together. That brought me an outpouring of more than 100 personal letters. The thing that stunned me most in this correspondence was the number of responses critical of day care that I received from current or former day care workers.

A single mother from Spokane, Washington wrote: "I know that the abdication of parents' responsibility to raise their children begins at a very young age in this country. I know that

and set up child care practices based on the very latest knowledge of child psychology. Conditions, all in all, were about as good as modern science and social concern could create.

What, then, were the results for their young charges? The truly crippling effects produced by average institutions were mostly eliminated. But in several vital areas children reared under these prime group conditions fared less well than children tended by average families. In speech, for example, the typical Hampstead two-year-old was six-months retarded compared with typical children looked after in their own homes. The Hampstead children were more aggressive and had less control of their impulses. They were late in achieving their toilet training. They were less cooperative. Many became listless.

In an attempt to soften these effects the nursery eventually grouped children into artificial "families," small groups of infants and toddlers with one or two adults serving as the exclusive "parents." "The result of this arrangement was astonishing in its force and immediacy. The need for individual attachment...which had been

parents abdicate this right even in the first few weeks after birth, during the critical bonding stage for infants. I know this because I am a nanny recruiter. I send nannies to the East Coast states and to Florida. I like my job, mostly because I deal with the really fine people we send, who are truly nurturing people, but I am alarmed by what I see happening at the end of my job placements, in the family itself. I am seriously thinking about altering my profession."

A woman named Cherie Johnson sent a note saying, "I am the Assistant Director of Rainbow Corners Child Care Center in Papillion, Nebraska. This one job I would cheerfully give up if all these kids could stay at home with Mom or Dad. We really try to give them

lying dormant, came out of a rush," wrote Freud and Burlingham. "The violent attachment to the mother substitutes...was anything but peaceful." Eventually, however, there was a positive effect on speech development and on toilet training. Overall, results were better but still far from optimal.

So here we had a model institution, directed by two international experts in child development as their contribution to the nation in a time of emergency. And the outcomes were literally less successful than those produced by a statistically average family with an average baby. This, incidentally, did not come as a surprise to Freud or Burlingham. They had long recognized that professional wisdom, for all its usefulness, could never supplant intimate family ties as the spur to human development. Results like those from the Hampstead Nurseries stand not as criticisms of the techniques of the child development profession but rather as, in psychoanalyst Selma Fraiberg's words, "an appreciation of the family as the point of departure for all sound psychological thinking."

—*KZ*

warm personal care but with so many I know most of our full-timers do not get the attention they really need."

Judy Hodges, a college-educated mother of two from Columbus, Ohio, wrote to report that after working in a day care center and keeping children in her home while her own daughters were young, she felt very uncomfortable with the idea of extended separations of young children from their parents. A woman who had worked at the Siemens Corporation day care center in Oslo wrote me from Norway to describe a "survival of the fittest environment" characterized by "fresh talk, aggressive behavior, a feed 'em and get 'em out to play" attitude.

Along these same lines, a different article I wrote on day care for the *Washington Post* produced a response from an intelligent 33-year-old mother of two living in Falls Church, Virginia. "I am a home day care provider," she began.

I care for a 19-month-old girl, the daughter of close friends of mine, who I've cared for since she was four months old. I normally have her four days a week, 8:30 A.M. to 4:30 P.M.... For many months this child cried and held her arms out to me every time her mother came to pick her up. I know her parents very well and feel certain that nothing resembling abuse or neglect was going on. After ruling that out it seemed that the child had made a conscious choice and preferred me to her mother. This has been difficult for both me and my friend.... This baby, unlike a child at home full time with his mother, was given another option and chose not to bond with her mother, to instead bond with me. I think this is an awful situation to put an infant in. To deprive a baby of the close, intense relationship with one caring, loving person, which I believe is critical in infancy, both for the child and the adult, negates the very basis from which emotional security derives.

One of the most compelling letters I've received on this subject came from a former day care worker from Wisconsin named Donna Briesemeister. She wrote as follows:

I am a public school music teacher, and the mother of two nearly grown sons.... In 1983, when I was between teaching positions, I took a job as a day care worker in Deerfield, Illinois. Baxter Laboratories made us nationally famous, and made history for themselves, by becoming the first corporation in the country to subsidize their employees's use of child care at an approved facility. We were housed in an unused public school building, and had in our care approximately 280 children between the ages of 6 weeks and 6 years. I was assigned to a room for infants, and for nine hours a day I, and three wonderful young women, tried to give "mother's care" to 12 precious souls.

This experience was one of the most poignant of my life, because it was impossible for us even to approach the level of care we believed a child needed.... I watched children being traumatized as workers came and went. I observed the disenchantment they suffered, and the hostility they developed. [Noted psychologist] Burton White even came to visit us, and to speak to us of his belief that children, if they are to grow up healthy and happy, need to be under the care of their own mothers, at least until they are three years of age. I couldn't agree more....

I could go on and on, because I have been haunted these past several years by the images I carry from this "best of all possible" institutional day care centers.... I can tell you that before my year in day care work was over, my co-workers and I were able to convince five of the 12 mothers whose children we cared for that they would be happier, and that their parent-child relationships would be healthier, if they would quit their jobs and would stay at home with their children. Our "babies" are five years old now, and we still stay in touch with their parents. That early bonding—unfortunately between us and the babies, instead of between the babies and their parents—is such a powerful human emotion that it never goes away, no matter

how many years pass or how circumstances change. No parent or child should miss out on that experience.

Fully half of all day care arrangements turn over in the course of a year.

Though it is obviously very difficult for workers to speak frankly on this charged subject, a great deal of uneasiness of this sort exists on day care's front lines today. There is a strong tendency in the popular press to censor such testimony for fear of "offending" some listeners. Nonetheless, warnings have worked their way into some established media outlets. In a feature article in the politically left magazine *The Progressive*, Dorothy Conniff, head of city day care programs in Madison, Wisconsin, describes day care as "mostly crowd control," and "a troubling social experiment." The *Washington Post* has quoted Jeree Pawl, director of the infant-parent program at the University of California-San Francisco, saying, "in most day cares, it's a pecking order; it's like a bunch of wild chickens in a hen yard." The loudest, most obnoxious behavior is what gets rewarded with attention from overloaded adult caretakers and intimidated peers both, stated Pawl.

The *Wall Street Journal* ran an interview in which the head of an Illinois day care center serving 300 children—250 from families where both parents work, 50 from single-parent families—worried aloud about her mission. An excerpt:

Demand is so great that Elaine Lombardo, the center's founder and executive director, could sign up many more parents for care ranging up to $120 a week if she wanted to.

She doesn't want to. Mrs. Lombardo has ambivalent feelings about her job. She knows she is providing a valuable and necessary service, but she worries about the family life and future of her charges. Many children are dropped off at 6:15 A.M. and don't see their parents again until 6 at night—even later, sometimes. One parent, a model, left her four-year-old until 8 P.M. It's not unheard of, either, for parents to drop off children who are obviously ill.

Under the circumstances, it's not surprising that the children come to look upon their teachers and Mrs. Lombardo as mother figures. "The kids kiss me good night," she says. "I'm torn. I want them to feel safe and secure, but this is not their home. Parents think we can substitute for family, but we can't."

In one of her books, bestselling child care author Penelope Leach also reports hearing such reservations among day care workers.

At a recent talk I gave to a group of nursery worker trainees, one girl recounted her worries about the lack of individual attention received by children in her unit. She finished with these words: "I suppose it's true that they are better off with us. We are taught and we do know what we are doing. But when I have children of my own I will use everything I know to look after them myself. I'd die rather than put a child of mine in the place where I work."

Coming as they do from talented and well-intentioned individuals right within the substitute-care industry itself, statements like these reflect much more than occasional dissatisfactions. They grow out of fundamental problems that exist at the very core of the childrearing-by-proxy experiment. In the sections that follow we'll look at some of those inherent problems.

MUSICAL CAREGIVERS

Remember Meryl Frank? She of the ten babysitters in two years, whose story started this article? Well, Meryl Frank has lots of company.

The *Washington Post Magazine* ran an admiring profile of a fine day care teacher working in a Maryland Kinder-Care center. In the body of the article, as part of a short description of the teacher's first weeks adjusting to her job, the reporter described how one mother angrily approached the new teacher with the news that "she was the ninth woman to work in her son's room in eight months." The mother demanded to know, "How long are you gonna be here?"

An article from *New York* magazine provides a snapshot of this same, central problem hitting a different part of the socio-economic spectrum. It chronicles the experiences of a "mergers-and-acquisitions specialist at Paine Webber" who went through six nannies in the first six months of her child's life. Nanny Number One was arrogant, while Number Two was overfanatic about housekeeping, and Number Three didn't stimulate the child. Nanny Number Four was great but left abruptly without notice. Number Five was an *au pair* whose inability to speak English led to nutritional problems for the infant, and nanny Number Six was a Haitian who turned out to be paranoid and a baby disliker. Number Seven was doing fine. As of the story's writing, anyway.

In the interview grapevine and the statistical studies alike, caretaker turnover turns out to be a very serious problem for hired day care. A pair of investigations by UCLA psychologist Carollee Howes of 18- to 24-month-olds in good quality home-based day care found that most of the children had already experienced two or three changes in caregivers, and some had had as many as six.

By its very nature, day care produces instability and discontinuities in a baby's life. A child in purchased care, Penelope Leach points out, must regularly rely on "somebody who, even if she was there yesterday because it wasn't her day off, doesn't know what happened to that child in the 12 hours previous." This can have negative effects:

> When a child is growing and changing and developing and working very hard at particular areas of his development, even 12 hours can put you totally out of step. Caring for a baby non-continuously is a constant process of experiment.... It may not hurt the baby for one afternoon, but it's awful bad for babies if all of their infant lives they are having to communicate with people to whom their language is foreign.

Yet this is what day care children are required to do all the time, as Leach notes:

> Split shifts to cover the long nursery day double the number of people with whom babies must interact. Lunch breaks, sick leave, vacations and in-service training courses produce such constant staff movement that case studies suggest an average of seven different people a day and 15 a week (some of them strangers "filling in") handle each child.

This is the *built-in* churning, Leach notes. On top of that you must add all the turnover that occurs whenever there is a change of center or arrangements.

There is widespread agreement among child development experts that instability in caretaking can seriously interfere with a young child's development. Howes' studies showed that the more changes a youngster had experienced, the more trouble he had adjusting to first grade. Other research shows that caregiver departures can cause breakdowns in toilet training and speech skills. Repeated disappointments will cause some youngsters to withdraw from adult contact. Other children will act out their resentment and disappointment by disrupting the classroom.

"The child is thrust into the care of some strange person, disrupting the bonds established with the mother. And just when he sends out some tender, new shoots of affection, he gets a new sitter," explains child psychiatrist Jack Raskin. "The child can't shout, 'My heavens, every attempt I'm making to get the closeness I need is sabotaged. What the hell is being done here?' But you'll see the results, perhaps five years later when he's disruptive in school, or ten years later when he's on drugs."

A baby who "is cared for by many well-meaning strangers in turn, or one who is cared for sketchily and without concentration, sharing his caretaker with other needful small people, is like an adult who moves from country to country, knowing the language of none," writes psychologist Leach. Some youngsters learn not to attach themselves to any caregiver. They lose the ability to feel or express warmth, and develop a shallow and indiscriminate emotional life. Certain such children end up without any sense of personal connectedness, and thus lack concern for winning any other person's approval. This leaves them unaccountable, and sometimes socially dangerous.

To understand why shifting parent-surrogates can be so disruptive to a youngster, consider that a child's feelings "acquire the strength and variety of adult love" by the age of two, according to experts. Take this fully-developed capacity to feel the thrills and pangs of love and then overlay it with a child's fundamental uncertainty about the larger world and you can see where the potential for hurt and insecurity comes from. As one mother I know asked when facing her own daughter's separation from her day care provider:

> How do I explain to Susannah that very soon she will leave the woman she has known and loved for three-fourths of her life? That she will be taken away from what has become her second family? That the children who are closer to her than her cousins, whose names were among the first words she learned, will be gone from her world?

Fear of abandonment is a primal human worry. There are fairy tales and ballads and novels aplenty to attest to that. The oldest theme in literature is that people can't simply be interchanged one for another in affairs of the heart. So is it really so hard to understand why children might suffer from being disconnected from the people they love most? And as wrenching as lost loyalty and love are for grown-ups, they are even harder for children—because children are

forming their very first attachments and have no other bonds or sense of worth to fall back on.

Though most parents are aware that harm can come from day care instability, it is not at all uncommon for children to be regularly moved to new settings. Census Bureau figures show that about one child out of every five in day

care has changed programs within the last four months. Other studies show that fully half of all day care arrangements change over the course of a year.

There are dozens of reasons for rapid day care turnover. The child or parent may have had a bad experience. There may have been a sickness. The child may have gotten too old for a

Longstanding Warnings from Experts

"It's very hard to become a sensitively responsive mother if you're away from your child ten hours a day," says distinguished child developmentalist Mary Ainsworth. "It really is." Margaret Mead, the scholar and champion of progressive causes, emphasized the same point. "A little baby needs continuity of care; all our studies suggest that too frequent changes of the mothering person are hard on children. If a woman works full time, it is very difficult for her to provide this continuity." Toward the end of her life, Mead argued explicitly that thoughtful women shouldn't be having children with the idea of placing them in someone else's care all day.

From her experience of recent years, Princeton, N.J. child therapist Isabel Paret concludes that "there's no question that infants don't do well in daycare, no matter how much modern families would like to think they do." Eleanor Galenson, a prominent New York child psychiatrist, states unequivocally that "putting infants into full-time daycare is a dangerous practice. Psychiatrists have been afraid to come out and tell the public this, but many of us certainly believe it to be true." Stanford psychologist Bryna Siegel concurs, noting that "clinician colleagues are reporting an increase in the number of children with unstable, extensive daycare histories in their practices." An article in the *Journal of the American Psychoanalytic Association* reports that among "patients with an early history of surrogate mothering," "estrangement from biological mothers, and intolerance of

intimate relationships" is a significant problem. Many teachers, physicians, and youth workers likewise report seeing more and more disturbance traceable to early non-parental care.

Lillian Katz, the 1994 president of the National Association for the Education of Young Children, describes this decade's findings on daycare effects as "very frightening." "Children under three don't belong in institutions," she states straightforwardly. Samuel Sava, executive director of the National Association of Elementary School Principals, likewise urges that "each child deserves at least three good years at home with a full-time parent."

Penelope Leach, the British psychologist and author of today's most influential childraising manuals, is an opponent of the trans-Atlantic trend toward viewing childraising as a sideline practiced by parents busy at jobs. She insists that newborns need the concentrated attention of their parents for at least their first couple years, and she speaks with passion against group care for children under two. Someone caring for a child out of love will do a far better job than someone doing it for pay, she argues, and it should be a major aim of modern society to make full-time parenting easier.

Another child advocate who refuses to pull his punches on the daycare issue is the prominent pediatrician William Sears. He insists that "when mother and baby are separated, both of them miss out on the full benefits of a continuous mother-infant attachment." A baby in substitute care, he says, is "re-

quired to bounce his cues and affections back and forth between various caregivers. His needs may not be consistently met, and his developing sense of trust may be compromised."

The granddaddy of parent counselors, of course, is the recently deceased Benjamin Spock. Dr. Spock had for years opposed infant daycare, arguing that "a day nursery...is no good for an infant. There's nowhere near enough attention or affection to go around." Spock has argued that children need responsive, full-time parental love in their first years, and that it makes no sense for parents to "pay other people to do a poorer job of bringing up their children."

Despite a good deal of backtracking in successive editions of his book to placate feminist criticisms, Spock still pointed out in recent years that "even at six months babies will become seriously depressed, losing their smile, their appetite, their interest in things and people, if the parent who has cared for them disappears.... Small children...may lose some of their capacity to love or trust deeply, as if it's too painful to be disappointed again and again." He adds that "it is stressful to children to have to cope with groups, with strangers, with people outside the family. That has emotional effects, and, if the deprivation of security is at all marked, it will have intellectual effects, too."

For the first three years of his life, Spock argued, a child needs individualized care from the same person. Only in the small number of cases where a childcare arrangement fits

particular group. The location may have turned out to be inconvenient. The cost may have been too high. Someone may have come to dislike someone else. Perhaps the family moved, or changed jobs.

And even when the parent and child stay put, providers very often move out from underneath them. The National Child Care Staffing Study, which examined a sample of 227 childcare centers in five regions of the country, reported that fully 41 percent of all caregivers quit their position each year. (Other studies show comparable results.) "To give you an idea of how bad it is," stated the director of the project, "during our study, we had tiny children coming up to our researchers and asking them, 'Are you my teacher?'"

And that's just in centers. Among *home* day care workers, the average turnover is even higher. Nationwide, 62 percent of all in-home workers flip over in the course of a year.

What's more, the situation is get-

that description can it substitute "pretty well" for parental care. He registered his urgent hope that "there will always be men and women who feel that the care of children...is at least as important and soul satisfying as any other activity." And he insisted that no parent should ever "feel the need to apologize for deciding to make that their main career."

Burton White, former director of the Harvard Preschool Project and one of the world's leading authorities on the first three years of life, has also written explicitly on the subject of nonparental care. "After more than 30 years of research on how children develop well, I would not think of putting an infant or toddler of my own into any substitute care program on a full-time basis," he reports, "especially a center-based program." White suggests that except for occasional baby-sitting, parents ought not use substitute care at all during the first six months of a child's life. A newborn "has to be responded to intensely in this period." From six months to three years of age, he says, the parent can use some part-time child-care, but the youngster should spend most of his waking time with a parent or grandparent. White concludes, "Unless you have a very good reason, I urge you not to delegate the primary child-rearing task to anyone else during your child's first three years of life.... Babies form their first human attachment only once. Babies begin to learn language only once.... The outcomes of these processes play a major role in shaping the future of each new child."

After studying hired child care in depth, in both its non-profit and for-profit forms, White pronounces it "a total disaster area," with "no feasible way of turning it into a model industry." Most families will find only "pretty poor substitutes" for parental care when they look outside the home, he warns. Therefore, "government should resist the cries for free full-time substitute baby care for all who want it."

If you are surprised to learn of this consensus against early full-time daycare, there is a good reason: Political fashions have made criticisms of daycare so off-limits that unfavorable evidence has been muted, downplayed, or ignored, in academic circles and mass media both. Michael Meyerhoff, director of the Center for Parent Education, explains that "over 90 percent of the professionals we deal with would agree with our basic position—that full-time substitute care for children under age three is not ordinarily in the best interests of the child. But many of these professionals are involved in situations where it's economically or politically unrealistic to maintain that position. Because of the strong attacks they'd be likely to get, many people are not saying anything."

Penelope Leach warns parents "there is a cover-up going on." The deep need of young children for individual care is seldom stated publicly and unequivocally for "fear of upsetting the parents who don't provide it." This, says Leach, is a serious error on the part of responsible authorities.

I am sorry for mothers who cannot look after their babies themselves, but I do not believe that it is helpful to conceal from them the fact that group care is a bad alternative. They are entitled to the facts as we understand them.... I am sympathetic, too, with mothers who could provide full-time care themselves but do not wish to. But they too are entitled to a true picture of the conflict between what they want and what their children need.

Rather than dispense information which could ruffle feathers, many pediatricians, psychologists, and other public advice-givers have fallen scandalously silent on this touchy subject. The result is that knowledgeable criticism of daycare is fading from popular view. And fewer and fewer parents are even aware that there exists a large body of research and clinical experience associating serious problems with early daycare.

But if public warnings on this subject have been muffled, the reservations of experts nonetheless remain strong. A 1990 poll of U.S. pediatricians conducted by the Thomas Jefferson School of Medicine in Philadelphia, for example, showed that 77 percent believe infants six months or younger ought to be cared for only at home. A different survey of 1,100 baby doctors carried out that same year by the American Academy of Pediatricians reported that a substantial majority of physicians consider full-time daycare harmful for children under age 4.

—*KZ*

ting worse. Surveys show that as the demand for day care and the size of the industry have risen, staff turnover has accelerated sharply over the last decade.

Anyone who does any research on day care today hears repeated stories of nomadism. "While Mrs. Freebing says she's had good luck with the two nannies she's hired, one from Utah and one from Montana, she's in the process of hiring her third nanny in 18 months. The first two are going back to school," reads a typical history. Parents finally find an acceptable childcare provider after a long ordeal, only to lose her. Left for a better position. Got married. Going to school to learn computers. Deported by the immigration service. These are experiences I've come across over and over.

Hardly any family relying on day care is safe from this sudden turmoil, not even those who pay for the costliest forms of care. An interview printed by Fredelle Maynard in her book on day care tells a representative story. Maynard quotes a Canadian mother describing an in-home day care arrangement she is satisfied with:

> They have a routine, the two of them. Victoria comes in the mornings and does toast and eggs for the baby; we leave while she's eating. Then they both watch "Polka Dot Door." Peggy recognizes the music, skips to the living room. After that the baby plays in her room, with the gate hooked, while Victoria cleans. Nap is from 11 to 1, lunch at one. Afternoons they go for a walk, shop, visit friends, watch some more TV (There's probably too much TV, but that's something I have to accept). Sometimes Peggy has a second nap while Victoria makes supper; they eat together, not with us (Victoria's choice). Peggy cries when she leaves.
>
> Everything considered, it's an ideal arrangement. I'm free to concentrate on my job, my child has a mother-substitute who's absolutely conscientious and devoted. Let me tell you I wake every morning and pray she won't leave us. Not that I really worry. The young nannies from

For children, the daily experience is "like enduring a nine-hour cocktail party."

Jamaica or the British Isles often don't take their jobs seriously; they meet a man, or get a better job, often, and they're off. For Victoria, stability is a central value. She regards this as her home.

One week after this interview, Victoria left without giving Riva, the mother, any notice. Her immigrant papers had come through. And "in the three months since," Maynard reveals, "Riva (pregnant again) has had one nanny who lasted two weeks and a series of makeshift arrangements. Now she and her husband are sponsoring a nanny from Hong Kong."

LOST IN A GROUP

For all of the problems associated with nannydom, it is still probably the least harmful form of hired caretaking in most cases, because it at least allows lots of one-on-one attention. Relatively few children, however, have their own nanny. And few ever will—because the average parent with average earning potential simply can't afford to hire someone to stand in for them full time.

Professionalized childcare, as Penelope Leach points out, "depends for its viability on economies of scale, because if one professional cares for only one baby then she is a direct swap for the mother." There is no great supply of willing and qualified workers making themselves available for such a swap,

and even if there were, this wouldn't "free up" any adults overall. Parents would be released, as Leach puts it, "only by leaving babies with less-skilled, or at least less well paid, adults—an uncomfortably colonialist thought."

In order to be affordable, mainstream day care will always require several children to share a single caretaker. Which brings us to the next inherent flaw that plagues paid childrearing—the problem of lack of individual attention. Fredelle Maynard reminds us that "a mother of twins is hard pressed to give *two* babies all the cuddling they want. What can be expected of a caretaker who's in charge of four infants—or six? With the best will in the world, that caretaker will be obliged to give some infants a propped-up bottle, to let others cry while she performs essential tasks."

Consider that the birth of triplets is literally considered an emergency situation which automatically qualifies two parents for caretaking assistance and special social aid. Yet in hired day care, the very *best* institutional situations involve three or four infants assigned to a single caretaker. This is what gets called "high quality care."

In average cases, things are worse yet. The government's National Child Care Survey showed that among centers caring for one-year-olds, the average group size is currently ten, and the child/staff ratio is nearly 7:1. Even this is probably an underestimate, since the survey was based on voluntary responses from day care centers and the worst institutions usually don't cooperate.

For many readers, those dry numbers may seem unexceptional. They give no hint of what it's really like to be responsible for several infants or toddlers at once. I suggest anyone who thinks 7:1, or even 4:1, sounds like a reasonable ratio ought to try it someday with real babies. I can promise that you'll experience chaos and practice neglect. You will be lucky just to keep up with diaper changing. Very little real fostering will take place under such conditions.

Dorothy Conniff, the Wisconsin day care chief, did some calculations back in 1988 of how much time it took to provide an infant with just the barest maintenance. She then translated that into the very best day care settings: Consider the amount of physical care and attention a baby needs—20 minutes for feeding every three hours or so, and ten minutes for diapering every two hours or so, and time for the caregiver to wash her hands thoroughly and sanitize the area after changing each baby. In an $8^{1}/_{2}$ hour day, then, a caregiver working under the most stringent regulation—the 4:1 ratio—will have 16 diapers to change and 12 feedings to give.

Four diaper-changes and three feedings apiece is not an inordinate amount of care over a long day from the baby's point of view.

But think about the caregiver's day: Four hours to feed the babies, two hours and 40 minutes to change them. If you allow an extra two-and-a-half minutes at each changing to put them down, clean up the area, and thoroughly wash your hands...that makes seven hours and 20 minutes of the day spent just on physical care—if you're

lucky and the infants stay conveniently on schedule.

Since feeding and diaper-changing are necessarily one-on-one activities, each infant is bound to be largely unattended during the five-plus hours that the other three babies are being attended to. So if there's to be any stimulation at all for the child, the caregiver had better chat and play up a storm while she's feeding and changing.

Day Care and Big Brother

"By virtue of its privacy, the family is the primary shelter of human variety. In the very process of preparing its newborn for the world the family can...see to it that the world's standards do not impinge too closely upon the defenseless young and so do not mold them too precisely to the world's imperious demands.... In this lies the human potentiality for freedom." So writes author Walter Karp, one of many observers (from various parts of the political spectrum) troubled by the standardizing effects of mass day care.

The contrast between a family upbringing and "collective professionalized care of the young" is stark, Karp notes. "Instead of protecting the young from the world, such administrative child care would fasten the world's ways on the newborn with a strangler's grip." And "in a society where cash is too often the link between people," daycare makes "the child's primary experience of life the experience of being someone's job."

When the infant-mother-father relationship is changed, the very institution that forms human personality is altered. Eventually, society itself may be reoriented. Some years ago, a Smithsonian Institution project attempted to determine the early childhood sources of human creativity and leadership, and eventually concluded that a consistently close parental connection was the most critical factor. Two other important influences were minimizing the time a child spent with peers, and providing

opportunities for free exploration of the world under parental encouragement. None of these conditions, chief investigator Harold McCurdy pointed out, are advanced by group socialization.

Sociologist David Popenoe asserts that "childrearing is one of those aspects of human society that is not subject to improvement through modern techniques of efficiency and rationalization." It is, he says, a "cottage industry." What is required—an abundance of time, patience, and love on the part of caring parents—"has no substitute in the technological realm."

Despite claiming to serve and speak on behalf of the family, the hired child care industry "actually weakens its authority at every point," suggests left-wing critic Christopher Lasch. Author George Gilder sees the professionalization of childrearing as a tragic extension of earlier errors in American public policy. "The same people who paved the road to hell in America's inner cities," he says, now "want to take care of your small children."

New York State teacher of the year John Taylor Gatto warns that any standardized process which has children as its product will eventually yield bitter results. "Lives can be controlled by machine education, but they will always fight back with weapons of social pathology—drugs, violence, self-destruction, indifference." These, he says, are already "symptoms I see in the children I teach."

—*KZ*

While older preschoolers in day care require somewhat less maintenance, they also get crowded into larger groups—typically from eight to 15 youngsters per adult. This also results in inadequate care. The average toddler makes 10 overtures an hour to his primary caretaker, according to studies. A day care worker responsible for 10 toddlers would thus be faced with an overture every 35 seconds. Obviously most will be ignored or bluntly cut off. The assistance, praise, rule-teaching, discipline, and reinforcement that one- to three-years-olds need will often be unavailable.

The problem is not that day care workers are thoughtless, but rather that they work within a structure where fine-tuning and sensitivity are simply not possible. I have helped mind eight preschoolers many times in morning cooperative playschools, and I know that all you can usually aim for is to keep basic order, to avoid accidents, to survive. The life's lessons come few and far between in such settings. If children are gathered in such groups a couple times a week for two or three hours of play, this is not a serious problem. But when such a group becomes the child's primary residence all day long, not even the most conscientious caretaker can rescue the situation. The plain result is neglect.

Many observers say all that's needed is some new laws requiring higher adult-to-child ratios. But they overlook day care's basic nature. Getting the ratios up to a humane level would amount to recreating families artificially, and the reason day care exists to begin with is because there aren't enough adults currently willing to spend their days in families. Even if you *could* provide enough adult bodies in every day care setting, you would, as Penelope Leach points out, "have lost your economies of scale." Only a comparatively small number of rich families can afford to hire one parent surrogate for every child or two. In any mass form of day care, basic financial considerations and the limited number of substitute parents available make the kind of personal attention children crave impossible.

Childrearing of adequate quality is inherently resistant to streamlining. "Raising several children is a project that exacts a constant alertness and attention," comments writer George Gilder, something social engineers "don't remotely understand when they urge that 'society' do it." Pediatrician Herbert Ratner worries that "nature goes out of its way to give each baby a private tutor. We go out of our way to develop a litter situation." Substitution of group care for parent care is both unnatural and impractical, he argues, and it will eventually be regretted.

CHILDREN OF INSTITUTIONS

In recent years there has been a big shift toward institutional child care. If the Clintons have their way, even more of the future growth will be at institutions. Making institutionalization a common part of early childhood will have effects on American personality. As Deborah Fallows points out,

Life for a child in a day care center, good or bad, is different in certain ways from other kinds of life. There is more rigidity to it. The sheer number of children that day care centers handle necessarily means organization, scheduling, and rules.... Life in day care centers is also more homogeneous than life elsewhere. The day's format is always the same. Most of the time is spent in the same building or room, on the same playground....The need to manage large numbers of young children...accounts for the centers' emphasis on standardization and routine.

"Anyone who has spent time in a day care center knows that it is not a place where children can 'do their own thing,'" add Bill and Wendy Dreskin.

Every aspect of the day is regulated. They must lie on the mats, whether tired of not, for the prescribed number of minutes. If they are tired, they must still wake up at the end of rest time.... They must eat by the clock, even if they are hungry earlier, and there is no allowance for individual taste.... In some infant centers, babies are "color coded." The "green" baby has the green pacifier, the green bottle, the green crib, and so on. The uniqueness of each little human person is lost....

While "better" quality centers avoid horrors like walking toddlers in groups on leashes and putting infants in stacking kennel-like cribs, day care centers, like hospitals, asylums, and the military, are...a total institution.... Children quickly get the message that they must go along with the group and not make waves.

The Dreskins evoke hospitals and barracks. I suggest an even closer analogy for the typical day care atmosphere might be a nursing home. There is often the same well-intended but ultimately depressing air. As one mother described full-day centers, "you go in there, and all these children are clutching their little possessions, and they're looking around. They don't have any concept of time, so when a door opens, they all look up, and when they see you're not their mother, they look back."

Day care centers even tend to have a uniform emotional environment. This is Fallows' characterization:

The children live in an "on" atmosphere that differs from the tone of life at home. Even when caregivers are most gentle and children most mild-mannered, the pressure of numbers generates considerable noise, confusion, interruptions. Children have to respond, to react, to engage the social side of their personalities almost all day long. Time alone, to be quiet, to muse, to just be there, is minimal.

Almost all day care observers eventually comment on the constant hubbub. "I couldn't stand the noise. From sun-up to sun-down, voices talking, talking," writes Anne Husted Burleigh. "People," she argues, "were not made for babble." "For ten hours a day, these kids have to interact with about 20 or 30 kids," says day care worker Katie Humes. "Imagine if we adults had to constantly be trying to get along with that many people." For lots of children, suggested author Vance Packard after making a series of day care visits, the daily experience "must be like enduring a nine-hour cocktail party."

Perhaps the most undesirable aspect of the day care center is that, as child psychologist Arnold Samuels puts it, "the child must comply with the environment; the program doesn't always respond to the child." Dorothy Conniff characterizes this as "the most consistent drawback of day care centers."

Staff resort to forcing children into the same boring activity all at the same time to maintain control. Whatever children can learn from pasting a picture of a pumpkin on a pumpkin outline is not enhanced the next day by pasting a paper feather on a turkey. This kind of solution to the problem of what to do with young children is a terrible waste....[a] kind of repressive control.

Given the impossibility of true personal attention, the need to mark time, and the necessity of keeping control, even the most mundane activities on the day care schedule take on large significance. Fallows describes the discomfort she observed during hand-washing periods as lines of children had to wait for those in front of them to one at a time walk to the sink, wet their hands, grasp the soap, wash, replace the soap, rinse, pull out a towel, dry, throw the towel away, and then return to their seat—all with the deliberate, painful slowness of a toddler. In the course of a nine-hour day, mass coat-donning, bathroom-using, grace-saying, line-forming and so forth can become trials in depersonalization for two-, three- and four-year-old children.

For her book *The Erosion of Childhood*, Valerie Suransky observed several widely different day care settings and came away struck by the way each stressed time scheduling and the routinization of tasks. Suransky also noted the importance of *containment* in day care, and the role of locked doors, marching in line, and other measures used toward this end.

Regimentation pops up wherever custodial care of children is substituted for family care—even when the children involved are much older and more competent than infants and toddlers. When *Time* profiled some typical days of American children a few years ago, a third grader named Katie, the only child of a Seattle doctor and nurse practitioner, was included. "Katie is a day care child," began the profile. "To her generation of children, day care is as familiar a destination as Disneyland, if not nearly as magical." Katie still goes to day care before and after every school day. Until her teenaged half-sister recently moved into the house, Katie also "used to go to day care all summer. I didn't look forward to summer then."

Behold a picture of upper-income early childhood at the end of the twentieth century:

Katie spends ten hours away from home each day. After rising at 7 a.m. and downing a breakfast of Lucky Charms, she buckles herself into the front seat of her mother's Volkswagen Jetta for the two-minute ride [to] Montlake Elementary School. She stays for an hour in a kindergarten classroom where the Community Day School sets up shop each day before and after school. At 9 A.M. she joins her third-grade classmates at Montlake. When the school day finishes, Katie circles back to day care, where she stays until 6 P.M.

Katie clearly does not like day care. "A lot of times it gets really boring just going there," she says. "It's the same setting and usually the same things to do." ...She cannot invite friends over to her house, nor can she go to theirs. Worst of all, she cannot disappear by herself

Regimentation pops up wherever custodial care of children is substituted for family care.

into her bedroom and play with her toys or work on her next book. "I would love if I could just stay in the attic," she says. "There's a little room in my mom and dad's closet. There's this little door to get in. It is really fun in there. They have all these old literature books and poetry books and drawing books. It is like a big library, and I could just sit there and read all day."

Sometimes when she's feeling unhappy at day care, Katie starts to imagine that the other children do not like her. She suffers from attacks of what she calls "aloneness," a feeling she rarely has when she is at home alone....

No matter how creative the entertainment, the children find it hard to keep going, going, going as they head into the final stretch late each afternoon.... Toward the end of the day, the slightest twist on the doorknob is enough to get a sea of tired eyes to look up. As parents arrive to pick up their kids, Katie quickly looks up to see if it is her mom or dad. Most kids have a pretty good feeling for what time their parents normally appear, so when a parent is late, a child becomes anxious.

Institutionalization of this sort means several things for children, comments family researcher David Cayley. "It means separation from the day-to-day world of home and neighborhood, it means the loss of the opportunity to do what you want when you want to do it, including sometimes just doing nothing at all. And it means the loss of privacy and solitude."

This is not an exclusively American problem. All industrial societies are pushing their children in the same direction. The *Christian Science Monitor* carried an interview with an educated Parisian couple who discussed family

practices and childcare policies in France (which Mrs. Clinton and other liberals in the U.S. often laud). "I've never wanted to put children into these public systems," confessed Alexandra Doualle. "You can say what you want, but day care centers are collective institutions. The children are raised as a collective entity. The child will develop his collective self but will not necessarily develop his individual self." What happens, she asks, to a particularly sensitive child? To one who is easily influenced? To one who can be dominated? They suffer. "A little day care, a few hours a day, that's fine," suggests Mrs. Doualle. But spending more time than that in a group can damage a child's personality.

One of the great cultural ironies of our era, Bill and Wendy Dreskin have argued, is that this trend toward institutionalization in childhood is being driven primarily by social liberals—the great professed opponents of dehumanizing standardization.

Progressives are dedicated to increasing the number of children who must lead these regimented lives. They are lobbying for the public schools to include day care programs for preschool children or even infants and toddlers, and in some states they are working toward lowering the age for compulsory entrance into the school system.... Progressives push for year-round schools which would shift the responsibility of summer care from parents to the government.

The institutions produced by all this social activism have been characterized as "part-time orphanages" by worried skeptics. And like the full-time versions, they can wrench their charges poignantly. Writer Harry Stein illustrates this through the experiences of a friend. While wrestling with the decision of whether to have children, the friend—a successful broadcasting executive—decided to visit the best day care center in her neighborhood and draw some conclusions for herself. She came back with serious reservations. "I was quite taken aback when I saw them consoling a six-month-old with a *pho-*

tograph of his parents," the woman reported. "I don't know," she observed after a pause, "those people are betting a helluva lot on this experiment panning out."

This snippet from one of Deborah Fallows' center visits provides another glimpse of the impersonality that prevails in so much hired childcare.

The story line of the book was getting more complicated when the phone rang next door in the director's office. The teacher got up to answer it because the director was out. When she came back, Jason started complaining that he didn't feel well. She let the comment pass and went back to reading when the phone rang a second time. She went again to answer it. When she returned, [Jason] stumbled out of his seat and toward the bathroom, spitting up on me and a few children as he passed.... The teacher went off to clean up Jason, laid him down in the director's office, and tried unsuccessfully to call his mother. She pulled out coloring books and crayons to keep the children busy in her absence.... All but two of the children located their coloring books by their names on the covers. Andrew, the two-and-a-half-year-old, and Michele, a recently arrived five-year-old, didn't have books. They found some left over from children who were no longer at the center and started using them. Suddenly Andrea discovered that she in fact had the wrong book and little Andrew was scribbling in hers. She attempted a quick switch, which set Andrew off howling. When the teacher returned, Michele was pouting and complaining about not having her own book. The teacher, impatient by then, picked up the book Michele was using, scratched out the name "Carolyn" and wrote "Michele" over it. "Carolyn withdrew from school," she explained to me. But Michele did not look convinced.

One leading edge in day care today is special centers that only accept sick children. All around the country, institutions with cutesy names like

> **Infants under one in group care have eight times as many colds and other infections.**

Sneezles and Chicken Soup and Teddy Bearacks have sprung up, solely as places to park youngsters too ill to attend their regular centers. But there is nothing cute, or healthy, about this practice. When a youngster who is already feeling bad goes to an ill child center he is faced with a totally unfamiliar environment, where all the adults and all the other children are strangers. Instead of bringing extra security and comfort, his illness thus brings him extra strangeness and uncertainty. Penelope Leach puts it bluntly: "To put a sick baby into a stranger's hands is cruelty."

In many cases, it is employers who set up these centers. They then parade them as proof that the company is "family friendly." One cover story in *Fortune* chortled that "for sheer cost-effectiveness, nothing beats a facility for children too sick to go to school or day care centers. About 80 employers, up 50 percent from a year ago, have made some provisions so that the mommies and daddies of sufferers can still report for work."

Susan Wolfe, director of one Minneapolis ill-child center, does the math for *Fortune.* When a middle manager at First Bank, one of her supporting employers, misses a day of work to minister to a miserable child, it costs the company $154, Wolfe reports. If, on the other hand, the employee checks the child into her center at company expense, it costs the bank only about $20. Viola! An institution that "saves the company 87 percent, or almost $135 a day."

The growing regimentation of childhood involves more than just day care institutions. It includes things like more and more young children having to brave rush hour each day. I have be-

fore me an Associated Press piece entitled "The Littlest Commuter" that is typical of several I've seen. It profiles a mother and toddler who spend four hours a day traveling from suburban New Jersey to work and day care, respectively, in lower Manhattan.

This is Ashley's day: She gets up very early and is driven by her mother from Oakland, N.J. to the train station in Ramsey. They park. They board the 6:22 A.M. local to Hoboken. In Hoboken they jump a Trans-Hudson subway. From the top of the subway stairs they stroller several blocks to Ashley's day care center. She stays there all day, then reverses her commute. All told, Ashley's "workday" is 12 hours long.

Welcome to the baby rat race, Ashley.

HEALTH RISKS

Doctors warn that day care centers have become troublesome sources of health problems. The American Pediatric Association reckons that infants under one in group care have eight times as many colds and other infections as babies cared for by their families. A baby's immune system is not well developed until about his third month of life, and it does not reach adult-level disease-fighting capability until around age two. Take this fact, plus the research finding that an average toddler puts a hand or object in his mouth every three minutes, and you can see why concentrating together groups of these drooling, toy-sucking, low-immune children creates an ideal environment for disease transmission.

Add to this the reality of diapers and you have a recipe for recurring sickness. The U.S. Centers for Disease Control warn that "diaper changing is the highest risk procedure" associated with day care. Even in the highest-quality center with a 1:4 adult-to-child ratio, a worker taking care of babies will have to clean an average of 16 bottoms every day, supposedly sanitizing the changing area thoroughly each time. Dorothy

Conniff comments that if you "think about thoroughly washing your hands 16 times a day, you may begin to understand why epidemics of diarrhea and related diseases regularly sweep through infant-care centers."

A Memphis State University study of 800 children under age three found that compared to youngsters at home, children in day care centers suffered half-again as many infections and four-and-a-half-times as many hospitalizations. The *American Journal of Public Health* has reported that children in day care centers incur overall medical expenses that are two to three times as high as those of children cared for at home. This research showed them to be nearly three times as likely to require hospitalization. A RAND Corporation study which analyzed data on 3,841 children age six months to five years showed that attending a day care center "increases bed days for young children by 30 percent," while youngsters attending home-based day care have 19 percent more bed days (both compared to parent-reared children).

In the *Journal of the American Medical Association*, physician Stanley Schuman reports that day care transmission is responsible for recent "outbreaks of enteric illness—diarrhea, dysentery, giardiasis, and epidemic jaundice—reminiscent of the pre-sanitation days of the seventeenth century." Other serious day care hazards include cytomegalovirus, shigellosis, hepatitis, HiB, and ear infections. When we checked my son into Children's Hospital in Washington, D.C., to have a minor hernia repaired when he was young, I was struck to note that half of the children in the surgical ward were in for inner ear surgery, most to have mechanical drains installed to try to prevent eardrum ruptures. Increased day care transmission of disease is the major reason this has become a big problem among children today.

· Committees of the the American Academy of Pediatrics recommended in the 1980s that to avoid chronic infections and childhood epidemics, children under two should be cared for only in the company of their siblings if at all possible. When that is impossible, the doctors urge that a small group of no more than six children, from no more than three families be used. Large groupings and groups with turnover among the children ought to be avoided when children are young, they suggest. This, obviously, would exclude most day care centers.

And there are public health issues associated with day care beyond just those of disease transmission. Phyllis Weikart, a University of Michigan professor of physical education, has implicated increased day care use in the sharp decline over the last generation in the physical motor skills of children. Today's children have fewer opportunities for unrestricted outdoor movement and play, she explained. And youngsters are considerably less likely to learn physical skills and games from older siblings, playmates, and role models than they once were. Day care creates single-age ghettos where there is less transmission of skills and information of all sorts across age boundaries.

CAN GOVERNMENT MAKE DAY CARE GOOD?

Now a brief word about day-care "quality." In the national research (including the latest NICHD study that activists misrepresent as exonerating day care), two facts are clear. The first is that when you get right down to actual effects on individual children, the differences between "good" programs and "poor" programs are not large.

The second reality is that in even the very *best* full-time day care situations, large numbers of children (often a majority, depending on what is being measured) end up showing some sign of maladjustment. Problems occur not just where the care is of low quality but also among children in the most careful and expensive forms of hired care—one-on-one nannies, and university lab schools, for instance. This is quite clear in the research, and the best way to summarize it may be to say that excel-lent day care gets less disappointing results than crummy daycare.

Certainly not all children who go into day care will end up with weak parental bonds, aggressive tendencies, academic problems, personal insecurities, difficulties in peer relations, or other evidence of emotional or cognitive damage. Lots will bounce through with few obvious effects. Individual circumstances like a youngster's temperament, sex, and the status of his home influence how he fares. Older children are better equipped to adapt than infants and toddlers. Part-time care is much less risky than full-time.

It's a mistake, though, to assume that a child with nice concerned parents and a nice middle-class daycare arrangement will be immune from harm. What we've learned over the last decade or so is that all youngsters are vulnerable. Lasting effects will show up among some considerable portion of the youngsters who experience extensive out-of-home care in their first three years. Exactly how large a portion we can't say; long-term results aren't in, and in any case many of these effects will never be fully measurable.

But the ominous findings that have piled up so far give us clear reason to hesitate in our headlong plunge toward more and more childraising by hire.

Day care advocates often claim that the kinds of problems I've been discussing in this chapter can be eliminated via more licensing and regulation. The trouble is, there are already lots of fully regulated—and fully disappointing—day care homes and centers out there. That's because most of the things that really matter to young children, if we're honest about it, simply can't be covered by regulations.

Linda Burton admits she "never found an accurate way to evaluate the merit of a day care situation. Despite my most painstaking investigations, many environments that appeared loving and constructive on initial (and sometimes repeated) examination, turned out later to be something quite different." Anyone who would have the state "guarantee good childcare" must explain how regulators can make these judgments that even cautious parents find so elusive.

Since the things that are really wanted in a childcare provider are almost impossible to stipulate through rules, state regulations generally dwell uselessly, or obsessively on the material inputs that are easiest to measure. What good is the government regulation that reads (literally): "Infants and toddlers should be offered water at intervals"? What about "Infants shall not remain in cribs, baby beds or playpens all day"? It may or may not be useful to insist that every room in which day care is conducted have an 8-foot ceiling, and that there are covers on all the diaper pails. But none of those things have much to do with producing humane childhoods.

A 1991 RAND study of child care quality published in the *Journal of Social Issues* concludes that "the structural elements that are currently the focus of [child care] licensing are, in fact, largely irrelevant in terms of what parents demand." The same conclusion is spelled out in more popular language in the 1990 report *Mothers Speak Out on Child Care*. "Mothers do not believe that loving care can be created by legislative mandate, or bought with generous salaries and top-of-the-line play equipment," it reads. "When they demand 'quality care' they are not referring to adequate fire exits and teacher-to-child ratio."

And there is another problem with proposed regulatory fixes for day care: More rules lead to higher expenses and fewer providers. William Gormley observes in a 1990 Brookings Institution study that because regulation will "decrease the supply and raise the costs" of care, it can "ironically, result in fewer regulated facilities." And what good is "better" care if it's unaffordable or unavailable?

I've known several cases where warmhearted people stopped providing care for neighbors because the paperwork became such a burden, because the windows in their playroom weren't as large as the specifications dictated, or for similar reasons. In a strictly regulated environment, the advantage goes to cookie-cutter chains and other mass providers.

A few years ago, Maryland working mother Judy Kaplan Warner wrote me to describe how day care regulations can have perverse effects in this way.

A Final Test of Surrogate Parenting

If you think the lucky few families able to afford gold-standard day care—a private nanny in one's own home—can thereby avoid day care's problems, think again.

From the later-1800s until the 1930s, placing one's children in the hands of a hired nanny was one of the hallmarks of upper-class existence in Britain and a few other European countries. This was gold-standard care if it ever existed. The nannies were with their children nearly round the clock, typically living right in the children's rooms, and giving their whole life to their charges.

Nonetheless, these arrangements caused much human unhappiness. Among other problems, Jonathan Gathorne-Hardy notes in his book *The Unnatural History of the Nanny*, "the annals of nanny literature are filled with desperate descriptions of incomprehensible and brutal partings" when caretakers left their host families. And even where the connections between nanny and child were never severed, nanny life often brought suffering. Many writers suggest this peculiar institution left deep, raw marks on the entire British upper class.

One famous graduate of a nanny upbringing was Winston Churchill. "If it worked for Churchill, it can't be so bad for others," intone defenders of nannying. And in truth, Churchill's early rearing did have a lot to do with making him the great public man he was. But that rearing also left him privately tormented, and desperately unhappy at the end of his life. Churchill's case is interesting because it illustrates the remarkable closeness of the very best nanny-child relationships while simultaneously demonstrating that, even under optimal conditions, parental surrogacy is ultimately inadequate.

Churchill's father, Lord Randolph, was an ambitious and preoccupied politician, and his mother, Jennie Jerome, was a beautiful young woman caught up in the whirl of fashionable society. Winston's childhood letters show him pleading with his parents for attention.

Rescuing Churchill from this sore neglect was his nanny Mrs. Everest. For the first eight years of his life, Churchill was virtually never separated from Nanny Everest. He slept in her room, had every need attended to by her, and soaked up her calm, loving warmth. From birth until his twentieth year, when she died,

Mrs. Everest was "the principal confidante of his joys, his troubles, and his hopes," according to Churchill's son.

She in turn adored Churchill. The depth of their mutual love shines forth in their correspondence. Some samples from her letters found among Churchill's papers when he died (having then been saved by him for more than 70 years):

Winny dear, do try to keep the new suit expressly for visiting, the brown one will do for everyday wear, please do this to please me.

Thank you so much dearest for getting me a present.... It is very kind of you but you know my Lamb I would rather you did not spend your money on me.

My darling Precious Boy: I hope you will take care of yourself, my darling. I hear of your exploits at steeplechasing. I do so dread to hear of it. Remember Count Kinsky broke his nose once at that....

Churchill was at Everest's deathbed when she succumbed to peritonitis at her sister's house in North London. He describes the day in *My Early Life*.

She included an article she had written for the *Washington Post* after her daughter's "grandmotherly" home day care provider was raided by a county inspector because she wasn't licensed. In it, Warner complained that "in the name of protecting children, the state law has thrown me back into the pool of anguished parents searching for good day care, while a superbly competent day care provider is forbidden to care for children."

Warner argues that she and thousands of other parents who freely choose informal unlicensed care arrangements "believe we know better than anyone else—the state, the county, the federal government—what our children need to thrive." And surely she

is right. Only parents can judge what qualities are essential for their sons and daughters. The effect of most government norms dictated in the name of "quality control" will simply be to drive informal caregivers out of business.

Day care proponents have an almost blind faith in the ability of government to solve child care problems. One favorite tactic of American liberals is to point to Europe—where they claim that excellent day care systems flourish because public will and public money have been applied. The truth, however, as I discovered when I did research in several European countries in the mid-1980s, is rather different.

To begin, most of the European systems are not really day care structures

but rather parts of a much larger apparatus of family allowances and tax breaks set up to encourage births and population growth in countries rapidly growing gray. The United States doesn't have a problem with too few births, and thus is not about to copy these programs. Particularly since these European "Family Policies" are incredibly costly—setting up a U.S. equivalent to the French system, for instance, would cost around $300 billion.

More to the point, European child care systems don't do what American promoters claim they do. In Europe, most day care is not excellent, it is mediocre—just as day care is everywhere when practiced on a mass scale. More national effort and funding has

The Nanny

She knew she was in danger, but her only anxiety was for me. There had been a heavy shower of rain. My jacket was wet. When she felt it with her hands she was greatly alarmed for fear I should catch cold. The jacket had to be taken off and thoroughly dried before she was calm again. Her only desire was to see my brother Jack, and this unhappily could not be arranged. I set out for London to get a good specialist.... I returned to her bedside. She still knew me, but she gradually became unconscious. Death came very easily to her. She had lived such an innocent and loving life...she had no fears at all.... She had been my dearest and most intimate friend during the whole of the 20 years I had lived.

Churchill enjoyed, as one writer put it, "the total love and undiluted attention of this good woman concentrated entirely on his well-being." He was cared for with intense devotion—far more than most substitute-parented children will ever know—and this gave him an unshakeable base of self-assurance.

Yet Churchill was haunted, in spite of everything he got from Mrs. Everest, by the absence of his mother and his fa-

ther. His parents were in no way hostile—"My mother shone for me like the Evening Star," Winston wrote in later life—his problem was simply that they were not around much.

The anxiety this ingrained into Churchill wasn't always debilitating. Indeed, Oxford University psychiatrist Anthony Storr argues that the parental indifference of his youth may actually have helped prepare Churchill for his inspired wartime leadership of Britain. The boy's early emotional pain crystallized as an extraordinary pugnacity, and in the midst of a national life-and-death struggle, this rage found a complete and legitimate outlet. The prime minister's famous cry that "We shall fight in France, we shall fight on the seas and oceans, we shall fight...in the air, we shall...fight on the beaches" exemplifies the survivor's spirit that stood him and his nation so well in the heat of battle. The fact that Churchill had been repeatedly forced to master his own despair left him perfectly suited to rouse the nation when all the odds seemed against it, Storr suggests.

But the boy's upbringing eventually came back to bite him. A child who is rejected will lack "belief that the world is

predominantly a happy place, and that he has a favored place in it," says Storr.

Although such a child may experience periods of both success and happiness, these will neither convince him that he is lovable, nor finally prove to him that life is worthwhile.... No amount of external success can ultimately compensate him for this.

That, alas, is precisely the circumstance Winston Churchill found himself in. All through his life he was plagued with moods of deep depression—he referred to them famously as his "Black Dog." These he combatted with activity, and during the periods he was holding political office he mostly kept them in control. But in the end, the "Black Dog" conquered the great man. In his last years, Churchill would sit glumly for days and weeks, convinced of his failure and the uselessness of his life. Despite his magnificent achievements, he ultimately died unhappy.

Separation from mother and father was something not even the generous love of Nanny Everest could save him from.   —*KZ*

been expended in France than anywhere else, and the average center for three-year-olds has one teacher and one half-time aide for every 22 children. Even if every teacher was unusually gifted, this would amount to mere custodialism. Three-year-olds are simply not built for herding in flocks.

Belgium has a free government-run nursery school system for children aged three and over that is very similar to France's. It also has a network, like other European countries, for providing referrals and public subsidies to day care centers that cater to younger children. A typical Belgian center will be staffed by aides with the equivalent of a vocational high school diploma, and the average worker earns about $900 a month. The major source of day care workers is unemployed persons on the government dole, who are assigned to centers by state welfare agencies. On a normal day, a third of the teachers may be absent. "You understand the difference between theory and practice," explains the director of one Brussels child care center, acknowledging that morale among the country's hired caretakers is low.

The really striking thing about European young-child care is not the quantity or quality of publicly-funded centers, but rather *the clear preference of parents to take care of their own infants and toddlers at home*. In the European Union as a whole, fewer than half of all mothers with children under 10 are currently employed. In the United States, half-again as many mothers of children in that age range are absent from the home. Fully seven out of ten infants and toddlers are raised in their own home in France. Even in Sweden, where tax rules and heavy social pressures make it extremely difficult for families to survive without two incomes, four out of every ten children age six or younger are cared for by a parent at home, and another two out of ten are looked after by a relative or neighbor. And if the Swedish public had its druthers there might be even less day care. A 1988 poll showed that 83 percent of all Swedes feel children should stay at home until age three.

Even when European children do end up in non-parental care, public institutions are a distinct second choice. Of the Swedish children in subsidized day care, for instance, fully 40 percent are taken care of in family homes rather than centers. Even more popular among European parents are related caretakers. According to European Union figures, European children with employed mothers are more than twice as likely to be looked after by their grandmothers, for example, than are American children.

The common claim that Europe is carpeted with day care institutions that are consistently wonderful and highly popular is simply not true. Europeans strongly prefer parental and family care to the alternatives. Most still provide such care to their own children. And the institutional care funded by the European governments tends to be mediocre and impersonal just like institutional care everywhere else.

There is no easy way, public or private, to buy for individual children the kind of loving concern that has never been for sale.

What Matters? What Does Not?

Five Perspectives on the Association Between

Marital Transitions and Children's Adjustment

E. Mavis Hetherington, Margaret Bridges, and Glendessa ·M. Insabella
University of Virginia

This article presents an analysis of 5 views of factors that contribute to the adjustment of children in divorced families or stepfamilies. These perspectives are those that emphasize (a) individual vulnerability and risk; (b) family composition; (c) stress, including socioeconomic disadvantage; (d) parental distress; and (e) disrupted family process. It is concluded that all of these factors contribute to children's adjustment in divorced and remarried families and that a transactional model examining multiple trajectories of interacting risk and protective factors is the most fruitful in predicting the well-being of children.

In the past 30 years, there has been a significant decline in the proportion of two-parent families in first marriages and a complementary increase in the number of single-parent households and stepfamilies. These changes are the result of a rapid rise in the divorce rate that began during the 1960s (Simons, 1996) and also, to a lesser extent, of an increase in births to single mothers. Although there has been a modest decrease in the divorce rate since the late 1970s, almost one half of marriages end in divorce in the United States, and one million children experience their parents' divorce each year (U.S. Bureau of the Census, 1992). It is projected that between 50% and 60% of children born in the 1990s will live, at some point, in single-parent families, typically headed by mothers (Bumpass & Sweet, 1989; Furstenberg & Cherlin, 1991). Currently, stepfamilies make up approximately 17% of all two-parent families with children under 18 years of age (Glick, 1989).

Although the high divorce rate has been interpreted as a rejection of the institution of marriage, 75% of men and 66% of women eventually will remarry, suggesting that although people are rejecting specific marital partners, most are not rejecting marriage itself (Booth & Edwards, 1992; Bumpass, Sweet, & Castro-Martin, 1990; Cherlin & Furstenberg, 1994; Ganong & Coleman, 1994). Since the 1960s, however, the annual rate of remarriage has actually declined as the divorce rate has increased. Moreover, divorces are more frequent in remarriages and occur at a rate 10% higher than that in first marriages (Bumpass et al., 1990; Cherlin & Furstenberg, 1994). Couples with remarried wives are almost twice as likely to divorce as are couples with remarried husbands. This association may be attributable to the 50% higher rate of dissolution in remarriages in which children from previous marriages are present (Tzeng & Mare, 1995), although the presence of children appears to be less relevant to the marital quality of African American couples (Orbuch, Veroff, & Hunter, in press). As a result of their parents' successive marital transitions, about half of all children whose parents divorce will have a stepfather within four years of parental separation, and 1 out of every 10 children will experience at least two divorces of their residential parent before turning 16 years of age (Furstenberg, 1988). These numbers underestimate the actual number of household reorganizations to which children are exposed because many couples cohabit before remarriage or cohabit as an alternative to remarriage (Bumpass & Raley, 1995; Bumpass, Sweet, & Cherlin, 1991; Cherlin & Furstenberg, 1994; Ganong & Coleman, 1994).

The national figures for marital transitions and family structure mask very different patterns among racial and ethnic groups because the social context of marriage varies across communities (Orbuch et al., in press). African American children are twice as likely as White children to experience at least one parental divorce (National Center for Health Statistics, 1988) and also are more likely to bear children out of wedlock in adolescence and adulthood (Demo & Acock, 1996; Tzeng & Mare, 1995; U.S. Bureau of the Census, 1992). In addition, African Americans and Hispanic Whites are less likely to divorce after separation and to remarry than are non-Hispanic Whites (Castro-Martin & Bumpass, 1989; Cherlin, 1992). Thus, in comparison with White children, more African American children spend longer periods of time in single-parent households, which often include kin and cohabiting partners.

As marriage has become a more optional, less permanent institution in contemporary American society, children in all ethnic groups are encountering stresses

E. Mavis Hetherington, Margaret Bridges, and Glendessa M. Insabella, Department of Psychology, University of Virginia.

Correspondence concerning this article should be addressed to E. Mavis Hetherington, Department of Psychology, University of Virginia, 102 Gilmer Hall, Charlottesville, VA 22903-2477. Electronic mail may be sent to emh2f@virginia.edu.

From *American Psychologist*, February 1998, pp. 167-184. © 1998 by the American Psychological Association. Reprinted by permission.

and adaptive challenges associated with their parents' marital transitions. Children from divorced and remarried families, in contrast to those from never-divorced families, exhibit more problem behaviors and lower psychological well-being. Little agreement exists, however, about the extent, severity, and duration of these problems because there is great diversity in children's responses to parental marital transitions (Amato & Keith, 1991a; Emery & Forehand, 1994; Hetherington, 1991b; McLanahan & Sandefur, 1994). Furthermore, although it is clear that marital dissension and dissolution, life in single-parent households, and remarriage present families and children with new experiences, risks, and resources, there is some disagreement on how these factors undermine or enhance the well-being of children.

Theoretical Perspectives on Marital Transitions and the Adjustment of Children

Five main theoretical perspectives have been proposed to explain the links between divorce and remarriage and children's adjustment. These perspectives are those emphasizing (a) individual risk and vulnerability; (b) family composition; (c) stress, including socioeconomic disadvantage; (d) parental distress; and (e) family process.

Individual Risk and Vulnerability

It has been proposed that some characteristics of parents and children may influence their exposure and vulnerability to adversity. Some adults possess characteristics (e.g., antisocial behavior) that place them at increased risk for marital discord, multiple marital transitions, and other adverse life experiences (Capaldi & Patterson, 1991; Kitson & Morgan, 1990; Patterson & Dishion, 1988; Simons, Johnson, & Lorenz, 1996). Adults with psychological problems such as depression or antisocial behavior often select partners who also experience psychological difficulties (Merikangas, Prusoff, & Weissman, 1988), thereby increasing their risk for marital problems and dissolution. This is called the marital selectivity hypothesis. In addition, some children have attributes that increase their vulnerability or protect them from deleterious consequences of stresses associated with their parents' marital transitions (Amato & Keith, 1991a; Emery & Forehand, 1994; Hetherington, 1989, 1991b).

Family Composition

It is commonly assumed that two biological parents provide the optimal family environment for healthy child development and that any deviation from this family structure, such as single-parent families or stepfamilies, is problematic for children (Amato & Keith, 1991a; Kitson & Holmes, 1992; Simons, 1996). Much of the early theorizing about divorce and family structure focused on father absence.

Stress and Socioeconomic Disadvantage

This perspective emphasizes that marital transitions trigger a series of negative social and economic changes, stresses, and practical problems that can interfere with the well-being of parents and children. For custodial mothers and their children, divorce is related to a notable economic decline that is associated with living conditions that make raising children more difficult (McLanahan & Sandefur, 1994), whereas remarriage is associated with an increase in household income for single mothers. Although much of the research on stress has focused on economic stresses, both divorced and remarried families encounter other stresses related to changing family roles and relationships (Cherlin & Furstenberg, 1994; Hetherington & Stanley Hagan, 1995; Simons, 1996).

Parental Distress

This perspective suggests that stressful life experiences, including economic decline and adaptive challenges associated with divorce and remarriage, lead to parental strain, distress, and diminished well-being, which are reflected in psychological problems such as depression, anxiety, irritability, and antisocial behaviors, as well as stress-related health problems (Capaldi & Patterson, 1991; Forgatch, Patterson, & Ray, 1995; Hetherington, 1989, 1991b; Kiecolt-Glaser et al., 1987; Lorenz, Simons, & Chao, 1996; Simons & Johnson, 1996). There is great individual variability in response to negative life changes; some parents cope with such changes with apparent equanimity, whereas others exhibit marked affective disruption and distress.

Family Process

Finally, many researchers have emphasized that differences between nondivorced families and divorced and remarried families on process variables such as conflict, control, expression of positive and negative affect, and problem solving largely explain the effects of divorce and remarriage. It is argued that more proximal variables, such as discipline and child-rearing practices, are most important in affecting children's adjustment.

Although these perspectives often are presented as competing with each other, empirical support can be found for each, suggesting that they may best be considered as complementary hypotheses (Amato & Keith, 1991a; Simons, 1996). In this article, research on the five perspectives is reviewed, and the direct and indirect effects of the five factors on the adjustment of children and parents in divorced and remarried families are examined. Finally, a transactional model of marital transitions involving relationships among the factors is presented.

Adjustment of Children in Divorced and Remarried Families

There is general agreement among researchers that children, adolescents, and adults from divorced and remarried families, in comparison with those from two-parent, nondivorced families, are at increased risk for developing problems in adjustment (for meta-analyses, see Amato & Keith, 1991a, 1991b) and that those who have undergone multiple divorces are at a greater risk (Capaldi & Patterson, 1991; Kurdek, Fine, & Sinclair, 1995). For the most part, the adjustment of children from divorced and remarried families is similar (Amato & Keith, 1991a; Cherlin & Furstenberg, 1994). Children from divorced and remarried families are more likely than children from nondivorced families to have academic problems, to exhibit externalizing behaviors and internalizing disorders, to be less socially responsible and competent, and to have lower self-esteem (Amato & Keith, 1991a; Cherlin & Furstenberg, 1994; Hetherington, 1989). They have problems in their relationships with parents, siblings, and peers (Amato & Keith, 1991b; Hetherington, 1997).

Normative developmental tasks of adolescence and young adulthood, such as attaining intimate relationships and increasing social and economic autonomy, seem to be especially difficult for youths from divorced and remarried families. Adolescents from divorced and remarried families exhibit some of the same behavior problems found in childhood and, in addition, are more likely to drop out of school, to be unemployed, to become sexually active at an earlier age, to have children out of wedlock, to be involved in delinquent activities and substance abuse, and to associate with antisocial peers (Amato & Keith, 1991a; Conger & Chao, 1996; Demo & Acock, 1996; Elder & Russell, 1996; Hetherington & Clingempeel, 1992; McLanahan & Sandefur, 1994; Simons & Chao, 1996; Whitbeck, Simons, & Goldberg, 1996). Increased rates of dropping out of high school and of low socioeconomic attainment in the offspring of divorced and remarried families extend across diverse ethnic groups (Amato & Keith, 1991b); however, the effect is stronger for females than for males (Hetherington, in press).

Adult offspring from divorced and remarried families continue to have more adjustment problems (Chase-Lansdale, Cherlin, & Kiernan, 1995; Hetherington, in press), are less satisfied with their lives, experience lower socioeconomic attainment, and are more likely to be on welfare (Amato & Keith, 1991b). Marital instability also is higher for adults from divorced and remarried families (Amato & Keith, 1991b; Glenn & Kramer, 1985; Hetherington, in press; McLanahan & Bumpass, 1988; Tzeng & Mare, 1995), in part because of the presence of a set of risk factors for divorce, including early sexual activity, adolescent childbearing and marriage, and cohabitation (Booth & Edwards, 1990; Hetherington, 1997). In addition, in comparison with young adults from nondivorced families, young adults from divorced and remarried families exhibit more reciprocated, escalating, negative exchanges, including denial, belligerence, criticism, and contempt, and less effective problem solving during their marital interactions (Hetherington, in press). This pattern is probably related to the intergenerational transmission of divorce, which is reported to be 70% higher in the first five years of marriage for adult women from divorced families than for those whose parents have remained married (Bumpass, Martin, & Sweet, 1991).

Although there is considerable consensus that, on average, offspring from divorced and remarried families exhibit more problems in adjustment than do those in nondivorced, two-parent families, there is less agreement on the size of these effects. Some researchers report that these effects are relatively modest, have become smaller as marital transitions have become more common (Amato & Keith, 1991a), and are considerably reduced when the adjustment of children preceding the marital transition is controlled (Block, Block, & Gjerde, 1986, 1988; Cherlin et al., 1991). However, others note that approximately 20%–25% of children in divorced and remarried families, in contrast to 10% of children in nondivorced families, have these problems, which is a notable twofold increase (Hetherington, 1989, 1991b; Hetherington & Clingempeel, 1992; Hetherington & Jodl, 1994; McLanahan & Sandefur, 1994; Simons & Associates, 1996; Zill, Morrison, & Coiro, 1993). Because these difficulties in adjustment tend to co-occur and appear as a single behavior-problem cluster (Jessor & Jessor, 1977; Mekos, Hetherington, & Reiss, 1996), the vast majority of children from divorced families and stepfamilies do not have these problems and eventually develop into reasonably competent individuals functioning within the normal range of adjustment (Emery & Forehand, 1994). This argument is not intended to minimize the importance of the increase in adjustment problems associated with divorce and remarriage nor to belittle the fact that children often report their parents' marital transitions to be their most painful life experience. It is intended to underscore the research evidence supporting the ability of most children to cope with their parents' divorce and remarriage and to counter the position that children are permanently blighted by their parents' marital transitions.

We turn now to an examination of some of the individual, social, economic, and family factors that contribute to the diversity in children's adjustment in divorced and remarried families. Each factor is discussed as it relates to the five perspectives on marital transitions.

Individual Risk and Vulnerability of Parents Associated With Divorce and Remarriage

Some adults have attributes that increase their probability not only of having dysfunctional marital relationships but also for having other problematic social relationships within and outside of the family, displaying inept parenting behaviors, encountering stressful life events, and having decreased psychological well-being (Amato & Booth, 1996; Block et al., 1986). Longitudinal studies have found that, in adults as well as in children, many of the problems attributed to divorce and remarriage and their concomitant life changes were present before these transitions occurred.

Although psychological distress and disorders may increase after divorce, parents who later divorce are more likely preceding divorce to be neurotic, depressed, antisocial, or alcoholic; to have economic problems (Amato, 1993; Capaldi & Patterson, 1991; Forgatch et al., 1995; Gotlib & McCabe, 1990); and to have dysfunctional beliefs about relationships (Baucom & Epstein, 1990; Kelly & Conley, 1987; Kurdek; 1993). In their marital interactions, they exhibit poor problem-solving and conflict resolution skills, thus escalating reciprocation of negative affect, contempt, denial, withdrawal, and stable, negative attributions about their spouses' behavior, which in turn significantly increase their risk for marital dissolution and multiple divorces (Bradbury & Fincham, 1990; Fincham, Bradbury, & Scott, 1990; Gottman, 1993, 1994; Gottman & Levenson, 1992; Matthews, Wickrama, & Conger, 1996). Sometimes these patterns are later found in the marital relationships of their adult offspring (Hetherington, in press). In relationships with their children, parents whose marriages will later be disrupted are more irritable, erratic, and nonauthoritative as much as 8–12 years prior to divorce (Amato & Booth, 1996; Block et al., 1988). These factors contribute to problems in children's adjustment and family relations in nondivorced families, single-parent families, and stepfamilies.

Children's Individual Risk, Vulnerability, and Resiliency Associated With Adjustment to Divorce and Remarriage

In accord with the individual risk perspective, characteristics of children may make them vulnerable or protect them from the adverse consequences or risks associated with their parents' divorce or remarriage. Some of these attributes influence the experiences and adjustment of children long before marital transitions occur.

Children's Adjustment Preceding Divorce and Remarriage

Children whose parents later divorce exhibit poorer adjustment before the breakup (Amato & Booth, 1996; Amato & Keith, 1991a; Block et al., 1986; Cherlin et al., 1991). When antecedent levels of problem behaviors are controlled, differences in problem behaviors between children from divorced and nondivorced families are greatly reduced (Cherlin et al., 1991; Guidubaldi, Perry, & Nastasi, 1987). Several alternative interpretations of these findings can be made. First, it is likely that maladapted parents, dysfunctional family relationships, and inept parenting already have taken their toll on children's adjustment before a divorce occurs. Second, divorce may be, in part, a result of having to deal with a difficult child. Third, personality problems in a parent, such as emotionality and lack of self-regulation, that lead to both divorce and inept socialization practices also may be genetically linked to behavior problems in children (Jockin, McGue, & Lykken, 1996; McGue & Lykken, 1992).

Children in stepfamilies also exhibit more behavior problems before remarriage occurs, and some researchers have speculated that the adaptive difficulties of stepchildren may be largely the result of experiences in divorced families (Furstenberg, 1988). This seems unlikely, because there is an increase in adjustment problems immediately after a marital transition, and because children in newly remarried families show more problems than those in stabilized, divorced, one-parent households (Hetherington & Clingempeel, 1992) or than those in longer remarried, stabilized stepfamilies (Hetherington & Jodl, 1994).

Personality and Temperament

Children who have easy temperaments; who are intelligent, socially mature, and responsible; and who exhibit few behavior problems are better able to cope with their parents' marital transitions. Stresses associated with divorce and remarriage are likely to exacerbate existing problems in children (Block et al., 1986; Elder, Caspi, & Van Nguyen, 1992; Hetherington, 1989, 1991b). In particular, children with difficult temperaments or behavior problems may elicit negative responses from their parents

who are stressed in coping with their marital transitions. These children also may be less able to adapt to parental negativity when it occurs and may be less adept at gaining the support of people around them (Hetherington, 1989, 1991b; Rutter, 1987). Competent, adaptable children with social skills and attractive personal characteristics, such as an easy temperament and a sense of humor, are more likely to evoke positive responses and support and to maximize the use of available resources that help them negotiate stressful experiences (Hetherington, 1989; Werner, 1988).

Developmental Status

Developmental status and gender are the child characteristics most extensively researched in relation to adaptation to divorce and remarriage; however, the results of these studies have been inconsistent. Investigations of children's age at divorce must consider both age at the time of the marital transition and age at the time of assessment. In most studies, these variables are confounded with the length of time since the divorce or remarriage occurred. Some researchers have found that preschool-age children whose parents divorce are at greater risk for long-term problems in social and emotional development than are older children (Allison & Furstenberg, 1989; Zill et al., 1993). It has been suggested that younger children may be less able to appraise realistically the causes and consequences of divorce, may be more anxious about the possibility of total abandonment, may be more likely to blame themselves for the divorce, and may be less able to utilize extrafamilial protective resources (Hetherington, 1989). This greater vulnerability of young children to divorce has not been reported by other investigators (Amato & Keith, 1991a).

In contrast, early adolescence seems to be an especially difficult time in which to have a remarriage occur. Early adolescents are less able to adapt to parental remarriage than are younger children or late adolescents (Hetherington, 1993; Hetherington & Clingempeel, 1992), perhaps because the presence of a stepparent exacerbates normal early adolescent concerns about autonomy and sexuality. In addition, adolescence and young adulthood are periods in which problems in adjustment may emerge or increase, even when divorce or remarriage has occurred much earlier (Amato & Keith, 1991a, 1991b; Bray & Berger, 1993; Hetherington, 1993, in press; Hetherington & Clingempeel, 1992; Hetherington & Jodl, 1994).

Gender

Although earlier studies frequently reported gender differences in response to divorce and remarriage, with divorce being more deleterious for boys and remarriage for girls (Hetherington, 1989), more recent studies have found that gender differences in response to divorce are less pronounced and consistent than was previously believed (Amato & Keith, 1991a). Some of the inconsistencies may be attributable to the fact that fathers' custody, joint custody, and the involvement of noncustodial fathers are increasing and that involvement of fathers may be more important for boys than for girls (Amato & Keith, 1991a; Clarke-Stewart & Hayward, 1996; Lindner-Gunnoe, 1993; Zill, 1988).

Some research has shown that boys respond to divorce with increases in conduct disorders and girls with increases in depression (Emery, 1982); however, both male and female adolescents from divorced and remarried families show higher rates of conduct disorders and depression than do those from nondivorced families (Amato & Keith, 1991a; Hetherington, 1993; Hetherington & Clingempeel, 1992; Hetherington & Jodl, 1994). Female adolescents and young adults from divorced and remarried families are more likely than their male counterparts to drop out of high school and college. Male and female adolescents are similarly affected in the likelihood of becoming teenage parents; however, single parenthood has more adverse effects on the lives of female adolescents (McLanahan & Sandefur, 1994). Female young adults from divorced and remarried families are vulnerable to declining socioeconomic status because of the sequelae of adolescent childbearing and school dropout. These sequelae are compounded in stepdaughters by early home leaving, which they attribute to family conflict (Cherlin & Furstenberg, 1994; Hetherington, 1997, in press).

Some girls in divorced, mother-headed families emerge as exceptionally resilient individuals, enhanced by confronting the increases in challenges and responsibilities that follow divorce (Hetherington, 1989, 1991b; Werner, 1993). Such enhancement is not found for boys following marital transitions or for girls in stepfamilies (Hetherington, 1989, 1991b). Boys, especially preadolescent boys, are more likely than girls to benefit from being in stepfather families (Amato & Keith, 1991a; Hetherington, 1993). Close relationships with supportive stepfathers are more likely to reduce antisocial behavior and to enhance the achievement of stepsons than of stepdaughters (Amato & Keith, 1991a; Hetherington, 1993; Lindner-Gunnoe, 1993; Zimiles & Lee, 1991). Girls are at greater increased risk than are boys for poor adjustment and low achievement when they are in either stepfather or stepmother families rather than in nondivorced families (Lee, Burkam, Zimiles, & Ladewski, 1994; Zimiles & Lee, 1991).

Some research suggests that living in stepfamilies is more beneficial to Black adolescents than to White adolescents, although these effects vary by gender. In contrast to the findings for White youths, young Black women in stepfamilies have the same rate of teenage parenthood as do those in two-parent, nondivorced families, and young Black men in stepfamilies are at no greater risk to drop out of high school than are those in two-parent families (McLanahan & Sandefur, 1994). McLanahan and Sandefur proposed that the income, supervision, and role models provided by stepfathers may be more advantageous for Black children because they are more likely than White children to live in more disorganized neighborhoods with fewer resources and social controls.

Family Composition–Parental Absence and the Adjustment of Children

The family composition or parental absence perspective proposes that a deviation in structure from a family with two first-married parents, biologically related to their children, is associated with increases in problem behavior in children. Two parents can provide support to each other, especially in their child rearing, as well as multiple role models and increased resources, supervision, and involvement for their children (Amato, 1995; Demo & Acock, 1996; Dornbusch et al., 1985; Furstenberg, Morgan, & Allison, 1987; Lamb, 1997). If father unavailability or absence is a critical factor in divorce, father custody or contact with a noncustodial parent, stepfather, or father surrogate should enhance children's adjustment. Furthermore, children who experience loss of their fathers through divorce or death should exhibit similar adjustment problems. Less theorizing has focused on mother absence, although similar hypotheses might be proposed for mothers.

Children and adults from homes with an absent parent due to either divorce or death have more problems in adjustment than do those in nondivorced families; however, significantly more problems are found in academic achievement, socioeconomic attainment, and conduct disorders for offspring from divorced families (Amato & Keith, 1991a; Felner, Ginter, Boike, & Cowen, 1981; Felner, Stolberg, & Cowen, 1975; Hetherington, 1972). Although children of both divorced and widowed women suffer the loss of their fathers and economic declines, the finding suggests that other factors moderate the differences in their outcomes. One of these factors may be greater support and involvement with the extended family, especially that of the lost parent's family, following death but not divorce (Hetherington, 1972). Another may be the greater conflict in families preceding divorce but not the death of a parent (Amato & Keith, 1991a).

The parental absence hypothesis also suggests that contact with noncustodial parents or joint custody should promote children's well-being; however, contact with both noncustodial mothers and fathers diminishes rapidly following divorce. More than 20% of children have no contact with their noncustodial fathers or see them only a few times a year, and only about one quarter of children have weekly visits with their divorced fathers (Seltzer, 1991). Black noncustodial fathers have higher rates of both regular contact and no contact with their children than do non-Hispanic White fathers (McLanahan & Sandefur, 1994). Decreased paternal involvement is related to residential distance, low socioeconomic status, and parental remarriage (Seltzer, 1991). Seltzer and Brandreth (1994) noted that custodial mothers serve as "gatekeepers" (Ahrons, 1983), controlling noncustodial fathers' access to and the conditions of visits with their children. When conflict, resentment, and anger are high, the "gate" may be closed, and fathers may be discouraged or shut out. In contrast, when there is low conflict between divorced spouses, when mediation is used (Dillon & Emery, 1996), or when noncustodial fathers feel they have some control over decisions in their children's lives (Braver et al., 1993; Seltzer, 1991), paternal contact and child support payments are more likely to be maintained.

In contrast, noncustodial mothers are more likely than noncustodial fathers to sustain contact with their children and to rearrange their living situations to facilitate children's visits. They maintain approximately twice as much contact with their children as noncustodial fathers do and are less likely to completely drop out of their children's lives or to diminish contact when either parent remarries (Furstenberg & Nord, 1987; Furstenberg, Nord, Peterson, & Zill, 1983; Lindner-Gunnoe, 1993; Santrock, Sitterle, & Warshak, 1988; White, 1994; Zill, 1988). In addition, there is some evidence that noncustodial mothers, like noncustodial fathers, are more likely to maintain contact with sons than with daughters (Lindner-Gunnoe, 1993), although the preferential contact of fathers with sons is larger and more consistently obtained than that of mothers (Amato & Booth, 1991).

There is little support for the position that sheer frequency of contact facilitates positive adjustment in children (Amato & Keith, 1991a; King, 1994a, 1994b). However, as we discuss at greater length in the Family Process and the Adjustment to Divorce and Remarriage section, under conditions of low interparental conflict, contact with competent, supportive, authoritative noncustodial parents can have beneficial effects for children, and these effects are most marked for noncustodial parents and children of the same sex (Hetherington, 1989; Lindner-Gunnoe, 1993; Zill, 1988) Thus, it is the quality of contact, rather than the frequency, that is important (Amato, 1993; Emery, 1988; Furstenberg & Cherlin, 1991).

Research on custodial arrangements also has found few advantages of joint custody over sole residential custody. In a large study of custody in California, Maccoby and Mnookin (1992) found adolescents in the custody of their fathers had higher rates of delinquency, perhaps because of poorer monitoring by fathers. A meta-analysis of divorce by Amato and Keith (1991a), however, did not support the findings of poorer adjustment in children in families in which fathers have custody.

A corollary to the parental absence hypothesis would suggest that the addition of a stepparent might compensate for the loss of a parent. However, the family composition perspective implies that it is not only the presence of two parents but also biological relatedness to the parents that matter. Although divorce involves the exit of a family member, remarriage involves the restructuring of the family constellation with the entrance of a stepparent and sometimes stepsiblings. Predictions made about stepfamilies on the basis of the family composition hypothesis are unclear. On the one hand, the presence of a stepparent might compensate for the loss of the noncustodial parent by restoring a two-parent household. On the other hand, the child must confront an additional transition to another family with a nontraditional composition involving the addition of nonbiologically related family members to the household. In a family in which both divorced parents remarry, much more complex kin networks are created within and outside the household in a linked family system (Jacobson, 1982) or a binuclear family (Ahrons, 1979). A child's expanded kin networks may include stepsiblings, half siblings, and stepgrandparents, as well as stepparents and biologically related kin, and represent a marked deviation from the composition of the nondivorced nuclear family (Booth & Edwards, 1992; Bray, 1987, 1988; Bray, Berger, & Boethel, 1994; Burrell, 1995; Cherlin & Furstenberg, 1994; Giles-Sims, 1987).

Stress, Socioeconomic Disadvantage, and the Adjustment to Divorce and Remarriage

The stress perspective attributes problems in the adjustment of children from divorced and remarried families to the increased stresses experienced in these families. Parents and children living in divorced families encounter a diverse array of stressful life events (Hetherington, Cox, & Cox, 1985; Simons et al., 1996). Both custodial mothers and fathers complain of task overload and social isolation as they juggle household, child-care, and financial responsibilities that are usually dealt with by two parents (Hetherington & Stanley Hagan, 1997). Noncustodial parents express concerns associated with the establishment of new residences, social networks, and intimate relationships; loss of children; problems with visitation arrangements; and continued difficulties in relations with their exspouses (Hetherington, 1989, 1991b; Hetherington & Stanley Hagan, 1997; Hoffman, 1995; Minton & Pasley, 1996).

In spite of the diversity in stresses associated with divorce, most attention by sociologists and economists has focused on the marked decrement in the income of custodial mothers following marital dissolution and its accompanying risk factors. Those investigators who support a socioeconomic disadvantage perspective suggest that controlling for income will eliminate or greatly diminish the association between family structure and children's well-being (McLanahan & Sandefur, 1994). In addition, because custodial fathers do not encounter the financial decrements experienced by custodial mothers and because remarriage is the fastest way out of poverty for single mothers, it might be expected that children in father-custody families and stepfamilies will exhibit fewer behavior problems than those in divorced mother-custody households.

Because of increased enforcement of noncustodial fathers' child support payments and changes in the labor force for women, it has been speculated that custodial mothers and their children may no longer experience such drastic economic declines following divorce. A recent review (Bianchi, Subaiya, & Kahn, 1997) suggests, however, that custodial mothers still experience the loss of approximately one quarter to one half of their predivorce income in comparison to only 10% by custodial fathers following divorce (Arendell, 1986; Cherlin, 1992; Emery, 1994; McLanahan & Booth, 1989). For custodial mothers, this loss in income is accompanied by increased workloads; high rates of job instability; and residential moves to less desirable neighborhoods with poor schools, inadequate services, often high crime rates, and deviant peer populations (McLanahan & Booth, 1989; McLanahan & Sandefur, 1994).

Although father-only families have substantially higher incomes than do families with divorced custodial mothers, a significant number of father-only families (18%) live in poverty, and fathers rarely receive child support (Meyer & Garasky, 1993). However, most father-custody families have financial, housing, child-care, and educational resources not available to divorced custodial mothers. Custodial fathers report less child-rearing stress than do custodial mothers, and their children show fewer problems (Amato & Keith, 1991a; Clarke-Stewart & Hayward, 1996). This could be attributed to economic advantages in father-custody families; however, even with income controlled, children in father-custody families—especially boys—show greater well-being than those in mother-custody families (Clarke-Stewart & Hayward, 1996).

Newly repartnered parents and their children report higher levels of both positive and negative life changes than do those in never-divorced families (Forgatch et al., 1995; Hetherington et al., 1985). Although there is a marked increase in income for divorced mothers following remarriage, conflicts over finances, child rearing, and family relations remain potent problems in stepfamilies (Bray & Berger, 1993; Hetherington, 1993; Hetherington & Jodl, 1994). The economic improvement conferred by remarriage is not reflected in the improved adjustment of children in stepfamilies, and the new stresses associated with remarriage often counter the benefits associated with increased income (Amato & Booth, 1991; Bray & Berger, 1993; Cherlin & Furstenberg, 1994; Demo & Acock, 1996; Forgatch et al., 1995; Hetherington & Clingempeel, 1992; Hetherington & Jodl, 1994).

Parental Distress and the Adjustment to Divorce and Remarriage

Investigators taking the parental distress perspective propose that stressors affect children's adjustment through parental distress and diminished well-being (Bank, Duncan, Patterson, & Reid, 1993; Forgatch et al., 1995; Lorenz et al., 1996; Simons & Beaman, 1996; Simons, Beaman, Conger, & Chao, 1992; Simons & Johnson, 1996). In this view, it is the parents' response to stress, rather than the stress itself, that is most salient for children's adjustment.

Signs of diminished parental well-being and distress, including anger, anxiety, depression, loneliness, impulsivity, feelings of being externally controlled, and emotional lability, may emerge or increase in the immediate aftermath of divorce (Hetherington, 1989, 1993; Pearlin & Johnson, 1977). In addition, newly remarried parents are often depressed or preoccupied as they cope with the challenges of their new family life (Hetherington & Clingempeel, 1992; Hetherington & Jodl, 1994). The mental health of parents in divorced and remarried families is related to children's adjustment through diminished competence in their parenting (Clarke-Stewart & Hayward, 1996; Forgatch et al., 1995; Hetherington, 1993; Lorenz et al., 1996; Simons, 1996).

The stresses associated with marital transitions place both residential and nonresidential parents at risk not only for psychological disorders (Hetherington, 1989, 1991b; Kitson & Morgan, 1990; Stack, 1989; Travato & Lauris, 1989) but also for disruption in immune system functioning (Kiecolt-Glaser et al., 1988) and concomitant increased rates of illness and morbidity, which are notable in divorced adults, especially in men (Burman & Margolin, 1992; Hu & Goldman, 1990; Riessman & Gerstel, 1985). Nonresidential fathers engage in more health-compromising and impulsive behaviors, such as alcohol consumption, than do fathers in any other family type

(Umberson, 1987; Umberson & Williams, 1993) and are overrepresented among suicides and homicides (Bloom, Asher, & White, 1978).

Although depression remains higher in divorced women than in nondivorced women, by two years after divorce, women show less depression and more psychological well-being than do those who remain in conflict-ridden marriages with husbands who undermine their discipline and feelings of competence. The well-being of both men and women increases after the formation of a mutually caring, intimate relationship, such as a remarriage (Hetherington, 1993). Most parents do adapt to their new marital situation, with concomitant decreases in psychological and physical problems. In support of the parental distress perspective, even temporary disruptions in parents' health, social, and psychological functioning may make it difficult to be competent in parenting children who may be confused, angry, and apprehensive about a divorce or remarriage, and this inept parenting adversely affects children's adjustment (Chase-Lansdale & Hetherington, 1990; Emery, 1988; Emery & Dillon, 1994; Hetherington, 1989; Hetherington & Stanley Hagan, 1995; Maccoby & Mnookin, 1992).

Family Process and the Adjustment to Divorce and Remarriage

Divorce and remarriage confront families with changes and challenges associated with pervasive alterations in family roles and functioning. The changes in family relationships can support or undermine the efforts of children to adapt to their new family situations. Proponents of the family process perspective argue that the impact of parental attributes, changes in family structure, socioeconomic disadvantage, and parental distress on children's adjustment is largely mediated by disruptions in family relationships and interactions, such as those involved in discipline and child-rearing practices (Demo & Acock, 1996; Forgatch et al., 1995; Hetherington, 1993; Simons & Beaman, 1996; Simons & Johnson, 1996). Without disruptions in family functioning, the former risk factors are less likely to compromise children's adjustment.

Relationships Between Divorced Couples

Marital conflict is associated with a wide range of deleterious outcomes for children, including depression, poor social competence and academic performance, and conduct disorders (Amato & Keith, 1991a; Cowan & Cowan, 1990; Davies & Cummings, 1994; Forehand, Brody, Long, Slotkin, & Fauber, 1986; Gottman & Katz, 1989; Peterson & Zill, 1986). Conflict, contempt, anger, and acrimony often antecede divorce, and in the immediate aftermath of marital disruption, conflict may escalate. Consequently, one of the most frequently asked questions about divorce is whether parents should stay together in an unhappy, conflict-ridden marriage for the sake of the children.

The hypothesis that conflict is a major contributor to problems in divorced families is substantiated by evidence that children in high-conflict, nondivorced families have more problems in psychological adjustment and self-esteem than do those in divorced families or in low-conflict, nondivorced families (Amato & Keith, 1991a; Amato, Loomis, & Booth, 1995). In addition, longitudinal prospective studies of divorce indicate that divorce improves the adjustment of children removed from contentious marriages but is deleterious for children whose parents had less overtly conflictual relationships preceding divorce (Amato et al., 1995). When measures of marital dissatisfaction rather than conflict are used, the advantages of divorce over unhappy marital situations are less marked (Simons, 1996) because many couples in unsatisfying marriages may not exhibit overt conflict (Gottman, 1994).

Although contact and conflict between divorced couples diminish over time, they remain higher for couples with children as they attempt to negotiate coparenting relationships and economic responsibilities (Masheter, 1991). Despite the fact that cooperative, mutually supportive, and nonconfrontational coparenting relationships are advantageous to parents and children, only about one quarter of divorced parents attain such relationships and an approximately equal number maintain acrimonious relationships (Maccoby & Mnookin, 1992). Most coparenting relationships after divorce evolve into parallel coparenting relationships not only with little communication or coordination of parenting but also with lessened conflict because of the disengaged relationships. Cooperative coparenting is most likely to occur when family size is small and when there was little conflict at the time of divorce (Maccoby, Buchanan, Mnookin, & Dornbusch, 1993). With little conflict and cooperative coparenting, children adapt better not only to their parents' divorce but also to their parents' remarriages, and they tend to have more positive relations with their stepparents (Bray & Berger, 1993; Crosbie-Burnett, 1991).

The sheer frequency of conflict may not be as detrimental as the type of conflict. Conflicts in which children are caught in the middle while parents denigrate each other, precipitate loyalty conflicts, communicate through the children, or fight about the children are most destructive to children's well-being (Buchanan, Maccoby, & Dornbusch, 1991; Maccoby et al., 1993; Maccoby & Mnookin, 1992). Children in highly conflicted families not only are more distressed but also may learn to exploit and mislead their parents and to escape monitoring of their activities when they are older (Hetherington, Law, & O'Connor, 1992). Even when children are not directly involved in their parents' conflicts, the adverse effects of conflicts may be experienced through increased parental irritability and diminished monitoring, support, and involvement (Patterson, 1991).

Relationships of Custodial Mothers and Children

Children in both mother- and father-custody families show more problems than do children in nondivorced families; however, most offspring in both types of divorced families eventually are reasonably well-adjusted. Because approximately 84% of children reside with their mothers following divorce (Seltzer, 1994), most studies of parent–child relations following marital dissolution have involved custodial mothers. Close relationships with

supportive, authoritative mothers who are warm but exert firm, consistent control and supervision are generally associated with positive adjustment in children and adolescents (Bray & Berger, 1993; Forehand, Thomas, Wierson, Brody, & Fauber, 1990; Hetherington, 1989, 1993; Hetherington & Clingempeel, 1992; Maccoby et al., 1993; Simons & Johnson, 1996). In the immediate aftermath of divorce, there is a period of disrupted parenting characterized by irritability and coercion and diminished communication, affection, consistency, control, and monitoring (Hetherington, 1991a, 1991b, 1993; Simons & Johnson, 1996).

The parenting of divorced mothers improves over the course of the two years following divorce but remains less authoritative than that of nondivorced mothers, and problems in control and coercive exchanges between divorced mothers and sons may remain high (Hetherington, 1991a). Even in adulthood, relationships between sons and divorced mothers are less close than those in nondivorced families, whereas differences in closeness are not found for daughters (Booth & Amato, 1994). Preadolescent girls and their divorced mothers often have close, companionate, confiding relationships; however, in adolescence, there is a notable increase in conflict in these relationships (Hetherington, 1991a; Hetherington & Clingempeel, 1992). In comparison with adolescents in nondivorced, two-parent families, adolescents in divorced families and in stepfamilies experience the highest levels of mother–adolescent disagreements and the lowest levels of parental supervision (Demo & Acock, 1996). Both conflictive, negative parent–adolescent relationships and lack of monitoring are associated with involvement with antisocial peers—one of the most potent pathways to the development of delinquency, alcoholism, substance abuse, and teenage sexual activity and childbearing (Conger & Reuter, 1996; Hetherington, 1993; Simons & Chao, 1996; Whitbeck et al., 1996).

About one quarter to one third of adolescents in divorced and remarried families, in comparison with 10% of adolescents in nondivorced families, become disengaged from their families, spending as little time at home as possible and avoiding interactions, activities, and communication with family members (Hetherington, 1993; Hetherington & Jodl, 1994). This incidence is greater for boys in divorced families and for girls in stepfamilies. If disengagement is associated with lack of adult support and supervision and with involvement in a delinquent peer group, it leads to both antisocial behavior and academic problems in adolescents (Hetherington, 1993; Patterson, DeBaryshe, & Ramsey, 1989). However, if there is a caring adult involved with the adolescent outside of the home, such as the parent of a friend, a teacher, a neighbor, or a coach, disengagement may be a positive solution to a disrupted, conflictual family situation (Hetherington, 1993).

It has been noted that children in divorced families grow up faster, in part, because of early assignment of responsibilities (Weiss, 1979), more autonomous decision making (Dornbusch et al., 1985), and lack of adult supervision (Hetherington, 1991a; Thomson, McLanahan, & Curtin, 1992). Assignment of responsibility may be associated with resilience and unusual social competence in girls from divorced families; yet, if the task demands are beyond the children's capabilities, they also may be associated with low self-esteem, anxiety, and depression (Hetherington, 1989, in press). Furthermore, if adolescents perceive themselves as being unfairly burdened with responsibilities that interfere with their other activities, they may respond with resentment, rebellion, and noncompliance.

The restabilizing of family relations following a remarriage takes considerably longer than that following a divorce (Cherlin & Furstenberg, 1994). Whereas a new homeostasis is established in about two to three years following divorce, it has been estimated that the adjustment to remarriage may take as long as five to seven years (Cherlin & Furstenberg, 1994; Papernow, 1988; Visher & Visher, 1990). Because more than one quarter of remarriages are terminated within five years, with higher rates for families with children, restabilization never occurs in many stepfamilies.

In the first year following a remarriage, custodial mothers engage in less affective involvement, less behavior control and monitoring, and more negativity than nondivorced mothers (Bray & Berger, 1993; Hetherington, 1993; Hetherington & Clingempeel, 1992). Negative mother–child interactions are related to more disengagement, dysfunctional family roles, poorer communication, and less cohesion in stepfamilies (Bray, 1990). However, in long-established remarriages, the parenting of custodial mothers with their biological offspring becomes increasingly similar to that in nondivorced families (Bray & Berger, 1993; Hetherington, 1993; Hetherington & Clingempeel, 1992; Hetherington & Jodl, 1994).

Relationships of Custodial Fathers and Children

Although children usually live with their mothers following the dissolution of their parents' marriage, father-headed families have tripled since 1974, making them the fastest growing family type in the United States (Meyer & Garasky, 1993). Arrangements about physical custody are often made on the basis of personal decisions by parents and not on judicial decree, and the preponderance of maternal physical custody, even when joint legal custody has been granted, may reflect concerns fathers have about assuming full-time parenting (Maccoby et al., 1993; Maccoby & Mnookin, 1992). Boys and older children are more likely to be placed in father-only custody, but some girls and young children do live with their fathers. In contrast to custodial mothers, custodial fathers are a very select group of fathers who may be more child-oriented than most fathers. Fathers who seek custody of their children are more involved and capable than those fathers who have custody thrust on them because the mothers were unwilling or incompetent to parent (Hanson, 1988; Mendes, 1976a, 1976b). Once their families have restabilized, custodial fathers report less child-rearing stress, better parent–child relations, and fewer behavior problems in their children than do custodial mothers (Amato & Keith, 1991a; Clarke-Stewart & Hayward, 1996; Furstenberg, 1988).

There are different strengths and weaknesses in the parenting of custodial mothers and fathers. Although custodial mothers and custodial fathers are perceived to be similarly warm and nurturing with younger children (Warshak, 1986), mothers have more problems with control and with assignment of household tasks, whereas fathers have more problems with communication, self-disclosure, and monitoring of their children's activities (Chase-Lansdale & Hetherington, 1990; Furstenberg, 1988; Warshak, 1986). Moreover, fathers have special difficulties with monitoring adolescents' behavior, especially that of daughters (Buchanan, Maccoby, & Dornbusch, 1992; Maccoby et al., 1993).

Recent evidence indicates that adolescent adjustment is more predictable from the parenting of a custodial parent of the same sex than one of the opposite sex (Lindner-Gunnoe, 1993). This evidence parallels findings of the greater salience of same-sex parents in the adjustment of adolescents in nondivorced families (Furman & Buhrmester, 1992; Kurdek & Fine, 1993). In spite of this greater influence of same-sex custodial parents, both sons and daughters report feeling closer to their custodial parent than to their noncustodial parent, regardless of whether the parent is a mother or a father (Hetherington & Clingempeel, 1992; Maccoby et al., 1993; White, Brinkerhoff, & Booth, 1985).

As has been found with mothers, when custodial fathers remarry, there are disruptions in father–child relationships, especially with daughters (Clingempeel, Brand, & Ievoli, 1984). Fathers may alter their caretaking relationships more radically than mothers do because fathers are more likely to expect a stepmother to play a major role in household tasks and parenting (Hetherington & Stanley Hagan, 1995). However, in long-established stepfamilies, there are few differences in parent–child relations between remarried fathers and their residential biological children and those fathers and children in nondivorced families (Hetherington & Jodl, 1994).

Relationships of Noncustodial Mothers and Children

Although less is known about noncustodial mothers than noncustodial fathers, nonresidential mothers maintain more contact with their children than do nonresidential fathers. It is not only in the quantity but also in the quality of parent–child relationships that these mothers and fathers differ. Noncustodial mothers are less adept than custodial mothers in controlling and monitoring their children's behavior, but they are more effective in these parenting behaviors than are noncustodial fathers (Furstenberg & Nord, 1987; Lindner-Gunnoe, 1993). Children report that noncustodial mothers are more interested in and informed about their activities; are more supportive, sensitive, and responsive to their needs; and are more communicative than noncustodial fathers (Furstenberg & Nord, 1987; Lindner-Gunnoe, 1993; Santrock & Sitterle, 1987). Therefore, it is not surprising that children report talking more about their problems and activities and feeling closer to noncustodial mothers than to noncustodial fathers (Lindner-Gunnoe, 1993), nor that noncustodial mothers have more influence over their children's development, especially their daughters' adjustment, than do noncustodial fathers (Brand, Clingempeel, & Bowen-Woodward, 1988; Lindner-Gunnoe, 1993; Zill, 1988). Noncustodial mothers' warmth, support, and monitoring enhance their children's scholastic achievement and diminish antisocial, externalizing problems (Lindner-Gunnoe, 1993). In appraising some research findings that children have fewer problems in the custody of fathers than in the custody of mothers (Amato & Keith, 1991a; Clarke-Stewart & Hayward, 1996), it must be considered that part of this effect may be attributable to the more active involvement of noncustodial mothers.

When a custodial father remarries, closeness to the noncustodial mother can have some disadvantages because it is related to children's lack of acceptance of a stepmother. In contrast, there is no association between the relationship with a noncustodial father and building a close relationship with a stepfather (Hetherington, 1993; Hetherington & Jodl, 1994; White, 1994).

Relationships of Noncustodial Fathers and Children

In contrast to mothers' behavior, the postdivorce parenting behavior of fathers is less predictable from their predivorce behavior (Hetherington et al., 1985). Some previously attached and involved fathers find the enforced marginality and intermittent contact in being noncustodial fathers to be painful, and they drift away from their children. Other fathers, especially custodial fathers, rise to the occasion and increase their involvement and parenting competence. However, most nonresidential fathers have a friendly, egalitarian, companionate relationship rather than a traditional parental relationship with their children (Arendell, 1986; Furstenberg & Nord, 1987; Hetherington, Cox, & Cox, 1979; Munsch, Woodward, & Darling, 1995). They want their visits to be pleasant and entertaining and are hesitant to assume the role of disciplinarian or teacher. They are less likely than nondivorced fathers to criticize, control, and monitor their children's behavior or to help them with tasks such as homework (Bray & Berger, 1993; Furstenberg & Nord, 1987; Hetherington, 1991b).

Frequency of contact with noncustodial fathers and the adjustment of children are usually found to be unrelated (Amato & Keith, 1991a). Although obviously some degree of contact is essential, it seems to be the quality of the relationship and the circumstances of contact rather than frequency of visits that are most important (Amato, 1993; Emery, 1988; Furstenberg & Cherlin, 1991; Simons & Beaman, 1996). When noncustodial fathers are not just "tour guide" fathers but maintain more parent-like contact, participate in a variety of activities with their children, and spend holidays together, the well-being of children is promoted (Clarke-Stewart & Hayward, 1996). Under conditions of low conflict, the involvement of authoritative noncustodial fathers can enhance children's adjustment (Hetherington, 1989), especially that of boys (Lindner-Gunnoe, 1993). It can even, to some extent, protect the children from the adverse consequences of rejecting or incompetent noncustodial mothers (Hetherington, 1989). In contrast, under conditions of high conflict, frequent contact with noncustodial parents

may exacerbate children's problems (Kline, Johnston, & Tschann, 1991).

Relationships Between Stepparents and Stepchildren

Papernow (1988) commented that the typical starting point for a stepfamily involving "a weak couple subsystem, a tightly bonded parent–child alliance, and potential interference in family functioning from an outsider" (p. 56) would be considered problematic in a traditional non-divorced family. Clinicians have remarked that any stepfamily that uses a traditional nuclear family as its ideal is bound for disappointment (Visher & Visher, 1990). Similar patterns of relationships in traditional families and stepfamilies may lead to different outcomes. Patterns of functioning and family processes that undermine or promote positive adjustment may differ in the two types of families (Bray & Berger, 1993). The complex relationships between families following remarriage may require less rigid family boundaries and more open, less integrated relations among the family subsystems.

Although both stepfathers and stepmothers feel less close to stepchildren than do nondivorced parents to their children, they, if not the stepchildren, want the new marriage to be successful (Brand et al., 1988; Bray & Berger, 1993; Hetherington, 1993; Kurdek & Fine, 1993). In the early stages of a remarriage, stepfathers have been reported to be like polite strangers, trying to ingratiate themselves with their stepchildren by showing less negativity but also less control, monitoring, and affection than do fathers in nondivorced families (Bray & Berger, 1992; Hetherington & Clingempeel, 1992). In longer established stepfamilies, a distant, disengaged parenting style remains the predominant one for stepfathers, but conflict and negativity, especially between stepparents and stepdaughters, can remain high or increase, especially with adolescents (Brand et al., 1988; Bray & Berger, 1993; Hetherington, 1993; Hetherington & Jodl, 1994). Some of the conflict in stepfamilies is due to the negative rejecting behavior of stepchildren toward stepparents (Bray & Berger, 1993; Hetherington & Clingempeel, 1992; Hetherington & Jodl, 1994). Even stepparents with the best intentions may give up in the face of persistent hostile behavior by stepchildren.

Conflict between stepfathers and stepchildren is not necessarily precipitated by the children. In fact, rates of physical abuse perpetrated by stepfathers on their stepchildren are 7 times higher than those by fathers on their biological children, and homicide rates for stepfathers are 100 times higher than those for biological fathers (Daly & Wilson, 1996; Wilson, Daly, & Weghorst, 1980). These differential rates are most marked with infants and preschool-age children (Daly & Wilson, 1996).

Stepmothers have a more difficult time integrating themselves into stepfamilies than do stepfathers. Remarried fathers often expect that the stepmothers will participate in child rearing, forcing the stepmothers into more active, less distant, and more confrontational roles than those required of stepfathers (Brand et al., 1988). Support by the fathers for the stepmothers' parenting and parental agreement on child rearing are especially important in promoting effective parenting in stepmothers (Brand et al., 1988). The assumption of the dominant disciplinarian role is fraught with problems for stepparents (Brand et al., 1988; Bray & Berger, 1993; Hetherington, 1991a), and although authoritative parenting can have salutary effects on stepchildren's adjustment, especially with stepfathers and stepsons, authoritative parenting is not always a feasible option in stepfamilies (Bray & Berger, 1993). When custodial parents are authoritative and when stepparents are warm and involved and support the custodial parents' discipline rather than making independent control attempts, children can be responsive and adjust well (Bray & Berger, 1993; Hetherington, 1989).

It is not only parent–child relationships but also relationships between siblings that are more conflictual and less supportive in divorced families and stepfamilies than in nondivorced families (Hetherington, 1991a). These effects are more marked for biologically related siblings than for stepsiblings (Hetherington & Jodl, 1994). Less involved, harsher parenting is associated with rivalrous, aggressive, and unsupportive sibling relationships in divorced and remarried families (Conger & Conger, 1996; Hetherington, 1991a, 1993; Hetherington & Clingempeel, 1992), and, in turn, these negative sibling relations lead to low social competence and responsibility and to more behavior problems in children (Hetherington & Clingempeel, 1992).

Conclusion: What Matters? What Doesn't?

In reviewing the five perspectives, it is clear that each may influence children's adjustment. The first perspective, the individual risk and vulnerability hypothesis, is supported by evidence suggesting that children and their parents have attributes that directly contribute to their experiencing marital transitions and to having more difficulties in adjusting to them. These problems may be transmitted genetically from parents to children, or the effect on children's adjustment may be indirect, due to parents' ineffective child-rearing strategies. However, individual vulnerability to the adverse outcomes of divorce and remarriage seems to involve a complex interaction among an array of individual attributes, including personality, age, gender, and ethnicity, and the effects of these interactions have been difficult to differentiate.

The family composition–parental absence hypothesis is not as well supported by the evidence. Generally, children in never-divorced families with two parents are more competent than children whose parents have divorced. However, this theory would suggest that children's adjustment should benefit from the addition of a stepparent, yet there are few indications of lower levels of problems in children in stepfamilies as compared with children in divorced families. Furthermore, some studies indicate that especially in the early stages of a remarriage, stepchildren exhibit more difficulties than do children in stabilized, divorced, single-parent families (Amato & Keith, 1991a; Hetherington, 1993; Hetherington & Clingempeel, 1992; Hetherington & Jodl, 1994).

These comments must be qualified by findings indicating that the presence of a stepfather, especially with preadolescent boys, can attenuate problems in adjustment for stepsons, whereas the presence of either a stepmother or a stepfather may be associated with higher levels of problem behaviors for girls (Amato & Keith, 1991a; Hetherington, 1989; Hetherington & Jodl, 1994; Lee et al., 1994). These results, in conjunction with the somewhat inconsistent evidence that boys may also fare better in a father-custody family than in a mother-custody family (Amato & Keith, 1991a; Clarke-Stewart & Hayward, 1996; Zill, 1988), indicate that the presence of a father may have positive effects on the well-being of boys. Rather than rejecting the family composition–parental absence perspective, it should be concluded that there is not a simple main effect of family composition or parental absence but that it is modified by the reason for parental unavailability, the quality of family relationships, and the child's gender.

The findings thus far yield only modest support for marked direct effects of life stress and economic deprivation on children's adjustment. Even when income is controlled, children in divorced families show more problems than do those in nondivorced families (Amato & Keith, 1991a; Clarke-Stewart & Hayward, 1996; Demo & Acock, 1996; Guidubaldi et al., 1987; Hetherington, 1997, in press; Simons & Associates, 1996). In addition, although the income in stepfamilies is only slightly lower than that in nondivorced families, children in these families show a similar level of problem behavior to that in divorced mother-custody families (Amato & Keith, 1991a; Demo & Acock, 1996; Forgatch et al., 1995; Henderson, Hetherington, Mekos, & Reiss, 1996; Simons & Johnson, 1996). Thus, the effects of income do not seem to be primary and are largely indirect.

Some investigators using large-scale survey data report that as much as half of the effects of divorce on children's adjustment is attributable to economic factors (McLanahan & Sandefur, 1994); others find no direct effects of income but a major effect of the quality of family relationships that may alter children's adjustment (Demo & Acock, 1996). Furthermore, in studies in which income has been controlled, differences between offspring in divorced and nondivorced families remain (Amato & Keith, 1991a; Clarke-Stewart & Hayward, 1996; Demo & Acock, 1996; Guidubaldi et al., 1987; Hetherington, in press; Simons & Associates, 1996). Some of the inconsistencies in findings are due to methodological differences in studies. Surveys often have large representative samples but inadequate measures, sometimes involving only two or three items and single informants, to assess parental and family characteristics and family process variables. Studies using smaller, less representative samples but more reliable multimethod, multi-informant assessment, including observations, have found that much of the effects of family structure and economic stress are mediated by inept parenting (Forgatch et al., 1995; Simons & Johnson, 1996). Furthermore, there is some support in the research on stress, economic deprivation, and marital transitions for the individual risk position. As stated earlier, antisocial individuals are at greater risk not only for job instability, economic problems (Simons et al., 1992), and stressful life events but also for divorce (Capaldi & Patterson, 1991; Kitson & Holmes, 1992; Lahey et al., 1988), problems

Figure 1

A Transactional Model of the Predictors of Children's Adjustment Following Divorce and Remarriage

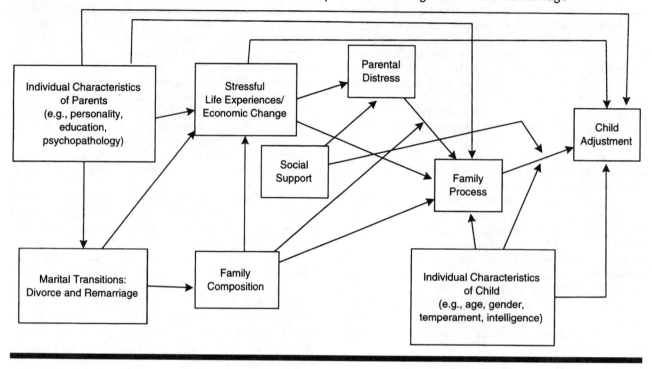

in successive marital relationships (Capaldi & Patterson, 1991), and incompetent parenting (Forgatch et al., 1995; Simons & Johnson, 1996).

Although it is true that parental distress increases in the aftermath of a divorce, research indicates that the effect of parents' well-being is largely mediated through their parenting. Even temporary disruptions in parents' physical and psychological functioning due to a marital transition interfere with their ability to offer support and supervision at a time when children need them most.

Although attributes of parents and children, family composition, stress and socioeconomic disadvantage, and parental distress impact children's adjustment, their effects may be mediated through the more proximal mechanism of family process. Dysfunctional family relationships, such as conflict, negativity, lack of support, and nonauthoritative parenting, exacerbate the effects of divorce and remarriage on children's adjustment. Certainly if divorced or remarried parents are authoritative and their families are harmonious, warm, and cohesive, the differences between the adjustment of children in these families and those in nondivorced families are reduced. However, marital transitions increase the probability that children will not find themselves in families with such functioning. Research on the relationships between family members in nondivorced families and stepfamilies supports the family process hypothesis, suggesting that, in large part, it is negative, conflictual, dysfunctional family relationships between parents, parents and children, and siblings that account for differences in children's adjustment.

It has become fashionable to attempt to estimate the relative contributions of individual attributes, family structure, stresses, parental distress, and family process to the adjustment of children in divorced and remarried families. These attempts have led to conflicting results, futile controversies, and misleading conclusions because the amount of variance explained by the factors differs from sample to sample and varies with the methods and the data analytic strategies used. Moreover, different risk and vulnerability factors are likely to come into play and to vary in salience at different points in the transitions from an unhappy marriage to divorce, to life in a single-parent household, through remarriage, and into subsequent marital transitions. These risk factors will be modified by shifting protective factors and resources.

A transactional model of risks associated with marital transitions is perhaps most appropriate (see Figure 1). Divorce and remarriage increase the probability of parents and children encountering a set of interrelated risks. These risks are linked, interact, and are mediated and moderated in complex ways. These effects are illustrated in the model in different ways. For example, parental distress (e.g., maternal depression) does not have a direct effect on children's adjustment, which is not to say it does not have an impact. Instead, its influence is mediated through its link to family process, specifically the depressed mothers' diminished ability to effectively parent. In contrast, some variables moderate the relationship between other variables, such that the relationship depends on the level of the moderator. For example, children with difficult temperaments are expected to be more adversely affected by disruptions in family functioning than are children with easy temperaments. Thus, individual variables such as temperament can moderate the effect of family process on children's adjustment.

All family members encounter stresses associated with marital transitions, and it may be the balance between risks and resources that determines the impact of stresses on divorced and remarried parents and their children. All five of the factors described at the beginning of this article are associated with divorce and remarriage and with adverse outcomes for children. Studies using path analyses (e.g., Conger & Conger, 1996; Forgatch et al., 1995; Simons & Associates, 1996) have helped illuminate the patterns of linkages among these risks and have suggested that many of the risk factors are mediated by proximal experiences such as disruptions in parent–child or sibling relationships. However, the fact that a path is indirect does not reduce its importance. Figure 1 presents the theoretical model describing the linkages among these factors. A set of individual attributes, such as antisocial behavior, is associated with an increased risk of divorce and an unsuccessful remarriage; problems in social relationships, including parent–child relationships; and stressful life events. All family members encounter stresses as they deal with the changes, challenges, and restructuring of the family associated with marital transitions, but these vary for different family members and for divorce and remarriage. Divorce usually leads to the loss or the diminished availability of a father and the economic, social, and emotional resources he can provide, which increases the probability of poverty and its concomitant environmental and experiential adversities for divorced custodial mothers and their children. Although some of the effects of stresses, such as living in neighborhoods with high crime rates, poor schools, antisocial peers, and few job opportunities or resources, may impact directly on children's adjustment and attainment, other effects of stress in divorced families may be indirect and mediated through parental psychological distress, inept or altered parenting, and disrupted family processes. Stresses associated with the changes and complexities in stepfamilies may also lead to distress and dysfunctional family functioning. Children, because of individual characteristics such as gender, temperament, personality, age, and intelligence, vary in their influence on family process and their vulnerability or resilience in dealing with their parents' divorce and remarriage and concomitant changes in family roles, relationships, and process. Thus, effects of the earlier risk factors on children's adjustment are mediated or moderated by associated transactional risk factors and often eventually by disruptions in family functioning. These indirect or mediated effects do not negate the importance of the earlier risk factors as a link in the transactional path of adversity leading to problems in child adjustment.

Static, cross-sectional slices out of the lives of parents and children in divorced or remarried families give a misleading picture of how risk and protective factors combine to influence the adjustment of children. An examination of the dynamic trajectories of interacting risk and protective factors associated with divorce and remarriage will yield a more valid and fruitful view of the multiple pathways associated with resiliency or adverse outcomes for children who have experienced their parents' marital transitions.

REFERENCES

Ahrons, C. R. (1979). The binuclear family: Two households, one family. *Alternative Lifestyles, 2,* 499–515.

Ahrons, C. R. (1983). Predictors of paternal involvement postdivorce: Mothers' and fathers' perceptions. *Journal of Divorce, 6,* 55–69.

Allison, P. D., & Furstenberg, F. F., Jr. (1989). How marital dissolution affects children: Variations by age and sex. *Developmental Psychology, 25,* 540–549.

Amato, P. R. (1993). Children's adjustment to divorce: Theories, hypotheses, and empirical support. *Journal of Marriage and the Family, 55,* 23–38.

Amato, P. R. (1995). Single-parent households as settings for children's development, well-being, and attainment: A social network/resources perspective. *Sociological Studies of Children, 7,* 19–47.

Amato, P. R., & Booth, A. (1991). Consequences of parental divorce and marital happiness for adult well-being. *Social Forces, 69,* 895–914.

Amato, P. R., & Booth, A. (1996). A prospective study of divorce and parent–child relationships. *Journal of Marriage and the Family, 58,* 356–365.

Amato, P. R., & Keith, B. (1991a). Parental divorce and adult well-being: A meta-analysis. *Journal of Marriage and the Family, 53,* 43–58.

Amato, P. R., & Keith, B. (1991b). Parental divorce and the well-being of children: A meta-analysis. *Psychological Bulletin, 110,* 26–46.

Amato, P. R., Loomis, L. S., & Booth, A. (1995). Parental divorce, marital conflict, and offspring well-being during early adulthood. *Social Forces, 73,* 895–915.

Arendell, T. (1986). *Mothers and divorce: Legal, economic, and social dilemmas.* Berkeley: University of California Press.

Bank, L., Duncan, T., Patterson, G. R., & Reid, J. (1993). Parent and teacher ratings in the assessment and prediction of antisocial and delinquent behaviors. *Journal of Personality, 61,* 693–709.

Baucom, D. H., & Epstein, N. (1990). *Cognitive–behavioral marital therapy.* New York: Brunner/Mazel.

Bianchi, S. M., Subaiya, L., & Kahn, J. (1997, March). *Economic well-being of husbands and wives after marital disruption.* Paper presented at the annual meeting of the Population Association of America, Washington, DC.

Block, J. H., Block, J., & Gjerde, P. F. (1986). The personality of children prior to divorce: A prospective study. *Child Development, 57,* 827–840.

Block, J. H., Block, J., & Gjerde, P. F. (1988). Parental functioning and the home environment in families of divorce: Prospective and concurrent analyses. *Journal of the American Academy of Child and Adolescent Psychiatry, 27,* 207–213.

Bloom, B. L., Asher, S. J., & White, S. W. (1978). Marital disruption as a stressor: A review and analysis. *Psychological Bulletin, 85,* 867–894.

Booth, A., & Amato, P. R. (1994). Parental marital quality, parental divorce, and relations with parents. *Journal of Marriage and the Family, 56,* 21–34.

Booth, A., & Edwards, J. N. (1990). Transmission of marital and family quality over the generations: The effects of parental divorce and unhappiness. *Journal of Divorce, 13,* 41–58.

Booth, A., & Edwards, J. N. (1992). Starting over: Why remarriages are more unstable. *Journal of Family Issues, 13,* 179–194.

Bradbury, T. N., & Fincham, F. D. (1990). Attributions in marriage: Review and critique. *Psychological Bulletin, 107,* 3–33.

Brand, E., Clingempeel, W. G., & Bowen-Woodward, K. (1988). Family relationships and children's psychosocial adjustment in stepmother and stepfather families. In E. M. Hetherington & J. D. Arasteh (Eds.), *Impact of divorce, single parenting, and stepparenting on children* (pp. 299–324). Hillsdale, NJ: Erlbaum.

Braver, S. L., Wolchik, S. A., Sandler, I. N., Sheets, V. L., Fogas, B., & Bay, R. C. (1993). A longitudinal study of noncustodial parents: Parents without children. *Journal of Family Psychology, 7,* 9–23.

Bray, J. H. (1987, August–September). *Becoming a stepfamily: Overview of The Developmental Issues in Stepfamilies Research Project.* Paper presented at the 95th Annual Convention of the American Psychological Association, New York.

Bray, J. H. (1988). Children's development during early remarriage. In E. M. Hetherington & J. D. Arasteh (Eds.), *Impact of divorce, single parenting, and stepparenting on children* (pp. 279–288). Hillsdale, NJ: Erlbaum.

Bray, J. H. (1990, August). *The developing stepfamily II: Overview and previous findings.* Paper presented at the 98th Annual Convention of the American Psychological Association, Boston.

Bray, J. H., & Berger, S. H. (1992). Nonresidential family–child relationships following divorce and remarriage. In C. E. Depner & J. H. Bray (Eds.), *Nonresidential parenting: New vistas in family living* (pp. 156–181). Newbury Park, CA: Sage.

Bray, J. H., & Berger, S. H. (1993). Developmental Issues in Stepfamilies Research Project: Family relationships and parent–child interactions. *Journal of Family Psychology, 7,* 76–90.

Bray, J. H., Berger, S. H., & Boethel, C. L. (1994). Role integration and marital adjustment in stepfather families. In K. Pasley & M. Ihinger-Tallman (Eds.), *Stepparenting: Issues in theory, research, and practice* (pp. 69–86). Westport, CT: Greenwood Press.

Buchanan, C. M., Maccoby, E. E., & Dornbusch, S. M. (1991). Caught between parents: Adolescents' experience in divorced homes. *Child Development, 62,* 1008–1029.

Buchanan, C. M., Maccoby, E. E., & Dornbusch, S. M. (1992). Adolescents and their families after divorce: Three residential arrangements compared. *Journal of Research on Adolescence, 2,* 261–291.

Bumpass, L. L., Martin, T. C., & Sweet, J. A. (1991). The impact of family background and early marital factors on marital disruption. *Journal of Family Issues, 12,* 22–42.

Bumpass, L. L., & Raley, R. K. (1995). Redefining single-parent families: Cohabitation and changing family reality. *Demography, 32,* 97–109.

Bumpass, L. L., & Sweet, J. A. (1989). *Children's experience in single-parent families: Implications of cohabitation and marital transitions* (National Study of Families and Households Working Paper No. 3). Madison: University of Wisconsin, Center for Demography and Ecology.

Bumpass, L. L., Sweet, J. A., & Castro-Martin, T. (1990). Changing patterns of remarriage. *Journal of Marriage and the Family, 52,* 747–756.

Bumpass, L. L., Sweet, J. A., & Cherlin, A. (1991). The role of cohabitation in declining rates of marriage. *Journal of Marriage and the Family, 53,* 913–927.

Burman, B., & Margolin, G. (1992). Analysis of the association between marital relationships and health problems: An interactional perspective. *Psychological Bulletin, 112,* 39–63.

Burrell, N. A. (1995). Communication patterns in stepfamilies: Redefining family roles, themes, and conflict styles. In M. A. Fitzpatrick & A. L. Vangelisti (Eds.), *Explaining family interactions* (pp. 290–309). Thousand Oaks, CA: Sage.

Capaldi, D. M., & Patterson, G. R. (1991). Relation of parental transitions to boys' adjustment problems: I. A linear hypothesis. II. Mothers at risk for transitions and unskilled parenting. *Developmental Psychology, 27,* 489–504.

Castro-Martin, T., & Bumpass, L. (1989). Recent trends and differentials in marital disruption. *Demography, 26,* 37–51.

Chase-Lansdale, P. L., Cherlin, A. J., & Kiernan, K. E. (1995). The long-term effects of parental divorce on the mental health of young adults: A developmental perspective. *Child Development, 66,* 1614–1634.

Chase-Lansdale, P. L., & Hetherington, E. M. (1990). The impact of divorce on life-span development: Short and long term effects. In P. B. Baltes, D. L. Featherman, & R. M. Lerner (Eds.), *Life-span development and behavior* (Vol. 10, pp. 105–150). Hillsdale, NJ: Erlbaum.

Cherlin, A. (1992). *Marriage, divorce, remarriage: Social trends in the U.S.* Cambridge, MA: Harvard University Press.

Cherlin, A. J., & Furstenberg, F. F. (1994). Stepfamilies in the United States: A reconsideration. In J. Blake & J. Hagen (Eds.), *Annual review of sociology* (pp. 359–381). Palo Alto, CA: Annual Reviews.

Cherlin, A. J., Furstenberg, F. F., Chase-Lansdale, P. L., Kiernan, K. E., Robins, P. K., Morrison, D. R., & Teitler, J. O. (1991). Longitudinal studies of effects of divorce in children in Great Britain and the United States. *Science, 252,* 1386–1389.

Clarke-Stewart, K. A., & Hayward, C. (1996). Advantages of father custody and contact for the psychological well-being of school-age children. *Journal of Applied Developmental Psychology, 17,* 239–270.

Clingempeel, W. G., Brand, E., & Ievoli, R. (1984). Stepparent–stepchild relationships in stepmother and stepfather families: A multimethod study. *Family Relations, 33,* 465–473.

Conger, R. D., & Chao, W. (1996). Adolescent depressed mood. In R. L. Simons & Associates (Eds.), *Understanding differences between divorced and intact families: Stress, interaction, and child outcome* (pp. 157–175). Thousand Oaks, CA: Sage.

Conger, R. D., & Conger, K. J. (1996). Sibling relationships. In R. L. Simons & Associates (Eds.), *Understanding differences between divorced and intact families: Stress, interaction, and child outcome* (pp. 104–124). Thousand Oaks, CA: Sage.

Conger, R. D., & Reuter, M. A. (1996). Siblings, parents, and peers: A longitudinal study of social influences in adolescent risk for alcohol use and abuse. In G. H. Brody (Ed.), *Sibling relationships: Their causes and consequences* (pp. 1–30). Norwood, NJ: Ablex.

Cowan, P. A., & Cowan, C. P. (1990). Becoming a family: Research and intervention. In I. Sigel & G. A. Brody (Eds.), *Family research* (pp. 246–279). Hillsdale, NJ: Erlbaum.

Crosbie-Burnett, M. (1991). Impact of joint versus sole custody and quality of the co-parental relationship on adjustment of adolescents in remarried families. *Behavioral Sciences and the Law, 9,* 439–449.

Daly, M., & Wilson, M. I. (1996). Violence against stepchildren. *Current Directions in Psychological Science, 5,* 77–81.

Davies, P. T., & Cummings, E. M. (1994). Marital conflict and child adjustment: An emotional security hypothesis. *Psychological Bulletin, 116,* 387–411.

Demo, D. H., & Acock, A. C. (1996). Family structure, family process, and adolescent well-being. *Journal of Research on Adolescence, 6,* 457–488.

Dillon, P. A., & Emery, R. E. (1996). Divorce mediation and resolution of child custody disputes: Long-term effects. *American Journal of Orthopsychiatry, 66,* 131–140.

Dornbusch, S. M., Carlsmith, J. M., Bushwall, S. J., Ritter, P. L., Liederman, H., Hastrof, A. H., & Gross, R. T. (1985). Single parents, extended households, and the control of adolescents. *Child Development, 56,* 326–341.

Elder, G., Caspi, A., & Van Nguyen, R. (1992). Resourceful and vulnerable children: Family influences in stressful times. In R. K. Silbereisen & K. Eyferth (Eds.), *Development in context: Integrative perspectives on youth development* (pp. 165–194). New York: Springer.

Elder, G. H., Jr., & Russell, S. T. (1996). Academic performance and future aspirations. In R. L. Simons & Associates (Eds.), *Understanding differences between divorced and intact families: Stress, interaction, and child outcome* (pp. 176–192). Thousand Oaks, CA: Sage.

Emery, R. E. (1982). Interpersonal conflict and the children of discord and divorce. *Psychological Bulletin, 92,* 310–330.

Emery, R. E. (1988). *Marriage, divorce, and children's adjustment.* Newbury Park, CA: Sage.

Emery, R. E. (1994). *Renegotiating family relationships.* New York: Guilford Press.

Emery, R. E., & Dillon, P. A. (1994). Conceptualizing the divorce process: Renegotiating boundaries of intimacy and power in the divorced family system. *Family Relations, 43,* 374–379.

Emery, R. E., & Forehand, R. (1994). Parental divorce and children's well-being: A focus on resilience. In R. J. Haggerty, L. R. Sherrod, N. Garmezy, & M. Rutter (Eds.), *Stress, risk, and resilience in children and adolescents* (pp. 64–99). Cambridge, England: Cambridge University Press.

Felner, R. D., Ginter, M. A., Boike, M. F., & Cowen, E. L. (1981). Parental death or divorce and the school adjustment of young children. *American Journal of Community Psychology, 9,* 181–191.

Felner, R. D., Stolberg, A., & Cowen, E. L. (1975). Crisis events and school mental health referral patterns of young children. *Journal of Consulting and Clinical Psychology, 43,* 305–310.

Fincham, F. D., Bradbury, T. N., & Scott, C. K. (1990). Cognition in marriage. In F. D. Fincham & T. N. Bradbury (Eds.), *The psychology of marriage* (pp. 118–149). New York: Guilford Press.

Forehand, R., Brody, G., Long, N., Slotkin, J., & Fauber, R. (1986). Divorce/divorce potential and interparental conflict: The relationship to early adolescent social and cognitive functioning. *Journal of Adolescent Research, 1,* 389–397.

Forehand, R., Thomas, A. M., Wierson, M., Brody, G., & Fauber, R. (1990). Role of maternal functioning and parenting skills in adolescent functioning following divorce. *Journal of Abnormal Psychology, 99,* 278–283.

Forgatch, M. S., Patterson, G. R., & Ray, J. A. (1995). Divorce and boys' adjustment problems: Two paths with a single model. In E. M. Hetherington & E. A. Blechman (Eds.), *Stress, coping, and resiliency in children and families* (pp. 67–105). Mahwah, NJ: Erlbaum.

Furman, W., & Buhrmester, D. (1992). Age and sex differences in perceptions of networks of personal relationships. *Child Development, 63,* 103–115.

Furstenberg, F. F., Jr. (1988). Child care after divorce and remarriage. In E. M. Hetherington & J. D. Arasteh (Eds.), *Impact of divorce, single parenting, and stepparenting on children* (pp. 245–261). Hillsdale, NJ: Erlbaum.

Furstenberg, F. F., Jr., & Cherlin, A. J. (1991). *Divided families: What happens to children when parents part.* Cambridge, MA: Harvard University Press.

Furstenberg, F. F., Jr., Morgan, S. P., & Allison, P. D. (1987). Paternal participation and children's well-being after marital dissolution. *American Sociological Review, 52,* 695–701.

Furstenberg, F. F., Jr., & Nord, C. W. (1987). Parenting apart: Patterns of childrearing after marital disruption. *Journal of Marriage and the Family, 47,* 893–904.

Furstenberg, F. F., Jr., Nord, C. W., Peterson, J. L., & Zill, N. (1983). The life course of children of divorce: Marital disruption and parental contact. *American Sociological Review, 48,* 656–668.

Ganong, L. H., & Coleman, M. (1994). *Remarried family relationships.* Thousand Oaks, CA: Sage.

Giles-Sims, J. (1987). Social exchange in remarried families. In K. Pasley & M. Ihinger-Tallman (Eds.), *Remarriage and stepparenting: Current research and theory* (pp. 141–163). New York: Guilford Press.

Glenn, N. D., & Kramer, K. B. (1985). The psychological well-being of adult children of divorce. *Journal of Marriage and the Family, 47,* 905–912.

Glick, P. C. (1989). Remarried families, stepfamilies, and stepchildren: A brief demographic profile. *Family Relations, 38,* 24–27.

Gotlib, I., & McCabe, S. B. (1990). Marriage and psychopathology. In F. D. Fincham & T. N. Bradbury (Eds.), *The psychology of marriage* (pp. 226–257). New York: Guilford Press.

Gottman, J. M. (1993). A theory of marital dissolution and stability. *Journal of Family Psychology, 7,* 57–75.

Gottman, J. M. (1994). *What predicts divorce?* Hillsdale, NJ: Erlbaum.

Gottman, J. M., & Katz, L. F. (1989). Effects of marital discord on young children's peer interaction and health. *Developmental Psychology, 25,* 373–381.

Gottman, J. M., & Levenson, R. W. (1992). Marital processes predictive of later dissolution: Behavior, physiology, and health. *Journal of Personality and Social Psychology, 63,* 221–233.

Guidubaldi, J., Perry, J. D., & Nastasi, B. K. (1987). Growing up in a divorced family: Initial and long-term perspectives on children's adjustment. In S. Oskamp (Ed.), *Applied social psychology annual: Vol. 7. Family processes and problems* (pp. 202–237). Newbury Park, CA: Sage.

Hanson, S. M. H. (1988). Single custodial fathers and the parent–child relationship. *Nursing Research, 30,* 202–204.

Henderson, S. H., Hetherington, E. M., Mekos, D., & Reiss, D. (1996). Stress, parenting, and adolescent psychopathology in nondivorced and stepfamilies: A within-family perspective. In E. M. Hetherington & E. H. Blechman (Eds.), *Stress, coping, and resiliency in children and families* (pp. 39–66). Mahwah, NJ: Erlbaum.

Hetherington, E. M. (1972). Effects of father absence on personality development in adolescent daughters. *Developmental Psychology, 7,* 313–326.

Hetherington, E. M. (1989). Coping with family transitions: Winners, losers, and survivors. *Child Development, 60,* 1–14.

Hetherington, E. M. (1991a). Families, lies, and videotapes. *Journal of Research on Adolescence, 1,* 323–348.

Hetherington, E. M. (1991b). The role of individual differences in family relations in coping with divorce and remarriage. In P. Cowan & E. M. Hetherington (Eds.), *Advances in family research: Vol. 2. Family transitions* (pp. 165–194). Hillsdale, NJ: Erlbaum.

Hetherington, E. M. (1993). An overview of the Virginia Longitudinal Study of Divorce and Remarriage with a focus on early adolescence. *Journal of Family Psychology, 7,* 39–56.

Hetherington, E. M. (1997). Teenaged childbearing and divorce. In S. Luthar, J. A. Burack, D. Cicchetti, & J. Weisz (Eds.), *Developmental psychopathology: Perspectives on adjustment, risk, and disorders* (pp. 350–373). Cambridge, England: Cambridge University Press.

Hetherington, E. M. (in press). Social capital and the development of youth from nondivorced, divorced, and remarried families. In A. Collins (Ed.), *Relationships as developmental contexts: The 29th Minnesota Symposium on Child Psychology.* Hillsdale, NJ: Erlbaum.

Hetherington, E. M., & Clingempeel, W. G. (1992). Coping with marital transitions: A family systems perspective. *Monographs of the Society for Research in Child Development, 57*(2–3, Serial No. 227).

Hetherington, E. M., Cox, M., & Cox, R. (1979). Family interaction and the social, emotional, and cognitive development of children following divorce. In V. Vaughn & T. Brazelton (Eds.), *The family: Setting priorities* (pp. 89–128). New York: Science and Medicine.

Hetherington, E. M., Cox, M., & Cox, R. (1985). Long-term effects of divorce and remarriage on the adjustment of children. *Journal of the American Academy of Child Psychiatry, 24,* 518–539.

Hetherington, E. M., & Jodl, K. M. (1994). Stepfamilies as settings for child development. In A. Booth & J. Dunn (Eds.), *Stepfamilies: Who benefits? Who does not?* (pp. 55–79). Hillsdale, NJ: Erlbaum.

Hetherington, E. M., Law, T. C., & O'Connor, T. G. (1992). Divorce: Challenges, changes, and new chances. In F. Walsh (Ed.), *Normal family processes* (2nd ed., pp. 219–246). New York: Guilford Press.

Hetherington, E. M., & Stanley Hagan, M. S. (1995). Parenting in divorced and remarried families. In M. Bornstein (Ed.), *Handbook of parenting* (pp. 233–255). Hillsdale, NJ: Erlbaum.

Hetherington, E. M., & Stanley Hagan, M. S. (1997). The effects of divorce on fathers and their children. In M. Bornstein (Ed.), *The role of the father in child development* (pp. 191–211). New York: Wiley.

Hoffman, C. D. (1995). Pre- and post-divorce father–child relationships and child adjustment: Noncustodial fathers' perspectives. *Journal of Divorce and Remarriage, 23,* 3–20.

Hu, Y., & Goldman, N. (1990). Mortality differentials by marital status: An international comparison. *Demography, 27,* 233–250.

Jacobson, D. S. (1982, August). *Family structure in the age of divorce.* Paper presented at the 90th Annual Convention of the American Psychological Association, Washington, DC.

Jessor, R., & Jessor, S. L. (1977). *Problem behavior and psycho-social development.* New York: Academic Press.

Jockin, V., McGue, M., & Lykken, D. T. (1996). Personality and divorce: A genetic analysis. *Journal of Personality and Social Psychology, 71,* 288–299.

Kelly, E. L., & Conley, J. J. (1987). Personality and compatibility: A prospective analysis of marital stability and marital satisfaction. *Journal of Personality and Social Psychology, 52,* 27–40.

Kiecolt-Glaser, J. K., Fisher, L. D., Ogrocki, P., Stout, J. C., Speicher, C. E., & Glaser, R. (1987). Marital quality, marital disruption, and immune function. *Psychosomatic Medicine, 49,* 13–34.

Kiecolt-Glaser, J. K., Kennedy, S., Malkoff, S., Fisher, L. D., Speicher, C. E., & Glaser, R. (1988). Marital discord and immunity in males. *Psychosomatic Medicine, 50,* 213–229.

King, V. (1994a). Nonresidential father involvement and child well-being: Can dads make a difference? *Journal of Family Issues, 15,* 78–96.

King, V. (1994b). Variation in the consequences of nonresidential father involvement for children's well-being. *Journal of Marriage and the Family, 56,* 964–972.

Kitson, G. C., & Holmes, W. M. (1992). *Portrait of divorce: Adjustment to marital breakdown.* New York: Guilford Press.

Kitson, G. C., & Morgan, L. A. (1990). The multiple consequences of divorce. *Journal of Marriage and the Family, 52,* 913–924.

Kline, M., Johnston, J. R., & Tschann, J. M. (1991). The long shadow of marital conflict: A model of children's post-divorce adjustment. *Journal of Marriage and the Family, 53,* 297–309.

Kurdek, L. A. (1993). Predicting marital dissolution: A 5-year prospective longitudinal study of newlywed couples. *Journal of Personality and Social Psychology, 64,* 221–242.

Kurdek, L. A., & Fine, M. A. (1993). Parent and nonparent residential family members as providers of warmth, support, and supervision to young adolescents. *Journal of Family Psychology, 7,* 245–249.

Kurdek, L. A., Fine, M. A., & Sinclair, R. J. (1995). School adjustment in sixth graders: Parenting transitions, family climate, and peer norm effects. *Child Development, 66,* 430–445.

Lahey, B. B., Hartdagen, S. E., Frick, P. J., McBurnett, K., Connor, R., & Hynd, G. W. (1988). Conduct disorder: Parsing the confounded relation to parental divorce and antisocial personality. *Journal of Abnormal Psychology, 97,* 334–337.

Lamb, M. E. (1997). Fathers and child development: An introductory overview and guide. In M. E. Lamb (Ed.), *The role of the father in child development* (pp. 1–18). New York: Wiley.

Lee, V. E., Burkam, D. T., Zimiles, H., & Ladewski, B. (1994). Family structure and its effect on behavioral and emotional problems in young adolescents. *Journal of Research on Adolescence, 4,* 405–437.

Lindner-Gunnoe, M. (1993). *Noncustodial mothers' and fathers' contributions to the adjustment of adolescent stepchildren.* Unpublished doctoral dissertation, University of Virginia.

Lorenz, F. O., Simons, R. L., & Chao, W. (1996). Family structure and mother's depression. In R. L. Simons & Associates (Eds.), *Understanding differences between divorced and intact families: Stress, interaction, and child outcome* (pp. 65–77). Thousand Oaks, CA: Sage.

Maccoby, E. E., Buchanan, C. M., Mnookin, R. H., & Dornbusch, S. M. (1993). Post-divorce roles of mothers and fathers in the lives of their children. *Journal of Family Psychology, 7,* 24–38.

Maccoby, E. E., & Mnookin, R. H. (1992). *Dividing the child: Social and legal dilemmas of custody.* Cambridge, MA: Harvard University Press.

Masheter, C. (1991). Post-divorce relationships between ex-spouses: The roles of attachment and interpersonal conflict. *Journal of Marriage and the Family, 53,* 101–110.

Matthews, L. S., Wickrama, K. A. S., & Conger, R. D. (1996). Predicting marital instability from spouse and observer reports of marital interaction. *Journal of Marriage and the Family, 58,* 641–655.

McGue, M., & Lykken, D. T. (1992). Genetic influence on risk of divorce. *Psychological Science, 6,* 368–373.

McLanahan, S. S., & Booth, K. (1989). Mother-only families: Problems, prospects, and politics. *Journal of Marriage and the Family, 51,* 557–580.

McLanahan, S. S., & Bumpass, L. (1988). Intergenerational consequences of family disruption. *American Journal of Sociology, 94,* 130–152.

McLanahan, S., & Sandefur, G. (1994). *Growing up with a single parent: What hurts, what helps?* Cambridge, MA: Harvard University Press.

Mekos, D., Hetherington, E. M., & Reiss, D. (1996). Sibling differences in problem behavior and parental treatment in nondivorced and remarried families. *Child Development, 67,* 2148–2165.

Mendes, H. A. (1976a). Single fatherhood. *Social Work, 21,* 308–312.

Mendes, H. A. (1976b). Single fathers. *Family Coordinator, 25,* 439–444.

Merikangas, K. R., Prusoff, B. A., & Weissman, M. M. (1988). Parental concordance for affective disorders: Psychopathology in offspring. *Journal of Affective Disorders, 15,* 279–290.

Meyer, D. R., & Garasky, S. (1993). Custodial fathers: Myths, realities, and child support policy. *Journal of Marriage and the Family, 55,* 73–89.

Minton, C., & Pasley, K. (1996). Fathers' parenting role identity and father involvement: A comparison of nondivorced and divorced, nonresident fathers. *Journal of Family Issues, 17,* 26–45.

Munsch, J., Woodward, J., & Darling, N. (1995). Children's perceptions of their relationships with coresiding and non-custodial fathers. *Journal of Divorce and Remarriage, 23,* 39–54.

National Center for Health Statistics. (1988). *Current estimates from the National Health Interview Survey: United States, 1987* (DHHS Publication No. 88-1594). Washington, DC: U.S. Government Printing Office.

Orbuch, T. L., Veroff, J., & Hunter, A. G. (in press). Black couples, White couples: The early years of marriage. In E. M. Hetherington (Ed.), *Coping with divorce, single-parenting, and remarriage: A risk and resiliency perspective.* Mahwah, NJ: Erlbaum.

Papernow, P. L. (1988). Stepparent role development: From outsider to intimate. In W. R. Beer (Ed.), *Relative strangers: Studies of stepfamily processes* (pp. 54–82). Totowa, NJ: Rowman & Littlefield.

Patterson, G. (1991, March). *Interaction of stress and family structure and their relation to child adjustment.* Paper presented at the biennial meetings of the Society for Research on Child Development, Seattle, WA.

Patterson, G., DeBaryshe, B., & Ramsey, E. (1989). A developmental perspective on antisocial behavior. *American Psychologist, 44,* 329–335.

Patterson, G., & Dishion, T. J. (1988). Multilevel family process models: Traits, interactions, and relationships. In R. Hinde & J. Stevenson-Hinde (Eds.), *Relationships within families: Mutual influences* (pp. 283–310). Oxford, England: Clarendon Press.

Pearlin, L. I., & Johnson, J. S. (1977). Marital status, life-stresses and depression. *American Sociological Review, 42,* 704–715.

Peterson, J. L., & Zill, N. (1986). Marital disruption, parent–child relationships, and behavior problems in children. *Journal of Marriage and the Family, 48,* 295–307.

Riessman, C. K., & Gerstel, N. (1985). Marital dissolution and health: Do males or females have greater risk? *Social Science and Medicine, 20,* 627–635.

Rutter, M. (1987). Psychosocial resilience and protective mechanisms. *American Journal of Orthopsychiatry, 57,* 316–331.

Santrock, J. W., & Sitterle, K. A. (1987). Parent–child relationships in stepmother families. In K. Pasley & M. Ihinger-Tallman (Eds.), *Remarriage and stepparenting: Current research and theory* (pp. 273–299). New York: Guilford Press.

Santrock, J. W., Sitterle, K. A., & Warshak, R. A. (1988). Parent–child relationships in stepfather families. In P. Bronstein & C. P. Cowan (Eds.), *Fatherhood today: Men's changing roles in the family* (pp. 144–165). New York: Wiley.

Seltzer, J. A. (1991). Relationships between fathers and children who live apart: The father's role after separation. *Journal of Marriage and the Family, 53,* 79–101.

Seltzer, J. A. (1994). Consequences of marital dissolution for children. *Annual Review of Sociology, 20,* 235–266.

Seltzer, J. A., & Brandreth, Y. (1994). What fathers say about involvement with children after separation. *Journal of Family Issues, 15,* 49–77.

Simons, R. L. (1996). The effect of divorce on adult and child adjustment. In R. L. Simons & Associates (Eds.), *Understanding differences between divorced and intact families: Stress, interaction, and child outcome* (pp. 3–20). Thousand Oaks, CA: Sage.

Simons, R. L., & Associates. (Eds.). (1996). *Understanding differences between divorced and intact families: Stress, interaction, and child outcome.* Thousand Oaks, CA: Sage.

Simons, R. L., & Beaman, J. (1996). Father's parenting. In R. L. Simons & Associates (Eds.), *Understanding differences between divorced and intact families: Stress, interaction, and child outcome* (pp. 94–103). Thousand Oaks, CA: Sage.

Simons, R. L., Beaman, J., Conger, R. D., & Chao, W. (1992). Childhood experience, conceptions of parenting, and attitudes of spouse as determinants of parental behavior. *Journal of Marriage and the Family, 55,* 91–106.

Simons, R. L., & Chao, W. (1996). Conduct problems. In R. L. Simons & Associates (Eds.), *Understanding differences between divorced and intact families: Stress, interaction, and child outcome* (pp. 125–143). Thousand Oaks, CA: Sage.

Simons, R. L., & Johnson, C. (1996). Mother's parenting. In R. L. Simons & Associates (Eds.), *Understanding differences between divorced and intact families: Stress, interaction, and child outcome* (pp. 81–93). Thousand Oaks, CA: Sage.

Simons, R. L., Johnson, C., & Lorenz, F. O. (1996). Family structure differences in stress and behavioral predispositions. In R. L. Simons & Associates (Eds.), *Understanding differences between di-*

vorced and intact families: Stress, interaction, and child outcome (pp. 45–63). Thousand Oaks, CA: Sage.

Stack, S. (1989). The impact of divorce on suicide in Norway, 1951–1980. *Journal of Marriage and the Family, 51,* 229–238.

Thomson, E., McLanahan, S. S., & Curtin, R. B. (1992). Family structure, gender, and parental separation. *Journal of Marriage and the Family, 54,* 368–378.

Travato, F., & Lauris, G. (1989). Marital status and mortality in Canada: 1951–81. *Journal of Marriage and the Family, 51,* 907–922.

Tzeng, J. M., & Mare, R. D. (1995). Labor market and socioeconomic effects on marital stability. *Social Science Research, 24,* 329–351.

Umberson, D. (1987). Family status and health behaviors: Social control as a dimension of social integration. *Journal of Health and Social Behavior, 28,* 306–319.

Umberson, D., & Williams, C. L. (1993). Divorced fathers: Parental role strain and psychological distress. *Journal of Family Issues, 14,* 378–400.

U.S. Bureau of the Census. (1992). *Marital status and living arrangements: March, 1992* (No. 468, Tables G & 5, Current Population Reports, Series P-20). Washington, DC: U.S. Government Printing Office.

Visher, E. B., & Visher, J. S. (1990). Dynamics of successful stepfamilies. *Journal of Divorce and Remarriage, 14,* 3–11.

Warshak, R. A. (1986). Father custody and child development: A review and analysis of psychological research. *Behavioral Sciences and the Law, 4,* 185–202.

Weiss, R. S. (1979). Growing up a little faster: The experience of growing up in a single-parent household. *Journal of Social Issues, 35,* 97–111.

Werner, E. E. (1988). Individual differences, universal needs: A 30-year study of resilient high-risk infants. *Zero to Three: Bulletin of National Center for Clinical Infant Programs, 8,* 1–15.

Werner, E. E. (1993). Risk, resilience, and recovery: Perspectives from the Kauaii Longitudinal Study. *Development and Psychopathology, 54,* 503–515.

Whitbeck, L. B., Simons, R. L., & Goldberg, E. (1996). Adolescent sexual intercourse. In R. L. Simons & Associates (Eds.), *Understanding differences between divorced and intact families: Stress, interaction, and child outcome* (pp. 144–156). Thousand Oaks, CA: Sage.

White, L. (1994). Stepfamilies over the life course: Social support. In A. Booth & J. Dunn (Eds.), *Stepfamilies: Who benefits? Who does not?* (pp. 109–137). Hillsdale, NJ: Erlbaum.

White, L. K., Brinkerhoff, D. B., & Booth, A. (1985). The effect of marital disruption on children's attachment to parents. *Journal of Family Issues, 6,* 5–22.

Wilson, M. I., Daly, M., & Weghorst, S. J. (1980). Household composition and the risk of child abuse and neglect. *Journal of Biosocial Science, 12,* 333–340.

Zill, N. (1988). Behavior, achievement, and health problems among children in stepfamilies. In E. M. Hetherington & J. D. Arasteh (Eds.), *Impact of divorce, single parenting, and stepparenting on children* (pp. 324–368). Hillsdale, NJ: Erlbaum.

Zill, N., Morrison, D. R., & Coiro, M. J. (1993). Long-term effects of parental divorce on parent–child relationships, adjustment, and achievement in young adulthood. *Journal of Family Psychology, 7,* 91–103.

Zimiles, H., & Lee, V. E. (1991). Adolescent family structure and educational progress. *Developmental Psychology, 27,* 314–320.

WHEN TO SPANK

BY LYNN ROSELLINI

ad and Mom are no fools: They know their '90s parenting manuals. So when 4-year-old Jason screams, "No!" and darts under the dining room table when it's time to leave Grandma's, Dad patiently crouches down. "Remember, Jason," he says soothingly, "when we talked earlier about leaving?" Jason, scowling, doesn't budge. His mother shifts uneasily and riffles through her mental Rolodex of tips garnered from all those child-rearing books. She offers Jason choices ("Would you like to come out by yourself, or shall I get you?"), then rewards ("I've got a cookie for you to eat in the car"), and finally consequences ("Get out or no *Arthur* tomorrow!"). Jason retreats further and cries, "I don't want to!" His parents look at each other wearily. Jason is a bright, cheerful child who, like most spirited kids, is gifted at pushing limits. He is often well-behaved, but lately, when his parents ask him to do something, he seems to melt down entirely, screaming and even biting. Now he sticks out his tongue and announced, "I hate you!" His father hauls the tiny tyrant, kicking and flailing, out from under the table. Jason lets loose an earspitting yell. Dad, red-faced, finally loses it, raising his hand over his son's rear end.

Now stop the action. If Jason's father reads the newspapers and listens to TV news, he knows spanking is one of the more destructive things he can do to his kid, that it could turn Jason into an angry, violent child—and perhaps, some day, a depressed, abusive adult. He may even have heard the familiar refrain of child-development specialists, who contend that a parent who uses corporal punishment "is a parent who has failed." Yet he also feels instinctively that a mild pop on the rear might get Jason's attention in a way negotiating won't. Besides, *his* dad spanked *him* occasionally, and he didn't turn into an ax-wielding monster.

In fact, the notion advanced by a slew of American child-raising authorities that a couple of well-placed swats on the rear of your beloved preschooler irreparably harms him or her is essentially a myth. Antispanking crusaders relied on inconclusive studies to make sweeping overgeneralizations about spanking's dangers. This week, even the American Academy of Pediatrics is expected to tone down its blanket injunction against spanking, though it still takes a dim view of the practice and encourages parents to develop discipline alternatives. An AAP conference on corporal punishment in 1996 concluded that in certain circumstances, spanking may be an effective backup to other forms of discipline. "There's no evidence that a child who is spanked moderately is going to grow up to be a criminal or antisocial or violent," says S. Kenneth Schonberg, a pediatrics professor who co-chaired the conference. In fact, the reverse may be true: A few studies suggest that when used appropriately, spanking makes small children less likely to fight with others and more likely to obey their parents.

Some caveats are in order. By "spanking," the AAP and other authorities mean one or two flat-handed swats on a child's wrist or read end, *not* a sustained whipping with Dad's belt. Neither the AAP nor the other child-development specialists believe that spanking should be the sole

For decades, parenting experts have said spanking irreparably harms kids. But a close look at the research suggests otherwise

 From *U.S. News & World Report*, April 13, 1998, pp. 52-58.

or preferred means of child discipline, or that it should be administered when a parent is very angry, or that it should be used with adolescents or children under 2 years old. Most experts who approve a spanking suggest it be used sparingly, as an adjunct to other discipline techniques.

Children are people. The origins of the antispanking prohibition have a lot to do with two social phenomena of postwar America: the rise of popular psychology and the breakup of the extended family. In years past, grandparents used to inundate a new mother with child-raising tips on everything from burping to bed-wetting. One of them was likely to be "spare the rod and spoil the child," an adage some adults used to justify repeated spankings as the only form of discipline—and not just in the home. Half a century ago, corporal punishment in schools was legal in all but one state. But by the early 1950s, young couples increasingly began to look to child-rearing "experts"—authors like Benjamin Spock, whose manual *Baby and Child Care* counseled against the punitive child-raising practices of earlier generations. Spock, a believer in firm and consistent parenting, did not rule out spanking in his book's early editions. But he salted his manual with concepts borrowed from Freudian theory, stressed the impact that parents have on their kids' development, and introduced what at the time was a radical notion: Children are individual little people, with a host of psychic needs.

The psychologists and child-development authorities who churned out parenting guides in the 1970s and 1980s took Spock one step further, advocating a new, child-centered view of family. The locus of power should shift, these experts seemed to suggest, so that kids are equal members of the household. Many writers, such as T. Berry Brazelton, warned that strict parenting, and particularly punishments like spanking, could promote aggression and discourage children from cooperating with others. One of the most popular of the new crop of books was Thomas Gordon's 1970 million-plus seller, *Parent Effectiveness Training*, which advised parents to stop punishing kids and to start treating them "much as we treat a friend or a spouse." More recently, writers like Nancy Samalin and Barbara Coloroso counseled an end to punishment altogether. And while such books helped open parents' eyes to the importance of listening to children and respecting their individuality, some warm, fuzzy—and not very reasonable—ideas about discipline also began to gain popularity. (One author suggested that if a child refused to get dressed in the morning, parents should send him to school in pajamas.)

This onslaught of advice did not, on the surface, appear to alter parents' attitudes toward spanking very much. Last year, 65 percent of Americans approved of spanking, not much less than the 74 percent who did so in 1946. But the modest overall shift in numbers concealed a marked change in opinion among the American elite. By the 1990s, the refusal to spank had, in some quarters, become a sign of enlightened parenting. In a 1997 poll, 41 percent of college-educated Americans disapproved of spanking children, compared with only 20 percent of those who didn't complete high school. Whites were more than twice as likely to disapprove of spanking as blacks, and the rich were less likely to favor the practice than the poor.

"Parents became intimidated by expertise," argues Kevin Ryan, director of the Center for the Advancement of Ethics and Character at Boston University, who thinks the antispanking movement has become too absolutist. "Psychologists and educators corrupted parents, saying that all it takes are rational appeals to a child's better side." Danielle Crittenden, a mother of two and editor of the *Women's Quarterly,* a conservative journal, adds that "if you say you swat your kid, people now look at you like you're a child abuser. You can't even talk about it because people are so hysterical."

Against spanking. Compounding parents' guilt were two books published in the mid-'90s by researchers Irwin A. Hyman and Murray A. Straus that seemed to solidify the antispanking consensus. In *Beating the Devil Out of Them*, Straus, a respected sociologist at the University of New Hampshire who has done groundbreaking research on child and spouse abuse, concluded that spanking children is a "major psychological and social problem" that can doom a child to a lifetime of

necting seemingly disparate social problems. "We really want to get rid of violence," Hyman said last year in an interview on CNN. "And we really want to improve children's self-esteem and behavior. We should pass a law against spanking." Straus went even further, asserting that spanking helps foster punitive social attitudes, such as support for bombing raids to punish countries that support terrorists. If parents stop spanking, Straus said on ABC-TV news last year, "we'll have ... lower costs to deal with crime and with mental illness."

The problem with Straus and Hyman's pronouncements was that they were based on a body of research that is at best inconclusive and at worst badly flawed. It is virtually impossible to examine the effects of spanking in isolation, uncontaminated by other influences on behavior and development, such as the overall quality of parenting and the varying temperaments of the children in question. A "pure" study, in which researchers randomly assign children to one of two conditions—either spanking or discipline with nonphysical methods—and then track their behavior over a number of years, is for obvious reasons impractical: Few parents would agree to participate in such research.

As a result, the vast majority of studies on spanking have instead been carried out in one of two other ways. Some rely on retrospective interviews with adults, who are asked decades later to recall if they were spanked as children, and how often. Researchers then attempt to link the spanking with current behaviors like depression or spouse abuse. In the second type of study, mothers are interviewed about how often their kids misbehave and how often they spank them, and

Timeout. Parents should develop a range of discipline strategies. In timeouts, children are seated in a boring spot—facing a wall, for example—for several minutes

difficulties ranging from juvenile delinquency to depression, sexual hangups, limited job prospects, and lowered earnings. Straus's 1994 book won raves from well-known child-development experts like Brazelton and Penelope Leach, who applauded him for spotlighting a link between spanking and violence in society. Hyman, a psychologist at Temple University, made much the same point in his 1997 manual, *The Case Against Spanking*, and promoted his views in numerous appearances on the talk-show circuit.

For Straus and Hyman, spanking became almost a unified field theory con-

researchers look for a relationship between the two behaviors.

Neither type of study is very effective in teasing out exactly what is going on. In the case of the interview studies, it is impossible to tell if the spanking led to the misbehavior or the misbehavior led to the spanking. In the case of the retrospective studies, it is anyone's guess how accurate the adult subjects' memories are of their parents' discipline techniques. In some cases, the researchers also failed to adequately control for other factors that might have influenced the results. For instance, most of the studies conducted by

Straus himself include many people who were spanked as teenagers, which most child-rearing experts agree is too old for corporal punishment. Other studies failed to distinguish between one or two taps on the rear end of a preschooler and, say, beating a child with a strap. One 1977 study of 427 third graders who were re-interviewed 10 years later found that those who had been punished more also were more likely than others to push, shove, or start fights over nothing. But "punishment" was defined as including everything from nonphysical disciplinary steps like reasoning with children or isolating them, to slapping their faces, washing their mouths out with soap, or spanking them until they cried.

The shortcomings in the research aren't just methodological quibbles—they go right to the heart of what worries parents about spanking. To take one example, one of parents' biggest fears is that spanking might lead to child abuse. Common sense suggests—and studies confirm—that child abuse typically starts from situations where a parent is attempting to discipline a child. But no study demonstrates that spanking a child leads to abuse—indeed, it may be the other way around. Parents who end up abusing their children may misuse all forms of discipline, including spanking. Sweden, often cited as a test case, hasn't borne out the spanking prohibitionists' fears, either. After Sweden outlawed spanking by parents in 1979, reports of serious child abuse actually increased by more than 400 percent over 10 years, though the actual number of reports—583 cases in 1994—was still quite small. Sweden's experience does not prove that banning spanking creates more child abuse, but it does suggest that outlawing the practice may do little to lower the rate of child abuse.

Why take a chance? Straus and Hyman and other parenting experts concede that much research on spanking is flawed, but they believe its collective weight supports their claims. "There's enough evidence to decide we don't need it [spanking]," says Hyman, "even if the evidence isn't that strong." Besides, he asks, given the stakes, is it worth taking a chance? "The question should be turned around. We should say, 'Give me a good reason why you *should* hurt kids.'"

Journalists, reporting on child-rearing trends, seem to have adopted a similar approach to spanking, rarely bothering to scrutinize the claims of prohibitionists. Consider the news media coverage of a much touted study by Straus, published last year in the *Archives of Pediatrics & Adolescent Medicine*. His research indicated that frequent spanking (three or more times a week) of children 6 to 9 years old, tracked over a period of two

years, increased a child's antisocial behavior, measured in activities like cheating, bullying, or lying. The American Medical Association, which publishes *Archives of Pediatrics & Adolescent Medicine*, issued a news release headlined "Spanking Makes Children Violent, Antisocial," and Straus's findings were reported by the three major networks and included in at least 107 newspaper and magazine stories. But neither the press release nor many of the news reports mentioned the study's gaps: that 9-year-olds who are spanked at the rate of every other day may have serious behavioral problems quite apart from their being spanked, and that the 807 mothers in the survey were just 14 to 24 years old at the time they gave birth—hardly a representative sample. Typically, news accounts reported simply that Straus's study determined that "spanking children causes [a] 'boomerang' of misbehavior," as the Associated Press put it.

Remarkably, the same issue of *Archives* carried another, longer-term study by psychologist Marjorie Lindner Gunnoe that came to quite different conclusions. Unlike Straus, Gunnoe used data that tracked somewhat more children (just over 1,100) for five years (not two years), sampled older parents as well, and relied on reports from both children and adults. The researcher concluded that "for most children, claims that spanking teaches aggression seem unfounded." Gunnoe found that children ages 4 to 7 who had been spanked got in fewer, not more, fights at school. (The reverse was true with white boys ages 8 to 11 in single-mother families, who Gunnoe suggested might be less accepting of parental authority.) Yet there was no AMA press release on the Gunnoe study, and none of the network reports and only 15 of the 107 newspaper and magazine stories on Straus's research mentioned Gunnoe's contrary findings.

Outside the not-so-watchful eye of the media, researchers have been reassessing the conventional wisdom on spanking for several years. In 1996, psychologist Robert E. Larzelere, director of residential research at Boys Town in Nebraska, which does not allow spanking, published the results of a sweeping review of spanking research, in which he examined 166 studies and came to several unexpected conclusions. Rejecting research that was not peer-reviewed, that included overly se-

vere or abusive punishment (causing bruises or other injuries), or in which the child's behavior was not clearly preceded by the spanking, Larzelere ferreted out the 35 best studies. Among these, he failed to find any convincing evidence that nonabusive spanking, as typically used by parents, damaged children. Even more surprisingly, Larzelere's review revealed that no other discipline tech-

Don't yell. In all forms of discipline, how you do it is important as what you do. Parenting experts say ver abuse can be as harmful to children as physical abus

nique—including timeout and withdrawal of privileges—had *more* beneficial results for children under 13 than spanking, in terms of getting children to comply with their parents' wishes.

When Larzelere and others presented their research at the 1996 AAP conference on spanking, it prompted a quiet wave of revisionism. The two conference organizers, S. Kenneth Schonberg and Stanford B. Friedman, both pediatrics professors at Albert Einstein College of Medicine in New York, wrote afterward in *Pediatrics*, "We must confess that we had a preconceived notion that corporal punishment, including spanking, was innately and always 'bad.'" Yet by the end of the conference, the two skeptics acknowledged that "given a relatively 'healthy' family life in a supportive environment, spanking in and of itself is not detrimental to a child or predictive of later problems."

The spanking controversy may be an abstract debate among academics, but it is a real-life dilemma for parents of young children who wrestle daily—and sometimes hourly—with disciplining their small charges. A study of 90 mothers of 2-years-olds found that they interrupted them an average of every 6 to 8 minutes to induce them to change their behavior. Shellee Godfrey, a mother of two from High Point, N.C., swore she'd never spank her kids. "I figured, I'm gonna talk to my children," she says. Then came the day when she was late for work and Jake, her strong-willed 2-year-old, refused to get dressed, repeatedly ripping off his diaper. "I was desperate. I finally popped him and said, 'You're putting this diaper on!' He looked at me, and he did it. He was fine. But I felt really bad, like I had hurt him."

Naturally, no child-development specialist is about to run out to write a book called *Why You Should Spank Your Kid*—which may be one reason why the news media have buried the notion that spanking might in some cases be a useful discipline technique. After ethicist Ryan was quoted in the *New York Times* a few years ago saying, "Mild physical punishment is appropriate in extreme cases," he says, "I never got so much hate mail about anything."

One lesson of the spanking controversy is that whether parents spank or not matters less than *how* they spank. "If parents use it as an occasional backup for, say, a timeout," says Larzelere, "and as part of discipline in the context of a loving relationship, then an occasional spanking can have a beneficial role." The welter of child-raising books of the past 30 years has also provided a host of alternatives to spanking that allow children to express their feelings—a radical idea earlier in this century—while at the same time preserving firm limits on behavior. The best disciplinary approach, experts say, is to use a number of methods, including reasoning, timeouts, rewards, withdrawals of privileges, and what some experts term "natural consequences" (e.g., if a child refuses to eat his breakfast, he goes hungry that morning). Spanking seems to work best in conjunction with some of these techniques. For example, another analysis of spanking studies by Larzelere shows that when spanking is used among 2- to 6-year-olds to back up other discipline measures—such as reasoning—that have failed, it delays the next recurrence of misbehavior for twice as long as the use of reasoning alone.

For parents who choose to spank, there are appropriate and inappropriate ways to do so. Kids under 2 years old should not be spanked, because the danger of causing physical injury is too great. As for adolescents, research suggests a fairly sol-id correlation between spanking and increased misbehavior; grounding teens has proven more effective. The age when spanking is most useful appears to be between 2 and 6, and parents should take into account the nature of the child. A single disapproving word can bring a sensitive child to tears, while a more spirited youngster might need stronger measures. Finally, spankings should be done in private to spare children humiliation, and without anger. A parent who purposefully includes spanking as one of a range of discipline options may be less likely to use it impulsively and explosively in a moment of rage.

As for how to spank, the AAP warns against using anything other than an open hand, and only on the child's rear end or extremities. The intention should be to modify behavior, not cause pain. "A spanking is nothing more than a nonverbal way of terminating the [bad] behavior," says psychologist John Rosemond, author of *To Spank or Not To Spank*. It secures "the child's attention, so that you can send the child a clear message of disapproval and direction."

Plenty of parents feel they can deliver that message without striking their child. "Our belief is that spanking, hitting, any overt physical punishment isn't an effective technique for encouraging positive behavior," says Gerrie Nachman, a Manhattan mother of an 11-year-old son. "The last thing we want to do is model to our son physical abuse as a way of dealing with inappropriate behavior in other people."

Parental abuse. At the other extreme are parents who deliver far more than a tap on the rear. In response to a 1995 poll, almost

Rewards. Rewarding children's good behavior with everything from TV shows to allowances to special desserts is a time-honored behavior modification tool

20 percent of parents said they had hit a child on the bottom with a brush, belt, or stick in the past year; another 10 percent said they had spanked the child with a "hard object." One valuable lesson to come out of the antispanking movement is an awareness of how many parents abuse spanking. Straus found that two thirds of mothers of children under 6, for instance, spank them at least three times a week, which most experts would say is too much.

The current state of knowledge about spanking may cut two ways: Parents who use spanking appropriately can relax and stop feeling that they are causing ineluctable harm to their child. But parents who overspank—and mistakenly believe that their firm thwacks are benefiting little Samantha—should scale back their spankings. Somewhere in between parents' guilt and parents' denial lies a happier medium.

With Anna Mulrine

Boys will be Boys

Developmental research has been focused on girls; now it's their brothers' turn. Boys need help, too, but first they need to be understood.

BY BARBARA KANTROWITZ AND CLAUDIA KALB

I T WAS A CLASSIC MARS-VENUS ENCOUNter. Only in this case, the woman was from Harvard and the man—well, boy—was a 4-year-old at a suburban Boston nursery school. Graduate student Judy Chu was in his classroom last fall to gather observations for her doctoral dissertation on human development. His greeting was startling: he held up his finger as if it were a gun and pretended to shoot her. "I felt bad," Chu recalls. "I felt as if he didn't like me." Months later and much more boy-savvy, Chu has a different interpretation: the gunplay wasn't hostile—it was just a way for him to say hello. "They don't mean it to have harsh consequences. It's a way for them to connect."

Researchers like Chu are discovering new meaning in lots of things boys have done for ages. In fact, they're dissecting just about every aspect of the developing male psyche and creating a hot new field of inquiry: the study of boys. They're also producing a slew of books with titles like "Real Boys: Rescuing Our Sons From the Myths of Boyhood"

and "Raising Cain: Protecting the Emotional Life of Boys" that will hit the stores in the next few months.

What some researchers are finding is that boys and girls really are from two different planets. But since the two sexes have to live together here on Earth, they should be raised with special consideration for their distinct needs. Boys and girls have different "crisis points," experts say, stages in their emotional and social development where things can go very wrong. Until recently, girls got all the attention. But boys need help, too. They're much more likely than girls to have discipline problems at school and to be diagnosed with attention deficit disorder (ADD). Boys far outnumber girls in special-education classes. They're also more likely to commit violent crimes and end up in jail. Consider the headlines: Jonesboro, Ark.; Paducah, Ky.; Pearl, Miss. In all these school shootings, the perpetrators were young adolescent boys.

Even normal boy behavior has come to be considered pathological in the wake of

the feminist movement. An abundance of physical energy and the urge to conquer—these are normal male characteristics, and in an earlier age they were good things, even essential to survival. "If Huck Finn or Tom Sawyer were alive today," says Michael Gurian, author of "The Wonder of Boys," "we'd say they had ADD or a conduct disorder." He says one of the new insights we're gaining about boys is a very old one: boys will be boys. "They are who they are," says Gurian, "and we need to love them for who they are. Let's not try to rewire them."

Indirectly, boys are benefiting from all the research done on girls, especially the landmark work by Harvard University's Carol Gilligan. Her 1982 book, "In a Different Voice: Psychological Theory and Women's Development," inspired Take Our Daughters to Work Day, along with best-selling spinoffs like Mary Pipher's "Reviving Ophelia." The traditional, unisex way of looking at child development was profoundly flawed, Gilligan says: "It was like having a one-dimensional perspective on a

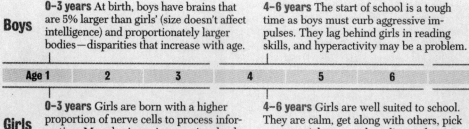

The Wonder (and Worry) Years

There may be no such thing as *child* development anymore. Instead, researchers are now studying each gender's development separately and discovering that boys and girls face very different sorts of challenges. Here is a rough guide to the major phases in their development.

Boys

0-3 years At birth, boys have brains that are 5% larger than girls' (size doesn't affect intelligence) and proportionately larger bodies—disparities that increase with age.

4-6 years The start of school is a tough time as boys must curb aggressive impulses. They lag behind girls in reading skills, and hyperactivity may be a problem.

| Age 1 | 2 | 3 | 4 | 5 | 6 | 7 |

Girls

0-3 years Girls are born with a higher proportion of nerve cells to process information. More brain regions are involved in language production and recognition.

4-6 years Girls are well suited to school. They are calm, get along with others, pick up on social cues, and reading and writing come easily to them.

Some Tips for Parents

- **Common sense helps.** So does a sense of humor. Most of all, boys need to know that the two most important people in their lives, their parents, are there for them.
- **Boys need hugs, too.** Don't try to turn him into Clint Eastwood at the age of 4. You're not coddling him by showing tenderness; you're developing emotional solidarity with your son and teaching him empathy.
- **Don't sweat the gun issue.** Even if you ban all guns, chances are your son will find a way to play at fighting: fingers or carrots work equally well. There's no evidence that this kind of play will turn your boy into a killer any more than playing with trucks will make him a truckdriver.
- **It's OK to get mad.** When he's at an appropriate age, you can help him understand the difference between legitimate feelings of anger and expressing it by hitting, kicking or screaming.
- **Stay in touch.** As they get older, boys still need their parents. Look for opportunities to communicate, like picking him up at school. He'll be strapped in a seat belt, so you know he can't get away.

two-dimensional scene." At Harvard, where she chairs the gender-studies department, Gilligan is now supervising work on males, including Chu's project. Other researchers are studying mental illness and violence in boys.

While girls' horizons have been expanding, boys' have narrowed, confined to rigid ideas of acceptable male behavior no matter how hard their parents tried to avoid stereotypes. The macho ideal still rules. "We gave boys dolls and they used them as guns," says Gurian. "For 15 years, all we heard was that [gender differences] were all about socialization. Parents who raised their kids through that period said in the end, 'That's not true. Boys and girls can be awfully different.' I think we're awakening to the biological realities and the sociological realities."

But what exactly is the essential nature of boys? Even as infants, boys and girls behave differently. A recent study at Children's Hospital in Boston found that boy babies are more emotionally expressive; girls are more reflective. (That means boy babies tend to cry when they're unhappy; girl babies suck their thumbs.) This could indicate that girls are innately more able to control their emo-

tions. Boys have higher levels of testosterone and lower levels of the neurotransmitter serotonin, which inhibits aggression and impulsivity. That may help explain why more males than females carry through with suicide, become alcoholics and are diagnosed with ADD.

The developmental research on the impact of these physiological differences is still in the embryonic stage, but psychologists are drawing some interesting comparisons between girls and boys (chart). For girls, the first crisis point often comes in early adolescence. Until then, Gilligan and others found, girls have an enormous capacity for establishing relationships and interpreting emotions. But in their early teens, girls clamp down, squash their emotions, blunt their insight. Their self-esteem plummets. The first crisis point for boys comes much earlier, researchers now say. "There's an outbreak of symptoms at age 5, 6, 7, just like you see in girls at 11, 12, 13," says Gilligan. Problems at this age include bed-wetting and separation anxiety. "They don't have the language or experience" to articulate it fully, she says, "but the feelings are no less intense." That's why Gilligan's student Chu is

studying preschoolers. For girls at this age, Chu says, hugging a parent goodbye "is almost a nonissue." But little boys, who display a great deal of tenderness, soon begin to bury it with "big boy" behavior to avoid being called sissies. "When their parents drop them off, they want to be close and want to be held, but not in front of other people," says Chu. "Even as early as 4, they're already aware of those masculine stereotypes and are negotiating their way around them."

It's a phenomenon that parents, especially mothers, know well. One morning last month, Lori Dube, a 37-year-old mother of three from Evanston, Ill., visited her oldest son, Abe, almost 5, at his nursery school, where he was having lunch with his friends. She kissed him, prompting another boy to comment scornfully: "Do you know what your mom just did? She kissed you!" Dube acknowledges, with some sadness, that she'll have to be more sensitive to Abe's new reactions to future public displays of affection. "Even if he loves it, he's getting these messages that it's not good."

There's a struggle—a desire and need for warmth on the one hand and a pull toward independence on the other. Boys like Abe are going through what psychologists long ago declared an integral part of growing up: individualization and disconnection from parents, especially mothers. But now some researchers think that process is too abrupt. When boys repress normal feelings like love because of social pressure, says William Pollack, head of the Center for Men at Boston's McLean Hospital and author of the forthcoming "Real Boys," "they've lost contact with the genuine nature of who they are and what they feel. Boys are in a silent crisis. The only time we notice it is when they pull the trigger."

No one is saying that acting like Rambo in nursery school leads directly to tragedies like Jonesboro. But researchers do think that boys who are forced to shut down positive emotions are left with only one socially acceptable outlet: anger. The cultural ideals boys are exposed to in movies and on TV still emphasize traditional masculine roles—warrior, rogue, adventurer—with heavy

7-10 years While good at gross motor skills, boys trail girls in finer control. Many of the best students but also nearly all of the poorest ones are boys.

11-13 years A mixed bag. Dropout rates begin to climb, but good students start pulling ahead of girls in math skills and catching up some in verbal ones.

14-16 years Entering adolescence, boys hit another rough patch. Indulging in drugs, alcohol and aggressive behavior are common forms of rebellion.

8	9	10	11	12	13	14	15	16

7-10 years Very good years for girls. On average, they outperform boys at school, excelling in verbal skills while holding their own in math.

11-13 years The start of puberty and girls' most vulnerable time. Many experience depression; as many as 15% may try to kill themselves.

14-16 years Eating disorders are a major concern. Although anorexia can manifest itself as early as 8, it typically afflicts girls starting at 11 or 12; bulimia at 15.

SOURCES: DR. MICHAEL THOMPSON, BARNEY BRAWER. RESEARCH BY BILL VOURVOULIAS—NEWSWEEK

doses of violence. For every Mr. Mom, there are a dozen Terminators. "The feminist movement has done a great job of convincing people that a woman can be nurturing and a mother and a tough trial lawyer at the same time," says Dan Kindlon, an assistant professor of psychiatry at Harvard Medical School. "But we haven't done that as much with men. We're afraid that if they're too soft, that's all they can be."

And the demands placed on boys in the early years of elementary school can increase their overall stress levels. Scientists have known for years that boys and girls develop physically and intellectually at very different rates (time-line). Boys' fine motor skills—the ability to hold a pencil, for example—are usually considerably behind girls. They often learn to read later. At the same time, they're much more active—not the best combination for academic advancement. "Boys feel like school is a game rigged against them," says Michael Thompson, coauthor with Kindlon of "Raising Cain." "The things at which they excel—gross motor skills, visual and spatial skills, their exuberance—do not find as good a reception in school" as the things girls excel at. Boys (and girls) are also in academic programs at much younger ages than they used to be, increasing the chances that males will be forced to sit still before they are ready. The result, for many boys, is frustration, says Thompson: "By fourth grade, they're saying the teachers like girls better."

A second crisis point for boys occurs around the same time their sisters are stumbling, in early adolescence. By then, say Thompson and Kindlon, boys go one step further in their drive to be "real guys." They partake in a "culture of cruelty," enforcing male stereotypes on one another. "Anything tender, anything compassionate or too artistic is labeled gay," says Thompson. "The homophobia of boys in the 11, 12, 13 range is a stronger force than gravity."

Boys who refuse to fit the mold suffer. Glo Wellman of the California Parenting Institute in Santa Rosa has three sons, 22, 19 and 12. One of her boys, she says, is a "nontypical boy: he's very sensitive and caring and creative and artistic." Not surprisingly, he had the most difficulty growing up, she says. "We've got a long way to go to help boys... to have a sense that they can be anything they want to be."

In later adolescence, the once affectionate toddler has been replaced by a sulky stranger who often acts as though torture would be preferable to a brief exchange of words with Mom or Dad. Parents have to try even harder to keep in touch. Boys want and need the attention, but often just don't know how to ask for it. In a recent national poll, teenagers named their parents as their No. 1 heroes. Researchers say a strong parental bond is the most important protection against everything from smoking to suicide.

For San Francisco Chronicle columnist Adnir Lara, that message sank in when she was traveling to New York a few years ago with her son, then 15. She sat next to a woman who told her that until recently she would have had to change seats because she would not have been able to bear the pain of seeing a teenage son and mother together. The woman's son was 17 when his girlfriend dumped him; he went into the garage and killed himself. "This story made me aware that with a boy especially, you have to keep talking because they don't come and talk to you," she says. Lara's son is now 17; she also has a 19-year-old daughter. "My daughter stalked me. She followed me from room to room. She was yelling, but she was in touch. Boys don't do that. They leave the room and you don't know what they're feeling." Her son is now 6 feet 3. "He's a man. There are barriers. You have to reach through that and remember to ruffle his hair."

With the high rate of divorce, many boys are growing up without any adult men in their lives at all. Don Elium, coauthor of the best-selling 1992 book "Raising a Son," says that with troubled boys, there's often a common theme: distant, uninvolved fathers, and mothers who have taken on more responsibility to fill the gap. That was the case with Raymundo Infante Jr., a 16-year-old high-school junior, who lives with his mother, Mildred, 38, a hospital administrative assistant in Chicago, and his sister, Vanessa, 19. His parents divorced when he was a baby and he had little contact with his father until a year ago. The hurt built up—in sixth grade, Raymundo was so depressed that he told a classmate he wanted to kill himself. The classmate told the teacher, who told a counselor, and Raymundo saw a psychiatrist for a year. "I felt that I just wasn't good enough, or he just didn't want me," Raymundo says. Last year Raymundo finally confronted his dad, who works two jobs—in an office and on a construction crew—and accused him of caring more about work than about his son. Now the two spend time together on weekends and sometimes go shopping, but there is still a huge gap of lost years.

Black boys are especially vulnerable, since they are more likely than whites to

Trouble Spots: Where Boys Run Into Problems

Not all boys are the same, of course, but most rebel in predictable patterns and with predictable weapons: underachievement, aggression and drug and alcohol use. While taking chances is an important aspect of the growth process, it can lead to real trouble.

When Johnny Can't Read
Girls have reading disorders nearly as often as boys, but are able to overcome them. Disability rates, as identified by:

CLINICAL TESTS	SCHOOLS
Boys 8.7%	Boys 13.6%
Girls 6.9%	Girls 3.2%

SOURCE: DR. SALLY SHAYWITZ, CONN. LONGITUDINAL STUDY

Suicidal Impulses
While girls are much more likely to try to kill themselves, boys are likelier to die from their attempts.

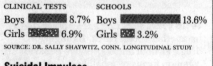

SUICIDE ATTEMPTS*	SUICIDE FATALITIES
Boys 3,000	Boys 260
Girls 23,000	Girls 77

1995, AGES 5-14. *NEWSWEEK ESTIMATE. SOURCES: NCHS, CDC

Binge Drinking
Boys binge more on alcohol. Those who had five or more drinks in a row in the last two weeks:

1997, BY GRADE

40% Boys

30

20 Girls

10

8th   10th   12th

SOURCE: MONITORING THE FUTURE STUDY

Aggression That Turns to Violence
Boys get arrested three times as often as girls, but for some nonviolent crimes the numbers are surprisingly even.

Arrests of 10- to 17-year-olds: ■ Boys ▩ Girls

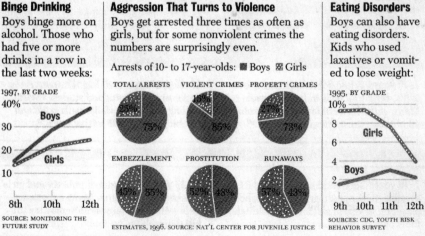

TOTAL ARRESTS	VIOLENT CRIMES	PROPERTY CRIMES
25% / 75%	15% / 85%	27% / 73%

EMBEZZLEMENT	PROSTITUTION	RUNAWAYS
45% / 55%	52% / 48%	57% / 43%

ESTIMATES, 1996. SOURCE: NAT'L CENTER FOR JUVENILE JUSTICE

Eating Disorders
Boys can also have eating disorders. Kids who used laxatives or vomited to lose weight:

1995, BY GRADE

10%

8 Girls

6

4

2 Boys

9th   10th   11th   12th

SOURCES: CDC, YOUTH RISK BEHAVIOR SURVEY

grow up in homes without fathers. They're often on their own much sooner than whites. Black leaders are looking for alternatives. In Atlanta, the Rev. Tim McDonald's First Iconium Baptist Church just chartered a Boy Scout troop. "Gangs are so prevalent because guys want to belong to something," says McDonald. "We've got to give them something positive to belong to." Black educators like Chicagoan Jawanza Kunjufu think mentoring programs will overcome the bias against academic success as "too white." Some cities are also experimenting with all-boy classrooms in predominantly black schools.

Researchers hope that in the next few years, they'll come up with strategies that will help boys the way the work of Gilligan and others helped girls. In the meantime, experts say, there are some guidelines. Parents can channel their sons' energy into constructive activities, like team sports. They should also look for "teachable moments" to encourage qualities such as empathy. When Diane Fisher, a Cincinnati-area psychologist, hears her 8- and 10-year-old boys talking about "finishing somebody," she knows she has mistakenly rented a violent videogame. She pulls the plug and tells them: "In our house, killing people is not entertainment, even if it's just pretend."

Parents can also teach by example. New Yorkers Dana and Frank Minaya say they've never disciplined their 16-year-old son Walter in anger. They insist on resolving all disputes calmly and reasonably, without yelling. If there is a problem, they call an official family meeting "and we never leave without a big hug," says Frank. Walter tries to be open with his parents. "I don't want to miss out on any advice," he says.

Most of all, wise parents of boys should go with the flow. Cindy Lang, 36, a full-time mother in Woodside, Calif., is continually amazed by the relentless energy of her sons, Roger Lloyd, 12, and Chris, 9. "You accept the fact that they're going to involve themselves in risky behavior, like skateboarding down a flight of stairs. As a girl, I certainly wasn't skateboarding down a flight of stairs." Just last week, she got a phone call from school telling her that Roger Lloyd was in the emergency room because he had fallen backward while playing basketball and school officials thought he might have a concussion. He's fine now, but she's prepared for the next emergency: "I have a cell phone so I can be on alert." Boys will be boys. And we have to let them.

With KAREN SPRINGEN *in Chicago,* PATRICIA KING *in San Francisco,* PAT WINGERT *in Washington,* VERN E. SMITH *in Atlanta and* ELIZABETH ANGELL *in New York*

Unit 5

Key Points to Consider

❖ Do you know what it's like to be a latchkey child? If you were a working parent confronted with inadequate child care for your school-age children, what arrangements would you be prepared to make for your children? How could you help children to be active and responsible participants in their own care?

❖ Due to changes in family structure, many American children are at risk and living in poverty. What should our nation do to help children? If family breakdown is related to numerous problems for children, should public policy be designed to help reduce the enormous number of children living in poverty in our country?

❖ What is the role of television in child development? How might television contribute to many of children's and society's problems? What advantages does television have for children's development? What can parents and schools do to help children become more "media literate" to protect them from negative influences in television and advertising? How do you balance our First Amendment rights to free speech with the data showing a correlation between media violence and murder rates in this country? Is censorship warranted or necessary?

❖ As a child, did you ever suffer from some form of victimization or exploitation? What were the responses of the adults and peers around you? What suggestions would you have to prevent what appears to be a very high incidence of childhood victimization? Why do you think some children make it against all odds and go on to thrive despite acute victimization?

❖ Imagine dressing up a newborn baby boy in pink taffeta and bows; would the newborn baby protest? Now imagine dressing this same boy in girl's clothing at age eight; what would his reaction likely be now? Gender identity and development clearly undergo developmental change with age and socialization. Why do you think the boy in the reading, "A Boy without a Penis," had difficulty in assuming a different gender identity? Growing up, what do you remember most vividly about being male or female?

DUSHKIN ONLINE Links   www.dushkin.com/online/

These sites are annotated on pages 4 and 5.

Social scientists and developmental psychologists have come to realize that children are influenced by a multitude of social forces that surround them. In this unit we present articles to illuminate how American children are influenced by broad factors such as economics, culture, politics, and the media. These influences also affect the family, which is a major context of child development, and many children are now faced with more family challenges than ever. In addition, analysis of exceptional or atypical children gives the reader a more comprehensive account of child development. Thus, articles are presented on special challenges of development, such as poverty, violence, sexual abuse, and learning disabilities.

"Buried Alive" raises difficult and provocative issues about how American children today are faced with the challenge of unprecedented levels of change in the family, society, and larger popular culture. For example, the connection between broader societal values and the concomitant pressures exerted on educational practices has placed more demands on schools. At the same time, while we may espouse the need to hold onto certain core societal values, our popular culture often appears to directly contradict these core values. This essay helps us to take stock of the complex ways in which our society sometimes sends conflicting messages to our unsuspecting children.

Another influence on children is television, the "electronic family member." Nearly all American homes have a television set, and two-thirds of homes have at least two. In fact, more families in the United States have a television set than a telephone. Given that by the time children graduate from high school they will have spent more time watching television than attending school, their exposure to television is likely to affect many aspects of development. "Of Power Rangers and V-Chips" discusses legislative changes regarding violent programming and the potentially negative and dangerous effects of television violence on children's development.

Some children all around the world are faced with challenges such as attention deficit disorder, autism, sexual abuse, and other forms of exploitation. These children are often misunderstood and mistreated and pose special challenges to parents, teachers, and society. Are schools and families prepared to deal with such children? Teachers and parents need information to be better able to identify and deal with these children. These issues are discussed in "Victimization of Children," "Resilience in Development," and "The Effects of Poverty on Children."

BURIED ALIVE

Our children and the avalanche of crud.

DAVID DENBY

MAX, my older son, who just turned thirteen, once had a thick green carpet in his room, a tufted and matted shag that my wife and I inherited from the previous owners of our West End Avenue apartment, in New York. When Max was six or seven, we spent a good deal of time kneeling in the carpet, cleaning up his toys, and down there in the green we got to thinking about the moral nature of his education. Pennies, rubber bands, paper clips, marbles, peanut shells, dirty socks, toy soldiers, wooden blocks, G.I. Joes, crayons, dollops of synthetic slime—a sort of kiddies' bouillabaisse, a thickening brew of plastic and metallic stuff—gathered in the shag. It was the landscape of the American child.

One day, the carpet was covered with hundreds of pieces of plastic, and I sat among them, overwhelmed. A friend of Max's had just been over, and the boys had dumped boxes of toys on the floor. There were Legos, of course—the plugged and stamped modular pieces that fit together in innumerable combinations—but also the mobile olive-green figures of the Teenage Mutant Ninja Turtles, along with He-Man and Skeletor, and odd figures from "Sesame Street" and two or three toy groups I couldn't identify. On the floor was the plastic detritus of half a dozen . . . what? Not toys, exactly, but toy systems, many of which were also available as a television show or a movie, or both, with links to computer games, video-arcade games, comic books, regular children's books, clothes, and cereal boxes. Each part of the toy system sold another part, and so Max was encased in fantasy props—*stuff*—virtually to the limits of his horizon.

Idly, I extracted one of the superheroes from the carpet and broke off its arm.

To my surprise, I find myself welcoming, or at least not opposing, the advent of the V-chip—the little device that is to be installed in new television sets sold from 1998 on and that will allow parents to block out programs they don't want their children to see. Many parents I know have similar feelings, and quite a few are surprised by the depths of their ambivalence and in some cases misery on the subject of the plastic on the carpet—upset by the way pop culture in all its forms has invaded their homes, and the habits, manners, and souls of their children. My friends are drawn from a small circle of well-educated New Yorkers; we are a fairly compact and no doubt privileged group. Yet our anguish about bringing up children is, I believe, widely shared by parents of all kinds. Child-rearing is at once the most prosaic and the most mesmerizing subject in the world. The nagging, repetitive tasks it requires—and the wrenching obsessions—reach across regional, class, and political lines. "Married . . . with Children" and the computer game Doom are the same in Montana and in Manhattan.

No one I know expects that the V-chip will make much difference. The chip is no more than a finger in a dike that has already sprung a thousand leaks. In the past two decades or so, pop has triumphed, defeating all but a few pockets of resistance, absorbing or marginalizing the older, "high" arts, humbling the schools, setting the tone for an entire society. The children live in it, but, of course, their parents also live in it, and this is part of the confusion. How can you fight what you enjoy yourself? I am

a film critic and I see more than a hundred movies every year, which puts me in the worst possible position when I berate my children for watching too many movies. My wife, a novelist, loves the new crop of girl rockers. In our family, "The Simpsons" is a source of wonder and "The Empire Strikes Back" an endlessly repeated pleasure.

Even parents who enjoy their share of pop are feeling wary and sore, as if someone has made fools of them. And a few parents I know have given themselves over to bitter rage and are locked in an unwinnable struggle to shut out pop culture and the life of the streets—the two are now indistinguishable—from their children's experience. Acting out of fear and love, and perhaps out of spiritual ambition, too, they have turned themselves into authoritarians, banning television, banning many kinds of "unsuitable" movies. There is so much to forbid—perhaps a whole culture to forbid! And in so doing, these parents risk making the forbidden glamorous and dangerous; they risk cutting the children off from their friends and bringing them up as alienated strangers in the electronic world of the future.

I don't want to be like them, but I understand their absolutism. We are all in the same boat, afloat in the boundless sea. For both relaxed and authoritarian parents, the real issue is much larger than bad TV shows and movies. (There are always some good ones.) We all believe in "choice," but our children, to our chagrin, may no longer have the choice *not* to live in pop. For many of them, pop has become not just a piece of reality—a mass of diversions, either good or bad, brilliant or cruddy—but the very ground of reality. The danger is not mere exposure to occasional violent or prurient images but the acceptance of a degraded environment that devalues everything—a shadow world in which our kids are breathing an awful lot of poison without knowing that there's clean air and sunshine elsewhere. They are shaped by the media as consumers before they've had a chance to develop their souls.

The usual response to such complaints is a sigh or a shrug or, alternatively, exhortations like "Get tough with them. Take control of what they see, what they read and listen to." Parents who think of themselves as conservatives often say this, and their assumptions give them a tactical advantage: they don't have to make so many choices; they are more likely to establish inflexible general principles for what their children can see and do and to insist on parental authority regardless of any contrary evidence or argument. If sex is something children should not see in movies, that's the end of the discussion. Yet the issue is not so simple, especially for parents like me and my wife, who are not eager to stand over the children, guiding their progress all day long like missionaries leading the savages to light. To assume control over their habits and attitudes, we would have to become bullies.

In fact, our two boys are far from addicted to television, but like many American children they consider themselves entitled to a certain amount of TV and to video games and movies as well. As far as they are concerned, such pleasures come with the territory: consuming media, they think, is part of what children do. No doubt I should have been tougher with them; I should have made it clear when they were younger that watching TV was not an entitlement but a privilege. (The awful word makes me wince, but I'm sorry now that I didn't say it.) At this point, we are stuck with the usual compromise, which the children accept in principle: We establish limits—only so much TV, only certain movies, and so on. But there are always arguments, discussions, trades, and other negotiations, and we have come to realize that asserting control over the boys' tastes is no longer possible be-

yond a certain point. How can you control what they breathe?

MANDATED as part of the Telecommunications Act (signed earlier this year), the V-chip is an attempt to give parents more control (or, realists would say, the illusion of control). At this moment, the Motion Picture Association of America, which has administered the movie ratings since 1968, is hoping to get a workable system in place by next January, a year before the V-chipped sets come out. Just like movies, television shows will be rated according to their suitability for children. Parents at home, using a secret code and a remote control, will set their new TVs at whatever rating level they are comfortable with. Any show rated above that level will automatically be shut out.

But how do you rate an endless sea? There are broadcast network and broadcast local shows, network cable and local cable shows, and public television, too: perhaps a thousand hours or more a day of programming. It is less a series of discrete shows than a nation's shared environment—our communal glop, our feed, our ether, our *medium*. Movies are currently rated by a group of thirteen Los Angeles–area citizens with experience as parents, but no group of ten, twenty, or fifty citizens, not even one chained to the spot like the inhabitants of Plato's cave, can sit and rate all the shows. What to do? Jack Valenti, who is the head of the M.P.A.A., and an industry advisory board have decided that the distributors of programming—networks, stations, cable operators—perhaps in consultation with the writers and producers of the shows, will assign the ratings to themselves.

Can the producers and distributors rate themselves? It seems a dubious procedure. In any case, the sheer amount of stuff overwhelms any rational attempt to assess it. Such criteria as intelligence, dramatic interest, and style will not play much of a role in the ratings. A few shows that I might want my older son to see are likely to receive the equivalent of an R—for instance, the occasional PBS series "Prime Suspect," made by England's Granada Television, and starring Helen Mirren as the London police detective Jane Tennison. One recent episode, "The Scent

of Darkness," detailed with grim intensity and admirable British levelheadedness the pursuit and capture of a serial killer. Most of Tennison's colleagues doubt her judgment in the case, and the true subject of the episode—and of Mirren's performance—is the moral gallantry of a woman fighting the coldness of male contempt. Burrowing deep within its peculiar, mazelike world, the drama was so convincing and intelligent that when my older son drifted in, my wife and I let him watch. (We shooed away Thomas, who is nine.) Mirren's fierce, driving anger, her sense that she has an obligation not only to the job but to herself—an obligation not to betray herself—is the essence of modern heroism, and Max, who has seen his share of thoughtlessly violent movies and TV shows, was impressed. Afterward, we talked it over. He wanted to go deeper into the plot and the characters, to understand everyone's motives. With the V-chip in place, however, viewers unfamiliar with the special qualities of "Prime Suspect" will probably not let their thirteen-year-olds see it.

POP culture hardly takes up all of my sons' lives. Their school gives them plenty of work. They read, though not as much as we'd like. (We also read to them and tell them stories and bits of history constantly.) They play basketball, go snowboarding, collect things, make friends everywhere; Max blades and rides, and Thomas plays the piano. If we put on Toscanini's recording of Beethoven's Seventh, they twirl and jump around the living room and carom off the furniture. They seem busier and more active than I was at nine or thirteen. Nevertheless, their absorption in pop is very intense.

When Max is at home on a Saturday, or on vacation, he may hit the computer as soon as he gets up, ignoring repeated entreaties to eat breakfast, and finally ignoring bowls of cereal placed under his nose as he plays one of the war-strategy games that he currently loves—Caesar II, say, set in ancient Rome, or Warcraft II, in which the player, in charge of the Humans, builds forts, towns, farms, and mills, all for the purpose of defeating the unspeakable Orcs, ardent little creatures who attack from many sides and emit anguished groans as they are hacked, maced, and cannonaded into the world below. (Children with a taste for perversity can take the side of the Orcs, or two kids can play against each other.) Warcraft is a big advance in complexity over the point-and-shoot games like Wolfenstein 3-D or Doom, in which the player passes through three-dimensional corridors and mows down endless assailants. (In Wolfenstein, after killing all the S.S. guards, one finally kills Hitler; I have played the game myself with a certain amount of pleasure.) In Warcraft, having won a particular battle, the player graduates to a more difficult level, and is greeted there by the game's narrator, who speaks the medieval fustian that seems to have spread from the Emperor in the "Star Wars" trilogy to many areas of the kiddie culture. "A great host of Orcs have reconstructed the Dark Portal and now lay siege to the land of Nethergarde," the narrator says. The voice rings out in the house like some lugubrious fake who won't go home after a dinner party.

Max may then meet some friends and go for some lunch at the nearest Burger King, where he will eat a Double Whopper and drink a Coke and sternly ignore (I hope) the free dolls and other promotional appeals for "The Hunchback of Notre Dame." Afterward, the group of boys may drift to a violent special-effects debauch like "Mission: Impossible." Later, they may play some basketball in the park (baseball is not the game of choice for media kids), or just hand out at home and (if we let them) watch TV or a rented movie. As the kids sit watching, we shove plates of raw vegetables and roast chicken in their faces, which they sample, all the while demanding chips, Fritos, and Pop-Tarts. And so on, into the night. We intervene, pulling Max away from his friends, but on these occasions when we're at work and can't intervene, he's spent his whole day in media junk, including the food—a day of pleasure, companionship, and maybe heightened alertness, but little else.

Crashing into the kitchen, my sons talk in the private languages they've worked up from exposure to the shows, movies, computer games, rap music, and basketball players that matter to them. Children have always spoken in tongues, living inside their jokes and insults—my

friends and I did it forty years ago—but in recent years the talk has grown quicker, more jangled and allusive, shifting at near-electronic speeds from, say, imitations of Apu, the Kwik-E-Mart manager in "The Simpsons," to Darth Vader, then to Snoop Doggy Dogg and on to jaw-jutting taunts from "Ace Ventura" and other Jim Carrey movies. The children channel-surf their own minds. They can talk logically and soberly, but they seem at their happiest bopping through the apartment, like Robin Williams on a roll, the older one with his high, serious forehead and dark-brown hair parted in the middle, like a German scientist from 1912, and the younger one singing and crowing and then tumbling over his own lines.

"Whooha! Whooha! It is *you*, young Skywalker, who are mistaken. Alrightee then! Power and the money, money and the power. Minute after minute, hour after hour. Thank you, come again!"

SOMEONE is bound to say, "It was ever thus," meaning that, as far as their elders are concerned, every generation of children is immersed in something that's no good for them. New York kids in the eighteen-sixties grew up in a rough city with gangs, street violence, and prostitutes, and most of them were no doubt familiar with such raucous and unenlightening entertainments as cockfighting and bare-knuckle boxing. It was ever thus. After all, many of us watched a good bit of TV as children, yet we wound up O.K., didn't we? What has changed? In a famous essay from 1954, "Paul, the Horror Comics, and Dr. Wertham," the cultural critic Robert Warshow deplored the violence and nihilistic goofiness of such pulp as "The Vault of Horror" and "Crime Suspen-Stories," but concluded that parents were worrying too much about horror comics. Children, like his son Paul, were resilient; most of them would outgrow comic books and would pass on to more complex narratives.

In the nineties, a great deal more than horror comics is jabbing at children, but we can agree with Warshow that the kids stay interested in nothing for very long. The computer games and TV shows, for instance, mark and cut the path of their own extinction, quickly

creating a restlessness that causes the child to turn against the games and the shows themselves. Children go from one craving to another, discarding—I don't know—"Looney Tunes" for "Superman," and "Superman" for "MacGyver," and "MacGyver" for "The Wonder Years," and "The Wonder Years" for Wolfenstein, and Wolfenstein for Sim City, and Sim City for Myst, and Myst for Doom, and Doom for Doom II. Nothing lasts. The restlessness produced by each station on this Via Dolorosa annihilates any chance for real devotion, and the child passes on. Finally the child passes *out:* he emerges at the other end of the media tunnel—though perhaps still ungratified.

My boys, after all, do not seem to be in dire trouble. They can be determinedly earnest on moral questions; they stand up for their friends and for powerless people. They are not, I think, likely to behave violently or commit crimes (the rewards for staying straight are too obvious), and if they screw up they will, like most white upper-middle-class children, be given a second chance, and a third, and they will probably do all right—they will probably come through.

But with what internal injuries along the way? It is a miserable question. Social scientists, looking for quantifiable results, have devised clinical experiments that measure the different effects of violence on children. These effects, which are apparently greater on boys, can be placed in three categories: direct imitation, which is rare, and the more frequent effects of desensitization (acceptance of violence as the way of the world) and a generalized fearfulness, a learned distrust and wariness. But as I write these words, I realize that the test results, however disturbing, are not the point. No social scientist need prove a direct effect on children's behavior for some of us to hate the bullying, conformist shabbiness of the worst pop and the way it consumes our children. If children are living in pop culture, and a good part of it is ugly and stupid, that is effect enough; the sheer cruddiness is an affront.

Individually, the games or shows may have little effect—or, at least, no effect that can't be overcome. But collectively, I'm not so sure. Even if the child's character is not formed by a single TV show, movie, video game, or computer game, the endless electronic assault obviously leaves its marks all over him. The children grow up, but they become ironists—ironists of waste. They know that everything in the media is disposable. Everything on television is just for the moment—it's just television—and the kids pick up this devaluing tone, the sense that nothing matters. Sold a bill of goods from the time they are infants, many of today's children, I suspect, will never develop the equipment to fight off the system of flattery and propitiation which soothes their insecurities and pumps their egos. By the time they are five or six, they've been pulled into the marketplace. They're on their way to becoming not citizens but consumers.

It was not ever thus. Our reality has changed. The media have become three-dimensional, inescapable, omnivorous, and self-referring—a closed system that seems, for many of the kids, to answer all their questions. The older children teach the younger ones the games and movie references, so they have something to talk about when they're alone. I've just run into a three-year-old girl who knew the names of the characters in "Hunchback" before the movie opened. Disney has already claimed her. Pop has also absorbed the oppositional energies that used to be associated with the avant-garde and with minority cultures, making once brave gestures empty gestures, commodifying discontent, inbreeding it with the edgy, in-your-face tone that teen-agers adopt as the sound of independence. That jeering tone has spread like a rash through the whole culture. It's awesome. It sucks.

When my older boy lets fly a stream of epithets in the rancorous tones of an inner-city black teen-ager, I know that the joke is on me—the white liberal. But the joke is not on me alone, of course: rap is very popular in the suburbs. One of the most remarkable social transactions of our time is the widespread assumption by white middle-class boys of the attitudes of a genuinely dispossessed class of young black men. Commodification of rage plays strange tricks. When the triumphal or despairing rant leaves its source, where it serves as a passionate expression of survival and protest, and goes into the heads of middle-class white children, it serves very different needs, fuelling the emotional demands of pre-teens and teens who may be afraid of women and of the adult world in general. The kids know that the profane rap lyrics are a violation; they speak the words with an almost ecstatic sense of release. Their parents, however, experience those words as an angry assault, and they can either roll with the punches, in which case they feel they've become teen-agers themselves, or sternly disapprove, like the squares in a fifties teen-rebel movie. "Make a stand," I tell myself as I disapprove and forbid, but dignity is not much to fall back on.

Some sort of commercialized aggression is always putting parents on the defensive—Jim Carrey with ketchup coming out of his ears in movie after movie, or Sylvester Stallone machine-gunning the population of Cleveland, or video arcades with so many shooting games that the noise level exceeds that of the Battle of the Somme. "Beavis and Butt-head" is a clever show—it mocks the cruddy teen culture even as it sells it to teens. The show brilliantly sends itself up. Still, it's hard to take. You have to listen to that warthog snort-giggle-snort, so reminiscent of advanced lunacy, as well as the frequent butthole-buttwipe exchanges. Hip parents may appreciate the wryness of B. & B.'s self-extinction, but it's dismaying that everything on teen TV—even irony—is a commodity.

The kids in the dating-game programs treat each other as commodities, the girls swinging their shoulders and smiling as they show themselves off, the audience whooping as the boys pull off their shirts and reveal their pecs and tattoos. Hardly the end of Western civilization, I admit, but the way the shows force teens to stereotype one another is awful. Children don't understand vulgarity as a concept, and the makers of commercial culture would be happy if they never understood it. Parents have to teach them what vulgarity is somehow. When I have the energy, I argue, I satirize, I get the boys to agree that the shows are stupid. Yet I don't turn off the set, because doing that would only cause them to turn it back on when I'm not there. I want *them* to turn it off.

Whether the sets are off or on, the cruddy tone is in the air and on the streets. The kids pick it up and repeat it, and every week there are moments when I feel a spasm of fury that surges back and forth between resentment and self-contempt. In those moments, I don't like the way my boys talk—I don't like the way they think. The crude, bottom-line attitudes they've picked up, the nutty obsessive profanity, the echo chamber of voices and attitudes, set my teeth on edge. The stuff fits, and they wear it. What American parent hasn't felt that spasm? Your kid is rude and surly and sees everything in terms of winning or losing or popularity and becomes insanely interested in clothes and seems far, far from courage and selfhood.

Aided by armies of psychologists and market researchers, the culture industries reach my children at every stage of their desires and their inevitable discontent. What's lost is the old dream that parents and teachers will nurture the organic development of the child's own interests, the child's own nature. That dream is largely dead. In this country, people possessed solely by the desire to sell have become far more powerful than parents tortuously working out the contradictions of authority, freedom, education, and soul-making.

IN "The Republic" Plato declares that the young should hear nothing—not even a few discordant lines from Homer—that would form their characters improperly. Plato can mischievous, but he appears to be saying that young people will adopt only the behavior that they have heard about. Today, fundamentalists have taken up this concept of education like a cudgel. Salman Rushdie's impressionistic, dream-filled novel "The Satanic Verses," in which the narrator makes fun of Muhammad, is an attack on all Islam. Kill the novelist! An American commercial movie—say, "Sleeping with the Enemy"—that has a bad marriage in it is seen not as the dramatization of a single, fictional marriage but as an attack on the institution of marriage itself. Save the institution of marriage! Well-educated American conservatives who vilify popular culture for political ends appear to want entertainment that is didactic, improving, hygienic.

In a true liberal-arts education, however, children are exposed to many stories, from many sources. They hear about all sorts of behavior—wickedness and goodness and the many fascinating varieties in between—and are taught what a narrative is and what its moral relation to life might be. Narratives give many pleasures, one of which, surely, is the working out of the story's moral significance, either simple and redundant or complex, layered, and exploratory. Parents and teachers still hope that a complicated narrative will serve as a prelude, preparing children for the complexities of life. They will learn good by studying evil as well as good.

Thinking back to my own lazy days at thirteen, I remember noodling around the house and eating my way through boxes of chocolate-chip cookies and watching old movies on TV—thirties comedies and musicals, forties thrillers and war movies, the narrative achievements of a studio system that, whatever else it did wrong, invariably managed to tell stories that pulled the viewer in. I was more passive, and certainly more isolated, than Max, but I was luckier in my movies: the movies were still a narrative medium.

The computer games, I suppose, offer a kind of narrative, but one that yields without resistance to the child's desire for instant gratification. Affording a momentary—and spurious—feeling of power, the summer's new big-budget action movies like "Mission: Impossible" and "The Rock" (and last year's "Batman Forever") offer larger versions of the same thing—increasingly jangled and incoherent narratives that also yield instantly to pleasure. I believe in pleasure, but I hate the way my boys are jacked up by the new movies without ever being drawn into the more enveloping and transforming enchantments of a beautifully worked-out story. They get used to feeling nothing but excitement. ("I don't like *drama*," I once heard one of Max's friends say with considerable exasperation.) An American adventure movie is now simply a violent movie—and, increasingly, an impersonally violent movie whose thrills refer almost entirely to earlier movie images. The Hollywood studios need to top last

year's explosions, so they keep the children bucking on a roller-coaster ride to nowhere.

I wouldn't mind the boys' seeing a certain amount of violence in movies or on TV if the violence were dramatized as serious or tragic, or even playful—anything more than an electric prod to their already overstimulated nerves. Children need secrets and hidden places, they need to tempt the forbidden. And they can really learn from tasting temptation. The thrill of danger is good for them: many of the classic stories and movies for children are about danger. But in the big new action movies, no one humanly vulnerable—no one children could identify with—is placed in jeopardy, so there's actually little sense of danger.

Because they haven't been touched or shaken, children think that having seen one violent film justifies seeing another. A parent who vetoes a movie is likely to be told, "I've seen much more violent things than this," by which he means "and yet I've survived." The kid wants to test himself against the movie, as if it were a wild ride at an amusement park, and the parent who doesn't utter an immediate and final "no" either argues endlessly, or allows himself to be dragged along with a heavy heart.

Film critics who are parents have a particularly rough time of it. A friend of mine who is also a film critic was confronted by her older son holding the videotape of a horror movie.

"Can I look at this?"

"No, you cannot."

"Why not?"

"Because it's scary, I didn't like it, and I don't want you to see it."

At that point, the child turned over the box and read aloud a rave quote from his mother's review.

My own personal calvary: Without my permission, Max saw "Pulp Fiction" on tape at a friend's house a few months ago, and enjoyed it as a bizarre collection of wicked thrills. I told him I wished he hadn't seen it, but I suppose that in one way I should have been relieved. He wasn't yet far enough along in his education in media irony to see how funny the movie was. "Pulp Fiction" is play, a mocking commentary on old genres, a celebration of pulp flagrancy and violation as pleasure—the

sport of a declining movie culture in which sincerity is the only unforgivable sin. Habitual moviegoers savor the fizz in the drink, including the S & M scene, which is deliberately absurd. But I didn't explain this to Max. I saw no reason to expand a twelve-year-old's interest in "Pulp Fiction."

But then, having seen "Pulp Fiction," he wanted to leverage himself into seeing Quentin Tarantino's earlier and much nastier (and more pointless) "Reservoir Dogs." No, I said. But why not? he asked. After all, his friends had seen it. I told him I couldn't stop him from seeing it at someone else's house, but I would prefer that he not. In such exchanges, Max is saying to me (in effect), "If I'm not old enough to see the movie, how come I'm old enough to understand the reasons I'm not supposed to see it?" That is the ultimate question posed to the parents of a media child.

Sometimes we win, but often we give in, because there are moments when my wife and I want to talk to each other or to a friend on the telephone, or read, or work. A hundred dollars for a moment of peace! It's the eternal parental cry. And in those moments and hours I let the kids watch what's on TV or play some inane point-and-shoot computer game. I am grateful that the boys have something that bottles them up for a time. The media have suffused the children with pleasure and their parents with guilt.

CONSERVATIVE critics attack the media easily and comfortably. But do they acknowledge any culpability for allowing pop culture and consumerism to become such an overwhelming force in our country's habits of child-rearing? Conservatives would like to believe that capitalism and its extraordinary executive tool, the marketplace, are not only productive and efficient but *good*. Thus they may criticize the "excesses" of a company like Time Warner; they may even criticize "greed," as if greed were some bizarre aberration normally unknown to capitalism. But they can rarely bring themselves to admit that capitalism in its routine, healthy, rejuvenating rampage through our towns, cities, and farmlands forces parents to work at multiple jobs, substitutes malls for small-city commercial streets and neighborhoods, and dumps formerly employed groups (like blacks in the inner cities) onto the street or into dead-end jobs. Or that these developments loosen parental control, and help create the very nihilism and anomie—the rootlessness of nowhere men—that find release in junk movies, rap, pornography, and the rest.

When it comes to pop culture, conservatives are the last innocents. Surely there's something pathetic about Bob Dole's calling for restraint from Time Warner, when it's precisely the unrestrained nature of capitalism that conservatives have always celebrated. Conservatives would make a lot more sense on the subject of popular culture if they admitted that the unregulated marketplace, in its abundant energy, is amoral, that it inspires envy and greediness, that it shreds "values" and offers little space or encouragement for what William Bennett calls "virtues." Parents deserve better than such ideologically motivated hypocrisies.

Nearly every parent, consciously or not, cherishes a kind of idealized timetable that proposes a mood—a state of readiness—in which a child can best be introduced to a new experience. Children's first responses—to nature, to death, to sex, to violence, to the arts, to the news that this world is often a dark and dirty place—obsess parents almost as much as providing proper food and education. In hoping to maintain a reasonable schedule, parents do not necessarily want to protect children's innocence. The schedule, after all, is a way of regulating the *loss* of innocence—opening up the world to children in a way that makes sense.

Parents can still control some of the schedule, but a large part of it has been wrenched out of their hands by pop culture. Is this a calamity? Not really. Middle-class parents are often squeamish and overprotective. Some children may be better off if they escape their parents' grip, healthier if they grow up wild and free and sort things out on their own. Still, the schedule is a lovely idea—one of the enduring talismans of middle-class family life. And parents, however discouraged they may have become, will always try to impose it.

They consider imposing it their right. For parents, the early responses are central to the poetry and moral charm of childhood. And to have those intimate moments and pleasures preëmpted by someone's marketing scheme is like receiving a blow to the chest.

If conservatives are going to oppose any sort of government regulation of the marketplace, they can't be surprised that the market overwhelms parents, and that parents then complain that they have lost control. When toys, movies, books, and television shows are all devoted to the same product or performer and are marketed by different branches of the same company, can we rationally speak of free choice in the marketplace? The producers and the distributors may be free, but are the children?

LIBERALS, too, have an accounting to make. There is a strain of opinion regarding the arts which has reigned during the last few decades in most of the bourgeois democracies—in the United States, Australia, Great Britain, France, Germany, and the rest of Western Europe. Let us call it cultural libertarianism (its god is John Stuart Mill). Cultural libertarianism insists on the paramount importance of free expression. Therefore, cultural libertarianism, when it has to, defends, as a corollary, the right of artists to use violence and sex in their work. That exploiters will use violence and sex, too, is exasperating, but such is the price of freedom. There is no way *in law* of curtailing exploiters without also curtailing artists. The market is tawdry, corrupt, and corrupting; it is also exhilarating. In a free society, art and schlock come joined together like ship and barnacle. The way to separate the two is with education and criticism.

Any other approach, cultural libertarians will argue, leads to censorship or (just as bad) self-censorship. In any case, politicized criticism of the media, whether from the left or the right, is often a form of self-righteous hysteria that inflames people against imaginary or relatively harmless dangers while diverting them from genuine social problems. In the United States, we should be less obsessed with popular culture than with the unequal distribution of goods and opportunities in an increasingly stratified society. Anyone can bring pres-

sure on Time Warner, but how do you change an inner-city neighborhood?

So goes the orthodoxy of enlightenment practiced for decades by many people (including me). Many cultural libertarians would agree, of course, that a different set of rules should be brought into play when we are talking about children. The children should be protected; they don't have the right to see and hear everything. But *can* they be protected anymore? Has our social reality changed so much that the automatic celebration of freedom in itself puts children at risk? Cultural libertarians are now faced with a number of unnerving challenges to their self-esteem.

For one thing, the tone of our common culture has coarsened in the last couple of decades. Everyone has said so, and everyone is right. The boasting polygamists on trash TV, the rap lyrics, the rancorous and openly racist talk-radio shows—these are just the most obvious examples. We left-wing types popularized rudeness and slangy candor as a style of public discourse thirty years ago—our language, we thought, would discredit the official hypocrisies—and now everyone is going in for it. With depressing effect: even those who love profanity may be dismayed to hear a former mayor of New York calling someone a "schmuck" on the radio. It is not the words that matter so much as the ravaging lack of dignity. The rout of gentility, which cultural libertarians sparked, has now been followed by the rout of self-respect. On ragged and exhausted nights, the wised-up tone of everything wears one down. As I go to sleep in our second-floor bedroom, I can hear couples dully cursing one another on the street, the words landing like blows. (That women now give as much as they get makes the sound no less melancholy.) When the clock radio clicks on in the morning, giggles and hoots accompany anyone trying to talk about a subject more serious than the weather. In the nineties, sarcasm is no longer a resistance to the marketplace; it *is* the marketplace. The constant atmosphere of selling creates a common ironic consciousness, the derisiveness of people in the know. And what do they know? That everyone is out for himself, that greed is what drives life forward. Derision has become the spirit of the jammed, crazy, relentless talk, the needling spritz of radio, of late-night TV, of kids teasing and threatening on the street. In these worlds, in our common world, no other kind of talk takes hold. If you aren't derisive, you're out of it. You're not in the market.

Adults learn to screen a lot of this out, but children don't necessarily do so. They enjoy it. They imitate it—and who can blame them? The media and the streets are far more exciting than school, where virtue so often comes packaged as learning.

Then there's the problem of pop growth: the huge increases in the formidability and quantity of mass culture—the new Fox network, the local and national cable operators, the Sony PlayStation and Sega and Nintendo systems, the innumerable computer games, and the rest. The problem is not simply that the stuff comes flooding in on children from all sides. The problem is that easy entertainment and self-serving communication of one sort or another (political speech, commercial messages, infotainment, advertorials, ego rants, self-promoting "confessions") increasingly push everything else to the margins. If you click through the channels, including the zillion cable channels, at different times of day, you will discover that serious communication of any sort is a tiny portion of what's available. One of the comedies of intellectual life in recent years has been the spectacle of the cultural left in the universities complaining that the words of women or minorities have been suppressed, when the exponential growth of mass communication has swamped just about anything of real consequence.

Cultural libertarians have been too complacently self-regarding in their defense of free expression. It's a noble position, a necessary position, never to be relinquished, but at this point it isn't enough. How valuable is the latest constitutional victory for freedom of speech if the general level of speech continues to be degraded? Moreover, some of the cultural libertarians, including me, have a minor crime to answer for—the too-easy use of such loaded words as "subversive" and "transgressive" to praise movies and rock albums that offer a little more sex and violence than other good movies and albums. A few years ago, liberal-minded cultural critics, terrified of standing with the squares, got bullied out of any sort of principled public resistance to pop. They took themselves out of the game, and left the field open for William Bennett's iron moralism.

THOMAS becomes annoyed when I question him about the Saturday morning kiddies' shows, in which, it seems, the world is always being saved by uniformed teens from some basso-voiced monster and his wicked female companion. Whatever I may think about the homogenized nature of these shows, however, Thomas sees important differences among them. What he loved six months ago, for instance, he now regards as beyond the pale. The market has moved him along and made him contemptuous of what he has discarded. He's a very easygoing child, but, as far as he's concerned, his entertainment choices are not our business. Shyly, like suitors with hat in hand, we question his tastes and try to introduce him to the older arts, to the things we love. It may be ridiculous, but parents suffer a narcissistic wound when their children don't care about their favorite pictures, their books and music. Five years ago, we heard, on the car radio, Chuck Berry singing "Johnny B. Goode," and Max, who was then in the depth of his Billy Joel phase, said he liked it. We were absurdly happy. He likes Chuck Berry! When Tommy popped out of bed at eleven o'clock recently and, half asleep, asked me if we could listen immediately to all nine of the Beethoven symphonies, I began playing the "Eroica," and he fell back to sleep on the couch, a warrior at rest, as the music swirled over him.

Choice! It has to mean more for parents than an endless opening to the market. An active and engaged liberalism, while rejecting censorship, would encourage the breaking up of such vertically integrated culture monoliths as Disney, Sony, and Time Warner. It would ask for more regulation. (The V-chip is only the beginning.) It would, for instance, support the attempt of Reed Hundt, the reform-minded F.C.C. chairman, to require broadcasters to put on three hours of educational television a week. (Which might mean three fewer hours of trash.) And it would go far beyond the mere celebration of choice. It would insist on discrimination—not in the racial sense but in the cultural arena, where liberals, so eager to appreciate everyone's point of view, are often milky and weak. If parents are not to feel defeated by the media and pop culture, they must get over their reluctance to make choices that are based on clear assertions of moral values. They cannot leave to the "virtuecrats" the defense of religion, high culture, the meritocracy, the Western literary classics, or anything else that implies a hierarchy of taste. They have to join the discourse and make it aesthetically and morally alive.

ON vacation, away from Media City, without a television or a movie theatre in sight, I read to Max the novel that begins, "My father's family name being Pirrip, and my Christian name Philip, my infant tongue could make of both names nothing longer or more explicit than Pip. So I called myself Pip, and came to be called Pip." The same novel was read to me at the same age—not by my father but by an elderly teacher who entertained her students after lunch by reciting both "Oliver Twist" and "Great Expectations" in a Midwesterner's gentle version of a thick Cockney accent. On vacation, Max became completely absorbed in the book, his eyes turning dreamy and inward-looking, and we read a great deal, for ninety minutes at a time. I was happy, too, because I was not on the carpet anymore, down there in the plastic rubble.

But then we returned to the metropolis. TV sets and computers, as well as school and friends, pressed in on all sides, and the reading slowly petered out. We read less every night, and after a while Dickens, who only weeks earlier had enchanted so tenderly, now seemed slow, laborious, convoluted, even boring. We've picked the book up a few times since, and my son is slowly climbing back into it—that he enjoys it, I have no doubt—but I don't know if we'll ever finish it. I would like to, and so would he, but Dickens's long, rolling sentences require peace and time, and the air is just too charged around here.

It's 4:00 p.m.

Do You Know Where Your Children Are?

The most dangerous time of day for kids isn't late at night. It's from 2 p.m. to 8 p.m., when children are out of school and their parents are still working. This can be crime time, and prime time to get them on the right path.

BY JONATHAN ALTER

I'T'S 4 P.M., AND SGT. MIKE GWYNES of the Jacksonville, Fla., police department is maneuvering his squad car past Jack Horner and Goldilocks toward Cinderella Street, where some teens are hanging out at a bus stop. Down in the Sweetwater section of town, the streets have fairy-tale names, but it's the kids who risk turning into pumpkins. And not at midnight. "The problem's 3 p.m. till about 8 p.m., when they go home unsupervised and get in with the wrong crowd," Gwynes says, making a sharp left. Over on Bo Peep, a few teenagers are playing some rough basketball in a driveway; on Tinkerbell, the activity looks a bit more suspicious. Drugs are a big problem here.

Up on Wilson Boulevard sits a big solution. An old National Guard armory restored by the Jacksonville Children's Commission now serves as an innovative charter school, a police substation and a Boys & Girls Club all rolled into one. At 4 p.m. the 5- to 9-year-olds are playing kickball, the 10- to 12-year-olds are playing board games or finishing up "Power Hour" homework help and the older kids are in the teen center, playing pool and flirting,

Jacob Inlong
CALIFORNIA

SEVEN-YEAR-OLD JACOB was worried about the rain. For the first half of the school year, the second grader had to hang around the playground of his school for two hours every afternoon until his folks could pick him up. His working parents hated leaving him without activities, but had to spend their child-care resources on Jacob's 2-year-old brother. After months on a waiting list, Jacob was admitted to one of his city's best after-school programs—one inside the school, 40 yards from his playground.

under adult supervision. Cursing risks a fine (25 cents) and boomboxes aren't allowed, which means some kids won't show up. But plenty of others do, including some just out of juvenile detention. Youth crime in the area has plummeted.

It doesn't take a Ph.D. to figure out that young people need some place positive to go after school to stay off the streets and out of their empty homes. If they end up in jail, in drug treatment or pregnant, we all pay. And even if they're good kids from good neighborhoods, we're anxious. A NEWSWEEK Poll shows that the number of Americans who worry "a lot" that their kids will get involved with troublemakers or use drugs or alcohol was up by a full one third since 1990. With 17 million American parents scrambling to find care for their school-age children during work hours, the problem keeps growing.

More than a decade after the media discovered "latchkey kids," the answers are still elusive. When budgets get tight, after-school programs—wrongly dismissed as "frills"—are often cut first. When talk turns to society's worst problems, it's easy to

shrug off concerns about kids home alone watching afternoon television or hanging with friends. After all, many of their parents did the same, and turned out just fine.

BUT TIMES HAVE CHANGED, and not just because "Jerry Springer" has replaced Jerry Mathers (the star of "Leave It to Beaver") as the TV babysitter. Among cops, social-service types and policymakers, there's a new awareness that structured activity during out-of-school hours is absolutely critical to confronting many of the country's most vexing social problems. For years, local TV-station public-service announcements sternly intoned: "It's 10 p.m. Do you know where your children are?" It was the wrong question. The answer was usually yes; relatively few kids are allowed to roam freely at that hour. Only one seventh of all juvenile crime is committed in the late night and early morning. But substitute "4 p.m." and millions of parents would have to answer no.

If idle hands are the Devil's workshop, the hellish consequences are being felt in the American heartland. Crime is down in metropolitan areas, but up in hundreds of small communities, especially among kids. Drug use in surburban middle schools is surging. Many rural counties now report teen-pregnancy rates equal to those in big cities. Sixty percent of the cases of sexually transmitted diseases are contracted by teens. The absence of parents from the home in the afternoon has made it much more convenient to get into trouble. More than three quarters of first-time sexual encounters occur at someone's house (usually the boy's). "We had to use Chevys," says criminologist James Alan Fox of Northeastern University. "Now kids don't need cars. When the cat's away, the mice will have sex."

And commit crimes, both petty and serious. Juvenile crime *triples* starting at 3 p.m. In fact, the 2 p.m. to 8 p.m. period—"Crime Time"—now accounts for more than 50 percent of all youth offenses. Not your kid, you

Jeremy Reese
ALABAMA

JEREMY (PEEWEE) REESE has a wide choice of after-school programs in and around the Metropolitan Gardens housing project—he just doesn't always feel like joining in. The sixth grader sometimes drops by an inner-city athletic club for a little basketball or pool, but the volunteers won't hesitate to kick him out if he gets out of line. When that happens, he heads over to Marconi Park, even though he says two Disciples gang members approached him there last summer. "I told them 'I don't want to'," says Peewee, who lives with his grandmother. "They'll get you in trouble." He doesn't want to be in a gang, but he says he's not interested in the homework teachers assign him for the afternoons, and he doesn't often feel like following the rules. What *does* he want? "If I can't be a ballplayer, I want to be a judge. I want to be the one that makes the decisions."

Anthony Scimeca
Kelsey Kordas
ILLINOIS

"NO HUGGING!" SHOUTS ONE of a dozen teenagers at Vanessa Swanson's suburban house, and everyone laughs. "I guess it's reasonable that we can't hug at school," says Anthony, 12—but here there are fewer rules for him and his buddy (*not* girlfriend, they insist) Kelsey, 13, to follow. The kids know to call in and tell their folks where they are and what they are doing. This usually amounts to playing Nintendo 64, jumping on the trampoline and blasting dance music. "If I didn't come here, I'd probably be at the mall," says another 13-year-old. "But it's a cool place to hang out." Vanessa's working mom, Victoria, thinks it's worth investing in a case of soda a day to give the group a place to go. "At first I had some concerns," she says. "But at least I know where my kids are."

America's Promise, an umbrella group for hundreds of nonprofits and corporations that's working to secure millions more "safe places" for kids (sidebar).

The struggle starts in the schools, which in many places still close in midafternoon. Even wealthy communities are beginning to recognize the folly of locking buildings for large chunks of the day when they're needed for recreation, tutoring and arts. Some districts embrace change: for years, Murfreesboro, Tenn., has kept schools open from 6 a.m. to 6 p.m. Others are actually moving in the wrong direction. Recently, Atlanta horrified child-development experts by canceling recess on the theory that there wasn't "enough time" for a break between classes. But the school day extends only until 2:30 p.m. Why? The current school schedule—six hours a day, nine months a year—was invented when the United States was an agrarian nation and children were needed in the fields.

Today, three out of four mothers of school-age children work outside the home. So it's not so surprising that by the time they are 12 years old, nearly 35 percent of American children are regularly left on their own. For the rest—the lucky ones—parents work by remote control to pull together a patchwork of supervised activities: soccer on Tuesdays, Scouts on Wednesday. Some child-care programs provide terrific enrichment; others amount to little more than warehousing. TV and videogames usually fill the gap. The average American child spends 900 hours a year in school—and 1,500 hours a year watching television.

For the working poor, having their kids watch TV at home is often the *best* option—far better than the streets. But the child-care arrangements can be alarming. According to a study sponsored by Wellesley College, more than 15 percent of low-income parents reported that their 4- to 7-year-old children regularly spent time all by themselves, or in the care of a sibling under the age of 12. Neighbors—who for generations helped out absent parents by shushing the kids—are no longer around much, either.

The schools that poor children attend are unlikely to have after-care. Currently only 30 percent of American schools offer after-hours supervision, and the vast majority of them charge fees. The average cost to parents is $45 a week per child, or more than $2,000 a year, which is too much for many who need it most. The YMCA, the largest provider of after-school activities, serves half a million kids a day from all backgrounds. But even Y's cost an average of $36 a week. The equation is straightforward: "If parents are well off, they purchase after-school care. If they're poor, [the kids] often get nothing," says Indianapolis Mayor Stephen Goldsmith, one of many mayors now trying to find new solutions.

say? Well, he or she might be a victim; they outnumber perpetrators of crime by 10 to 1. Juvenile homicide, which has doubled in a decade, is usually connected to after-school fights, not late-night crime. But even for those who don't worry about a potential Jonesboro massacre in their neighborhood, everyday teen problems of all kinds get worse when the last school bell rings.

The research confirms common sense. According to one University of Southern California study, eighth graders looking after themselves were more likely to smoke, drink and use marijuana than those who have some supervision after school. Another study of sixth graders showed those in "self care" were more likely to get poor grades or behave badly.

Good youth-development programs not only keep kids safe, they often change their lives. Finally, social policymakers are getting the message. Last week Vice President Al Gore stumped for the administration's after-school initiative and foundations funded by Charles Stewart Mott and George Soros planted some seed money. Organizations like Save the Children (which until recently concentrated its efforts overseas) are also turning to this issue. So is Colin Powell's

Among the biggest backers of after-school programs are the nation's police chiefs, who argue that recent reductions in crime, while gratifying, are temporary. "We've come to the realization that we're not going to arrest our way out of this problem," says Salt Lake City Police Chief Ruben Ortega, who heads an association of big-city police chiefs. "If we don't change our strategy, we'll be complaining in five or 10 years about how bad crime has gotten again."

Los Angeles is a good object lesson. Until Proposition 13 in 1978, all L.A. schools offered after-school enrichment programs. By 1992, when riots broke out in the wake of the Rodney King verdict, not one public high school had anything after school except interscholastic sports. The riots erupted in mid-afternoon. Would as many kids have been on the streets to join in if they had had somewhere else to go? Would the city's gang problem have gotten so out of hand? A program called L.A.'s Best is now trying to bring back after-school programs in a few schools. The waiting lists are long.

This is not touchy-feely do-gooder territory. A survey of 548 police chiefs showed them favoring prevention programs by an astonishing four-to-one margin over tougher sentencing and more cops on the street. But their lobbying often falls short in Washington and state capitals. When it comes to crime, "politicians believe in the three R's: Retribution, Revenge and Retaliation, which they think takes them to the fourth R—Re-Election," says Fox.

There are signs that the politics of prevention might be changing. Gore, for example, has seen how the after-school issue resonates, and he's grabbing it. After a town meeting in New Orleans last week, he held a teleconference with local officials from Atlanta to Anchorage, Alaska, who are working on answers. One common worry: the organizational headaches involved in bringing schools, churches, parents, nonprofits, corporations and different levels of government together. That takes a new breed of leader at the local level.

In Washington, Republican attacks on "midnight basketball" as liberal waste helped sink prevention programs in 1994. But the stigma is wearing off. As part of its child-care plan, the Clinton administration wants to spend $200 million a year for after-school programs. The idea is to get schools and community nonprofits working together to serve an additional 500,000 kids a year on school grounds. At best, however, even with matching contributions from nonprofits, that's only one tenth of the 5 million "latchkey" kids.

'I Wasn't Left to Myself'

When I was a kid, the safety net protected me. Here's how to put it back in place. BY GEN. COLIN POWELL

WHEN I WAS growing up in the South Bronx, I was as liable to be led astray by the temptations of the street as any other inner-city youth, then or now. Left to myself, I could have ended up on Rikers Island rather than chairman of the Joint Chiefs of Staff.

But I wasn't left to myself. The tough neighborhood of Banana Kelly where I grew up had a heart: people cared about kids. I was surrounded by family, church and a wonderful public-school system. And when I set off to school each morning, I had an aunt in every other house, stationed at the window with eyes peeled, ready to spot the slightest misbehavior on my part and report it back to my parents. The instant communication of today's Internet pales in comparison to the "Aunt-Net" I remember from my childhood.

My relations weren't the only caring adults who took an interest in my welfare. I think of Jay Sickser, the kindly merchant who gave me my first job—helping out at his store after school. Or the folks at the Young Men's Hebrew Association who provided me with a place where I could spend time in a secure environment. Given a safety net with a mesh that fine, it took *work* for even the most rambunctious kid to get into real trouble.

Fast-forward several decades. Today our society is materially richer, but it is easier than ever for kids to go wrong—in the suburbs as in the cities. Because many of the social structures that once kept our kids secure have broken down, we have today's appalling data on juvenile crime, gangs, drug abuse, pregnancy and dropouts. We know juvenile crime and other pathologies are at their worst in the hours immediately after school lets out. It is just common sense that if we don't provide young people with some kind of sanctuary—I call them "safe places"—and give kids something constructive to do once the last bell rings, they are going to be easy marks for drug dealers, gang recruiters and other predators.

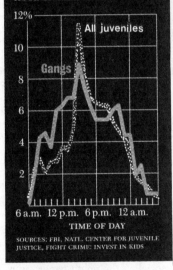

The Troubled Hours
PERCENTAGE OF VIOLENT JUVENILE CRIME OCCURRING BY HOUR ON SCHOOL DAYS

All juveniles

Gangs

6 a.m. 12 p.m. 6 p.m. 12 a.m.
TIME OF DAY

SOURCES: FBI, NATL. CENTER FOR JUVENILE JUSTICE, FIGHT CRIME: INVEST IN KIDS

A safe place can be a YMCA, a Boys & Girls Club, a rec room at a house of faith, a playground or a school. Ronald McDonald House Charities has donated $4 million to keep a hundred Chicago schools open after hours so that children can have a safe place until their parents pick them up. Not long ago I visited St. Elizabeth's Hospital in Beaumont, Texas. St. Elizabeth's is part of a program called Health Adventures, in which hospital staff members mentor needy youngsters. While I was there, one young man proudly told me about the medical skills he had acquired by learning to suture an orange. He might just grow up to be a brain surgeon.

Safe places do not have to cost a lot of money. In many instances, the building or location already exists; all you need are volunteers to donate their time. A few dollars contributed to a local youth service organization—or a few hours invested in being a mentor—can make a safer world for kids today and a better world for all of us tomorrow.

POWELL *is chairman of America's Promise—The Alliance for Youth. Those interested in volunteering should call 888-55-YOUTH.*

In the NEWSWEEK Poll, **64%** of parents worry at least a little about their children's getting hurt or into trouble if a parent can't be with them after school

FOR THIS NEWSWEEK POLL, PRINCETON SURVEY RESEARCH ASSOCIATES INTERVIEWED 500 PARENTS OF CHILDREN AGE 6–17 JAN. 16–26. THE MARGIN OF ERROR IS +/- 5 PERCENTAGE POINTS. THE NEWSWEEK POLL © 1998 BY NEWSWEEK, INC.

Benny Morales
OREGON

WHEN 8-YEAR-OLD Benny gets home from school, it's not his mom but his brother Cesar who is waiting at the door to their mobile home. Cesar, 16, does his best to keep both Benny and Eloy, 13, occupied until their mother comes home from her waitressing job around 9 p.m. "I feel safe with my brothers," says Benny. "All you do at day care is play Legos, and I don't like Legos." Twice a week, Eloy walks the second grader to T-Ball practice, but most afternoons in this economically depressed rural town are extremely quiet. When it starts to get dark, the boys sit down in the kitchen to do homework and help Benny with his school projects, dishing up dinner from a pot their mother Edith Sanchez has left bubbling on the stove whenever they get hungry. Cesar says he doesn't mind the way things are. How long will he be the caretaker? "As long as it takes."

THE REPUBLICAN LEADERSHIP in Congress opposes the Clinton plan, but doesn't want to go into the November midterm elections with no after-school program in hand. As a result, Congress is giving $20 million a year directly to the Boys & Girls Clubs of America. That's better than nothing, but the money will build only a few new clubs a year—and address one hundredth of the after-school problem. Unlike many social challenges, this one is not hugely expensive; $2 billion or $3 billion a year would go a long way toward solving it.

Skeptics say that even the best programs can't attract tougher kids who prefer life on the streets. Maybe so. Gang members very rarely quit their gangs. But predators can be made less dangerous. In Ft. Worth, Texas, 1,000 gang members go to "Coming Up" programs at eight Boys & Girls Clubs for late-night recreation and counseling. The police, at first dubious, are now pleased with the decline in gang-related violence.

But programs to reach out to the estimated 650,000 gang members across the country are still scarce. The key: when programs are established, they must be well run—or risk driving gang members away for good. "We need to make sure positive things will happen for the kids who are there, or they'll leave," says Sanford Newman of a Washington, D.C., group called Fight Crime/Invest in Kids.

The stakes couldn't be higher, and not just for the kids themselves. The larger society has a huge financial interest in confronting this problem. Juvenile crime surges at 14 and drops off at 18. Experts agree that if kids can get through this four-year period, the chances are good they will stay out of serious trouble. If they don't, the aggregate fiscal consequences are astronomical. Combining jail costs and lost taxes, career criminals cost taxpayers an estimated $1 million each during their lives. The United States now has 15 million at-risk children, several million of whom are in danger of going off track in the next 10 years. According to Ray Chambers, a financier and chair of America's Promise (which grew out of last year's Presidents' Summit in Philadelphia), that sends the stakes in this crisis into the hundreds of billions of dollars.

Back at the converted armory in Jacksonville, it's nearly 5 p.m. Some cops are talking about taking a few kids to a Go Kart track, or maybe to play some pinball. Navy Lt. Cmdr. Robert Sanders, who helped start the youth center, is reflecting back on his own life. "I think back to the kids I grew up

Stephen Ruggs
MASSACHUSETTS

ASK STEPHEN RUGGS WHERE he would be without the Rev. Eugene Rivers's after-school program, and he doesn't hesitate. "I'd be at the park somewhere, where people beat up on other people just for looking at them." Or worse—the 14-year-old had a friend who he says was killed over a $2 I.O.U. Instead, Stephen is bent over a table at the Ella J. Baker House, a renovated Victorian building in the rough Boston neighborhood of Dorchester, working hard at an anti-smoking campaign he and his friends in the program will be presenting to younger children. Stephen's grandparents, both of whom work for the city transit authority and have raised him since he was a baby, see Baker House as "a haven," and the boy agrees. "The kids here are the lucky ones," he says.

with who are not dead or in jail. What did we have in common? Those who succeeded had some kind of structure that let us go to the next level. A few years ago, the big thing was to say that kids had to have food in their stomachs to think. But that's not enough. We have 8-year-olds raising 3-year-olds and they're supposed to grow up to compete in the world economy? Our whole future, our national security, depends on what kids can do tomorrow." And that depends on what they do this afternoon.

With T. TRENT GEGAX, CLAUDIA KALB, DEBRA GWARTNEY *and* ADRIAN MAHER

46% of parents say it is very important that schools stay open all day; **43%** think after-school activities should be a high priority despite limited education budgets

Child Labor in Pakistan

Pakistan has recently passed laws greatly limiting child labor and indentured servitude—but those laws are universally ignored, and some 11 million children, aged four to fourteen, keep that country's factories operating, often working in brutal and squalid conditions.

JONATHAN SILVERS

Jonathan Silvers is a writer and an independent television producer specializing in international affairs and human-rights issues.

No two negotiations for the sale of a child are alike, but all are founded on the pretense that the parties involved have the best interests of the child at heart. On this sweltering morning in the Punjab village of Wasan Pura a carpet master, Sadique, is describing for a thirty-year-old brick worker named Mirza the advantages his son will enjoy as an apprentice weaver. "I've admired your boy for several months," Sadique says. "Nadeem is bright and ambitious. He will learn far more practical skills in six months at the loom than he would in six years of school. He will be taught by experienced craftsmen, and his pay will rise as his skills improve. Have no doubt, your son will be thankful for the opportunity you have given him, and the Lord will bless you for looking so well after your own."

Sadique has given this speech before. Like many manufacturers, he recruits children for his workshop almost constantly, and is particularly aggressive in courting boys aged seven to ten. "They make ideal employees," he says. "Boys at this stage of development are at the peak of their dexterity

and endurance, and they're wonderfully obedient—they'd work around the clock if I asked them." But when pressed he admits, "I hire them first and foremost because they're economical. For what I'd pay one second-class adult weaver I can get three boys, sometimes four, who can produce first-class rugs in no time."

The low cost of child labor gives Sadique and his fellow manufacturers a significant advantage in the Western marketplace, where they undersell their competitors from countries prohibiting child labor, often by improbable amounts. Not surprisingly, American and European consumers are attracted to low-price, high-quality products, and imports of child-made carpets from Pakistan have trebled in the past two decades. Pakistan's carpet makers have satisfied this surging demand by expanding production at existing factories and opening new ones wherever they can. To maximize their returns, virtually all these factories employ children, and an increasing number do so exclusively. Somewhere between 500,000 and one million Pakistani children aged four to fourteen now work as full-time carpet weavers. UNICEF believes that they make up 90 percent of the carpet makers' work force.

Sadique delivers his speech at volume and accompanies it with an assort-

ment of gestures—nods, waves, raised eyebrows—that are as theatrical as they are out of place in his shambles of a workshop. He concludes with a smile and, just in case Mirza does not appreciate his generosity, adds a wistful coda: "I wish my father had given me such an opportunity." Mirza seems doubtful, perhaps because his son is

EACH YEAR MILLIONS OF CHILDREN IN PAKISTAN ENTER THE LABOR FORCE, WHERE THEY COMPETE WITH ADULTS—OFTEN EVEN WITH THEIR PARENTS —FOR WHAT LITTLE WORK IS AVAILABLE. AT LEAST HALF THESE CHILDREN ARE UNDER THE AGE OF TEN.

seven years old, perhaps because he has seen too many of his neighbors' children suffer through similar opportunities. But he returns Sadique's smile and says in a faint voice that he hopes Nadeem will learn enough to work one day as a journeyman weaver or, better still, to open a workshop of his own.

Whatever misgivings Mirza has at the moment are overshadowed by his poverty, which is extreme and worsening. He supports a family of five by working at a nearby kiln, molding bricks by hand for up to eighty hours a week. The work pays poorly at the best of times, and on occasion it does not pay at all. Three weeks earlier a monsoon destroyed several thousand unfired bricks that had been left drying on factory grounds. The kiln owner held the workers accountable for the damage and refused to pay them for the two weeks they had spent making the bricks. The "fine," as the owner called it, proved ruinous. Already months behind on their rent and in debt to the village merchants, Mirza and his wife concluded that the only way to avoid eviction was to bond their eldest child to one of the district's manufacturers. Sadique was their first choice: he was prosperous, his workshop was near their home, and he was rumored to have an urgent need for child laborers, which they believed would translate into a high price for Nadeem.

They were half right. The workshop has a perpetual need for children, but Sadique is unwilling to pay a premium for them. For that matter, he is unwilling to pay market rates. Having dispensed with the niceties, he offers Mirza 5,000 rupees ($146) for five years of his son's labor. It's a paltry sum—roughly two months' earnings for an adult weaver. Mirza was expecting an offer at least three times as high. "Business is off this year," Sadique says, by way of preempting Mirza's objections. "When things improve, I may be able to give you another two or three hundred. Many fathers would be glad to get half this amount."

Mirza is distressed. He is a small man, stooped and wasted from his years at the kiln, his skin and tunic flecked with soot. Like most laborers, he is

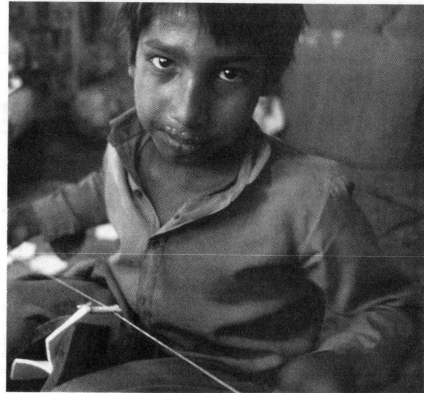

Stitching soccer balls in a factory in Sialkot

acutely aware of his caste, and in the presence of those whom he deems his betters is deferential to the point of abjectness. Bravely he asks Sadique for another thousand rupees, though he couches the request in the most self-deprecating terms he knows. "Sir, my family's survival depends on your charity. You will always be remembered in our prayers as our savior from beggary and destitution." To his relief, Sadique agrees at once, extending a manicured hand with a speed that suggests he was prepared to pay more and got a bargain. In any event, he can afford to be generous. The money he offers Mirza, called a *peshgi*, will be paid in installments, and he will deduct from it all costs associated with Nadeem's maintenance and training. Many of the deductions are contrived and inflated. Parents are charged for their children's food and tools, the raw materials they use, the errors they make, the amount of time the master spends "educating" them. Throughout Pakistan parents consider themselves fortunate if at the end of their child's service the master has paid them one third of the *peshgi*.

Mirza is unaware of these deductions and, eager to make his escape, does not ask questions that might complicate the proceedings. He consummates the deal by shaking Sadique's hand (after wiping his own on his tunic) and accepting from him a first installment of 200 rupees. The parties are bound only by their word: no contracts are signed; no witnesses are present. "Your boy now belongs to me," Sadique says as Mirza pockets the banknotes. "Please understand that so long as he works under my roof he is answerable only to me. Inform him that the needs of my shop take priority over those of his family, and he must do all he can to please me. If he does not, we will all be disappointed, him most of all." Mirza thanks the master for his kindness, bows low, and runs off to relay this information to his son.

An Inexhaustible Labor Pool

CHILD labor has assumed epidemic proportions in Pakistan. Statistics are unreliable, but the Human Rights Commission of Pakistan

(HRCP) last year estimated the number of Pakistani working children to be "realistically in the region of 11–12 million." At least half these children are under the age of ten. Despite a recent series of laws prohibiting child labor and indentured servitude, children make up a quarter of the unskilled work force, and can be found in virtually every factory, every workshop, every field. They earn on average a third of the adult wage. Certain industries, notably carpet making and brick making, cannot survive without them. One World Bank economist maintains that Pakistan's economic viability correlates with the number of children in its factories. The child labor pool is all but inexhaustible, owing in part to a birth rate that is among the world's highest and to an education system that can accommodate only about a third of the country's school-age children. Each year millions of children enter the labor force, where they compete with adults—often even with their parents—for what little work is available. In many regions the surplus of cheap child labor has depressed the already inadequate adult wage to the point where a parent and child together now earn less than the parent alone earned a year ago. As long as children are put to work, poverty will spread and standards of living will continue to decline.

To be sure, child labor is an institution throughout the Third World, and its incidence has been increasing in countries that are usually described as advanced. The worldwide population of children under fourteen who work full-time is thought to exceed 200 million. But few countries have done less to abolish or to contain the practice than Pakistan. And fewer still have a ruling class that opposes workplace reform and human-rights initiatives as vigorously. Given its relative prosperity, its constitutional prohibition against child labor, and its leaders' signatures on every UN human- and child-rights convention, Pakistan's de facto dependency on child labor is troubling and to its critics inexcusable.

"Inaction speaks louder than words," says I. A. Rehman, the director of the HRCP. "This government is in continuous violation of the Convention on the Rights of the Child, and has consistently refused to enforce those very laws it enacted to protect its most vulnerable citizens. We have far more in the way of resources and legal remedies than China, India, and Indonesia, and we do far less for our young than they. The problem is lack of political will. The problem is greed."

The median age of children now entering the Pakistani work force is seven. Two years ago it was eight. Two years from now it may be six. In the lowest castes, children become laborers almost as soon as they can walk. Much of the nation's farmland is worked by toddlers, yoked teams of three-, four-, and five-year-olds who plough, seed, and glean fields from dawn to dusk. On any given morning the canal banks and irrigation ditches in rural villages are lined with urchins who stand no taller than the piles of laundry they wash for their wealthier neighbors. Even the world-class industries of Islamabad, the modern capital, are staffed in large part by children and adolescents; politicians traveling to the National Assembly can't help noticing the ragged youths entering and exiting the brick factories, steel mills, and stone-crushing plants at all hours of the day and night. These children work with a minimum of adult supervision. An overseer comes by periodically to mark their progress and to give them instructions or a few encouraging blows, but for the better part of the workday they are left to themselves. "Children are cheaper to run than tractors and smarter than oxen," explains one Rawalpindi landowner. He prefers field hands between seven and ten years old, "because they have the most energy, although they lack discipline."

In rural areas children are raised without health care, sanitation, or education; many are as starved for affection as for food. As soon as they're old enough to have an elementary understanding of their circumstances, their parents teach them that they are expected to pay their

way, to make sacrifices, and, if necessary, to travel far from home and live with strangers. "When my children were three, I told them they must be prepared to work for the good of the family," says Asma, a Sheikhupura villager who bonded her five children to masters in distant villages. "I told them again and again that they would be bonded at five. And when the time came for them to go, they were prepared and went without complaint."

Bonding is common practice among the lower castes, and although the decision to part with their children is not made lightly, parents do not agonize over it. Neither, evidently, do the children, who regard bonding as a rite of passage, the event that transforms them into adults. Many look forward to it in the same way that American children look forward to a first communion or getting a driver's license. They are eager to cast off childhood, even if to do so means taking on adult burdens. Irfana, a twelve-year-old schoolgirl who spent four years as a brick worker before she was freed by an anti-slavery organization, remembers feeling relieved when her father handed her over at age six to a kiln owner. "My friends and I knew that sooner or later we'd be sent off to the factories or the fields. We were tired of doing chores and minding infants. We looked forward to the day when we'd be given responsibilities and the chance to earn money. At the time work seemed glamorous and children who worked seemed quite important."

She soon learned otherwise. "For the masters, bonded children are a commodity. My master bought, sold, and traded us like livestock, and sometimes he shipped us great distances. The boys were beaten frequently to make them work long hours. The girls were often violated. My best friend got ill after she was raped, and when she couldn't work, the master sold her to a friend of his in a village a thousand kilometers away. Her family was never told where she was sent, and they never saw her again."

Early in this decade the Pakistan National Assembly enacted two labor laws meant to curb such practices. The first, The Employment of Children Act of 1991, prohibited the use of child labor in hazardous occupations and environments. The second, The Bonded Labor Act of 1992, abolished indentured servitude and the *peshgi* system. As progressive as these laws were, the government failed to provide for their implementation and enforcement. It also neglected to inform the millions of working children and indentured servants that they were free and released from their debts. "We prefer to leave enforcement to the discretion of the police," says a Ministry of Labor official. "They understand best the needs of their community. Law is not an absolute. We must expect a certain flexibility on the part of those who enforce it. Could this sometimes mean looking the other way? Absolutely."

A Diminutive Entrepreneur

THE farther authorities are from a major city in Pakistan, the less likely they are to pursue violators of the child-labor laws. To leave Lahore, the nation's intellectual and commercial center, is to enter a land populated and run by children. The change is as abrupt as it is extreme. The roads just beyond the city limits are congested with donkey carts, all of them driven by teamsters of eight or nine. Boys seem to have a monopoly on roadside attractions: gas stations, auto-repair centers, restaurants. When I pull into the Star Petroleum station on the Ferozpur Road, five miles from Lahore, three boys rush out of the garage to service my car. They are twelve, eight, and seven, and wear uniforms intended for men twice their size. The eldest has rolled up his pants and sleeves, but his colleagues helplessly trail theirs in the dirt. While the older boys fill my tank with a rusted hand pump, the youngest climbs into the hood and cleans the windshield with a dangling sleeve. When I pull away, the boys rush back to the garage and to a diesel engine they are at-tempting to rebuild between fill-ups. No adults are visible on the premises.

Adults are also in short supply at the crossroads markets that provide villagers with everything from prayer mats to surgical instruments. Twelve of the fifteen stands at the Tohkar Road market are managed by children under fourteen. The fruit stand is run by a tyrannical eight-year-old boy and his four- and five-year-old sisters. The boy spends his morning slicing melons with a knife half his size, while behind him the girls sort cartloads of fruit. At the next stall two eleven-year-old cousins fashion sandals out of discarded tires. They work from dawn to dusk six days a week, and make more than 1,200 pairs each week. Behind the last stall another boy is struggling to unload a stack of carpets from his donkey cart. He weighs seventy pounds. The twenty-odd carpets in his cart weigh sixty pounds apiece, and it takes him ten minutes of yanking, hefting, and cursing to get each one into the stall. The stall's proprietor watches him with interest, but his concern is strictly for the merchandise. He is a tall, heavyset forty-year-old who looks as if he could unload the entire cart in fifteen minutes without breaking a sweat. But he makes no move to help the boy, and seems to regard his exertions as routine. So do the passersby. And, for that matter, so does the boy.

His name is Faiz. A lively nine-year-old, he has been working as a hauler since he was six. He attended school for two years, but dropped out when an elderly neighbor offered him an advantageous lease on the cart and donkey. He runs the business alone, and spends his days scrounging for hauling jobs and shuttling produce, scrap metal, and crafts around six villages. He averages sixty miles a week—no easy feat with a donkey that trots at three miles an hour. "The work is painful and the days are long, but I earn enough to feed myself and tend the donkey," Faiz says with an entrepreneur's pride. The key to his success is underbidding the competition; his rates are a tenth of his pre-decessor's. "It is reasonable that people should pay me less. My equipment is the same as an adult's, but I am small and have a fraction of an adult's strength. I take longer to make deliveries, so I must charge less. My hope is that the more goods I move, the stronger I will get and the more I can charge."

Soon after I arrived in Pakistan, I arranged a trip to a town whose major factories were rumored to enslave very young children. I found myself hoping during the journey there that the children I saw working in the fields, on the roads, at the marketplaces, would prepare me for the worst. They did not. No amount of preparation could have lessened the shock and revulsion I felt on entering a sporting-goods factory in the town of Sialkot, seventy miles from Lahore, where scores of children, most of them aged five to ten, produce soccer balls by hand for forty rupees, or about $1.20, a day. The children work eighty hours a week in near-total darkness and total silence. According to the foreman, the darkness is both an economy and a precautionary measure; child-rights activists have difficulty taking photographs and gathering evidence of wrongdoing if the lighting is poor. The silence is to ensure product quality: "If the children speak, they are not giving their complete attention to the product and are liable to make errors." The children are permitted one thirty-minute meal break each day; they are punished if they take longer. They are also punished if they fall asleep, if their workbenches are sloppy, if they waste material or miscut a pattern, if they complain of mistreatment to their parents or speak to strangers outside the factory. A partial list of "infractions" for which they may be punished is tacked to a wall near the entrance. It's a document of dubious utility: the children are illiterate. Punishments are doled out in a storage closet at the rear of the factory. There, amid bales of wadding and leather, children are hung upside down by their knees, starved, caned, or lashed. (In the interests of economy the foreman uses a lash made from scrap soccer-ball leather.) The punishment room is a standard feature of a Pakistani factory, as common as a lunchroom at a Detroit assembly plant.

The town's other factories are no better, and many are worse. Here are brick kilns where five-year-olds work hip-deep in slurry pits, where adolescent girls stoke furnaces in 160° heat. Here are tanneries where nursing mothers mix vats of chemical dye, textile mills where eight-year-olds tend looms and breathe air thick with cotton dust.

When confronted with questions from a foreigner about their use of child labor, industrialists respond in one of two ways: they attack the questioner or they deliver a lengthy lecture about the role of children in Pakistan's development. The attacks are not always verbal. Last June a Norwegian trade-union delegation was attacked at the Sialkot sporting-goods factory by three or four armed men who were believed to work for the factory's owner. The delegation's guide and cameraman were severly beaten and the latter required hospitalization. The police characterized the attackers as "civic-minded" and warned the delegation against inspecting other area factories and "unnecessarily antagonizing factory owners."

More common, though, is the industrialist who ushers the foreign investigator into his office, plies him with coffee and cake, and tells him in his friendliest manner that child labor is a tradition the West cannot understand and must not attempt to change. "Our country has historically suffered from a labor shortage, a deficit of able-bodied men," says Imran Malik, a prominent Lahore carpet exporter and the vice-chairman of the Pakistan Carpet Manufacturers and Exporters Association. "Children have compensated for this shortage. They have worked when adults could not. They have helped construct Pakistan's infrastructure and advanced its industry. For thousands of years children have worked alongside their parents in their villages. The work they now do in fac-

tories and workshops is an extension of this tradition, and in most ways an improvement on it. The children earn more than they would elsewhere. They contribute significantly to their family's security and raise their standard of living."

The industrialist's argument is accurate only in its assertion that Pakistani children have traditionally worked with their families. But children seldom worked *outside* the family until the 1960s, when the Islamic Republic made

a dramatic effort to expand its manufacturing base. This led to a spectacular and disproportionately large increase in the number of children working outside the home, outside the village, at factories and workshops whose owners sought to maximize profits by keeping down labor costs. The rise in child abuse was as meteoric as the rise in child labor. The children working in these

factories were beyond the reach or care of their families and were increasingly the victims of industrial accidents, kidnapping, and mistreatment.

A Mixed Curse

"IF employers would apply as much ingenuity to their manufacturing processes as they do to evading labor laws, we'd have no child-labor problem," says Najanuddin Najmi, the director general of the Work-

At the carpet looms of Wasan Pura

ers Education Program, a government agency. "There's little doubt that inexpensive child labor has fueled Pakistan's economic growth. Entire industries have relocated to Pakistan because of the abundance of cheap child labor and our lax labor laws. At the same time, child labor has hindered our industrial development, especially in the use of advanced technologies.

Why should a manufacturer invest in labor-saving technology when labor-intensive mechanisms are so much cheaper? We are discovering more and more factories that have been redesigned and retooled so that only children can work there."

Child labor has been a mixed curse for all of southern Asia, expanding its industrial capacity while generating an unprecedented assortment of social problems. Not surprisingly, Pakistan's leaders are of two minds on the subject. Speaking officially, they deplore the practice and have nothing but pity for the roughly 11 million children working in factories, in fields, and on the streets. Speaking pragmatically, they regard the practice as a distasteful but unavoidable part of an emerging economy which time and prosperity will end. They are quick to take offense (and quicker to take the offensive) when human-rights activists suggest that they have ignored the problem.

"Westerners conveniently forget their own shameful histories when they come here," says Shabbir Jamal, an adviser to the Ministry of Labor. "Europeans addressed slavery and child labor only after they became prosperous. Pakistan has only now entered an era of economic stability that will allow us to expand our horizons and address social concerns. Just as we are catching up with the West in industrial development, so we are catching up in workplace and social reforms. We are accelerating the pace of reform and have resolved to create viable welfare and educational structures that will eradicate child labor in the foreseeable future."

Foreseeable may be a long way off. At the moment Prime Minister Benazir Bhutto seems more interested in outfitting her army than in reforming Pakistani society; her government has embarked on an ambitious military buildup that has already imperiled the region. Its first victims have been Pakistan's lower castes, the working poor who are accustomed to receiving little in the way of social services and must now make do with less. In 1994 military spending was 240 percent as high as spending on health and education combined; the disparity is expected to widen in years to come. Spending on education remains among the world's lowest. Only 37 percent of Pakistan's 25 million school-age children complete primary school—as compared with a world average of 79 percent and a South Asian average of approximately 50 percent. By the year 2000 less than a third of Pakistani children will attend school. The rest will enter the work force or become beggars.

Behind these statistics lurks an unpleasant truth: despite its modern views on warfare and industrialization, Pakistan remains a feudal society, committed to maintaining traditions that over the centuries have served its upper castes well. The lords—factory owners, exporters, financiers—reflexively oppose any reforms that might weaken their authority, lower their profit margins, or enfranchise the workers. "There is room for improvement in any society," the industrialist Imram Malik says. "But we feel that the present situation is acceptable the way it is. The National Assembly must not rush through reforms without first evaluating their impact on productivity and sales. Our position is that the government must avoid so-called humanitarian measures that harm our competitive advantages." On those rare occasions when a reform does squeak through, the backlash is fierce. For example, when the legislature last year approved a modest tax on bricks to fund an education program, brick-kiln owners staged a ten-day nationwide protest and threatened to suspend production, crippling construction, until the tax was repealed. Trade associations have used similar strong-arm tactics to fight minimum-wage legislation, occupational-safety regulations, and trade-union activity.

"The Charter of Freedom"

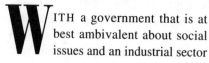

WITH a government that is at best ambivalent about social issues and an industrial sector resistant to workplace reform, the task of abolishing child labor has fallen to the human-rights community. But in a country where corruption is pervasive and education scarce, social activists are everyone's natural enemy. The ruling class despises them for assaulting its profitable traditions. The lower castes suspect them of ulterior motives. (Laborers are forever asking activists, "Why would an educated man trouble himself with the poor?") Consequently, activists are frequent targets of slander, police harassment, and lawsuits. They are beaten just as frequently, and on occasion they are killed.

Yet they persist, and sometimes they prevail. If human-rights organizations are judged by the number of people they have helped, the Bonded Labor Liberation Front is probably the most successful in Pakistan. Since its founding, in 1988, the BLLF has led the fight against bonded and child labor, liberating 30,000 adults and children—frequently entire families—from brick kilns, carpet factories, and farms, and placing 11,000 children in its own primary school system (its motto: "Struggle against slavery through education"). At the same time, it has won 25,000 high-court cases against abusive and unscrupulous employers, and helped to push the recent labor legislation through the National Assembly.

"Our victories amount to a hardship," says Ehsan Ulla Khan, the BLLF's founder and guiding force. "The state has done nothing to enforce the anti-slavery laws or even to inform the public that child and bonded labor have been outlawed. It's evident that if the enslaved workers are to be delivered from bondage, private citizens will have to do the delivering. That is, we will have to proclaim the end of slavery, educate workers, monitor employer compliance, and take legal action when necessary, because the state lacks the will and resources to do so."

With little funding, the BLLF wages a two-front war against enterprises that use child and bonded labor. While its legal advisers engage the courts and the legislature, its field staff shuttles around the country, informing workers of their recently acquired rights and distributing a pamphlet known as "The Charter of Freedom," which enumerates those rights in simple language. If a bonded laborer—child or adult—asks for its help, the BLLF takes whatever legal action is necessary to secure his or her release.

These days a surprising number of workers are refusing the pamphlet and turning their backs on BLLF staff members. This is an expression less of ingratitude than of fear. Employers throughout Pakistan are cautioning their workers against consorting with reformers who spread "false rumors" about the end of bonded labor. Many workers have been threatened with dismissal or violence if they speak with "the abolitionists" or are caught with "illegal communist propaganda."

So effective is the factory owners' disinformation campaign that workers literally flee when approached by BLLF staff members. This happened recently outside a Muridke brick factory to a BLLF leader I'll call Tariq. The fifty-odd kiln workers leaving the factory at the end of the workday scattered in all directions when they noticed Tariq lingering outside the factory gate, pamphlets in hand. One soot-covered girl of eight, left behind in the confusion, burst into tears when Tariq asked if she needed help. Between sobs the girl pleaded, "Please, sir, I have nothing to tell you. Please let me go."

Tariq did, albeit reluctantly. He has witnessed scenes like this countless times; they happen more and more often. If they discourage him (how could they not?), he takes care not to let anyone know. He describes his work as "an outgrowth of my patriotism." "What we do is meant not to shame Pakistan before the world but to create a Pakistan that respects the rights of all its peoples and encourages human potential." Tariq is a tall, pensive thirty-nine-year-old, an artist by training and by temperament. He traces his interest in child labor to an afternoon five years ago when an anti-slavery activist entered his graphic-de-

sign study in need of a brochure for his struggling organization. "Ehsan Ulla Khan had little money to spare, and he intimated that he'd rather not pay at all for the design work," Tariq told me. "I was just starting out in business and had no interest in politics or human rights. But I was moved by his photos of the children and agreed to do the work." Within six months Tariq was preparing all, of the BLLF's documents; within a year he was overseeing its operations. Today he is its factotum: equal parts tactician, recruiter, instructor, fundraiser, morale booster.

IN THE LOWEST CASTES, CHILDREN BECOME LABORERS ALMOST AS SOON AS THEY CAN WALK. BY THE YEAR 2000 LESS THAN A THIRD OF PAKISTANI CHILDREN WILL ATTEND SCHOOL. THE REST WILL ENTER THE WORK FORCE OR BECOME BEGGARS.

Some days he is also part spy. In addition to their assigned duties, the BLLF's 600 staff members are encouraged to spend their free time scrounging for leads on factory owners who are especially abusive to children. All ru-

mors are passed on to the BLLF's Lahore headquarters. Tariq does what he can to substantiate the worst of them, usually by touring the factories. It's a duty he dislikes. For one thing, it's exhausting: there are too many leads, too many rumors to verify. For another, it's dangerous: he's had numerous clashes with publicity-shy employers and their thugs. He prefers to travel alone, reasoning that one man is less conspicuous and less of a threat than is a group. And despite his reservations he is adept at subterfuge, at gaining entry to factories by masquerading as a laborer, a wholesaler, an exporter. "I do not misrepresent myself," he says. "But if a foreman mistakes me for a businessman or a wholesaler, I don't correct him."

His first stop one day last summer was a carpet workshop in a village twenty-four miles from Lahore. The village amounted to thirty brick huts, and the workshop was small in proportion—about the size of a subway car, and about as appealing. The long, narrow room contained a dozen upright looms. On each rough-hewn workbench between the looms squatted a carpet weaver. The room was dark and airless. Such light as there was came from a single ceiling fixture, two of its four bulbs burned out. A thermometer read 105°, and the mud walls were hot to the touch. A window promised some relief, but it was closed against fabric-eating insects.

Tariq entered quietly, in slacks, shirt, and patent-leather loafers. This outfit is uncommon in the provinces; he hoped it marked him as a person with Western tastes, and his vehicle, a Toyota Land Cruiser (donated to the BLLF by UNICEF), which he had parked conspicuously close to the entrance, marked him as a man of means—a buyer, a broker, an exporter. The weavers smiled at him, and a few bowed, but no one dared speak to him. Tariq took advantage of their reverence—and the master's absence—by circling the room, noting its conditions. After two circuits he began guessing the ages of the young weavers: "Are you twelve?" The boy nodded. Tariq pointed to the next.

"Fourteen?" Another nod and a smile. "Ten?" This time the nod was shy, and someone mentioned that the day before had been the boy's birthday. Tariq wished him health and happiness.

Of the twelve weavers, five were eleven to fourteen, and four were under ten. The two youngest were brothers named Akbar and Ashraf, aged eight and nine. They had been bonded to the carpet master at age five, and now worked six days a week at the shop. Their workday started at 6:00 A.M. and ended at 8:00 P.M., except, they said, when the master was behind on his quotas and forced them to work around the clock. They were small, thin, malnourished, their spines curved from lack of exercise and from squatting before the loom. Their hands were covered with calluses and scars, their fingers gnarled from repetitive work. Their breathing was labored, suggestive of tuberculosis. Collectively these ailments, which pathologists call captive-child syndrome, kill half of Pakistan's working children by age twelve.

Tariq and I watched Akbar in silence for some time. A hand-knotted carpet is made by tying short lengths of fine colored thread to a lattice of heavier white threads. The process is labor-intensive and tedious: a single four-by-six-foot carpet contains well over a million knots and takes an experienced weaver four to six months to complete. The finest, most intricate carpets have the highest density of knots. The smaller the knot, the more knots the weaver can cram into his lattice and the more valuable the finished carpet. Small knots are, of course, made most easily by small hands. Each carpet Akbar completed would retail in the United States for about $2,000—more than the boy would earn in ten years.

Observing a child carpet weaver at work generates in an American alternating currents of admiration and anger. At one moment the boy seems a prodigy, his carpet a lesson in geometry and colors. His patience is remarkable; his artistry seems effortless and of the highest order—comparable to, say, that of a great medieval tapestry

master. The next moment he fumbles with his scissors, and one notices a welt on his forearm. Suddenly the monotony of tying thousands of threads each hour seems like torture of the worst sort—like a death sentence, which in a way it is.

After ten minutes Tariq knelt by Akbar's side and said softly, "You're very good at this. The master must be quite pleased with you." The boy shook his head and grimaced. "The master says I am slow and clumsy."

Tariq placed a sympathetic hand on the boy's shoulder. "Have you been punished for poor work?" he asked. The boy shrugged and tied a red knot. Tariq repeated the question. This time the boy tied a dozen knots before answering him, in a conspiratorial whisper. "The master screams at us all the time, and sometimes he beats us," he said. "He is less severe with the younger boys. We're slapped often. Once or twice he lashed us with a cane. I was beaten ten days ago, after I made many errors of color in a carpet. He struck me with his fist quite hard on the face." By way of corroborating this, Akbar lifted a forelock, revealing a multicolored bruise on his right temple. Evidently the master did not consider the blow sufficient punishment: "I was fined one thousand rupees and made to correct the errors by working two days straight." The fine was added to Akbar's debt, and would extend his "apprenticeship" by several months.

"Do you like working here?"

"Oh, no, sir, staying here longer fills me with dread. I know I must learn a trade. But my parents are so far away, and all my friends are in school. My brother and I would like to be with our family. We'd like to play with our friends. This is not the way children should live."

Tariq listened to this outpouring without emotion. He has cultivated what he calls a surgeon's insensitivity to ravaged flesh, "because otherwise my heart would break ten times a day." Neither Akbar nor the others knew that child labor was illegal, that they were

free to leave the workshop whenever they wished.

Tariq left the factory and, on a whim, headed for the district police headquarters. As a rule BLLF members are closely observant of legal procedure, lest they be accused of subversive activity. The organization's legal advisers typically spend weeks drafting a formal complaint against a factory, based on members' espionage, before they register it with a high-court magistrate. Right now, however, Tariq was as interested in testing the responsiveness of the police as in penalizing the factory owner.

The nearest police station is a colonial relic on the Lahore road in Muridke. Tariq was caught up in the usual bureaucratic chaos on entering. The foyer was packed with police officers, soldiers, crime victims, and criminals, half of them shouting, the other half covering their ears against the noise. Every now and then the soldiers tried to impose order on the crowd, but with tattered uniforms and clipless rifles their authority went only so far. Familiar with such outposts, Tariq took his place in a line and forty minutes later was face-to-face with the district sergeant. It was ten in the morning. The sergeant had been at his post for two hours, but it could have been 200 for the way he looked. Tariq told him about the conditions in the workshop, about the children. The sergeant was perplexed. "Is this a crime?" he asked. "No one has ever complained before. What do you want us to do about it?" Tariq suggested sending officers to investigate, along with a medical-services crew for the children.

The sergeant left to consult his superior. Two minutes later he returned with the superintendent, a gracious, mustachioed man of fifty. "We are not unsympathetic to your complaint," the superintendent informed Tariq. "But the place you describe is registered as a home enterprise. It is run by a small landowner, and the workers are his immediate family. Family businesses are exempt from the labor laws. This enterprise is not illegal." The superintendent opened a binder and showed Tariq the workshop's registration certificate. Tariq attempted to correct him, but the superintendent said, "What you say may or may not be true. Unfortunately, our jurisdiction does not include child labor. I have no authority to investigate a private workplace. I have no evidence that the children are working there against their will or that their lives are in jeopardy. The mechanism for doing what you ask simply does not exist here."

Tariq was not disappointed, nor was he surprised. He expected no better, and was even pleased that he had rated an audience with the superintendent. Corruption is pervasive in the justice system: for a small consideration the police will look the other way when employers misuse their workers. In several districts the police are notorious for colluding with employers—supplying factories with children who have been abducted from itinerant poor families, orphanages, schools. Not long ago a boy of nine escaped from an abusive landowner and sought help from a police sergeant at this very station. The boy claimed that he had been held captive and tortured; he begged the police to return him to his parents. Instead the sergeant ordered the "fugitive" returned in shackles to the landowner. The sergeant later made the landowner a gift of the shackles, suggesting that they be used on other disruptive children.

The Death of Iqbal Masih

IN 1992 Pakistani carpet exports fell for the first time in two decades. The fall was slight in absolute terms—no more than three or four percentage points—but it indicated that Western consumers were shying away from luxury goods made by Third World children. Carpet makers' fears were confirmed when in 1993 and 1994 sales fell sharply in several of the largest markets for Pakistani exports. Since carpets were an important source of foreign currency, the decline sent shock waves throughout the Pakistani economy. At a 1993 conference, officials of the Pakistan Carpet Manufacturers and Exporters Association blamed the decline on "subversive domestic organizations which are conducting misleading and false international media campaigns abroad about the use of child labor in our manufacturing processes." The conference concluded on an optimistic note: "The memory of Western consumers is brief and our enemies' meager resources cannot sustain their destructive campaign for much longer."

Whatever hopes the carpet makers had for a reversal of their misfortunes were dashed in 1994, when human-rights organizations around the world acclaimed a twelve-year-old former slave named Iqbal Masih for his crusade against child labor. A small, sickly boy, Iqbal had been bonded at age four to a village carpet maker. He spent much of the next six years chained to a loom, which he worked fourteen hours a day, six days a week. He was fed just enough to keep him functioning, and was beaten more often than the other children at the workshop, because, unlike them, he defied the master time and again, refusing to work and on occasion attempting to escape. At ten he slipped his chains and sought the help of the BLLF, which secured him his freedom and a place in a primary school.

Frail as he was, Iqbal was a child of rare gifts, possessed of an intellectual maturity beyond his years and a precocious sense of justice. He applied these gifts to the anti-slavery movement, and achieved results that would be impressive for a Nobel laureate, let alone a schoolboy. By his twelfth birthday he had helped to liberate 3,000 children from bondage at textile and brick factories, tanneries, steelworks—industries at the heart of the Pakistani economy. He was subsequently honored by the International Labor Organization, in Sweden; by Reebok, which presented him with its prestigious Human Rights Youth in Action Award (for "his courage and ingenuity in righting a centuries-old wrong") in Boston in December of 1994; and by ABC News, which featured him as its Person of the Week. He used his unlikely celebrity status to remind consumers that "the world's two hundred million enslaved children are your responsibility." Subsequent to his travels millions of people in the United States and Europe searched their souls and decided that they could do without products of doubtful origin from Pakistan, India, and Bangladesh.

Iqbal attained a corresponding notoriety in Pakistan, particularly among the politicians and industrialists whose feudal practices he opposed. They responded with smear campaigns and the occasional threat of violence. Iqbal dismissed these threats, telling his friends that they encouraged him to work harder. He reasoned that grown men would harm a child only as a last resort, when their own position proved vulnerable.

IQBAL ATTAINED NOTORIETY IN PAKISTAN, PARTICULARLY AMONG THE POLITICIANS AND INDUSTRIALISTS WHOSE FEUDAL PRACTICES HE OPPOSED. HE DISMISSED THREATS AGAINST HIM, TELLING HIS FRIENDS THAT THEY ENCOURAGED HIM TO WORK HARDER.

On the evening of April 16, 1995, Easter Sunday, Iqbal Masih was shot dead while visiting relatives in a rural village. Immediately afterward Ehsan Ulla Khan declared that the slain youth was the victim of "a mafia conspiracy." In the days that followed, Khan embellished his conspiracy theory for anyone willing to listen. "I emphatically say that the carpet mafia is responsible for this brutal killing . . . Iqbal has become a symbol of our struggle against slavery and was not afraid to expose the inhuman practices prevailing in the carpet industry. I have no doubt that the police are also a part of the conspiracy." However, Khan did not support his fulminations with evidence. "I do not rely on evidence," he told his critics. "I have my instinct. How else do you explain how, in a village where no murder has occurred for a decade, the one child who poses a threat to the carpet owners is gunned down? Coincidence is never so cruel." To the claim of the local police that Iqbal's murder was an isolated incident Khan retorts, "The evidence can be found if the police could be bothered to look." The killing remains unsolved.

Eight hundred mourners crowded into the Muridke cemetery for Iqbal's funeral. A week later 3,000 protesters, half of them under twelve, marched through the streets of Lahore demanding an end to child labor. A few days after the funeral Khan left Pakistan to consult with children's-rights activists in Europe. There he repeated his accusations to great effect at conferences, on television, before lawmakers. Iqbal was proclaimed a "martyr for the cause of bonded labor"; his murder became a cause célèbre among the intelligentsia. Khan called upon the Human Rights Commission of the United Nations to ban the import and sale of all products made by children, especially carpets. "I appeal to importers and consumers: say no and only no to child-made carpets," he said. "This is the last message of Iqbal. It would be an insult to his blood and memory if people continue to buy child-made products in any part of the world."

Western consumers have responded to Khan's plea. Sales of imported carpets have fallen precipitously in recent months. Bowing to public pressure, importers in the United States, Sweden, Italy, Britain, France, and Germany by last June had canceled carpet orders collectively valued at $10 million. At the same time, human-rights groups and individual sympathizers have donated large sums to support and expand BLLF operations. Ironically, Iqbal's death opened doors and purses that were previously closed to Khan.

Westerners, who have seen economic weapons used to achieve social reforms, might expect canceled orders to result in negotiation and, with luck, accommodation between industrialists and activists. Pakistan's industrialists, however, have chosen the questionable tactic of denying the existence of bonded labor in their factories. Shahid Rashid Butt, the president of the Islamabad Carpet Exporters Association, told his colleagues, "Our industry is the victim of enemy agents who spread lies and fictions around the world that bonded labor and child labor are utilized in the production of hand-knotted carpets. They are not and have never been." He condemned the BLLF and its allies as Jewish and Indian enemies who had launched a systematic campaign to damage the reputation of Pakistan's carpet industry for their own profit. His remarks were enthusiastically endorsed by the Pakistan Carpet Manufacturers and Exporters Association and echoed in the National Assembly.

"These charges flew in the face not just of reason but also of an extraordinary amount of evidence," says I. A. Rehman, the director of the Human Rights Commission of Pakistan. "Anywhere else they would have been laughed at and dismissed. Here they were accepted as fact and acted on." At the urging of politicians and industrialists, Javed Mahmood, the assistant director of Pakistan's Federal Investigation Agency (FIA), last May launched an inquiry into the BLLF on the strength of information he had received from highly placed sources suggesting that the organization was supported by "Pakistan's enemies." He later said, "I consider the information credible and will do all I can to protect our country's commercial interests from unscrupulous enemies." At the same time, Pakistan's leading newspapers began running "exposés" of abolitionist leaders, the nicest of which characterized Ehsan Ulla Khan as a philandering bigamist with "indisputable ties to Jewish and Indian agencies hostile to Pakistan." The publishers of these newspapers are suspected of having large financial interests in industries employing child labor.

The FIA is a secret police force, and one of its best-kept secrets is whom it works for. Nominally an organ of the state, it is not above accepting freelance assignments from prominent individuals and commercial groups. The extent of its extralegal activities is anyone's guess, but a highly respected human-rights investigator believes that "there is close cooperation between carpet interests, feudal lords, segments of the police force, and the administration—district commissioners, the courts, and government officials. Financially resourceful drug barons are also a part of the scene." Whoever the client, the FIA provides an assortment of services straight out of the KGB handbook; wiretaps, tails, searches, arrests, harassment, and varying degrees of corporal punishment.

These services were very much in evidence on a Thursday afternoon in late June, when the FIA raided the BLLF's Lahore headquarters. The detail consisted of ten men, all in plain clothes, who scrambled up four flights of stairs to the tiny office in no time flat. These were not ordinary policemen; this was not the usual surprise "inspection" (read "intimidation") to which all nongovernment organizations are periodically subjected. These were professional agents, lithe and expert, commanded by a severe officer in a freshly pressed safari suit. After lining the BLLF workers up against a wall, he ordered his troops to "confiscate anything that may incriminate them." The agents took a liberal view of "incriminate," and packed up computers, filing cabinets, fax machines, photocopiers, telephones, stationery, posters, bicycles—and the cashbox containing the monthly payroll. Their depredations were supervised by a small man who was distinctly not a policeman. He represented, it turned out, the Pakistan Carpet Manufacturers and Exporters Association. His purpose, he said, was "to protect the interests of legitimate businessmen." Every so often he consulted with the commander.

When one BLLF worker tried to protest, an agent threw her against a wall and held a rifle butt inches from her face. When another worker demanded to see a search warrant, the commander informed her that none was necessary, because "we are acting to prevent terrorism." The association representative nodded in agreement.

Fifteen minutes later the detail was gone, along with the office equipment and furnishings. All that remained was a heap of broken furniture, a workers'-rights poster, and a BLLF flag dangling out an open window. Several staff workers had been taken away as well, to an FIA holding center, where they were interrogated for three days.

Two days later another FIA detail raided the BLLF's "Freedom Campus" training facility in Lahore, along with several of its primary schools around the country. Once again the agents were undiscriminating. They seized everything movable ("items used to obstruct valid commercial interests") and mistreated the staff without respect for position or age. Teachers, drivers, secretaries, and peasant families seeking refuge from violent employers were interrogated along with administrators, advocates, attorneys, and fundraisers.

After an earlier raid on BLLF headquarters Fatima Ghulam, the director of the BLLF's women's-education program, was held for two days. "An officer promised to release me immediately if I agreed to inform against Ehsan Ulla Khan and some of the others," Ghulam says. "He wanted me to testify that Khan is a subversive, an enemy

agent, and that the BLLF receives money from foreign governments. He said he had tapped my telephone conversations and had recordings of me discussing treasonable acts. If I wanted to avoid prosecution, I would have to cooperate with the FIA. I refused, and he kept me without food or water. When I wouldn't speak to him the next day, he slapped me and dragged me around the room."

Not to be outdone, the Pakistani press stepped up its campaign against the BLLF. Last summer a number of newspapers whose editorial pages conceded that they were "troubled by the carpet export crisis" reported the following "facts": Khan himself had murdered Iqbal Masih to win sympathy for the BLLF; Khan had misappropriated BLLF funds to support his own decadent lifestyle; Khan routinely used BLLF schoolchildren as sex partners and house slaves; Iqbal Masih was a twenty-one-year-old midget whom Khan paid to masquerade as a carpet child; the BLLF was an outpost of India's intelligence agency; Khan was an Indian agent working to disgrace the Pakistani carpet trade. These same papers also "revealed" that carpet workers enjoy a higher standard of living than the average citizen, along with better working conditions. "The few children working on carpets," one editorial assured its readers, "do so after school, in their own homes, under the supervision of loving parents."

In the wake of these attacks BLLF operations—child-welfare programs, schools, training and education programs—nearly shut down for lack of funds and staff. Membership has suffered, and many of the legal advisers and support staff, fearing reprisals, have fallen away. Those who remain are subject to almost constant harassment: the fortunate ones have their telephones tapped; the less fortunate are shadowed around the clock. At the same time, the courts have ignored their complaints

about child labor and abusive treatment by employers.

Just in case the intention of the Federal Investigation Agency was unclear, Assistant Director Mahmood in early June charged Ehsan Ulla Khan, who was still abroad, and a BLLF strategist named Zafaryab Ahmad with sedition and economic treason, capital offenses punishable by death. According to Mahmood, "The accused men conspired with the Indian espionage agency to exploit the murder of Iqbal Masih . . . causing a recurring huge financial loss to Pakistan's business interests abroad and paving the way for India to wage economic warfare against Pakistan." Ahmad was arrested and taken to a Lahore jail, where, after repudiating the charges (he called them "foolish and absurd"), he was denied bail. The FIA has since refused to provide BLLF attorneys with evidence supporting the charges, although Mahmood assures them that it consists of "videotapes and recordings of telephone conversations that amount to firm proof." Mahmood has vowed to arrest Khan "the very moment he returns to Pakistan, the moment his aircraft touches down."

Ehsan Ulla Khan remains in Europe, an unhappy exile. "They will jail me if I return to Pakistan," he told me shortly after he left his country. "Our attorneys tell me I am of greater use to the BLLF here, speaking out against the authorities, than I would be inside a Lahore cell. I fear for my people. The police have harassed many of them, and so many more have left us out of fear. We are demoralized. We cannot pay our bills and our staff. Our schools may close and our thousands of students may end up in the very factories we saved them from. Our offices and homes are under surveillance. Our telephones are tapped. We are fighting for our survival. If the attacks do not stop soon, it is possible that the BLLF will perish. That would be tragic. What will become of the children of Pakistan?"

Of *Power Rangers* and V-Chips

Chris J. Boyatzis

These are exciting times for people who care about children and what they watch on television. The latest wave of public and political debate about television has generated some encouraging outcomes. A major legal and political change is the Telecommunications Act of 1996, part of which calls for more educational programming for children, ratings for TV shows, and, beginning in early 1998, the inclusion in new television sets of the V-chip—a device that will allow parents to electronically block certain programs.

A major scientific change is the undertaking of the largest study ever on the effects of TV, the National Television Violence Study (NTVS), begun in 1994. The project is being conducted at four major universities across the country and is supervised by a council of representatives from 17 national organizations concerned about television. Their findings are informing public and political discussion about children and television (Federman 1997).

I have been particularly interested in these changes ever since coworkers and I conducted an experiment several years ago on *The Mighty Morphin Power Rangers*, the most popular children's program of the mid-90s. In our study (Boyatzis, Matillo, & Nesbitt 1995), children in an elementary after-school program were randomly assigned to one of two groups. One group of children was shown, on one day during their after-school program, one episode of *Power Rangers*. Following this viewing we observed the children at play with their peers and recorded the number of aggressive acts. On another day we observed the other group of children, who were not shown the program, in normal, ongoing play and recorded the number of aggressive acts toward their peers. We found that after viewing just one episode, children—especially boys—committed aggressive acts seven times more often than did control children who did not see the show. Children who viewed *Power Rangers* typically used karate chops and flying kicks against their peers in direct and obvious imitation of the Power Rangers' actions.

Given the popularity of *Power Rangers,* our study is important because it was, as far as we can tell, the first systematic assessment of the show's impact on children. The mix of the show's popularity and our findings—it made children aggressive—attracted extensive media attention for nearly two years.

When our findings were distributed through the media, we received many calls and letters from the public. A veteran kindergarten teacher in California lamented, "I can hardly do any teaching because of the time I spend on *Power Rangers* discipline problems." A grandfather from Michigan called to express worry about his two grandchildren who, after watching the show, were uncharacteristically hostile in their play. A mother wrote to say that after watching the show, her daughter kicked her in the legs, saying, "The Power Rangers do it."

The anecdotal testimony echoed the large majority (86%) of parents in a massive national survey who observed changes in their children's behavior after the children had watched a violent program (Levine 1994). But there were also defenders of *Power Rangers,* such as the mother who said the show offered heroic role models to children. Others claimed the show was merely the latest harmless fad for children. Some argued that the prior TV rage—*Teenage Mutant Ninja Turtles*—didn't inspire kids to kill each other; older critics charged that their countless childhood hours watching Superman and the Lone Ranger beating up bad guys didn't make them violent criminals. Finally, the producers of the program and the Fox network, which airs it, defended the show as a source of positive role models and prosocial messages (Weinstein 1994).

Recently *The Mighty Morphin Power Rangers* has undergone changes, mostly cosmetic (it is now titled *Power Rangers Turbo*, there is a new villainess, etc.). Concerns remain, however, about this and other violent shows. I offer some below, putting them into an empirical context from the social science research. Although I focus on this program, the criticisms apply to many other children's programs as well.

Chris J. Boyatzis, *Ph.D., is assistant professor of psychology at Bucknell University. Chris has conducted research on the effects of television on children. At home he has two young children and two old TVs.*

From *Young Children*, November 1997, pp. 74-79. © 1998 by the National Association for the Education of Young Children. Reprinted by permission.

Why worry about Power Rangers *and violent TV?*

1. The show is extremely violent, and it makes children aggressive.

In fact, according to the National Coalition on Television Violence, a nonprofit organization that has analyzed the content of children's programs since 1980, it is the most violent children's program ever (Kiesewetter 1993). The average Saturday morning cartoon has 20 to 25 violent acts per hour; *Ninja Turtles* had more than 90 violent acts an hour. Where did the original *Power Rangers* fit into this hierarchy of gratuitous violence? At the top, with 211 violent acts per hour. As recently as the 1995–96 season, the show was classified by one group in the NTVS project in the "sinister combat violence" category (Cole 1996).

Our first study (Boyatzis, Matillo, & Nesbitt 1995) provided direct evidence that children become more aggressive after watching *Power Rangers*. We then conducted a second study (Boyatzis, Matillo, Nesbitt, & Cathey 1995), surveying 263 parents of school children about their children's viewing habits and the parents' beliefs about *Power Rangers*. We also had children's teachers rate the children's aggressiveness and altruism. We found that the more girls watch the show, the more aggressive they become; for boys the correlations were in the expected direction but not significant.

Although this study was correlational and hence cannot prove causality, it suggests that *Power Rangers* is associated with aggression. Did parents notice an effect on their children? Across the four different schools in this study, 70–80% of the parents said that after watching the show their children acted more aggressively toward friends, siblings, and even the parents themselves.

Our findings are not surprising. Scientific research from the past 30 years has demonstrated that viewing TV violence increases real-life aggression in children and youth (for reviews see Stein & Freidrich 1975; Heller & Polsky 1976; Hearold 1986; Huesmann & Eron 1986; Liebert & Sprafkin 1988; Paik & Comstock 1994). However, our studies were important for demonstrating for the first time a strong link between *Power Rangers* viewing and children's aggression.

Despite these findings, I must offer two important qualifications and rejoinders to them. First, *not all children are influenced in the same way by TV violence.* Indeed, our first study (Boyatzis, Matillo, & Nesbitt 1995) found that boys but not girls became much more aggressive after viewing *Power Rangers;* further, not all boys showed heightened aggression.

But let us remember that research rarely, if ever, offers guaranteed deterministic relationships between variables (such as that violent TV makes *all* children aggressive). Instead, research provides probabilistic relations: rather than black-and-white absolutes, we get odds and expectations.

Research over three decades shows unequivocally that the odds are that watching violent TV *increases the likelihood* that children will be more aggressive. This statement is as true as saying, for example, that smoking cigarettes strongly increases the risk of serious health problems, even though smoking doesn't guarantee that all smokers will suffer them. Of course there are exceptions to the rule because individuals differ and other factors influence outcomes, but the general rule is clear: watching TV violence increases the risk for real-life aggression.

Second, *TV violence is not the only cause of aggression.* There are many causes, from societal to family factors (e.g., corporal punishment) to children's temperaments (see Eron 1987; Singer, Singer, & Rapaczynski 1989). Nevertheless, aggression is largely a learned behavior, and television is one of the teachers. Given that children watch so much TV—more than 25 hours a week on average—it is a pervasive and potent teacher.

How does viewing violent TV make children more aggressive? By watching others be aggressive, children learn new forms of hostile and dangerous behavior. This is *observational learning,* and it is perhaps the most long-confirmed mechanism for increased aggression (Bandura, Ross, & Ross 1961, 1963; Bandura 1965). Also, by watching others be aggressive, children become desensitized toward violence and more tolerant of real-life aggression (see Drabman & Thomas 1974; Thomas et al. 1977). Finally, watching violent TV promotes the internalization of aggressive scripts that can guide children's behavior (see Huesmann & Eron 1984; Eron 1987). These mental scripts are correlated with children's actual aggression (Huesmann & Guerra 1997), and they promote the use of some behaviors (e.g., hitting others to resolve conflicts) and inhibit the use of nonviolent alternatives.

2. The show's violence is unrealistic.

Despite violence that should leave the characters bloodied, immobile, or even dead, the Power Rangers seem immune to injury. This is typical for children's programs—consequences of violence are rarely shown (Potts & Henderson 1991)—and troubling, as

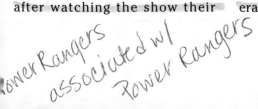
Power Rangers associated w/ Power Rangers

What Can Parents and Teachers Do?

Because our work received wide media attention—segments on *20/20*, *Entertainment Tonight*, and many local news stations; radio spots; extensive newspaper coverage—I would like to believe that our research on *The Mighty Morphin Power Rangers* contributed to the latest surge of public debate about television and children. For the sake of individual teachers and parents who feel they have little voice in this national discussion, I must note that the media attention was instigated by a single brief letter we wrote to the *Los Angeles Times* criticizing *Power Rangers*. Perhaps there's a moral here about "the power of one."

One concrete outcome of this public debate is the Telecommunications Act of 1996, which calls for, among other things, producers to provide more educational programming for children and ratings for their programs, and for TV manufacturers to build in V-chips. The 1996 act provides steps toward greater personal control of the medium in the home, in contrast to previous, less explicit telecommunications acts. The breadth of these legal actions reflects the complex ecology of factors in the role of TV in children's lives, which has been addressed by a number of researchers (e.g., Anderson & Bryant 1983; Pinon, Huston, & Wright 1989; Truglio et al. 1996; Cantor, Harrison, & Nathanson 1997).

Taking action

There are several ways that parents concerned about their children might mitigate the aggression-inducing impact of *Power Rangers* and other violent or undesirable programs. The most effective step would be to unplug or remove the family TV. However, this may not be possible or

even desirable since much of the educational programming for children has proven benefits. Presuming we keep the TV in the house, we need to strive for better TV management. At the very least, parents should not put television sets in children's bedrooms, where viewing time and programs are most difficult to monitor or discuss.

In the home, parents could "just say no" to programs that are offensive or unacceptable. While this can be justified in light of research on TV violence, it may not be feasible. For example, *Power Rangers* airs daily in many markets, which may make it more difficult to monitor. And exacerbating this problem is the fact that children frequently watch TV by themselves. In our survey study, 75% of parents said they do not watch *Power Rangers* with their children, a level of unmonitored children's viewing found by others for television in general (St. Peters et al. 1991).

Leave it to the V-chip?

Of course, the proposed V-chip technology, due in early 1998, should facilitate parents' prohibition of unwanted programs. But we can anticipate V-chip complications. Besides the obvious one—parents' difficulty in figuring out how to program the V-chip—there are other, more serious issues. For example, what percentage of parents will buy a new TV equipped with the chip? Will it be enough to make a difference? Further, how will we determine if the chip has the positive impact its proponents anticipate? I presume (and hope) researchers will study families to learn about family dynamics and child behavior before and after the chip. Such research will be necessary to demonstrate any positive change in children and, at a broader level, in society due to greater parental control over children's TV con-

sumption. If such changes do not materialize, the television industry and other defenders of the medium will wag an "I-told-you-so" finger and repeat their standard line: societal problems are due to many things, but what children and adults watch on TV isn't one of them.

I also foresee problems stemming from V-chip technology. Producers might use the availability of the technology as a defense for abdicating their own responsibility for programming, placing the burden fully on parents. The industry could take the position that if parents don't want their children to view a program because it's too violent, sexual, or adult, they can use the V-chip to block it. Thus, the television industry may use the existence of the V-chip as justification for producing programming that is more offensive than the current fare in terms of violence or sex. This could make the full spectrum of television programs worse and be especially problematic for those families without a chip-equipped TV. Finally, I worry that parents may come to rely on the technology as an easy fix, thereby reducing parent-child discussion about what is appropriate for children to watch and what isn't. If these scenarios are played out, the V-chip will be a solution that exacerbates the problem it was designed to remedy.

Another issue in banning unwanted shows—whether via V-chip or parental fiat—is that such action may create a forbidden-fruit syndrome: children will want even more to watch the programs because they are banned. Current research on the use of ratings for television programs supports this presumption. The television industry now applies the ratings of the Motion Picture Association of America (MPAA). These ratings (G, PG, PG-13, R) give guidance only on the age-appropriateness of programs. The National

Television Violence Study found that the more restrictive ratings ("PG-13: Parents strongly cautioned" and "R: Restricted") increase a show's attractiveness to 10- to 15-year-olds, whereas the rating of "G: General audiences" lowers interest in it (Cantor, Harrison, & Nathanson 1997; Federman 1997). Banning a program is not as simple or even as desirable as it may seem.

Strategies for parents

Parents can try several strategies for managing their children's TV viewing. One approach is to *put children on a "reduced Power Rangers diet"*: if children are watching *Power Rangers* four times a week, reduce their viewing to once or twice a week. Parents might also want to share responsibility with children by giving older school children a "TV ration" that allots a specific number of hours per week for viewing, leaving it primarily to the children to choose the programs.

I know several sets of *parents and children who have struck a deal*—the children can watch *Power Rangers* (or any other violent show) as long as they don't imitate its violence—leading to kids happy to watch the show and parents pleased that their children aren't behaving aggressively.

Another tactic is to *watch TV with your child and discuss the programs.* This approach probably enhances children's critical-viewing skills. In fact, Cantor and Harrison (1996) found that children whose parents watch and discuss programs with them are less interested in programs that carry restrictive warnings or ratings, perhaps because the discussions promote the child's internalization of the parents' standards.

In addition to discussing the programs, *parents can draw on their ingenuity.* To help her child recognize the level of violence in *Power Rangers,* one mother had her son

count the number of aggressive acts in a 10-minute segment. The child became exasperated, unable to keep track of the fighting. In another case, a creative father allowed his child to watch *Ninja Turtles* only if the child imagined an additional turtle named Gandhi who would settle conflicts with nonviolent means (Levine 1994).

I tried some of these tactics myself. When I first saw *Power Rangers,* its violence led me to ban it from my then-7-year-old's viewing options. After taking this just-say-no stance, I realized that discussing the show with her might be more beneficial. We watched several episodes together and generated nonviolent solutions for the Power Rangers' problems. We also discussed how unrealistic it was for them to emerge unscathed after so much fighting. Finally, watching the program together allowed me to highlight and reinforce the show's prosocial messages.

Such shared viewing and analysis might help children develop a form of TV literacy that will serve them as future viewers. Given the pervasiveness and influence of TV, media literacy should be part of the curriculum beginning in elementary school. And schools concerned about violence might also implement a violence-prevention curriculum for children (see Grossman et al. 1997).

Strategies for schools

At school, teachers, administrators, and parent-teacher organizations should consider taking a stance on offensive programs. One elementary school nurse, to ensure that parents were aware of *Power Rangers'* violent content, sent a letter to parents asking them to sign it to confirm that they had watched the show. Schools (teachers, school nurse) might record accidents and injuries related to *Power Rangers* or

other action shows. Parents and schools may be more motivated to confront the program's effects if they discover that many injuries or fights are related to the program.

A course of action for all

Finally, let your views be known. Parents, educators, and concerned citizens can write to local television stations, advertisers, politicians, and media to express concern. The new telecommunications act (Telecommunications Act of 1996) facilitates contacting TV stations because it requires stations to make available a staff person as liaison with viewers who want to comment on children's programs.

Just months after the current ratings system for TV programs was implemented, the television industry and child advocacy groups engaged in heated argument, moderated by the Federal Communications Commission, about revising the ratings to include specific information about a show's content (e.g., sex, violence, offensive language). This change is due largely to the outcry from parents and child advocacy groups for improvements in the ratings system.

Guidelines based on content will be better not only because they give parents more information about programs, but because content advisories such as "mild violence" or "graphic violence" actually reduce five- to nine-year-olds' interest in those programs (Cantor, Harrison, & Nathanson 1997).

Finally, parents and educators can stay informed on other TV-management approaches by reading available resources, such as *The Smart Parent's Guide to Kids' TV* (Chen 1994).

exposure to unrealistic depiction of violence and injury-free action increases children's risk-taking and injurious behavior (Potts, Doppler, & Hernandez 1994).

3. The show has high visibility.

For two solid years *Power Rangers* was the most popular children's TV program in the country for two- to eleven-year-olds. In many TV markets the show airs daily. This high visibility is reason to worry because, as many studies have shown, the more children are exposed to TV violence, the more likely they are to imitate it.

4. The Power Rangers are actually people, not cartoon characters.

Part of the show's appeal may be that the characters are played by real actors who "morph" into Power Rangers. This is unfortunate because children are more likely to imitate the behavior of real people than that of animated cartoon characters (Bandura, Ross, & Ross 1963).

5. The Power Rangers are heroes.

The Power Rangers are "the good guys," exalted for their violent tactics against their enemies. Even when the characters are their normal, nonmorphed teenage selves, they are admired by other characters (often for their expertise in martial arts). Such high status is reason to worry because the more a character is rewarded for performing an aggressive act, the more likely children are to imitate it (Bandura & Walters 1963).

6. The Power Rangers are mostly male role models.

The majority of the Power Rangers are male, and their action is highlighted in most episodes. Our first study found that boys who viewed *Power Rangers* were much more aggressive than were any of the other children, perhaps because of the surfeit of male role models to identify with and emulate.

7. The show offers unfavorable representation of females and minorities.

The source of evil in the show's first several seasons was a shrill and dastardly Asian female, Rita Repulsa, whereas the Power Rangers' leader was a more dignified White male. (Though no longer Asian, the current villain is still a female and is dressed in revealing clothes.) Such images may perpetuate racist and sexist notions and reinforce the idea that it is normal or even wise to distrust and suspect people who are different (Carlsson-Paige & Levin 1990; Levin & Carlsson-Paige 1994).

8. The Power Rangers' prosocial messages are lost amidst the violence.

A redeeming feature of the show is that the characters often state positive messages (e.g., "Express your anger responsibly," "Fight only in self-defense"). Some anecdotal evidence suggests that these messages might be working. A second-grade teacher wrote to say that some of her students endorsed the show because the characters "tell you good things, like not to pollute." A child remarked that the characters tell children, "Don't go on the evil side."

Unfortunately, research has found that children do not understand prosocial messages when the messages are embedded in violence. Instead, they attend to the fighting, which is troubling because "visual presentations of aggressive acts, independent of plot and dialogue, may be sufficient to engender aggression" (Huesmann et al. 1984, 771).

In our survey study we asked teachers to rate children's altruism. If *Power Rangers* is associated with altruistic, prosocial qualities, we would expect to find a positive correlation between viewing the show and children's altruism ratings. Instead, we found that the more children watched the show, the lower their altruism scores.

In addition, the large majority of parents we surveyed did not think their children learned anything positive from the show. The show's excessive violence squanders an opportunity to teach children appropriate means for conflict resolution.

When we surveyed parents regarding what they thought about the program, about 60% wrote comments to the effect that the show was too violent. This finding is all the more striking, given that the words "violent" and "violence" did not appear anywhere on the survey we gave parents. Thus we did not cue them to express this concern. In sum, if the show has any prosocial benefit for children, we have yet to find it in our research and the television industry has yet to offer a shred of evidence.

Conclusions

Recent developments, such as program ratings and V-chip technology, will surely evolve, and other unanticipated changes will come. It is unlikely, however, that a marked reduction in TV violence or even a significant decline in TV viewing by children will result from these developments. With the spread of cable, the growing number of stations, and the ubiquity of VCRs, the viewing options are greater than ever. Thus, it is all the more important that parents and teachers find ways to manage and use television so that it is a positive influence on children, not a negative one.

We cannot expect the television industry to do this, nor should we expect, or even want, the government to do so. But as both government and the industry itself take some encouraging legal and technological steps, let us put our own house in order. The harmful impact of *The Mighty Morphin Power Rangers* and other offensive programs may be mitigated by the types of action suggested here, which are likely to be effective only when undertaken in earnest. Assuming that the TV will continue to bring violence and other unwelcome fare into our homes, our children deserve at least these efforts from us.

References

Anderson, D.R., & J. Bryant. 1983. Research on children's television viewing: The state of the art. In *Children's understanding of television,* eds. J. Bryant & D.R. Anderson, 331–53. New York: Academic.

Bandura, A. 1965. Influence of models' reinforcement contingencies on the acquisition of imitative responses. *Journal of Personality and Social Psychology* 1: 589–95.

Bandura, A., D. Ross, & S.A. Ross. 1961. Transmission of aggression through imitation of aggressive models. *Journal of Abnormal and Social Psychology* 63: 575–82.

Bandura, A., D. Ross, & S.A. Ross. 1963. Imitation of film-mediated aggressive models. *Journal of Abnormal and Social Psychology* 66: 3–11.

Bandura, A., & R.H. Walters. 1963. *Social learning and personality development.* New York: Holt, Rinehart & Winston.

Boyatzis, C.J., G. Matillo, & K. Nesbitt. 1995. Effects of *The Mighty Morphin Power Rangers* on children's aggression with peers. *Child Study Journal* 25: 45–55.

Boyatzis, C.J., G. Matillo, K. Nesbitt, & G. Cathey. 1995. Effects of *The Mighty Morphin Power Rangers* on children's aggressive and prosocial behavior. Paper presented at the meeting of the Society for Research in Child Development, March, Indianapolis, Indiana.

Cantor, J., & K. Harrison. 1996. Ratings and advisories for television programming. In *National Television Violence Study,* vol. 1, ed. D. Kunkel, 361–410. Thousand Oaks, CA: Sage.

Cantor, J., K. Harrison, & A. Nathanson. 1997. Ratings and advisories for television programming. In *National Television Violence Study,* vol. 2, ed. B. Wilson, 267–322. Thousand Oaks, CA: Sage.

Carlsson-Paige, N., & D.E. Levin. 1990. *Who's calling the shots? How to respond effectively to children's fascination with war play and war toys.* Philadelphia: New Society.

Chen, M. 1994. *The smart parent's guide to kids' TV.* San Francisco: KQED Books.

Cole, J. 1996. *UCLA television violence report: 1996.* Los Angeles: UCLA Center for Communication Policy.

Drabman, R., & M. Thomas. 1974. Does media violence increase children's toleration of real-life aggression? *Developmental Psychology* 10: 418–21.

Eron, L.D. 1987. The development of aggressive behavior from the perspective of a developing behaviorism. *American Psychologist* 42: 435–42.

Federman, J., ed. 1997. *National television violence study, vol. 2: Executive summary.* Santa Barbara: University of California, Center for Communication & Social Policy.

Grossman, D.C., H.J. Neckerman, T.D. Koepsell, P.-Y. Liu, K.N. Asher, D. Beland, K. Frey, & F.P. Rivara. 1997. Effectiveness of a violence prevention curriculum among children in elementary school. *Journal of the American Medical Association* 277: 1605–11.

Hearold, S. 1986. A synthesis of 1,043 effects of television on social behavior. In *Public communications and behavior,* vol. 1, ed. G. Comstock, 65–133. New York: Academic.

Heller, M.S., & S. Polsky. 1976. *Studies in violence and television.* New York: American Broadcasting Companies.

Huesmann, L.R., & L.D. Eron. 1984. Cognitive processes and the persistence of aggressive behavior. *Aggressive Behavior* 10: 243–51.

Huesmann, L.R., & L.D. Eron, eds. 1986. *Television and the aggressive child: A cross-national comparison.* Hillsdale, NJ: Erlbaum.

Huesmann, L.R., L.D. Eron, M.M. Lefkowitz, & L.O. Walder. 1984. Stability of aggression over time and generations. *Developmental Psychology* 20: 1120–34.

Huesmann, L.R., & N.G. Guerra. 1997. Children's normative beliefs about aggression and aggressive behavior. *Journal of Personality and Social Psychology* 72: 408–19.

Kiesewetter, J. 1993. Top kids' show also ranks as most violent. *Cincinnati Enquirer,* 17 December, A1.

Levin, D.E., & N. Carlsson-Paige. 1994. Developmentally appropriate television: Putting children first. *Young Children* 49 (5): 38–44.

Levine, S.B. 1994. Caution: Children watching. *Ms.* July/August, 23–25.

Liebert, R., & J. Sprafkin. 1988. *The early window: Effects of television on children and youth.* New York: Pergamon.

Paik, H., & G.A. Comstock. 1994. The effects of television violence on antisocial behavior: A meta-analysis. *Communication Research* 21: 516–46.

Pinon, M.F., A.C. Huston, & J.C. Wright. 1989. Family ecology and child characteristics that predict young children's educational television viewing. *Child Development* 60: 846–56.

Potts, R., M. Doppler, & M. Hernandez. 1994. Effects of television content on physical risk-taking in children. *Journal of Experimental Child Psychology* 58: 321–31.

Potts, R., & J. Henderson. 1991. The dangerous world of television: A content analysis of physical injuries in children's television programming. *Children's Environments Quarterly* 8: 7–14.

Singer, J.L., D.G. Singer, & W.S. Rapaczynski. 1989. Family patterns and television viewing as predictors of children's beliefs and aggression. *Journal of Communication* 34: 73–89.

St. Peters, M., M. Fitch, A.C. Huston, J.C. Wright, & D.J. Eakins. 1991. Television and families: What do young children watch with their parents? *Child Development* 62: 1409–23.

Stein, A.H., & L.K. Freidrich, 1975. *Impact of television on children and youth.* Chicago: University of Chicago Press.

Telecommunications Act of 1996. U.S. Public Law 104, 105th Cong., 1st sess., 8 February 1996.

Thomas, M.H., R.W. Horton, E.C. Lippincott, & R.S. Drabman. 1977. Desensitization to portrayals of real-life aggression as a function of exposure to television violence. *Journal of Personality and Social Psychology* 35: 450–58.

Truglio, R.T., K.C. Murphy, S. Oppenheimer, A.C. Huston, & J.C. Wright. 1996. Predictors of children's entertainment television viewing: Why are they tuning in? *Journal of Applied Developmental Psychology* 17: 475–93.

Weinstein, S. 1994. Morphin mania: How—and why? *Los Angeles Times,* 26 February.

The Effects of Poverty on Children

Jeanne Brooks-Gunn
Greg J. Duncan

Jeanne Brooks-Gunn, Ph.D., is Virginia and Leonard Marx professor of child development and education, and is director of the Center for Young Children and Families at Teachers College, Columbia University.

Greg J. Duncan, Ph.D., is a professor of education and social policy, and is a faculty associate at the Institute for Policy Research, Northwestern University.

Abstract

Although hundreds of studies have documented the association between family poverty and children's health, achievement, and behavior, few measure the effects of the timing, depth, and duration of poverty on children, and many fail to adjust for other family characteristics (for example, female headship, mother's age, and schooling) that may account for much of the observed correlation between poverty and child outcomes. This article focuses on a recent set of studies that explore the relationship between poverty and child outcomes in depth. By and large, this research supports the conclusion that family income has selective but, in some instances, quite substantial effects on child and adolescent well-being. Family income appears to be more strongly related to children's ability and achievement than to their emotional outcomes. Children who live in extreme poverty and who live below the poverty line for multiple years appear, all other things being equal, to suffer the worst outcomes. The timing of poverty also seems to be important for certain child outcomes. Children who experience poverty during their preschool and early school years have lower rates of school completion than children and adolescents who experience poverty only in later years. Although more research is needed on the significance of the timing of poverty on child outcomes, findings to date suggest that interventions during early childhood may be most important in reducing poverty's impact on children.

In recent years, about one in five American children—some 12 to 14 million—have lived in families in which cash income failed to exceed official poverty thresholds. Another one-fifth lived in families whose incomes were no more than twice the poverty threshold.[1,2] For a small minority of children—4.8% of all children and 15% of children who ever became poor—childhood poverty lasted 10 years or more.[3]

From *The Future of Children*, Summer/Fall 1997, pp. 55-71. © 1997 by the Center for the Future of Children of the David and Lucile Packard Foundation. Reprinted by permission. *The Future of Children* journals and executive summaries are available free of charge by faxing mailing information to: Circulation Department (650) 948-6498.

Income poverty is the condition of not having enough income to meet basic needs for food, clothing, and shelter. Because children are dependent on others, they enter or avoid poverty by virtue of their family's economic circumstances. Children cannot alter family conditions by themselves, at least until they approach adulthood. Government programs, such as those described by Devaney, Ellwood, and Love in this journal issue, have been developed to increase the likelihood that poor children are provided basic necessities. But even with these programs, poor children do not fare as well as those whose families are not poor.[4]

What does poverty mean for children? How does the relative lack of income influence children's day-to-day lives? Is it through inadequate nutrition; fewer learning experiences; instability of residence; lower quality of schools; exposure to environmental toxins, family violence, and homelessness; dangerous streets; or less access to friends, services, and, for adolescents, jobs? This article reviews recent research that used longitudinal data to examine the relationship between income low-poverty and child outcomes in several domains.

Hundreds of studies, books, and reports have examined the detrimental effects of poverty on the well-being of children. Many have been summarized in recent reports such as *Wasting America's Future* from the Children's Defense Fund and *Alive and Well?* from the National Cenier for Children in Poverty.[5] However, while the literature on the effects of poverty on children is large, many studies lack the precision necessary to allow researchers to disentangle the effects on children of the array of factors associated with poverty. Understanding of these relationships is key to designing effective policies to ameliorate these problems for children.

This article examines these relationships and the consequences for children of growing up poor. It begins with a long, but by no means exhaustive, list of child outcomes (see Table 1) that have been found to be associated with poverty in several large, nationally representative, cross-sectional surveys. This list makes clear the broad range of effects poverty can have on children. It does little, however, to inform the discussion of the causal effects of income poverty on children because the studies from which this list is derived did not control for other variables associated with poverty. For example, poor families are more likely to be headed by a parent who is single, has low educational attainment, is unemployed, has low earning potential and is young. These parental attributes, separately or in combination, might

account for some of the observed negative consequences of poverty on children. Nor do the relationships identified in the table capture the critical factors of the timing, depth, and duration of childhood poverty on children.[6,7]

This article focuses on studies that used national longitudinal data sets to estimate the effects of family income on children's lives, independent of other family conditions that might be related to growing up in a low-income household. These studies attempt to isolate the effect of family income by taking into account, statistically, the effects of maternal age at the child's birth, maternal education, marital status, ethnicity, and other factors on child outcomes.[2,8] Many used data on family income over several years and at different stages of development to estimate the differential effects of the timing and duration of poverty on child outcomes. The data sets analyzed include the Panel Study of Income Dynamics (PSID), the National Longitudinal Survey of Youth (NLSY), Children of the NLSY (the follow-up of the children born to the women in the original NLSY cohort), the National Survey of Families and Households (NSFH), the National Health and Nutrition Examination Survey (NHANES), and the Infant Health and Development Program (IHDP). These rich data sets include multiple measures of child outcomes and family and child characteristics.

This article is divided into four sections. The first focuses on the consequences of poverty across five child outcomes. If income does, in fact, affect child outcomes, then it is important not only to identity these outcomes but also to describe the pathways through which income operates. Accordingly, in the second section, five pathways through which poverty might operate are described. The third section focuses on whether the links between poverty and outcomes can reasonably be attributed to income rather than other family characteristics. The concluding section considers policy implications of the research reviewed.

Effects of Income on Child Outcomes

Measures of Child Well-Being

As illustrated in Table 1, poor children suffer higher incidences of adverse health, developmental, and other outcomes than non-poor children. The specific dimensions of the well-being of children and youths considered in some detail in this article include (1) physical health (low birth weight, growth stunting, and lead poisoning), (2) cognitive ability (intelligence, verbal ability, and achievement test scores), (3) school achievement

Table 1
Selected Population-Based Indicators of Well-Being for Poor and Nonpoor Children in the United States

Indicator	Percentage of Poor Children (unless noted)	Percentage of Nonpoor Children (unless noted)	Ratio of poor to Nonpoor Children
Physical Health Outcomes (for children between 0 and 17 years unless noted)			
Reported to be in excellent health[a]	37.4	55.2	0.7
Reported to be in fair to poor health[a]	11.7	6.5	1.8
Experienced an accident, poisoning, or injury in the past year that required medical attention[a]	11.8	14.7	0.8
Chronic asthma[a]	4.4	4.3	1.0
Low birth weight (less than 2,500 grams)[b]	1.0	0.6	1.7
Lead poisoning (blood lead levels 10u/dl or greater)[c]	16.3	4.7	3.5
Infant mortality[b]	1.4 deaths per 100 live births	0.8 death per 100 live births	1.7
Deaths During Childhood (0 to 14 years)[d]	1.2	0.8	1.5
Stunting (being in the fifth percentile for height for age for 2 to 17 years)[e]	10.0	5.0	2.0
Number of days spent in bed in past year[a]	5.3 days	3.8 days	1.4
Number of short-stay hospital episodes in past year per 1,000 children[a]	81.3 stays	41.2 stays	2.0
Cognitive Outcomes			
Developmental delay (includes both limited and long-term developmental deficits) (0 to 17 years)[a]	5.0	3.8	1.3
Learning disability (defined as having exceptional difficulty in learning to read, write, and do arithmetic) (3 to 17 years)[a]	8.3	6.1	1.4
School Achievement Outcomes (5 to 17 years)			
Grade repetition (reported to have ever repeated a grade)[a]	28.8	14.1	2.0
Ever expelled or suspended[a]	11.9	6.1	2.0
High school dropout (percentage 16- to 24-year olds who were not in school or did not finish high school in 1994)[f]	21.0	9.6	2.2
Emotional or Behavioral Outcomes (3 to 17 years unless noted)			
Parent reports child has ever had an emotional or behavioral problem that lasted three months or more[g]	16.4	12.7	1.3
Parent reports child ever being treated for an emotional problem or behavioral problem[a]	2.5	4.5	0.6
Parent reports child has experienced one or more of a list of typical child behavioral problems in the last three months[h] (5 to 17 years)	57.4	57.3	1.0
Other			
Female teens who had an out-of-wedlock birth[i]	11.0	3.6	3.1
Economically inactive at age 24 (not employed or in school)[j]	15.9	8.3	1.9
Experienced hunger (food insufficiency) at least once in past year[k]	15.9	1.6	9.9
Reported cases of child abuse and neglect[l]	5.4	0.8	6.8
Violent crimes (experienced by poor families and nonpoor families)[m]	5.4	2.6	2.1

(years of schooling, high school completion), (4) emotional and behavioral outcomes, and (5) teenage out-of-wedlock childbearing. Other outcomes are not addressed owing to a scarcity of available research, a lack of space, and because they overlap with included outcomes.

While this review is organized around specific outcomes, it could also have been organized

around the various ages of childhood.[9-11] Five ag groups are often distinguished—prenatal to : years, early childhood (ages 3 to 6), late child hood (ages 7 to 10), early adolescence (ages 1 to 15), and late adolescence (ages 16 to 19). Facl age group covers one or two major transitions i a child's life, such as school entrances or exits biological maturation, possible cognitive changes

Indicator	Percentage of Poor Children (unless noted)	Percentage of Nonpoor Children (unless noted)	Ratio of poor to Nonpoor Children
Afraid to go out (percentage of family heads in poor and nonpoor families who report they are afraid to go out in their neighborhood)[n]	19.5	8.7	2.2

Note: This list of child outcomes reflects findings from large, nationally representative surveys that collect data on child outcomes and family income. While most data comes from the 1988 National Health Interview Survey Child Health Supplement, data from other nationally representative surveys are included. The rates presented are from simple cross-tabulations. In most cases, the data do not reflect factors that might be important to child outcomes other than poverty-status at the time of data collection. The ratios reflect rounding.

[a] Data from the 1988 National Health Interview Survey Child Health Supplement (NHS-CHS), a nationwide household interview survey. Children's health status was reported by the adult household member who knew the most about the sample child's health, usually the child's mother. Figures calculated from Dawson, D.A. *Family structure and children's health: United States, 1988*. Vital Health and Statistics, Series 10, n0. 178. Hyattsville, MD: U.S. Department of Health and Human Services, Public Health Service, June 1991; and Coiro, M.J., Zill, n., and Bloom, B. *Health of our nation's children*. Vital Health and Statistics, Series 10, n0. 191. Hyattsville, MD: U.S. department of Health and Human sErvices, Public Health Service, December 1994.

[b] Data from the National Maternal and Infant Health Survey, data collected in 1989 and 1990, with 1988 as the reference period. Percentages were calculated from the number of deaths and number of low birth weight births per 1,000 live births as reported in Federman, M., Garner, T., Short, K., et al. What does it mean to be poor in America? *Monthly Labor Review* (May 1996) 119, 5:10.

[c] Data from the NHANES III, 1988–1991. Poor children who lived in families with incomes less than 130% of the poverty threshold are classified as poor. All other children are classified as nonpoor.

[d] Percentages include only black and white youths. Percentages calculated from Table 7 in Rogot, E. *A mortality study of 1.3 million persons by demographic, social and economic factors: 1979–1985 follow-up*. Rockville, MD: National Institutes of Health, July 1992.

[e] Data from NHANES II, 1976–1980. For more discussion, see the Child Indicators article in this journal issue.

[f] National Center for Education Statistics. *Dropout rates in the United States: 1994*. Table 7, Status dropout rate, ages 16–24, by income and race ethnicity: October 1994. Available online at: http://www.ed.gov/NCES/pubs/r9410†t07.html.

[g] Data from the NHIS-CHS. The question was meant to identify children with common psychological disorders such as attention deficit disorder or depression, as well as more severe problems such as autism.

[h] Data from the NHIS-CHS. Parents responded "sometimes true," "often true,", or "not true" to a list of 32 statements typical of children's behaviors. Each statement corresponded to one of six individual behavior problems—antisocial behavior, anxiety, peer conflict/social withdrawal, dependency, hyperactivity, and headstrong behavior. Statements included behaviors such as cheating or lying, being disobedient in the home, being secretive, and demanding a lot of attention. For a more complete description, see Section P-11 of the NHIS-CHS questionnaire.

[i] Data from the Panel Study of Income Dynamics (PSID). Based on 1,705 children ages 0 to 6 in 1968; outcomes measured at ages 21 to 27. Haveman, R., and Wolfe, B. Succeeding generations: On the effect of investments in children. New York: Russel Sage Foundation, 1994, p. 108, Table 4, 10c.

[j] Data from the PSID. Based on 1,705 children ages 0 to 6 in 1968; outcomes measured at ages 21 to 27. In Succeeding generations: On the effect of investments in children. Haveman, R., and Wolfe, B. New York: Russel Sage Foundation, 1994, p. 108, Table 4, 10d. Economically inactive is defined as not being a full-time student, working 1,000 hours or more per year; attending school part time and working 500 hours; a mother of an infant or mother of two or more children less than five years old; a part-time student and the mother of a child less than five years old.

[k] Data from NHANES III, 1988–1991. Figures reflect food insufficiency, the term used in government hunger-related survey questions. For a more in-depth discussion, see Lewit, E.M., and Kerrebrock, N. Child indicators: Childhood hunger. *The Future of Children* (Spring 1997), 7, 1:128–37.

[l] Data from Study of National Incidence and Prevalence of Child Abuse and Neglect: 1988. In *Wasting America's future*. Children's Defense Fund. Boston: Beacon Press, 1994, pp. 5–29, 87, Tables 5–6. Poor families are those with annual incomes below $15,000.

[m] Data from the National Crime Victimization Interview Survey. Results are for households or persons living in households. Data were collected between January 1992 and June 1993 with 1992 as the reference period. Percentages are calculated from number of violent crimes per 1,000 people per year. Reported in Federman, M., Garner, T., Short, K., et al. What does it mean to be poor in America? *Monthly Labor Review*. (May 1996) 119,5:9.

[n] Data from the Survey of Income and Program Participation. Participation data collection and reference periods are September through December 1992. Reported in Federman, M., Garner, T., Short, K., et al. What does it mean to be poor in America? hly Labor Review (May 1996) 119,5:9.

role changes, or some combination of these. These periods are characterized by relatively universal developmental challenges that require new modes of adaptation to biological, psychological, or social changes.[10]

Somewhat different indicators of child and youth well-being are associated with each period. For example, grade retention is more salient in the late childhood years than in adolescence (since most schools do not hold students back once they reach eighth grade[12]). Furthermore, low income might influence each indicator differently. As an illustration, income has stronger effects on cognitive and verbal ability test scores than it has on indices of emotional health in the childhood years.

Physical Health

Compared with nonpoor children, poor children in the United States experience diminished physical health as measured by a number of indicators of health status and outcomes (see Table 1). In the 1988 National Health Interview Survey; parents reported that poor children were only two-thirds as likely to be in excellent health and almost twice as likely to be in fair or poor health as nonpoor children. These large differences in health status between poor and nonpoor children do not reflect adjustment for potentially confounding factors (factors, other than income, that may be associated with living in poverty nor do they distinguish between long- or short-term poverty or the timing of poverty. This section reviews research on the relationship of poverty to several key measures of child health, low birth weight and infant mortality, growth stunting, and lead poisoning. For the most part, the focus is on research that attempts to adjust for important confounding factors and/or to address the effect of the duration of poverty on child health outcomes.

Birth Outcomes

Low birth weight (2,500 grams or less) and infant mortality are important indicators of child health. Low birth weight is associated with an increased

> *Poverty status had a statistically significant effect on both low birth weight and the neonatal morality rate for whites but not for blacks.*

likelihood of subsequent physical health and cognitive and emotional problems that can persist through childhood and adolescence. Serious physical disabilities, grade repetition, and learning disabilities are more prevalent among children who were low birth weight as infants, as are lower levels of intelligence and of math and reading achievement. Low birth weight is also the key risk factor for infant mortality (especially death within the first 28 days of life), which is a widely accepted indicator of the health and well-being of children.[13]

Estimating the effects of poverty alone on birth outcomes is complicated by the fact that adverse birth outcomes are more prevalent for unmarried women, those with low levels of education, and black mothers—all groups with high poverty

rates. One study that used data from the NLSY to examine the relationship between family income and low birth weight did find, however, that among whites, women with family income below the federal poverty level in the year of birth were 80% more likely to have a low birth weight baby as compared with women whose family incomes were above the poverty level (this study statistically controlled for mothers' age, education, marital status, and smoking status). Further analysis also showed that the duration of poverty had an important effect; if a white woman was poor both at the time when she entered the longitudinal NLSY sample and at the time of her pregnancy (5 to 10 years later), she was more than three times more likely to deliver a low birth weight infant than a white woman who was not poor at both times. For black women in this sample, although the odds of having a low birth weight baby were twice the odds for white mothers, the probability of having a low birth weight baby was not related to family poverty status.[14]

Other studies that used county level data to examine the effects of income or poverty status and a number of pregnancy-related health services on birth outcomes for white and black women also found that income or poverty status had a statistically significant effect on both low birth weight and the neonatal mortality rate for whites but not for blacks.[15,16]

Growth Stunting

Although overt malnutrition and starvation are rare among poor children in the United States, deficits in children's nutritional status are associated with poverty. As described more fully in the Child Indicators article in this journal issue, stunting (low height for age), a measure of nutritional status, is more prevalent among poor than nonpoor children. Studies using data from the NLSY show that differentials in height for age between poor and nonpoor children are greater when long-term rather than single-year measures of poverty are used in models to predict stunting. These differentials by poverty status are large even in models that statistically control for many other family and child characteristics associated with poverty.[17]

Lead Poisoning

Harmful effects of lead have been documented even at low levels of exposure. Health problems vary with length of exposure, intensity of lead in the environment, and the developmental stage of the child—with risks beginning prior to birth. At very young ages, lead exposure is linked to stunted growth,[18] hearing loss,[19] vitamin D metabolism damage, impaired blood production, and toxic effects on the kidneys.[20] Additionally, even a small increase in blood lead above the Centers for Disease Control and Prevention (CDC) current intervention threshold (10 µg/dL) is associated with a decrease in intelligence quotient (IQ).[21]

Today, deteriorating lead-based house paint remains the primary source of lead for young children. Infants and toddlers in old housing eat the sweet-tasting paint chips and breathe the lead dust from deteriorating paint. Four to five million children reside in homes with lead levels exceeding the accepted threshold for safety,[22] and more than 1.5 million children under six years of age have elevated blood lead levels.[23]

Using data from NHANES III (1988–1991), one study found that children's blood lead levels declined as family income increased.[23] All other things being equal, mean blood lead levels were 9% lower for one- to five-year-olds in families with incomes twice the poverty level than for those who were poor. Overall blood levels were highest among one to five-year-olds who were non-Hispanic blacks from low-income families in large central cities. The mean blood lead level for this group, 9.7 µg/dL, was just under the CDC's threshold for intervention and almost three times the mean for all one- to five-year-olds.

Cognitive Abilities

As reported in Table 1, children living below the poverty threshold are 1.3 times as likely as non-poor children to experience learning disabilities and developmental delays. Reliable measures of cognitive ability and school achievement for young children in the Children of the NLSY and IHDP data sets have been used in a number of studies to examine the relationship between cognitive ability and poverty in detail.[6,24–26] This article reports on several studies that control for a number of potentially important family characteristics and attempts to distinguish between the effects of long- and short-term poverty.

A recent study using data from the Children of the NLSY and the IHDP compared children in families with incomes less than half of the poverty threshold to children in families with incomes between 1.5 and twice the poverty threshold. The poorer children scored between 6 and 13 points lower on various standardized tests of IQ, verbal ability; and achievement.[25] These differences are very large from an educational perspective and were present even after controlling for maternal age, marital status, education, and ethnicity. A 6- to 13-point difference might mean, for example, the difference between being placed in a special education class or not. Children in families with

incomes closer to, but still below, the poverty line also did worse than children in higher-income families, but the differences were smaller. The smallest differences appeared for the earliest (age two) measure of cognitive ability; however, the sizes of the effects were similar for children from three to eight. These findings suggest that the effects of poverty on children's cognitive development occur early.

The study also found that duration of poverty was an important factor in the lower scores of poor children on measures of cognitive ability. Children who lived in persistently poor families (defined in this study as poor over a four-year span) had scores on the various assessments six to nine points lower than children who were never poor.[25] Another analysis of the NLSY that controlled for a number of important maternal and child health characteristics showed that the effects of long-term poverty (based on family income averaged over 13 years prior to testing of the child) on measures of children's cognitive ability were significantly greater than the effects of short-term poverty (measured by income in the year of observation).[26]

> *The effects of long-term poverty on measures of children's cognitive ability were significantly greater than the effects of short-term poverty.*

A few studies link long-term family income to cognitive ability and achievement measured during the school years. Research on children's test scores at ages seven and eight found that the effects of income on these scores were similar in size to those reported for three-year-olds.[25] But research relating family income measured during adolescence on cognitive ability finds relatively smaller effects.[27] As summarized in the next section, these modest effects of income on cognitive ability are consistent with literature showing modest effects of income on schooling attainment, but both sets of studies may be biased by the fact that their measurement of parental income is restricted to the child's adolescent years. It is not yet possible to make conclusive statements regarding the size of the effects of poverty on children's long-term cognitive development.

School Achievement Outcomes

Educational attainment is well recognized as a powerful predictor of experiences in later life. A comprehensive review of the relationship between parental income and school attainment, published in 1994, concluded that poverty limited school achievement but that the effect of income on the number of school years completed was small.[28] In general, the studies suggested that a 10% increase in family income is associated with a 0.2% to 2% increase in the number of school years completed.[28]

Several more recent studies using different longitudinal data sets (the PSID, the NLSY and Children of the NLSY) also find that poverty status has a small negative impact on high school graduation and years of schooling obtained. Much of the observed relationship between income and schooling appears to be related to a number of confounding factors such as parental education, family structure, and neighborhood characteristics.[28-30] Some of these studies suggest that the components of income (for example, AFDC) and the way income is measured (number of years in poverty versus annual family income or the ratio of income to the poverty threshold) may lead

> *For low-income children, a $10,000 increase in mean family income between birth and age 5 was associated with nearly a full-year increase in completed schooling.*

to somewhat different conclusions. But all the studies suggest that, after controlling for many appropriate confounding variables, the effects of poverty per se on school achievement are likely to be statistically significant, yet small. Based on the results of one study, the authors estimated that, if poverty were eliminated for all children, mean years of schooling for all children would increase by only 0.3% (less than half a month).[30]

Why do not the apparently strong effects of parental income on cognitive abilities and school achievement in the early childhood years translate into larger effects on completed schooling? One possible reason is that extrafamilial environments (for example, schools and neighborhoods) begin to matter as much or more for children than family conditions once children reach school age. A second possible reason is that school-related

achievement depends on both ability and behavior. As is discussed in the Emotional and Behavioral Outcomes section, children's behavioral problems, measured either before or after the transition into school, are not very sensitive to parental income differences.

A third, and potentially crucial, reason concerns the timing of economic deprivation. Few studies measure income from early childhood to adolescence, so there is no way to know whether poverty early in childhood has noteworthy effects on later outcomes such as school completion. Because family income varies over time,[31] income measured during adolescence, or even middle childhood, may not reflect income in early childhood. A recent study that attempted to evaluate how the timing of income might affect completed schooling found that family income averaged from birth to age 5 had a much more powerful effect on the number of school years a child completes than does family income measured either between ages 5 and 10 or between ages 11 and 15.[7] For low-income children, a $10,000 increase in mean family income between birth and age 5 was associated with nearly a full-year increase in completed schooling. Similar increments to family income later in childhood had no significant impact, suggesting that income may indeed be an important determinant of completed schooling but that only income during the early childhood years matters.

Emotional and Behavioral Outcomes

Poor children suffer from emotional and behavioral problems more frequently than do nonpoor children (see Table 1). Emotional outcomes are often grouped along two dimensions: externalizing behaviors including aggression, fighting, and acting out, and internalizing behaviors such as anxiety, social withdrawal, and depression. Data regarding emotional outcomes are based on parental and teacher reports. This section reviews studies that distingnish between the effects of long- and short-term poverty on emotional outcomes of children at different ages.

One study of low birth weight five-year-olds using the IHDP data set found that children in persistently poor families had more internalizing and externalizing behavior problems than children who had never been poor. The analysis controlled for maternal education and family structure and defined long-term poverty as income below the poverty threshold for each of four consecutive years. Short-term poverty (defined as poor in at least one of four years) was also associated with more behavioral problems, though the effects were not as large as those for persistent poverty.[6]

Two different studies using the NLSY report findings consistent with those of the IHDP study. Both found persistent poverty to be a significant predictor of some behavioral problems.[26,32] One study used data from the 1986 NLSY and found that for four- to eight-year-olds persistent poverty (defined as a specific percentage of years of life during which the child lived below the poverty level) was positively related to the presence of internalizing symptoms (such as dependence, anxiety; and unhappiness) even after controlling for current poverty status, mother's age, education, and marital status. In contrast, current poverty (defined by current family income below the poverty line) but not persistent poverty was associated with more externalizing problems (such as hyperactivity; peer conflict, and headstrong behavior).[32]

The second study used NLSY data from 1978–1991 and analyzed children ages 3 to 11. On average children living in long-term poverty (defined by the ratio of family income to the poverty level averaged over 13 years) ranked three to seven percentile points higher (indicating more problems) on a behavior problem index than children with incomes above the poverty line. After controlling for a range of factors including mother's characteristics, nutrition, and infant health behaviors, the difference remained though it dropped in magnitude. This study also found that children who experienced one year of poverty had more behavioral problems than children who had lived in long-term poverty.[26]

The above studies demonstrate that problematic emotional outcomes are associated with family poverty. However, it is important to note that the effects of poverty on emotional outcomes are not as large as those found in cognitive outcomes. Also these studies do not show that children in long-term poverty experience emotional problems with greater frequency or of the same type as children who experience only short-term poverty. These studies analyzed data for young children. Few studies have examined the link between emotional outcomes and poverty for adolescents. One small study of 7th- to 10th-graders in the rural Midwest did not find a statistically significant relationship between poverty and emotional problems, either internalizing or externalizing.[33] Self-reporting by the adolescents rather than maternal reporting, as used in the data sets on younger children, may account for the differences found in the effects of income on emotional outcomes in this study as compared with the previously reviewed research. It may also be that younger children are more affected by poverty than older children.

These findings point to the need for further research to improve understanding of the link between income and children's emotional outcomes.

Teenage Out-of-Wedlock Childbearing

The negative consequences for both mothers and children associated with births to unwed teen mothers make it a source of policy concern.[34] Although the rate of out-of-wedlock births among poor teens is almost three times as high as the rate among those from nonpoor families (see Table 1), the literature on linkages between family income and out-of-wedlock childbearing is not conclusive. A recent review of the evidence put it this way: "[P]arental income is negative and usually, but not always, significant. . . . The few reports of the quantitative effects of simulated changes in variables suggest that decreases in parental income . . . will lead to small increases in the probability that teen girls will experience a nonmarital birth."[28]

Problematic emotional outcomes are associated with family poverty; however, the effects of poverty on emotional outcomes are not as large as its effects on cognitive outcomes.

A recent study, which used data from the PSID to investigate factors in teen out-of-wedlock births, found that variations in income around the poverty threshold were not predictive of a teenage birth but that the probability of a teenager's having an out-of-wedlock birth declined significantly at family income levels above twice the poverty threshold.[35] The duration and timing of poverty had no effect on the probability of a teen out-of-wedlock birth. These findings are somewhat different from those reported for cognitive outcomes and school achievement. In the case of cognitive outcomes for young children, the variation in income mattered most to children at very low levels of income; for school achievement, the timing and duration of poverty seemed to have important differential effects on outcomes.

Why should poverty status matter more for schooling than for childbearing? This difference is consistent with the more general result that parental income appears more strongly linked with ability and achievement than with behavior. The factors influencing teenage out-of-wedlock childbearing are less well understood than the factors influencing schooling completion: interventions have generally been much less successful in altering teen birthrates than in keeping teens in school.[36,37]

A child's home environment accounts for a substantial portion of the effects of family income on cognitive outcomes in young children.

Pathways Through Which Poverty Operates

The research reviewed thus far suggests that living in poverty exacts a heavy toll on children. However, it does not shed light on the pathways or mechanisms by which low income exerts its effects on children. As the term is used in this discussion, a "pathway" is a mechanism through which poverty or income can influence a child outcome. By implication, this definition implies that a pathway should be causally related to both income and at least one child outcome. Exploration of these pathways is important for a more complete understanding of the effects of poverty on children; moreover, exploration of pathways can lead to the identification of leverage points that may be amenable to policy intervention and remediation in the absence of a change in family income.

Research on the size and strength of the pathways through which income might influence child health and development is still scanty. In this section, five potential pathways are discussed:

(1) health and nutrition, (2) the home environment, (3) parental interactions with children, (4) parental mental health, and (5) neighborhood conditions. Space limitations preclude a discussion of other potential pathways such as access to and use of prenatal care, access to pediatric care, exposure to environmental toxins, household stability, provision of learning experiences outside the home, quality of school attended, and peer groups. Further, few studies have tested pathway models using these variables.

Health and Nutrition

Although health is itself an outcome, it can also be viewed as a pathway by which poverty influences other child outcomes, such as cognitive ability and school achievement. As discussed previously poor children experience increased rates of low birth weight and elevated blood lead levels when compared with nonpoor children. These conditions have, in turn, been associated with reduced IQ and other measures of cognitive functioning in young children and, in the case of low birth weight, with increased rates of learning disabilities, grade retention, and school dropout in older children and youths.

A 1990 analysis indicated that the poverty-related health factors such as low birth weight, elevated blood lead levels, anemia,[38] and recurrent ear infections and hearing loss contributed to the differential in IQ scores between poor and nonpoor four-year-olds.[39] The findings suggest that the cumulative health disadvantage experienced by poor children on these four health measures may have accounted for as much as 13% to 20%

© Steven Rubin

of the difference in IQ between the poor and non-poor four-year-olds during the 1970s and 1980s.[39]

As discussed in the Child Indicators article in this journal issue, malnutrition in childhood (as measured by anthropometric indicators) is associated with lower scores on tests of cognitive development. Deficits in these anthropometric measures are associated with poverty among children in the United States, and the effects can be substantial. One recent study found that the effect of stunting on short-term memory was equivalent to the difference in short-term memory between children in families that had experienced poverty for 13 years and children in families with incomes at least three times the poverty level.[26]

Home Environment

A number of studies have found that a child's home environment—opportunities for learning, warmth of mother-child interactions, and the physical condition of the home—account for a substantial portion of the effects of family income on cognitive outcomes in young children. Some large longitudinal data sets use the HOME scale as a measure of the home environment. The HOME scale is made up of items that measure household resources, such as reading materials and toys, and parental practices, such as discipline methods. The HOME scale has been shown to be correlated with family income and poverty, with higher levels of income associated with improved home environments as measured by the scale.[7,40]

Several studies have found that differences in the home environment of higher-and lower-income children, as measured by the HOME scale, account for a substantial portion of the effect of income on the cognitive development of preschool children and on the achievement scores of elementary school children.[6,26,37] In one study, differences in the home environment also seemed to account for some of the effects of poverty status on behavioral problems. In addition, the provisions of learning experiences in the home (measured by specific subscales of the HOME scale) have been shown to account for up to half of the effect of poverty status on the IQ scores of five-year-olds.[37,41]

Parental Interactions with Children

A number of studies have attempted to go beyond documentation of activities and materials in the home to capture the effects of parent-child interactions on child outcomes. Much of the work is based on small and/or community-based samples. That work suggests that child adjustment and achievement are facilitated by certain parental

practices. There is also some evidence that poverty is linked to lower-quality parent-child interaction and to increased use of harsh punishment. This research suggests that parental practices may be an important pathway between economic resources and child outcomes.

Parents who are poor are likely to be less healthy, both emotionally and physically, than those who are not poor.

Evidence of such a parental-practice pathway from research using large national data sets of the kind reviewed in this article is less consistent. One NLSY-based study found that currently poor mothers spanked their children more often than nonpoor mothers and that this harsh behavior was an important component of the effect of poverty on children's mental health.[32] Mothers' parenting behavior was not, however, found to be an important pathway by which persistent poverty affected children's mental health. A more recent study using the National Survey of Families and Households found that the level of household income was only weakly related to effective parenting and that differences in parent practices did not account for much of the association between poverty and child well-being.[42]

Among adolescents, family economic pressure may lead to conflict with parents, resulting in lower school grades, reduced emotional health, and impaired social relationships.[33,43] Other work suggests that it may be income loss or economic uncertainty due to unemployment, underemployment, and unstable work conditions, rather than poverty or low income per se, that is a source for conflict between parents and teens leading to emotional and school problems.[33,44]

Parental Mental Health

Parents who are poor are likely to be less healthy, both emotionally and physically, than those who are not poor.[45] And parental irritability and depressive symptoms are associated with more conflicted interactions with adolescents, leading to less satisfactory emotional, social, and cognitive development.[43,46,47] Some studies have established that parental mental health accounts for some of the effect of economic circumstances on child health and behavior. Additionally, poor parental mental health is associated with impaired parent-child interactions and less provision of learning experiences in the home.[33,41,48]

Neighborhood Conditions

Another possible pathway through which family income operates has to do with the neighborhoods in which poor families reside. Poor parents are constrained in their choice of neighborhoods and schools. Low income may lead to residence in extremely poor neighborhoods characterized by social disorganization (crime, many unemployed adults, neighbors not monitoring the behavior of adolescents) and few resources for child development (playgrounds, child care, health care facilities, parks, after-school programs).[49,50] The affluence of neighborhoods is associated with child and adolescent outcomes (intelligence test scores at ages 3 and 5 and high school graduation rates by age 20) over and above family poverty.[37,51] Neighborhood residence also seems to be associated with parenting practices, over and above family income and education.[52] Neighborhood ef-

> *Low income may lead to residence in extremely poor neighborhoods characterized by social disorganization and few resources for child development.*

fects on intelligence scores are in part mediated by the learning environment in the home.[52,53] Living in neighborhoods with high concentrations of poor people is associated with less provision of learning experiences in the homes of preschoolers, over and above the links seen between family income and learning experiences.

A key issue that has not been fully explored is the extent to which neighborhood effects may be overestimated because neighborhood characteristics also reflect the choices of neighborhood residents. One study that examined the effects of peer groups (as measured by the socioeconomic status of students in a respondent's school) on teenage pregnancy and school dropout behavior found that while student body socioeconomic status seemed to be an important predictor of both dropout and teen pregnancy rates, it did not appear to be related to those outcomes in statistical models that treated this peer characteristic as a matter of family choice.[54]

How Much Does Income Cause Child Outcomes?

It may seem odd to raise this question after summarizing evidence indicating that family income does matter—across the childhood and adolescent years and for a number of indicators of well-being. However, these associations have been demonstrated when a relatively small set of family characteristics are controlled through statistical analyses. It is possible, therefore, that other important family characteristics have not been controlled for and that, as a result of this omission, the effects of income are estimated incorrectly.... Distinguishing between the effects on children of poverty and its related events and conditions is crucial for public policy formulation. Programs that alter family income may not have intended benefits for children if the importance of family income has been mismeasured.

Despite the evidence reviewed in this article and elsewhere, there is an important segment of the population who believes that income per se may not appreciably affect child outcomes. This viewpoint sees parental income mainly as a proxy for other charateristics such as character (a strong work ethic) or genetic endowment that influence both children and parents. A recent book by Susan Mayer, *What Money Can't Buy: The Effect of Parental Income on Children's Outcomes,*[55] presents a series of tests to examine explicitly the effects of income on a set of child outcomes. In one test, measures of income *after* the occurrence of an outcome are added to statistical models of the effects of income and other characteristics on a child outcome. The idea behind this test is that unanticipated future income can capture unmeasured parental characteristics but cannot have caused the child outcome. The inclusion of future income frequently produced a large reduction in the estimated impact of prior parent income. Mayer also tries to estimate the effects on children of components of income (for example, asset income) that are independent of the actions of the family. Although these tests provide some support for the hypothesis that family income may not matter much for child outcomes, even Mayer admits that these statistical procedures are not without their problems. For example, prior income and future income are highly correlated, and if parents take reasonable expectations of future income into consideration in making decisions regarding the well-being of children, then the assumption that child outcomes are independent of future income, which underlies the first test, is violated.

A second approach to the problem that omitted variables may bias the estimation of the effects of income and poverty on children looks at siblings within families. Siblings reared in the same family share many of the same unmeasured family characteristics. Thus, comparing children at the same age within families makes it possible to look at the income of the family at different time points (for example, if a firstborn was five years of age in 1985 and the second child was five years of age in 1988, it is possible to look at their achievement levels at this age and the average family income between 1980 and 1985 for the firstborn and between 1983 and 1988 for the second child). One study that used this approach found that sibling differences in income were associated with sibling differences in completed schooling, which gave support to the notion that family income matters.[7]

Perhaps the most convincing demonstration of the effects of income is to provide poor families with income in the context of a randomized trial. In four Income Maintenance/Negative Income Tax Experiments in the 1960s and 1970s, experimental treatment families received a guaranteed minimum income. (These experiments are discussed in more detail in the article by Janet Currie in this journal issue.) Substantial benefits resulting from increased income effects were found for child nutrition, early school achievement, and high school completion in some sites but not in others. These results might be viewed as inconclusive; however, since the site with the largest effects for younger children (North Carolina) was also the poorest, one interpretation of the results is that income effects are most important for the very poorest families.[56,57]

Conclusion

The evidence reviewed in this article supports the conclusion that family income can substantially influence child and adolescent well-being. However, the associations between income and child outcomes are more complex and varied than suggested by the simple associations presented in Table 1. Family income seems to be more strongly related to children's ability and achievement-related outcomes than to emotional outcomes. In addition, the effects are particularly pronounced for children who live below the poverty line for multiple years and for children who live in extreme poverty (that is, 50% or less of the poverty threshold). These income effects are probably not due to some unmeasured characteristics of low-income families: family income, in and of itself, does appear to matter.

The timing of poverty is also important, although this conclusion is based on only a small number of studies. Low income during the preschool and early school years exhibits the strongest correlation with low rates of high school completion, as compared with low income during the childhood and adolescent years.[7,58] Poor-quality schooling, which is correlated with high neighborhood poverty, may exacerbate this effect.[59] These findings suggest that early childhood interventions may be critical in reducing the impact of low income on children's lives.

The pathways through which low income influences children also suggest some general recommendations. Nutrition programs, especially if they target the most undernourished poor, may have beneficial effects on both physical and cognitive outcomes. Lead abatement and parental education programs may improve cognitive outcomes in poor children residing in inner-city neighborhoods where lead is still an important hazard.

Because about one-half of the effect of family income on cognitive ability is mediated by the home environment, including learning experiences in the home, interventions might profitably focus on working with parents. An example is the Learningames curriculum in which parents are provided instruction, materials, and role playing in learning experiences.[60] Other effective learning-oriented programs might also be pursued.[61–63]

Finally, income policies (as discussed by Robert Plotnick in this journal issue) and in-kind support programs (as discussed by Devaney, Ellwood, and Love in this journal issue) can have immediate impact on the number or children living in poverty and on the circumstances in which they live. Most important, based on this review, would be efforts to eliminate deep and persistent poverty especially during a child's early years. Support to families with older children may be desirable on other grounds, but the available research suggests that it will probably not have the same impact on child outcomes as programs focused on younger children.

The authors would like to thank the National Institute of Child Health and Human Development Research Network on Child and Family Well-being for supporting the writing of this article. The Russell Sage Foundation's contribution is also appreciated as is that of the William T. Grant Foundation, and the Canadian Institute for Advanced Research. The authors are also grateful for the feedback provided by Linda Baker, Pamela K. Klebanov, and Judith Smith and would like to thank Phyllis Gyamfi for her editorial assistance.

1. Hernandez, D.J. America's children: Resources from family government and the economy. New York: Russell Sage Foundation, 1993.
2. Duncan, G.J., and Brooks-Gunn, J., eds. Consequences of growing up poor. New York: Russell Sage Foundation, 1997.
3. Duncan, G.J., and Rodgers, W.L. Longitudinal aspects of childhood poverty. Journal of Marriage and the Family (November 1988) 50,4:1007–21.
4. Chase-Lansdale, P.L., and Brooks-Gunn, J., eds. Escape from poverty: What makes a difference for children? New York: Cambridge University Press, 1995.
5. Children's Defense Fund. Wasting America's future. Boston: Beacon Press, 1994; Klerman, L. Alive and well? New York: National Center for Children in Poverty, Columbia University, 1991.
6. Duncan, G.J., Brooks-Gunn, J., and Klebanov, P.K. Economic deprivation and early-childhood development. Child Development (1994) 65,2:296–318.
7. Duncan, G.J., Yeung, W., Brooks-Gunn, J., and Smith, J.R. How much does childhood poverty affect the life chances of children? American Sociological Review, in press.
8. Hauser R., Brown, B., and Prosser W. Indicators of children's well-being. New York: Russell Sage Foundation, in press.
9. Brooks-Gunn,J., Guo, G., and Furstenberg, F.F.Jr. Who drops out of and who continues beyond high school?: A 20-year study of black youth. Journal of Research in Adolescence (1993) 37,3:271–94.
10. Graber, J.A., and Brooks-Gunn, J. Transitions and turning points: Navigating the passage from childhood through adolescence. Developmental Psychology (1996) 32,4:768–76.
11. Rutter, M. Beyond longitudinal data: Causes, consequences, changes and continuity. Journal of Counseling and Clinical Psychology (1994) 62,5:928–90.
12. Guo, G., Brooks-Gunn, J., and Harris, K.M. Parents' labor-force attachment and grade retention among urban black children. Sociology of Education (1996) 69,3:217–36.
13. For a review of the causes and consequences of low birth weight in the United States, see Shiono, P., ed. Low Birth Weight. The Future of Children (Spring 1995) 5,1:4–231.
14. Starfield, B., Shapiro, S., Weiss, J., et al. Race, family income, and low birth weight. American Journal of Epidemiology (1991) 134,10:1167–74.
15. Corman, H., and Grossman, M. Determinants of neonatal mortality rates in the U.S.: A reduced form model. Journal of Health Economics (1985) 4,3:213–36.
16. Frank, R., Strobino, D., Salkever, D., and Jackson, C. Updated estimates of the impact of prenatal care on birthweight outcomes by race. Journal of Human Resources (1992) 27,4:629–42.
17. Miller, J., and Korenman, S. Poverty and children's nutritional status in the United States. American Journal of Epidemiology (1994) 140,3:233–43.
18. Schwartz, J., Angle, C., and Pitcher, H. Relationship between childhood blood lead levels and stature. Pediatrics (1986) 77,3:281–88.
19. Schwartz, J., and Otto, D. Lead and minor hearing impairment. Archives of Environmental Health (1991) 46,5:300–05.
20. Agency for Toxic Substances and Disease Registry. The nature and extent of lead poisoning in the US.: A report to Congress. Washington, DC: U.S. Department of Health and Human Services, 1988, Section II, p. 7.
21. Schwartz, J. Low level lead exposure and children's IQ: A meta-analysis and search for threshold. Environmental Research (1994) 65,1:42–55.
22. Ronald Morony, Deputy Director, U.S. Department of Housing and Urban Development, Office of Lead Based Paint Abatement and Poisoning Prevention, Washington, DC. Personal communication, November 20, 1996.
23. Brody, D.J., Pirkle, L., Kramer, R., et al. Blood lead levels in the U.S. population. Journal of the American Medical Association (1994) 272,4:277–81.
24. Brooks-Gunn, J., McCarton, C.M., Casey, P.H., et al. Early intervention in low birth weight premature infants: Results through age 5 years from the Infant Health and Development Program. Journal of the American Medical Association (1994) 272,16:1257–62.
25. Smith, J.R., Brooks-Gunn, J., and Klebanov, P. The consequences of living in poverty for young children's cognitive and verbal ability and early school achievement. In Consequences of growing up poor. G.J. Duncan and J. Brooks-Gunn, eds. New York: Russell Sage Foundation, 1997.
26. Korenman, S., Miller, J.E., and Sjaastad,J.E. Long-term poverty and child development in the United States: Results from the National Longitudinal Survey of Youth. Children and Youth Services Review (1995)17,1/2:127–51.
27. Peters. E., and Mullis, N. The role of the family and source of income in adolescent achievement. In Consequences of growing up poor: G. Duncan and J. Brooks-Gunn, eds. New York: Russell Sage Foundation, 1997.
28. Haveman, R., and Wolfe, B. The determinants of children's attainments: A review of methods and findings. Journal of Economic Literature (1995) 33,3:1829–78.
29. Teachman,J., Paasch, K.M., Day, R., and Carver, K.P Poverty during adolescence and subsequent educational attainment. In Consequences of growing up poor: G. Duncan and J. Brooks-Gunn, eds. New York: Russell Sage Foundation, 1997.
30. Haveman, R., and Wolfe, B. Succeeding generations: On the effect of investments in children. New York: Russell Sage Foundation, 1994.

31. Duncan, G.J. Volatility of family income over the life course. In *Life-span development and behavior.* Vol. 9. P. Baltes, D. Featherman, and R.M. Lerner, eds. Hillsdale, NJ: Erlbaum, 1988, pp. 317–58.

32. McLeod, J.D., and Shanahan, M.J. Poverty, parenting and children's mental health. *American Sociological Review* (June 1993) 58,3:351–66.

33. Conger, R.D., Conger, K.J., and Elder, G.H. Family economic hardship and adolescent adjustment: Mediating and moderating processes. In *Consequences of growing up poor:* G. Duncan and J. Brooks-Gunn, eds. New York: Russell Sage Foundation, 1997.

34. Hotz, V.J., McElroy, S.W., and Sanders, S.G. Costs and consequences of teenage childbearing. *Chicago Policy Review.* Internet: http://www.spc.uchicago.edu/cpr/Teenage_Child.htm.

35. Haveman, R., Wolfe, B., and Wilson, K. Childhood poverty and adolescent schooling and fertility outcomes: Reduced form and structural estimates. In *Consequences of growing up poor.* G.J. Duncan and J. Brooks-Gunn, eds. New York: Russell Sage Foundation, 1997.

36. U.S. Department of Health and Human Services. *Report to Congress on out-of-wedlock childbearing.* PHS-95–1257. Hyattsville, MD: DHHS, September 1995.

37. Brooks-Gunn, J., Duncan, G.J., Klebanov, P.K., and Sealand, N. Do neighborhoods influence child and adolescent behavior? *American Journal of Sociology* (1993) 99,2:335–95.

38. Iron-deficiency anemia is an important health problem that was traditionally identified with child poverty. Iron-deficiency anemia has been associated with impaired exercise capacity, increased susceptibility to lead absorption, and developmental and behavioral problems; see Oski, F. Iron deficiency in infancy and childhood. *The New England Journal of Medicine.* (July 15, 1993) 329,3:190–93. The importance of iron-deficiency anemia and its sequelae among poor children in the United States today is unclear. Increased use of iron-fortified foods and infant formulas along with their provision through public nutrition programs such as the Special Supplemental Food Program for Women, Infants, and Children (see the article by Devaney, Ellwood, and Love in this journal issue) have contributed to a dramatic decline in anemia; see Yip, R., Binkin, N.J., Fleshood, L., and Trowbridge, F.L. Declining prevalence of anemia among low-income children in the U.S. *Journal of American Medical Association* (1987) 258,12:1623. Between 1980 and 1991, the prevalence of anemia among infants and children through age five declined from 7% to 3%. Still, low-income children participating in public health programs have a higher-than-average prevalence of anemia; see Yip, R., Parvanta, I., Scanlon, K., et al. Pediatric Nutrition Surveillance System—United States, 1980–1991. *Morbidity and Mortality Weekly Report* (November 1992) 41,SS-7:1–24. In part, this is because risk of anemia is a criterion for enrollment in these programs and also because these low-income children have low iron levels.

39. Goldstein, N. *Explaining socioeconomic differences in children's cognitive test scores.* Working Paper No. H-90-1. Cambridge, MA: Malcolm Wiener Center for Social Policy, John F. Kennedy School of Government, Harvard University, 1990.

40. Garrett, P., Ng'andu, N., and Ferron, J. Poverty experience of young children and the quality of their home environments. *Child Development* (1994) 65,2:331–45.

41. Bradley, R.H. Home environment and parenting. In *Handbook of parenting:* M. Bornstein, ed. Hillsdale, NJ: Erlbaum, 1995.

42. Hanson, T., McLanahan, S., and Thomson, E. Economic resources, parental practices, and child well-being. In *Consequences of growing up poor:* G.J. Duncan and J. Brooks-Gunn, eds. New York: Russell Sage Foundation, 1997.

43. Conger, R.D., Ge, S., Elder, G.H., Jr., et al. Economic stress, coercive family process and developmental problems of adolescents. *Child Development* (1994) 65,2:541–61.

44. McLoyd, V.C. The impact of economic hardship on black families and children: Psychological distress, parenting, and socioemotional development. *Child Development* (1990) 61,2:311–46.

45. Adler, N.E., Boyce, T., Chesney, M.A., et al. Socioeconomic inequalities in health: No easy solution. *Journal of the American Medical Association* (1993) 269:3140–45.

46. Liaw, F.R., and Brooks-Gunn, J. Cumulative familial risks and low birth weight children's cognitive and behavioral development. *Journal of Clinical Child Psychology* (1995) 23,4:360–72.

47. McLoyd, V.C., Jayaratne, T.E., Ceballo, R., and Borquez, J. Unemployment and work interruption among African American single mothers. Effects on parenting and adolescent socioemotional functioning. *Child Development* (1994) 65,2:562–89.

48. Brooks-Gunn, J., Klebanov, P.K., and Liaw, F. The learning, physical, and emotional environment of the home in the context of poverty: The Infant Health and Development Program. *Children and Youth Services Review* (1995)17,1/2.251–76.

49. Wilson, W.J. *The truly disadvantaged. The inner city, the underclass, and public policy.* Chicago. University of Chicago Press, 1987.

50. Sampson, R., and Morenoff, J. Ecological perspectives on the neighborhood context of urban poverty: Past and present. In *Neighborhood poverty: Conceptual, methodological, and policy approaches to studying neighborhoods.* Vol. 2. J. Brooks-Gunn, G. Duncan, and J.L. Aber, eds. New York: Russell Sage Foundation, in press.

51. Brooks-Gunn, J., Duncan, G.J., and Aber, J.L., eds. *Neighborhood poverty: Context and consequences for children.* Vol. 1. New York: Russell Sage Foundation, in press.

52. Klebanov, P.K., Brooks-Gunn, J., and Duncan, G.J. Does neighborhood and family poverty affect mother's parenting, mental health and social support? *Journal of Marriage and Family* (1994) 56,2:441–55.

53. Klebanov, P.K., Brooks-Gunn, J., Chase-Lansdale, L., and Gordon, R. The intersection of the neighborhood and home environment and its influence on young children. In *Neighborhood poverty: Context and consequences for children.* Vol. 1. J. Brooks-

Gunn, G.J. Duncan, and J.L. Aber, eds. New York: Russell Sage Foundation, in press.

54. Evans, W.N.. Oates, W.E., and Schwab, R.M. Measuring peer group effects: A study of teenage behavior. *Journal of Practical Economy* (1992) 100,5:966–91.

55. Mayer S.E. *What money can't buy: The effect of parental income on children's outcomes.* Cambridge, MA: Harvard University Press, 1997.

56. Kershwa, D., and Fair, J. *The New Jersey income maintenance experiment.* Vol. I. New York: Academic Press, 1976.

57. Salkind, N.J., and Haskins, R. Negative income tax: The impact on children from low-income families. *Journal of Family Issues* (1982) 3,2:165–80.

58. Baydar, N., Brooks-Gunn, J., and Furstenberg, E.F, Jr. Early warning signs of functional illiteracy: Predictors in childhood and adolescence. *Child Development* (1993) 64,3:815–29.

59. Alexander, K.L., and Entwisle, D.R. Achievement in the first 2 years of school: Patterns and proc-esses. *Monographs of the Society for Research in Child Development* (1988) 53,2:1–153.

60. Sparling, J.J., and Lewis, J. *Partner for learning.* Lewisville, NC: Kaplan, 1984.

61. Olds, D.L., and Kitzman, H. Review of research on home visiting for pregnant women and parents of young children. *The Future of Children* (Winter 1993) 3,3:53–92.

62. Brooks-Gunn, J., Denner, J., and Klebanov, P.K. Families and neighborhoods as contexts for education. In *Changing populations, changing schools: Ninety-fourth yearbook of the National Society for the Study of Education, Part II.* E. Flaxman and A. H. Passow, eds. Chicago, IL: National Society for the Study of Education, 1995, pp. 233–52.

63. Brooks-Gunn, J. Strategies for altering the outcomes of poor children and their families. In *Escape from poverty: What makes a difference for children?* P.L. Chase-Lansdale and J. Brooks-Gunn, eds. New York: Cambridge University Press, 1996.

Victimization of Children

David Finkelhor and Jennifer Dziuba-Leatherman

David Finkelhor and Jennifer Dziuba-Leatherman, Family Research Laboratory, University of New Hampshire.

Nadine M. Lambert served as action editor for this article.

We thank the Boy Scouts of America for financial support. We would also like to thank Kyle Ruonala for help in preparing the manuscript and Lucy Berliner, David Chadwick, Kathy Kaufer Christoffel, James Collins, Pat Crittenden, Howard Davidson, James Garbarino, Malcolm Gordon, Elizabeth Kandel, Kathy Kendall-Tackett, David Kerns, Ben Saunders, Murray Straus, James Tucker, members of the Family Violence Research Seminar, and several anonymous reviewers for helpful comments on the article.

Correspondence concerning this article should be addressed to David Finkelhor, Family Research Laboratory, University of New Hampshire, 126 Horton Social Science Center, Durham, NH 03824.

Children suffer more victimizations than do adults, including more conventional crimes, more family violence, and some forms virtually unique to children, such as family abduction. On the basis of national statistics, these victimizations can be grouped into three broad categories: the pandemic, *such as sibling assault, affecting most children; the* acute, *such as physical abuse, affecting a fractional but significant percentage; and the* extraordinary, *such as homicide, affecting a very small group. They can also be differentiated by the degree to which they result from the unique dependency status of children. A field called the victimology of childhood should be defined that adopts a developmental approach to understanding children's vulnerability to different types of victimizations and their different effects.*

Although the issue of child victimization has elicited considerable attention from professionals and the public, the interest has largely been fragmented. Writers and advocates have tended to confine themselves to certain specific topics, such as child abuse, child molestation, or stranger abduction, and few have considered the larger whole (for exceptions, see Best, 1990; Christoffel, 1990; McDermott, Stanley, & Zimmerman-McKinney, 1982; Morgan & Zedner, 1992). Unfortunately, this fragmentation has inhibited the recognition and development of what should be a very important field: the general victimology of childhood. Such a general victimology would highlight more clearly the true vulnerability of children to victimization, the overlap and co-occurrence of different types of victimization, and the common risk factors and effects. It is our goal to assemble disparate statistics and knowledge about the victimization and maltreatment of children in order to define such a field. We will review findings on the incidence, risk factors, and effects of child victimization and suggest integrative concepts.

Children Are More Victimized Than Adults

One reality, not widely recognized, is that children are more prone to victimization than adults are. For example, according to the 1990 National Crime Survey (NCS; Bureau of Justice Statistics, 1991), the rates of assault, rape, and robbery against those aged 12–19 years are two to three times higher than for the adult population as a whole (Table 1). Homicide is the only violent crime category for which teens are somewhat less vulnerable than adults.[1]

This disproportionate victimization of children is also confirmed in studies that gather information from adults on their lifetime experience with crime. For example, in the first national survey to ask adult women about their lifetime experiences of forcible rape, 61% of the rapes occurred before the age of 18 (Kilpatrick, 1992). This translates roughly into a fivefold higher rape risk for children.

The disproportionate victimization of children would be even more evident if the NCS and other studies were not so deficient in their counting of incidents of family violence (Garbarino, 1989), to which children are enormously more vulnerable than adults. For example, in the National Family Violence Survey (Straus, Gelles, & Steinmetz, 1980), adults reported that they inflicted almost twice as much severe violence (which includes beating up, kicking, hitting with a fist or object) against a child in their household than they did against their adult partner (Table 2). When to family violence we add the frequent occurrence of peer and sibling assaults against younger children—experiences that have virtually no equivalent among adults (Pagelow, 1989)—evidence strongly suggests that children are more victimized than adults are.

Statistics on Child Victimization

To illustrate the spectrum of child victimization, we have arrayed the national statistics gleaned from more than a dozen sources in Table 3 in rough order of magnitude. (See Appendix for list of sources.) We limited our notion

---

[1] Unfortunately, this contrast is muddied by the fact that the NCS does not have rates on children under 12 years of age, and, although they are usually classified as young adults, 18- and 19-year-olds—a very high-risk group—are treated as children. Even if one reclassifies 18- and 19-year-olds as adults and assumes no victimizations at all for children younger than 12, the overall rate for children, based on NCS data, would still be higher than the overall rate for adults.

of victimization to crimes, interpersonal violence (acts carried out with the intention or perceived intention of physically hurting another person, Gelles & Straus, 1979), child abuse, and certain related acts, such as abduction, that have been highlighted in the current wave of interest in child victimization. We included only forms of victimization for which there were scientifically defensible national estimates.

One of the interesting features of child victimology is that children suffer from certain types of violence that have been largely excluded from traditional criminologic concern. The first is assaults against young children by other children, including violent attacks by siblings. Prevailing ideology has tended to treat these as relatively inconsequential.[2] But from the point of view of the child, it is not clear, for example, why being beaten up by a peer would be any less traumatic or violative than it would be for an adult (Greenbaum, 1989).

An even more problematic type of noncriminalized violence toward children is spanking and and other forms of corporal punishment. There are signs that a normative transformation is in progress regarding corporal punishment (Greven, 1990). A majority of states have banned it in schools, and several Scandinavian countries have outlawed its use even by parents. Some social scientists have begun to study it as a form of victimization with short- and long-term negative consequences (Daro & Gelles, 1991; Hyman, 1990; Straus, in press).

This is far from an exhaustive inventory of all the victimizations children could be said to suffer. For example, bullying and emotional abuse by peers have received some deserved attention (Olweus, 1978). Moreover, children have been plausibly described as victims when crimes are committed against other members of their household (Morgan & Zedner, 1992). Finally, there are many types of criminal victimizations, such as involvement in child prostitution, for which we could identify no reliable national statistics.

Table 1

Crime Victimization Rate per 1,000:
Adolescents Versus Adults

Crime	Age in years	
	12–19	20+
Assault[a]	58.45	17.85
Robbery[a]	11.53	4.73
Rape[a]	1.60	0.50
Homicide[b]	0.09[c]	0.10

Note.   Some figures shown in this table did not appear in original source but were derived from data presented therein.
  [a] National Crime Survey, 1990 (Bureau of Justice Statistics, 1992).
  [b] Uniform Crime Report, 1991 (Federal Bureau of Investigation, 1992).
  [c] Rate is for ages 10–19.

Table 2

Family Violence Victimization Rate per 1,000:
Children Versus Adults, 1985

Perpetrator–victim relationship	Any violence	Severe violence[a]
Spouse to spouse	158	58
Parent to child	620	107

Note.   Source: National Family Violence Resurvey, 1985 (Straus & Gelles, 1990).
  [a] Includes kicking, biting, hitting with fist or object, beating up, using or threatening to use knife or gun.

Typology of Child Victimizations

Examining the figures in Table 3 and recognizing their methodological limitations, definitional imprecision, and variability, we nonetheless suggest that the types of child victimization reflected there should be broken into three broad categories according to their order of magnitude (Figure 1). First, there are the pandemic victimizations that occur to a majority of children in the course of growing up. At a minimum these include assault by siblings, physical punishment by parents, and theft, and probably also peer assault, vandalism, and robbery. Second, there are what might be called acute victimizations. These are less frequent—occurring to a minority, although perhaps a sizable minority, of children—but may be of generally greater severity. Among these we would include physical abuse, neglect, and family abduction. Finally, there are the extraordinary victimizations that occur to a very small number of children but that attract a great deal of attention. These include homicide, child abuse homicide, and nonfamily abduction.

Several observations follow from this typology. First, there has been much more public and professional attention paid to the extraordinary and acute victimizations than to the pandemic ones. For example, sibling violence, the most frequent victimization, is conspicuous for how little it has been studied in proportion to how often it occurs. This neglect of pandemic victimizations needs to be rectified. For one thing, it fails to reflect the concerns of children themselves. In a re-

---

[2] The following quote in a discussion of the meaning of the NCS statistics on adolescents is an example: "A student who is coerced into surrendering the Twinkies in his or her lunchbox to a school bully is, by strict definition, a victim of robbery. These events, although unpleasant and perhaps frightening, are not as alarming as suggested by the labels 'assault' and 'robbery'" (Garofalo, Siegel, & Laub, 1987, p. 331). This is common stereotypy of peer victimizations, even though the kind of chronic bullying, terrorizing, and intimidation that characterizes the lives of many children in school and in their neighborhood has almost no equivalent for adults, except perhaps in the case of battered wives (Greenbaum, 1989). There is also a tendency to see violence among children, particularly young children, as fighting and not as victimization. It is important to point out that this is not a distinction made in any of the statistics regarding adult victimization. That is, an adult who is assaulted in a fight he or she may have "started" (according to some observers) will nonetheless be counted as a victim in the NCS.

Table 3
Rate and Incidence of Various Childhood Victimization

Type of violence/age in years	Rate per 1,000	No. victimized	Year	Source	Report type[a]
Sibling assault					
3–17	800.0	50,400,000[b]	1975	NFVS-1	C
3–17	530.0	33,300,000[c]	1975	NFVS-1	C
Physical punishment					
0–17	498.6	31,401,329[d]	1985	NFVS-2	C
Theft					
11–17	497.0	—	1978	NYS	S
12–15	89.2	—	1990	NCS90	S
Assault					
11–17	310.6	—	1978	NYS	S
Grade 8	172.0	—	1988	NASHS	S
12–15	53.3	—	1990	NCS90	S
Vandalism					
11–17	257.6	—	1978	NYS	S
Robbery					
11–17	245.8	—	1978	NYS	S
Grade 8	160.9	—	1988	NASHS	S
12–15	13.6	—	1990	NCS90	S
Rape					
Grade 8	118.0	—	1988	NASHS	S
11–17	78.0	—[e]	1978	NYS78	S
12–15	1.8	—	1990	NCS90	S
Physical abuse					
0–17	23.5	1,480,007	1985	NFVS-2	C
0–17	10.5	673,500	1991	50-SS	A
0–17	4.9	311,500	1986	NIS-2	A
Neglect					
0–17	20.2	1,293,120	1991	50-SS	A
0–17	11.3	710,700[f]	1986	NIS-2	A
Sexual abuse					
0–17	6.3	404,100	1991	50-SS	A
0–17	2.1	133,600	1986	NIS-2	A
Family abduction					
0–17	5.6	354,100[g]	1988	NISMART	C
0–17	2.6	163,200[h]	1988	NISMART	C
Psychological maltreatment					
0–17	3.0	188,100	1986	NIS-2	A
0–17	2.5	161,640	1991	50-SS	A
Nonfamily abduction					
0–17	0.05–0.07	3200–4600[i]	1988	NISMART	A
0–17	0.003–0.005	200–300[i]	1988	NISMART	A
Homicide					
0–17	0.035	2,233	1991	UCR91	A
Abduction homicide					
0–17	0.001–0.002	43–147	1988	NISMART	A

Note. Some figures shown did not appear in original source but were derived from data presented therein. Dash = Unable to compute for entire population (0–17). NFVS-1 = National Family Violence Survey, 1975 (Straus & Gelles, 1990); NFVS-2 = National Family Violence Resurvey, 1985 (Straus & Gelles, 1990); NYS = National Youth Survey (Lauritsen, Sampson, and Laub, 1991); NCS90 = National Crime Survey, 1990 (Bureau of Justice Statistics, 1992); NASHS = National Adolescent Student Health Survey (American School Health Association, 1985); NYS78 = National Youth Survey, 1978 (Ageton, 1983); 50-SS = Annual Fifty State Survey, 1990 (Daro & McCurdy, 1991); NIS-2 = National Study of the Incidence and Severity of Child Abuse and Neglect, 1988 (Sedlak, 1991); NISMART = National Incidence Study of Missing, Abducted, Runaway and Thrownaway Children, 1990 (Finkelhor, Hotaling, & Sedlak, 1990); UCR91 = Uniform Crime Reports, 1991 (Federal Bureau of Investigation, 1992). Categories listed are not necessarily distinct and mutually exclusive. Under some victimization categories, estimates of several studies have been listed, sometimes showing widely divergent numbers. These differences stem from two factors in particular: the source of the report and the definition of the activity. Of the three main sources of reports—children themselves, caretakers knowledgeable about children's experiences, and agencies such as police and child protection services—children and caretakers are quite likely to provide many more accounts than are available from agencies alone. Estimates also diverge because some studies used more careful or restrictive definitions.
[a] Report type: A = agency; C = caretaker; S = self-report. [b] Any violence. [c] Severe violence. [d] Excludes corporal punishment in schools. [e] Girls only. [f] Physical and emotional neglect. [g] Broad scope. [h] Policy focal. [i] Legal definition. [i] Stereotypical kidnapping.

Figure 1
Typology of Child Victimization

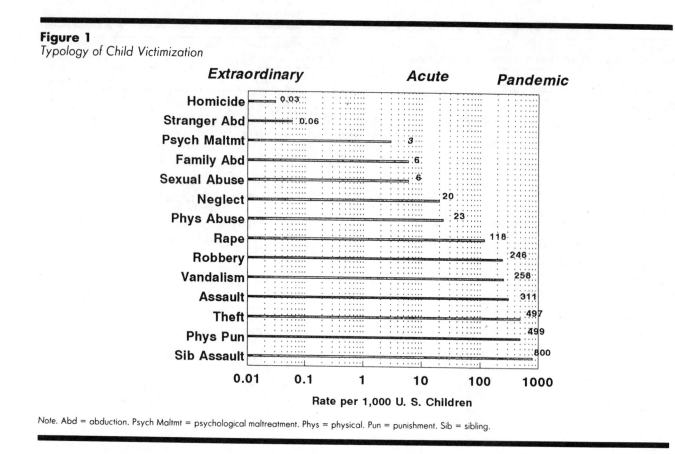

Note. Abd = abduction. Psych Maltmt = psychological maltreatment. Phys = physical. Pun = punishment. Sib = sibling.

cent survey of 2,000 children aged 10–16 years, three times as many were concerned about the likelihood of being beaten up by peers as were concerned about being sexually abused (Finkelhor & Dziuba-Leatherman, in press-b). The pandemic victimizations deserve greater attention, if only because of their alarming frequency and the influence they have on children's everyday existence.

Second, this typology can be useful in developing theory and methodology concerning child victimization. For example, different types of victimization may require different conceptual frameworks. Because they are nearly normative occurrences, the impact of pandemic victimizations may be very different from extraordinary ones, which children experience in relative isolation.

Finally, the typology helps illustrate the diversity and frequency of children's victimization. Although homicide and child abuse have been widely studied, they are notable for how inadequately they convey the variety and true extent of the other victimizations that children suffer. Almost all the figures in Table 3 have been promoted in isolation at one time or another. Viewed together, they are just part of a total environment of various victimization dangers with which children live.

Why Is the Victimization of Children So Common?

When the victimization of children is considered as a whole and its scope and variety more fully appreciated, it prompts a number of interesting and important theoretical questions. The first concerns why the victimization of children is so common. Obviously this is a complex question; a complete answer will undoubtedly require the explanation of elevated risks for different categories of children for different kinds of victimization. However, some generalizations may apply. Certainly the weakness and small physical stature of many children and their dependency status put them at greater risk. They cannot retaliate or deter victimization as effectively as can those with more strength and power. The social toleration of child victimization also plays a role. Society has an influential set of institutions, the police and criminal justice system, to enforce its relatively strong prohibitions against many kinds of crime, but much of the victimization of children is considered outside the purview of this system.

Another important generalization about why children are at high risk for victimization is that children have comparatively little choice over whom they associate with, less choice perhaps than any segment of the population besides prisoners. This can put them in more involuntary contact with high-risk offenders and thus at greater jeopardy for victimization. For example, when children live in families that mistreat them, they are not free or able to leave. When they live in dangerous neighborhoods, they cannot choose on their own to move. If they attend a school with many hostile and delinquent peers, they cannot simply change schools or quit. The absence of choice over people and environments affects children's vulnerability to both intimate victimization and street crime. Although some adults, like battered women and the poor, suffer similar limitations, many adults are able to seek divorce or change their residences in reaction to dangerous conditions. Adults also have more ready access to cars and sometimes have the option to live and work alone. Children are obliged to live with other people, to travel collectively, and to work in high density, heterogenous environments, which is what schools are. In short, children have difficulty gaining access to the structures and mechanisms in society that help segregate people from dangerous associates and environments.

Differential Character of Child Victimization

A second interesting theoretical question concerns how the victimization of children differs from the victimization of adults. Children, of course, suffer from all the victimizations that adults do (including economic crimes like extortion and fraud), but they also suffer from some that are particular to their status. The main status characteristic of childhood is its condition of dependency, which is a function, at least in part, of social and psychological immaturity. The violation of this dependency status results in forms of victimization, like physical neglect, that are not suffered by most adults (with the exception of those, like the elderly and sick, who also become dependent).

The dependency of children creates a spectrum of vulnerability for victimizations. Interestingly, the victim-

ization categories that we have identified in Table 3 can be arrayed on a continuum, according to the degree to which they involve violations of children's dependency status (Figure 2). At one extreme is physical neglect, which has practically no meaning as a victimization except in the case of a person who is dependent and needs to be cared for by others. Similarly, family abduction is a dependency-specific victimization because it is the unlawful removal of a child from the person who is supposed to be caring for him or her. Psychological maltreatment happens to both adults and children, but the sensitive psychological vulnerability of children in their dependent relationship to their caretakers renders such parental behavior a major threat to normal child development (Claussen & Crittenden, 1991; Hart & Brassard, 1987). This is why society considers psychological maltreatment of children a form of victimization that warrants an institutional response.

At the other end of the continuum are forms of victimization that are defined without reference to dependency and which exist in similar forms for both children and adults. Stranger abduction is prototypical in this instance because both children and adults are taken against their will and imprisoned for ransom or sexual purposes. Homicide is similar; the dependency status of the victim does little to define the victimization. In some cases, to be sure, children's deaths result from extreme and willful cases of neglect, but there are parallel instances of adult deaths resulting from extreme and willful negligence.

Finally, there are forms of child victimization that should be located along the midsection of the dependency continuum. Sexual abuse falls here, for example, because it encompasses at least two different situations, one dependency related, one not. Some sexual abuse entails activities, ordinarily acceptable between adults, that are deemed victimizing in the case of children because of their immaturity and dependency. But other sexual abuse

Figure 2
Dependency Continuum for Child Victimization Types

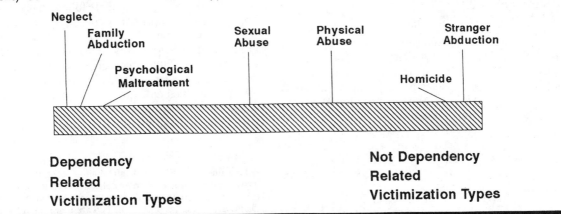

involves violence and coercion that would be victimizing even with a nondependent adult.

In the case of physical abuse, there is also some mixture. Although most of the violent acts in this category would be considered victimizing even between adults, some of them, like the shaken baby syndrome, develop almost exclusively in a caretaking relationship in which there is an enormous differential in size and physical control.

The dependency continuum is a useful concept in thinking about some of the unique features of children's victimizations. It is also helpful in generating hypotheses about the expected correlates of different types of victimization, such as variations according to age.

Developmental Victimology

Childhood is such an extremely heterogenous category—4-year-olds and 17-year-olds having little in common—that it is inherently misleading to discuss child victimization in general without reference to age. We would expect the nature, quantity, and impact of victimization to vary across childhood with the different capabilities, activities, and environments that are characteristic of different stages of development. A good term for this might be *developmental victimology*. Unfortunately, we do not have good studies of the different types of victimization across all the ages of childhood with which to examine such changes.

There are two plausible propositions about age and child victimization that could be a starting place for developmental victimology. One is that victimizations stemming from the dependent status of children should be most common among the most dependent, hence the youngest, children. A corollary is that as children grow older, their victimization profile should more and more resemble that of adults.

One can examine such propositions in a crude way with the data that are available. In fact, it is apparent (Table 4) that the types of victimization that are most concentrated in the under-12 age group are the dependency related ones (see the dependency continuum in Figure 2), particularly family abduction and physical neglect. Victimizations such as homicide and stranger abduction, which we grouped at the nondependency end of the continuum, involve a greater percentage of teenagers. However, not everything falls neatly into place; sexual abuse seems anomalously concentrated among teenagers, too. We believe this to be an artifact of the National Incidence Study (NIS) data on sexual abuse (National Center on Child Abuse and Neglect, 1981), which was based only on reported cases and thus undercounted sexual abuse of young children.[3] When the incidence of sexual abuse is based on data from retrospective self-reports, 64% of victimizations occur before age 12 (Finkelhor, Hotaling, Lewis, & Smith, 1990), a pattern more consistent with the hypothesis and the place of sexual abuse on the dependency continuum.

For additional insights about development and victimization, one can look also at child homicide, the type

Table 4
Victimization of Younger Children

Type of victimization	% of victims under 12 years of age	Source
Family abduction	81[a]	NISMART (R)
Physical neglect	70	NIS-2C
Psychological maltreatment	58[b]	NIS-2C, NSCANR
Physical abuse	56	NIS-2C
Sexual abuse	40	NIS-2C
Stranger abduction	27	NISMART (R)
Homicide	21[c]	UCR91

Note. Some figures shown in this table did not appear in original source but were derived from data presented therein. NISMART (R) = National Incidence Study of Missing, Abducted, Runaway and Thrownaway Children, 1990 (Authors' reanalysis of published data; Finkelhor, Hotaling, & Sedlak, 1990); NIS-2C = National Study of the Incidence and Severity of Child Abuse and Neglect, 1988 (Powers & Eckenrode, 1992); NSCANR = National Study on Child Abuse and Neglect Reporting, 1983 (American Association for Protecting Children, 1985); UCR91 = Uniform Crime Reports, 1991 (Federal Bureau of Investigation, 1992).
[a] Broad scope. [b] Reflects midpoint of two divergent estimates. [c] Age group for this category is under 10.

of victimization to which a developmental analysis has been most extensively applied (Christoffel, 1990; Crittenden & Craig, 1990; Jason, 1983). Child homicide has a conspicuous bimodal frequency, with high rates for the very youngest and oldest children (Figure 3). But the two peaks represent very different phenomena. The homicides of young children are primarily committed by parents, most often using their hands—so-called "personal weapons." In contrast, the homicides of older children are committed mostly by peers and acquaintances, most often with the use of firearms.

Although the analysts do not agree entirely on the number and age span of the specific developmental categories for child homicides, a number of propositions are clear. There is a distinct group of neonaticides, or children killed on the first day or within the first few weeks of life. Homicide at this age is generally considered to include many isolated mothers dealing with unwanted children. After the neonatal period, there follows a period in which homicides are still primarily committed by caretakers using personal weapons, but the motives and circumstances are thought to be somewhat different. These appear to be mostly cases of fatal child abuse that occur as a result of parents' attempts to control child behavior (Christoffel, 1990; Crittenden & Craig, 1990). As children become of school age and older, the nature of child homicide becomes incrementally more like adult homicide. Killings

---

[3] The undercount stems from two problems: (a) Most sexual abuse reports, unlike other forms of child maltreatment, start from children's own disclosures, which are more difficult for younger children to make. (b) Much sexual abuse goes on for extended periods of time before being disclosed, and the age data in the NIS are based on age at the time of report, not age at onset.

Figure 3
Relationship of Child Homicide Victims to Perpetrators

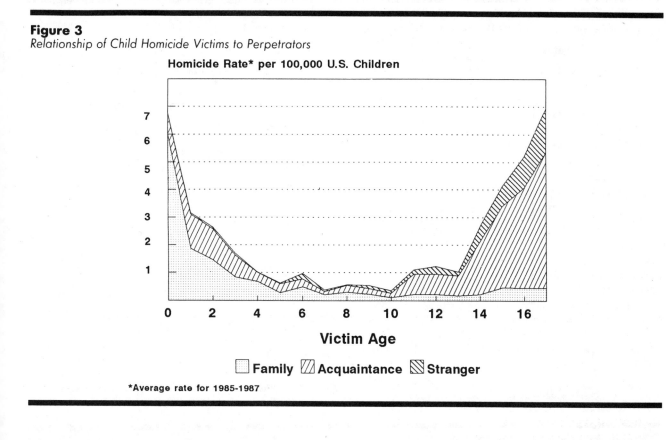

Homicide Rate* per 100,000 U.S. Children

Victim Age

☐ Family ▨ Acquaintance ◩ Stranger

*Average rate for 1985-1987

by parents and caretakers decline, and those by peers and acquaintances rise. Firearms become the predominant method.

These trends clearly suggest that the types of homicide suffered by children are related to the nature of their dependency and to the level of their integration into the adult world. These trends provide a good case for the importance and utility of a developmental perspective on child victimizations and a model of how such an approach could be applied to other types of victimization.

Intrafamily Victimization

Unlike many adults, children do not live alone; most live in families. Thus, another plausible principle of developmental victimology is that more of the victimization of children occurs at the hands of relatives. We illustrated this in Table 2 and also Table 3, showing the sheer quantity of victimization by relatives apparent in the elevated figures on sibling assault (Table 3), which outstrip any other kind of victimization.

The findings on homicide also suggest a developmental trend: Younger children have a greater proportion of their victimizations at the hands of intimates and correspondingly fewer at the hands of strangers. They live more sheltered lives, spend more time in the home and around family, and have less wealth and fewer valuable possessions that might make them attractive targets for strangers.

An additional possible principle is that the identity of perpetrators may vary according to the type of victimization and its place on the dependency continuum (Figure 2). Victimizations that are more dependency related should involve more perpetrators who are parents and family members. Accordingly, parents are 100% of the perpetrators of neglect and psychological maltreatment (Sedlak, 1991), the most dependency-related victimizations. However, they represent only 51% of the perpetrators of sexual abuse (Sedlak) and 28% of the perpetrators of homicide (Jason, Gilliand, & Taylor, 1983). This pattern occurs because the responsibilities created by children's dependency status fall primarily on parents and family members. They are the main individuals in a position to violate those responsibilities in a way that would create victimization. Thus, when a sick child fails to get available medical attention, it is the parents who are charged with neglecting the child, even if the neighbors also did nothing.

Gender and Victimization

Developmental victimology needs to take account of gender as well. On the basis of the conventional crime statistics available from the NCS and Uniform Crime Reports (UCR), boys would appear to suffer more homicide (2.3:1), more assault (1.7:1), and more robbery (2.0:1) than girls, whereas girls suffer vastly more rape (8.1:1). But this primarily pertains to the experience of adolescents and does not consider age and gender variations.

Figure 4
Gender Differences in Victimization Rates

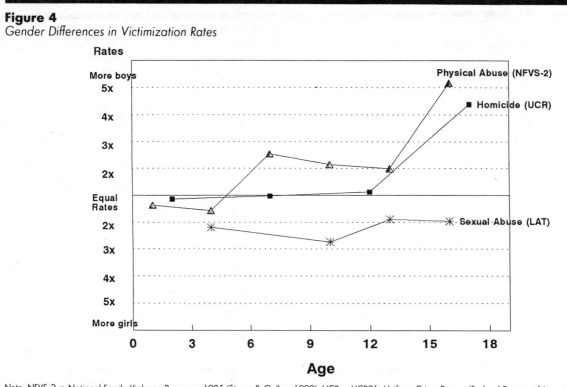

Note. NFVS-2 = National Family Violence Resurvey, 1985 (Straus & Gelles, 1990); UCR = UCR91, Uniform Crime Report (Federal Bureau of Investigation, 1992). LAT = *Los Angeles Times* Poll (Finkelhor, Hotaling, Lewis, & Smith, 1990).

Because gender differentiation increases as children grow older, a developmental hypothesis might predict that the pattern of victimization would be less gender-specific for younger children. That is, because younger boys and girls are more similar in their activities and physical characteristics, there might be less difference between sexes in the rate of victimization.

This pattern does indeed appear to be the case at least for homicide, the type of victimization for which we have the best data (Figure 4). Rates of homicide are quite similar for younger boys and girls, even up to age 14, after which point the vulnerability of boys increases dramatically.

However, this increased differentiation with age is less apparent for other types of victimization. In contrast to homicide, for example, for sexual abuse we might expect that it would be girls who would become increasingly vulnerable as they age. However, the national data do not

Table 5
Rate of Physical Injury Due to Childhood Victimization

Type of victimization	Rate of injury per 1,000 children	% of all victims sustaining injury	Source	Age in years
Assault	19.23	33	NCS90	12–19
Physical abuse	3.59	84	NIS-2	0–17
Robbery	2.71	24	NCS90	12–19
Physical neglect	1.39	52	NIS-2	0–17
Family abduction	0.22	04	NISMART	0–17
Sexual abuse	0.09	05	NIS-2	0–17
Stranger abduction	0.007–0.015	14–21	NISMART	0–17

Note. Some figures shown in this table did not appear in original source but were derived from data presented therein. NCS90 = National Crime Survey, 1990 (Bureau of Justice Statistics, 1992); NIS-2 = National Study of the Incidence and Severity of Child Abuse and Neglect, 1988 (Sedlak, 1991); NISMART = National Incidence Study of Missing, Abducted, Runaway and Thrownaway Children, 1990 (Finkelhor, Hotaling, & Sedlak, 1990).

show this. They show girls at roughly twice the risk of boys throughout childhood, with no increase during adolescence.

So it looks as though a developmental pattern in gender differentiation may apply to some forms of victimization but not others. This mixed picture in regard to gender and age merits more study. Some victimization types may have unique gender patterns reflecting their particular dynamics. However, we may also be suffering from inadequate data that are clouding the true situation.

Effects of Child Victimization

Homicide is currently one of the five leading causes of child mortality in the United States (Goetting, 1990). In addition to the more than 2,000 homicide deaths that occur each year (FBI, 1992), one needs to add a sizable proportion of 1,200 child abuse and neglect fatalities, an estimated two thirds of which are not often counted in the homicide statistics (Ewigman, Kivlahan, & Land, 1993). Victimization also results in a substantial toll of nonfatal injuries that are more difficult to count accurately. The NIS estimated that 317,700 children suffered serious or moderate physical injuries in one year (Table 5) as a result of physical abuse or neglect or sexual abuse, that is, injuries for which observable symptoms, such as bruises, lasted at least 48 hours. From the NCS, one can estimate that approximately 523,300 twelve- to 19-year-olds sustained physical injury due to an assault in 1990, and approximately 132,900 received hospital care as a result of any kind of violent crime. A Massachusetts study suggested that each year 1 in every 42 teenage boys receives hospital treatment for an assault-related injury (Guyer, Lescohier, Gallagher, Hausman, & Azzara, 1989).

Children's level of development undoubtedly influences the nature and severity of injuries resulting from victimization, although few analyses have taken such a developmental approach. An obvious example is the greater vulnerability of small children to death and serious harm as a result of inflicted blows. Another obvious example is the higher likelihood of older children to contract sexual-abuse-related HIV infection, because older children suffer more penetrative abuse (Kerns & Ritter, 1991).

In addition to physical injury, there is a growing literature documenting that victimization has grave short- and long-term effects on children's mental health. For example, sexually victimized children appear to be at a nearly fourfold increased lifetime risk for any psychiatric disorder and at a threefold risk for substance abuse (Saunders, Villeponteaux, Lipovsky, Kilpatrick, & Veronen, 1992; Scott, 1992). Scott estimated that approximately 8% of all psychiatric cases within the population at large can be attributed to childhood sexual assault.

Although they do not involve such specific epidemiological assessments, other studies have also demonstrated increased rates of mental health morbidity for other types of childhood victimization, including physical abuse (Kolko, 1992), psychological maltreatment (Briere

& Runtz, 1990), and physical punishment (Straus, in press).

In addition to general mental health impairments, a proposition that has been established across various types of victimization is that a history of such victimization increases the likelihood that someone will become a perpetrator of crime, violence, or abuse. Although this popular shibboleth has been criticized and qualified (Kaufman & Ziegler, 1987), evidence to support it comes from a wide variety of methodologies, such as longitudinal follow-ups (McCord, 1983; Widom, 1989a), studies of offender populations (Hanson & Slater, 1988), and surveys of the general population (Straus et al., 1980) and concerns a wide variety of perpetrations, including violent crime, property crime, child abuse, wife abuse, and sexual assaults (for review, see Widom, 1989b). An important qualification is that victims are not necessarily prone to repeat their own form of victimization. But the proposition that childhood victims are more likely to grow up to victimize others is firmly established.

Theory about posttraumatic stress disorder (PTSD) is being applied to, and may be a unifying concept for, understanding common psychological effects of a wide variety of child victimizations (Eth & Pynoos, 1985), including abuse in schools (Hyman, Zelikoff, & Clarke, 1988). Terr (1990) has made some effort to cast PTSD in a more developmental framework, but its application is mostly anecdotal.

Sexual abuse is the only area in which a developmental approach to the psychological impact of victimization has advanced on the basis of empirical studies (Kendall-Tackett, Williams, & Finkelhor, 1993). For example, in reaction to sexual abuse, symptoms of sexualization seem to appear more frequently among preschool than among school-age girls, who seem more aware of appropriate and inappropriate sexual conduct (Friedrich et al., 1992). This is the direction the whole area of child victimization needs to take.

Research Needs

The research needs in this field of child victimization are vast and urgent, given the size of the problem and the seriousness of its impact, and they range from studies of risk factors to studies of treatment efficacy. In the limited space of this review, we mention only three important points.

First, if we are to take child victimization seriously, we need much better statistics to document and analyze its scope, nature, and trends. We need comprehensive, yearly, national and state figures on all officially reported crimes against children and forms of child abuse. These need to be supplemented by regular national studies (one is currently in progress; Finkelhor & Dziuba-Leatherman, in press-a) to assess the vast quantity of unreported victimization, including family violence and child-to-child and indirect victimizations. Currently, the NCS records crime victimizations only down to age 12. The UCR in the past has made no age information available about crimes, with the exception of homicide. Because the national data collection system for child abuse fails to include all states and has severe methodological limitations, the information cannot be aggregated nationally or compared across states (National Center on Child Abuse and Neglect, 1992).

Second, we need theory and research that cuts across and integrates the various forms of child victimization. One example is the research illustrating how forms of victimization occur together (Claussen & Crittenden, 1991) or create vulnerability for one another (Russell, 1984). Another good example is the work on PTSD in children, which has been applied to the effects of various victimizations: sexual abuse, corporal punishment-related abuse in schools, stranger abduction, and the witnessing of homicide (Eth & Pynoos, 1985; Hyman et al., 1988; Terr, 1990). Similar cross-cutting research could be done on other subjects, such as what makes children vulnerable to victimization or how responses by family members buffer or exacerbate the impact of victimization. To be truly synthetic, this research needs to study the pandemic victimizations, not just the acute and the extraordinary, which have been the main foci in the past.

Finally, the field needs a more developmental perspective on child victimization. This would start with an understanding of the mix of victimization threats that face children of different ages. It would include the kinds of factors that place children at risk, including ecological factors, and the strategies for victimization avoidance that are appropriate at different stages of development. It would also differentiate how children, with all their individual differences, react and cope at different stages with the challenges posed by victimization. It is only through this more differentiated approach that we can understand how victimization leaves its mark on children's lives.

REFERENCES

Ageton, S. S. (1983). *Sexual assault among adolescents*. Lexington, MA: Lexington Books.
American Association for Protecting Children. (1985). *Highlights of official child neglect and abuse reporting, 1983*. Denver, CO: American Humane Association.
American School Health Association. (1985). *The national adolescent student health survey: A report on the health of America's youth*. Kent, OH: Author.
Best, J. (1990). *Threatened children: Rhetoric and concern about child-victims*. Chicago: University of Chicago Press.
Briere, J., & Runtz, M. (1990). Differential adult symptomatology associated with three types of child abuse histories. *Child Abuse and Neglect, 14*, 357–364.
Bureau of Justice Statistics. (1991). *Teenage victims: A national crime survey report* (NCJ-128129). Washington, DC: U.S. Department of Justice.
Bureau of Justice Statistics. (1992). *Criminal victimization in the United States, 1990: A national crime victimization survey report* (NCJ-134126). Washington, DC: U.S. Department of Justice.
Christoffel, K. K. (1990). Violent death and injury in U.S. children and adolescents. *American Journal of Diseases of Children, 144*, 697–706.
Claussen, A. I. E., & Crittenden, P. M. (1991). Physical and psychological maltreatment: Relations among types of maltreatment. *Child Abuse and Neglect, 15*, 5–18.

Crittenden, P. A., & Craig, S. E. (1990). Developmental trends in the nature of child homicide. *Journal of Interpersonal Violence, 5*, 202–216.
Daro, D., & Gelles, R. (1991). *Public attitudes and behaviors with respect to child abuse prevention 1987–1991* (Working paper No. 840). Chicago: National Center on Child Abuse Prevention Research, National Committee for Prevention of Child Abuse.
Daro, D., & McCurdy, K. (1991). *Current trends in child abuse reporting and fatalities: The results of the 1990 annual fifty state survey* (Working paper No. 808). Chicago: National Center on Child Abuse Prevention Research, National Committee for Prevention of Child Abuse.
Eth, S., & Pynoos, R. S. (1985). *Post-traumatic stress disorder in children*. Washington, DC: American Psychiatric Press.
Ewigman, B., Kivlahan, C., & Land, G. (1993). The Missouri Child Fatality Study: Underreporting of maltreatment fatalities among children younger than five years of age: 1983 through 1996. *Pediatrics, 91*, 330–337.
Federal Bureau of Investigation. (1992). *Crime in the United States, 1991: Uniform crime reports*. Washington, DC: U.S. Department of Justice.
Finkelhor, D., & Dziuba-Leatherman, J. (in press-a). Children as victims of violence: A national survey. *Pediatrics*.
Finkelhor, D., & Dziuba-Leatherman, J. (in press-b). Victimization prevention programs: A national survey of children's exposure and reactions. *Child Abuse and Neglect*.
Finkelhor, D., Hotaling, G. T., Lewis, I. A., & Smith, C. (1990). Sexual abuse in a national survey of adult men and women: Prevalence, characteristics, and risk factors. *Child Abuse and Neglect, 14*, 19–28.
Finkelhor, D., Hotaling, G. T., & Sedlak, A. (1990). *Missing, abducted, runaway, and thrownaway children in America: First report*. Washington, DC: Juvenile Justice Clearinghouse.
Friedrich, W. N., Grambsch, P., Damon, L., Hewitt, S. K., Koverola, C., Wolfe, V., Lang, R. A., & Broughton, D. (1992). Child Sexual Behavior Inventory: Normative and clinical comparisons. *Psychological Assessment, 4*, 303–311.
Garbarino, J. (1989). The incidence and prevalence of child maltreatment. In L. Ohlin & M. Tonry (Eds.), *Family violence* (pp. 219–261). Chicago: University of Chicago Press.
Garofalo, J., Siegel, L., & Laub, J. (1987). School-related victimizations among adolescents: An analysis of National Crime Survey narratives. *Journal of Quantitative Criminology, 3*, 321–338.
Gelles, R. J., & Straus, M. A. (1979). Determinants of violence in the family: Towards a theoretical integration. In W. R. Burr, R. Hill, F. I. Nye, & I. L. Reiss (Eds.), *Contemporary theories about the family* (Vol. 1). New York: Free Press.
Goetting, A. (1990). Child victims of homicide: A portrait of their killers and the circumstances of their deaths. *Violence and Victims, 5*, 287–296.
Greenbaum, S. (1989). *School bullying and victimization* (NSSC resource paper). Malibu, CA: National School Safety Center.
Greven, P. (1990). *Spare the child: The religious roots of punishment and the psychological impact of physical abuse*. New York: Knopf.
Guyer, B., Lescohier, I., Gallagher, S. S., Hausman, A., & Azzara, C. V. (1989). Intentional injuries among children and adolescents in Massachusetts. *The New England Journal of Medicine, 321*, 1584–1589.
Hanson, R. L., & Slater, S. (1988). Sexual victimization in the history of sexual abusers: A review. *Annals of Sex Research, 4*, 485–499.
Hart, S. N., & Brassard, M. R. (1987). A major threat to children's mental health: Psychological maltreatment. *American Psychologist, 42*, 160–165.
Hyman, I. A. (1990). *Reading, writing and the hickory stick: The appalling story of physical and psychological abuse in American schools*. Lexington, MA: Lexington Books.
Hyman, I. A., Zelikoff, W., & Clarke, J. (1988). Psychological and physical abuse in the schools: A paradigm for understanding post-traumatic stress disorder in children and youths. *Journal of Traumatic Stress, 1*, 243–267.
Jason, J. (1983). Child homicide spectrum. *American Journal of Diseases of Children, 137*, 578–581.

Jason, J., Gilliand, J. C., & Taylor, C. W. (1983). Homicide as a cause of pediatric mortality in the United States. *Pediatrics, 72,* 191–197.

Kaufman, J., & Ziegler, E. (1987). Do abused children become abusive parents? *American Journal of Orthopsychiatry, 57,* 186–192.

Kendall-Tackett, K. A., Williams, L. M., & Finkelhor, D. (1993). Impact of sexual abuse on children: A review and synthesis of recent empirical studies. *Psychological Bulletin, 113,* 164–180.

Kerns, D. L., & Ritter, M. L. (1991, September). *Data analysis of the medical evaluation of 1,800 suspected child sexual abuse victims.* Paper presented at the Ninth National Conference on Child Abuse and Neglect, Denver, CO.

Kilpatrick, D. (1992). *Rape in America: A report to the nation.* Charleston, SC: Crime Victims Research Center.

Kolko, D. J. (1992). Characteristics of child victims of physical violence: Research findings and clinical implications. *Journal of Interpersonal Violence, 7,* 244–276.

Lauritsen, J. L., Sampson, R. J., & Laub, J. H. (1991). The link between offending and victimization among adolescents. *Criminology, 29,* 265–292.

McCord, J. (1983). A forty year perspective on effects of child abuse and neglect. *Child Abuse and Neglect, 7,* 265–270.

McDermott, M. J., Stanley, J. E., & Zimmerman-McKinney, M. A. (1982). The victimization of children and youths. *Victimology, 7,* 162–177.

Morgan, J., & Zedner, L. (1992). *Child victims: Crime, impact, and criminal justice.* Oxford, England: Clarendon Press.

National Center on Child Abuse and Neglect. (1981). *Study findings, National Study of the Incidence and Severity of Child Abuse and Neglect* (OHDS Publication No. 81-30325). Washington, DC: Department of Health and Human Services.

National Center on Child Abuse and Neglect. (1992). *National child abuse and neglect data system* (Working paper No. 1): *1990 summary data component* (DHHS Publication No. ACF 92-30361). Washington, DC: Department of Health and Human Services.

Olweus, D. (1978). *Aggression in the schools: Bullies and whipping boys.* Washington, DC: Hemisphere.

Pagelow, M. D. (1989). The incidence and prevalence of criminal abuse of other family members. In L. Ohlin & M. Tonry (Eds.), *Family violence* (pp. 263–314). Chicago: University of Chicago Press.

Powers, J., & Eckenrode, J. (1992, March). *The epidemiology of adolescent maltreatment.* Paper presented at the Fourth Biennial Meeting of the Society for Research on Adolescence, Washington, DC.

Russell, D. (1984). *Sexual exploitation: Rape, child sexual abuse, and workplace harassment.* Beverly Hills, CA: Sage.

Saunders, B. E., Villeponteaux, L. A., Lipovsky, J. A., Kilpatrick, D. G., & Veronen, L. J. (1992). Child sexual assault as a risk factor for mental disorders among women: A community survey. *Journal of Interpersonal Violence, 7,* 189–204.

Scott, K. D. (1992). Childhood sexual abuse: Impact on a community's mental health status. *Child Abuse and Neglect, 16,* 285–295.

Sedlak, A. J. (1991). *Supplementary analyses of data on the national incidence of child abuse and neglect.* Rockville, MD: Westat.

Straus, M. A. (in press). Corporal punishment of children and depression and suicide in adulthood. In J. McCord (Ed.), *Coercion and punishment in long-term perspective.* Cambridge, England: Cambridge University Press.

Straus, M. A., & Gelles, R. J. (1990). *Physical violence in American families: Risk factors and adaptations to violence in 8,145 families.* New Brunswick, NJ: Transaction.

Straus, M., Gelles, R., & Steinmetz, S. K. (1980). *Behind closed doors: Violence in the American family.* Garden City, NY: Anchor Press.

Terr, L. (1990). *Too scared to cry.* New York: Harper/Collins.

Widom, C. S. (1989a). The cycle of violence. *Science, 244,* 160–166.

Widom, C. S. (1989b). Does violence beget violence? A critical examination of the literature. *Psychological Bulletin, 106,* 3–28.

APPENDIX

Sources of Data

Acronym	Survey
50-SS	Annual Fifty State Survey, 1990 (Daro & McCurdy, 1991).
LAECA	Los Angeles Epidemiologic Catchment Area data (Scott, 1992).
LAT	*Los Angeles Times* Poll (Finkelhor, Hotaling, Lewis, & Smith, 1990).
NASHS	National Adolescent Student Health Survey (American School Health Association, 1985).
NCS90	National Crime Survey, 1990 (Bureau of Justice Statistics, 1992).
NCSTEEN	National Crime Survey, 1979–1988 (as presented in Bureau of Justice Statistics, 1991).
NFVS-1	National Family Violence Survey, 1975 (Straus & Gelles, 1990).
NFVS-2	National Family Violence Resurvey, 1985 (Straus & Gelles, 1990).
NISMART	National Incidence Study of Missing, Abducted, Runaway and Thrownaway Children, 1990 (Finkelhor, Hotaling, & Sedlak, 1990).
NSCANR	National Study on Child Abuse and Neglect Reporting, 1983 (American Association for Protecting Children, 1985).
NIS-1	National Study of the Incidence and Severity of Child Abuse and Neglect, 1981 (National Center on Child Abuse and Neglect, 1981).
NIS-2	National Study of the Incidence and Severity of Child Abuse and Neglect, 1988 (Sedlak, 1991).
NIS-2C	National Study of the Incidence and Severity of Child Abuse and Neglect, 1988 (as presented in Powers & Eckenrode, 1992).
NYS	National Youth Survey (Lauritsen, Sampson, & Laub, 1991).
NYS78	National Youth Survey, 1978 (Ageton, 1983).
UCR91	Uniform Crime Reports, 1991 (Federal Bureau of Investigation, 1992).

Resilience in Development

Emmy E. Werner

Emmy E. Werner is Professor of Human Development at the University of California, Davis. Address correspondence to Emmy E. Werner, Department of Applied Behavioral Sciences, University of California, Davis, 2321 Hart Hall, Davis, CA 95616.

During the past decade, a number of investigators from different disciplines—child development, psychology, psychiatry, and sociology—have focused on the study of children and youths who overcame great odds. These researchers have used the term resilience to describe three kinds of phenomena: good developmental outcomes despite high-risk status, sustained competence under stress, and recovery from trauma. Under each of these conditions, behavioral scientists have focused their attention on protective factors, or mechanisms that moderate (ameliorate) a person's reaction to a stressful situation or chronic adversity so that his or her adaptation is more successful than would be the case if the protective factors were not present.[1]

So far, only a relatively small number of studies have focused on children who were exposed to biological insults. More numerous in the current research literature are studies of resilient children who grew up in chronic poverty, were exposed to parental psychopathology, or experienced the breakup of their family or serious caregiving deficits. There has also been a growing body of literature on resilience in children who have endured the horrors of contemporary wars.

Despite the heterogeneity of all these studies, one can begin to discern a common core of individual dispositions and sources of support that contribute to resilience in development. These protective buffers appear to transcend ethnic, social-class, and geographic boundaries. They also appear to make a more profound impact on the life course of individuals who grow up in adversity than do specific risk factors or stressful life events.

Most studies of individual resilience and protective factors in children have been short-term, focusing on middle childhood and adolescence. An exception is the Kauai Longitudinal Study, with which I have been associated during the past three decades.[2] This study has involved a team of pediatricians, psychologists, and public-health and social workers who have monitored the impact of a variety of biological and psychosocial risk factors, stressful life events, and protective factors on the development of a multiethnic cohort of 698 children born in 1955 on the "Garden Island" in the Hawaiian chain. These individuals were followed, with relatively little attrition, from the prenatal period through birth to ages 1, 2, 10, 18, and 32.

Some 30% of the survivors in this study population were considered high-risk children because they were born in chronic poverty, had experienced perinatal stress, and lived in family environments troubled by chronic discord, divorce, or parental psychopathology. Two thirds of the children who had experienced four or more such risk factors by age 2 developed serious learning or behavior problems by age 10 or had delinquency records, mental health problems, or pregnancies by age 18. But one third of the children who had experienced four or more such risk factors developed instead into competent, confident, and caring adults.

PROTECTIVE FACTORS WITHIN THE INDIVIDUAL

Infancy and Early Childhood

Our findings with these resilient children are consistent with the results of several other longitudinal studies which have reported that young children with good coping abilities under adverse conditions have temperamental characteristics that elicit positive responses from a wide range of caregivers. The resilient boys and girls in the Kauai study were consistently characterized by their mothers as active, affectionate, cuddly, good-natured, and easy to deal with. Egeland and his associates observed similar dispositions among securely attached infants of abusing mothers in the Minnesota Mother-Child Interaction Project,[3] and Moriarty found the same qualities among infants with congenital defects at the Menninger Foundation.[4] Such infants were alert, easy to soothe, and able to elicit support from a nurturant family member. An "easy" temperament and the ability to actively recruit competent adult caregivers were also observed by Elder and his associates[5] in the resourceful children of the Great Depression.

By the time they reach preschool

From *Current Directions in Psychological Science*, June 1995, pp. 81-85. © 1995 by the American Psychological Society.

age, resilient children appear to have developed a coping pattern that combines autonomy with an ability to ask for help when needed. These characteristics are also predictive of resilience in later years.

Middle Childhood and Adolescence

When the resilient children in the Kauai Longitudinal Study were in elementary school, their teachers were favorably impressed by their communication and problem-solving skills. Although these children were not particularly gifted, they used whatever talents they had effectively. Usually they had a special interest or a hobby they could share with a friend, and that gave them a sense of pride. These interests and activities were not narrowly sex typed. Both the boys and the girls grew into adolescents who were outgoing and autonomous, but also nurturant and emotionally sensitive.

Similar findings have been reported by Anthony, who studied the resilient offspring of mentally ill parents in St. Louis;[6] by Felsman and Vaillant, who followed successful boys from a high-crime neighborhood in Boston into adulthood;[7] and by Rutter and Quinton, who studied the lives of British girls who had been institutionalized in childhood, but managed to become well-functioning adults and caring mothers.[8]

Most studies of resilient children and youths report that intelligence and scholastic competence are positively associated with the ability to overcome great odds. It stands to reason that youngsters who are better able to appraise stressful life events correctly are also better able to figure out strategies for coping with adversity, either through their own efforts or by actively reaching out to other people for help. This finding has been replicated in studies of Asian-American, Caucasian, and African-American children.[2,9,10]

Other salient protective factors that operated in the lives of the resilient youths on Kauai were a belief in their own effectiveness (an internal locus of control) and a positive self-concept. Such characteristics were also found by Farrington among successful and law-abiding British youngsters who grew up in high-crime neighborhoods in London,[11] and by Wallerstein and her associates among American children who coped effectively with the breakup of their parents' marriages.[12]

PROTECTIVE FACTORS WITHIN THE FAMILY

Despite the burden of chronic poverty, family discord, or parental psychopathology, a child identified as resilient usually has had the opportunity to establish a close bond with at least one competent and emotionally stable person who is attuned to his or her needs. The stress-resistant children in the Kauai Longitudinal Study, the well-functioning offspring of child abusers in the Minnesota Mother-Child Interaction Project, the resilient children of psychotic parents studied by Anthony in St. Louis, and the youngsters who coped effectively with the breakup of their parents' marriages in Wallerstein's studies of divorce all had received enough good nurturing to establish a basic sense of trust.[2,3,6,12]

Much of this nurturing came from substitute caregivers within the extended family, such as grandparents and older siblings. Resilient children seem to be especially adept at recruiting such surrogate parents. In turn, they themselves are often called upon to take care of younger siblings and to practice acts of "required helpfulness" for members of their family who are ill or incapacitated.[2]

Both the Kauai Longitudinal

Study and Block and Gjerde's studies of ego-resilient children[9] found characteristic child-rearing orientations that appear to promote resiliency differentially in boys and girls. Resilient boys tend to come from households with structure and rules, where a male serves as a model of identification (father, grandfather, or older brother), and where there is some encouragement of emotional expressiveness. Resilient girls, in contrast, tend to come from households that combine an emphasis on risk taking and independence with reliable support from a female caregiver, whether mother, grandmother, or older sister. The example of a mother who is gainfully and steadily employed appears to be an especially powerful model of identification for resilient girls.[2] A number of studies of resilient children from a wide variety of socioeconomic and ethnic backgrounds have also noted that the families of these children held religious beliefs that provided stability and meaning in times of hardship and adversity.[2,6,10]

PROTECTIVE FACTORS IN THE COMMUNITY

The Kauai Longitudinal Study and a number of other prospective studies in the United States have shown that resilient youngsters tend to rely on peers and elders in the community as sources of emotional support and seek them out for counsel and comfort in times of crisis.[2,6]

Favorite teachers are often positive role models. All of the resilient high-risk children in the Kauai study could point to at least one teacher who was an important source of support. These teachers listened to the children, challenged them, and rooted for them—whether in grade school, high school, or community college. Similar findings have been reported by Wallerstein and her associates from their long-term observations of youngsters who coped effectively with their parents' divorces[12] and by Rutter and his associates from their studies of inner-city schools in London.[13]

Finally, in the Kauai study, we found that the opening of opportunities at major life transitions enabled the majority of the high-risk children who had a troubled adolescence to rebound in their 20s and early 30s. Among the most potent second chances for such youths were adult education programs in community colleges, voluntary military service, active participation in a church community, and a supportive friend or marital partner. These protective buffers were also observed by Elder in the adult lives of the children of the Great Depression,[14] by Furstenberg and his associates in the later lives of black teenage mothers,[15] and by Farrington[11] and Felsman and Vaillant[7] in the adult lives of young men who had grown up in high-crime neighborhoods in London and Boston.

PROTECTIVE FACTORS: A SUMMARY

Several clusters of protective factors have emerged as recurrent themes in the lives of children who overcome great odds. Some protective factors are characteristics of the individual: Resilient children are engaging to other people, adults and peers alike; they have good communication and problem-solving skills, including the ability to recruit substitute caregivers; they have a talent or hobby that is valued by their elders or peers; and they have faith that their own actions can make a positive difference in their lives.

Another factor that enhances resilience in development is having affectional ties that encourage trust, autonomy, and initiative. These ties are often provided by members of the extended family. There are also support systems in the community that reinforce and reward the competencies of resilient children and provide them with positive role models: caring neighbors, teachers, elder mentors, youth workers, and peers.

LINKS BETWEEN PROTECTIVE FACTORS AND SUCCESSFUL ADAPTATION IN HIGH-RISK CHILDREN AND YOUTHS

In the Kauai study, when we examined the links between protective factors within the individual and outside sources of support, we noted a certain continuity in the life course of the high-risk individuals who successfully overcame a variety of childhood adversities. Their individual dispositions led them to select or construct environments that, in turn, reinforced and sustained their active approach to life and rewarded their special competencies.

Although the sources of support available to the individuals in their childhood homes were modestly linked to the quality of the individuals' adaptation as adults, their competencies, temperament, and self-esteem had a greater impact. Many resilient high-risk youths on Kauai left the adverse conditions of their childhood homes after high school and sought environments they found more compatible. In short, they picked their own niches.

Our findings lend some empirical support to Scarr and McCartney's theory[16] about how people make their own environment. Scarr and McCartney proposed three types of effects of people's genes on their environment: passive, evocative, and active. Because parents provide both children's genes and their rearing environments, children's genes are necessarily correlated with their own environments. This is the passive type of genotype-environment effect. The evocative type refers to the fact that a person's partially heritable characteristics, such as intelligence, personality, and physical

attractiveness, evoke certain responses from other people. Finally, a person's interests, talents, and personality (genetically variable traits) may lead him or her to select or create particular environments; this is called an active genotype-environment effect. In line with this theory, there was a shift from passive to active effects as the youths and young adults in the Kauai study left stressful home environments and sought extrafamilial environments (at school, at work, in the military) that they found more compatible and stimulating. Genotype-environment effects of the evocative sort tended to persist throughout the different life stages we studied, as individuals' physical characteristics, temperament, and intelligence elicited differential responses from other people (parents, teachers, peers).

IMPLICATIONS

So far, most studies of resilience have focused on children and youths who have "pulled themselves up by their bootstraps," with informal support by kith and kin, not on recipients of intervention services. Yet there are some lessons such children can teach society about effective intervention: If we want to help vulnerable youngsters become more resilient, we need to decrease their exposure to potent risk factors and increase their competencies and self-esteem, as well as the sources of support they can draw upon.

In *Within Our Reach*, Schorr has isolated a set of common characteristics of social programs that have successfully prevented poor outcomes for children who grew up in high-risk families.[17] Such programs typically offer a broad spectrum of health, education, and family support services, cross professional boundaries, and view the child in the context of the family, and the family in the context of the community. They provide children with sustained access to competent and caring adults, both professionals and volunteers, who teach them problem-solving skills, enhance their communication skills and self-esteem, and provide positive role models for them.

There is an urgent need for more systematic evaluations of such programs to illuminate the process by which we can forge a chain of protective factors that enables vulnerable children to become competent, confident, and caring individuals, despite the odds of chronic poverty or a medical or social disability. Future research on risk and resiliency needs to acquire a cross-cultural perspective as well. We need to know more about individual dispositions and sources of support that transcend cultural boundaries and operate effectively in a variety of high-risk contexts.

Notes

1. A.S. Masten, K.M. Best, and N. Garmezy, Resilience and development: Contributions from the study of children who overcame adversity, *Development and Psychopathology, 2,* 425–444 (1991).

2. All results from this study that are discussed in this review were reported in E.E. Werner, Risk resilience, and recovery: Perspectives from the Kauai Longitudinal Study, *Development and Psychopathology, 5,* 503–515 (1993).

3. B. Egeland, D. Jacobvitz, and L.A. Sroufe, Breaking the cycle of child abuse, *Child Development, 59,* 1080–1088 (1988).

4. A. Moriarty, John, a boy who acquired resilience, in *The Invulnerable Child,* E.J. Anthony and B.J. Cohler, Eds. (Guilford Press, New York, 1987).

5. G.H. Elder, K. Liker, and C.E. Cross, Parent-child behavior in the Great Depression, in *Life Span Development and Behavior,* Vol. 6, T.B. Baltes and O.G. Brim, Jr., Eds. (Academic Press, New York, 1984).

6. E.J. Anthony, Children at risk for psychosis growing up successfully, in *The Invulnerable Child,* E.J. Anthony and B.J. Cohler, Eds. (Guilford Press, New York, 1987).

7. J.K. Felsman and G.E. Vaillant, Resilient children as adults: A 40 year study, in *The Invulnerable Child,* E.J. Anthony and B.J. Cohler, Eds. (Guilford Press, New York, 1987).

8. M. Rutter and D. Quinton, Long term follow-up of women institutionalized in childhood: Factors promoting good functioning in adult life, *British Journal of Developmental Psychology, 18,* 225–234 (1984).

9. J. Block and P.F. Gjerde, *Early antecedents of ego resiliency in late adolescence,* paper presented at the annual meeting of the American Psychological Association, Washington, DC (August 1986).

10. R.M. Clark, *Family Life and School Achievement: Why Poor Black Children Succeed or Fail* (University of Chicago Press, Chicago, 1983).

11. D.P. Farrington, *Protective Factors in the Development of Juvenile Delinquency and Adult Crime* (Institute of Criminology, Cambridge University, Cambridge, England, 1993).

12. J.S. Wallerstein and S. Blakeslee, *Second Chances: Men, Women and Children a Decade After Divorce* (Ticknor and Fields, New York, 1989).

13. M. Rutter, B. Maughan, P. Mortimore, and J. Ousten, *Fifteen Thousand Hours: Secondary Schools and Their Effects on Children* (Harvard University Press, Cambridge, MA, 1979).

14. G.H. Elder, Military times and turning points in men's lives, *Developmental Psychology, 22,* 233–245 (1986).

15. F.F. Furstenberg, J. Brooks-Gunn, and S.P. Morgan, *Adolescent Mothers in Later Life* (Cambridge University Press, New York, 1987).

16. S. Scarr and K. McCartney, How people make their own environments: A theory of genotype → environment effects, *Child Development, 54,* 424–435 (1983).

17. L. Schorr, *Within Our Reach: Breaking the Cycle of Disadvantage* (Anchor Press, New York, 1988).

Recommended Reading

Haggerty, R., Garmezy, N., Rutter, M., and Sherrod. L., Eds. (1994). *Stress, Risk, and Resilience in Childhood and Adolescence* (Cambridge University Press, New York).

Luthar, S., and Zigler, E. (1991). Vulnerability and competence: A review of research on resilience in childhood. *American Journal of Orthopsychiatry, 61,* 6–22.

Werner, E.E., and Smith, R.S. (1992). *Overcoming the Odds: High Risk Children From Birth to Adulthood* (Cornell University Press, Ithaca, NY).

A Boy Without a Penis

The experts had it all wrong, says the beleaguered survivor of a landmark 1960s sex-change operation

By CHRISTINE GORMAN

HE WAS ONE OF A SET OF INFANT TWIN boys when, in 1963, his penis was damaged beyond repair by a circumcision that went awry. After seeking expert advice at Johns Hopkins Medical School, the parents decided that the child's best shot at a normal life was as an anatomically correct woman. The baby was castrated, and surgeons fashioned a kind of vagina out of the remaining tissue. When "she" grew older, hormone treatments would complete the transformation from boy to girl.

The case became a landmark in the annals of sex research, living proof of the prevailing theory of the 1960s and early 1970s that sexual identity exists in a kind of continuum and that nurture is more important than nature in determining gender roles. Babies are born gender neutral, the experts said. Catch them early enough, and you can make them anything you want. Widely cited in medical and social-science textbooks, the baby's transformation helped pediatricians confidently advise other parents facing similar circumstances to rear their wounded boys as girls.

What these doctors and parents didn't know was that the celebrated sex-change success story was, in fact, a total failure. In a follow-up study published last week in the *Archives of Pediatric and Adolescent Medicine*, Milton Diamond, a professor of anatomy and reproductive biology at the University of Hawaii, and Dr. Keith Sigmundson, a psychiatrist with the Canadian Ministry of Health, report that the child, whom they called "Joan," never really adjusted to her assigned gender. In fact, Joan was surgically changed back to "John" in the late 1970s, and is now the happily married father of three adopted children.

Almost from the beginning, Diamond and Sigmundson write, Joan rebelled at her treatment. Even as a toddler, she felt different. When her mother clothed her in frilly dresses, she would try to rip them off. She preferred to play with boys and stereotypical boys' toys—in one memorable instance walking into a store to buy an umbrella and walking out with a toy machine gun. By second grade, she had come to suspect she would fit in better as a boy. But her doctors insisted that these feelings were perfectly normal, that she was just a tomboy. "I thought I was a freak or something," John told Diamond and Sigmundson in interviews conducted in 1994 and 1995. Although the other kids didn't know about Joan's surgical history, they teased her about her tomboyish looks and behavior. Public bathrooms proved to be a source of particular discomfort. Joan often insisted on urinating standing up, which usually made a mess. In junior high school she stood so often in the stalls of the girls' rest room that the girls finally refused to let her in anymore, forcing her to use the boys' room instead.

By this time, Joan was pretty sure she was a boy. But no matter what she told her doctors and psychiatrists, they kept pressing her to act more feminine. Eventually she gave up trying to convince them. "You can't argue with a bunch of doctors in white coats," John recalls. "You're just a little kid, and their minds are already made up. They didn't want to listen."

In 1977, when she was 14, Joan decided she had only two options: either commit suicide or live her life as a male. Finally, in a tearful confrontation, her father told her the true story of her birth and sex change. "All of a sudden everything clicked," John remembers. "For the first time things made sense, and I understood who and what I was." With the support of a new set of doctors, Joan underwent a pair of operations to reconstruct a penis—albeit a diminutive one without the sensitivity of a normal sex organ.

Following this second set of sex-change procedures, John's new doctors advised the family to move to a new town and another school and start over. This time however, John's parents rejected the expert advice. People would find out anyway, they reasoned. It was better to stay put and be open about what had happened. Their strategy seems to have worked. After a brief transition, John was accepted by his peers in a way that Joan never was. Once, when John first began dating, he confessed to a would-be girlfriend that he was insecure about his penis, and she started telling tales in school about his condition. But Joan's old schoolmates stuck loyally by John, refusing to be drawn into the girls' malicious gossip.

At its worst, this story could be read as a lesson in scientific hubris. At its best, it's a story about the courage of one boy who claimed the right to determine his own identity.

Unfortunately, no follow-up study reporting that John had rejected his initial sex change was ever published. As a result, say Diamond and Sigmundson, dozens of other boys may have been needlessly castrated. In defense of the original team, Johns Hopkins says it wasn't able to conduct a follow-up because the family stopped coming to see its doctors.

Diamond and Sigmundson suspect that most boys-made-girls will, like John, reject their female identity by the time they reach puberty. Other experts are not so sure. "We don't have the answers," says Dr. William Reiner, a surgeon and psychiatrist at Johns Hopkins (who was not involved in the original case). "Let's listen to these kids. They eventually are going to give us the answer."—*Reported by Dick Thompson/Washington*

gender: and developmental research on boys, 160–163; education and, 108–117; and parents' marital transitions, 142–143; play and, 103; sex-change operations and, 224; and victimization of children, 215–217
generalizations, categorization and, 54
genes: brain development and, 21–22; cognitive skills and, 29–35; personality and, 8–12
Gerken, LouAnn, 40
Gilder, George, 131
Gilligan, Carol, 160–161
glial cells, 20
Goldman, William, 28
Goldsmith, Stephen, 174
Goleman, Daniel, 90–96
Goodman, Corey, 21, 22
Goodwin, Frederick, 9
Gordon, Thomas, 157
Gore, Al, 174
Gormley, William, 136
grammar, language learning and, 36–42
Greenough, William, 12, 24
Greenspan, Stanley, 21, 23
grief, children and, 88–89
Grollman, Earl, 88
growth cone, 22
Gunnar, Megan, 28, 85–86, 87
Gunnoe, Marjorie Lindner, 158
Gurian, Michael, 160

Hamer, Dean, 11
Hare, Robert, 94
Harlow, Harry, 85
Harris, Maxine, 88
health risks: of day care, 135; of poverty, 194–208
hedgehog gene, 21
heights, development of wariness of, 80–83
heredity. See genes
heroes, Power Rangers and, 192
Heyl, Peter, 13
Hillman, Catherine, 88
hippocampus, 28
Homer, 169
homicide, and victimization of children, 209–219
homosexuality, genes and, 8–12
Howes, Carollee, 127
human rights, and child labor in Pakistan, 177–187
Hundt, Reed, 172
Huttenlocher, Janellen, 27, 42
Huttenlocher, Peter, 22
Hyman, Irwin A., 157, 158
Hyman, Stephen, 12

in vitro fertilization, 13
individual risk and vulnerability hypothesis, and children of divorce, 149

intelligence: breastfeeding and, 28; emotional, 90–96; genes and, 29–35

James, William, 51
Jessell, Thomas, 21
Jusczyk, Peter, 36, 38

Kagan, Jerome, 86, 91
Kamin, Leon, 8
Kandel, Eric, 22
Katz, Lillian, 128
Kegl, Judy, 41, 42
Khan, Ehsan Ulla, 182, 183, 185–186, 187
Kitcher, Philip, 11
Klaus, Marshall, 15
Klima, Edward, 41
Koren, Gideon, 17
Kosofsky, Barry, 16
Kranzler, Elliot, 89
Kuhl, Patricia, 23, 26

language: brain development and, 25–28, 36–42; categorization and, 54–55
Lara, Adnir, 162
Larzelere, Robert E., 158, 159
Lasch, Christopher, 131
Le Doux, Joseph, 91
Le Vay, Simon, 10–11
Leach, Penelope, 120, 126, 127, 129, 130, 134, 157
lead poisoning, 198–199
Lesch-Nyhan syndrome, 34
Lester, Barry, 16, 17
Levitt, Pat, 16
limbic system, 28, 87, 91
Lipton, Rose, 124
locomotor experience, and development of wariness of heights, 80–83
locus ceruleus, 28
Loehlin, John C., 32
logic, brain development and, 25–28
love, bonding and, 84–87
Lovejoy, Owen, 14
Lucas, Alan, 28

Malik, Imram, 182
manic depression, 9–10
Mann, Alan, 15
marital transitions, effect of, on children, 139–155
Masih, Iqbal, 185–187
math: Asian methods of teaching, 66–77; brain development and, 25–28
Mayer, John, 91
Mayer, Susan, 204

Mayes, Linda, 27–28
Maynard, Fredelle, 130
McClearn, Gerald E., 30
McCurdy, Harold, 131
McGue, Matthew, 31
McHugh, Paul, 91, 95, 96
Mead, Margaret, 124
media, influence of, on children, 166–172, 188–193
Melmed, Matthew, 24
memory, 28, 86
mental illness, as brain disease, 8–12
mental retardation, 21, 32, 33, 34, 86
metamood, 92
Meyerhoff, Michael, 129
Mills, Debra, 41
Mischel, Walter, 96
Mott, Charles Stewart, 174
mourning, children and, 88–89
multiple births, 13
multiple solutions, use of, in math lessons, 73–74
muscular dystrophy, 34
music, brain development and, 25–28

nannies, 136–137
National Association for the Education of Young Children (NAEYC), guidelines for developmentally appropriate practice of, 58–65
nature vs. nurture: brain development and, 21–22; personality and, 8–12
neglect, and victimization of children, 209–219
neocerebellum, 39
neocortex, 91
neural networks, 40
neural tube, 21
neurofibromatosis, 34
Newman, Frank, 21
Newport, Elissa, 37, 40
Nichols, Robert C., 32

observational learning, 189
Ortega, Ruben, 174
out-of-wedlock births, 196, 201–202

Pakistan, child labor in, 177–187
pandemic, victimization of children as, 209
parentese, 23
Paret, Isabel, 128
Pawl, Jeree, 126
Pedersen, Nancy L., 31
Peele, Stanton, 10
peer nomination, as measure of acceptance, 97
Perry, Bruce, 23, 27, 28, 86

AE Article Review Form

We encourage you to photocopy and use this page as a tool to assess how the articles in **Annual Editions** expand on the information in your textbook. By reflecting on the articles you will gain enhanced text information. You can also access this useful form on a product's book support Web site at **http://www.dushkin.com/ online/.**

NAME: DATE:

TITLE AND NUMBER OF ARTICLE:

BRIEFLY STATE THE MAIN IDEA OF THIS ARTICLE:

LIST THREE IMPORTANT FACTS THAT THE AUTHOR USES TO SUPPORT THE MAIN IDEA:

WHAT INFORMATION OR IDEAS DISCUSSED IN THIS ARTICLE ARE ALSO DISCUSSED IN YOUR TEXTBOOK OR OTHER READINGS THAT YOU HAVE DONE? LIST THE TEXTBOOK CHAPTERS AND PAGE NUMBERS:

LIST ANY EXAMPLES OF BIAS OR FAULTY REASONING THAT YOU FOUND IN THE ARTICLE:

LIST ANY NEW TERMS/CONCEPTS THAT WERE DISCUSSED IN THE ARTICLE, AND WRITE A SHORT DEFINITION

ANNUAL EDITIONS revisions depend on two major opinion sources: one is our Advisory Board, listed in the front of this volume, which works with us in scanning the thousands of articles published in the public press each year; the other is you—the person actually using the book. Please help us and the users of the next edition by completing the prepaid article rating form on this page and returning it to us. Thank you for your help!

ANNUAL EDITIONS: Child Growth and Development 99/00

ARTICLE RATING FORM

Here is an opportunity for you to have direct input into the next revision of this volume. We would like you to rate each of the 32 articles listed below, using the following scale:

1. Excellent: should definitely be retained
2. Above average: should probably be retained
3. Below average: should probably be deleted
4. Poor: should definitely be deleted

Your ratings will play a vital part in the next revision. So please mail this prepaid form to us just as soon as you complete it. Thanks for your help!

We Want Your Advice

RATING

ARTICLE

1. Politics of Biology
2. Multiplying the Risks
3. Putting a New Spin on the Birth of Human Birth
4. Hope for 'Snow Babies'
5. Fertile Minds
6. How to Build a Baby's Brain
7. The Genetics of Cognitive Abilities and Disabilities
8. Baby Talk
9. How Do Infants Learn about the Physical World?
10. Categories in Young Children's Thinking
11. What Have We Learned about Developmentally Appropriate Practice?
12. How Asian Teachers Polish Each Lesson to Perfection
13. Early Experience and Emotional Development: The Emergence of Wariness of Heights
14. Babies, Bonds, and Brains
15. How Kids Mourn
16. The EQ Factor
17. Children without Friends

RATING

ARTICLE

18. Teacher Response to Superhero Play: To Ban or Not to Ban?
19. Girls and Boys Together . . . but Mostly Apart: Gender Arrangements in Elementary Schools
20. Why Johnny Can't Sleep
21. The Problem with Day Care
22. What Matters? What Does Not? Five Perspectives on the Association between Marital Transitions and Children's Adjustment
23. When to Spank
24. Boys Will Be Boys
25. Buried Alive
26. It's 4:00 p.m. Do You Know Where Your Children Are?
27. Child Labor in Pakistan
28. Of Power Rangers and V-Chips
29. The Effects of Poverty on Children
30. Victimization of Children
31. Resilience in Development
32. A Boy without a Penis

(Continued on next page)

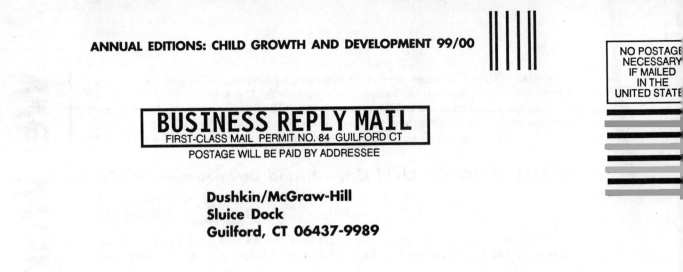

BUSINESS REPLY MAIL
FIRST-CLASS MAIL PERMIT NO. 84 GUILFORD CT

POSTAGE WILL BE PAID BY ADDRESSEE

Dushkin/McGraw-Hill
Sluice Dock
Guilford, CT 06437-9989

NO POSTAGE
NECESSARY
IF MAILED
IN THE
UNITED STATE

ABOUT YOU

Name   Date

Are you a teacher? ☐ A student? ☐
Your school's name

Department

Address   City   State   Zip

School telephone #

YOUR COMMENTS ARE IMPORTANT TO US!

Please fill in the following information:
For which course did you use this book?

Did you use a text with this *ANNUAL EDITION*? ☐ yes ☐ no
What was the title of the text?

What are your general reactions to the *Annual Editions* concept?

Have you read any particular articles recently that you think should be included in the next edition?

Are there any articles you feel should be replaced in the next edition? Why?

Are there any World Wide Web sites you feel should be included in the next edition? Please annotate.

May we contact you for editorial input? ☐ yes ☐ no
May we quote your comments? ☐ yes ☐ no